HISTORICAL DICTIONARY OF THE NEW DEAL

HISTORICAL DICTIONARY OF THE NEW DEAL

From Inauguration to Preparation for War

Edited by
JAMES S. OLSON

Greenwood Press
Westport, Connecticut • London, England

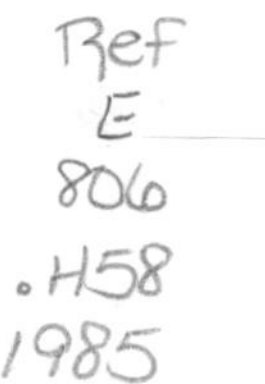

Library of Congress Cataloging in Publication Data

Main entry under title:

Historical dictionary of the new deal.

Bibliography: p.
Includes index.
1. New Deal, 1933-1939—Dictionaries. 2. United States—History—1933-1945—Dictionaries. I. Olson, James Stuart, 1946-
E806.H58 1985 973.917′03′21 84-19792
ISBN 0-313-23873-1 (lib. bdg.)

Library of Congress Catalog Card Number: 84-19792
ISBN: 0-313-23873-1

First published in 1985

Greenwood Press
A division of Congressional Information Service, Inc.
88 Post Road West
Westport, Connecticut 06881

Printed in the United States of America

The paper in this book complies with the Permanent Paper Standard issued by the National Information Standards Organization (Z39.48-1984).

10 9 8 7 6 5 4 3 2 1

CONTENTS

PREFACE

For nearly fifty years, historians have debated the nature of public policy during the 1930s, concentrating on such questions as the "First New Deal," the "Second New Deal," the "watershed of 1933," the shortcomings of Herbert Hoover, the differences between the Populists, progressives, and New Dealers, the origins and merits of various New Deal programs, and the significance of the New Deal for American society. What historians have generally agreed on is that by 1945 the public policy landscape in the United States had been transformed. Anyone comparing the political economy of 1945 with its 1920 counterpart notices two dramatic changes. First, the "bureaucratic state" had appeared and claimed responsibility for stable prices and full employment by managing the economy through the coordination and regulation of more centralized institutions. Second, Keynesian fiscal policies had largely replaced more traditional monetary techniques in stimulating purchasing power, production, and employment. Without question, the New Deal was a critical watershed in the history of public policy in the United States.

This *Historical Dictionary of the New Deal* is designed to provide a ready reference tool for students and scholars. The major focus of the *Dictionary* is on domestic policy between 1933 and 1940. Foreign policy questions have been ignored unless they directly affected domestic policies or programs. The *Dictionary* provides brief descriptive essays on most of the people, agencies, and legislation important to the New Deal. They are arranged in alphabetical order, with four appendixes at the end of the book providing a chronology of the New Deal, a list of key personnel, a bibliography of New Deal programs, and a table of acronyms commonly used to describe New Deal agencies. To aid in finding related items, there are cross-references within the texts of most entries. These are designated by an asterisk (*).

I wish to express my thanks to the scholars who contributed essays to the *Dictionary*. Their names appear at the end of the entries they wrote. All unsigned entries were written by me. I would also like to thank the librarians who assisted me in locating hard-to-find material. I am especially grateful to J. Larry Murdock, Ann Holder, Paul Culp, Bill Bailey, and Jaspyr Sanford, all of the Sam Houston

State University Library staff. Finally, I am indebted to my wife, Judy, for her patience in tolerating what has seemed an endless task in producing the *Dictionary*.

James S. Olson

THE DICTIONARY

A

ABBOTT, GRACE Born in 1878 in Nebraska, Grace Abbott played an influential role concerning women's issues during the New Deal.* She came from a politically active family: her father had been involved in Nebraska politics and her mother had worked actively for women's suffrage and abolition. Abbott graduated from Grand Island College in 1898 and then took a master's degree in political science at the University of Chicago in 1909. Her own interests in reform followed those of her parents, except hers were directed toward the problems of urban society. Abbott worked at Hull House in Chicago and in 1917 joined the Children's Bureau of the Department of Labor. In 1919 she left the bureau to work for the Illinois State Immigrants Commission, but she came back to Washington as head of the Children's Bureau in 1921. Abbott was active in the National Consumers' League and the Women's Trade Union League, and in 1923 and 1924 she was president of the National Conference of Social Work. Close to Eleanor Roosevelt* as well as several other influential women in the New Deal, Abbott served on the Consumers' Advisory Board* of the National Recovery Administration* in 1933 and 1934; and after she left the Children's Bureau to return to the University of Chicago, President Franklin D. Roosevelt* appointed her to the Committee on Economic Security.* She died in Chicago on June 19, 1939. (Susan Ware, *Beyond Suffrage: Women in the New Deal*, 1981.)

ACHESON, DEAN GOODERHAM Dean Acheson was born on April 11, 1893, in Middletown, Connecticut. Coming from a prosperous New England family, he graduated from Yale in 1915 and the Harvard Law School in 1918. Acheson served as private secretary to Supreme Court Justice Louis Brandeis* until 1921, when he joined the law firm of Covington, Burling and Rublee in Washington, D.C. He stayed there until 1933. An ardent Democrat, Acheson campaigned actively for Franklin D. Roosevelt's* candidacy in 1932, especially among the New England upper crust. In return, the president named him under secretary of the treasury in May 1933. Later in the year, Acheson became a political liability for Roosevelt because of rumors linking him with the J. P.

Morgan banking firm and because of Acheson's opposition to the gold-buying program.* On November 15, 1933, Acheson resigned his treasury post and returned to private law practice. His personal relations with President Roosevelt, however, remained quite cordial, and he frequently advised the president on economic and monetary matters. On February 1, 1941, Roosevelt brought Acheson back into the administration as assistant secretary of state to Cordell Hull.* Acheson became under secretary of state in August 1945 and secretary of state in July 1949. He left the State Department in January 1953 and returned to private law practice. Dean Acheson died of a heart attack on October 12, 1971. (Dean Acheson, *Present at the Creation*, 1969.)

ADAMS, ALVA BLANCHARD Alva B. Adams was born in Del Norte, Colorado, on October 29, 1875, the son of Alva Adams and Ella Nye. He was educated at Phillips Academy and at Yale, graduating there in 1896, and then took a law degree at Columbia. He practiced law in Pueblo, Colorado, and served briefly in the United States Senate in 1923-1924, filling the vacancy caused by the death of Samuel Nicholson. Adams was elected to the United States Senate by 28,000 votes in the Democratic landslide of 1932. During his career there he developed a reputation for hard work and political conservatism, continually advocating government efficiency and cuts in federal spending. Because he found many New Deal* relief programs wasteful, he became a thorn in President Franklin D. Roosevelt's* side, especially when he bitterly attacked the "court-packing"* scheme. Roosevelt tagged Adams as one of the Democrats he wanted "purged" in 1938,* and he saw to it that Colorado Supreme Court Justice Benjamin C. Hilliard opposed him in the Democratic primary. Although Hilliard ran as the "New Deal candidate," Adams won the primary and reelection. Alva B. Adams died of heart failure on December 1, 1941. (*New York Times*, December 2, 1941.)

ADJUSTED COMPENSATION ACT OF 1936 In 1924 Congress had issued adjusted compensation certificates to veterans of World War I as a payment for their loyalty and services. The certificates were due to mature in 1945 and serve as a cash reward for some and a small pension for others. When the stock market crashed, however, and unemployment became severe, many veterans' groups began demanding immediate payment of the bonuses. In June 1932 a large group of veterans had marched on Washington, D.C., demanding their bonuses, and in July President Herbert Hoover* had used the army to disperse them. By the time of the New Deal,* with many conservatives concerned about government spending, cash payments to veterans seemed a likely place to make cuts. The Economy Act of 1933* had made cuts in pension payments to veterans suffering from non-service-related disabilities. Veterans organizations had protested the cuts, and in 1934, with the Independent Offices Appropriations Act,* Congress restored $228 million in veteran allowances. President Franklin D. Roosevelt* had vetoed the bill, but in the election year, Congress had successfully managed to override it.

Congressman Wright Patman* of Texas, one of the more vociferous congressional advocates of veterans' rights, sponsored a new bonus bill in 1935. It provided for immediate payment of the adjusted compensation certificates by issuing $2.2 billion in greenbacks. The president viewed the measure as inflationary, and he appeared before a joint session of Congress to deliver his veto message. Under Patman's leadership, the House overrode the veto by a vote of 322 to 98, but the Senate sustained the veto. The Patman bonus bill* was dead, despite the bitter complaints of World War I veterans.

Its death was short-lived. Early in 1936, with the congressional primaries of 1936 looming ahead, the question of veterans' bonuses once again surfaced in Congress. The Senate passed the Adjusted Compensation Act of January 20, 1936, and the House passed it on January 22. The bill provided for full cash payment of the adjusted compensation certificates by having the treasury issue nine-year interest-bearing bonds redeemable in cash at any time. President Roosevelt also vetoed the Adjusted Compensation Act, but Congress immediately overrode him. The election-year power of veterans' groups was impossible for most congressmen and senators to resist. On June 15, 1936, more than $1.5 billion in bonus bonds were distributed to more than 3 million veterans of World War I. (James MacGregor Burns, *Roosevelt: The Lion and the Fox*, 1956.)

AGEE, JAMES RUFUS Born in Knoxville, Tennessee, in 1909, James Rufus Agee was educated at Phillips Exeter Academy, and at Harvard where his sensitivity to language was heightened by the theories of I. A. Richards. Although his career as critic and writer was often frustrated by turmoils of self-evaluation and ambivalence about his art, Agee's work as poet, journalist, film critic, and writer of screen adaptations was fastidious and original. His *Let Us Now Praise Famous Men* (1941), despite its complex form, will remain one of the great books of the Depression Era. *A Death in the Family*, published posthumously in 1957, was awarded the Pulitzer Prize in 1958. *Agee on Film* (2 vols.: 1958, 1960) and *Letters to Father Fly* (1962) allowed access to his film reviews and also revealed the intensity of his aesthetic and moral deliberations.

In 1936 Agee was sent as a staffwriter for *Fortune* magazine to rural Alabama to study the lives of indigent sharecroppers, the local unions, and leadership of New Deal* programs. Shortly before this assignment, Agee had written an article on the TVA,* and his editor had praised his writing generously. When he returned from his larger assignment, however, the manuscript he submitted was held by *Fortune* for a year, then rejected. Not until 1941 was Agee's response to an eight-week stay with three sharecropper families published. *Let Us Now Praise Famous Men* was his tour de force in experimental style, a book in which Walker Evans'* photographs were co-equal with the written text. Published out of its own time, the book was received with mixed appreciation. Although it is often called one of the great "social documents" of the depression, such patent classification is ironic, because it was Agee and Evans' prime intention that their work would escape facile labeling and generalizations. Agee's turbulent but earnest morality was always hostile to the trend, as he saw it, for readers to patronize poverty, to see such documents as "artistic" or "picturesque." What he wanted, he said, was "to portray unimagined reality."

Walker Evans' "Foreword" to the 1960 edition of *Famous Men* pictured Agee at work during the year of the book's making. The young writer, irrepressible in talk and work, established an easy intimacy with the Alabama people that was an almost psychic contact, possibly an innate response to his own blood heritage, especially in his father's land origins. Agee's explicit anti-art, anti-authoritarian voice in his own preface is certainly counter-balanced by an affection for his subject that is near sacramental. As Evans says, "to him, human beings were at least possibly immortal and literally sacred souls."

Such words partially explained both the genius and the difficulty of Agee's style in *Famous Men*. His effort to present a "pure" realism based on his eight-week experience with the sharecroppers was a modernist's aesthetic imperative. For him, art was a dynamic interaction between subject, artist, and audience, allowing ever-changing perspectives to its human participants. Thus, his book strove to break down all preconceptions about subject, structure, typography, points of view, and time frames. Essentially, Agee wanted to capture the states of his own subjective experience while recalling and refashioning his subject. Subsequently, he hoped to jar the reader into examining his own preconceptions about the "reality" of any subject.

The results of such efforts was a book whose form has been described in a hearty miscellany of labels: a grab bag, a prose poem, a symphony, an incantation of facts, a sonata, minimal art, action painting, a covert autobiography, and more. Agee's instruction that his book has two subjects: the "nominal subject" and the "reader's expectation of its proper treatment," which has the tone of a goading, taunting Walt Whitman who wanted his readers to see life with new eyes. Agee's style, in fact, had been called Whitmanesque, but more often it was compared to the poetic and prose experiments of such early modernists as John Dos Passos, Robinson Jeffers, Wallace Stevens, and James Joyce.

During the 1940s and 1950s, Agee restricted almost all his writing to movie reviews and columns for *Time* and *The Nation*, as well as to screenplays and adaptations. The latter included such familiar titles as *The Blue Hotel*, *The African Queen*, and *Key Largo*. After his death critics often spoke about Agee's failure of talent during these years of film writing and reviewing, about his seeming victimization by the corporate publishing world and by Hollywood. Since the 1960s, however, a reassessment of the significance of American films has prompted scholars to place increasing value on Agee's work in these genres. In 1948 Agee left *Time* in order to work on his autobiographical novel, *A Death in the Family*, which was unfinished when he died in 1955, but published posthumously in 1957. It was adapted for the stage in 1960 as "All the Way Home" and filmed in that form in 1963. Along with *Famous Men*, it best represents the rare quality of Agee's aesthetic and his talent. (James Agee and Walker Evans, *Let Us Now Praise Famous Men*, 1960; Alfred T. Barson, *A Way of Seeing: A Critical Study of James Agee*, 1972.)

BARBARA M. TYSON

AGRICULTURAL ADJUSTMENT ACT OF 1933 Ever since the late nineteenth century, the major problem facing American agriculture had been overproduction. Commodity prices were usually low because supplies consistently exceeded domestic demand. During the 1920s, the problem had become especially acute. Farm leaders and politicians proposed a variety of solutions, including marketing cooperatives, foreign dumping, and government-financed surplus storage. Nothing worked. Late in the 1920s, a proposal known as the "Domestic Allotment Plan"* began gaining momentum among agricultural economists. In 1927 farm expert William J. Spillman wrote *Balancing the Farm Output* and proposed acreage reductions to individual farmers by government allotment. Picking up on the idea, Professor John Black* of the University of Minnesota wrote *Agricultural Reform in the United States* in 1929 and refined the idea. Professor M. L. Wilson* of Montana State College then suggested financing the payments to farmers for reducing acreage through a tax at the processing level. Wilson called it the "Voluntary Domestic Allotment Plan." Henry A. Wallace,* editor of *Wallace's Farmer*, converted to the idea in 1930 and began publicizing it widely. In 1931 and 1932 Wallace helped convene a conference in Chicago of farm leaders and farm economists, including Rexford G. Tugwell* of Columbia, and both years the group endorsed the Voluntary Domestic Allotment Plan.

After the inauguration of Franklin D. Roosevelt* in 1933, with Wallace now secretary of agriculture and Tugwell assistant secretary, the allotment plan became a New Deal* priority. They sponsored a National Agricultural Conference in March 1933, where the American Farm Bureau Federation* and the National Farmers' Union* endorsed the basic concept, and Wallace then assigned Frederic P. Lee, Mordecai Ezekiel,* Jerome Frank,* Rexford G. Tugwell, Chester Davis,* and George Peek* to draft the necessary legislation. Marvin Jones,* chairman of the House Committee on Agriculture, introduced the measure to Congress. It encountered challenges from two sources. John Simpson,* head of the National Farmers' Union, wanted the bill to guarantee farmers their entire cost of production, and Senator George Norris* of Nebraska supported him. Roosevelt and Wallace, however, rejected the concept, and it never became part of the law. Second, inflationists in Congress, led by Senators Elmer Thomas* of Oklahoma and Burton Wheeler* of Montana, wanted the law to greatly expand the currency. John Simpson supported them in this populistic quest for higher commodity prices. Realizing the power of western mining and farming interests, Roosevelt decided to appease Wheeler and Thomas and accepted what became the Thomas Amendment giving the president the right, but not requiring him, to expand the money supply. Introduced on March 16, 1933, the Agricultural Adjustment Act became law on May 12, 1933.

Title I of the Agricultural Adjustment Act stated the goal of "relieving the existing national economic emergency by increasing agricultural purchasing power." It designated wheat, cotton, tobacco, corn, hogs, rice, and milk as basic commodities, and called on the secretary of agriculture to enter into "marketing agreements" with individual farmers to reduce their production. The law appropriated $100 million to finance the program initially, but thereafter imposed a tax on processors to sustain the program. Title II focused on the problem of rural credit, primarily the question of mortgage debt. It incorporated into the Agricultural Adjustment Act the legislation entitled the Emergency Farm Mortgage Act.* Title III of the Agricultural Adjustment Act gave the president power, when he saw it necessary, to inflate the money supply by issuing up to $3 billion in paper currency, reducing the gold content of the dollar, or freely coining silver. (Van L. Perkins, *Crisis in Agriculture. The Agricultural Adjustment Administration and the New Deal, 1933*, 1969.)

AGRICULTURAL ADJUSTMENT ACT OF 1938 Ever since the nineteenth century, the most consistent problem affecting American agriculture had been overproduction and its associated depressed prices. Farmers had approached the problem from a number of directions, asking the federal government to expand the money supply, inflate the currency, dump surpluses on foreign markets, purchase surpluses, make loans to allow farmers to store crops during bumper years, and pay farmers not to grow as a means of cutting surpluses. The Agricultural Adjustment Act of 1933* had paid farmers to reduce production, with a tax on processors used to finance the program, but in 1936 the Supreme Court* declared the AAA unconstitutional. Congress responded with the Soil Conservation and Domestic Allotment Act,* which paid farmers to make improvements in soil quality. The measure was financed by congressional appropriations rather than through a processor tax.

But the Soil Conservation and Domestic Allotment Act proved insufficient because not enough farmers were voluntarily cooperating to limit production. The cotton crop in 1936 reached 18 million bales, driving prices down. Wheat, corn, and tobacco farmers faced similar problems. Farm bloc lobbyists were demanding higher and higher subsidies, few production restrictions, and export dumping; but administration officials, particularly Secretary of Agriculture Henry Wallace,* shied away from such radical demands. In the summer of 1937, the House Committee on Agriculture held meetings throughout the United States, and both houses of Congress began to debate the issue in December 1937 and January and February of 1938. In the final bill which President Franklin D. Roosevelt* signed on February 16, 1938, the farm bloc got much of what it had demanded. Titles I and II of the law reinforced and made permanent the soil conservation features of the Soil Conservation and Domestic Allotment Act. Title III established the "ever-normal granary"* principle. The secretary of agriculture could set marketing quotas whenever the price of a particular crop was threatened by surplus production. Acreage allotments for individual farmers went into effect once two-thirds of the affected farmers had approved them in referendum elections. The Commodity Credit Corporation* would make loans on surplus crops at prices just below the parity* levels of 1909-1914. If market prices went above the value of the loan, the farmer could sell his produce at a profit and repay the government. If crop prices fell below the value of the loan, the farmer surrendered the crop to the Commodity Credit Corporation, which would absorb the loss. The individual farmer kept a minimum income. Title IV of the act dealt with specific problems of cotton operations. Title V established the Federal Crop Insurance Corporation,* with a capital stock of $100 million, to insure wheat crops. The FCIC would accept wheat in payment for the insurance premiums covering crop losses of 50 to 75 percent of average yield for unavoidable causes. It also authorized the secretary of agriculture to establish a Surplus Reserve Loan Corporation with $100 million in capital to provide assistance to farmers. Finally, four regional research laboratories were established in Albany, California; Peoria, Illinois; New Orleans, Louisiana; and Wyndmoor, Pennsylvania. They would specialize in agricultural research designed to improve soil quality and productivity.

In March 1938 farmers participated in government sponsored elections to approve the compulsory marketing quotas. The results were overwhelmingly favorable with 1,189,000 cotton growers approving them and only 97,000 opposed. Tobacco farmers favored the quotas by 251,000 to 43,000. But even with the Agricultural Adjustment Act of 1938, the farm problem was not resolved. Crop surpluses continued to mount, so much so that large volumes of wheat and cotton had to be dumped abroad in 1938 and 1939. Despite six years of effort, the New Deal* farm program was a failure, and an agricultural disaster was averted only by the outbreak of World War II. (William E. Leuchtenburg, *Franklin D. Roosevelt and the New Deal, 1932-1940*, 1963; Edward L. Schapsmeier and Frederick H. Schapsmeier, *Henry A. Wallace of Iowa: The Agrarian Years, 1910-1940*, 1968.)

AGRICULTURAL ADJUSTMENT ADMINISTRATION On May 12, 1933, President Franklin D. Roosevelt* signed the Agricultural Adjustment Act* into law, making the Voluntary Domestic Allotment Plan the federal government's major agricultural policy. The long-range goal of the law was to attain "parity"* for farmers—an economic balance between the prices received for farm commodities and the prices paid for manufactured goods equivalent to the mix existing between 1909 and 1914 (1919 to 1929 for cotton). The secretary of agriculture was to enter into "marketing agreements" with individual farmers to reduce their production. Wheat, cotton, corn, hogs, rice, tobacco, and milk were designated as "basic commodities." By reducing the supply of those basic commodities, the administration hoped to raise commodity prices toward parity levels. The Agricultural Adjustment Administration was established to administer the program, and Secretary of Agriculture Henry Wallace* named George N. Peek,* the veteran leader of the McNary-Haugen plan for dumping surpluses abroad, as AAA administrator. He named Charles J. Brand as co-administrator.

Chester Davis* was given control of the Division of Production; M. L. Wilson,* the Wheat Section; Howard R. Tolley,* the Special Crops Section; and Mordecai Ezekiel* was designated economic adviser to the secretary of agriculture.

The AAA was immediately embroiled in controversy, both from external criticism and internal struggles. The delay in passing the legislation left Wallace with a dilemma: sows had already farrowed and cotton had already been planted during the congressional debates over the farm program. Huge surpluses already abounded in those commodities, and Wallace feared that another bumper year would completely undermine prices and saddle the AAA with an impossible burden. So he decided to order the destruction of 6 million little pigs and 200,000 sows and the plow-up of 10 million acres of cotton. The decision was a realistic one given the administration's commitment to production cutbacks, but it generated a storm of protest. Critics never let Wallace forget the decision. The AAA also encountered criticism from the left, particularly from John Simpson* of the National Farmers' Union* and Milo Reno* of the National Farmers' Holiday Association. Both accused the AAA of being the tool of the American Farm Bureau Federation,* of ignoring the suffering of millions of small farmers, and of producing no tangible results. The pressure applied by Simpson and Reno forced the administration to broaden farm programs, leading to passage of the Federal Farm Bankruptcy Act of 1934* and establishment of the Commodity Credit Corporation,* Federal Surplus Relief Corporation,* and increased spending activities by the Farm Credit Administration.*

Internally, the AAA was also caught up in a bitter struggle over policy. George Peek and Charles Brand immediately became critics of the idea of crop reduction. For years they had campaigned for exporting farm surpluses to foreign markets, with the government making up the difference between the domestic and foreign prices received. This had been the central theme of the unsuccessful McNary-Haugen plan during the 1920s. Wallace tried to convince Peek and Brand of the futility of foreign dumping and the rationality of production controls, but neither could be converted. Both became obstacles to the success of the Agricultural Adjustment Administration. Brand resigned in September 1933 and Peek in December 1933. Peek then became Roosevelt's "Special Adviser on Foreign Trade." Chester Davis was named chief of the AAA and Howard R. Tolley his assistant.

By early 1934 more than 3 million farmers were participating in the AAA program. They had also been organized into more than 4,000 local associations on the county level to implement production control. The elected committees were composed of more than 100,000 farmers, and they determined allotments for their areas. County agents from the land-grant colleges worked with the committees, which greatly enhanced the power of the American Farm Bureau Federation. The program evolved in 1933 and 1934 with farmers and government agents negotiating the differences between needs and resources. In the Midwest, where corn and hog production was the greatest concern, the government asked farmers to reduce corn production by 20 percent from 1932-1933 levels and hog production by 25 percent. In return, the government would pay them 30¢ a bushel for corn they did not raise and $5 a head for the pigs not produced. Similar quotas were developed for tobacco, cotton, potatoes, milk, rice, and wheat. The major problem, however, was that farmers exaggerated the size of their 1932-1933 crop, hoping to maximize their production for 1933-1934 as well as receive government checks. Farmers protested when the AAA questioned their 1932-1933 estimates, and out of the negotiations the final quotas were considerably less than 25 percent for most crops. The great droughts of 1934 further complicated the picture by dramatically driving up feed prices and forcing the AAA to allow the production of forage crops on contracted acreage. Despite the controversy, however, corn and hog producers ratified the AAA program by a three to one margin in their elections in October 1934. Tens of thousands of farmers were saved from ruin by the government checks in 1934. The Jones-Connally Farm Relief Act of 1934* added barley, rye, peanuts, flax, cattle, and grain sorghum as basic "commodities" covered by the AAA,* and the Jones-Costigan Sugar Act of 1934 did the same for sugar beets and sugar cane.

But the AAA had not been nearly as successful in achieving parity because huge surpluses still dominated agricultural markets in the United States. In the South, the AAA had negotiated 1,030,433 contracts, reducing the total cotton acreage by 10,487,991 acres, which supposedly meant 4,489,467 fewer bales. The contracts had asked farmers to reduce production by 25 to 50 percent, and in 1934-1935 the government wanted a 55 to 65 percent reduction. But because the program was voluntary, the AAA had experienced a great deal of trouble getting farmers to comply with their contracts. So in 1934 the AAA moved to a more regulated program through the Bankhead Cotton Control Act of 1934.* Under the law, growers received tax-exempt certificates for their contracted crop. The total of all tax-exempt certificates would equal the predetermined adjusted crop quota of ten million, 500 pound bales. A heavy tax was imposed on cotton at the ginning level. The Kerr-Smith Tobacco Control Act of 1934* and Warren Potato Control Act of 1935* did the same for those crops as a means of reducing cheating on the contracts. Like the corn and hog producers, cotton, tobacco, and potato producers had complained about the small quotas they received, but they still ratified the program.

A major problem facing the AAA, however, was the general problem of southern agriculture. Most of the farm leaders and agricultural economists who had developed the domestic allotment concept had been the products of mid-western agriculture where farm tenancy was not a significant question. But in the South, more than 700,000 farms were operated by sharecroppers and tenants, and when landlords signed the acreage reduction contracts, tens of thousands of tenant families were thrown off the land. Jobless and homeless, their plight became a national scandal. In 1934 Norman Thomas,* leader of the Socialist Party of America,* helped form the Southern Tenant Farmers' Union* to organize tenant farmers in an association capable of entering into collective bargaining arrangements with landlords. Inside the AAA, a group of liberal reformers became sympathetic to the tenant farmer situation. Jerome Frank,* head of the AAA Legal Division, along with other lawyers and AAA leaders like Gardner Jackson,* Victor Rotnem, Francis Shea, Frederick C. Howe,* Lee Pressman,* and Alger Hiss,* began campaigning to shift the AAA away from its large commercial farm and landlord orientation toward a greater concern for tenant farmers and farm laborers. In 1935, when Chester Davis was out of town, Frank and the others wrote a new interpretation for cotton reduction contracts making it illegal for landlords to displace any tenants. Enraged about what he considered insubordination and worried that southern landlords might no longer back the AAA, Chester Davis fired Frank, Shea, Pressman, and Jackson on February 5, 1935. Howe and Hiss resigned later. This "purge of 1935" only increased criticism of the AAA's insensitivity to the plight of poor people. In May 1935 Roosevelt responded to the criticism by creating the Resettlement Administration,* under the direction of Rexford Tugwell,* to give concrete assistance to displaced tenants. In 1936 Roosevelt also appointed a Special Committee on Farm Tenancy,* with Wallace as chairman, to study the problem of the increasing number of landless tenants. The recommendations of the Special Committee became the foundation for the Bankhead-Jones Farm Tenancy Act of 1937* creating the Farm Security Administration.*

Although criticisms from the left helped shape AAA policy between 1933 and 1937, criticism from the right all but destroyed the agency. Many conservatives described the AAA as "socialistic agriculture," but the real threat came from people who viewed the AAA as unconstitutional. In particular, the AAA had attempted to collect processing taxes from William H. Butler and his associates, receivers of the bankrupt Hoosac Mills Corporation. They rejected the claim and sued in the federal courts. On January 6, 1936, the United States Supreme Court* declared the AAA unconstitutional, claiming that agricultural problems were local, not national, issues, and therefore beyond federal control. Consequently, the AAA was a violation of the Tenth Amendment. The Court also complained that the federal program did not operate on the basis of voluntary contracts but on coercion.

Enraged about the Court's unwillingness to let the federal government deal with the economic crisis, the Department of Agriculture prepared new legislation which became law on February 29, 1936, as the Soil Conservation and Domestic Allotment Act.* The law allowed the Agricultural Adjustment Administration to continue to control agricultural output by benefit payments to farmers who practiced soil conservation in cooperation with government guidelines. Farmers who joined the program leased to the government the land they had removed from the production of soil-depleting crops and received government checks for the lease. Chester Davis, whose relationship with Wallace had soured since the "purge of 1935," resigned from the AAA, and Howard R. Tolley became the new administrator.

But despite the controversies over quotas, tenants, and constitutionality and the general support of the commercial farming community for the AAA, it had not made much headway toward its goal of achieving parity. The Soil Conservation and Domestic Allotment Act proved insufficient because not enough farmers voluntarily limited production. The cotton crop in 1936 had reached an unprecedented 18 million bales, driving prices down, and similar forces were at work on wheat, corn, and tobacco. Farm lobbyists were demanding increases in subsidies, fewer production restrictions, and export dumping, but Henry Wallace still wanted to achieve parity and his idea of the "ever-normal granary."* The Agricultural Adjustment Act of 1938* addressed farm demands and Wallace's vision. To avoid problems with the Supreme Court, the act eliminated all processing taxes and funded the program from the federal treasury, allowed the AAA to set compulsory production quotas once two-thirds of the affected farmers had approved in referenda elections, and recognized the idea of the "ever-normal granary" by allowing the Commodity Credit Corporation to make loans on surplus crops at prices slightly below the parity levels of 1909-1914. Bumper crops would be stored under government auspices, with farmers repaying the loans and selling the surplus during low production years when prices were above parity. The act also established a Federal Crop Insurance Corporation.* In March 1938 farmers overwhelmingly approved the plan in referenda elections. But even that legislation did not solve the problem. The Agricultural Adjustment Administration, by getting badly-needed money into the hands of farmers, greatly relieved suffering, but it had not restructured the farm economy as Henry Wallace had originally envisioned. Farm surpluses still abounded, and only the outbreak of World War II, with its tremendous demand for food and fibre, absorbed those surpluses and achieved the goal of parity. (Dean Albertson, *Roosevelt's Farmer. Claude R. Wickard in the New Deal*, 1961; Edward L. Schapsmeier and Frederick H. Schapsmeier, *Henry A. Wallace of Iowa: The Agrarian Years, 1910-1940*, 1968.)

AIR MAIL ACT OF 1934 With the introduction of air mail in 1918, the Post Office Department assumed responsibility for flying the mail; but in 1925, when the Kelly Act was passed, the actual carrying of air mail was handed over to commercial lines holding government contracts. Although the contracts were awarded to the low-bidders, government subsidies to air mail carriers became commonplace in the late 1920s and early 1930s to help companies cover high operating costs. By 1931 the Post Office was awarding contracts to a few large companies without competitive bidding, and in 1933 a Senate investigation led by Senator Hugo Black* of Alabama exposed the practice. As the scandal surfaced, President Franklin D. Roosevelt* blamed the previous Republican administration, had Postmaster General James Farley* cancel all contracts, and in February 1934 turned air mail carrying over to the U.S. Army Air Corps. Republicans began accusing Roosevelt of trying to "socialize" America, and their charges became even more hostile when several army pilots died in crashes while carrying the mail. In May 1934, pending federal legislation, Roosevelt turned the air mail back over to private carriers. Dozens of bills were presented in Congress to solve the crisis, some advocating complete laissez-faire and others wanting to use the scandal to bring about complete federal regulation of the airline industry through an independent agency. In June, Congress passed an interim measure—the Air Mail Act of 1934. It outlawed monopolistic holding companies in the air mail business, required competitive bidding for contracts, established maximum rates and mail loads, and gave the Interstate Commerce Commission* certain regulatory powers. (Thomas T. Spencer, "The Air Mail Controversy of 1934," *Mid-America*, LXII:161-172, 1980.)

ALDRICH, WINTHROP WILLIAMS Winthrop Aldrich was born in Providence, Rhode Island, on November 2, 1885. He graduated from Harvard in 1907 and from the Harvard Law School in 1910. Aldrich began practicing law in 1912, joined the firm of Byrne, Cutcheon & Taylor in 1916, and served in the naval reserve during World War I. After the war Aldrich returned to his law practice, this time as a partner in Murray, Aldrich & Webb, where he remained until 1929, specializing in banking and finance law. In 1929 he was named president of the Equitable Trust Company. One year later, he rose to the peak of American banking when named president of Chase National Bank. Aldrich possessed a vision of national economic planning, as long as it was part of the private sector, and in 1933 he joined the Business Advisory Council,* a New Deal* group of businessmen ready to advise the federal government on economic matters. Aldrich felt comfortable with the National Recovery Administration* and urged its extension in 1934 and 1935, just before it was declared unconstitutional in the *Schechter** case. After 1934, however, he grew increasingly disenchanted with the New Deal. He opposed the Banking Act of 1935,* which he viewed as a dangerous form of bureaucratic centralization, fought against the "court-packing" proposal* in 1937, called for an end of work relief in 1936 and 1937, and resisted the reorganization plans of 1938 and 1939. In 1935 Aldrich became chairman of the board of Chase National Bank and remained there until 1953 when President Dwight Eisenhower named him ambassador to England. Aldrich served at the Court of St. James until 1957. He died on February 25, 1974. (*New York Times*, February 26, 1974.)

ALEXANDER, WILL WINTON Will W. Alexander, authority on race relations and farm poverty, was born in Marrisville, Missouri, in 1884. He graduated from Scarritt-Morrisville College in 1908 and went into the Methodist ministry. Alexander had parishes in Nashville and Murfreesboro, Tennessee, between 1911 and 1917, but he gradually became interested in more direct forms of social action. Particularly concerned about rural black poverty, Alexander grew frustrated with the ministry's inability to make much difference in the fight against poverty. He left the ministry in 1917 and became executive director of the Commission on Interracial Cooperation in 1919. In 1930 Alexander was appointed president of Dillard University in New Orleans.

Alexander left Dillard University in 1935 to become assistant administrator of the Resettlement Administration,* where he worked under the direction of Rexford G. Tugwell.* Shortly before his appointment, his book *The Collapse of Cotton Tenancy* was published, where he vigorously argued that the only answer for the problem of farm tenancy in America was government programs to assist the poor in buying their own land. Tugwell was impressed with Alexander's grasp of the problem and made him his assistant. During the 1920s Alexander had also been an outspoken critic of the Ku Klux Klan and had served as chairman of the Social Science Research Council's Advisory Commission on Racial Problems. He was eminently qualified for work in the Resettlement Administration. In 1937, when the Resettlement Administration was absorbed by the new Farm Security Administration,* President Franklin D. Roosevelt* named Alexander to head the agency.

Alexander's tenure with the Farm Security Administration was a mirror image of the agency's history. The FSA was the most radical of any New Deal* program because it looked to the elimination of migratory labor, farm tenancy, and sharecropping, and the creation of a new rural social order based on widespread ownership of property. While it may have inspired hope among many poor tenant farmers, academic liberals, and social workers, the FSA enraged vested interests, especially large landowners dependent on cheap labor and merchants able to exploit debt-ridden tenants. The Farm Security Administration inspired no end of criticism about its radicalism and "communist-leanings" and was phased out in 1942. Will Alexander retired as head of the FSA in 1940 and returned to private life. He died on January 13, 1956. (Sidney Baldwin, *Poverty and Politics: The Rise and Decline of the Farm Security Administration*, 1968; *New York Times*, January 14, 1956.)

ALSBERG, HENRY Born in 1881, Henry Alsberg was a journalism graduate of Columbia in 1900 and then took his law degree. He spent one year at Harvard studying literature, three years in private law practice, and five years as an editorial writer for the New York *Evening Post*. Alsberg then became secretary to the American ambassador to Turkey in 1916 and travelled widely throughout Europe and the Middle East. His intense concern with the plight of European Jews made him a bitter critic of the young Soviet regime. During those years he also represented a number of American publications as a foreign correspondent, including the *Nation* and the socialist *Call*. A friend of Jacob Baker, who was director of Work Relief for the Federal Emergency Relief Administration,* Alsberg joined the agency in 1934 and became supervisor of reports. He was especially concerned about the plight of unemployed journalists, researchers, and writers, and used FERA funds to employ them to draft community geography and culture reports. In August 1935 Alsberg was named national director of the Federal Writers' Project,* where he presided over the American Guide.* More editor than administrator, Alsberg was politically naive and not a very successful defender of the FWP against congressional critics. His own anti-Soviet attitudes early in the1920s did help him defend the FWP against charges of Communist infiltration, but he still had to leave the project in 1938. Henry G. Alsberg died in Palo Alto, California, on November 2, 1970. (William F. McDonald, *Federal Relief Administration and the Arts*, 1969; *New York Times*, November 3, 1970.)

ALTMEYER, ARTHUR JOSEPH Arthur J. Altmeyer was born in De Pere, Wisconsin, on May 8, 1891. He graduated from the University of Wisconsin in 1914, and after working as a teacher and principal, he accepted appointment as statistician for the Wisconsin Tax Committee. Altmeyer became chief statistician in 1920. He wrote *The Industrial Commission* in 1932 and *General Accident Statistics for Wisconsin* in 1933, after which President Franklin D. Roosevelt* named him to head the NRA* Compliance Division. After the NRA was declared unconstitutional in 1935, Altmeyer went to work on Roosevelt's Committee on Economic Security,* and became chairman of the committee in 1937. While on the committee Altmeyer advocated coordination of unemployment insurance programs and employment agencies, as well as extending the old-age and survivors' insurance programs to cover temporary disability. He also wanted to lower the retirement age for women to sixty and extend coverage to millions of people exempted because they were domestic workers, self-employed, or employees of religious institutions. Altmeyer also served as a member of the Social Security Board between 1935 and 1937 and as chairman of the board between 1937 and 1946. His title was changed to commissioner of Social Security, and he served there until 1953. After leaving the federal government, Altmeyer served on a number of international social insurance commissions and taught as a visiting professor at several universities, including the University of Utah, the University of Chicago, and the University of Wisconsin. Arthur J. Altmeyer died on October 17, 1972. (*New York Times*, October 18, 1972.)

AMERICAN CHRISTIAN DEFENDERS Led by Colonel Eugene Nelson Sanctuary, the American Christian Defenders campaigned against Franklin D. Roosevelt* and the New Deal* because they believed the president was intent on sabotaging America in order to bring about a "world Jewish state where only Jews will own property and reap profits." Anti-Semitic and anti-black, the American Christian Defenders were openly pro-fascist and pro-Nazi during the 1930s. (George Wolfskill and John A. Hudson, *All but the People. Franklin D. Roosevelt and His Critics, 1933-1939*, 1969.)

AMERICAN COALITION OF PATRIOTIC, CIVIC, AND FRATERNAL SOCIETIES The American Coalition of Patriotic, Civic, and Fraternal Societies was an umbrella organization of patriotic, fascist, and anti-New Deal groups in the mid-1930s. Its leader was John B. Trevor, and the coalition had ninety-four organizations in 1934 and 125 in 1939. Strongly anti-Semitic in tone as well as intensely anti-Roosevelt, the coalition consisted of a wide range of people, including Bainbridge Colby, secretary of state under Woodrow Wilson, and

George Sylvester Viereck, a Nazi propagandist. (George Wolfskill and John A. Hudson, *All but the People. Franklin D. Roosevelt and His Critics, 1933-1939*, 1969.)

AMERICAN COMMONWEALTH POLITICAL FEDERATION The American Commonwealth Political Federation was established in 1935 in Chicago by several left-wing organizations, including the League for Independent Political Action,* Farmer-Labor Political Federation, Wisconsin Progressive party,* and Minnesota's Farmer-Labor party.* A number of farm leaders, intellectuals, socialists, and union leaders supported the federation. Thomas Amlie* was elected chairperson, with John H. Bosch, vice-chairperson; Paul H. Douglas, treasurer; Howard Y. Williams, national organizer; and Alfred Bingham, executive secretary. Their hope was to form a new coalition third-party to unite liberal Democrats, progressive Republicans, and socialists. They called for public ownership of major industries, more public works projects for the unemployed, unemployment and old-age insurance, veterans' bonuses, nationalization of banks, redistribution of national income, civil rights for minorities, federal aid to education, and a mortgage moratorium. Hopes for a third-party never materialized. Not only did the various liberal interest-groups argue over public policies, but the New Deal's* own shift to the left after 1934 tended to undermine the American Commonwealth Political Federation's membership. The organization dissipated in 1937. (Donald R. McCoy, *Angry Voices: Left-of-Center Politics in the New Deal*, 1958.)

AMERICAN FARM BUREAU FEDERATION The American Farm Bureau Federation, under the leadership of President Edward A. O'Neal* and Vice-President Earl C. Smith, was the most influential farm organization in the United States during the New Deal.* By 1933 the farm bureau had evolved from a local educational agency into a national political organization. The first local bureau was formed in 1911; the first state federation of county bureaus, in 1915. These early associations were dedicated to the dissemination of scientific methods in farming and to improved standards of rural living. The Smith-Lever Act of 1914 created the federal-state Agricultural Extension Service and provided grants for the states to support county agricultural extension agents, who generally worked in close cooperation with local farm bureaus. The formation in 1919-1920 of the American Farm Bureau Federation united the state organizations. Although some state federations emphasized economic cooperation and the national organization offered such economic benefits as group insurance, the main purpose of the national federation was to influence federal agricultural policy.

With the coming of the Great Depression, membership in the farm bureau dropped to just 163,000, but the organization carried a firm set of tenets into the 1930s. The first was that it should speak primarily to questions of economic policy, not social concerns. The AFBF represented commercial farmers, generally the more prosperous ones. Its chief goal was "parity"—the re-establishment of the purchasing power of farmers to what it had been between 1909-1914 through political lobbying. The AFBF was effective in the early years of the New Deal for several reasons. O'Neal, a southern Democrat, and Smith, a midwestern Republican, brought together the two major agricultural regions in a non-partisan format. The AFBF was a general farm organization, not one specialized around a particular commodity. The AFBF was willing to work with Franklin D. Roosevelt's* administration and its secretary of agriculture, Henry A. Wallace,* to forge a farm program addressing the pressing questions of commodity surpluses and farm mortgage debt.

The AFBF quickly swung its support to the concept of a voluntary domestic allotment program to curtail production, and the United States Department of Agriculture wrote the goal of parity into its legislation, omitting reference to the "cost of production" goal advocated by the National Farmers' Union.* As the Agricultural Adjustment Act* went to Congress in 1933, the AFBF supported its passage; afterward, local bureaus worked to secure farmer cooperation. After disallowance of the AAA by the Supreme Court* in 1936, the AFBF labored to ensure that the program's successor, the Soil Conservation and Domestic Allotment Act of 1936,* retained effective controls on production. The AFBF continued to work for the principle of parity achieved through production controls during passage of the Agricultural Adjustment Act of 1938,* obtaining in addition the issuance of "parity payments" to supplement farmers' incomes when prices were below parity levels.

By this time, however, the working relationship between the AFBF and the USDA had deteriorated. After 1935 the two entities frequently disagreed over such issues as the USDA's determination to remove administration of AAA programs from the extension service; the USDA's practice of developing farm program proposals in-house, within the Bureau of Agricultural Economics, instead of merely soliciting them from farm organizations; suspicions on the part of the AFBF that the USDA was seeking closer alliance with the National Farmers' Union, especially through the credit policies of the Farm Security Administration;* the belief by the AFBF that the Department of Agriculture should advocate the interests of farmers exclusively rather than attempt to shape farm policy for larger social goals; and attempts by Secretary Wallace during the election of 1940 to claim for the Democratic party* exclusive credit for New Deal farm policy. The AFBF, however, had prospered during the 1930s. Its membership, which stood at 163,000 in 1933, continued to grow, reaching 1.3 million by 1948 and 3.3 million by 1983. (Christiana M. Campbell, *The Farm Bureau and the New Deal: A Study of the Making of National Farm Policy, 1933-1940*, 1962.)

THOMAS D. ISERN

AMERICAN FEDERATION OF LABOR Since before the Civil War, skilled workers had tried to organize at the national level, and in the process they had distanced themselves from semi-skilled and unskilled workers who lacked the bargaining power and job control that craftsmen had. Organized in 1886 as a coalition of many national unions, and directed by Samuel Gompers, the American Federation of Labor became the dominant force in the United States labor movement. Eschewing radical politics and socialism in favor of more conservative wages, hours, and working-conditions demands, the AFL confined its organizational activities to skilled workers or strategic, semi-skilled workers in a wide variety of industries. By 1933 there were more than 2,317,000 members in the AFL affiliate unions. Under the direction of William Green,* the AFL was a major supporter of New Deal* relief, recovery, labor, and social welfare legislation. At the same time, despite the defection of the CIO* unions, the AFL made major membership gains in the 1930s. Between 1936 and 1937 the AFL lost 1,104,900 members because of the suspension of the CIO unions, but at the same time recruited 760,000 new members. Between 1937 and 1945 another 4 million workers joined AFL affiliates. The major gains came in the construction, transport, communications, and service industries where small firms were still dominant. Capable of adapting to technological and organizational change and prospering in the pro-labor atmosphere of the National Labor Relations Act of 1935,* the AFL played a critical role in the expansion of the labor movement. (Christopher L. Tomlins, "AFL Unions in the 1930s: Their Performance in Historical Perspective," *Journal of American History*, LXV:1021-1042, 1979.)

AMERICAN GUARD, THE WHITE MAN'S PARTY The American Guard was headed by Olov E. Tietzow, an intense anti-Semite, and based in Chicago during the 1930s. Tietzow was fanatically anti-Roosevelt, and in his work *Aryan Americanism* he openly accused the administration of being the "Jewish New Deal." As far as Tietzow was concerned, America had fallen prey to the "international Jewish conspiracy." He also predicted that if Franklin D. Roosevelt* was not stopped, the United States would eventually find itself in a civil war between Jews and New Dealers on the one side and "Gentile Americans" on the other. Bloodshed would be enormous, but the Gentiles would eventually triumph. (George Wolfskill and John A. Hudson, *All but the People. Franklin D. Roosevelt and His Critics, 1933-1939*, 1969.)

AMERICAN GUIDE (See the FEDERAL WRITERS' PROJECT.)

AMERICAN LABOR PARTY Because of the National Labor Relations Act* and other pro-union legislation, President Franklin D. Roosevelt* and the New Deal* had won the solid support of organized labor by 1936. The Republicans nominated Alf Landon* for president, and to support Roosevelt's candidacy, John L. Lewis* and other union leaders had established Labor's Non-Partisan League.* Unlike any previous election in United States history, the unions were using their political power in behalf of a single candidate. In New York, Sidney Hillman* of the Amalgamated Clothing Workers and David Dubinsky* of the International Ladies Garment Workers had helped to organize the American

Labor party. The needle trades unions in New York had traditionally had powerful Socialist ties, but the New Deal had captured their loyalties. Dubinsky had even resigned from the Socialist Party.* But although many socialists wanted to vote for Roosevelt, they did not want to endorse the Democratic party,* which they saw as a stooge of southern Democrats and Tammany Hall. The American Labor party, with Roosevelt as its nominee, gave them the alternative of voting for the president without voting for a Democrat. In the election of 1936,* Roosevelt won 274,924 votes in New York on the American Labor party ticket. Nationwide, the Socialist candidate Norman Thomas* won only 187,720 votes. Although largely confined to New York City, the American Labor party was influential politically, contributing to the mayoral victories of Fiorello H. La Guardia* in 1937 and 1941 and the congressional victory of Vito Marcantonio* in 1938. (Max D. Danish, *The World of David Dubinsky*, 1957.)

AMERICAN LIBERTY LEAGUE The American Liberty League, an unappeasable foe of Franklin D. Roosevelt* and the New Deal,* was the voice of political conservatism in the decade of the 1930s. It drew to its membership a substantial cross-section of the leaders of American business, industry, finance, law, and the professions. It is no exaggeration to say that, to that time, no one organization in the history of the United States marshalled so much wealth, prestige, and managerial skill to unhorse a president as the American Liberty League did in the fight against Roosevelt.

The formation of the ALL was announced to the press on August 22, 1934. Its goals were "to defend and uphold the Constitution . . . to teach the necessity of respect for the rights of persons and property . . . to preserve the ownership and lawful use of property when acquired." But regardless of its laudable goals, everyone understood that the ALL, from the outset, was formed to oppose the New Deal.

The president of the ALL was Jouett Shouse.* Shouse, a power in the Democratic party,* was a former congressman from Kentucky, floor leader for William Gibbs McAdoo* at the Democratic National Conventions of 1920 and 1924, and executive chairman of the Democratic National Committee from 1928 to 1932. The five member board of directors included: John W. Davis* and Alfred E. Smith,* Democratic presidential nominees in 1924 and 1928; Republicans James W. Wadsworth,* a former senator and representative; Nathan Miller, former governor of New York; and Irenee du Pont. Du Pont had been a Republican, but he had voted for Al Smith in 1928 and Franklin Roosevelt in 1932.

Organizing the ALL was fairly easy because many, maybe most, of the leading members of the ALL had worked together in an earlier organization, the Association Against the Prohibition Amendment,* that had carried on a spectacularly successful campaign resulting in the repeal of the Eighteenth Amendment. When plans for the ALL were being discussed, it was widely agreed that former members of the Association Against the Prohibition Amendment offered "the best nucleus around which to build such a new organization.'' Jouett Shouse, it should be noted, had also been the president of the AAPA.

The ALL never received significant popular support. It reached its maximum membership of 124,856 during the summer of 1936 then tailed off badly after the presidential election that fall. What it lacked in numerical strength, however, it tried to make up in wealth and influence. During its six-year history, 1934-1940, the ALL collected and disbursed $1,200,000. Half of this amount was spent during the 1936 election year. The ALL raised almost as much money as each of the two major parties during 1935 and 1936, and most of the money came from a modest group of prominent business men, two dozen at the most. In 1936, for example, one of every four dollars spent came from the du Pont family.

Most of the money went into a massive publicity campaign. The ALL, using the techniques that had been tried and tested by the AAPA, launched an extensive pamphlet series. Between August 1934 and November 1936, the ALL issued some 135 pamphlets, approximately one a week. Copies were supplied in advance were they would do the most good. The Washington bureau of some 350 newspapers, the press associations, and well-known editors and columnists received advance copies, resulting in wide publicity. In addition to the pamphlets, the ALL distributed both a monthly bulletin and a leaflet series, and used the radio extensively for speeches, documentaries, and forums. The most notable of these activities was a 1936 dinner in Washington, D.C., sponsored by the ALL, at which Al Smith, before a national radio audience, charged the New Deal with being communistic.

The ALL combined criticism of the New Deal with a concise and thorough summary of conservative political thought. The chief argument was simply that the New Deal endangered the Constitution. Moreover, the centralization of government power under the New Deal would eventually produce tyranny; economic planning and economic regulation were based on false economic assumptions that retarded natural recovery; tax policies damaged private enterprise; spending and unbalanced budgets were producing a dangerous inflation; banking policies were politicizing banking; monetary policies were threatening the credit of the United States; and most New Deal measures were socialistic, fascistic, or both. In summary, the cure for these New Deal excesses lay in the Congress and in its willingness to reassert its responsibility for preserving the Constitution and the traditional form of government.

If the object of the ALL was to stop the New Deal and rid the country of Franklin Roosevelt, it was a failure. It probably failed because it represented economic and political conservatism at a time when both were under attack and out of favor. Defeating the ALL was comparatively simple for Roosevelt and the New Dealers. Because the ALL leaders inevitably supported Alf Landon* and the Republican party* in the election of 1936,* Democratic strategy was, according to Democratic National Chairman James A. Farley,* ''to ignore the Republican Party and to concentrate fire on the Liberty League.'' ''It was simple,'' said another member of the administration; what we did was "parade their directorate before the people."

The ALL severely curtailed its activities after the defeat in the election of 1936. Soon foreign affairs and the threat of war diverted the attention of the administration from domestic affairs. By 1938 the domestic New Deal was most certainly over. The ALL, which was concerned almost entirely with domestic affairs, had now outlived its usefulness. In 1940 the organization officially dissolved. (George Wolfskill, *The Revolt of the Conservatives: A History of the American Liberty League, 1934-1940*, 1962.)

GEORGE WOLFSKILL

AMERICAN VIGILANT INTELLIGENCE FEDERATION Led by Harry A. Jung, the American Vigilant Intelligence Federation was an intensely anti-Semitic, anti-Roosevelt organization. The Federation frequently distributed the phony "Protocols of the Elders of Zion" and argued that Franklin D. Roosevelt* was Jewish, and there was a Jewish conspiracy to take over the world. Throughout the 1930s, Harry A. Jung and the American Vigilant Intelligence Federation maintained a continuous criticism of Roosevelt, the New Deal,* and Jews. (George Wolfskill and John A. Hudson, *All but the People. Franklin D. Roosevelt and His Critics, 1933-1939*, 1969.)

AMLIE, THOMAS RYUM Thomas Amlie, the radical progressive congressman from Wisconsin during the New Deal,* was born on a farm near Binford, North Dakota, on April 17, 1897. Amlie attended the University of North Dakota and the University of Minnesota and graduated from the University of Wisconsin Law School in 1923. After law school Amlie practiced law in Beloit and then Elkhorn, Wisconsin, and became a political organizer for the Nonpartisan League.* Influenced by the writings of Karl Marx and Thorstein Veblen, Amlie's progressivism developed consistently to the left in the 1920s; when the depression swept through the country in 1930, he saw it as evidence of the weaknesses of capitalism. In 1931 and 1932 Amlie served as president of the Walworth County Bar Association and was elected as a Republican, albeit a progressive one, to fill the congressional seat vacated by the death of Henry Allen Cooper. He lost that seat in the Democratic landslide of 1932 but continued his own political development, becoming president of the Farmer-Labor Political Federation in 1933. In those early years of the New Deal, Amlie called for an end to a profit-based economy and establishment of a production-for-use economy, elimination of absentee-owned property, and national economic planning. At the same time, Amlie opposed communism as an irrelevant movement in the United States.

Amlie became involved in the Wisconsin Progressive party* in 1934 and was returned to the House of Representatives. During his two terms in Congress, Amlie joined a small group of radical congressmen which included Maury Maverick* of Texas, Vito Marcantonio* of New York, and Ernest Lundeen* of Minnesota. They consistently advocated increases in government spending, national economic planning, confiscation of excess corporate profits, social welfare legislation, and protection of labor rights. But as anti-New Deal sentiments developed in the late 1930s, Amlie's point of view became politically vulnerable. Along with Progressive Governor Philip La Follette* of Wisconsin, Amlie was swept out of office in the election of 1938* when Republicans seized so many electoral offices there. President Franklin D. Roosevelt* nominated Amlie for a position on the Interstate Commerce Commission* in 1939, but in the ensuing storm of protest from conservatives, Amlie had his name withdrawn and returned to private law practice. (S. L. Wise, "Thomas Amlie and the New Deal," *Mid-America*, LIX:19-38, 1977.)

ANDERSON, MARIAN Born in Philadelphia in 1902, Marian Anderson became internationally known for her dramatic and versatile contralto voice. A student of Guiseppi Boghetti, she appeared with the New York Philharmonic in 1925 after winning a major competition. Soon after, she was awarded a fellowship to continue her musical training. In 1930 she made her European debut at a concert in Berlin, Germany. Under the guidance of Sol Hurok, she travelled throughout Europe in the early 1930s and earned praise from such celebrated musicians as Arturo Toscanini. Her success in Europe established her as one of the world's premier opera singers. She returned to the United States in 1935 and performed in a highly acclaimed tour that included a recital in New York City's Carnegie Hall.

In 1939 Anderson became the center of a controversy that reached all the way to the White House. Her planned concert in Washington, D.C., was cancelled when the Daughters of the American Revolution refused her permission to sing in their Constitution Hall because of her race. Incensed by the actions of the DAR, Eleanor Roosevelt,* a life member of the organization, resigned in protest.

Since a large crowd had been expected to attend the concert, Constitution Hall had been considered the only suitable facility in the town for such a performance. As an alternative, Eleanor Roosevelt helped arrange for a special Easter concert at the Lincoln Memorial. There Anderson sang to a crowd, estimated at 75,000, that stretched from the memorial steps, down along the reflecting pool toward the Washington Monument.

Through her open support of Marian Anderson, Eleanor Roosevelt made a symbolic gesture for all blacks, at a time when such action significantly contributed to the public awareness of racial inequality. Her actions also reflected favorably on the New Deal* policies of President Franklin D. Roosevelt,* who had made equal opportunity one of his administration's goals.

Marian Anderson continued her successful musical career and in 1955 became the first black to perform at the Metropolitan Opera in New York City. She also made lasting contributions to the United States through participation in programs sponsored by the State Department. In 1958 President Dwight Eisenhower named her as a delegate to the United Nations General Assembly. (Marian Anderson,

My Lord, What a Morning, 1956; W. Augustus Low and Virgil A. Clift, eds., *Encyclopedia of Black America*, 1981.)

DAN K. UTLEY

ANDERSON, MARY Mary Anderson was born in Sweden in 1872 and immigrated to the United States in 1888. Her family settled in Chicago, and Anderson went to work in the garment and shoe industries there and became active in union politics. In 1905 Anderson joined the Women's Trade Union League. She was active in the WTUL league for the rest of her life. In 1919 President Woodrow Wilson appointed her director of the new Women's Bureau of the Department of Labor, and she headed the bureau until 1944. Anderson was an active supporter of the NRA's* industry codes because she strongly believed they allowed great advances in labor standards for women. Although she was disappointed in the level of commitment of Secretary of Labor Frances Perkins* toward women's issues, Anderson faithfully worked to enforce Section 7(a), the National Labor Relations Act of 1935,* the Walsh-Healey Public Contracts Act of 1936,* and the Fair Labor Standards Act of 1938.* Mary Anderson retired as head of the Women's Bureau in 1944. She died in January 1964. (Susan Ware, *Beyond Suffrage: Women in the New Deal*, 1981.)

APPLEBY, PAUL HENSON Paul H. Appleby, a longtime assistant to Secretary of Agriculture Henry A. Wallace,* was born on September 13, 1891, in Greene County, Missouri. He graduated from Grinnell College in 1913 and began a journalism career which brought him to Des Moines, Iowa, in 1924 as an editorial writer for the *Des Moines Register and Tribune*. In Des Moines Appleby became socially acquainted with Henry A. Wallace. In 1926 Appleby went to Radford, Virginia, after purchasing two weeklies—the *News Journal* in Radford and the *News Messenger* in Christiansburg. Donald Murphy and Dante M. Pierce, both Wallace's associates on *Wallace's Farmer*, recommended Appleby to serve as an administrative assistant. Wallace offered the job to Appleby, and he accepted in March 1933.

As Wallace's administrative assistant in the Department of Agriculture, Appleby took a broad view of federal government authority. He did not like George Peek's* role in the Agricultural Adjustment Administration* because Peek opposed acreage reduction, and he wanted the Department of Agriculture to move beyond a mere research institution assisting commercial farmers. Appleby became quite sympathetic to the plight of tenant and low-income farmers, and he became closely associated in the department with Jerome Frank* and the urban liberals. When the "purge" of those liberals came in 1935, Appleby managed to stay on as Wallace's assistant, even though AAA administrator Chester Davis* was somewhat upset with his role in the affair. Appleby's survival was largely due to his close relationship with Henry A. Wallace and his consistent habit of adopting a low public profile in the Department of Agriculture. By 1940 Appleby had played an important role in changing the Department of Agriculture from a research to an action agency of the federal government: one concerned with the needs of poor farmers as well as those of large commercial farmers. Paul Appleby died on October 22, 1963 (Gladys L. Baker, " 'And to Act for the Secretary': Paul H. Appleby and the Department of Agriculture, 1933-1940," *Agricultural History*, XLV:235-258, 1971.)

ARNOLD, THURMAN WESLEY Thurman Wesley Arnold was the New Deal's* trustbuster. Born June 2, 1891, in Laramie, Wyoming, Arnold was the son of Constantine and Annie Brockway Arnold. A plain-spoken, generous man, Arnold graduated Phi Beta Kappa from Princeton University in 1911. He received a law degree from Harvard in 1914. Arnold practiced law in Chicago and served in Mexico in Company C, Illinois National Guard, and in World War I as a first lieutenant, 101st Field Artillery. Discharged in 1919, Arnold rejoined his wife, Frances Longan Arnold, whom he had married in New York City on September 4, 1917. Returning to Laramie, he became a homesteader, a sheep rancher, and an attorney-at-law. Arnold served as Laramie's mayor and president of the Lion's Club, taught law at the University of Wyoming, and was the only Democrat in Wyoming's state legislature in 1922. He guided Wyoming's National Guard as judge-advocate general from 1924 to 1927. In 1927 Arnold became dean of the University of West Virginia Law School. He taught three years before becoming a professor of law at Yale in 1930. While at Yale, Arnold served as counsel to the Agriculture Department, as legal adviser to the governor general of the Philippines, and as a trial examiner for the Securities and Exchange Commission.* He wrote *The Symbols of Government* in 1935 and *The Folklore of Capitalism* in 1937, both of which brought him a national reputation.

Arnold departed Yale in March 1938 to assume new duties as assistant attorney general in charge of the Anti-trust Division of the Department of Justice. Arnold's views on the anti-trust issue marked a complete reversal of the government's position. His insistence that direct action set the government's policy, plus stressing consumer protection and increasing consumer purchasing power earned him his trustbuster reputation. Arnold perceived the size of corporations to be meaningless and he preferred to use the "rule of reason" when dealing with trusts. Under his leadership a major effort was instituted to establish an effective national anti-trust program. In order to implement this program, the Anti-trust Division increased from forty to over 280 investigators and lawyers. Arnold moved the government toward large-scale national investigation, use of consent decrees, and evaluation of prospective cases. Director of the Anti-trust Division for five years, Arnold filed 230 suits for monopoly practices or restraint of trade. He resigned from the Department of Justice in 1943 amid allegations that his anti-trust activities obstructed the war effort. Immediately appointed to the United States Court of Appeals for the District of Columbia by President Franklin D. Roosevelt,* Arnold served for two years. Arnold resigned his lifetime court appointment in 1945 to start a private law practice.

Arnold established the firm Arnold, Fortas, and Porter, with Abe Fortas* and

Paul Porter. Arnold undertook the defense in many civil liberties suits. He was particularly active during the McCarthy period and regarded Congressional loyalty investigations as an intrusion on free speech. Arnold reorganized his firm in 1965 when Abe Fortas was appointed to the United States Supreme Court.* He continued to practice law in Washington, D.C., until his death on November 7, 1969, in Alexandria, Virginia. (Ellis W. Hawley, *The New Deal and the Problem of Monopoly; A Study in Economic Ambivalence*, 1966; *New York Times*, November 8, 1969.)

CHARLES E. DARBY, JR.

ASHWANDER ET AL. V. TENNESSEE VALLEY AUTHORITY The Tennessee Valley Authority,* created by an act of Congress on May 18, 1933, (amended August 31, 1935) had entered into a contract with Alabama Power Company (January 4, 1934) to buy certain transmission lines and substations from the power company. The lines in question extended from Wilson Dam at TVA's Muscle Shoals* plant into seven counties within a radius of fifty miles, serving a population of about 190,000 and about 10,000 individual customers. The TVA's objectives were to provide an interchange of hydroelectric energy for the sale of its surplus power to the Alabama Power Company and for mutual restrictions as to the areas to be served in the sale of the power.

The holders of preferred stock in Alabama Power Company first complained to the board of directors of the power company and then to the parent company, Commonwealth and Southern Corporation. But both bodies refused to take any action. The stockholders then brought suit against TVA, contending that TVA's contract with Alabama Power was injurious to the corporate interests and invalid as it exceeded the power of the federal government under the Constitution.

The district court found for the plaintiffs and issued a decree annulling the contract. The circuit court of appeals limited its consideration to the questions of the constitutional authority of Congress to build the Wilson Dam and to the subsequent authority to dispose of the surplus power produced there. The circuit court found that the judgment of the district court was erroneous and reversed the decision.

The Supreme Court* of the United States accepted the case on appeal. The case was argued and submitted on December 19 and 20, 1935, and decided on February 17, 1936. In its deliberations the Supreme Court also confined itself to the narrow issues considered by the circuit court of appeals. The Supreme Court concurred with the judgment of the circuit court, upholding the authority of the federal government to build Wilson Dam under the war and commerce powers of Congress (National Defense Act of June 3, 1916).

On the question of the constitutional authority of TVA to dispose of electric power generated at the Wilson Dam, the Court found that the energy produced there constituted property belonging to the United States and that Section 3, Article 4 of the Constitution expressly gave Congress the power to dispose of such property. In the opinion of the majority, this was a broad grant of power and could be applied to electric energy no less than to mineral resources and real property.

On the question of the authority of TVA to acquire transmission lines, the Court found no constitutional objections. In the opinion of the Court, such lines were simply a facility necessary for disposal of the surplus energy which would otherwise be wasted.

On those narrow issues, the Supreme Court affirmed the decree of the circuit court. Although the decision was hailed by some contemporary commentators as a great victory for the federal government, the Court avoided the larger constitutional issue of government competition with private business by confining its deliberations to those questions raised by the circuit court. (Gerald O. Dykstra and L. G. Dykstra, *Selected Cases on Government and Business*, 1937; Alfred H. Kelly and Winfred A. Harbison, *The American Constitution*, 1970; *Supreme Court Reporter*, LVI:466-480, 1936.)

JOSEPH M. ROWE, JR.

ASSOCIATION AGAINST THE PROHIBITION AMENDMENT Although the Association Against the Prohibition Amendment began meeting informally in 1918 during the ratification process for the Eighteenth Amendment, it was not formally organized until 1920. Its founder was William H. Stayton, a former naval captain with conservative political views. The major political philosophy of the AAPA was that prohibition was dangerous not because it outlawed alcohol but because it represented a centralizing force which destroyed state and local rights. By 1926 the AAPA had a membership of more than 700,000 people in twenty-five states, and it focused most of its energy on lobbying activities. John J. Raskob,* chairman of the Democratic National Committee, and Jouett Shouse,* head of the Democratic National Committee's executive council, were prominent members of the AAPA. Shouse became head of the association in 1932 and campaigned for the election of Franklin D. Roosevelt.* After the Democratic landslide of 1932, the AAPA pressured Congress for approval of the Twenty-First Amendment* and immediate legalization of beer and wine with less than 3.2 percent alcohol content. The AAPA version of the Twenty-First Amendment was the one passed, and twenty-five states used AAPA instructions for ratification. One day after the Twenty-First Amendment was ratified, the AAPA directors formally dissolved the organization. Many of them, however, later joined the American Liberty League* when they became frightened that the New Deal* too was centralizing power in the United States. (David E. Kyvig, "In Revolt against Prohibition: The Association against the Prohibition Amendment and the Movement for Repeal, 1919-1933," Ph.D. dissertation, Northwestern University, 1971.)

ASTOR, WILLIAM VINCENT Born November 15, 1891, in New York City, William Vincent Astor inherited the Astor fortune in 1912 when his father, John Jacob Astor IV, drowned with the sinking of the *Titanic*. He married Helen D.

Huntington in 1914. Astor served as a naval officer during World War I and then returned to private business. Politically, the Astor family had long been staunchly conservative, and Astor supported Warren Harding and Calvin Coolidge during the 1920s, but by 1928 he was gravitating toward the Democrats, supporting Al Smith's* presidential campaign. When Franklin D. Roosevelt* ran for president in 1932, Astor served on the Democratic Finance Committee and contributed $35,000 to the campaign. For several years he was an enthusiastic New Dealer. Together with Mary Harriman Rumsey* and Averell Harriman, he invested in a weekly news magazine, *Today*. Raymond Moley,* assistant secretary of state and a member of Roosevelt's "brain trust,"* edited the magazine, and many people assumed *Today* reflected White House policy. But on June 19, 1935, when President Roosevelt sent a message to Congress expressing the belief that the "transmission from generation to generation of vast fortunes by will, inheritance, or gift is not consistent with the ideals and sentiments of the American people," Astor broke with the administration. Astor and Harriman merged *Today* with *News-Week* in 1937, and they titled the new magazine *Newsweek*. During World War II, Astor served as a convoy commodore carrying war material to Europe and bringing wounded soldiers back home. He died on February 2, 1959. (Lucy Kavaler, *The Astors, An American Legend*, 1966.)

AUSTIN, WARREN ROBINSON Warren R. Austin was born in Highgate, Vermont, on November 12, 1877. He graduated from the University of Vermont in 1899 and studied law privately, working for the firm C. G. Austin & Sons in St. Albans between 1899 and 1902. Austin was admitted to the Vermont bar in 1902. He worked with his father's law firm between 1902 and 1916 and moved to Burlington to practice in 1917. Austin maintained his practice there until 1931, when he was elected as a Republican to the United States Senate. During the New Deal* years, Austin was part of the conservative coalition in the Senate which opposed Franklin D. Roosevelt's* administration, particularly deficit spending, capital gains taxes, pro-labor legislation, executive reorganization, "court-packing",* and relief appropriations. In 1937 Austin worked with Senator Arthur Vandenberg* of Michigan to draft what became known as the "conservative manifesto" opposing the New Deal. After leaving the Senate in 1946, Austin became a special ambassador to the United Nations, where he represented the United States until his retirement in 1953. Warren Austin died on December 25, 1962. (*New York Times*, December 26, 1962.)

AUTOMOBILE LABOR BOARD Section 7(a) of the National Industrial Recovery Act of 1933* had guaranteed the right of labor to bargain collectively with representatives of their own choosing, but it quickly became a source of great controversy when business resisted the idea. President Franklin D. Roosevelt* established a National Labor Board* under the National Recovery Administration* to mediate labor-management disputes and to try to implement Section 7(a), but the business community was more than reluctant to cooperate. The crisis came in the automobile industry in March 1934 when General Motors and Hudson workers threatened to strike unless management agreed to recognize the AFL's* United Automobile Workers Union. Workers also demanded a 20 percent pay increase and reinstatement of workers fired for union activity. When the National Labor Board attempted to mediate, the companies refused to even deal with the government. The National Automobile Chamber of Commerce openly repudiated Section 7(a). Afraid that a strike would stop the modest recovery underway in the automobile industry, Roosevelt wanted a settlement, so instead of supporting the NLB, he appointed a tripartite Automobile Labor Board on March 25, 1934. Leo Wolman* was the impartial board member, with Nicholas Kelley representing management and Richard Byrd representing labor. Roosevelt openly supported management in the ALB's decisions: to employ seniority privileges in hiring and firing, to give legal sanction to company unions and to endorse proportional representation instead of majority rule in choosing bargaining agents. The automobile industry was in effect exempted from Section 7(a) as well as the "Reading formula,"* and the settlement all but destroyed the National Labor Board. The Automobile Labor Board expired after the *Schechter** decision in May 1935 which declared the National Industrial Recovery Act unconstitutional. (Bernard Bellush, *The Failure of the NRA*, 1975; Lewis L. Lorwin and Arthur Wubnig, *Labor Relations Boards*, 1935.)

B

BAILEY, JOSIAH WILLIAM Josiah William Bailey was born on September 14, 1873, in Warrenton, North Carolina. The son of a Baptist preacher, Bailey graduated from Wake Forest College in 1893 and immediately became editor of a Baptist magazine, *The Biblical Recorder*. He remained editor there until 1907. After studying law at Trinity College and Wake Forest in 1907 and 1908, he began to practice law at Raleigh, North Carolina. In 1913, as a loyal Wilsonian Democrat, Bailey received an internal revenue collectorship, which he kept until 1921. During the 1920s, Bailey joined a group of North Carolina Democrats opposed to the political machine of Senator Furnifold M. Simmons. When Simmons mistakenly opposed Alfred E. Smith* in the presidential election of 1928, he lost his hold on the machine, and Bailey defeated him in the senatorial primary of 1930. By the early 1930s Bailey's power in North Carolina almost rivaled what Simmons' had been.

During the 1930s Bailey developed into one of President Franklin D. Roosevelt's* most implacable opponents. Although he professed loyalty to the New Deal* and tried to maintain his patronage connections, Bailey hated the large-scale federal expenditures and the political power which seemed to be gravitating to the executive branch. He privately was anti-New Deal. After the election of 1936,* Bailey's antipathy toward the New Deal became even clearer. He frequently criticized the National Labor Relations Act* and the activities of the National Labor Relations Board*; denounced the whole idea of deficit spending and pump-priming; saw the "court-packing"* scheme as a bald attempt by Roosevelt to take over the Supreme Court* as he had already done the Congress; viewed the executive reorganization plans of 1939 as a move by the president to assume dictatorial authority in the United States; and bitterly opposed the New Deal's willingness to include blacks in the various relief programs. He was also an opponent of the federal anti-lynching bill* because he viewed it as an unnecessary infringement on state prerogatives. During the late 1930s, Bailey became one of the leaders of the conservative Democratic coalition in the Senate. In the elections of 1938* he openly endorsed the men Roosevelt wanted to purge and thus earned Roosevelt's deep resentment. Bailey was a man of strong, moralistic convictions who felt the New Deal was leading the country down the road to totalitarianism, socialism, and perhaps even communism. Yet, when the world went to war in the 1940s, Bailey became one of Roosevelt's strongest supporters. Bailey was re-elected to the Senate in 1942 and died in office on December 15, 1946. (John Robert Moore, *Senator Josiah William Bailey of North Carolina: A Political Biography*, 1968.)

BAKER, NEWTON DIEHL, II Newton D. Baker was born on December 3, 1871, in Martinsburg, West Virginia. He attended the Episcopal High School near Alexandria, Virginia, and graduated from Johns Hopkins in 1892. While at Johns Hopkins he took a class from Woodrow Wilson, who periodically lectured there, and lived at the same boarding house where Wilson stayed during his visits to Baltimore. Baker received a law degree at Washington and Lee University in 1894. After a brief period practicing law in Martinsburg, Baker took a job in Washington, D.C., as private secretary to Democratic Congressman William L. Wilson of West Virginia, who was postmaster general in the second Grover Cleveland administration. Baker lost that job in 1897 when the Republicans took over the White House. He returned to law practice. In 1899 Baker moved his practice to Cleveland, Ohio.

In Cleveland, Baker became involved in local Democratic politics and supported the progressive reforms of Mayor Tom Johnson. Baker became city solicitor under Mayor Johnson in 1901 and remained there until 1912, when he won the mayoralty race. He had also been a vigorous supporter of Woodrow Wilson that year. Four years later President Wilson named Baker as secretary of war in his cabinet, a position he held until 1921. During the 1920s Baker was an advocate of United States entry into the World Court and League of Nations; and with the onset of the Great Depression, he began giving some reluctant thought to running for the presidency. But his interests had shifted from domestic to foreign policy over the years, and he did not project a clear public image on economic questions. In 1932 Baker assumed the role of dark horse candidate but proved unable to stop Franklin D. Roosevelt's* nomination. He campaigned for Roosevelt during the election and was at first pleased with the New Deal,* particularly with its energy and vitality during the first "one hundred days."* But as a nineteenth-century liberal, Baker believed in limited government. Gradually he became alienated from the New Deal bureaucracy and spending programs. The NRA* and TVA* frightened him. Although he never joined such anti-New Deal groups as the American Liberty League,* he found it difficult to be very supportive of President Roosevelt. He was too much a Cleveland Democrat—committed to sound money, fiscal conservatism, tariff reduction, and small government. Newton D. Baker died of heart failure on December 25, 1937. (C. H. Carmer, *Newton D. Baker. A Biography*, 1961.)

BALDWIN, CALVIN BENHAM C. B. Baldwin was born in Radford, Virginia, on August 19, 1902. He was a student at Virginia Polytechnic Institute between 1920 and 1923 and then went to work as a railway shop inspector, rising to assistant to the general foreman. In 1928 Baldwin became manufacturer and owner of the Electric Sales & Service Company of East Radford. Baldwin served between 1933 and 1935 as an assistant to Secretary of Agriculture Henry Wallace,* assistant to Rexford G. Tugwell* in the Resettlement Administration* in 1935 and 1936, and assistant to Will Alexander* in the Farm Security Administration* between 1937 and 1939. In 1940 President Franklin D. Roosevelt* appointed him head of the Farm Security Administration, and Baldwin desperately and unsuccessfully tried to protect the FSA from conservative criticism. After its demise in 1942, Roosevelt appointed Baldwin to a State Department post in Italy, and late in 1943 he became assistant chairman of the CIO* Political Action Committee. A close supporter of Henry Wallace throughout the 1930s and 1940s, Baldwin served as executive vice-chairman of the Progressive Citizens of America in 1947 and 1948, national secretary of the Progressive party in 1948, and campaign manager for Wallace's presidential bid in 1948. Calvin B. Baldwin died on May 12, 1975. (Sidney Baldwin, *Poverty and Politics: The Rise and Decline of the Farm Security Administration*, 1968.)

BANISTER, MARION GLASS Born in 1875 to the Virginia family which included Senator Carter Glass and Meta Glass, later president of Sweet Briar College, Marion Glass married Blair Banister. During World War I, she wrote publicity releases for the Committee on Public Information and then stayed on during the 1920s working for the Democratic party.* Banister was widowed in the mid-1920s and became a founder of the Women's National Democratic Club in 1924. She supported herself during these years working as a publicity agent for the Mayflower Hotel in Washington, D.C. Banister actively supported Franklin D. Roosevelt* in the election of 1932,* and in return he named her assistant treasurer of the United States in 1933. Banister stayed in that position until her death in 1951. (Susan Ware, *Beyond Suffrage: Women in the New Deal*, 1981.)

BANKHEAD COTTON CONTROL ACT OF 1934 The Bankhead Cotton Control Act was passed by Congress on April 21, 1934, to increase participation in the cotton programs of the Agricultural Adjustment Administration.* Senator John H. Bankhead* and his brother, Representative William B. Bankhead,* both Democrats from Alabama, wrote the bill. Cotton had become a chief concern of the Agricultural Adjustment Administration because of severely fluctuating prices on the world market. Prices of cotton had been falling steadily since the early 1920s while farmers continued to provide huge surpluses. The Agricultural Adjustment Act* was designed to reduce those surpluses.

The AAA required farmers to sign contracts agreeing to plow under from 25 to 50 percent of their crops in 1933 in return for cash rental payments or cash plus options. The second series of contracts were on the 1934-1935 crop, and required the growers to limit their production to 55 to 65 percent of their base acreage, a figure determined as the average acreage planted for the crops from

1928-1932. However, since the program was voluntary, the administration had difficulty getting farmers to comply with their contracts as well as attracting farmers to participate in the program. Thus in 1934 the Bankhead proposal was adopted to penalize non-participants and contract violators.

Under the Bankhead Act individual growers received tax-exempt certificates for their contracted crop. The total of all tax-exempt certificates would equal the predetermined adjusted crop quota of 10 million, 500 pound bales. Allotment of tax-exempt certificates was determined by past production. Small producers were given certificates covering their entire production. (Small producers were designated as those who farmed up to five acres in 1934 or produced up to two bales in 1935.) There were also other exemptions allowed in special cases. According to the Bankhead Act, a tax would be levied on "the ginning of cotton equal to 50 percent of the average price of the standard grade on the 10 principal spot markets, but not under 5 cents per pound." Therefore, the tax penalized any cotton ginned in excess of individual allotments and tended to limit production. The act was intended to force a larger percentage of growers into the "voluntary contract" system and was successful. The program was to be mandatory for only one year; thereafter the decision to extend the program for another one-year period would be decided by referendum of the local producers. Cotton producers did extend the controls of the Bankhead Act through 1935, but it died when the Supreme Court* declared the AAA unconstitutional in January 1936. Congress formally repealed the Bankhead Cotton Control Act on February 10, 1936. Although the Bankhead Act was short-lived, it served its purpose as an emergency action designed to quickly raise prices and lower production. It was enforced easily by monitoring the places of ginning and marketing of cotton. Methods for controlling production developed under the Bankhead Act later became an important aspect of farm policy. (Edwin G. Nourse et al, *Three Years of the Agricultural Adjustment Administration*, 1937.)

CATHERINE EGGERS

BANKHEAD, JOHN HOLLIS John Bankhead was born in Moscow, Alabama, on July 8, 1872. He graduated in 1891 from the University of Alabama. From 1891-1893 he worked as his father's secretary in Washington, D.C., and studied law at Georgetown University, where he received his degree in 1893. After practicing law for twelve years, John and his brother, William B. Bankhead,* established their own law firm. John H. Bankhead was also involved in coal mining operations in Alabama, serving as president of the Bankhead Coal Company from 1911-1925. From 1903 to 1907 he served as a member of the Alabama legislature, during which time he authored the Alabama Election Law.

In 1930 Bankhead was elected to the United States Senate from Alabama, an office which he held until his death on June 12, 1946. During his tenure in office he worked to support most of President Franklin D. Roosevelt's* policies, especially defense. He did not, however, support President Roosevelt's tactics against the Supreme Court* in 1937. But he helped the Agricultural Adjustment

Administration's* program requiring producers to plow under a large percentage of their cotton crop after planting in 1933. Bankhead supported the idea of providing government loans on agricultural commodities which ultimately resulted in the Commodity Credit Corporation.* Along with his brother, William B. Bankhead, he wrote the Bankhead Cotton Control Act,* which applied the idea of manipulating the supply of a commodity to meet the demands of the market by compulsory control of acreage and marketing. In 1936 he co-authored the Soil Conservation and Domestic Allotment Act,* which appropriated funds to provide benefit payments to farmers involved in soil conservation. John H. Bankhead also wrote the Subsistence Homestead* section of the National Industrial Recovery Act of 1933* which eventually led to the Resettlement Administration.* He co-authored the Bankhead-Jones Farm Tenancy Act of 1937* to aid certain farm tenants and workers in acquiring homes as well as rehabilitation loans to refinance indebtedness and for family subsistence. The Tenancy Act also worked toward development of soil conservation and land-use programs. In further aid to farmers, Bankhead co-authored the Agricultural Adjustment Act of 1938* with special emphasis on the cotton program. Other legislation co-authored by John H. Bankhead included such bills as the Bankhead-Fulmer Bill which provided government insurance of cotton crops, the Lucas-Bankhead Amendment which provided soil conservation money for basic crop producers, and the Bankhead-Jones Act authorizing more money for land grant colleges. John Bankhead died on June 12, 1946, in Bethesda, Maryland. (*New York Times*, June 13, 1946.)

CATHERINE EGGERS

BANKHEAD-JONES FARM TENANCY ACT OF 1937 For several decades farm tenancy had been increasing and by 1935 42 percent of the nation's farms were operated by tenants. This problem had been caused in part by the increasing amount of capital required for farm ownership and the purchase of equipment necessary for profitable commercial agriculture. The Great Depression increased the trend, causing many farmers to lose their lands and fall into tenancy, or day labor, particularly in cotton areas. For example, in Texas, 57.2 percent of all farms and 70 percent of the cotton farms were operated by tenants, of which one-third were blacks. To provide a federal solution to this problem, in November 1936 President Franklin D. Roosevelt* appointed a Special Committee on Farm Tenancy.* Simultaneously, he asked Senator John Bankhead* of Alabama and Representative Marvin Jones* of Texas to draft tenancy legislation. By mid-February 1937, the committee had presented its report, and parts of it were incorporated into legislation introduced in Congress.

Some farm officials and congressmen wanted the government to purchase large tracts of land, but the idea was blocked by the House Agriculture Committee because it appeared "socialistic." In keeping with traditional American attitudes and practical politics of the times, Jones favored a financial credit approach in which local committees would purchase farms with limited government funds and sell them at low interest loans to worthy tenants selected by local committees.

Jones' idea was written into the Bankhead-Jones Farm Tenancy Act. It authorized rehabilitation loans for operating expenses and education, and it appropriated $50 million for conservation programs on submarginal lands. The Farm Security Administration* was created to administer the act. The bill became law on July 22, 1937.

The Bankhead-Jones Farm Tenancy Act never intended to achieve total relief to all tenants, but from 1937 through 1947, the FSA made loans of $293 million to 47,104 farmers. Nevertheless, the legislation was a small step forward for the tenants. Perhaps its most important result came during World War II when FSA families, representing only 7 percent of the nation's farmers, accounted for a much larger increase in food production. (Sidney Baldwin, *Poverty and Politics: The Rise and Decline of the Farm Security Administration*, 1968; Irvin M. May, Jr., *Marvin Jones: The Public Life of an Agrarian Advocate*, 1980; Theodore Saloutos, *The American Farmer and the New Deal*, 1983.)

IRVIN M. MAY, JR.

BANKHEAD, WILLIAM BROCKMAN William B. Bankhead was born in Moscow, Alabama, on April 12, 1874, to a politically prominent family. His father, John Hollis Bankhead, had served in the United States Senate as had his brother, John Hollis II. William grew up in the tradition of Southern Democracy and its strong emphasis on states' rights. Bankhead attended the University of Alabama and graduated in 1893, took a master's degree there in 1896, and received a law degree from Georgetown University in 1895. He practiced law privately before becoming active in local politics and won a seat in Congress in 1917. He stayed there until his death in 1940, representing the 7th Alabama Congressional District. During the 1930s Bankhead was a New Deal* supporter in his position as chairman of the powerful House Rules Committee. His willingness to expedite New Deal legislation was so strong that Republicans in the House accused him of supporting "gag rules" to prevent legitimate debate. When Speaker of the House Henry Rainey* died in 1935 and Joseph W. Byrns* became the new Speaker, Bankhead was named the new majority leader. A strong supporter of cotton interests and the prerogatives of the states, Bankhead nevertheless was loyal to the New Deal, even though he frequently took issue with President Franklin D. Roosevelt's* tactics, especially in the "court-packing" scheme,* a measure he was sympathetic to but felt the president had mismanaged. William B. Bankhead died on September 14, 1940. (*New York Times*, September 15, 1940.)

BANK HOLIDAY On March 6, 1933, President Franklin D. Roosevelt* signed a proclamation declaring a moratorium on all banking operations in the United States, climaxing a financial panic which had been building since late in 1932 when depositors began demanding their cash. The concept of a national bank holiday did not originate with the New Deal.* As early as 1918, Milton Elliott, a lawyer with the Federal Reserve Board,* suggested the potential need for a banking and currency moratorium if any war-related financial crisis struck the nation. The Trading-With-the-Enemy Act of 1917 authorized the president to impose such an embargo during financial emergencies. In January 1932, during the liquidity crisis preceding establishment of the Reconstruction Finance Corporation,* Secretary of the Treasury Ogden Mills and President Herbert Hoover* considered declaring a national bank holiday; they did so again in June when the Central Republic Bank of Chicago closed. By February 1933, with the banking system rapidly approaching a state of collapse after the severe crises in Louisiana and Michigan, several of Hoover's advisers, including Ogden Mills and Walter Wyatt of the Federal Reserve Board staff, urged him to consider declaring a national holiday as the only way of preventing a complete liquidation of the money markets. Although reluctant to use the federal government in such a way, Hoover moved ahead, asking Attorney General DeWitt Mitchell for an opinion on the constitutionality of such a declaration. Mitchell had some doubts about it and urged Hoover to secure the cooperation of President-elect Franklin D. Roosevelt* before making the declaration. During the first two days of March 1933, President Hoover had Walter Wyatt draft a holiday proclamation, but Roosevelt refused to join in the declaration, agreeing only to support Hoover's proposal up to the moment of his inauguration, after which he wanted a free hand to develop his own approach. So nothing happened. On March 6, 1933, however, two days after his inauguration, President Roosevelt signed Wyatt's proclamation closing banks throughout the country, and on March 9, 1933, included it as Title I of the Emergency Banking Act of 1933.*

At first, the administration had little sense of how they would go about reopening all the nation's banks, but they were certain that only sound banks should return to business. Otherwise new failures would only trigger another panic and liquidity crisis. By March 11 government banking officials had decided to open only individual banks sound enough to operate profitably without restrictions. Only assurance by the federal government that every reopened bank was sound could restore public confidence. Under a crash program, bank examiners from the Reconstruction Finance Corporation, comptroller of the currency, Treasury Department, and Federal Reserve Board began analyzing the assets of national banks throughout the country. All national banks whose capital was unimpaired received licenses permitting them to reopen. Banks whose capital was impaired but whose assets were valuable enough to repay all depositors in full remained closed until the crisis had passed and they could reopen with RFC assistance. Banks whose capital was gone and had no hope of providing a full return to depositors were placed in the hands of conservators who could reorganize them with RFC funds, liquidate their assets, and give an equitable return to depositors. State banking authorities followed the same basic procedure for reopening their closed banks. On March 14, the eve of the reopening, President Roosevelt went on radio in a "fireside chat"* explaining what would happen the next day and assuring the public that any bank open at the end of the day would be sound and reliable.

On March 15, 1933, 12,756 banks reopened, 69 percent of the total of 18,390 banks which had been open before the holiday. Of the 6,816 member banks of the Federal Reserve System, 5,038 received licenses. In the first week after the reopening, public confidence in the banking system returned, as did more than $660 million in hoarded currency. That increased to $1 billion by the end of the month. During the rest of 1933, only 221 banks suspended operations: nine of them were national banks, six state member banks of the Federal Reserve, and 206 state non-member banks. Between March 15 and April 15, another 1,300 banks reopened with RFC assistance. All of the remaining 4,215 closed banks were placed in the hands of conservators or state banking authorities. More than 1,100 of them were so weak that they had to be liquidated. Between May 1 and December 31, 1933, another 1,200 closed banks were reorganized and reopened with RFC loans and investment capital. By December 31, 1933, there were still approximately 2,000 banks without licenses, but because the Federal Deposit Insurance Corporation* was ready to begin operations on January 1, Secretary of the Treasury Henry Morgenthau, Jr.,* agreed to reopen them and place them in the FDIC if Jesse Jones* and the RFC agreed to provide them with the cash loans and investment capital necessary to make them solvent. Jones agreed. The bank holiday, officially terminated on March 15, 1933, was finally over. (Susan Estabrook Kennedy, *The Banking Crisis of 1933*, 1973.)

BANKING ACT OF 1933 After more than a century of haphazard evolution, the American banking system in 1920 was the most complicated in the world. By then there were more than 30,000 commercial banks in the country, with 8,000 possessing federal charters and approximately 22,000 possessing state charters. The national banks were supervised by the comptroller of the currency and state banks by individual state banking authorities. All national banks were also members of the Federal Reserve System, as were 1,374 state banks. In addition to commercial banks, there were another 20,000 financial institutions in the money market—investment banks, credit unions, savings banks, industrial banks, building and loan associations, private banks, and insurance companies. Many commercial banks had gone into the investment banking business by creating security affiliates during the 1920s, and the development of group and chain banking gave rise to the creation of branch banks. The American banking system was complicated, poorly supervised, and given to inconsistent management.

During the 1920s, demands for bank reform became more and more intense. Some people wanted a federally-owned central bank, not the decentralized regional arrangement of the Federal Reserve System. Others wanted to preserve the dual banking system, feeling that states had the right to manage their own financial institutions. Many people worried about the security operations of commercial banks, while small banks were concerned about the branch-banking plans of larger institutions, fearing for the future of their own local markets. The failure of 5,600 banks during the 1920s had also frightened many people, giving rise to the suggestion that the federal government establish some way of insuring bank deposits. The financial panic of 1931 and 1932, when several thousand more banks went under, only magnified all these concerns. During 1932, a whole series of bills to reform the banking system were introduced to Congress, the most important of them by Senator Carter Glass* of Virginia and Congressman Henry Steagall* of Alabama. But the political problems surrounding Herbert Hoover's* last year in office stalled most of them. The Glass-Steagall Act of 1932 liberalized Federal Reserve discount provisions but left untouched the major problems facing the banking system. The panic of 1932-1933 and the complete collapse of the banking system that winter, followed by the bank holiday* and inauguration of Franklin D. Roosevelt,* generated an irresistible momentum for reform. Fueled by public outrage over the Pecora investigations into bank fraud, demand for reform was unprecedented.

Throughout March and April 1933, the administration, with the constant advice of Carter Glass and Henry Steagall, studied the problem and developed a legislative approach. In mid-May Glass and Steagall introduced bills to Congress. Together, they called for an increase in Federal Reserve control over bank credit, coordination of Federal Reserve open market operations, and legal recognition of the Open Market Committee. The Federal Reserve Board* acquired control of all the foreign operations of member banks. Commercial banking was separated from investment banking to prevent future speculative fevers and loss of assets which had so recently occurred. Commercial banks could underwrite only the securities of state and local governments, and member banks had one year to divorce themselves from security affiliates. The officers of national banks had until July 1, 1935, to divest themselves of any loans granted to them by their own institutions. National banks could establish branches on a statewide basis in those states already allowing state banks to do so. To control chain and group banking, the law gave the comptroller of the currency authority to regulate the stock voting rights of the holding company affiliate of national banks. The law also raised the capital requirements for national banks and provided for the establishment of a Federal Deposit Insurance Corporation.*

The last proposal raised the ire of most private bankers. Some of them, especially those connected with state banks, resisted the proposal because it abrogated states' rights and amounted to federal intervention into a broader area of American life. They saw the FDIC as a first step toward the destruction of the dual banking system. Other bankers, especially those with large national banks, worried that creation of the FDIC would only add to the already complicated array of bank regulatory agencies. Still others resisted because they feared the FDIC would only delay the unification of all commercial banks under the Federal Reserve System. Many bankers also resented the assessment they would have to pay for membership in the FDIC. But bankers were out of favor with the public and their complaints fell on deaf ears. The bill created a Federal Deposit Insurance Corporation, using $150 million of federal money and the premiums of each member bank to finance operations. The FDIC would begin operation on January 1, 1934. All national banks had to join, as did state banks in the Federal Reserve System. State banks not in the Federal Reserve System could join the FDIC, with the provision that they would become part of the Federal Reserve System by July 1, 1936. The full bill passed through Congress in mid-June, and President Franklin D. Roosevelt signed the Banking Act of 1933 into law on June 16. (Helen M. Burns, *The American Banking Community and New Deal Banking Reforms: 1933-1935*, 1974.)

BANKING ACT OF 1935 On August 23, 1935, President Franklin D. Roosevelt* signed into law one of the most significant pieces of banking legislation in United States history—the Banking Act of 1935. A compromise measure between the private banking community resisting centralization and federal banking authorities committed to acquiring more rational control over the nation's banking system, the Banking Act of 1935 was a logical outgrowth of the Great Depression. After a century of explosive growth, there were approximately 50,000 banks and private financial institutions in the United States in 1920, and many of them were dangerously undercapitalized and overextended. The agricultural depression of the 1920s devastated thousands of rural banks, and the stock market crash eroded the assets of thousands of others. When the banking system collapsed in the late winter of 1933, a sense of paralysis gripped the financial community. President Franklin D. Roosevelt's bank holiday* stopped the panic; the Emergency Banking Act of 1933* provided a careful process of examining and reopening closed banks, as well as supplying them with RFC* capital; and the Banking Act of 1933* had separated commercial from investment banking and created the Federal Deposit Insurance Corporation* to guarantee bank deposits and protect the money supply. By 1934 the reconstruction of the American banking system was well underway.

But a number of problems still concerned many private bankers and government economists. The Banking Act of 1933 had required the officers of national banks to divest themselves of all loans granted to them from their own institutions by July 1, 1935. Many private bankers wanted a time extension, and J. F. T. O'Connor,* comptroller of the currency, agreed with them. Also, the FDIC, after operating on an emergency basis since January 1, 1934, was to begin formal operations on January 1, 1935, but most private bankers believed that the insurance rates charged were too high. Leo Crowley,* head of the FDIC, supported the proposal. Marriner Eccles,* the new chairman of the Federal Reserve Board* and an early New Deal* advocate of Keynesian economics, wanted to change the Federal Reserve System, centralizing power with the Federal Reserve Board in Washington, D.C., rather than at the regional Federal Reserve Banks. Concerned that a modern industrial economy required central control of the money supply in order to guarantee stable prices and full employment, Eccles wanted the Federal Reserve Board in Washington, D.C., to assume responsibility for all open market operations, instead of having the regional Federal Reserve Banks independently buying or selling securities to manipulate the money supply.

President Roosevelt realized that private bankers would support the proposals of J. F. T. O'Connor and Leo Crowley, but he also knew they would oppose any attempt to centralize banking power in Washington. So he had his staff draft an omnibus bill including all three provisions, hoping that private bankers would want the proposals for reduced FDIC assessments and a time extension on liquidating the prohibited loans so much that they would swallow the centralization feature. Roosevelt was personally committed to the legislation, not only because his relief proposals for 1935 and 1936 would require large-scale federal spending and cooperation from the Federal Reserve Board, but because the landslide Democratic victory in the congressional elections of 1934* had given him the political clout to achieve banking reform. Roosevelt's assessment of the political situation was correct. Private bankers along with Senator Carter Glass* of Virginia strongly opposed the Federal Reserve idea but were seduced by the other provisions. The bill moved through the House and Senate in the summer, and President Roosevelt signed the Banking Act of 1935 on August 23.

Title I of the Banking Act of 1935 reduced the assessments on members of the FDIC and helped the corporation begin operations. Title II provided major changes in the Federal Reserve System. The Federal Reserve Board was replaced by the board of governors of the Federal Reserve System, with seven members appointed by the president and confirmed by the Senate. The original appointments were scheduled from two to fourteen years so that not more than one position would expire every two years. At the regional Federal Reserve Banks, the title of governor was changed to president, the president to be appointed to a five-year term by the local Federal Reserve Bank board of directors, subject to approval by the board of governors in Washington, D.C. The old Federal Open Market Committee, consisting of the twelve governors of the Federal Reserve Banks, was replaced by a new Federal Open Market Committee composed of the board of governors and five representatives from Federal Reserve Banks. The new Federal Open Market Committee controlled open market operations and policy. Federal Reserve Banks, with approval of the board of governors, could also make advances to member banks on "satisfactory" as well as eligible paper. Title III extended the deadline for officers of national banks to divest themselves of loans from their own institutions.

Along with the Federal Deposit Insurance Corporation, the Banking Act of 1935 was a milestone in the history of public policy in the United States. Because of the new power of the Federal Reserve Board and the supervising authority of the FDIC, the federal government had the responsibility for monetary management and credit control. More than ever before, the nation's banks were part of a larger, more coordinated system. Ever since 1935 the Federal Reserve Board has played a critical role in federal economic policy, working to achieve stable prices and full employment. (Helen M. Burns, *The American Banking Community and New Deal Banking Reforms: 1933-1935*, 1974.)

BANK OF AMERICA (See GIANNINI, AMADEO PETER.)

BANKS FOR COOPERATIVES (See FARM CREDIT ACT OF 1933 and FARM CREDIT ADMINISTRATION.)

BARKLEY, ALBEN WILLIAM Born in Graves County, Kentucky, on November 24, 1877, Alben W. Barkley graduated from Marvin College in Clinton, Kentucky, in 1897. His father had been a former tenant farmer and railroad section hand. Alben Barkley studied law for one year at Emory University in Oxford, Georgia, and then changed to the University of Virginia Law School. In 1901 he began practicing law in Paducah, Kentucky. He entered local politics as a Democrat in 1905, serving until 1909 as prosecuting attorney for McCracken County and then for four years as judge of the county court. In 1912 he began his fourteen-year-term in the United States House of Representatives, and in 1926 he won a seat in the United States Senate. He won three successive terms in the Senate, where he was an outspoken advocate of the New Deal.* Between 1937 and 1947, Barkley was the Senate majority leader. He vigorously supported work relief measures, a federal anti-lynching bill,* and Franklin D. Roosevelt's* foreign policies. He resigned as majority leader in 1944 over a dispute about President Roosevelt's revenue proposals but was shortly re-elected to the position. At the Democratic conventions of 1932, 1936, and 1940, Barkley was a keynote speaker, and in 1948 President Harry S Truman* selected him as his vice-presidential running mate. Barkley was an active and popular vice-president and tried to secure the Democratic presidential nomination in 1952, but he failed when labor refused to support him. In 1954 he wrote a book, *That Reminds Me*, and regained his seat in the United States Senate. Alben W. Barkley was serving in the Senate when he died on April 30, 1956. (Jane R. Barkley and F. S. Leighton, *I Married the Veep*, n.d.; *New York Times*, May 1, 1956.)

BARUCH, BERNARD MANNES Born in 1870, Bernard Mannes Baruch eventually became a minor adviser to Franklin D. Roosevelt,* albeit a giant influence upon Democratic congressional leaders and certain New Deal* administrators. A man of fabled wealth gained from speculation on Wall Street—who used it to advance his power in the Democratic party* during the 1920s—Baruch's only governmental positions had been chairman of the War Industries Board in 1918 and economic adviser to President Woodrow Wilson at the Paris Peace Conference of 1919. In 1932 Baruch hoped to be the next secretary of state, but Roosevelt allowed Baruch to come no closer to influencing foreign affairs than a brief service as a coordinator of American strategy during the London Economic Conference of 1933.*

Baruch's influence upon the New Deal was indirect. He had been an *eminence grise* with Democratic lawmakers during 1926-1932, thereby helping to formulate the bi-partisan congressional consensus that passed Herbert Hoover's* program in 1932, including the Reconstruction Finance Corporation.* Roosevelt respected that power. Rexford Tugwell* recalled Roosevelt's telling him at the outset that "Baruch owned—he used the word—sixty congressmen. That, he said, was power around Washington. . . . Those sixty congressmen had to be kept in line."

It was that apparent power which compelled Roosevelt to add Baruch's crony, Hugh S. Johnson,* to the brain trust* during the 1932 campaign. Moreover, Baruch's influence with Democratic lawmakers barely abated during the 1930s. Late in the New Deal Roosevelt would tell Frances Perkins* that Baruch had "lots of influence on the Congress still. We kind of need him to keep [congressmen] in line. . . . He helps out tremendously in keeping the more wild members of Congress, the Southern members of Congress, kind of down and reconciled."

Baruch himself was reconciled to the New Deal. A conservative opposed to New Deal policies of inflation, sharing power with labor, and instituting the welfare state, he nevertheless rationalized the New Deal as a humane and political necessity. Besides, Roosevelt shrewdly saw to it that Baruch had an indirect stake in the New Deal's industrial and agricultural recovery programs. The National Recovery Administration* was modeled on the industrial cooperation strategy of the War Industries Board and was led by Hugh Johnson, a member of the WIB and a business associate of Baruch's since then. Like the NRA, the Agricultural Adjustment Administration* also stressed cartelistic cooperation among producers and was headed by George N. Peek,* another member of the WIB and longtime friend of Baruch. Yet Baruch had not recommended either man for their New Deal posts and had doubted the wisdom of giving them such responsibilities. Rather, Roosevelt had chosen them because each was an articulate advocate for cooperation policies favored by Roosevelt and because they ensured that Baruch would not oppose the inflationary, cartelistic producer strategies. Neither Johnson nor Peek lasted out Roosevelt's first term. By 1936 Baruch was on the fringes of power and a symbol of Bourbon Democrats who were New Deal pariahs.

However, Baruch's influence endured with Congress and expanded to include Eleanor Roosevelt* and various administrators who respected his views on rearmament to meet the rise of fascism in Europe and Asia. Still, he was never a New Dealer and, through his support for the repeal of the undistributed profits tax in 1938, dealt a blow to its liberal supporters. However his friendship with Eleanor Roosevelt and financial support for her projects such as the Arthurdale community experiment softened the sting of his conservative opposition. Also, he publicized the cash-and-carry provision of the 1937 neutrality act. To symbolize his disagreement with the speed, comprehensiveness, and methods of Roosevelt's preparedness program during 1938-1941 and his exclusion from its policymaking and administration, Baruch would tell reporters that his Washington office was a park bench in Lafayette Square across the street from the White House. During World War II—in his seventies—he would be at the height of his fame as "adviser to presidents" and the "Park Bench Statesman." Bernard Baruch died in 1965. (Jordan A. Schwarz, *The Speculator: Bernard M. Baruch in Washington, 1917-1965*, 1981.)

JORDAN A. SCHWARZ

BEER TAX ACT The Democratic party* platform of 1932 had called for the repeal of the Eighteenth Amendment. While the amendment was in progress,

Congress acted in accordance with President Franklin D. Roosevelt's* suggestion to hasten the end of prohibition by passing the Beer Tax Act. The measure, which became law on March 22, 1933, legalized the manufacture of alcoholic beverages containing not more than 3.2 percent alcohol by weight. (Alfred Kelly and Winfred Harbison, *The American Constitution*, 1970; *U.S. Statutes at Large*, Vol. XXXXVIII:16-20, 1933.)

JOSEPH M. ROWE, JR.

BELL, DANIEL WAFENA Daniel W. Bell was born in Kinderhook, Illinois, on July 23, 1891. He received a LL.B. from National University in Washington, D.C., in 1924, and a B.C.S. from Southeastern University in 1927. Bell had gone to work for the Treasury Department in 1911 as a bookkeeper, and he steadily rose through the civil service ladder, becoming the accountant in charge of foreign loans in 1919, executive assistant to the assistant secretary of the treasury in 1920, assistant commissioner of accounts and deposits in 1924, and commissioner of accounts and deposits in 1931. When President Franklin D. Roosevelt* decided to create the Bureau of the Budget* as a means of centralizing the financial operations of the federal government, he asked Secretary of the Treasury Henry Morgenthau, Jr.,* to name a director of the bureau, and Morgenthau selected Bell, at the same time making him his own executive assistant. Bell served as acting director of the Bureau of the Budget until 1939, always refusing to accept a regular appointment because it meant the surrender of his civil service protection. In 1940 Bell became the undersecretary of the treasury. He retired from government service in 1945 and between 1946 and 1959 served as president of the American Security and Trust Company in Washington, D.C. Bell died on October 3, 1971. (*New York Times*, October 4, 1971.)

BENNETT, HUGH HAMMOND Born in 1881, Hugh Hammond Bennett was raised on a farm in North Carolina and graduated from the University of North Carolina in 1903. Immediately employed by the Department of Agriculture as a chemist in the Bureau of Soils, he spent most of the next twenty-five years conducting soil surveys, thereby acquiring familiarity with agricultural conditions throughout the United States. He also took part in a number of foreign missions, investigating agricultural resources and conditions in the Panama Canal Zone (1909), in Honduras and Guatemala (1919), and in Cuba (intermittently 1926-1932).

During this time with the Bureau of Soils, Bennett established a national reputation as a soils expert but not as a conservationist. His observations, however, convinced him that soil erosion was a problem demanding national programs to remedy it, a conclusion he expressed in his landmark bulletin of 1928, *Soil Erosion: A National Menace*. Congress in that year appropriated funds for establishment of erosion control stations by the Department of Agriculture. Heading the new program, Bennett between 1929 and 1933 established ten such stations across the United States. Personnel of the stations surveyed soil erosion in their areas and tested methods for its control, including contouring, terracing, crop rotation, and planting of cover crops.

In 1933, under the National Industrial Recovery Act,* Congress allocated new funds for soil conservation to the Department of the Interior. Secretary of Interior Harold Ickes* thereupon selected Bennett to serve as director of the new Soil Erosion Service. Under Bennett's direction the service constructed numerous public works, both on public land and, with the cooperation of farmers, on private property.

During 1934 and 1935, as dust storms on the Great Plains raised public and Congressional consciousness of the need for conservation, Bennett lobbied effectively for increased appropriations and broader programs. In 1935 with the Soil Conservation Act,* Congress transferred soil conservation work back to the Department of Agriculture, and Bennett returned to that department to direct the new Soil Conservation Service. The Soil Conservation Service continued construction of conservation projects, utilizing labor from the Civilian Conservation Corps* and other federal work-relief agencies.

Bennett believed that conservation work would be successful only by the efforts of farmers themselves. During the late 1930s, when successful demonstration projects had been situated across the nation, he engineered the decentralization of soil conservation work through the establishment of local soil conservation districts. It was on his urging that President Franklin D. Roosevelt* in 1937 pressed the individual states to enact legislation establishing such districts and placing them under the governance of locally-elected boards. Thereafter Bennett guided the service into the provision of scientific, technical, and organizational assistance to the districts in the execution of their own projects.

Bennett, who became known as "father of soil conservation," received the Distinguished Service Award of the Department of Agriculture in 1947 and retired from the department in 1951. He died in 1960. (Wellington Brink, *Big Hugh: The Father of Soil Conservation*, 1951.)

THOMAS D. ISERN

BENSON, ELMER AUSTIN Elmer Austin Benson was born to Norwegian immigrant parents in Appleton, Minnesota, on September 22, 1895. His father, Tom, was a Republican until the rise of the Farmer-Labor party* in Minnesota, when his politics took a turn toward the left. Elmer assumed many of his father's political attitudes. He graduated from high school in 1915 and entered the St. Paul College of Law. World War I interrupted his studies, but he passed the bar exam in 1919. By then he had been a clerk at the First National Bank in Appleton and did not practice law. While working as a banker, Benson became an active supporter of the Farmer-Labor party and in 1924 endorsed Robert W. La Follette for president. He also endorsed Floyd Olson's* political candidacy in 1930 and 1932, calling for more work relief, social security, and reduction in farm taxes. In 1932 Olson appointed Benson to become commissioner of securities for Minnesota. Benson was a strong supporter of the idea of bank deposit insurance and wholeheartedly endorsed the Federal Deposit Insurance Corporation* provision of the Banking Act of 1933.* In December 1935 Governor Olson appointed Benson to fill the U.S. Senate seat vacated by the death of Thomas Schall.* There Benson became a loyal New Dealer.

He ran for governor in 1936 and won a landslide victory, quickly establishing a "little New Deal"* which supported the right to strike, increased relief expenditures, tax relief, prison reform, and social security. Benson was often critical of the New Deal,* not because of its basic philosophy and goals but because of what he considered poor administration. But Benson was soon victimized by the Republican revival of 1938, when he lost the governorship to Harold Stassen. Benson lost again in 1940 and unsuccessfully ran for the Senate in 1942. In 1944 he became head of the CIO's* National Citizen's Political Action Committee, and in 1948 he served as the national chairman for Henry A. Wallace's* Progressive party candidacy for the presidency. (James M. Shields, *Mr. Progressive. A Biography of Elmer Austin Benson*, 1971.)

BERLE, ADOLF AUGUSTUS One of the original "brain trust"* trio of advisers to Franklin D. Roosevelt* with Raymond Moley* and Rexford Tugwell* during the 1932 campaign for the presidency, Adolf Augustus Berle was acknowledged as one of the most brilliant and creative of the New Dealers. Born in 1895, a son of a Congregational minister, Berle was a child prodigy who graduated from Harvard at eighteen and its law school at twenty-one. He did intelligence work for the army during World War I and at the Paris Peace Conference. A corporation lawyer and law professor at Columbia University, he was the principal author with economist Gardiner Means* of *The Modern Corporation and Private Property* (1932), one of the most influential books of the decade because it suggested a trend toward concentration of power in 200 corporations which were increasingly divorced from stockholder or public control. Concentration of corporation power was one of the principal issues of the New Deal,* and it brought Berle into political conflict with an old personal enemy, Felix Frankfurter,* who, along with Justice Louis Brandeis,* argued for enforcement of anti-trust laws against the biggest corporations while Berle and others advocated their control. He wrote Roosevelt's Commonwealth Club speech, which more than any other campaign address suggested the progressivism and governmental activism of the New Deal.

Yet Berle chose to fight these New Deal philosophy battles from New York. Except for a brief role with the Reconstruction Finance Corporation* in 1933, he refused several offers of positions in the New Deal and became chamberlain of New York City under Mayor Fiorello La Guardia* during 1934-1937. Even so, he remained among the most influential of Roosevelt's advisers through frequent meetings and letters that began with the jocular salutation "Dear Caesar." (He was asked to desist from it during the "court-packing"* fight of 1937.) Moreover, Roosevelt valued Berle's New York role as the architect of the city's financial recovery from the brink of bankruptcy in 1934-1935. Berle built a political base in New York City among labor liberals that gave him independence from the New Deal, but in 1938 he returned at Roosevelt's insistence to be assistant secretary of state. Roosevelt intended that Berle should use that foreign affairs position for advising on a broad range of problems including dealing with the recession of 1937-1938.* At a time when anti-trust sentiment was growing in Washington, Roosevelt chose to bring aboard a spokesman for planning and control.

Berle was assistant secretary of state through 1944 and served as ambassador to Brazil until early 1946. He remained interested in hemispheric problems and foreign intelligence, serving as chairman of President John Kennedy's Latin American Task Force which originated the Alliance for Progress in 1961. He also was chairman of the board of the Twentieth Century Fund, 1949-1971. He died in 1971. (*New York Times*, February 19, 1971; Elliott A. Rosen, *Hoover, Roosevelt, and the Brains Trust: From Depression to New Deal*, 1977.)

JORDAN A. SCHWARZ

BERRY, GEORGE LEONARD George L. Berry was born on September 12, 1882, in Lee Valley, Tennessee. The son of Thomas Berry and Cornelia Trent, he went to work in the printing offices of the Jackson, Mississippi, *Evening News* in 1891, and during the next several years he held a number of jobs with several regional newspapers. He joined the Press Assistants Union in 1899, and eight years later was elected president of the AFL's* International Pressmen and Assistants Union. An active Democrat, Berry unsuccessfully tried to secure the vice-presidential nomination in 1924. He became a strong supporter of President Franklin D. Roosevelt* and the New Deal* during the 1930s. Berry served as a member of the National Labor Board* and the Cotton Textile National Industrial Relations Board,* divisional administrator of the National Recovery Administration,* and coordinator for Industrial Cooperation in the NRA.* During the elections of 1936,* Berry joined with United Mine Worker President John L. Lewis* in forming Labor's Non-Partisan League* to support Roosevelt. In 1937 Berry was appointed U. S. senator from Tennessee to fill the unexpired term of Nathan Bachman. George Berry died on December 4, 1948. (*Who Was Who in America*, II:60, 1963.)

BETHUNE, MARY McLEOD Mary McLeod Bethune was born in 1875 to former South Carolina slaves. She was educated at the Scotia Seminary in Concord, North Carolina, and at the Moody Bible Institute in Chicago. After graduating in 1895, Bethune returned to the South, where she was a teacher in several church schools. Led by her concern for the problems of black railroad workers in Florida, Bethune established a normal and industrial school for black girls at Daytona Beach in 1904. In 1923 the school merged with Cookman Institute of Jacksonville to form Bethune-Cookman College. As president of the school, Bethune gained national prominence as an educator and civil rights leader. Her stature in education was matched by her leadership in such organizations as the National Council of Negro Women, which she founded in 1935, the National Business League, the National Urban League, and the National Association for the Advancement of Colored People.* She also served on the National Child Welfare Commission during Calvin Coolidge's and Warren Harding's administrations.

Bethune joined the New Deal* in 1935 as a special adviser on minority affairs. The following year she was named director of the Division of Negro Affairs in the National Youth Administration.* As director, she was responsible for overseeing various projects of the NYA, the New Deal agency established to assist young people. She was also instrumental in the distribution of NYA funds to black schools. The degree of Bethune's influence in the New Deal was enhanced by her personal friendship with Eleanor Roosevelt.* In addition, she was an organizer of the informal "black cabinet,"* a group of black leaders in Franklin D. Roosevelt's* administration that advised the president on racial problems. With the support of the black cabinet and the National Youth Administration, Bethune organized two national conferences that focused on civil rights.

The National Youth Administration was discontinued in 1943, but Bethune continued to serve as an important leader through her writing and public speaking and through her contributions to national civil rights organizations. In 1945 she served as an adviser to the San Francisco conference which established the United Nations. That same year she also assisted the War Department in the selection of candidates to the Women's Army Corps. Mary McLeod Bethune died in 1955. (Rackman Holt, *Mary McLeod Bethune, A Biography*, 1964; Rayford R. Logan and Michael R. Winston, *Dictionary of American Negro Biography*, 1982.)

DAN K. UTLEY

BEYER, CLARA MORTENSON Born in California in 1892 to Danish immigrant parents, Clara M. Beyer graduated from the University of California in 1915 and took a master's degree there in 1916. She went East to teach labor economics at Bryn Mawr for one year and then joined the War Labor Policies Board during World War I. She married Otto Beyer in 1920 and between 1921 and 1925 had three children while working part-time as an executive secretary for the National Consumers' League. During her years with the National Consumers' League, Beyer formed close friendships with Mary Dewson* and Frances Perkins.* She came to the Children's Bureau of the Department of Labor in 1928, served as director of its Industrial Department between 1931 and 1934, and then became associate director of the Division of Labor Standards in the Department of Labor. Beyer remained with the Division until her retirement in 1957. (Susan Ware, *Beyond Suffrage: Women in the New Deal*, 1981.)

BIDDLE, FRANCIS Born on May 9, 1886, in Paris, France, Francis Biddle was raised amidst the wealth of a patrician Philadelphia family. He graduated from the Harvard Law School in 1911 and quickly found a position as secretary to Supreme Court* Justice Oliver Wendell Holmes. Despite the conservative background of his family, Biddle developed a progressive philosophy. He supported Theodore Roosevelt's "Bull Moose" campaign in 1912 and was unsuccessful in his own bid for a seat in the Pennsylvania state senate. He entered private law practice in 1912 and remained there until the 1930s, except for a four-year stint between 1922 and 1926 as assistant United States attorney for the eastern district of Pennsylvania. During the depression, Biddle was overwhelmed by the suffering of the poor and unemployed, changed his political affiliation to the Democratic party,* and became an enthusiastic supporter of Franklin D. Roosevelt.*

In 1935 the president appointed Biddle to chair the National Labor Relations Board,* an agency established to implement the National Labor Relations Act* promoting collective bargaining. Under Biddle's leadership, the federal government secured three major gains for organized labor: the right to secret elections conducted by the government permitting workers to select their union; the union chosen by a majority of workers had exclusive bargaining rights for all workers; and employers had to bargain with unions in good faith, and that bargaining must lead to an agreement. Biddle resigned his position after the Supreme Court declared the National Industrial Recovery Act* unconstitutional in 1935 and returned to private law practice. He served as chief counsel for the joint congressional investigation of the Tennessee Valley Authority* in 1938 and 1939 and accepted Roosevelt's nomination of him as United States solicitor general in 1940. The next year Roosevelt named him attorney general. Biddle resigned as attorney general in 1945 and later served as a member of the International Military Tribunal which tried former Nazi leaders at Nuremberg, as head of the liberal Americans for Democratic Action between 1950 and 1953, and as chairman of the Franklin Delano Roosevelt Memorial Commission from 1956 to 1966. He wrote a number of books, including *The Fear of Freedom and Justice Holmes*, *Natural Law*, and *The Supreme Court*. Francis Biddle died on October 4, 1968. (Peter H. Irons, *The New Deal Lawyers*, 1982; *New York Times*, October 5, 1968.)

BIGGS, JAMES CRAWFORD J. Crawford Biggs was born in Oxford, North Carolina, on August 29, 1872. He graduated from the University of North Carolina in 1893, studied law there for two years, and was admitted to the bar in 1894. Biggs began practicing law in Oxford, taught law at the University of North Carolina between 1898 and 1900, and served a term in the state legislature in 1905. Biggs was a Supreme Court* reporter between 1905 and 1907 and a justice on the North Carolina Superior Court between 1907 and 1911. He resigned in 1911 and returned to private practice in Raleigh, North Carolina. In 1917 President Woodrow Wilson appointed him a special assistant in the Justice Department to work on the oil litigation case against the Southern Pacific Railroad in California. During the 1920s he continued practicing law in North Carolina and working in local politics. Between 1929 and 1932 he served as the chairman of the North Carolina Board of Elections. In 1933 President Franklin D. Roosevelt* appointed Biggs soliciter general of the United States, a position Biggs held until 1935. It was a difficult time for him because the government lost ten of the seventeen cases he argued before the Supreme Court. Biggs resigned to become a special assistant in the Justice Department again and returned to private practice in 1938. J. Crawford Biggs died on January 30, 1960. (*Who Was Who In America*, III:75, 1960.)

BLACK, ALBERT GAIN Albert G. Black was born in Peoria, Illinois, on April 2, 1896. He received a B.S. from the University of Illinois in 1920 and an M.A. and Ph.D. from the University of Minnesota in 1925 and 1927. He went to work for the Federal Farm Loan Bureau in 1921 and 1922, the Dayton Joint Stock Land Bank from 1922 to 1924, and joined the faculty of the Department of Agricultural Economics at the University of Minnesota in 1924. From there he went on to Iowa State College in 1929 and became chairman of the department of economics and sociology in 1930. In 1933 Secretary of Agriculture Henry A. Wallace* brought Black to Washington, D.C., to head up the corn and hog production section of the Agricultural Adjustment Administration.* After the "purge of 1935" in the Department of Agriculture, Black became director of the AAA's Division of Livestock and Feed Grains and later in the year chief of the Bureau of Agricultural Economics for the USDA. In 1939 President Franklin D. Roosevelt* named him to head the Farm Credit Administration,* where he stayed until 1944. After the war Black was part of the American Financial Mission to Iran (1945-1946), assistant to the secretary of commerce (1946-1947), and a lecturer at Harvard (1947-1948). He served on a wide variety of international agricultural agencies and died on May 19, 1966. (W. Gifford Hoag, *The Farm Credit System: A History of Financial Self-Help*, 1976; *Who Was Who in America*, IV:89, 1968.)

BLACK CABINET Black cabinet was a term that originally referred to any group of black leaders who had some influence on the party in power in Washington, D.C. The term was first used to describe the influence of Frederick Douglass on Republican party* politics in the last half of the nineteenth century. The black cabinet or black brain trust was revived during the administration of Franklin D. Roosevelt.* Blacks were not appointed to high posts in the government; the appointments they did receive were unique because they were not the result of patronage or politics. Most black appointees were middle-class college graduates and professionals. They were chosen because of their ability to identify issues which affected the black community.

The ability of blacks to enter the administration, and thus be in a position to influence New Deal* policies, depended a great deal on the benevolence of the various agency heads. Harold Ickes,* the head of the Interior Department, had once served as president of the Chicago chapter of the National Association for the Advancement of Colored People.* Because of his ties with the black community, Ickes served as Roosevelt's informal secretary of Negro relations.

For his part, Ickes ended segregation at the Interior Department. He hired black lawyers, engineers, and architects. Ickes made the black lawyer William Hastie* assistant solicitor and Robert C. Weaver* an adviser on black problems. Many other blacks served as racial advisers in other New Deal agencies. Harry Hopkins* appointed many black assistants to administer his relief programs. Mary McLeod Bethune* served as director of Minority Affairs within the National Youth Administration.* By 1940 over 100 blacks had served the New Deal, although one fourth of them had left the administration by 1939 because their appointments had been to temporary agencies. Also included in the ''black cabinet'' was Robert L. Vann,* editor of the *Pittsburgh Courier*, who was a special assistant in the Justice Department.

Many of these black members of the New Deal came together for the black cabinet, an informal lobbying group. Its two leading members were Robert Weaver and Mary McLeod Bethune. The black community which initially had not benefited from New Deal programs demanded tangible results from the black cabinet. This pressure from the black community was used to enhance the black cabinet's influence in the administration. The influence of the black lobby, however, was not strong enough to get a federal anti-lynching bill* through Congress nor could it get any major civil rights legislation passed. Although Roosevelt voiced support for black issues, he was not willing to risk his other economic programs pending before Congress by actively fighting for civil rights legislation. Mary McLeod Bethune was able to provide funds to thousands of young blacks because of her position in NYA. The Works Progress Administration* also put many thousands of unemployed black people to work. It would be hard to find many tangible successes wrought by the black cabinet. Most New Deal actions toward blacks were merely symbolic gestures and discrimination continued to be a pervasive problem in all New Deal programs. But for people accustomed to getting nothing, even minor successes meant a great deal. (Robert H. Brisbane, *The Black Vanguard: Origins of the Negro Social Revolution, 1900-1960*, 1970; John B. Kirby, *Black Americans in the Roosevelt Era: Liberals and Race*, 1980.)

MICHAEL G. DENNIS

BLACK-CONNERY BILL In the early days of the New Deal,* administration officials were preoccupied with banking, agriculture, and relief, ignoring for a while the problem of industrial recovery. Labor leaders and social reformers grew restless in the absence of New Deal recovery proposals, and Senator Hugo Black,* Democrat from Alabama, moved in to fill the vacuum. In December 1932 he had introduced his thirty-hour workweek bill to Congress. Black believed that a shorter workweek would more widely distribute available jobs, increase worker purchasing power, and stop the erosion of labor standards. The bill prohibited the interstate shipment of products made in factories or mines employing workers for more than thirty hours in a five-day week. William Green* of the AFL* endorsed the idea and even threatened a general strike if it did not pass. On March 30, 1933, the Senate Judiciary Committee endorsed the bill, and on

April 6, 1933, the Senate passed it by 53 to 30. Afraid of losing the initiative in formulating industrial policy and convinced that the Supreme Court* would declare the law unconstitutional, President Franklin D. Roosevelt* decided to create an alternative. William Connery,* chairman of the House Labor Committee, was ready to call up his version of the Black bill, so Roosevelt appointed a cabinet committee headed by Secretary of Labor Frances Perkins* to study the Black-Connery proposal and offer amendments. He also asked Raymond Moley* to prepare an alternative recovery measure. Nearly three weeks later, Perkins testified before the House Labor Committee and endorsed the thirty-hour idea along with minimum wage boards in the Department of Labor and the granting of power to the secretary of labor to restrict production and prevent cutthroat competition by relaxing anti-trust laws and formulating trade agreements. On May 10, the House Labor Committee unanimously approved the Black-Connery bill, but Roosevelt mobilized all of his resources to oppose it. He began vigorously promoting the administration proposal which would eventually become the National Industrial Recovery Act,* and the Black-Connery bill was then buried in the House Rules Committee. (Bernard Bellush, *The Failure of the NRA*, 1975.)

BLACK, EUGENE ROBERT Eugene R. Black was born in Atlanta, Georgia, in 1872. He graduated from the Boys High School in Atlanta and attended the University of Georgia and the University of Georgia Law School, but he left before graduating. Eventually he read law privately and was admitted to the Georgia bar. Black practiced law for more than twenty years before becoming president of the Atlanta Trust Company in 1921. Six years later he was appointed governor of the Federal Reserve Bank of Atlanta. During the repeated banking crises of the late 1920s and early 1930s, Black consistently warned that a nationwide liquidity crisis was imminent, and he gained national respect when his predictions were realized. A conservative who was widely respected in banking circles, Black also had the friendly ear of President Franklin D. Roosevelt* and served as an able liaison between the White House and the financial community. Roosevelt appointed Black head of the Federal Reserve Board* in May 1933, and Black played a critical role in the bank reopening process and in drafting legislation creating the Securities Act of 1933,* Banking Act of 1933,* extension of the Reconstruction Finance Corporation,* and the Securities Exchange Act of 1934.* After a brief illness, Eugene Robert Black died on December 19, 1934. (*New York Times*, December 20, 1934.)

BLACK, HUGO LA FAYETTE Hugo La Fayette Black was born on February 27, 1886. His family lived in the heart of Alabama cotton country. When Hugo was three, the family moved to Ashland, a town of about 350, where his father bought and operated a general store. He attended Ashland College and from there he went to the University of Alabama to pursue a medical career. But after one year he switched to law and graduated with an LL.B. in 1906. He practiced law in Ashland and then Birmingham. In addition to his private clients, he served as legal counsel to the miners' union and the carpenters' union. In 1910 he was appointed police court judge, a part-time position which he retained for about eighteen months. Then in 1915 he was elected county solicitor (prosecutor) for Jefferson County. When the United States entered World War I, Black resigned his position to join the army. He rose to the rank of captain in the 81st Field Artillery and also served as adjutant of the 19th Artillery Brigade. After the war he returned to Birmingham.

When Senator Oscar Underwood announced his intention to retire in 1926, Black decided to run for the Senate. He simply took off on his own, covering the back country alone in his Model-T, speaking anywhere he could find listeners and staying with anyone who would put him up. His vigorous campaign won him the nomination over three opponents, and at that time in Alabama the Democratic nomination was tantamount to election. In his first term Black did what was expected of junior members. He remained discreetly in the background while he studied the legislative process to learn how the system worked. At the same time he began a life-long habit of reading extensively to make up for the deficiencies of his early education, concentrating on history, economics, and philosophy. He consumed the writings of Thomas Jefferson and studied the accounts of the Federal Convention of 1787 as well as the records of the state ratifying conventions. It gave him a deep reverence for the Constitution.

When he felt prepared, he plunged into the work of the Senate by joining Senator George W. Norris* of Nebraska in the fight for public operation of Muscle Schoals* in his home state of Alabama. Elected to a second term in the Democratic sweep of 1932, Black soon emerged as a conspicuous figure in the Senate. He was an enthusiastic backer of the New Deal,* voting for all the major measures proposed in Congress during Franklin D. Roosevelt's* first term, except one—he strongly opposed the National Industrial Recovery Act,* which he felt from the first was doomed to failure. During the New Deal, he was also a staunch friend of labor. In 1933 Black launched a series of investigations into the policies, costs, and salaries of the United States Shipping Board, a matter which had interested him since the late 1920s. He was extremely critical of subsidies. In 1935 Black was given credit for passing the Public Utility Holding Company Act.* He created an uproar when, as chairman of the Senate Lobby Investigating Committee, he tried to subpoena some 5 million telegrams as evidence of the high pressure tactics of lobbyists. He was rebuffed by the courts and roundly criticized in the press.

His relatively brief career in the Senate was cut short when President Roosevelt nominated him for the Supreme Court* on August 12, 1937, to replace conservative Justice Willis Van Devanter.* The Senate voted confirmation, and on the same day Mr. Justice Black took the oath of office. He then sailed for Europe on vacation. While he was still abroad a new controversy swirled around Black. A series of articles in the Pittsburgh *Post-Gazette* revealed that he had joined the Ku Klux Klan on September 11, 1923, and resigned on July 9, 1925, as he began his campaign for the Senate. These revelations set off a new round of denunciation and defense. Black himself said nothing from Europe, but after his return to the United States he explained in a radio address that he joined the Klan but resigned and never rejoined. In an interview not published until after his death, Black explained that because many lawyers in Birmingham and many jurors belonged to the Klan he too had to join to have an equal advantage with juries.

He took his seat on the Court and quickly emerged as a consistent dissenter. His minority opinions prompted continued attack by conservatives and support by liberals. If there was any lingering doubt about his ''Klanism'' he soon dispelled it with his strong defense of individual and minority rights. In 1940 he wrote the majority opinion in the case of *Chambers v. Florida*, vacating the conviction of four blacks whose confessions had been obtained under duress, a violation of the Fourteenth Amendment. Also in 1940 in *Smith v. Texas*, Justice Black wrote the majority opinion that a black defendant had not received a fair trial because blacks were excluded from the jury. Justice Black found himself in frequent conflict with Justice Felix Frankfurter* over the Bill of Rights. Black insisted that the guarantees contained in the First and Fifth Amendments were absolute, that there was nothing equivocal about the language in the Bill of Rights. When the First Amendment said, ''Congress shall make no law . . . ,'' it meant precisely that—*no law*. Justice Frankfurter rejected such a concept. He believed that the guarantees of the Bill of Rights had to be balanced against other considerations. Thus, the two men were often in conflict over the issue of individual rights.

Occasionally, Justice Black aroused the wrath of liberals for his opinions. In *Korematsu v. United States* (1944), he upheld the authority of the federal government to remove the Japanese from along the Pacific coast. Especially in his later years, liberals accused him of turning conservative because he declined to defend civil rights demonstrations under First Amendment rights, upheld the constitutionality of the Virginia poll tax, and refused to overturn an anti-birth control law in Connecticut. But Justice Black insisted that these opinions were consistent with his views on constitutional guarantees. On Sunday, September 26, 1971, Justice Hugo Black died at age eighty-five from inflammation of the arteries and a stroke that he had suffered the previous Sunday. Eight days before his death, he had resigned from the Supreme Court after thirty-four years of service as one of the foremost champions of individual rights in the Court's history. (John P. Frank, *Mr. Justice Black*, 1949; James J. Magee, *Mr. Justice Black: Absolutist on the Court*, 1980.)

JOSEPH M. ROWE, JR.

BLACK, JOHN DONALD John Donald Black was born on June 6, 1883, in Jefferson County, Wisconsin. With a keen interest in agricultural economics, Black took all of his higher education at the University of Wisconsin, receiving the B.A. in 1909, M.A. in 1910, and Ph.D. in 1918. He held a number of academic positions before joining the staff of Harvard University, including

Western Reserve University (1910-1911), Michigan College of Mines (1911-1915), University of Wisconsin (1917-1918), and the University of Minnesota (1918-1927). He joined the staff of Harvard in 1927 and shortly thereafter published his influential *Agricultural Reform in the United States* (1929), the book proposing acreage reductions as a means of lifting farm commodity prices. The book became extremely popular among liberal agricultural economists and became the basis for the Agricultural Adjustment Act of 1933.* Other books included *The Dairy Industry and the AAA* (1935), *Parity, Parity, Parity* (1942), and *Three Years of the AAA* (1938). Black retired from Harvard in 1956 as Henry Lee Professor of Economics and continued to write and consult on agricultural problems. He died on April 12, 1960. (*New York Times*, April 13, 1960.)

"BLACK MONDAY" The term "black Monday" was used by many New Dealers to describe the events of May 27, 1935, when the Supreme Court,* in three unanimous decisions, invalidated the National Industrial Recovery Act,* overturned the Frazier-Lemker Farm Bankruptcy Act of 1934,* and declared that the president's removal of William E. Humphrey* from the Federal Trade Commission* was illegal. The judicial assault on the New Deal* helped inspire President Franklin D. Roosevelt's* unsuccessful "court-packing"* scheme of 1937 and his subsequently successful reorientation of the Supreme Court through a number of new appointments. (Bernard Bellush, *The Failure of the NRA*, 1975).

BLAIR, EMILY NEWELL Emily Newell Blair was born in Joplin, Missouri, in 1877. She was educated at Goucher College and the University of Missouri, and she married Harry Blair in 1900. Blair had two children, in 1903 and 1907, and after 1910 became very active in the women's suffrage movement. During World War I, Blair worked with Anna Howard Shaw in the Women's Committee on National Defense, and from that base she became prominent in Democratic party* politics during the 1920s. In 1922 Blair became one of the first women to gain prominence in the Democratic party, serving as vice-chairman of the Democratic National Committee from 1922 to 1928. There she became friendly with Eleanor Roosevelt.* Blair was a founding member of the Women's National Democratic Club and served as president of the club in 1928. She supported Franklin D. Roosevelt's* campaign in 1932 and joined the Consumer's Advisory Board* of the National Recovery Administration* in 1933. Blair retired for a time from government service after the NRA was declared unconstitutional but then returned during the war with the Public Relations Department of the War Department. Emily Newell Blair died in 1951. (Susan Ware, *Beyond Suffrage: Women in the New Deal*, 1981.)

BLUE EAGLE (See NATIONAL RECOVERY ADMINISTRATION.)

BOILEAU, GERALD JOHN Gerald Boileau was born on January 15, 1900, in Woodruff, Wisconsin. After graduating from high school, he joined the army and served overseas during World War I, returning home to enter the Marquette University Law School. He received his law degree in 1923 and began practicing in Wausau, Wisconsin. Between 1926 and 1931 Boileau was the district attorney of Marathon County, Wisconsin. He had earlier become a Republican, but his politics were hardly a reflection of the national GOP's approach to modern industrial society. Boileau was a committed progressive, suspicious of the motives of corporate capitalism and always anxious to restrict and limit its power. In 1930 he was elected to Congress as a Republican and then re-elected in 1932. He allied himself there with the young group of liberal Democrats like Maury Maverick* and progressive Republicans like Vito Marcantonio.* In 1934, along with Philip La Follette* and other progressive Republicans in Wisconsin, Boileau switched his party affiliation to the new Wisconsin Progressive party* and was re-elected again. He endorsed Franklin D. Roosevelt* for president in 1936 and was re-elected himself. Boileau was a consistent advocate of increased relief spending, social security and unemployment compensation, regulation of public utilities, increased taxes on corporations and wealthy individuals, and federally-protected labor standards. But in the Republican resurgence of 1938, Boileau's political career went down with those of Philip La Follette and other Wisconsin Progressives. He tried unsuccessfully to regain his seat in 1940 but was elected circuit judge in Wisconsin in 1942 and re-elected in 1945, 1951, 1957, and 1963. He retired in 1970. (*Biographical Directory of Congress, 1774-1971*, 1972.)

BONNEVILLE POWER ADMINISTRATION To handle the electric power produced by the recently completed Bonneville Dam in Oregon, President Franklin D. Roosevelt* created the Bonneville Power Administration in August 1937 under the authority of the Bonneville Power Administration Act. J. D. Ross, head of the Seattle city light program, was appointed its first administrator. By executive order in 1940, Roosevelt designated the BPA as the marketing agency for all power generated by the Grand Coulee Dam. The PWA provided money and manpower to construct transmission lines. J. D. Ross died in March 1939, and Paul Raver became the new administrator; by then BPA was the chief producer of electric power in the Northwest. The Bonneville Power Administration sold that power wholesale, and it brought to an end for two decades the establishment of private power installations. (Richard Lowitt, *The New Deal and the West*, 1984.)

"BOONDOGGLING" "Boondoggling" was a term widely used in the 1930s to criticize New Deal* relief projects as useless, "make-work" programs. The term was attributed to Robert H. Link, a scoutmaster, who first used it in 1925 to describe crafts made by Boy Scouts. Alternatively, "boondoggle" was attributed to the western frontier where it referred to practical gadgets or useful handcrafted products such as belts, knife sheaths, and ax handles. The term came into use for the New Deal by a relief administrator testifying before the Aldermanic Committee for the Investigation of Relief in New York City. He used the term to mean the employment of individuals on relief to make marketable items out of discarded materials. The word was rapidly adopted by the public, however, to describe pointless, unnecessary, or wasteful work created by the government to occupy individuals while keeping them off the relief rolls. Soon New Deal critics used the term to describe the Civil Works Administration* and the Works Progress Administration,* especially the arts projects of Federal One.* ''Boondoggle'' was also used to imply misuse of public funds for private benefit. Although President Franklin D. Roosevelt* tried to speak of the nation ''boondoggling'' its way out of the depression, the term retained its pejorative meaning. (''Boondoggling,'' *The Christian Century*, LII:1231-1233, 1935; Henry G. Leach, ''In Praise of Boondoggling,'' *Forum*, XCIII:321-322, 1935.)

VIRGINIA F. HAUGHTON

BORAH, WILLIAM EDGAR William E. Borah was a United States senator from Idaho between 1907 until his death on January 19, 1940. Borah was born on June 29, 1865, in rural southern Illinois, near Fairfield. Of Pennsylvania Dutch stock, Borah's family had also lived in Kentucky. Borah's father, William Nathan, was a farmer and stock raiser, who married Eliza West of Indiana. William E. was the seventh child in a family of ten. Borah had an unusual childhood and education. His father was a stern and disciplined man who demanded compliance and made life miserable for his young namesake. William E. Borah attended public schools in Illinois and Kansas before entering the University of Kansas at age twenty. Borah, who once joined a travelling Shakespearean troupe, found academia to his liking, except for the expense and a bout with tuberculosis. Unable to complete a freshman year, he decided to read law in his brother-in-law's office. After passing the bar in 1887, young Borah decided to move to the Pacific Northwest. On the train trip west, he was persuaded to settle in Idaho, so he got off in Boise. The year was 1890, and the young lawyer had less than $20.

Quickly establishing himself as a criminal lawyer and special prosecutor, and named chairman of the Republican State Central Committee, Borah rapidly rose to prominence in the young state of Idaho. He married Mary McConnell, the daughter of Governor William McConnell, and they created a great political and personal partnership. As a lawyer, Borah was instrumental in gaining a conviction of ''Diamondfield Jack'' Davis for the murder of two sheepherders. He prosecuted ''Big Bill'' Haywood, George Pettibone, and Charles Moyer for conspiring to murder former Idaho governor, Frank Steunenberg. Clarence Darrow,* Borah's legal opponent in the case, won an acquittal, but Borah's eloquence received national attention.

Elected to the U.S. Senate in 1906, he established himself as a Progressive Republican. He sponsored legislation to create the Department of Labor, an eight-hour day for government contracts, and better working conditions in the steel industry. A dedicated opponent of big trusts, he fought for the income tax and the direct election of senators amendment. Although his progressivism waned somewhat under Woodrow Wilson, he claimed it was because Wilson tried to create a greater bureaucracy and centralize too much power in the federal government. During the 1920s, Borah served as chairman of the Foreign Relations Committee. Although a powerful opponent of the League of Nations and entangling alliances, Borah did work on disarmament conferences during the decade. In some respects both the Washington Naval Conference of 1921 and the Kellogg-Briand Pact of Paris were his handiwork.

Although a Republican, Borah gave considerable support to New Deal* legislation. The TVA,* SEC,* Social Security Act,* National Labor Relations Act,* and Wealth Tax Act* were supported by the Idaho senator. He consistently bolted his own party to vote for increased relief spending and bills to expand currency. Borah opposed Franklin D. Roosevelt's* NRA,* the "court-packing"* scheme, the FEPC,* and other items. His main opposition to Roosevelt was over foreign policy issues of the 1930s. He became the leader of the isolationists and was able to get the neutrality legislation passed. He even flirted with the Republican presidential nomination in 1936 but decided against a full-fledged attempt. Borah died in Washington, D.C., on January 19, 1940. (Claudius O. Johnson, *Borah of Idaho*, 1965; Marian C. McKenna, *Borah*, 1961.)

F. ROSS PETERSON

BOWERS, CLAUDE GERNADE Claude G. Bowers was born in Westfield, Indiana, in 1878. After graduating from high school, he became a journalist in Indianapolis and in Terre Haute and became involved in local Indiana Democratic politics. In 1911 he went to Washington, D.C., as an assistant to Senator John Worth Kern. There he broadened his political connections, and in 1913 he met Franklin D. Roosevelt.* Bowers returned to Terre Haute in 1917, where he wrote the popular, partisan column "Kabbages and Kings." In 1923 he joined the editorial staff of the *New York World*. During the 1920s, Bowers wrote history—*The Party Battles of the Jackson Period* (1922), *Jefferson and Hamilton* (1925), and *The Tragic Era* (1929). These books and his syndicated columns established his reputation as one of the foremost scholars of the Democratic party.* Bowers viewed history, politics, government, economics, and international relations in terms of a Hamiltonian/Jeffersonian conflict between the forces of aristocracy which benefited the few and those of democracy which benefited the many.

Bowers was called upon to make numerous addresses in the 1920s, including the major speech at the 1928 Jackson Day Dinner in Washington. His success there led to his selection as keynote speaker at the 1928 Democratic National Convention. At the convention Bowers renewed his acquaintance with Roosevelt, and, during the Herbert Hoover* administration, he served as occasional speechwriter and political adviser for the New York governor. Following his election in 1932, Roosevelt appointed Bowers ambassador to Spain, where he sympathized with the Loyalists. After the fall of the Loyalist government, Bowers was reassigned to Chile. Following the Republican victory in 1952, Bowers resigned from the diplomatic corps and returned to the United States. He died in January 1958. (Merrill D. Peterson, "Bowers, Roosevelt, and the 'New Jefferson,' " *Virginia Quarterly Review*, XXXIV:530-534, 1958.)

VIRGINIA F. HAUGHTON

"BRAIN TRUST" During his early political career, Franklin D. Roosevelt* had frequently consulted academics and intellectuals on important policy issues, and he had continued the tradition during his governorship in New York between 1929 and 1933. Early in 1932, as he was planning his presidential campaign, he and some of his advisers were worried about issues and themes. They were as confused as everyone else about the problem of depression and recovery. In March 1932 Roosevelt's general counsel, Samuel Rosenman,* suggested that he assemble a group of advisers to develop campaign themes, but they should not be drawn from the business community. Rosenman urged Governor Roosevelt to turn to the universities, and Roosevelt agreed. Rosenman took the initiative and recruited Raymond Moley,* a political scientist at Barnard College who had written speeches for Roosevelt and frequently offered political advice. For expertise on agriculture, Moley then recruited Rexford Guy Tugwell,* another Columbia professor. For advice on corporate and economic affairs, they both turned to Adolf Berle, Jr.,* a Columbia professor and author of *The Modern Corporation and Private Property* (1932). Basil O'Connor, Roosevelt's law partner, joined them. Moley assumed leadership of the group, wrote up the list of topics they discussed, and presided at their meetings. They met frequently throughout 1932, and in September James Kieran of *The New York Times* dubbed them the "brains trust," a term the public later shortened to "brain trust."

In their meetings, which frequently included Roosevelt, the "brain trust" argued and debated a number of policy issues. Moley, Berle, and Tugwell all rejected the Wilsonian-Brandeisian description of economic reality. They believed that bigness in business was here to stay and that the key was regulation not anti-trust activity. Society could benefit from economies of scale if the federal government was willing to regulate the abuses of concentrated economic power. Tugwell was also a strong advocate of national economic planning and the underconsumption theory of the depression. Their ideas helped lead the way to the National Industrial Recovery Act of 1933* and to the Agricultural Adjustment Act of 1933.* After the election in November 1932, the "brain trust" dissolved as a formal group. All five men continued to play significant roles in the New Deal,* but as a formal group meeting frequently, they disbanded. Beyond helping Franklin D. Roosevelt formulate his major campaign ideas and stimulating a policy momentum which carried right through the "hundred days,"* they established the tradition of the "service intellectual" on the federal level. (Elliott A. Rosen, *Hoover, Roosevelt, and the Brains Trust: From Depression to New Deal*, 1977.)

BRANDEIS, LOUIS DEMBITZ European revolutionaries forced the Brandeis family to leave Czechoslovakia in 1848, and eight years later, when Louis was born in 1856, Adolf Brandeis was established as a successful grain commission merchant in Louisville, Kentucky. Louis was educated at the German and English Academy in Louisville, and attended school in Dresden, Germany, before entering Harvard Law School in 1875. His brilliance and judicial philosophy quickly became apparent. Brandeis viewed the Constitution as a flexible instrument that allowed people to govern themselves democratically. In order for the courts to interpret the Constitution properly, they had to consider legal precedents, common sense, and social realities. This method of jurisprudence came to national attention in 1908 when Brandeis submitted to the Supreme Court* what came to be known as a Brandeis brief. In *Muller v. Oregon*, Brandeis persuaded the Supreme Court to accept sociological statistics as evidence in upholding a law.

While arbitrating the New York garment workers' strike in 1910, Brandeis discovered his Jewish identity and eventually became head of the powerful American Zionist movement. He saw Zionism as an extension of the American ideal. Brandeis was also a fervent believer in freedom of business enterprise. He felt that the great enemy of freedom was monopoly and special privileges, such as tariffs and subsidies. He also opposed the union demand for closed shops. To force laborers to join a union in order to secure employment violated his ideas of democracy.

In 1912 Woodrow Wilson asked Brandeis to serve as his campaign adviser. Brandeis helped the future president shape a program which they called the "New Freedom." It called for regulating competition and creating a federal trade commission to supervise business practices. Wilson appointed Brandeis to the Supreme Court in 1916. He served on the Supreme Court for twenty-three years, during the administrations of five presidents. For almost the entire time, Brandeis' views were expressed in minority opinions.

The Great Depression brought a new popularity to his opinions. Inexpensive editions of his book *Other People's Money* were published during the campaign of 1932 and Franklin D. Roosevelt* frequently referred to the book in his fireside chats*. Brandeis differed sharply with the planning philosophy behind early New Deal* measures such as the National Recovery Administration* and the Agricultural Adjustment Act.* However, he voted against specific New Deal measures only three times: in the *Schechter** case which struck down the NRA, the *Panama** decision which repudiated a section of the NIRA,* and the Louisville land bank* case, which struck down the Frazier-Lemke Act.* He acknowledged that the federal government had a role to play in the recovery but advocated that as many duties as possible should devolve upon the states. Brandeis advocated "breaking up business to the point where the states could regulate them;" championed the Wisconsin plan as a model for state action in handling unemployment compensation; criticized the Social Security Act* for retaining too large a role for the federal government; and opposed the court-packing* scheme as dangerous to an independent judiciary.

Through the influence of Felix Frankfurter,* one of his disciples, many of Brandeis' economic and labor reforms became reality during the New Deal. The prudent investment theory of valuation set forth by Brandeis in a 1923 dissent became constitutional doctrine in 1933. The National Labor Relations Act of 1935* embodied Brandeis' dissents in the *Hickman, Duplex Printing* and other cases. Brandeis' arguments as an attorney in the 1914 *O'Hara* case finally became law of the land when the Court upheld the validity of minimum wage legislation in *West Coast Hotel v. Parrish.**

He suffered a heart attack in January 1939 and retired one month later. To Brandeis' immense satisfaction, Roosevelt named William O. Douglas,* chairman of the Securities and Exchange Commission,* to the vacant seat. He continued meeting with government officials and reformers, intervening when he could on Jewish matters with Roosevelt. The president often referred to Brandeis as "Isaiah." He died on October 5, 1941, a month before his eighty-fifth birthday. (Melvin I. Urofsky, *Louis Brandeis and the Progressive Tradition*, 1981.)

ANITA PILLING

BRICKER, JOHN WILLIAM John W. Bricker was born on September 6, 1893, in Madison County, Ohio. He graduated from Ohio State University in 1916, served in the army during World War I, and then took a law degree at Ohio State in 1920. A Republican active in local party politics, Bricker was appointed assistant attorney general for Ohio in 1923 and in 1929 became a member of the Ohio Public Utilities Commission. Between 1929 and 1932 he greatly increased his popularity among the voters of Ohio by travelling widely and insisting on a doctrine of strict law enforcement and close adherence to a literal interpretation of the United States Constitution. In 1932 John Bricker announced his candidacy for the office of state attorney general. Although the severity of the Great Depression in Ohio gave Franklin D. Roosevelt* a landslide victory in the state's presidential election and a Democrat took over the governor's mansion, Bricker defied the odds and won his election. During his years as attorney general he continued to insist on a strict view of the Constitution and a very literal view of law enforcement. His tenure as attorney general was lackluster but he was able to become one of the more prominent Republicans in Ohio. Bricker also became a staunch critic of the New Deal.* In October 1935 he attacked the Roosevelt administration's policies, particularly the NRA* and increasing deficit expenditures. During 1936 he assailed Roosevelt's support for a minimum wage for industrial workers. Although a popular Republican in Ohio by this time, he lost his bid for the governor's mansion to Martin L. Davey* in the election of 1935. Instead, he had to be content with remaining the attorney general and a well-known critic of the New Deal. Then he tried his hand at national politics. On January 17, 1937, Bricker delivered a stinging attack on the New Deal before the Women's National Republican Club, where he claimed that Roosevelt had damaged small businessmen and farmers in Ohio and the South. In 1938 he announced his candidacy for governor and because of internal dissension within the Democratic party* he defeated Martin Davey. Bricker was governor of Ohio between 1939 and 1945. An avowed isolationist, Bricker espoused neutrality and criticized Roosevelt's support of the Allied powers in Europe. In May 1940 Bricker announced his candidacy for the Republican presidential nomination. A dark horse candidate from the outset, Bricker assailed Roosevelt and the New Deal, but he lost the nomination to Wendell Willkie.* Bricker returned to his gubernatorial duties, but he had lost much of his popularity. In the election of 1944, the Democrats ousted Bricker and elected Frank J. Lausche as governor of Ohio. Bricker returned to his legal practice for a short time. But in 1947 he was elected to the U.S. Senate, and he remained there until his death in March 1956. (Denis W. Brogan, *The Era of Franklin Roosevelt*, 1950; *New York Times*, November 13, 1938.)

JOHN S. LEIBY

BROWDER, EARL Browder was born on May 20, 1891, in Wichita, Kansas, one of ten children of a struggling farmer. Leaving school after the third grade, Browder helped to support the family as an errand boy, a telegraph clerk, and a bookkeeper. In 1906 he joined the Socialist party,* and by 1912 he was associated with William Z. Foster's* Syndicalist League of North America. Late in 1914 Browder organized the League for Democratic Control to oppose the United States' entry into World War I. He was arrested in 1917 and sentenced to a year in Platte County jail for draft evasion and two years in Leavenworth for conspiracy to block the draft. In 1921 Browder attended the first congress of the Red International of Labor Unions in Moscow. For the next five years, he edited the *Labor Herald*, the paper of the Trade Union Educational League and worked with the Workers Party of America, a political organization that agitated for trade unionism. In 1926 he went to China, where he organized Communist labor unions and edited the publication of the Pan-Pacific Trade Union Secretariat.

Shortly before the stock market crash, Browder returned to America to find the Party rife with sectarianism. His distance from factional strife made him an attractive candidate for Party leadership. In 1930 Browder was appointed to a three-man ruling council. He was named general secretary four years later. Browder declared a "united front" between the Communist* and Socialist parties* "to fight off the imminent danger of fascism and war." This coalition remained frankly anti-capitalist and anti-New Deal until August 1935 when the Comintern's Seventh Congress shelved its revolutionary model for a moderate "People's Front" cooperation between all anti-fascists. Suddenly, communism was, according to Browder's slogan, "Twentieth Century Americanism," and the New Deal* was no longer foot-dragging reformism but rather a viable middle course between reaction and progressive strategies. In 1936 Browder received 80,159 votes for president, but his vigorous campaign was aimed mainly at defeating Alf Landon's* Republican ticket. A year later Browder applauded

Franklin D. Roosevelt's* proposed quarantine of the fascist nations. The CPUSA's official attitude toward the president had grown very cordial.

Browder's public support of New Deal policies continued until August 1939 when the Soviet Union and Germany signed a non-aggression pact. Browder accommodated himself to this disastrous turn, though only weeks earlier he had guessed that such an agreement was as likely as "Earl Browder being elected President of the Chamber of Commerce." He quickly condemned the war against Germany as "imperialist" and "phony" and would soon denounce the Lend-Lease Bill. In 1940 he received 46,251 votes for president, but this time he attacked Roosevelt, whom he claimed was a war-monger and stooge of Wall Street. But by summer 1941, after Germany's invasion of the Soviet Union, the Comintern was supporting the war effort, and Browder again found himself scrambling to keep up with its ever-twisting line. Relations with Roosevelt were again amiable, but the CPUSA would never fully recover from such vertiginous shifting of its position.

In 1940 Browder was sentenced to four years in federal prison for passport violations but was pardoned by Roosevelt in May 1942. Two years later, badly misreading both Stalin's dissolution of the Comintern and the Teheran agreements between the United States, Britain, and the Soviet Union, Browder replaced the CPUSA with the Communist Political Association, an organization designed to contribute to "national unity." For disbanding the Party, Browder was attacked publicly by Jacques Duclos, a leading French Communist, replaced as general secretary by William Z. Foster when the CPUSA was reestablished in 1945, and expelled from the Party in 1946. Browder died on June 27, 1973, no longer a Marxist and largely remembered by his former comrades as a "right deviationist." (Philip J. Jaffe, *The Rise and Fall of American Communism*, 1975; James Gilbert Ryan, "The Making of a Native Marxist: The Early Career of Earl Browder," in *Review of Politics*, XXXIX:332-362, 1977.)

ART CASCIATO

BROWNLOW COMMITTEE (See the REORGANIZATION ACT OF 1939.)

BROWNLOW, LOUIS Louis Brownlow was born in Buffalo, Missouri, on August 29, 1879. He was educated at home by his parents and worked as a reporter for the *Nashville Banner* (1900-1902), *Louisville Courier-Journal* (1902), and the *Louisville Times* (1903). Brownlow was Washington correspondent for the *Nashville Banner* in 1904, and he became editor of the *Paducah News-Democrat* in 1905. Between 1906 and 1915, Brownlow was a writer and foreign correspondent for the Haskin Syndicate, and then he went into administrative politics. He served as a commissioner of Washington, D.C., between 1915 and 1917, and president of the board of commissioners between 1917 and 1920. Brownlow's career in public administration began there. In 1920 he became city manager of Petersburg, Virginia, and moved to Knoxville, Tennessee, in the same position in 1924. In 1928 Brownlow became a consultant to the City

Housing Corporation of New York, and he remained in that position until 1931 when he became director of the Public Administration Clearing House in Chicago. Brownlow was director of the PACH until 1949.

In 1936 President Franklin D. Roosevelt* appointed a three-man President's Committee on Administrative Management to examine the problems of management, economy, and efficiency in government. The chairman was Louis Brownlow, and Luther Gulick* and Charles E. Merriam* were the other members. It became known as the Brownlow Committee.* Brownlow was a strong New Deal* supporter. In January 1937 he presented his report to the president. Eventually, it became the Reorganization Act of 1939.* Louis Brownlow wrote several books, including *The President and the Presidency* (1949), *Passion for Politics* (1955), and *A Passion for Anonymity* (1958). He died on September 28, 1963. (Barry D. Karl, *Executive Reorganization and Reform in the New Deal: The Genesis of Administrative Management, 1900-1939*, 1963; *Who Was Who in America*, IV:128, 1968.)

BULKLEY, ROBERT JOHNS Robert J. Bulkley was born in Cleveland, Ohio, on October 8, 1880. He graduated from Harvard University in 1902 and from the Harvard Law School in 1906, practiced law for five years in Cleveland, and was elected to Congress on the Democratic ticket in 1910. During World War I, Bulkley served as chief of the legal section of the War Industries Board, came to know Bernard Baruch,* and then practiced law in the 1920s and remained active in Democratic politics. He was a delegate to every Democratic national convention between 1912 and 1960. In 1930 Bulkley was elected to fill the Senate seat vacated by the death of Theodore E. Burton. He was re-elected in 1932 but was unsuccessful in 1938. During the 1930s, Bulkley was generally a Franklin D. Roosevelt* supporter, although he did oppose the Agricultural Adjustment Administration* and the suspension of gold payments. President Roosevelt endorsed him in the Democratic primary of 1938, which Bulkley won, but the anti-New Deal tide swept him out of office in the general election. Bulkley then returned to private law practice, maintained some interest in the banking and construction industries, and died on July 21, 1965. (*Biographical Directory of the American Congress, 1774-1971*, 1971; James T. Patterson, *Congressional Conservatism and the New Deal*, 1967.)

BURDICK, USHER LLOYD Usher L. Burdick was born in Owatonna, Minnesota, on February 21, 1879, and moved with his parents to the Dakota Territory in 1882, where he was raised among the Sioux Indians. After graduating from the state normal college at Mayville in 1900, Burdick went into education, serving as deputy superintendent of schools for Benson County between 1900 and 1902. He graduated from the University of Minnesota Law School in 1904 and then began practicing in Munich, North Dakota. Burdick entered politics in 1907 as a state representative and stayed in the legislature until 1911, when he became lieutenant governor. He was not re-elected in 1912 and became state attorney for Williams County (1913-1915). Burdick then retired from politics for more than a decade but in 1929 began working as assistant U.S. district attorney for North Dakota. He tried for Congress as a Republican in 1932 but lost in the Democratic landslide. Burdick came back and won a congressional seat in the election of 1934,* and was re-elected in 1936, 1938, 1940, and 1942. In Congress he was an eccentric figure but usually faithful to the small group of liberal Democrats and progressive Republicans in the House who looked to Maury Maverick* and Vito Marcantonio* for leadership. Burdick lost the Republican primary for the Senate in 1944, retired from politics for four years, but then was elected once again to Congress in 1948 and re-elected in 1950, 1952, 1954, and 1956. He was not a candidate for re-election in 1958, and died on August 19, 1960. (*New York Times*, August 20, 1960.)

BUREAU OF RECLAMATION Because of Secretary of the Interior Harold L. Ickes'* desire for an ''inland empire'' of federally coordinated water, wildlife, and resources conservation and development programs, the Bureau of Reclamation during the 1930s enjoyed a marked increase in its available funds. Before 1933 the bureau's average annual expenditures were $8.9 million, but between 1933 and 1940 they averaged $52 million. Bureau engineers emphasized the multipurpose approach and combined hydro-electric power development with irrigation programs in their planning, much like the Tennessee Valley Authority* approach. Bureau engineers also considered flood control, drainage, and recreation in their major projects. Ickes regularly allowed the Bureau of Reclamation to use PWA,* CCC,* and WPA* labor on projects, and in 1938 Congress permitted the Department of the Interior to divert half of the proceeds from naval petroleum reserves to the Reclamation Fund. The Reclamation Project Act of 1939 set a ten-year period before repayment on reclamation projects was to begin and shifted costs of some reservoir projects to flood control and navigation programs. The Wheeler-Case Act of 1939 stipulated that labor costs on irrigation projects using WPA or CCC employees would not be passed on to settlers unless they could afford to pay for them. These laws allowed for the construction of many reclamation projects which could not qualify for the 100 percent reimbursement terms of the Reclamation Act of 1902.

By 1937 the Bureau of Reclamation was engaged in seventy-two projects totalling $87.8 million, and their effect would be to increase reservoir storage capacities to 56.6 million acre-feet. In addition to massive, multipurpose projects, the bureau constructed dozens of smaller earthen dams to catch and store flood waters in smaller rivers and streams. Their goal was to stabilize the water needs of western areas where hurried settlement, overgrazing, range plowing, and speculation had depleted resources. The Bureau of Reclamation during the 1930s wanted to help farm families by irrigating acreage not ready for dry commercial farming, restore depleted water supplies, and assist in the development of dry farming. (Richard Lowitt, *The New Deal in the West*, 1984.)

BUREAU OF THE BUDGET The 1921 Budget and Accounting Act created a Bureau of the Budget located "in but not of" the Treasury Department. The Bureau of the Budget was charged with preparing the president's annual spending proposals to Congress and studying economy and efficiency in government operations. The efficiency mission was largely ignored under the succeeding Republican administrations in favor of budget preparation and economy. The director of the Bureau of the Budget was also to be a personal assistant appointed by the president without Senate confirmation. Upon taking office in 1933, President Franklin D. Roosevelt* immediately upgraded the role of the Bureau of the Budget, placing in it considerable responsibility for management and coordination of the executive branch, including the New Deal* emergency agencies. This emphasis reflected the president's interest in budgetary matters, executive branch reorganization, economy, and efficiency.

Lewis W. Douglas,* a former banker and businessman, resigned from Congress to become director of the Bureau of the Budget. He was invited to all cabinet meetings and had a daily appointment with President Roosevelt. Roosevelt initially sought to reduce expenditures and balance the budget, goals which the conservative Douglas shared. But Douglas finally resigned in 1934 because of rising government expenditures. He opposed the New Deal public works and relief programs, as well as abandonment of the gold standard. After that the president minimized the bureau's role and began to rely more on his White House assistants.

Upon the recommendation of Treasury Secretary Henry Morgenthau, Jr.,* the president appointed Daniel W. Bell* as acting director. Bell was a civil servant who had entered the treasury in 1911 as a bookkeeper and risen to be commissioner of accounts and deposits. He insisted on acting director status because it permitted him to retain his civil service status and seniority; he also served as assistant to the secretary of the treasury for fiscal and auditing matters. Bell did not usually attend cabinet meetings. During his tenure some significant changes occurred in bureau operations. In 1933 the president had required that all executive orders drafted by agencies for his consideration be submitted through the Bureau of the Budget, which handled interagency clearance as well as policy review. Subsequently, he extended this central clearance procedure to all appropriations proposals (1933) and then all legislative proposals (1937), including agency reports and testimony to Congress. Such proposals had to be consistent with the president's program. Beginning in 1934 the Bureau of the Budget was also directed to expand its clearance of bills approved by Congress for the president's consideration. By 1938 the Bureau of the Budget was reviewing virtually all congressional measures going to the president. Still, the bureau was largely a treasury agency rather than a staff agency for the president. It was located in the treasury, had a restricted view of its role based on an economy approach, lacked the resources and organization to serve as a presidential staff agency, and following the Douglas era lacked President Roosevelt's confidence.

All that changed after the Reorganization Act of 1939.* The 1937 Report of the President's Committee on Administrative Management* emphasized the Bureau of the Budget's importance as a presidential staff agency to help manage the executive branch. Reorganization Plan No. 1 in April 1939 transferred the Bureau of the Budget to the new executive office of the president. Roosevelt nearly doubled the 1939 appropriation and more than doubled the staff of the bureau, which became responsible for reorganization plans. In March 1939 he appointed Harold D. Smith* as the director of the Bureau of the Budget. Smith established a good personal relationship with Roosevelt. Executive Order 8248 on September 8, 1939, broadly defined the duties assigned to the Bureau of the Budget, including keeping the president informed on work in progress throughout the executive branch. Within two years the Bureau of the Budget had doubled its funding and personnel. U.S. entry into World War II greatly expanded its management role. In 1940 the agency was drastically reorganized into six functional divisions: estimates, fiscal, legislative, reference, administrative management, and statistical standards. A special war projects unit was added in 1941.

The New Deal had stimulated a revolution in the mission, role, and status of the Bureau of the Budget. It was transformed from a treasury bureau focused on budget preparation and economy recommendations to a presidential staff agency for the management of the executive branch. The role of the federal budget was greatly increased by New Deal emergency spending and World War II. The Bureau of the Budget became the lead agency in central clearance and executive branch reorganization. (Larry Berman, *The Office of Management and Budget and the Presidency, 1921-1979*, 1979; Percival Brundage, *The Bureau of the Budget*, 1970.)

DUANE WINDSOR

BURKE, EDWARD RAYMOND Edward R. Burke was born in Runningwater, South Dakota, on November 28, 1880. He graduated from Beloit College in 1906 and received a law degree from Harvard in 1911. For more than twenty years Burke practiced law privately and was active in local Democratic politics, winning a seat in Congress in 1932. Known as a conservative Democrat, Burke enjoyed a close friendship with Arthur Mullen, former Nebraska Democratic national committeeman and President Franklin D. Roosevelt's* floor manager at the 1932 national convention in Chicago. Burke loyally supported early New Deal* legislation as a congressman, but after he won the senatorial nomination and election in 1934, he veered away from Roosevelt's forces. Mullen was by then representing electric utility forces in Nebraska, and he complained frequently about Harold Ickes'* friendship with progressive Republican Senator George Norris.* In fact, large numbers of Nebraska Democrats were upset that Roosevelt was so supportive of Norris. Burke also sympathized with business and manufacturing interests in Nebraska and was bitterly opposed to the Committee for Industrial Organization. Consequently, he voted against the National Labor Relations Act,* the Public Utility Holding Company Act,* pump-priming and deficit spending, and the "court-packing"* scheme. He was a thorn in Roosevelt's side, and after losing his attempt at renomination in 1940, he endorsed Republican Wendell Willkie's* candidacy for the presidency. Burke continued to practice law after his political career ended and served on the boards of directors of a number of banking and manufacturing concerns. He died on November 4, 1968. (James T. Patterson, *Congressional Conservatism and the New Deal*, 1967; *New York Times*, November 5, 1968.)

BURNS, EVELINE Born in London, England, in 1900, to a lower middle class family, Eveline Richardson attended Streatham School in London; and while working during the day at the British Ministry of Labor, she attended the London School of Economics at night, graduating with honors in 1920. She entered graduate school there in 1920, married fellow graduate student Arthur R. Burns in 1922, and received a doctorate in 1926. With a Social Science Research Council fellowship, she travelled throughout the United States between 1926 and 1928, and in 1928 she joined the faculty in the Department of Economics at Columbia University. Burns' early work involved research into the unemployment insurance systems of Great Britain and Germany. At Columbia she met Mary Dewson,* head of the National Consumers' League, and Dewson introduced her to members of the New York Consumers' League. They soon elected her president of the league in New York. One of Burns' first students, Abraham Epstein,* interested her in old-age assistance and unemployment compensation reform. Epstein was the founder of the American Association for Social Security, and Burns served as vice-president from 1935 to 1943.

In June 1934 President Franklin D. Roosevelt* established the Committee on Economic Security* to study the problem of social security. Burns was a critical staff member who advocated the Ohio plan of a national unemployment system, but the final draft of the Social Security Act* contained mostly the federal-state system pioneered in Wisconsin. During congressional hearings on the bill, Burns delivered many speeches and wrote articles defending the measure and trying to educate the public about the need for the proposed legislation. Roosevelt signed the Social Security Act on August 14, 1935.

After passage of the bill, Burns wrote a brief work explaining the social security system which was published early in 1936 as *Toward Social Security*. The head of the research division of the new Social Security Board asked Burns to come to Washington, D.C., to serve as a consultant on long-range research. Upon her arrival, Burns concluded that the greater need involved training new administrators for implementing the complicated system of old-age assistance, unemployment insurance, and public assistance programs. Using her wide knowledge of social insurance systems around the world as a base and her recently published book as a text, Burns co-directed three-week training sessions for the administrators in the spring and summer of 1936.

Throughout the New Deal* years Burns continued her teaching and research at Columbia University, broadening her knowledge of social insurance laws, practices, financing, and administration. In the summer of 1939, William Haber, director of the recently established Committee on Long-Range Work and Relief Policies of the National Resources Planning Board,* asked Burns to submit a memorandum on how to organize that committee's review of New Deal relief, work relief, and public works programs. Shortly thereafter Burns became research director of the committee which conducted its investigation between late 1939 and late 1941. In addition to providing the most comprehensive review of New Deal relief programs, the committee also submitted recommendations for social security and relief reforms for the postwar period. Though the planning board tried to encourage Roosevelt to release the final report in early 1942, the president delayed submitting it to Congress until March 1943.

When the committee's report, *Security, Work, and Relief Policies*, was finally released, it appeared as Part III of the planning board's 1943 postwar planning report. Heralded and damned as the American equivalent of the British Beveridge Report, *Social Insurance and Allied Services* (1942), the Burns-written report came at a bad time. Congress conducted appropriation hearings for the planning board at the same time as the release of the report. Critics of the planning board, hoping to attack Roosevelt indirectly and redress a perceived imbalance of power between executive and legislative branches, began calling the three-part report a "cradle to grave" plan that would bring socialism to America. Burns came under personal attacks which called her everything from a "Fascist" to a "Communist." Her report advocated a national system of unemployment insurance and intervention by the federal government in other relief programs when states did not create their own. Congress abolished the planning agency effective August 31, 1943, burying the relief report with it. Burns remained with the National Planning Commission until 1945. During the 1950s, she worked as a consultant to the Department of Health, Education, and Welfare; served as vice-president of the American Economic Association (1953-1954); and wrote several books, including *The Social Security System* (1949) and *Social Security and Public Policy* (1956). (Vera Shlakman, "Eveline M. Burns: Social Economist," in Shirley Jenkins, ed., *Social Security in International Perspective*, 1969; Susan Ware, *Beyond Suffrage: Women in the New Deal*, 1981.)

PATRICK D. REAGAN

BUSINESS ADVISORY COUNCIL Formed in June 1933 as the Business Advisory and Planning Council (renamed Business Advisory Council in 1935), the BAC was the brainchild of Daniel Roper,* secretary of commerce. He hoped the council would provide President Franklin D. Roosevelt* with an advisory group from the business community to help cement relations with the New Deal* and hasten economic recovery. The BAC included forty-one prominent businessmen, among whom were Myron Taylor of U.S. Steel, Alfred Sloan* of General Motors, Robert Wood* of Sears Roebuck, Walter Gifford of AT&T, and Pierre du Pont. Gerard Swope* of General Electric was chairman. In addition to making a variety of proposals about American business, the BAC membership staffed the NRA's* Industrial Advisory Board on a rotating basis. When Hugh

Johnson* left the NRA in November 1934, S. Clay Williams* left the BAC to replace him.

But the days of real cooperation were short-lived. As the National Recovery Administration became bogged down in dissension and bureaucratic infighting, the members of the Business Advisory Council grew frustrated, and they became positively angry with such New Deal measures as the Securities Exchange Act of 1934* and the National Labor Relations Act of 1935.* In 1935, when President Roosevelt tried to use the BAC to attack the U.S. Chamber of Commerce,* many members resigned because they felt the president had used them to create the impression that the chamber was alone in its opposition to the New Deal. In 1936 and 1937, the Business Advisory Council called for fiscal retrenchment and a balanced budget. They never really adjusted to the Keynesian ideas gaining ground among New Dealers. Still, the Business Advisory Council remained a bastion of those who dreamed of a business commonwealth—national planning and regulation of industry, with government cooperation but not government control. Supporting such measures as the National Recovery Administration and the Social Security Act,* they were not at all a laissez-faire interest group representing conservative businessmen. (Robert M. Collins, ''Positive Business Responses to the New Deal: The Roots of the Committee for Economic Development, 1933-1942,'' *Business History Review*, LII:369-391, 1978.)

BUTLER, PIERCE Pierce Butler, an associate justice of the Supreme Court* between 1922 and 1938, was born on March 17, 1866, in Northfield, Minnesota. His parents were Roman Catholics who had immigrated to the United States during the Irish potato famine of the 1840s. Saving money he had earned working at a dairy, Butler attended Carleton College and graduated in 1887. After reading law for one year in St. Paul with the firm of Pinch & Twohy, he was admitted to the Minnesota bar. Butler began practicing law with Stan Donnelly, son of Ignatius Donnelly, the Minnesota congressman and later vice-presidential candidate for the People's Party. In 1891 Butler was elected assistant attorney of Ramsey County and later served as county attorney. During the William Howard Taft administration, Attorney General of the United States George Wickersham hired Butler to represent the federal government in several anti-trust suits. He had also earned a reputation as a conservative railroad attorney for representing the interests of the Northern Pacific, Great Northern, and Chicago, Burlington, and Quincy Railroads. In 1922 Chief Justice William Howard Taft suggested Butler's name to President Warren G. Harding to fill the vacancy on the Supreme Court. Senate liberals opposed the nomination, arguing that Butler's conservative philosophy would turn the Supreme Court into a reactionary institution, but he was confirmed nonetheless.

During the 1920s and 1930s, Butler's conservative reputation was fulfilled again and again. On the Taft Court, he regularly aligned himself with the chief justice as well as with Justices James McReynolds,* George Sutherland,* and Willis Van Devanter* to form a conservative majority; and during the 1930s he maintained that position, then forming a coalition with the new Chief Justice Charles Evans Hughes* and Justices Owen Roberts,* George Sutherland, Willis Van Devanter, and James McReynolds to destroy the Agricultural Adjustment Administration,* the National Recovery Administration,* and other New Deal* programs. Indeed, Butler was perhaps the most conservative justice on the Supreme Court during the 1920s and 1930s, voting with Justice James McReynolds more than 94 percent of the time. He completely rejected sociological jurisprudence because he believed in interpreting the Constitution "as it is written," without confusing issues at hand with "irrelevant social and economic data." Butler firmly believed that the federal courts should not concern themselves with the internal affairs of a corporation foreign to the state where it sits, nor did he believe the federal government was in the business of promoting the general welfare. Blessed with a ready wit, Butler was a congenial colleague on the Supreme Court, but after the "court-packing"* fight in 1937 and Franklin D. Roosevelt's* new appointments, he was increasingly isolated into a small conservative minority. Pierce Butler died suddenly on November 16, 1939, in Washington, D.C. (*Guide to the U.S. Supreme Court*, 1979; Alpheus Thomas Mason, *The Supreme Court from Taft to Warren*, 1958.)

BYRD, HARRY FLOOD Harry F. Byrd was born in Martinsburg, West Virginia, on June 10, 1887. He went to public schools and the Shenandoah Valley Academy in Winchester, Virginia, and at the age of fifteen went to work for the family newspaper, the *Winchester Star*. Over the years he rose to become publisher of the *Star* and the *Harrisonburg Daily News Record*, managed prosperous fruit orchards, and served as president of the Valley Turnpike Company between 1908 and 1918. His interest in politics came naturally, since his uncle, "Hal" Flood, had been the state boss of Virginia politics during the Wilson era. Byrd served in the state senate between 1915 and 1925 and a term as governor of Virginia between 1926 and 1930. A protégé of Senator Carter Glass,* Byrd was appointed to fill the unexpired term of Senator Claude Swanson in 1933 when President Franklin D. Roosevelt* named Swanson secretary of the navy.

Early into the New Deal,* Harry Byrd became one of its most intense conservative critics. Both the NRA* and the AAA* raised his ire. For personal reasons, he found the NRA wage regulations too expensive for his apple operations, and he also resented the AAA processing taxes. On a more philosophical level, Byrd was the most forceful spokesman for fiscal conservatism in the nation and a proud advocate of states' rights and congressional prerogatives. Throughout the 1930s, the New Deal's deficit spending enraged Byrd, as did its commitment to executive power and centralization of authority in Washington, D.C. He bitterly fought the "court-packing"* scheme in 1937 and executive reorganization plans in 1938, opposed Roosevelt's renomination in 1940, and constantly fought patronage wars with Roosevelt during the 1930s. Byrd won those wars. As head of the Senate Finance Committee, he also made life difficult for some New Deal legislation. In 1938, when the president tried to appoint Floyd Roberts, an opponent of Byrd and Glass, to a federal judgeship in Virginia, Byrd fought the measure and the Senate refused to confirm him. By the time the New Deal years ended, Byrd was in complete political control in Virginia, still a conservative opponent of New Deal spending and labor legislation, and yet a victor in the patronage wars. He offered similar opposition to Presidents Harry S Truman,* John F. Kennedy, and Lyndon Johnson. Byrd retired from the Senate in 1965 and died on October 20, 1966. (James T. Patterson, *Congressional Conservatism and the New Deal*, 1967; A. Cash Koeniger, "The New Deal and the States: Roosevelt versus the Byrd Organization in Virginia," *Journal of American History*, LXVIII:876-896, 1982.)

BYRNES, JAMES FRANCIS A native son of South Carolina, James Byrnes was born in 1879 and went on to a distinguished career as a congressman, U.S. senator, Supreme Court* justice, secretary of state, and governor of his home state. His eleven years in the Senate coincided with the Great Depression, and as a self-styled "conservative, liberal Democrat," he placed his stamp on the New Deal.* After fourteen years in Congress, Byrnes campaigned unsuccessfully for a seat in the Senate in 1924 and then successfully in 1930. He was a charter member supporting Franklin D. Roosevelt's* presidential aspirations in 1932, and during the campaign he was a frequent political consultant and occasional speechwriter.

Having Roosevelt's ear after the inauguration, Byrnes supported the emergency measures which characterized the "first hundred days."* Of the fifteen major legislative enactments of that period, Byrnes was directly involved in the Economy Act,* the Thomas amendment to the Agricultural Adjustment Act,* the Securities Act,* the Home Owners' Refinancing Act,* and the Independent Offices Appropriations Act.* Ever mindful of his South Carolina constituents, he also focused his attention on the Santee-Cooper public power project and employment and agricultural problems in the state. He was very popular at home, and in the 1936 senatorial primary, he took 87 percent of the vote and was re-elected easily in November.

During Roosevelt's second term, some differences developed between the two men. Byrnes supported the "court-packing"* scheme but resisted the federal anti-lynching bill,* the use of sit-down strikes, Roosevelt's interference in a Senate contest between Alben Barkley* and Pat Harrison* for the majority leadership post and the attempted "purge"* of undeserving Democrats in 1938. Although Byrnes was convinced that northern liberals, labor unions, and blacks were exerting too much influence on the later New Deal, he was still counted among the administration's strongest supporters. As such he manuevered the administration's Reorganization Act of 1939* through the Congress as part of the concessions to economy. During the Democratic convention of 1940, Byrnes served as Roosevelt's "floor manager" in securing the third-term nomination. In June 1941 Roosevelt appointed him to the Supreme Court, but Byrnes was not comfortable in the judicial isolation and resigned in 1942 to head up the

Office of Economic Stabilization (1942-1943) and then the Office of War Mobilization (1943-1945). Byrnes accompanied Roosevelt to Yalta in February 1945, and in June 1945 President Harry S Truman* named him secretary of state, a post he held until 1947. From 1951 to 1955, he served as governor of South Carolina. Jamcs Byrnes died on April 9, 1972. As spokesman for the New South during the 1930s, he had exhibited legislative talents *par excellence*. He straddled successfully the liberal-conservative dichotomy in the fashion which served the nation's and the region's interests in combating the Great Depression and in assuming a worldwide responsibility. His stature is such that he ranks with John C. Calhoun as South Carolina's most effective statesman. (James F. Byrnes, *All in One Lifetime*, 1958; Winfred B. Moore, Jr., *New South Statesman*, 1976.)

ROBERT A. WALLER

BYRNS, JOSEPH WELLINGTON Joseph W. Byrns was born in Cedar Hill, Tennessee, on July 20, 1869. He received a law degree from Vanderbilt University in 1890 and began practicing law in Nashville. Byrns served in the state legislature between 1895 and 1901 and was elected to Congress in 1908. He was re-elected to Congress in each of the next fourteen election years, rising to majority leader in 1932 and Speaker of the House in 1935. Byrns was loyal to the early New Deal,* particularly to agricultural issues. He died suddenly on June 4, 1936. (*New York Times*, June 5, 1936.)

C

CAHILL, HOLGER Born in 1893 in St. Paul, Minnesota, Holger Cahill was educated at Columbia and the New School for Social Research. Over the years he came to view art as an expression of folk culture. Cahill's first book, *Profane Earth*, was published in 1927 and was followed three years later by *A Yankee Adventurer*. Cahill joined the staff of the Newark Museum in 1922. Under the direction of John Cotton Dana, he developed a democratic approach to art by emphasizing the connection between art, popular culture, and everyday life. During his years with the Newark Museum he also wrote *Geo. O "Pop" Hart* (1928) and *Max Weber* (1930). Cahill became director of exhibitions at the American Museum of Modern Art in New York in 1932 and stayed there until President Franklin D. Roosevelt* appointed him to head the Federal Art Project* in 1935. Cahill proved to be one of the most effective New Deal* administrators. He understood public relations and journalism, loved art, but was not an artist himself, so he could be very political in the best sense of the word, compromising when necessary and anticipating problems before they arose. Finally, Cahill's love of popular and folk art made him the ideal choice to administer a federal art program to employ poor artists while sustaining public support for the project. Under his direction, the FAP employed 4,300 artists to work on 327 projects in forty states. He remained with the Federal Art Project until 1943. After World War II, Cahill continued writing and won national acclaim with *The Shadow of His Hand* (1956). Holger Cahill died of a cerebral hemorrhage on July 8, 1960. (William F. McDonald, *Federal Relief Administration and the Arts*, 1969; *New York Times*, July 9, 1960.)

CALDWELL, ERSKINE Erskine Caldwell was born in 1903 in White Oak, Georgia, the only child of a liberal Presbyterian minister and a schoolmistress. After a one-year stint at Erskine College in South Carolina and sporadic attendance at the University of Virginia over a four-year period, Caldwell got a job as a reporter for *The Atlantic Journal* and began to write short stories in his spare time. He moved to Maine in 1926 and devoted more time to his fiction. His first "break" as an author came when Maxwell Perkins, the well-known editor-in-chief of Scribner's, read some of his early short stories in little magazines and encouraged him to submit any of his unpublished stories to *Scribner's Magazine*. Eventually Scribner's published his first two important books, a volume of short stories entitled *American Earth* (1930) and the novel *Tobacco Road* (1932).

Tobacco Road describes the cavortings of the degenerate, poverty-stricken Georgia sharecropper Jeeter Lester and his family. The novel contains several unforgettable episodes: Jeeter robs his neighbor, Lov Benson (married to Jeeter's twelve-year-old daughter Pearl), while Lov is distracted by another daughter, the harelipped Ellie May; Jeeter's lustful sister, the preacher Bessie Rice, bribes his sixteen-year-old son Dude to marry her by purchasing an $800 automobile (which Dude wrecks, killing his grandmother); Pearl runs away from Lov, and Ellie May takes her place. Jeeter's attempt to borrow money to improve the soil-exhausted land he lives on comes to naught, and Jeeter and his wife Ada die when a fire consumes their shack. *Tobacco Road* gained enormous popularity from the dramatized version (1933), which enjoyed an exceptionally long run on Broadway.

Another of Caldwell's chief novels is *God's Little Acre* (1933). Like *Tobacco Road*, it depicts impoverished Georgians. For fifteen years a mountaineer, protagonist Ty Ty Walden, has dug for the gold he is convinced lies underneath his land. A series of family calamities leaves Ty grief stricken, but only temporarily: he soon resumes his monomaniacal prospecting. Less well known are several excellent text-picture books published jointly by Caldwell and his second wife, the famous photographer Margaret Bourke-White. The most significant of these, insofar as depression America is concerned, is *You Have Seen Their Faces* (1937), which captures the misery and despair in the faces of black and white southern farmers and which invites government investigation of their plight.

During the 1930s, Caldwell's literary efforts helped familiarize large numbers of Americans with rural southern poverty and helped provide the intellectual and cultural rationale for such organizations as the Resettlement Administration* and the Farm Security Administration.* After the 1930s, Caldwell's critical reputation began to decline, although he continued to publish prolifically (roughly 150 short stories and over twenty-five volumes of longer fiction by the late 1970s). Actually the basic question of Caldwell's literary worth—even in the case of the fiction for which he is best-known—remains unsettled. Detractors claim that Caldwell succumbs to sensationalism and fails to create a coherent tragic vision out of the wildly comic antics of his characters. Defenders argue that Caldwell makes effective use of crude characters and grotesque situations to suggest the moral degradation engendered by poverty. (James Korges, *Erskine Caldwell*, 1969; Scott MacDonald, *Critical Essays on Erskine Caldwell*, 1981.)

DONALD V. COERS

CANNON, CLARENCE Clarence Cannon was born in Elsberry, Missouri, on April 11, 1879. He graduated from William Jewell College in 1903 and took a master's degree there in 1904. Between 1904 and 1908 Cannon was a history teacher at Stephens College, studying law privately. He began practicing law at Troy, Missouri, in 1908, and was elected as a Democrat to Congress in 1922. Between 1920 and 1960, Cannon was parliamentarian for the Democratic National Conventions; and during his service in the House of Representatives between 1923 and 1962, Cannon was a tireless advocate of farm interests. During the New Deal,* he served as a member of the House Appropriations Committee and always had farm income and interests as his major priority. Cannon died on May 12, 1964. (*Who Was Who in America*, IV:152, 1968.)

CAPPER, ARTHUR Born on July 14, 1865, in Garnett, Kansas, Arthur Capper graduated from high scool in 1884 and went to work for the Topeka *Daily Capital*. He reported on local and state politics and joined the Republican party.* In 1891 he became the Washington, D.C., correspondent for the *Capital*. Two years later Capper purchased the *Topeka Mail*, a small weekly, and over the years built a midwestern business empire by prudent purchases of ailing newspapers. By the early 1900s his progressive Republicanism was being echoed in the editorial policies of the Capper newspapers. He ran for governor in 1912 on the Republican ticket while maintaining open sympathy for Theodore Roosevelt's Bull Moose candidacy. He lost a close election to Democrat George H. Hodges but then overwhelmingly defeated Hodges in the 1914 election. In 1918 Capper won a seat in the United States Senate. He emerged as a leader of the farm bloc in the 1920s, sponsored legislation to ease the marketing of farm products, and unsuccessfully tried to push the McNary-Haugen plan. Capper was known also as a foreign policy isolationist and critic of Republican presidents during the 1920s. He found them too conservative. During the 1930s, Capper was an early supporter of the New Deal,* especially its work relief, agricultural, and Social Security measures. He became known as a Republican New Dealer, even though he remained loyal to his own party. Capper became somewhat critical of President Franklin D. Roosevelt* after 1936 because of the "court-packing"* scheme and the drift toward an internationalist foreign policy. Arthur Capper remained in the Senate until 1949. He died on December 19, 1951. (Homer E. Socolofsky, *Arthur Capper. Publisher, Politician, and Philanthropist*, 1962.)

CARAWAY, HATTIE OPHELIA WYATT Hattie Ophelia Wyatt was born on February 1, 1878, near Bakerville, Tennessee. The family moved to Hustburg, Tennessee, in 1882, and in 1896 she graduated from Dickson Normal College with a B.A. degree. She married Thaddeus Caraway in 1902, and they settled in Jonesboro, Arkansas. She worked as a mother and homemaker while her husband practiced law, was elected to Congress in 1912, and served in the United States Senate from 1921 to 1931. When he died in 1931, Governor Harvey Parnell named Hattie Caraway as an interim appointment to fill the vacant seat. On December 9, 1931, she became the first woman to serve in the United States

Senate. She was re-elected in 1932 and 1938 and was one of the New Deal's* most faithful supporters, sharing the concern of many others for the plight of poor people during the Great Depression. After losing the Democratic primary in 1944, she accepted President Franklin D. Roosevelt's* appointment to the Employees Compensation Commission. Hattie Caraway died on December 21, 1950. (Diane D. Kincaid, *Silent Hattie Speaks. The Personal Journal of Senator Hattie Caraway*, 1979.)

CARDOZO, BENJAMIN NATHAN Benjamin N. Cardozo, noted jurist and associate justice of the Supreme Court,* was born in New York City on May 24, 1870, to Sephardic Jewish parents whose forebears could be traced to pre-Revolutionary New York. He graduated from Columbia College at age nineteen. While attending Columbia Law School, he took his masters degree at age twenty. He was admitted to the bar in 1891. Most of Cardozo's legal career was unusual in that he was a barrister in the British tradition—he was a lawyer's lawyer. Operating behind the scenes, this shy and retiring man gained the respect and admiration of his colleagues for the brilliance of his advice, his legal briefs, and his scholarly publications on the law. His forte was commercial law. An offer of a district court appointment by President William Taft was refused by Cardozo because of the inadequate pay. But in 1913 he was nominated and elected as a justice of the New York Supreme Court. His tenure, however, was brief. After a few months the governor of New York asked him to serve temporarily on the Court of Appeals, a post for which his legal brilliance and experience suited him. The temporary stint turned into a more permanent service when he was elected to a fourteen-year term. In 1926 he won unopposed election to the post of chief judge.

Judge Cardozo served with great distinction on the Court of Appeals. The legal mastery exhibited in his opinions and his publications spread his fame far beyond his native state. During his tenure, the New York Court of Appeals came to be regarded as the most distinguished court in the nation after the United States Supreme Court. It was not surprising, therefore, that such a man should be selected for the ultimate distinction available to his profession, nomination to the Supreme Court of the United States. In 1932 President Herbert Hoover* named Cardozo to take the place of the retiring Justice Oliver Wendell Holmes, a friend whom Cardozo held in the greatest admiration. But there were obstacles. Two New Yorkers already served on the Court (Chief Justice Charles Evans Hughes* and Justice Harlan Fiske Stone*), and there was already one Jewish member on the Court (Justice Louis Brandeis*). With the staunch support of such powerful Senate leaders as William E. Borah,* however, the geographic and ethnic objections were overcome and Cardozo won confirmation.

Justice Cardozo entered upon his service at a critical time in United States history. The nation was mired in depression; President Hoover would soon be out of office; the new administration of Franklin D. Roosevelt* launched one of the most ambitious programs of economic rejuvenation and social reform in the history of the Republic. In all this the Supreme Court would play a pivotal role, a Court in which conservatives held a four to three edge over the liberals, with two swing votes in the middle. Justice Cardozo quickly emerged as the most persuasive member of the liberal faction. Unlike his conservative colleagues, who essentially saw the Constitution as a dead body of precedent sanctified and fastened by the past on the present, Cardozo viewed it as a living organism which must expand and grow to accommodate changed times and conditions. In his great decisions, many in dissent against the narrow interpretation of the conservative bloc, he would light the path which constitutional interpretation would take in the next decades. His efforts toward reaching that goal, however, were cut short by death. After a brief service of six years on the Court, Justice Cardozo died of a coronary thrombosis on July 9, 1938. His reputation has endured. He and Justice Holmes are regarded as the two greatest jurists to serve on the United States Supreme Court in the twentieth century. (*Dictionary of American Biography*, XI:93-96, Supp. 2, 1958.)

JOSEPH M. ROWE, JR.

CARMODY, JOHN MICHAEL John M. Carmody was born in 1881 in Bradford County, Pennsylvania. He attended the Elmira (N.Y.) Business College and the Lewis Institute in Chicago and attended Columbia University for a short time in 1926. Carmody began work as a bookkeeper and worked for a number of structural steel manufacturers between 1900 and 1914 and then for several garment manufacturers between 1914 and 1923. Between 1923 and 1926 Carmody worked as vice-president of industrial relations for the Davis Coal and Coke Company. In 1927 he became editor of *Coal Age*, a trade journal, and later of *Industrial and Factory Management*. He became active in the New Deal* when he was named to chair the Bituminous Coal Labor Board. Late in 1933 he became chief engineer for the Civil Works Administration* and later for the Federal Emergency Relief Administration.* President Franklin D. Roosevelt* placed Carmody on the National Labor Relations Board* in 1935 and then selected him to head the Rural Electrification Administration* in 1936. After the Reorganization Act of 1939,* Carmody took over the newly created Federal Works Agency.* A warm man who avoided publicity and worked well with people, Carmody was the quintessential bureaucrat. Because of a 1931 trip to the Soviet Union as part of a McGraw-Hill survey of industrial development there, Carmody frequently had trouble with extreme right-wing activists who accused him of being a Communist, but he remained a loyal follower of President Roosevelt and the president remained loyal to him. John M. Carmody died on November 11, 1963. (*New York Times*, November 12, 1963.)

CARTER V. CARTER COAL COMPANY When the Supreme Court* outlawed the National Industrial Recovery Act of 1933* with its *Schechter** decision in May 1935, Franklin D. Roosevelt's* administration quickly responded with the Guffey-Snyder Bituminous Coal Stabilization Act,* a measure designed to bring industrial self-regulation and rationalization to the soft coal industry. President Franklin D. Roosevelt signed the measure on August 30, 1935. The Guffey bill guaranteed collective bargaining in the industry, provided uniform scales of wages and hours throughout the country, established a national commission to fix coal prices and control production, permitted the closing of less profitable mines, and imposed a production tax to pay for the mines and to assist in the retraining of unemployed miners. The Guffey bill amounted to reenactment of the bituminous coal code of the outlawed National Recovery Administration.*

No sooner had the law been passed than lawsuits were filed against it, and in January 1936 the Supreme Court agreed to hear the *Carter v. Carter Coal Company* case, which claimed that the production tax was a government imposed penalty and therefore a violation of Fifth and Tenth Amendment property rights. In May 1936 the Court announced its decision and hammered another nail into the coffin of the New Deal's* industrial recovery program. As in its other anti-New Deal decisions, the court's majority was 6 to 3, with Justices Willis Van Devanter,* Owen Roberts,* Pierce Butler,* George Sutherland,* and James McReynolds* voting against the Guffey bill and Chief Justice Charles Evans Hughes* concurring, and Justices Louis Brandeis,* Benjamin Cardozo,* and Harlan Fiske Stone* dissenting. George Sutherland's majority opinion held that the law's price-fixing and labor provisions were inextricably connected, that the price-fixing violated the Fifth Amendment and the labor provisions violated the Tenth Amendment by having Congress intervene into purely local matters. In a concurring opinion, Chief Justice Hughes felt that the price-fixing did not violate the Fifth Amendment but that the labor provisions violated the Tenth Amendment. He added that if Americans wanted to give Congress the power to regulate intrastate commerce, they should go through the process of amending the Constitution. In writing the dissenting opinion, Justice Cardozo argued that in a modern industrial economy labor problems inevitably affected interstate commerce and, by invalidating the Guffey coal act, the Supreme Court was blocking the right of people to govern themselves. The decision then forced Congress to respond with the Guffey-Vinson Bituminous Coal Act of 1937.* (James P. Johnson, *The Politics of Soft Coal: The Bituminous Industry from World War I through the New Deal*, 1979.)

CENTRAL STATISTICAL BOARD Soon after his inauguration, President Franklin D. Roosevelt* became frustrated with conflicting statistical data he was receiving from various government agencies. To remedy the problem, he created the Central Statistical Board by Executive Order No. 6225 on July 27, 1933. The board had one representative from the Departments of Interior, Agriculture, Commerce, and Labor, the Federal Reserve Board,* the National Recovery Administration,* and others at the president's discretion. The Public Works Administration* funded the board. (Samuel I. Rosenman, ed., *The Public Papers and Addresses of Franklin D. Roosevelt*, II:307-308, 1938.)

CHANDLER ACT OF 1938 Because of the large numbers of corporate bankruptcies and reorganizations during the 1930s, there was a growing concern among New Dealers that the interests of many small investors were not being protected. To deal with that concern, the Chandler Act passed through Congress in June 1938 and amended existing federal bankruptcy law. In addition to streamlining a number of procedural questions, the act gave the Securities and Exchange Commission* power to participate in corporate reorganizations and to act as technical adviser to federal courts as a means of protecting the interests of small and inarticulate securities owners. Chapter Thirteen of the measure also permitted wage earners to arrange for amortization of their debts over a period of years under protection of federal bankruptcy legislation. At the time, President Franklin D. Roosevelt* considered the Chandler Act an important addition to federal securities regulatory power. (*New York Times*, June 17, 1938.)

CIVIL AERONAUTICS ACT OF 1938 Beginning in 1926, the Aeronautics Branch in the Department of Commerce supervised the development and regulation of commercial aviation and promoted the rise of airmail, passenger, and freight services. The agency also stressed the licensing of all pilots, establishment of safety rules, and drafted regulations for flight crews, aircraft manufacturers, airport operators, and ground employees. The Aeronautics Branch also investigated accidents. In 1933 President Franklin D. Roosevelt* appointed Eugene L. Vidal of South Dakota to take over the Aeronautics Branch, and in 1934 they changed the agency's name to the Bureau of Air Commerce. Vidal left the post in 1937 and was succeeded by Fred Fagg, Jr. After considerable debate over the agency's status, Congress passed the Civil Aeronautics Act in 1938 removing the Bureau of Air Commerce from the Department of Commerce and renaming it the Civil Aeronautics Authority. A Civil Aeronautics administrator directed the former responsibilities of the Bureau of Air Commerce and enjoyed the new responsibility of regulating commercial air carriers economically. An independent Air Safety Board assumed responsibility for investigating accidents. Finally, in 1940 President Roosevelt placed the economic regulation and accident investigation under the new Civil Aeronautics Board and renamed the remainder the Civil Aeronautics Administration and returned it to the Department of Commerce. (Nick A. Komons, *Bonfires to Beacons: Federal Civil Aviation Policy Under the Air Commerce Act, 1926–1938*, 1978; Donald R. Whitnah, *Safer Skyways: Federal Control of Aviation, 1926-1966*, 1966.)

CIVIL AERONAUTICS AUTHORITY (See CIVIL AERONAUTICS ACT OF 1938.)

CIVILIAN CONSERVATION CORPS As soon as the banking crisis had been stabilized during the first week of his administration, President Franklin D. Roosevelt* turned his attention to emergency conservation work; and on March 21, 1933, he asked Congress to establish the Civilian Conservation Corps. Not only would it be able to perform valuable conservation work, it would also help alleviate the severe unemployment problem among young men. By late 1932 more than 25 percent of single men between the ages of fifteen and twenty-four were out of work, and another 29 percent were only working part-time. Very much the "brain-child" of the president, the Civilian Conservation Corps was among the first of the New Deal* agencies. Authorized under the Civilian Conservation Corps Reforestation Relief Act of March 31, 1933, the CCC was expected to provide jobs for young men between the ages of seventeen and twenty-four who came from families already on relief. Organized labor initially opposed creation of the CCC, arguing that the pay-scale of $30 per month was too low and that administrative control by the U.S. Army would lead to undeirable regimentation and control of the work force. However, very little opposition surfaced in Congress, and the CCC went on to become one of the most successful of the New Deal programs.

By the end of June 1933 over 239,000 young men had been organized into companies of 200 and either assigned to a camp or already were in one. Ultimately, some 2.5 million men would serve in the CCC and many early restrictions on age or family status would be lifted. For example, over 225,000 veterans of World War I joined the CCC, as did nearly 15,000 American Indians. Moreover, by the terms of the act which created the CCC, the agency was open to all races and some 200,000 blacks ultimately served in it. That more blacks did not, despite their plight, join the CCC was due to CCC director Robert Fechner,* who insisted that segregation be maintained. Thus, most blacks who served did so in all black camps, and new enrollees appeared only when vacancies in those camps occurred.

The CCC proved to be one of the most expensive New Deal agencies on a per capita basis. Nevertheless, most analysts agree that the projects completed during the agency's nine-year existence more than justified the expense. CCC workers restored national historic sites, built national park facilities, cleaned and enlarged reservoirs, assisted in fighting forest fires, and undertook an immense reforestation effort. Eventually, the CCC planted over 2 billion trees, earning their nickname of "Roosevelt's Tree Army." The CCC also assisted in topsoil conservation efforts in the midwest, under the authority of the TVA.* Over 200 million trees were planted on these soil preservation projects alone. Within the camps, the CCC also encouraged educational programs and some 35,000 men learned to read and write while in the corps.

At its peak in 1935, the CCC had over 500,000 men working in over 2,500 camps. However, its numbers declined after that and although the agency remained popular, it failed to overcome its image as a temporary, relief-oriented organization and never became permanent. In 1939 the life of the CCC was extended to July 1943, but improvements in the civilian economy followed by the coming of the war spelled its earlier demise. Robert Fechner had died on December 31, 1939, and the CCC was then directed by James J. McEntee.* In June 1942 Congress simply refused to appropriate any more operating funds for the agency, giving only the money necessary to close down its camps. (John A. Salmond, *The Civilian Conservation Corps, 1933-1942: A New Deal Case Study*, 1967.)

ROBERT S. BROWNING III

CIVIL WORKS ADMINISTRATION On November 9, 1933, seeing the early signs of a potentially devastating winter, President Franklin D. Roosevelt* signed Executive Order 6420-B establishing the Civil Works Administration. Roosevelt appointed Federal Emergency Relief* Administrator Harry L. Hopkins* as its director and announced that the CWA would function under Title II of the National Industrial Recovery Act.* Unlike FERA,* CWA operated entirely as a federal program, with Hopkins' staff dispensing paychecks and recruiting workers from relief lists and the ranks of the unemployed. Hopkins persuaded Roosevelt that public work rather than straight relief was superior because "able bodied people should work for their existence." Roosevelt transferred $400 million from Harold Ickes'* Public Works Administration* to initiate the experimental plan. By February 1934 the CWA employed over 4,200,000 workers who received minimum wages rather than relief payments.

The Civil Works Administration was an immediate success. In the West, the CWA helped people cope with a destructive drought that exacerbated agricultural conditions. Hopkins' special field representative, Lorena Hickok,* noted that it was a "a godsend," excavating prehistoric Indian mounds, hiring unemployed teachers in Boston, and sending opera singers on a tour of the Ozarks. When Roosevelt questioned the validity of some of these projects, Hopkins and Eleanor Roosevelt* reinforced the need to provide work for artists and actors. Its political impact did not escape either Franklin Roosevelt or Harry Hopkins. The primary payoff stemmed from its boost to the nation's psychological morale. On Christmas eve, 1933, nearly 4 million CWA workers and their families crowded the nation's streets to spend their recently-earned cash. This combination of public work and economic pump-priming became a principal tenet of the New Deal's* approach to unemployment. But the CWA also carried political liabilities. "Half way between a lemon and an orange is a grapefruit," commented Al Smith,* who thought the CWA was illegal, that it would further depress the private construction industry. When Smith cracked that a civil work existed "half way between a public work and a relief work," Hopkins could not resist retorting that if creating 4 million federal jobs involved "going into the grapefruit business, then I'm delighted to be in it."

Despite these problems, Roosevelt and Hopkins wanted to exclude politics from the administration of the CWA. But rumors of politicians attempting to convert CWA jobs into personal patronage generated controversy. Furthermore, reports circulated that businessmen exerted a corrupting influence by extracting illegal profits from materials sold to the government. Hopkins reacted quickly, firing seventy-two "political employees" in Wisconsin and chastising state governors who attempted to interfere with the federal process. Hopkins made a national example of Governor Eugene Talmadge* of Georgia, characterized as "that guy [who] wants headlines. He doesn't contribute a dime but he's always yapping. Some people can't stand to see others making a living wage."

Although the program generated political controversy, most observers judged it a success. "Give the Roosevelt administration a dozen Hopkins and a few more years," wrote the editor of the *Portland Oregonian*, "and you will see them establish a new standard of efficiency in public service, a standard comparable to the pre-war German public service or to the British civil service at its best in integrity and immunity to political interference." The CWA constructed 40,000 schools, 469 airports, 255,000 street and road miles, and pumped a billion dollars into the ailing economy through the hiring of 4 million persons. Most of all, the CWA played a vital role in bringing some desperate Americans through the bitter winter of 1933-1934.

Although impressed by these considerable accomplishments, Franklin Roosevelt did not wish to continue CWA beyond the spring of 1934. Political interference by state and local officials constituted a major reason, as well as Roosevelt's fear of creating a lasting underclass of poor people. Expressing concern with the growing costs involved with maintaining a work relief program of CWA's size, Roosevelt made a determined effort to end federal welfare. Finally, improved economic conditions in the spring of 1934 reinforced his hopes that no permanent, massive federal work relief program would be necessary. When the program ended, it constituted a great domestic achievement and paved the way for the subsequent creation of the Works Progress Administration.* (Forrest A. Walker, *The Civil Works Administration: An Experiment in Federal Work Relief*, 1979.)

J. CHRISTOPHER SCHNELL

CLAPPER, RAYMOND Raymond Clapper, a newspaper correspondent and radio commentator, was born on a farm near La Cynge, Kansas, on May 30, 1892, the son of John William and Julia (Crow) Clapper. The family soon moved to Kansas City so that the father could earn enough to support his wife and only son. The father and mother were a kindly, frugal couple with narrow Protestant views. Since there were no books in the house, young Ray developed his own library of clippings from the *Kansas City Star*, including everything from baseball to politics. His adolescent hero was William Allen White,* the famous editor of the *Emporia Gazette*. After graduation from grade school, Clapper was forced to work three years before entering high school at the age of seventeen. In 1913, two months before his twenty-first birthday, he married Olive Ewing, who was only seventeen. In September the young couple walked forty miles, with knapsacks on their backs, to Lawrence, Kansas, to enter the University of Kansas. At the university, where they remained until 1916, they supported themselves with Ray's earnings as college correspondent to the *Kansas City Star* and his wife's small income as a piano teacher.

In 1916 Clapper became a staff member of the *Star*. Later that year he was hired by the United Press to work in Chicago. In 1929 he became manager of

UP's Washington bureau. He held that position until 1933, when he became chief of the *Washington Post*'s capital bureau. When his contract expired in 1936, he was hired by the Scripps-Howard papers to write a daily column. Clapper's ability to write with insight and clarity about complex political issues made his column popular, and it was soon being distributed nationwide by the United Features Syndicate. After September 1942, when he started his radio program with the Mutual Broadcasting System, Clapper was able to reach an even larger audience.

Clapper, who characterized himself as a "seventy-five percent New Dealer," supported most of President Franklin D. Roosevelt's* measures. One of his most notable columns was his description in 1940 of a National Youth Administration* project at West Texas State Normal College. "I as a taxpayer consider it a good investment," he wrote. Later that year, however, he severely criticized Roosevelt's decision to run for a third term. "If I were God," he told a meeting of publishers, "I would make Cordell Hull* the presidential candidate for the Democratic party."*

When the war came Clapper deemphasized politics and, like his good friend and fellow columnist Ernie Pyle, began to focus his writings and broadcasts on the human side of the war. He spent part of 1943 in the Mediterranean theater and was aboard one of the American planes in the first bombing of Rome. In January 1944 he again left his Washington headquarters for a first-hand look at the war in the Pacific. On February 3, 1944, Clapper, covering the invasion of the Marshall Islands, was a passenger on a plane that collided with another plane while forming up. In the words of the terse announcement issued by the Navy later that morning, "Both planes crashed in the lagoon. There were no survivors." (Raymond Clapper, *Watching the World*, 1944: *New York Times*, February 4, 1944.)

JOHN PAYNE

CLARK, GRENVILLE Born on November 5, 1882, in New York City, Grenville Clark graduated Phi Beta Kappa from Harvard University in 1903 and received his law degree there in 1906. In 1906, he went to work for the New York law firm of Carter, Ledyard and Milburn, where Franklin D. Roosevelt* was also clerking, and in 1909 he opened his own firm along with Francis W. Bird and Elihu Root, Jr. A Bull Moose Progressive, Clark initiated the "Plattsburgh Plan" in 1915 where business and professional men received military training to form an officer pool in the event of war. During World War I he rose to the rank of lieutenant colonel and served in the adjutant general's office. After the war he returned to private practice, serving as a member of the Emergency Committee on Railroad Investigations of Life Insurance Companies and Mutual Savings Banks and formed the National Economy League in 1931 to oppose increases in veterans' pensions. During the first "hundred days"* of the New Deal,* he helped draft the Economy Act of 1933.* Clark remained in private practice, serving periodically as an adviser to the New Deal until the "court-packing"* scheme, when he organized wide-spread opposition among the legal community. He helped draft the Selective Service Act of 1940, served as chairman of the Citizens Committee for the National War Service during World War II, and was vice-president of United World Federalists, an international peace group, after the war. Grenville Clark died on January 11, 1967. (*New York Times*, January 12, 1967.)

CLARK, JOEL BENNETT The son of Champ Clark, famous Speaker of the House of Representatives, Joel Bennett "Champ" Clark was born January 8, 1890, and raised on a steady diet of Democratic party* politics. He attended Pantops Academy in Charlottesville, Virginia, and Eastern High School in Washington, D.C., and took a bachelor's degree from the University of Missouri in 1913. Clark received a law degree from George Washington University in 1914. Before completing law school, Clark was made parliamentarian of the House of Representatives while his father was speaker. Admitted to the bar in 1914, Clark set up a practice in his home town of Bowling Green. Moving to St. Louis to join a larger firm, he gained a great deal of legal experience in banking, insurance, railroad, utilities, and industrial issues. In 1933, when Harry B. Hawes resigned as United States senator from Missouri, Clark received an appointment to the unexpired term, despite the opposition of the Tom Pendergast* machine and his own opposition to Prohibition.

Blessed with an independent, "maverick" streak, Clark was never a consistent supporter of the New Deal.* Indeed, he frequently was a thorn in Franklin D. Roosevelt's* side. Although he voted for the TVA* and the National Labor Relations Act,* he opposed Roosevelt on the NRA,* the AAA,* the court-packing* scheme, and executive reorganization; and he supported the 1939 cuts in WPA* funding. Clark was suspicious of the White House and the growing power of the executive branch, and he was a rabid isolationist who early in the 1930s decided that Roosevelt would lead the country into difficult, entangling foreign adventures. In 1939, 1940, and 1941, Clark opposed all aid to Great Britain, the draft, Lend-Lease, and anything else likely to lock the United States into international commitments. His roots were in the anti-trust, isolationist tradition of early twentieth century progressivism, and Clark never made the transition to the idea of the modern bureaucratic state. A long-time colleague and friend of Harry S Truman,* Clark was appointed as an associate justice of the United States Court of Appeals for the District of Columbia in 1945. He died on July 13, 1954. (*New York Times*, July 14, 1954; James T. Patterson, *Congressional Conservatism and the New Deal*, 1967.)

COAL ARBITRATION BOARD In July 1933 John L. Lewis* of the United Mine Workers called a strike in the coal fields, charging that the coal operators were discouraging workers from affiliating with the UMW. Disorder was widespread and at times Governor Gifford Pinchot of Pennsylvania had to call out the state militia to preserve order. With the strike threatening to spread to all 200,000 workers in the bituminous industry, General Hugh S. Johnson* of the National Recovery Administration* suggested to President Franklin D. Roosevelt* the creation of a Coal Arbitration Board to settle the dispute. Roosevelt agreed and appointed a three-person board composed of Gerard Swope* of General Electric, George L. Berry* of the AFL,* and Louis Kirstein of Filene's in Boston. The board quickly secured an agreement to postpone the strike until the National Recovery Administration had developed the bituminous coal code. John L. Lewis agreed, and the strike was averted. President Franklin D. Roosevelt announced the agreement on August 4, 1933. (Samuel I. Rosenman, ed., *The Public Papers and Addresses of Franklin D. Roosevelt*, II:317, 1938.)

COHEN, BENJAMIN VICTOR Benjamin Victor Cohen was born in Muncie, Indiana, on September 23, 1894, the son of Polish Jewish immigrants. As a child he "neglected marbles for Descartes and Spencer," and he went on to a brilliant academic career at the University of Chicago, receiving a bachelor of philosophy and a doctorate in jurisprudence. His law school grades were the highest ever recorded at Chicago, and he decided to pursue graduate studies at the Harvard Law School. There he met Professor Felix Frankfurter,* who almost twenty years later would be responsible for bringing Cohen to Washington as a legal and legislative adviser. Between 1916 and 1933 Cohen pursued a distinguished career in corporate law and public service. He served as secretary to Judge William Mack (federal circuit court, New York City); attorney for the United States Shipping Board during World War I; and counsel for the American Zionists negotiating the Palestine Mandate at the London and Paris peace conferences. Afterwards he practiced law privately in New York City, specializing in corporate reorganization cases and acting at the same time as unpaid counsel to the National Consumers League.

Cohen came to Washington in 1933 with James Landis* to work on the Truth-in-Securities Act,* which eventually became the Securities Act of 1933.* It was while working on this legislation that he met Thomas Corcoran,* then counsel to the Reconstruction Finance Corporation.* Together Cohen and Corcoran wrote the more comprehensive Securities Exchange Act of 1934,* and the team of Cohen and Corcoran was born. Theirs was an extraordinary collaboration, responsible in whole or in part for a host of New Deal* laws, including the acts establishing the Federal Housing Administration* and the Tennessee Valley Authority*; the RFC extension; and the Public Utility Holding Company Act of 1935.* Cohen was also responsible for the lend-lease program before World War II and contributed to the development and implementation of the wage and price control programs during the war. He earned a reputation as a superb legislative draftsman whose work left lawyers searching in vain for loopholes.

Cohen and Corcoran worked largely behind the scenes throughout the New Deal, displaying a "passion for anonymity." They worked incessantly; not only did they write legislation, but they shepherded their bills through Congress and helped defend the finished products in court. Of the two, Cohen was the chief draftsman; Corcoran, the head lobbyist. The two men shared a Georgetown townhouse with other New Deal lawyers and developed a reputation for late-night work sessions at home or at the office. Cohen's favorite diversion was an occasional motion picture, though it was said that he typically fell asleep before the credits were over.

The Cohen and Corcoran partnership was an unlikely one. Cohen was Jewish, with a methodical and scholarly temperament; Corcoran was Irish, with a vivacious and effervescent style. Cohen was shy, Corcoran outgoing; Cohen was happiest indoors, working or reading, Corcoran was more robust and more inclined to enjoy the outdoors. Rather than causing friction between the two men, their contrasting styles blended them into a highly efficient team and led to deep friendship and mutual respect. ''He is the high priest,'' Corcoran said of Cohen late in life, ''he is the saint.''

Though Cohen and Corcoran were hardly known to the general public, their record of successes and their behind-the-scenes style quickly captured the attention of Washington insiders. The two men earned the title of the ''gold dust twins'' after a popular soap advertisement which encouraged the householder to ''let the gold dust twins do your work.'' They were also called ''Frankfurter's two chief little hot dogs'' and ''the brain twins.''

During the war, Cohen served as adviser to the United States embassy in London and as an adviser to James F. Byrnes* in the Office of Economic Stabilization and in the State Department. He left government service for a brief period in 1947 but returned when asked by President Harry S Truman* to join the U.S. delegation to the United Nations, a post he remained in until 1952. Never a man to seek the public spotlight, Cohen was nonetheless one of the most influential of all those who shaped the course of the New Deal. To many, he was the ''top brain'' in the later Franklin D. Roosevelt* group of counselors. Upon his death in 1983, Cohen was eulogized as a gentle, passionate man ''whose mind was one of the main portals through which ideas entered the New Deal.'' (Katie Louchheim, ed., *The Making of the New Deal. The Insiders Speak*, 1983; *New York Times*, September 5, 1983.)

WILLIAM LASSER

COLLIER, JOHN Born in Atlanta, Georgia, on May 4, 1884, John Collier was the fourth child in a family of seven children. His father, a banker and politician, was instrumental in shaping Collier's belief that only through cooperative, communal efforts could the social ills of society be reformed. Although he never received a formal degree, Collier was well educated, studying at Columbia University and at the College de France. He became secretary of the People's Institute in New York City in 1907, where he worked on behalf of immigrants and came to the conclusion that rejecting one's heritage was not necessary to the process of Americanization.

Collier resigned from the People's Institute in 1919 after federal support for the program evaporated, and he became director of adult education in California.

The state legislature eliminated the position in 1920, fearing that Collier's approach was too "bolshevik." Mabel Dodge, a friend of Collier's from New York, learned of his misfortune and invited him to Taos, New Mexico, where he viewed firsthand the problems confronting the Pueblo Indians. After living among them for several months, Collier realized that these people still maintained a sense of unity—a community spirit, in spite of generations of attacks on their culture. Collier saw them as a symbol of his philosophy. He had discovered his "red Atlantis."

Convinced he could help American Indians, Collier became research agent for the Indian Welfare Committee of the General Federation of Women's Clubs in 1922. There he gained national attention in blocking the Bursum Bill which threatened Spanish land grants to the Pueblo Indians. In 1923 he organized and became executive director of the American Indian Defense Association, a group which called for termination of the Dawes Act, preservation of Indian cultures, and certain guarantees of political and economic rights for all Indians. For the next ten years Collier continued his efforts to help Indian people. And in April 1933 Collier became commissioner of Indian Affairs, a position he held until 1945.

As Indian commissioner Collier promised Indian America a "New Deal." For example, he secured enactment of the Pueblo Relief Bill to give compensation to Pueblo Indians for lands lost to non-Indian settlers; channeled millions of dollars from New Deal* relief agencies to help destitute Indians; and cancelled Indian debts to the federal government for irrigation projects and highways. Collier's "Indian New Deal"* further resulted in the passage of the Johnson-O'Malley Act of 1934,* which gave the federal government the power to make contracts with states to provide for Indian educational, medical, and social welfare services. Also in 1934 the cornerstone of the "Indian New Deal" was passed in the form of the Indian Reorganization Act.* Although not as comprehensive as Collier envisioned, this measure ended the policy of land allotments in severalty; restored surplus lands to tribes; permitted voluntary exchanges of restricted trust lands for tribal corporation shares; and provided for the creation of tribal governments and corporations. Additional provisions concerned appropriations for land purchases, tribal corporations and organizing tribal self-governments, and financial aid for Indian students. Indians also received preferential treatment in securing jobs with the Bureau of Indian Affairs. Finally, in 1935 the Indian Arts and Crafts Board* was created to encourage and improve Indian-made products and protect them by a government trademark.

By 1939 Collier's "Indian New Deal" was besieged by financial cuts and congressional critics who saw these programs as impediments to assimilation. And with the advent of World War II, attention was shifted from domestic reforms to foreign affairs. Collier realized his growing ineffectiveness and tendered his resignation in February 1945. After his resignation he taught at the City College of New York and at Knox College. John Collier died on May 8, 1968, in Talpa, New Mexico. (Lawrence C. Kelly, *The Assault on Assimilation: John*

Collier and the Origins of Indian Policy Reform, 1983; Kenneth R. Philp, *John Collier's Crusade for Indian Reform, 1920-1954*, 1977.)

RAYMOND WILSON

COLUMBIA RIVER BASIN ANTI-SPECULATION ACT OF 1937 Concerned about speculators making a fortune off Columbia River Basin land, which was soon to enjoy the benefits of federal water development, Congress passed the Columbia River Basin Anti-Speculation Act on May 27, 1937. The federal government also wanted to break up large, dry-farms in regions that could be irrigated. The Department of the Interior estimated that over 1 million acres were involved, and the act decreed that farms exceeding eighty acres per family would be designated excess land. Owners of excess land would not receive irrigation water on any part of their property until they had sold excess land at prices the federal government considered fair market value. The law also gave the federal government the option to purchase excess land. (Richard Lowitt, *The New Deal in the West*, 1984.)

COMMITTEE FOR THE NATION In 1921 the economist Irving Fisher* organized the Stable Money Association to promote the idea of a dollar whose purchasing power was stable. Prominent members of the association were Henry A. Wallace,* later secretary of agriculture, and Frank A. Vanderlip, president of the National City Bank of New York. They worked for the concept of the "commodity dollar"* and found a good deal of support for it among farmers and some businessmen. In the summer of 1932, Frank Vanderlip brought together a group of prominent businessmen to discuss the problem of collapsing prices, and early in 1933 they formed the Committee for the Nation to Rebuild Prices and Purchasing Power.* The committee took up where Fisher's Stable Money Association left off. Included in its membership were James H. Rand, Jr.,* of Remington, Rand; General Robert E. Wood* and Lessing Rosenwald of Sears, Roebuck and Company; newspaperman Frank Gannett;* and economists Irving Fisher and George Warren.* During the 1930s, the committee campaigned for the gold-buying* scheme, silver inflation, and manipulation of the value of the dollar, and in doing so represented new businesses hoping inflation would create new investment capital, mining interests interested in stimulating employment and profits, and farmers convinced that the schemes of the 1890s were still relevant.

During the early years of the New Deal,* the Committee for the Nation to Rebuild Prices and Purchasing Power offered general support for the National Recovery Administration* except Section 7(a) of the NIRA*, the Agricultural Adjustment Act of 1933,* Banking Act of 1933,* Civilian Conservation Corps,* Reciprocal Trade Agreements Act of 1934,* and the Securities Exchange Act of 1934.* Members of the committee broke with Franklin D. Roosevelt* and the New Deal after 1935. The shift to the "Second New Deal,"* with its emphasis on anti-trust, regulation, and taxation of the wealthy, alienated most members of the committee; and they were unable to endorse Roosevelt in the election of 1936.* (H. M. Bratter, "The Committee for the Nation," *Journal of Political Economy*, IL:531–553, 1941.)

COMMITTEE FOR THE NATION TO REBUILD PRICES AND PURCHASING POWER (See COMMITTEE FOR THE NATION.)

COMMITTEE ON ECONOMIC SECURITY By 1934 pressure was mounting in labor and social welfare circles for some type of unemployment and old-age insurance. Those demands eventually led to the Social Security Act of 1935.* Senator Robert Wagner* of New York and Congressman David J. Lewis of Maryland had submitted an unemployment compensation bill to Congress, and Senator Clarence Dill of Washington and Representative William Connery* of Massachusetts did the same with a pension bill. Inside the Franklin D. Roosevelt* administration, a host of prominent New Dealers—including Frances Perkins,* Louis Brandeis,* Benjamin Cohen,* Thomas Corcoran,* and Rexford Tugwell*—were urging federal legislation. So on June 8, 1934, President Franklin D. Roosevelt submitted a message to Congress raising the idea of social insurance, and late in the month he appointed a cabinet-level Committee on Economic Security to investigate the major policy issues and economic needs and to make a recommendation before December 1934. He named Secretary of Labor Frances Perkins as chairman of the committee, and she appointed Professor Edwin Witte of the University of Wisconsin as executive director and Arthur J. Altmeyer* as head of the Technical Board on Economic Security.

The committee had to resolve two conflicting positions on both the question of unemployment insurance and the question of old-age pensions. As for unemployment insurance, the basic question was to have a state-based plan, based on the Wisconsin unemployment compensation system, with basic minimum standards or a national plan administered and financed by the federal government. After intense debate and negotiation, the Committee on Economic Society recommended the former, with each state required to establish an unemployment insurance system adhering to some fundamental basic standards. As for the question of old-age pensions, the major debate was over its financing—whether to have the federal government finance it out of general revenues, which would have had the effect of redistributing income, or whether to have employers and employees make equal contributions so that workers could gradually accumulate annuities rights in their old age. The committee opted for the latter, much to the dismay of liberals who wanted to redistribute national income. The committee also recommended that the federal government make grants-in-aid to states for assisting the contemporary elderly who had no pension reserves. Finally, the committee decided on supplementary benefits to the blind and to dependent children. Although the committee debated the question of national health insurance, it made no recommendation. Opposition from the American Medical Association and the business community appeared so overwhelming that the proposal might damage the chances of success for the other provisions.

The Committee on Economic Security submitted its report to the president on January 15, 1935, with Arthur J. Altmeyer drafting the message. President Roosevelt then submitted his request to Congress for social security legislation on January 17. Senator Robert Wagner introduced the bill to the Senate and Representatives David J. Lewis and Robert Doughton* of North Carolina introduced it into the House. The Social Security Act became law on August 14, 1935. (Arthur M. Schlesinger, Jr., *The Age of Roosevelt. Vol. III. The Politics of Upheaval, 1935-1936*, 1960.)

COMMODITY CREDIT CORPORATION The central problem of American agriculture in the 1930s was overproduction and depressed commodity prices. The New Deal* tried to solve the overproduction problem with the Agricultural Adjustment Administration,* but members of Franklin D. Roosevelt's* administration were also concerned about the farmer claim that low prices were also a consequence of marketing conditions. Because crops came on the market soon after harvest, prices were artificially low on a seasonal basis. Farmers demanded that some scheme for the orderly marketing of farm commodities be developed. On October 18, 1933, President Franklin D. Roosevelt responded to their demands with Executive Order 6340 creating the Commodity Credit Corporation. The origins of the Commodity Credit Corporation went back to the subtreasury plans of the Populists in the 1890s, but in the recent past they extended back to the Herbert Hoover* administration when stabilization corporations had been established and the Reconstruction Finance Corporation* had made loans to banks and agricultural credit corporations for the orderly marketing of farm products. The Commodity Credit Corporation took over the RFC's loan program for farmers with the hope of bringing relief by allowing them to hold their crops off the market until more favorable marketing conditions had appeared. The Commodity Credit Corporation also hoped to stimulate farm loans by private banks through loan guarantees. To maintain normal channels of credit, the Commodity Credit Corporation urged private bankers to make the loans with the guarantee that upon demand the corporation would purchase all of the marketing loans they had extended. When banks refused to make the loans, the Commodity Credit Corporation would loan directly. Between 1933 and 1935, while the Commodity Credit Corporation was a subsidiary of the RFC, Lynn P. Talley* was general manager and John D. Goodloe was vice-president. Goodloe became president of the Commodity Credit Corporation in 1935 and stayed there until 1939 when the corporation became an independent agency.

During the next several years, the Commodity Credit Corporation loaned funds on cotton, corn, wheat, turpentine, rosin, figs, peanuts, raisins, butter, dates, cowhides, wool, and tobacco. The number of loans made directly by the Commodity Credit Corporation was inconsequential; the directors preferred to have private bankers make the loans, after which the corporation would buy the loans on demand. By 1936 loans totaling $628 million had been extended to farmers, but only $2 million had been loaned directly by the Commodity Credit Corporation. The state of agricultural prices was just too unstable to give bankers the assurance that farmers would be able to repay the loans or that the value of collateral would remain high enough to cover any losses. So the Commodity Credit Corporation made the loans itself through private financial institutions. Demand for loans was so high that between 1933 and 1939 the Commodity Credit Corporation gained the authority to borrow $900 million against its $100 million capital. The money was used to enable farmers to hold crops off the market. By absorbing the surplus of bumper crops and meeting deficiencies in short years, the Commodity Credit Corporation would be able to help farmers achieve price stability. With passage of the Agricultural Adjustment Act of 1938,* the Commodity Credit Corporation became the major vehicle in achieving Secretary of Agriculture Henry Wallace's* goal of an "ever-normal granary."*

By June 30, 1940, the Commodity Credit Corporation had loaned $889 million on 16,674,000 bales of cotton; $470 million on 897,776,000 bushels of corn; $166 million on 253,391,000 bushels of wheat; and $46 million on 253,249,000 pounds of tobacco. (Jesse Jones, *Fifty Billion Dollars*, 1951.)

"COMMODITY DOLLAR" (See GOLD RESERVE ACT OF 1934.)

COMMONS, JOHN ROGERS Born on October 13, 1862, in Hollendsburg, Ohio, John R. Commons graduated from Oberlin College in 1888 and took an A.M. there in 1890. He studied at Johns Hopkins, and between 1890 and 1904 he taught economics and sociology at Wesleyan, Indiana, Oberlin, and Syracuse. He began his career at the University of Wisconsin. An optimistic utilitarian, Commons believed a stable capitalist system would generate the greatest good for the greatest number of Americans. Economically powerful organizations had become a permanent feature of the American economy. The key to economic stability and growth depended on efficient "working rules" permitting mutual accommodation between such powerful economic interests as business and labor. Government could induce business to develop "working rules" through high premiums for permitting industrial accidents and higher taxes for avoidable layoffs. Business could then prevent unsafe working conditions and unemployment.

Commons translated these principles into policy through scholarship and policy debate. He actively served as an officer in the National Civic Federation and the American Association for Labor Legislation. He drafted a plan for stabilizing employment through the maintenance of individual company reserves to be distributed after a layoff; the plan was funded by taxes based on the employer's record in maintaining a stable payroll. Enacted by Wisconsin in 1932, Commons' proposal became the nation's first unemployment compensation law and heavily influenced the Social Security Act.* As a member of the U.S. Commission on Industrial Relations (1913-1915), Commons shaped that body's agenda of its final reports. His report anticipated the kind of industry self-regulation later authorized by the National Industrial Recovery Act.*

Commons also produced influential students. John B. Andrews, his most loyal student, stands out. Ensconced by Commons as executive secretary of the A.A.L.L. in 1906, Andrews held that position until 1943. With Commons, he co-authored a frequently used labor law text; he also wrote in 1914 a "Practical Program for the Prevention of Unemployment," a widely read progressive manifesto advocating a nationwide system of public employment exchanges, systematic distribution of public works projects, stabilization of industries, and unemployment insurance. During the 1930s, Andrews found in Senator Robert Wagner* a willing sponsor for such measures, and most of the "Practical Program" became law; in addition, the AALL actively mobilized social welfare intellectuals to lobby for this legislation.

Many other students of Commons influenced the New Deal* as well. William Leiserson, an expert on labor relations, served as executive secretary of the National Labor Board* under the NIRA, testified on behalf of the National Labor Relations Act,* and in 1935 became chairman of the National Mediation Board. Edwin Witte served as executive director of the Committee on Economic Security,* which drafted the Social Security Act. Arthur Altmeyer,* Commons' research assistant in 1918, served Franklin D. Roosevelt's* administration in the National Recovery Administration,* the Labor Department, and as chairman of the Social Security Board. Other New Deal participants such as Ewan Clague and Wilbur Cohen also had studied with Commons. Though none of these figures uncritically accepted all of Commons' ideas, the contribution of each to social policy reflected Commons' pragmatism and his aspiration to render more responsible an economic system inevitably dominated by powerful institutions. John R. Commons died on May 11, 1944. (Lafayette Harter, *John R. Commons*, 1962.)

DAVID BRIAN ROBERTSON

COMMUNICATIONS ACT OF 1934 (See the FEDERAL COMMUNICATIONS COMMISSION.)

COMMUNIST PARTY Leaders of the Communist party entered the 1930s with their hopes high. Marxist theories that capitalism would eventually collapse under the weight of its own inequities seemed ripe for fulfillment as the depression deepened. In the presidential election of 1928, Communist party candidate William Z. Foster* had polled only 21,603 votes, but he had improved that total in 1932, winning 102,785 votes. Early in 1933 with unemployment reaching 25 percent, the banking system collapsing, and insurgent protest movements like the National Farmers' Holiday Association* in the Midwest, Communists thought their time had come. Franklin D. Roosevelt* and the New Deal,* however, transformed their dreams into nightmares. New Deal relief, reform, and recovery legislation captured the national attention just as President Roosevelt captured the public heart. Communist party leader Earl Browder,* watching the New Deal erase public frustration, charged Roosevelt with "carrying out more thoroughly and brutally than even [Herbert] Hoover* the capitalist attack against the living standard of the masses."

Between 1933 and 1935, Browder and the Communist party saw the New Deal as the savior of capitalism. The NRA,* in their view, was simply a sophisticated government technique for increasing business consolidation and corporate power, while the AAA* rewarded large commercial farmers at the expense of sharecroppers, tenants, and small farmers. After 1935, however, the Communist party changed its tune and began to offer a limited praise of the New Deal. Although the New Deal had turned more to the left in 1935, becoming more overtly anti-business and pro-labor, the real source of the Communist change was part of the Moscow-inspired "Popular Front" era when Joseph Stalin hoped to create a coalition between radicals and liberals in the United States. Earl Browder began issuing peaceful overtures to Socialists and liberal Democrats and even offered cautious praise of the New Deal. Popular Frontists hoped to forge a new party in the United States, one with a reformist exterior and a hard-core radical interior. It was an incredibly naive notion. In the presidential election of 1936,* Browder received only 80,869 votes.

Popular Front values dominated the late 1930s as well, with most American Communists praising the New Deal while urging more of the same—more relief to the poor and more control and regulation of big corporations. They occasionally criticized the Roosevelt administration when relief appropriations were cut or when Loyalist Spain was hurt by the neutrality legislation, but they generally supported the president. In 1939 Browder even began urging the president to seek a third term. But the Party's fortunes received a shock in August 1939 when the Germans and Soviets signed the Non-Aggression Pact. After years of condemning internationalism and fascism, American Communists found themselves obligated to praise internationalism and support Nazism. In the process the party sustained huge defections from disillusioned intellectuals; the dependence of the American Communist party on Moscow's whims had become all too blatant. In the election of 1940,* Browder received only 46,251 votes.The hopes for a depression-inspired political revolution in America were gone. (Irving Howe and Lewis Coser, *The American Communist Party. A Critical History (1919-1957)*, 1957.)

CONGRESS OF INDUSTRIAL ORGANIZATIONS By the early 1930s, the American Federation of Labor* was the premier union in the country, resting on a half-century of success. When Samuel Gompers organized the AFL in the early 1880s, he succeeded where others had failed by eschewing mass organization and focusing on skilled workers in the craft trades. In the twentieth century Gompers, and his successor William Green,* formed federal labor unions for the increasing numbers of mass production workers but clearly treated them as second-class citizens. The mass production workers chafed at the AFL's anti-industrial attitude; and at the 1934 convention, a group of perhaps 30 percent of the union membership called on the AFL to organize mass production factory workers into industrial unions. John L. Lewis,* president of the United Mine Workers, led the rebellion. They got little satisfaction in 1934 but renewed their demands at the 1935 convention. There the rank-and-file membership delegates voted them down by a vote of 18,464 to 10,987. John L. Lewis, Sidney Hillman* (Amalgamated Clothing Workers), David Dubinsky* (International Ladies Garment Workers), Thomas McMahon (Textile Workers), and Charles Howard (Typographers) formed the Committee for Industrial Organization as a formal entity within the AFL. In 1936 the AFL suspended the CIO unions, and after two years of legal disputes, Lewis and the others formed the Congress of Industrial Organizations.

Protected by the provisions of the National Labor Relations Act,* the CIO became a potent political and economic force in the United States. In the 1936 presidential election, they contributed nearly one million dollars to Franklin D. Roosevelt's* re-election campaign and established the Labor's Non-Partisan League and American Labor party* to campaign for him. Economically, the CIO then assaulted the major corporate bastions of industrial America in mass organization drives. In June 1936, Philip Murray,* Lewis' assistant with the United Mine Workers, formed the Steel Workers Organizing Committee. Sidney Hillman established the Textile Workers Organizing Committee. Later in 1936 the United Automobile Workers launched their "sit-down" strikes which shut down the industry. In February 1937 General Motors capitulated, recognized the union, and met its wage-and-hours demands. By the end of 1937 the UAW membership had jumped from less than 30,000 to more than 400,000 workers. In March 1937 United States Steel Corporation recognized the Steel Workers Organizing Committee and agreed to its demands. By mid-summer of 1937, the SWOC membership stood at nearly 350,000 people. The United Rubber Workers, United Electrical and Radio Workers, and the Textile Workers Organizing Committee enjoyed a similar triumph in 1937. Only Henry Ford,* the "little steel" companies, and the major packinghouses remained unorganized; but their independence was doomed. By 1940 the CIO had a total membership of 2,654,000 in forty-one affiliated unions. More than 71 percent of the CIO membership was concentrated in the United Mine Workers, United Automobile Workers, Steel Workers Organizing Committee, Amalgamated Clothing Workers, Textile Workers, and United Electrical, Radio, and Machine Workers. John L. Lewis' role in the CIO ended in 1940 when he endorsed Wendell Willkie* for president and had to resign when Roosevelt was re-elected. Philip Murray then succeeded him as head of the CIO. (Irving Bernstein, *Turbulent Years. A History of the American Worker 1933-1941*, 1970.)

CONNALLY ACT OF 1935 In its early drive to stabilize price levels and stimulate business confidence, Congress in 1933 had passed the National Industrial Recovery Act.* Section 9(c) of the NIRA was the so-called "hot-oil" section, permitting the president to regulate the interstate shipment of illegally-produced oil exceeding state production quotas. By regulating oil production, the administration hoped to stop the price declines so endemic to the early 1930s. But in January 1935 the Supreme Court,* in the *Panama Refining Company** and *Amazon Petroleum* cases, declared unconstitutional Section 9(c) because of the discretionary authority it gave the executive branch over interstate commerce. Oil producers in Texas, Louisiana, and Oklahoma, afraid that illegally produced and exported oil would undermine prices, insisted on some protection; and in February 1935 Senator Thomas Connally* sponsored legislation to prohibit the practice. President Franklin D. Roosevelt* signed the Connally Act into law on February 22, 1935. The law prohibited the interstate transportation of ''hot oil'' (oil in excess of state production quotas); authorized the president to lift the prohibition on such crude oil if a disparity developed between supply and demand; and called for federal confiscation of illegal petroleum taken across state lines. Along with the Bituminous Coal Conservation Act, Guffey-Vinson Act,* Robinson-Patman Act,* Walsh-Healey Act,* and Miller-Tydings Act,* the Connally Act of 1935 has been considered by historians as part of the ''Little NRA''* legislation passed by Congress in the wake of the Supreme Court's* destruction of the National Recovery Administration.* (Bernard Bellush, *The Failure of the NRA*, 1975.)

CONNALLY, THOMAS TERRY Thomas T. Connally was born on a farm in McLennan County, Texas, on August 19, 1877. He attended public schools in Eddy, Texas, graduated from Baylor College in 1896, and earned his law degree at the University of Texas in 1898. He served in the United States Army during the Spanish-American War and then went into private law practice. While serving in the Texas legislature between 1900 and 1904, as well as a term as county attorney in Falls County in 1906 and 1908, Connally earned a reputation as a ''young progressive,'' at least within the context of Texas politics. Elected to Congress in 1916, Connally resigned to serve in the army during World War I and was re-elected in 1918. Connally stayed in the House until 1929. In the election of 1928, he defeated Earl Mayfield in the Democratic primary for the United States Senate and began a career there which lasted until 1953.

Until the dispute over the ''court-packing''* scheme, Connally had been a loyal supporter of the New Deal.* At the 1932 Democratic convention he played an influential role in persuading John Nance Garner* to back Franklin D. Roosevelt.* Except for his opposition to the National Recovery Administration* and the Guffey-Snyder Bituminous Coal Conservation Act of 1935,* which he viewed as anti-southern bills, he voted for New Deal legislation. Still, he was a conservative Democrat in the context of the 1930s. As his political base in Texas rested on oil and banking interests, Connally could not afford to move too far to the left. He was uncomfortable with the Wealth Tax Act of 1935* and the Public Utility Holding Company Act of 1935,* but it was the court-packing plan which enraged him. Connally had an enormous respect for the law, and he saw the plan as an attempt on the part of President Roosevelt to alter fundamental

American institutions. He had felt much the same way about the president's elimination of the two-thirds rule* at the 1936 Democratic national convention. Connally openly denounced the court-packing scheme, and he and Roosevelt refused to talk to one another for the next two years. Connally similarly denounced the administration's willingness to let the "sit-down strikes" occur in 1936 and 1937, and he opposed the Reorganization Act of 1939.* A leading Democratic moderate in the Senate, Connally was symbolic of the disintegration of the faithful coalition Roosevelt had enjoyed during his first term. Thomas T. Connally remained in the Senate until 1953. He died on October 28, 1963. (James T. Patterson, *Congressional Conservatism and the New Deal*, 1967.)

DAN K. UTLEY

CONNERY, WILLIAM PATRICK, JR. William Patrick Connery, Jr., was born on August 24, 1888, in Lynn, Massachusetts. He attended Holy Cross College between 1904 and 1908, acted and toured with the George M. Cohan production group, and served with the American Expeditionary Force in France during World War I. After the war Connery returned home and went to work at the General Electric plant in East Boston, eventually rising to the position of foreman. Later he opened a candy manufacturing business. Active in Democratic politics and imbued with the urban liberalism then emerging out of the working-class Irish Catholic communities, he ran for Congress in 1922 and won the election. When the Democrats took over the House of Representatives after the 1930 congressional elections, Connery became chairman of the House Labor Committee, a position he held until his death. A devout New Dealer, Connery was close to President Franklin D. Roosevelt* and piloted most New Deal* labor legislation through the House. Along with Senator Hugo Black* of Alabama, Connery sponsored the famous "Thirty-Hour Bill" which played an instrumental role in establishing the National Industrial Recovery Act* as law. A lifelong opponent of child labor and proponent of labor rights, Connery was especially proud of the role he played in passage of the National Labor Relations Act of 1935.* He also had supported a wide variety of public works, relief, and labor laws central to the New Deal. After a short illness from food poisoning, William Connery, Jr., died on June 15, 1937. (*New York Times*, June 16, 1937.)

CONSERVATION OF FISH ACT OF 1934 Because of President Franklin D. Roosevelt's* life-long interest in wildlife conservation and because of concern among conservationists that federal public works and public power projects might harm fish populations, Congress passed the Conservation of Fish Act in 1934. The law specifically directed Secretary of the Interior Harold L. Ickes* to cooperate with local fish and game management groups to make sure that native fish populations were not harmed by federal water development projects. (Ira N. Gabrielson, *Wildlife Conservation*, 1959.)

CONSUMERS' ADVISORY BOARD At its inception, the National Recovery Administration* intended to be an impartial arbiter of industrial, labor, and consumer interests. To protect the interests of those groups, the NRA established an Industrial Advisory Board, Labor Advisory Board,* and Consumers' Advisory Board. The Consumers' Advisory Board was directly under the control of Hugh S. Johnson,* head of the NRA. Appointed on June 26, 1933, it consisted of Mary Harriman Rumsey,* Frank P. Graham of the University of North Carolina, economist William F. Ogburn of the University of Oregon, Belle Sherwin of the League of Women Voters, Professor Alonzo Taylor of Stanford University, and Mrs. Joseph Daniels of the Indiana League of Women Voters. A number of other people, including economist Paul H. Douglas and sociologist Robert S. Lynd, later served on the Consumers' Advisory Board. Without any organized consumer constituency in the country, the board had very little power and was generally ignored by General Johnson and the NRA staff. (Bernard Bellush, *The Failure of the NRA*, 1975.)

COOKE, MORRIS LLEWELLYN Born on May 11, 1872, in Carlisle, Pennsylvania, Morris L. Cooke graduated from Lehigh University in 1895, after having worked for a number of newspapers for several years. He then became a consulting engineer, with specialties in public works and electric power. Cooke was named director of the Department of Public Works of Philadelphia in 1911 and during World War I worked first with the War Industries Board and then as executive assistant to the chairman of the U.S. Shipping Board. A progressive Republican for most of his life, Cooke served as an economic adviser to Governor Gifford Pinchot of Pennsylvania and came to the attention of Governor Franklin D. Roosevelt* of New York. Roosevelt appointed him to the Power Authority of the State of New York in 1929, and by 1932 Cooke had switched political allegiance to the Democratic party.* Roosevelt appointed him to chair the Mississippi Valley Committee of the Public Works Administration* in 1933 and then to the National Power Policy Committee.* In March 1935 the president selected Cooke to head the new Rural Electrification Administration.* An advocate of national economic planning and ecological awareness, Morris Cooke was years ahead of his time, especially during the Great Depression when economic growth seemed the only priority. In 1937 he became chairman of the Great Plains Drought Area Committee,* a government body designed to plan a twenty-five-year program to restore the economy and ecological balance of the Midwest. During World War II, Cooke served as a consultant to the Office of Production Management and headed an American technical mission to Brazil. His last major government appointment came in 1950 when President Harry S Truman* selected him to chair the President's Water Resources Policy Committee. Morris L. Cooke died on March 5, 1960. (Jean Christie, *Morris Llewellyn Cooke: Progressive Engineer*, 1982.)

COOLIDGE, MARCUS ALLEN Marcus Coolidge, Democratic senator from Massachusetts, was born on October 6, 1865, in Westminister, Massachusetts.

He attended public schools and the Bryant & Stratton Commercial College in Boston and then went to work in his father's furniture manufacturing business. Coolidge moved to Fitchburg, Massachusetts, in 1895 and started a very successful heavy construction business. He served as mayor of Fitchburg in 1916, supported Woodrow Wilson's presidential campaigns in 1912 and 1916, and served as a delegate to Poland in 1919. Coolidge was chairman of the Democratic state convention in 1920, and ten years later he was elected to the United States Senate. He served one term between 1931 and 1937 and was considered one of the more unreliable northeastern Democrats, at least in terms of his support of the New Deal.* Coolidge opposed the Tennessee Valley Authority,* Franklin D. Roosevelt's* gold buying policy,* and the Public Utility Holding Company Act of 1935.* He decided not to stand for re-election in 1936 and returned home to his business interests. Coolidge died on January 23, 1947. (*New York Times*, January 24, 1947.)

COPELAND, ROYAL SAMUEL Royal S. Copeland was born on November 7, 1868, on a farm in Dexter, Michigan. He graduated from Michigan State Normal College and then took a medical degree at the University of Michigan in 1889. Copeland specialized in ophthalmology and taught at the University of Michigan Medical School until 1908. As a Republican, he also served a term as mayor of Ann Arbor in 1901-1903 and then president of the board of education between 1903 and 1908. He moved to New York City in 1908 as dean of the New York Flower Hospital and Medical School, and became a widely syndicated medical columnist for the Hearst press. He also established a personal friendship with William Randolph Hearst.* Interested in politics but realizing that his tradition of Republicanism would not serve him well in New York City, Copeland switched parties and in 1918 was appointed commissioner of health for the city. In 1922, when Al Smith* refused to accept any suggestion of William Randolph Hearst representing the New York Democratic party as a candidate for the U.S. Senate, Copeland got the nod because of his friendship with Hearst. He won the general election and was re-elected in 1928 and 1934.

During the 1930s, Copeland gradually became a critic of the New Deal.* Although he had initially supported the NRA,* the Economy Act of 1933,* and the various relief proposals, he soon became disaffected. Copeland hated the monetary tinkering and abandonment of the gold standard in 1933, opposed the "court-packing"* proposal of 1937, and fought Franklin D. Roosevelt's* executive reorganization plan in 1938. Copeland's real love was food and drug legislation. Between 1933, when Rexford Tugwell* wrote it, and 1938, when it was passed, the Food, Drug, and Cosmetic Act* had the undivided support of Senator Copeland. Royal Copeland died suddenly on June 17, 1938. (Charles O. Jackson, *Food and Drug Legislation in the New Deal*, 1970; *New York Times*, June 18, 1938.)

CORCORAN, THOMAS GARDINER Thomas "The Cork" Corcoran, the brilliant, witty legislative strategist behind much of the New Deal,* was born

December 29, 1900, in Pawtucket, Rhode Island. Corcoran graduated Phi Beta Kappa from Brown University in 1922, and then went on to the Harvard Law School. At Cambridge he quickly impressed Professor Felix Frankfurter* with his wit and unparalleled analytical skills, becoming the future Supreme Court* justice's "favorite pupil." Corcoran graduated from the Harvard Law School in 1925, took a doctorate of juristic science in 1926, and then went, on Frankfurter's recommendation, to serve one year as secretary to Supreme Court Justice Oliver Wendell Holmes, Jr. Between 1927 and 1932 Corcoran practiced law privately in New York with the firm of Colton and Franklin, specializing in corporate reorganization and new stock issues. Although a loyal Democrat in the tradition of millions of Irish Catholics, Corcoran first went to work for the federal government in 1932, when President Herbert Hoover* appointed him counsel to the Reconstruction Finance Corporation.* In 1933 Felix Frankfurter introduced him to newly-elected Franklin D. Roosevelt,* and the president made him a special assistant to both Secretary of Treasury William Woodin* and to Attorney General Homer Cummings.* In 1934 Corcoran returned to the RFC as special counsel, and he remained there until his return to private practice in 1941.

Corcoran's influence, however, was hardly confined to the RFC. Roosevelt frequently used him on a wide variety of legislation. While working on the Truth-in-Securities* legislation in 1933 which became the Securities Act,* Corcoran met Benjamin Cohen,* who had come to Washington with Harvard Law School professor James Landis* to work on the bill. Together, they wrote the more comprehensive Securities Exchange Act of 1934,* and the team of Cohen and Corcoran was born. Theirs was an extraordinary collaboration, responsible in whole or in part for a wealth of New Deal legislation, including the Federal Housing Administration,* Tennessee Valley Authority,* the RFC extension, and the Public Utility Holding Company Act of 1935.* The two of them worked behind the scenes in New Deal Washington, displaying a "passion for anonymity," which actually enhanced their influence. The two men shared a Georgetown townhouse with several other New Deal lawyers and worked incessantly, with Cohen serving as the chief legislative draftsman and Corcoran using his effervescent personality to shepherd the bills through Congress. The two men earned the title of the "gold dust twins," after a popular soap advertisement which encouraged the householder to "let the gold dust twins do your work." They were also called "Frankfurter's two chief little hot dogs" and "the brain twins."

Beyond his role as a legislative lobbyist for the New Deal, Corcoran also played an extraordinary role in placing bright young lawyers into important New Deal positions. Although he was nominally housed in the RFC, Corcoran operated widely throughout Washington. Frankfurter had been his entrée into the White House, and there Corcoran impressed the president because of his enormous personal charm, single-minded commitment to the New Deal, ability to direct a team effort, and his uncanny understanding of the law and the Constitution. Over the course of seven years, between 1933 and 1941, Corcoran placed hundreds of Ivy League and Wall-Street attorneys in government jobs, and all of them were people he had known through, or had recommended to him by, Felix Frankfurter. His only requirements were a penchant for hard work, legal expertise, and commitment to the New Deal.

Corcoran's influence, however, peaked in 1937 during the "court-packing"* controversy. Although he personally disagreed with the president's approach to the problem of the conservative, even reactionary, Supreme Court, he completely invested his energies in trying to maneuver the legislation through Congress in 1937. When public opposition to the proposal eventually destroyed any chance of passage, the president held Corcoran somewhat responsible, even though he had done all that was humanly possible to promote the measure. Frustrated about not getting any higher appointments in the federal government, Corcoran resigned from the RFC in 1941 and began a lucrative law practice in Washington. The thousands of contacts he had made during the 1930s served him well, as did his brilliance, wit, and hard work. Although in later years people accused him of influence-peddling in Washington, no charges were ever filed against him. Thomas Gardiner Corcoran, one of the most influential people in the United States during the 1930s, died on December 6, 1981. (*New York Times*, December 7, 1981; Peter Irons, *The New Deal Lawyers*, 1982.)

CORPORATE BANKRUPTCY ACT OF 1934 As part of their recovery efforts and to extend to businessmen the same opportunities that farmers, railroads, and cities had already received, the Franklin D. Roosevelt* administration began pushing amendments to federal bankruptcy laws in 1934. Similar measures had reached Congress in 1932, only to be opposed by the Democratic majority. But by 1934, with the National Recovery Administration* in full gear, many New Dealers hoped that more liberal bankruptcy rules for private corporations would facilitate their reorganization and prepare them to hire workers once again and increase production. One problem with the existing bankruptcy regulations was that a minority of stockholders unwilling to accept an adjustment of their assets could block, as could a minority of creditors, any attempts at refinancing or scaling down of debts. In the spring of 1934, Senator Frederick Van Nuys of Indiana and Representative Tom D. McKeown of Oklahoma jointly sponsored a corporate reorganization measure to prevent such minority delays. The measure provided for an application for reorganization by an insolvent corporation if it was approved by 25 percent of the stockholders. All creditors were bound to a reorganization plan sanctioned by a federal court and accepted by 67 percent of the holders of the total amount of claims. The law also specifically prohibited corporations applying for reorganization from interfering with the rights of their employees to join labor unions. The bill enjoyed the widespread support of the business community and President Roosevelt signed it into law on June 7, 1934.

Four years later, on June 22, 1938, President Roosevelt signed into law the Chandler Act,* which amended the Federal Bankruptcy Act of 1898 to allow financially-distressed people, partnerships, and corporations to petition the federal courts for settlement, refinancing, or debt reduction if such a step was agreeable to a majority of creditors in each class of debt and if it was necessary to avoid liquidation. (*New York Times*, June 8, 1934 and June 23, 1938.)

COSTIGAN, EDWARD PRENTICE Edward Prentice Costigan was a leading figure in Colorado progressivism for nearly three decades. Born on July 1, 1874, in King William County, Virginia, he moved to Colorado with his family when still a boy. In 1897 he received the A.B. degree from Harvard and then practiced law in Denver and Salt Lake City. Costigan early established his credentials as a progressive, serving as an attorney for the Denver Honest Election League and the Anti-Saloon League in the early 1900s and president of the Denver Civil Service Reform Association. Costigan helped found the Progressive party in Colorado in 1912, endorsed the Bull Moose campaign, and failed to win the governorship in 1912 and 1914. In 1916 he endorsed Woodrow Wilson for the presidency, and Wilson rewarded him with an appointment to the Tariff Commission in 1917. Costigan kept the post until 1928, always campaigning for flexible, and usually lower, tariff schedules. He resigned in protest in 1928, and two years later won a seat in the United States Senate as a Democrat. He supported the candidacy of Franklin D. Roosevelt* in 1932 and became an avid New Dealer, aligning himself in the Senate with the progressive bloc led by Senators George Norris* and Robert La Follette, Jr.* Costigan was a consistent advocate of the need for relief, public works, and social security legislation; demanded protection of the right of workers to bargain collectively; and unsuccessfully fought for a federal anti-lynching bill.* Ill health kept him from running for re-election in 1936, and he died on January 17, 1939. (*New York Times*, January 18, 1939.)

COTTON TEXTILE NATIONAL INDUSTRIAL RELATIONS BOARD On July 9, 1933, President Franklin D. Roosevelt* signed the NRA* code of fair competition for the cotton textile industry. As part of the agreement, a Cotton Textile National Industrial Relations Board was established. Economist Robert W. Bruere served as the chairman of the board, and the other two members were George L. Berry* of the AFL* and B. E. Greer of Furman University, who fervently represented the interests of southern textile mills. The purpose of the Cotton Textile Industrial Relations Board was to settle labor disputes in the industry. The board proved to be ineffective. Chairman Bruere refused to confront the industry whenever serious charges were raised, and the board came under the influence of George A. Sloan, head of the Cotton Textile Institute. Labor frustration with the NRA code mounted in 1933 and 1934 because of what they considered repeated violations of Section 7(a) of the National Industrial Recovery Act* and of its minimum wage provisions. In August 1934, after the mill owners announced a 25 percent reduction in wages and hours for workers, the United Textile Workers of America voted for a nationwide strike to take place on September 1, 1934. Ever since June 1933 the UTWA had frequently forwarded complaints from workers to the board, but Bruere simply sent them on to George Sloan's Cotton Textile Institute, which "investigated" them and decided against workers. To avert the strike and deal with some of the union complaints, President Roosevelt called for a reduction in the weekly hours of 200,000 cotton-garment workers by 10 percent and raising their wages by 10 percent.

Manufacturers bitterly protested the president's decision, and the strike went forward by the UTWA. The strike proved to be a failure. Cotton inventories in the mill inventories were bulging so the Cotton-Textile Institute refused to submit to arbitration. The Cotton Textile National Industrial Relations Board was completely unable to deal with the crisis, the AFL refused to give the UTWA any financial support, and state governors called out the national guard in several areas to restore order. Roosevelt appointed a three-man board headed by Republican Governor John G. Winant* of New Hampshire to conduct arbitration. Still, the industry refused to arbitrate and the strike collapsed. Roosevelt agreed to create a new Textile Labor Relations Board* to work out future disputes, but wages remained unchanged and employers did not have to rehire striking workers. (Bernard Bellush, *The Failure of the NRA*, 1975; Lewis L. Lorwin and Arthur Wubnig, *Labor Relations Boards*, 1935.)

COUGHLIN, CHARLES EDWARD Charles E. Coughlin, the "radio priest" during the 1930s, was born October 25, 1891. He was raised in Hamilton, Ontario, and studied theology at the University of Toronto before entering the Roman Catholic priesthood. Coughlin taught for ten years at Assumption College in Windsor, Ontario, and in 1926 was transferred to the Diocese of Detroit, where he took over a parish in Royal Oaks, Michigan. A few weeks after he arrived, the Ku Klux Klan burned a cross in the churchyard, and Coughlin started a weekly radio broadcast from his church—The Shrine of the Little Flower. In 1930 he began warning listeners about the dangers of communism, and his popularity soared. Soon he had a nationwide CBS contract for weekly broadcasts. In 1932 he endorsed Franklin D. Roosevelt* for president, telling his listeners it was a choice between "Roosevelt or ruin."

Father Coughlin combined skillful manipulation of the medium with considerable personal charisma to achieve by 1934 a position of real political power. In that year he received more mail than any other American, including the president. And it has been estimated that during the early 1930s between 30 and 45 million Americans each week listened to his CBS radio show called "The Golden Hour of the Little Flower." Coughlin appealed to people who were lost in the economic and social complexities of modern life. He offered simple explanations and equally simple solutions, and his offering was served up with just the right seasoning of humanity. In addition, Coughlin appealed to a side of the American character which was then little understood. As William Manchester observed, Coughlin exploited "American innocence, the nation's yearning for simple solutions, its joiner complex, and the carnival instinct for collecting shiny junk."

A salesman, Coughlin peddled hate, suspicion, and prejudice. The depression, he argued, was the work of "bad" people, primarily international bankers, Communists, and Jews. Heavily invested in silver futures, he made the purchase and monetization of silver his central doctrine. He waged war against the "pagan god of gold." As he once claimed, "Silver is the key to world prosperity—silver that was damned by the Morgans." If his rantings had any sort of consistent ideology, then it tended to be fascist. He greatly admired the work of Hitler and Mussolini, and he often advocated a political system similar to that of Italian corporatism.

Coughlin continued to support Roosevelt and the New Deal* throughout 1933, telling his radio listeners that "the New Deal is Christ's deal," and that "Gabriel is over the White House, not Lucifer." But the romance, never based on any positive bonds, did not last long. By the spring of 1934, Coughlin was becoming more critical of individual New Deal measures. He attacked the NRA* and AAA,* and he was particularly incensed over Secretary of the Treasury Henry Morgenthau's* economic programs. By late 1934 there could be little doubt that Coughlin had changed his earlier opinions concerning the New Deal. In 1935 he began speaking of the New Deal as the "Jew Deal" and labelled Roosevelt as "a liar," an "anti-God." He even suggested that Roosevelt should be eliminated by "the use of bullets."

On November 11, 1934, Coughlin announced the formation of the National Union for Social Justice. Its stated purpose was to promote social and economic reforms for the benefit of the poor and bewildered masses. He used his radio show and his magazine *Social Justice* to publicize the NUSJ's programs. Specifically, he called for an inflationary monetary policy, redistribution of the national wealth, and enactment of widespread welfare measures. At its peak, the National Union for Social Justice had over 500,000 members. With that political base, Coughlin in 1935 allied with other New Deal critics. Joining with Senator Huey P. Long* and Francis Townsend,* Coughlin laid the groundwork for the Union party.* They hoped Long would run for president on the party's ticket in 1936, but the assassination of Long in September 1935 ended that plan. Instead, the Union party nominated Representative William Lemke* of North Dakota. Coughlin confidently announced he would attract at least 9 million votes for Lemke, or he would quit broadcasting and retire from politics. During the campaign, Coughlin's attacks on Roosevelt became so vitriolic and uncontrolled that his own church intervened to restrain him. Lemke polled less than one million votes, about 2 percent of the total, and Coughlin did retire from broadcasting, but only for seven weeks.

After the election of 1936,* Coughlin's influence began to decline. He became increasingly anti-Semitic, pro-Hitler, and isolationist in his political opinions. In 1937 Archbishop Edward Mooney of Detroit publicly condemned Coughlin for his attacks on labor and the New Deal, and Rome publicly concurred. By 1942 Coughlin was claiming that World War II was a "Roosevelt-British-Jewish" conspiracy. That year the church formally ended his radio broadcasts and the United States government banned *Social Justice* from the mail. Coughlin continued to work as a priest at The Shrine of the Little Flower, and in 1944 the National Union for Social Justice disbanded. After the war Coughlin was known for his hatred of communism and his resentment about the changes Vatican II brought to the Roman Catholic church. He died on October 27, 1979. (*New York Times*, October 28, 1979; Charles J. Tull, *Father Coughlin and the New Deal*, 1965.)

RANDY ROBERTS

"COURT-PACKING" BILL After a landslide victory in the election of 1936,* President Franklin D. Roosevelt* indicated in his second inaugural address that he was planning some radical changes in the federal judiciary. The Supreme Court* had already declared the National Recovery Administration,* the Agricultural Adjustment Administration,* and the Guffey-Snyder Bituminous Coal Conservation Act* unconstitutional. In the *Morehead** case, the Supreme Court had held by a five to four vote that the New York state minimum wage law was invalid. Roosevelt and other New Dealers feared that the National Labor Relations Act,* the wages and hours legislation, and other reform measures might be in jeopardy from the Supreme Court.

For two years Roosevelt had sought some means to make the Supreme Court more amenable to New Deal* legislation. After considerable investigation on ways to alter the high court constitutionally, he concluded that "court-packing" was the only feasible solution. But Roosevelt and his advisers also decided that any attempt to pack the court had to be masked by raising the broader issue of judicial reform. This would hopefully divert attention away from Roosevelt's real objective, the liberalization of the Supreme Court. He sought historical precedent in a document drafted in 1913 by then Attorney General James McReynolds.* The McReynolds plan would have made provision for younger men to be appointed to the federal judiciary. The president believed this principle could be applied to the Supreme Court. He could expand the high court by nominating men who were friendly toward the New Deal, and he could avoid the need for a constitutional amendment to change the Supreme Court.

On February 5, 1937, Roosevelt sent Congress his plan for reorganizing the federal judiciary. Among his stated reasons for introducing this plan was his claim that the federal docket was overcrowded. In one year, he claimed, the Supreme Court had denied 87 percent of petitions for hearings on appeal without citing reasons. Roosevelt further raised doubts about the mental capacity of the justices. The proposal included provisions for an increase in the membership of the court from nine to a maximum of fifteen members if justices reaching the age of seventy decided not to retire; the addition of not more than fifty judges to all levels of the federal court system; and assignment of district judges to congested areas in order to make the court system more efficient.

When the plan was made public, a storm of criticism descended on the administration. Opponents of the plan immediately mounted an offensive, labelling the charge of court inefficiency a false one and demonstrating that the president was actually seeking a more responsive court. They accused the president of dictatorial behavior, wanting to subvert the independence of the Court, tampering with the separation of powers, and trying to "pack" the Court for his own purposes. Among Roosevelt's opponents were those who had disliked his economic policies and now found justification to break with him and not incur public disapproval. Many conservative Democrats were outraged at his actions. Most people, however, opposed him out of genuine fear that his actions might weaken the Supreme Court's ability to protect civil liberties. Senator Burton K. Wheeler* led the fight against the plan, and Roosevelt had already weakened his position by not lining up cabinet and congressional support before pushing the measure. The Senate Judiciary Committee reported negatively on the plan.

In March President Roosevelt personally tried to promote the bill in an address to the Democratic Victory Dinner in Washington, D.C., and a fireside chat* with the nation, where he claimed that the Court was preventing the federal government from dealing with the economic crisis.

By the end of May, the urgency of the court reform bill had dissipated. On March 29, in a five to four decision, the Court upheld Washington's minimum wage law, one similar to the New York statute that had been struck down earlier. During April and May, the court also upheld the Frazier-Lemke Farm Mortgage Moratorium Act of 1935, the Social Security Act,* and the National Labor Relations Act,* primarily because Justice Owen Roberts* began to vote in favor of the Roosevelt programs. Also, Justice William Van Devanter,* a New Deal opponent on the Court, announced his impending retirement on May 18, a decision which would give Roosevelt a six to three split. The president pressed on with the fight, but on July 14, Senator Joseph Robinson* of Arkansas, leader of the fight for the bill, died. The bill then lost whatever momentum it had left in the face of such concerted opposition. On July 22, Senator Marvel Logan of Kentucky moved that the bill be recommitted, and it was by a vote of 70 to 20. It died there in the Senate Judiciary Committee. As a compromise measure, the president signed the Judicial Procedures Reform Act on August 26, 1937, reforming some lower court procedures but doing nothing about the appointment of new justices in the federal court system.

In one sense Roosevelt had achieved his objective: the Supreme Court no longer declared his programs unconstitutional, and by the end of 1941 he had appointed seven new justices: Hugo Black* (1937), Stanley Reed* (1938), Felix Frankfurter* (1939), William O. Douglas* (1939), Frank Murphy* (1940), Robert Jackson* (1941), and James F. Byrnes* (1941). But in achieving the victory, the president had driven a permanent wedge into the Democratic coalition, alienating conservatives and compromising his ability to secure congressional support. (Leonard Baker, *Back to Back: The Duel Between FDR and the Supreme Court*, 1967.)

MICHAEL DENNIS

COUZENS, JAMES JOSEPH, JR. James Joseph Couzens, Jr., was born on August 26, 1872, in Chatham, Ontario, Canada. His father was an independent businessman, manufacturing soap and selling coal and ice. Couzens worked briefly in the family business but left home and moved to Detroit in 1890. He went to work for the Michigan Central Railroad and in 1895 for the Malcomson Fuel Company. Alex Malcomson became an early investor in some of Henry Ford's* first enterprises, and Couzens became Malcomson's chief clerk. Ford, Couzens, Malcomson, and several others became founding members and original stockholders of the Ford Motor Company in 1903. Couzens was named secretary of the new company and soon business manager. His fortunes rose with those of Ford Motor Company—a fortune based on mass production and the emerging car culture. Because of personal differences with Henry Ford, Couzens resigned from the company in 1915. By then a multimillionaire, Couzens turned to politics.

He became police commissioner of Detroit in 1916, mayor in 1918, and United States senator from Michigan in 1922. By then he had well-established credentials as a progressive, though independent, Republican. During the 1920s, he supported George Norris'* proposals for Muscle Shoals,* opposed Prohibition, outspokenly criticized Secretary of the Treasury Andrew Mellon's tax proposals, and called for unemployment insurance and old-age pensions. During the New Deal,* Couzens helped lead the Pecora investigations of the banking and investment community, served as a delegate to the World Economic and Monetary Conference in 1933, and became known as a "New Deal Republican," supporting the CCC,* NRA,* Social Security,* the National Labor Relations Act,* the Public Utility Holding Company Act,* WPA* appropriations, and Franklin D. Roosevelt's* tax proposals. Though a Republican, Couzens became a public critic of the Republican Old Guard, conservative Democrats, the Hearst press, and the American Liberty League.* When he endorsed Roosevelt's re-election bid before the Republican primary in Michigan, his own Senate career was doomed. He lost the primary to Wilbur Brucker. After a short illness from uremic poisoning, James Joseph Couzens, Jr., died on October 22, 1936. (Harry Barnard, *Independent Man: The Life of Senator James Couzens*, 1958.)

COX, EDWARD EUGENE Edward E. Cox was born near Camilla, Georgia, on April 3, 1880. He attended Mercer University for four years and received a law degree there in 1902. Cox began practicing law in Camilla, served as mayor there between 1904 and 1906 and was a superior court judge between 1912 and 1916. He ran unsuccessfully as a Democrat for Congress in the election of 1916 but was elected in 1924. During the New Deal,* Cox was an intense opponent of many of Franklin D. Roosevelt's* policies. Although he had favored the Public Utility Holding Company Act of 1935,* he became a bitter opponent of the New Deal after 1936. A believer in individual rights and private property, he was incensed when Roosevelt did nothing about the "sit-down" strikes, and viewed the president's tolerance of the new CIO* as proof of his radicalism. During the last half of the New Deal, Cox opposed the court-packing* scheme, executive reorganization, deficit spending, the WPA,* and the National Labor Relations Board.* A leader among southern Democrats in the House, Cox proved to be a critical figure in the coalition of southerners and northern Republicans who fought the New Deal in the later 1930s. He served in the House of Representatives until his death on December 24, 1952. (*New York Times*, December 25, 1952; James T. Patterson, *Congressional Conservatism in the New Deal*, 1967.)

COYLE, DAVID CUSHMAN David Cushman Coyle, a civil engineer turned economist during the New Deal,* was born on May 24, 1887, in North Adams, Massachusetts. He graduated from Princeton in 1908 and then took a civil engineering degree from Rensselaer Polytechnic Institute in 1910. Coyle took a job after leaving Rensselaer with the Gunvald Company, a group of consulting engineers in New York City. He worked both with them and independently for the rest of his life. In 1933 Secretary of the Interior Harold Ickes* named Coyle to the Technical Board of Review of the Public Works Administration,* and between 1933 and the end of World War II Coyle worked as a consulting engineer with several federal agencies, including the PWA, Rural Electrification Administration,* Works Progress Administration,* and the Federal Works Agency.*

During the 1930s, Coyle also turned his attention to economics and became a popular writer as well as an advocate of economic decentralization. Convinced that the national planning inherent in the National Recovery Administration* would lead to a tyranny of economic discipline and corporate control, Coyle began calling for higher income and inheritance taxes to prevent the wealthy from oversaving and creating stagnation; for strict federal control of bank credit; for anti-trust activity to prevent the destruction of competition; and for tight federal regulation of the securities markets. He also was an exponent of large-scale public works spending as a means of stimulating the economy. His views, connected to the thinking of Louis Brandeis* and John Maynard Keynes,* symbolized the New Deal's drift to the left after 1935. Coyle's 1935 article ''Decentralize Industry'' in the *Virginia Quarterly Review* and his books *Waste* (1936) and *The American Way* (1938) were widely read by and influential for New Dealers, including Franklin D. Roosevelt,* Harold Ickes, Harry Hopkins,* Jerome Frank,* Rexford Tugwell,* and Leon Henderson.* After World War II, Coyle continued to work as an engineering consultant and author, writing *The United States Political System* (1954), *The United Nations* (1955), *Conservation* (1957), and *Ordeal of the Presidency* (1959). He died in Washington, D.C., on July 15, 1969. (Arthur M. Schlesinger, Jr., *The Age of Roosevelt. Vol. III. The Politics of Upheaval, 1935-1936*, 1960; *Who Was Who in America*, V:156, 1973.)

CREEL, GEORGE Born on December 1, 1876, in Lafayette County, Missouri, George Creel attended local public schools until the tenth grade, when he decided to move away from the state. He settled in Kansas and went to work for the *Kansas City World* before trying to publish his own newspaper, the *Kansas City Independent* in 1903. Later he moved to Colorado where he worked for the

Denver Post and the *Rocky Mountain News*. Creel's pro-Wilson editorials for the *Rocky Mountain News* gained the president's attention, and in 1917 Woodrow Wilson appointed him head of the newly-created Committee on Public Information. During World War I, the Committee on Public Information helped censor anti-American and pro-German publications and published a great deal of pro-allied and anti-German propaganda. When the war ended, Creel returned to private life. In 1933 he became head of the San Francisco Regional Labor Board and in 1934 unsuccessfully challenged Upton Sinclair* for the Democratic gubernatorial nomination. An early supporter of the New Deal,* Creel served on the National Advisory Committee of the Works Progress Administration* in 1936 and the San Francisco International Exposition in 1939. He remained a vocal supporter of President Franklin D. Roosevelt* until the early 1940s when he began to question the inefficiency of the new federal bureaucracies. After World War II, Creel continued writing, particularly for *Collier's* magazine. He died of a liver ailment in 1953. (George Creel, *How We Advertised America*, 1920; *Current Biography*, 1944.)

CROP LOAN ACT OF 1934 (See FARM CREDIT ADMINISTRATION.)

CROSSER-DILL RAILWAY LABOR ACT OF 1934 (See RAILWAY LABOR ACT OF 1934.)

CROWLEY, LEO THOMAS Leo Thomas Crowley was born in 1889 in Milton Junction, Wisconsin, but was raised in Madison. Because of his family's poverty, Crowley had to quit school and go to work, but in 1910 he bought part-interest in a wholesale paper and supply company. By 1918 he was president of the General Paper and Supply Company and a major investor in a variety of real estate and banking concerns. During the 1920s he also became president of the State Bank of Wisconsin and director of First Wisconsin Bankshares Corporation. A devout Roman Catholic and fervent Democrat, Crowley supported the presidential candidacy of Al Smith* in 1928 and Franklin D. Roosevelt* in 1932. Crowley's own finances took a sharp turn downward in 1932 when the State Bank of Wisconsin failed. The fact that the bank had made him a large number of personal loans would plague Crowley throughout his political career.

Crowley had a reputation as a conservative Democrat, and in 1932, after supporting and leading the election campaign of Governor Albert G. Schmedeman, he gained great influence in Wisconsin. Crowley helped draft Wisconsin's banking holiday proclamation early in March 1933 and even managed to get President-elect Franklin D. Roosevelt's blessing on it. In October 1933 Henry Morgenthau, Jr.,* appointed Crowley to be coordinator of the Seventh Farm District for the Farm Credit Administration,* and in February 1934 Roosevelt brought Crowley to Washington, D.C., to head the newly-created Federal Deposit Insurance Corporation.* He stayed with the FDIC for about twelve years, leading the examination process which brought so many troubled banks into the new insurance program. Despite constant rumors about his financial debts and problems, Crowley kept Roosevelt's favor, and in 1942 the president appointed him Alien Property Custodian. In 1943 he became head of the Office of Economic Warfare and the Foreign Economic Administration, which controlled all foreign economic operations, including lend-lease. After President Roosevelt's death in 1945, Crowley lost his real source of power in Washington, D.C., and Harry S Truman* did not reappoint him. Leo T. Crowley died on April 15, 1972. (Stuart Weiss, "Leo T. Crowley: Pragmatic New Dealer," *Mid-America*, LXIV:33-52, 1982.)

CRUSADERS FOR ECONOMIC LIBERTY The Crusaders for Economic Liberty was an anti-Roosevelt, anti-New Deal group convinced that the president was leading the country down the road to communism. Founded by George W. Christians in 1934, the crusaders had a small but vocal following in the South. Members of the Crusaders for Economic Liberty called themselves "White Shirts" and railed against the national debt, deficit spending, federal bureaucracy, and diplomatic recognition of the Soviet Union. With his headquarters in Chattanooga, Tennessee, Christians periodically forayed out through the Middle West calling for a new civilization "based upon the Constitution as it is written with Economic Liberty." (George Wolfskill and John A. Hudson, *All but the People. Franklin D. Roosevelt and His Critics, 1933-1939*, 1969.)

CUMMINGS, HOMER STILLE Homer Cummings was born in Chicago, Illinois, on April 30, 1870. He received his undergraduate and law degrees from Yale in 1891 and 1893 and went into private practice in Stamford, Connecticut. Cummings was active in local Democratic politics, serving three terms as mayor of Stamford between 1902 and 1908 and as state attorney for Fairfield County between 1914 and 1924. He was elected vice-chairman of the Democratic National Committee in 1913 and ran unsuccessfully for the United States Senate in 1916. In 1919 and 1920 Cummings served as chairman of the Democratic National Committee and was appointed attorney general in the cabinet of President Franklin D. Roosevelt* in 1933. He filled that position until January 1, 1939. After his resignation he returned to private law practice. Cummings wrote two books: *Liberty under Law and Administration* (1934) and *We Can Prevent Crime* (1937). He died on September 10, 1956, in Washington, D.C. (*New York Times*, September 11, 1956.)

CUMMINGS, WALTER J. Walter J. Cummings was born on June 24, 1879, in Springfield, Illinois. He was educated at Northwestern University and Loyola University and entered the banking business in Chicago. An active Democrat, Cummings became a prominent, conservative party leader. In 1933 Secretary of the Treasury William Woodin* named Cummings as his administrative assistant. Cummings left that position after Woodin's death in January 1934, but later in the year President Franklin D. Roosevelt* named him to become the first chairman of the Federal Deposit Insurance Corporation.* Cummings headed the FDIC during its formative stage but left it in 1934 to become chairman of the board of the Continental Illinois Bank & Trust Company and treasurer of the Democratic National Committee. Cummings remained with the Democratic National Committee until 1936 and then returned exclusively to banking endeavors. He died on August 20, 1967. (*New York Times*, August 21, 1967.)

CURRIE, LAUCHLIN Lauchlin Currie was born October 8, 1902, in West Dublin, Nova Scotia. He received his education at St. Francis Xavier University (1920-1922) and graduated from the London School of Economics in 1925. Currie received a Ph.D. in economics at Harvard in 1936. Currie's early professional career involved an instructorship in economics at Harvard University (1927-1934) and a professorship in international economics at the Fletcher School of Law and Diplomacy in Medford, Massachusetts. Currie's major interest lay in the area of monetary policy. He argued in a 1934 article that Federal Reserve Board* policy in the 1920s had contributed to the monetary contraction which helped bring on the depression. Yet by the early 1930s, Currie began advocating increased federal expenditures for public works in that monetary policy could no longer bring about economic recovery. In 1934 Currie received an invitation from University of Chicago economist Jacob Viner to come to Washington, D.C., to work for the Department of the Treasury. While at the treasury, Currie met and became a close friend to Marriner Eccles,* then secretary of the treasury Henry Morgenthau's* special assistant on monetary and credit matters. When Eccles became head of the Federal Reserve Board in Washington in November 1934, he asked Currie to transfer to the board to work as assistant director of the Research and Statistics Division.

There Currie helped draft the Banking Act of 1935,* which centralized control of the reserve system in the new board of governors in Washington. It also gave the board greater control over reserve requirements and policymaking in the Open Market Committee. In late 1935, with the aid of reserve board economist Martin Krost, Currie developed the "Net Contribution of the Federal Government to National Buying Power" series of monthly calculations, a statistical tool that made possible policymaking advances in what later became known as Keynesian economics. Currie argued that citing figures of actual government expenditures told policymakers little about the impact of federal deficit spending on increasing purchasing power. Rather total government expenditures and receipts had to be compared to arrive at a net figure for the government's contribution to national purchasing power.

Currie's statistical work, building on the national income series developed by Dr. Simon Kuznets, helped in building an explanation for the recession of 1937.* Increased costs and prices alongside lagging private investment meant that federal expenditures should be increased. Loss of the net expenditures created by the bonus bill of 1936 and the deflationary impact of social security taxes had the effect of decreasing the net contribution of federal expenditures to purchasing power with government cutbacks in 1937. Currie's most important work took the form of unpublished memoranda which Eccles used to persuade Franklin D. Roosevelt* to resume federal spending to meet the crisis of the recession of 1937. Along with WPA* economist Leon Henderson* and Commissioner of Labor Statistics Isador Lubin, Currie wrote the memorandum which Roosevelt read on November 8, 1937. Eccles' knowledge of John M. Keynes'* *The General Theory of Employment, Interest, and Money* (1936) came from a ten-page analysis written by Currie for the reserve board.

Currie functioned as an economic expert advising Chairman Eccles of the board of governors of the Federal Reserve Board. Currie also took part in policy discussions in Washington, D.C., among the Eccles spending group. In the Temporary National Economic Committee* hearings in the spring of 1939, Currie and Alvin Hansen* presented the Keynesian case for compensatory government spending policy. Passage of the Reorganization Act of 1939* created six new administrative assistants and the Executive Office of the President. Roosevelt appointed Currie as one of the six with responsibility for economic affairs. As Currie later phrased it, he "became the first economist in the White House." Though Currie may have felt slighted when Roosevelt passed on his memoranda to Secretary of the Treasury Morgenthau and Budget Director Harold Smith,* his entry into the executive branch paved the way for the postwar Council of Economic Advisers.

Currie did not agree with all of Keynes' economic analysis, but he became known as one of the first Keynesian economists to work for the federal government in the late New Deal.* During World War II, Currie increasingly moved away from domestic economic policy advising and toward foreign affairs work. During the war, Currie was joined by a number of other Keynesian economists who worked in mobilization agencies. After the war, Currie headed the International Bank for Reconstruction and Development and served as economic and diplomatic consultant to the federal government and a number of major corporations. (Byrd L. Jones, "The Role of Keynesians in Wartime and Postwar Planning," *American Economic Review*, LXII:116-133, 1972; Dean May, *From New Deal to New Economics*, 1982; Herbert Stein, *The Fiscal Revolution in America*, 1969.)

PATRICK D. REAGAN

CUTTING, BRONSON MURRAY Born on June 23, 1888, in Oakdale, New York, to a wealthy family, Bronson Cutting went his own way to become a journalist and a United States senator. Cutting attended Groton and entered Harvard with the class of 1910, but because of ill-health he moved to the New Mexico Territory. Troubled by the social and economic problems of the region as well as by the political corruption of the territorial administration, Cutting adopted a progressive political philosophy. Mastering the Spanish language, he became a champion of the Spanish-speaking people of New Mexico. Cutting purchased a newspaper, the *Santa Fe New Mexican*, in 1912 and also published a Spanish edition, *El Nuevo Mexicano*. He used both as forums for his commitment to good government and democracy. Cutting supported Theodore Roosevelt's "Bull Moose" candidacy in 1912 and remained in the Progressive party until 1916, when he returned to the Republican fold. He served as assistant military attaché at the United States embassy in London during World War I and then returned to New Mexico in 1919. He served as regent of the New Mexico Military Institute in 1920 and chairman of the state penitentiary board in 1925, and Governor Richard C. Dillon appointed Cutting to fill the unexpired term of Senator Andrieus A. Jones. Cutting was elected in his own right in 1928 and again in 1934. He was an avid supporter of the New Deal,* breaking with Franklin D. Roosevelt* only on questions of veterans' benefits, which Cutting wholeheartedly supported. Bronson Cutting, a progressive Republican and a New Dealer, was killed in a plane crash on May 6, 1935. (*New York Times*, May 7, 1935.)

D

DARROW, CLARENCE Clarence Darrow was born in Kinsman, Ohio, on April 18, 1857. He attended Allegheny College and the University of Michigan Law School and was admitted to the Ohio bar in 1878. In 1887 Darrow moved to Chicago and joined the law firm of John Peter Altgeld. An opponent of capital punishment, Darrow earned a reputation as one of the country's most successful trial lawyers, especially in first-degree murder cases. Among his more prominent clients were Eugene V. Debs, "Big Bill" Haywood, Nathan Leopold, and Richard Loeb. Darrow became an expert in the use of psychiatric evidence. He also gained national attention in 1925 when he defended John Scopes in the famous "Monkey Trial" in Dayton, Tennessee. By 1933 Darrow was known throughout the country as a defender of the poor and oppressed. In 1934, when criticism of the National Recovery Administration* as a bastion of big business began to surface among liberal Democrats, labor leaders, and progressive Republicans, President Franklin D. Roosevelt* established the National Recovery Review Board to investigate. Senator Gerald P. Nye* of North Dakota, who was publicly expressing his suspicions about the NRA, was given the right to name several board members, and Donald Richberg* had the president appoint Darrow to head the board. The investigation went on for four months, involving sixty public hearings and thousands of complaints. Darrow concluded that the NRA was indeed dominated by monopolies and that only a planned economy with socialized ownership would ever resolve the problem. Hugh Johnson* and Donald Richberg were outraged with Darrow, and for several weeks in the early summer of 1934 public battle between NRA officials and the administration, on the one hand, and Darrow's National Recovery Review Board was bitter and intense and fueled labor's suspicions, as well as those of small businessmen. The dispute with the Roosevelt administration was the last major controversy of Darrow's career. He died on March 13, 1938. (Arthur Weinberg and Lola Weinberg, *Clarence Darrow. A Sentimental Rebel*, 1980.)

DAVEY, MARTIN LUTHER Martin L. Davey was born on July 25, 1884, near Kent, Ohio. He worked in his father's tree surgery business and later became general manager and national president of the Davey Tree Expert Company. In 1914 Davey ran successfully for mayor of Kent, Ohio, and in 1918 won a seat in Congress. He was defeated in his gubernatorial bid of 1928 in the Herbert Hoover* landslide but remained active in Democratic politics and won election as governor of Ohio in 1934 and 1936. He was widely known during his administration as an anti-Roosevelt, anti-labor, anti-New Deal Democrat. He feuded frequently with Harry Hopkins* over relief matters, used National Guard troops against workers in the ''Little Steel'' strike of 1937, and was a bitter critic of the National Labor Relations Board.* President Franklin D. Roosevelt* was so frustrated with Davey that he had Harry Hopkins bypass the Ohio state government in administration of all federal relief programs. In the election of 1938,* Roosevelt opposed Davey's renomination, and the governor lost the primary. Although he won the Democratic primary in 1940, he lost the general election and retired from politics. Martin L. Davey died on March 31, 1946. (*New York Times*, April 1, 1946.)

DAVIS, CHESTER CHARLES Chester Charles Davis was born near Linden, Iowa, on November 17, 1887. He attended Grinnell College and graduated in 1911, beginning a career in journalism, agricultural economics, and government service. Davis served as managing editor of *The Montana Farmer* from 1917 to 1921 and then went into the state civil service as commissioner of agriculture and labor. Davis specialized in grain production and marketing and in 1925 went to work as director of grain marketing for the Illinois Agricultural Association. Along with George Peek,* Davis became one of the leading advocates in the 1920s for the McNary-Haugen plan to dump farm surpluses abroad after they had been purchased from farmers at fair market value by the federal government. In 1928 Davis endorsed Al Smith* for president and played a critical role in getting the Democratic National Convention to support the McNary-Haugen plan. Soon after, Davis became enamored with the domestic allotment ideas of Professors John Black* and Milburn Wilson* to raise farm prices by restricting production. Between 1929 and 1933 Davis was vice-president of the Maizewood Products Corporation and stayed there until 1933 when George Peek, new head of the Agricultural Adjustment Administration,* named him director of the AAA Division of Production. Peek's tenure with the AAA was short-lived because he much preferred a marketing approach to farm prices rather than acreage reduction, and in December 1933 he resigned. Secretary of Agriculture Henry A. Wallace* then turned to Davis and selected him as the new administrator of the AAA.

A warm, affable, and fair man, Davis inspired trust and loyalty in his subordinates. His background was in family farm and commercial agriculture, and Davis was oriented to rural life. A major problem he faced inside the AAA was with urban liberals like Jerome Frank,* Gardner Jackson,* Alger Hiss,* and Frank Shea. They were especially concerned about the plight of tenant farmers thrown out of work and their homes by the AAA acreage reductions. Convinced that Davis was a pawn of large corporate farmers and the American Farm Bureau

Federation,* they tried in 1935, during a western trip Davis had taken, to write a new AAA policy forbidding tenant displacement in any new cotton reduction contracts. Davis was incensed when he found out about the policy and insisted, on threat of his own resignation, that the urban liberals be dismissed. Secretary of Agriculture Wallace agreed, and the "purge of 1935" in the USDA occurred. After that Davis' relationship with Wallace slowly deteriorated, and in 1936 he resigned to accept a position on the board of governors of the Federal Reserve Board.* Davis remained with the Federal Reserve Board until 1941 when he accepted the presidency of the Federal Reserve Bank of St. Louis. Except for a brief stint with the War Food Administration in 1943, Davis stayed with the Federal Reserve Bank of St. Louis until 1951, when he became an associate director of the Ford Foundation. Chester C. Davis died on September 25, 1975. (Dean Albertson, *Roosevelt's Farmer. Claude R. Wickard in the New Deal*, 1961; Edward L. Schapsmeier and Frederick H. Schapsmeier, *Henry A. Wallace of Iowa. The Agrarian Years, 1910-1940*, 1968.)

DAVIS, JAMES JOHN James J. Davis was born on October 27, 1873, in Tredegar, South Wales. He immigrated with his parents to the United States in 1881 and went to work in the steel mills of Pittsburgh and the surrounding area at the age of eleven. Davis moved to Elwood, Indiana, in 1893 and continued working in steel and tin plate mills. In 1898 he became city clerk for Elwood. In 1903 he became the recorder for Madison County, Indiana, and in 1906 director general of the Loyal Order of Moose. A Republican and a member of the Amalgamated Association of Iron, Steel and Tin Workers, Davis served as secretary of labor in the cabinets of Presidents Warren G. Harding, Calvin Coolidge, and Herbert Hoover* and in 1930 was elected to the United States Senate to fill an unexpired term. He was re-elected in 1932 and 1938, serving in the Senate from 1930 until 1945. During the New Deal,* Davis found himself in a difficult position. Because of the strength of labor unions in Pennsylvania and his own labor background, he was quite responsive to New Deal legislation supporting minimum wages, maximum hours, collective bargaining, and unemployment assistance. But New Dealers could not rely on his support elsewhere, and he openly opposed the "court-packing"* proposal and executive reorganization. He also criticized the size of the federal bureaucracy and the continuing budget deficits. James J. Davis left the Senate in 1945 and died on November 22, 1947. (*New York Times*, November 23, 1947; James T. Patterson, *Congressional Conservatism in the New Deal*, 1967.)

DAVIS, JOHN WILLIAM John W. Davis was born on April 13, 1873, in Clarksburg, West Virginia, and received undergraduate and law degrees from Washington and Lee in 1892 and 1895. After teaching law for two years at Washington and Lee, Davis went into private practice and became active in local Democratic politics. He served one term in the West Virginia House of Delegates in 1899 and a term as a U.S. congressman between 1911 and 1913. He left the

House when President Woodrow Wilson named him solicitor general in 1913. Because of his intense hatred of Germany and his personal friendship with Secretary of State Robert Lansing, Davis was named ambassador to Great Britain in 1918, a position he held until 1921. Although he secured the Democratic presidential nomination after the tumultuous convention in New York City in 1924, he lost the general election to Calvin Coolidge. Davis returned to private law practice after the election. During the 1930s, he became deeply alienated from Franklin D. Roosevelt* and the New Deal.* As a fiscal conservative, Davis could not tolerate the increasing power of the federal government or the deficit spending. His opposition to the New Deal was so bitter that he helped organize the American Liberty League* in 1934 and supported Wendell Willkie's* presidential campaign in 1940. John W. Davis died on March 24, 1955, in Charleston, South Carolina. (William Henry Harbaugh, *Lawyer's Lawyer. The Life of John W. Davis*, 1973.)

DELANO, FREDERIC ADRIAN Frederic A. Delano, the uncle and close political associate of President Franklin D. Roosevelt,* was born in Hong Kong, China, on September 10, 1863. He grew up in Newburgh, New York, and graduated from Harvard in 1885. He moved up the corporate ladder of the Chicago, Burlington, and Quincy Railroad between 1885 and 1905 and in the process became interested in urban and regional planning. In 1914 Delano secured an appointment to the Federal Reserve Board,* but he resigned that in 1918 to enter the army as an executive officer in the Engineering Corps. Before the war he had also served a stint as promoter of the Burnham City Plan of Chicago (1908). During the 1920s, Delano helped work with Franklin D. Roosevelt on his political career and recovery from polio, chaired the League of Nations' International Commission on the Production of Opium, and was director of the Regional Plan of New York and Its Environs (1923-1932). Delano was also founder and director of Washington, D.C.'s National Capital Park and Planning Commission (1924-1943). Roosevelt appointed him head of the National Planning Board* in 1933 and 1934, chairman of the National Resources Board* from 1935 through 1938, and chairman of the National Resources Planning Board* from 1939 to 1941. Frederic A. Delano died on March 28, 1953. (*New York Times*, March 29, 1953; Philip Warken, *A History of the National Resources Planning Board, 1933-1943*, 1979.)

DEMOCRATIC PARTY During the 1930s, because of major structural changes in American life and the effects of the Great Depression, the Democratic party entered a generation of political supremacy. Ever since the Civil War, the Democratic party had suffered a long period of minority status, isolated in the "Solid South" and the northern cities. The Republican party,* dominating small towns, the farmbelt, and city suburbs, controlled American politics because most Americans lived in the areas of their constituency. But the late nineteenth- and early twentieth-century rise of the big cities—fueled by mass immigration from Europe, the black South, and the rural farmbelt—joined hands with industrialization to bring a majority of Americans into the Democratic party. By the 1920s the Democratic party was becoming the home for immigrants, their ethnic descendants, and union members, as well as southerners. The mass unemployment of the Great Depression then destroyed Republican credibility and began bringing large numbers of northern blacks and middle-class whites into Democratic ranks. In the election of 1932,* Franklin D. Roosevelt* inherited all these gains and defeated Herbert Hoover* by 22,809,638 votes to 15,758,901. Democrats also took over Congress with 310 House seats and 60 Senate seats.

During the next four years, the party only magnified its control of American politics. The dynamic personality of Franklin D. Roosevelt, the unprecedented programs of the New Deal,* and the enormous funds dispensed by the relief agencies gave the Democratic party tremendous momentum. Millions of workers owed their jobs to agencies like the Civilian Conservation Corps,* Civil Works Administration,* Federal Emergency Relief Administration,* Public Works Administration,* and Works Progress Administration*; and they came to view the Democratic party as their savior. The famous "New Deal coalition"—the political combination of left-wing socialists, urban liberals, southerners, immigrants and ethnic groups, Roman Catholics, intellectuals, and union members—had taken over American politics. "Old Guard" Republicans and some disgruntled Democrats in groups like the American Liberty League* complained about the changes occurring in public policy, but the public was not listening. In the congressional elections of 1934* the Democrats defied history by increasing their House contingent to 319 and their Senate numbers to 69. Not since the Civil War had American politics been so completely controlled by one party. During 1935 and 1936, the New Deal's shift leftward—symbolized by such measures as the National Labor Relations Act of 1935,* the Public Utility Holding Company Act of 1935,* the Social Security Act of 1935,* the Wealth Tax Act of 1935,* and creation of the Works Progress Administration—only consolidated their political power. In the election of 1936,* Roosevelt secured the support of many socialists as well as progressive Republicans and defeated Alf Landon* of Kansas by 27,752,869 to 16,674,665 votes, the largest presidential plurality in American history. Landon and the Republicans, sensing the New Deal's popularity, had been reduced to endorsing most of the relief programs while condemning deficit spending and federal bureaucracy.

Not until 1937 and 1938 did the New Deal coalition experience its first major defections. Franklin D. Roosevelt's "court-packing"* proposal of 1937 stirred up a hornet's nest of opposition, leading to a break in the support of progressive Republicans and southern Democrats. Many Americans began to worry about Roosevelt's intentions, whether he was grasping for too much power. They viewed the Reorganization Act* proposals in the same light. The serious recession of 1937 and 1938,* which destroyed much of the public credibility of New Deal recovery efforts, further undermined support for the Democratic party. Finally, the president's ill-advised "purge of 1938"*—the unsuccessful attempt to defeat conservatives like Senators Guy Gillette,* Ellison "Cotton Ed" Smith,* Walter George,* and Millard Tydings*—in the Democratic primaries of 1938 triggered even more public opposition. In the congressional elections of 1938,* the Democrats suffered a major defeat, losing 70 seats in the House and 7 in the Senate.

Throughout 1938, 1939, and 1940, the coalition of southern Democrats and rejuvenated northern Republicans became a roadblock for the New Deal, limiting its effectiveness, cutting relief appropriations, and preventing the president from reorganizing the executive branch of the government as completely as he hoped. Republicans, sensing victory in the presidential election of 1940,* increased the level of their criticisms of the president and his domestic record. Democratic conservatives like John Nance Garner,* Cordell Hull,* and James Farley* began to lust after the presidential nomination; but other New Dealers like Harold Ickes,* Thomas Corcoran,* and Harry Hopkins,* along with a number of city bosses, urged the president to seek a third term. Although Roosevelt hoped to be drafted by acclamation at the 1940 convention, conservatives like Farley denied him the pleasure. Still, he won the nomination easily and then dumped Vice-President John Nance Garner from the ticket, replacing him with a committed New Dealer, Secretary of Agriculture Henry A. Wallace,* Republicans nominated utilities executive Wendell Willkie* for president. Willkie tried to make political profit over the size of the federal bureaucracy, the waste of so many programs, and the weakened state of national defense, but in the end, the war crisis in Europe underwrote the Roosevelt campaign. The president defeated his Republican challenger by a vote of 27,307,819 to 22,321,018 and 449 electoral votes to 82. The New Deal coalition had held together. (David Burner, *The Politics of Provincialism. The Democratic Party in Transition, 1918-1932*, 1967; Ralph M. Goldman, *Search for Consensus. The Story of the Democratic Party*, 1979.)

DENNIS, LAWRENCE Lawrence Dennis, prominent fascist writer during the 1930s, was born in Atlanta, Georgia, on December 25, 1893. Although he worked as a boy evangelist for several years, he changed directions and entered Exeter Academy in 1913 and Harvard University in 1916. After graduating from Harvard in 1920, Dennis served as a foreign service officer in Romania, Nicaragua, Haiti, and Paris, where he became increasingly critical of how American diplomacy was used to underwrite corporate expansion. Strangely enough, he resigned from the foreign service in 1927 to go into the very business he despised—investment banking—with J & W Seligman & Company. He resigned in 1930, served as a witness against Wall Street for the Pecora investigations, and continued a writing career which had begun with the publication of *Is Capitalism Doomed* in 1932. Dennis argued that capitalism was in serious trouble because of the power of investment bankers to control the flow of money and assets in the United States. In 1936 he wrote *The Coming American Fascism*, a book which argued that capitalism was indeed doomed and that when given a choice between communism and fascism, Americans should definitely choose the latter. Big business had prepared America for fascism, so he called for a dictatorship which would nationalize banks and fundamental monopolies, guarantee employment through massive spending, eliminate women from the work force, abolish states' rights, and outlaw all but one political party. Hopelessly romantic and unrealistic about the nature of American institutions, Dennis nevertheless enjoyed some vogue in intellectual circles in the mid-1930s. He rejoined the brokerage business in 1936 with E. A. Pierce & Company, and resigned in 1939 to edit and publish *The Weekly Foreign Letter*. He also tried to search for potential leaders to promote American fascism, but his dreams were destroyed by American entry into World War II. Dennis wrote *The Dynamics of War and Revolution* in 1940 and *A Trial on Trial* in 1946. He died on August 20, 1977. (Arthur M. Schlesinger, Jr., *The Age of Roosevelt. Vol. III. The Politics of Upheaval, 1935-1936*, 1960; *Who Was Who In America*, V:150, 1978.)

DERN, GEORGE HENRY George H. Dern was born in Dodge County, Nebraska, on September 8, 1872. He graduated from Fremont Normal College in 1888 and then attended the University of Nebraska for two years in 1893 and 1894. Dern left the university to take a job with the Mercur Gold Mining & Milling Company in Utah, and he stayed there until 1900 when he became general manager of Consolidated Mercur Gold Mines Company. He held that post until 1913 when he became vice-president of Holt Christensen Process Company. Between 1915 and 1923 Dern served as a Democrat in the Utah state legislature and was elected governor of Utah in 1924. Dern remained governor of Utah until 1933. After the election of 1932,* President-elect Franklin D. Roosevelt* selected Dern to join his cabinet as the new secretary of war. Dern accepted and remained in that position until his death on August 27, 1936. (*New York Times*, August 28, 1936.)

DEWSON, MARY WILLIAMS Mary W. Dewson was born February 18, 1874, in Quincy, Massachussets. She graduated from Wellesley College in 1897 and then worked as an economic researcher for the Women's Educational and Industrial Union in Boston until 1900. Between 1900 and 1912 Dewson served as superintendent of the Massachusetts Girls' Parole Department. From 1912 to 1917 she operated an experimental, scientific dairy in Massachusetts. Dewson left the dairy when World War I broke out and became a zone chief in charge of immigrant refugees for the American Red Cross in Europe. Upon her return, she joined the National Consumers' League as a research secretary and became president of the Consumers' League of New York in 1925. Dewson stayed in that position until 1931. An intimate friend of the Roosevelt family, Dewson worked closely with Eleanor Roosevelt,* organizing women's groups in the Democratic party* in the 1920s. In 1933 James Farley* named her head of the Women's Division of the Democratic National Committee. She was an active political campaigner for Franklin D. Roosevelt,* and in 1934 the president appointed her to the Committee on Economic Security,* which drafted the Social

Security Act of 1935.* Dewson was appointed to the Social Security Board in 1937 and served there until 1938, when ill health forced her to resign. She retired from public life in 1940 and died on October 24, 1962. (*New York Times*, October 25, 1962; Susan Ware, *Beyond Suffrage: Women in the New Deal*, 1981.)

DICKINSON, JOHN John Dickinson was born in Greensboro, Maryland, on February 24, 1894. He graduated from Johns Hopkins in 1913, took a master's degree at Princeton in 1915, and a Ph.D. there in 1919. Dickinson then entered the Harvard Law School, where he became a student of Felix Frankfurter.* After graduating from Harvard in 1921, Dickinson went into private practice in California with the law firm of William Gibbs McAdoo,* specializing in the defense of corporations facing anti-trust suits. He returned to academic life as a lecturer on government at Harvard in 1924, assistant professor of politics at Princeton in 1927, and professor of law at the University of Pennsylvania, a position he held until 1948. With his corn-cob pipes, tweedy suits, and bald head, Dickinson had a professorial manner which seemed to fit his moderate political views. During the early New Deal,* Dickinson served as a liaison between the government and the business community through his 1933 appointment as assistant secretary of commerce. President Franklin D. Roosevelt* asked Dickinson to head an interdepartmental committee to propose new exchange legislation. Completed in January 1934, the report advocated licensing only of the exchanges instead of a regulatory commission. James Landis,* Benjamin Cohen,* and Felix Frankfurter found the approach too moderate and went well beyond it when they drafted the Securities Exchange Act of 1934.* In 1934 Roosevelt named Dickinson head of the Central Statistical Board* and in 1935 appointed him assistant attorney general. Dickinson left government service in 1937 to become general solicitor and then general counsel for the Pennsylvania Railroad. John Dickinson died on April 9, 1952. (Peter H. Irons, *The New Deal Lawyers*, 1982; *Who Was Who In America*, III:227, 1960.)

DICKSTEIN, SAMUEL Samuel Dickstein was born near Vilna, Russia, on February 5, 1885, and immigrated to the United States in 1887. His family settled in New York City. Dickstein attended the College of the City of New York and graduated from the New York City Law School in 1906. After practicing privately for several years, Dickstein became special deputy attorney general of the state of New York in 1911. He stayed there until 1914. Dickstein was a city alderman in 1917 and a member of the state legislature in 1919. Dickstein won a congressional seat as a Democrat in 1922 and stayed in the House of Representatives until 1945. During the New Deal* years, Dickstein was a consistent supporter of Franklin D. Roosevelt's* administration, particularly in social and labor legislation, and chaired the House committee on immigration. Along with John McCormack* of Massachusetts, Dickstein headed the special investigation of "un-American" activities in 1934, but his own highly developed sense of civil liberties prevented the committee from becoming a "witch-hunting" agency as it did in later years. Dickstein left the House in 1945 to become a justice of the New York State Supreme Court, and he worked there until his death on April 22, 1954. (*New York Times*, April 23, 1954.)

DIES COMMITTEE (See DIES, MARTIN, JR.)

DIES, MARTIN, JR. Martin Dies, Jr., was born in Colorado, Texas, on November 5, 1900. He studied at Wesley College in Greenville and later at the University of Texas and received a law degree from the National University in Washington, D.C. Dies practiced law during the early 1920s, first in Marshall, Texas, and later in Orange, Texas. However, he soon moved into politics, winning a seat in the House of Representatives and serving there from 1931 to 1945 and then again from 1953 to 1959. During the late 1930s and early 1940s, he came to the national forefront as chairman of the special House Committee on Un-American Activities. Before 1937 Dies was generally a supporter of the New Deal,* but after the election of 1936* he came to be more and more critical, particularly of President Franklin D. Roosevelt's* friendship with CIO* leaders. Intensely anti-union and anti-immigrant, Dies' notoriety resulted from his attitude toward civil liberties and the threat of subversive activities. He did not believe that anyone who belonged to subversive groups should be allowed to work for the government or in defense industries. Rather than risk potential sabotage, it was better to bar potential subversives from government-related positions. Specifically, he believed Congress should outlaw the Communist party,* eliminate Communists from government jobs, demand that all government employees sign a loyalty pledge, and refuse to sanction government negotiations with labor unions which were "Communist-controlled."

Roosevelt's attitude toward civil liberties was less direct and more complex than Dies'. Although conceding that an individual's associates could disqualify him for appointment to a sensitive position, Roosevelt believed that loyalty should be measured by performance rather than belief. The distinction between sensitive and non-sensitive government positions is a nicety that Dies did not recognize. He withdrew support from the later New Deal because of what he perceived to be a liberal change of direction. He could barely stand the presence of such New Deal leaders as Frances Perkins,* Harry Hopkins,* and Harold Ickes;* hated labor standards legislation; opposed the Works Progress Administration;* and fought against the monetary tinkering of the New Deal. Still, Roosevelt never broke completely with Dies, primarily because the House Committee on Un-American Activities had too much support. By 1939 the committee's attacks on the Nazis in the United States pleased the president. In his book, *The Trojan Horse in America* (1940), Dies devoted 303 pages to the menace of communism but only forty-one to the threat of fascism. His committee listed 640 organizations, 438 newspapers, and 280 labor groups as possible Communist fronts, and the list of targets ranged from the American Civil Liberties Union and the

American League for Peace and Democracy to the Boy Scouts, Girl Scouts, and Shirley Temple. Martin Dies died on November 14, 1972. (*New York Times*, November 15, 1972; Richard Polenberg, "Franklin Roosevelt and Civil Liberties: The Case of the Dies Committee," *Historian*, XXX:165-178, 1968.)

RANDY ROBERTS

DOMESTIC ALLOTMENT PLAN (See AGRICULTURAL ADJUSTMENT ACT OF 1933.)

DOUGHTON, ROBERT LEE Robert L. Doughton was born on November 7, 1863, in Laurel Springs, North Carolina. He attended local public schools and took a J.D. degree at Catawba College. A farmer and livestock rancher, Doughton served on the North Carolina State Board of Agriculture between 1903 and 1909 and then in the state senate during 1908 and 1909. He received the appointment as director of the state prison system in 1909, and he served there until his election to Congress in 1911. Doughton was a member of the House of Representatives until 1953, enjoying one of the longest congressional careers in American history and exerting great power through his chairmanship of the House Ways and Means Committee. During the New Deal,* Doughton was a conservative Democrat like so many of his southern colleagues, but he was generally considered a Franklin D. Roosevelt* loyalist. Frequently during the 1930s, Doughton played a central role in compromising the interests of southern and northern Democrats. In 1935, for example, he held long hearings on Roosevelt's controversial tax proposal, and in order to get it through Congress, Doughton eliminated its intercorporate dividend tax and reduced the progressive corporate tax rates. A reasonable and reliable man, Doughton served in the House of Representatives until 1953, finally deciding before his ninetieth birthday not to run for re-election. He died on October 1, 1954. (*New York Times*, October 2, 1954.)

DOUGLAS, LEWIS WILLIAM Lewis William Douglas was born July 2, 1894, in Bisbee, Arizona. He graduated from Amherst College in 1916 and then did some graduate work at MIT in 1916 and 1917. Douglas served in the Arizona state legislature between 1923 and 1925 and in 1927 began a career as a Democrat in the House of Representatives. A well-known fiscal conservative, Douglas was by 1933 convinced that only drastic cuts in government expenditures could restore confidence to the business community, stimulate increases in investment, and lift the country out of the depression. In that sense, Douglas was a traditional Cleveland Democrat: committed to free trade, sound money, and a balanced federal budget. In February 1933, at the suggestion of Senator James F. Byrnes* of South Carolina, President Franklin D. Roosevelt* named Douglas his new director of the budget. Although reluctant to end his congressional career, Douglas accepted the appointment because he felt the president was sincerely interested in cutting federal spending and preserving sound money principles. When Roosevelt decided during the special congressional session of the "hundred days''* to promote the Economy Act* by cutting government spending, Douglas was encouraged that he had made the right decision. An ''insider'' in New Deal policymaking circles, Douglas played a critical role in the formulation of public policy, always advocating efficiency in government and always warning about new spending programs.

But after passage of the Economy Act of 1933, Douglas and the president began to drift apart. Four days after signing the Economy Act, Roosevelt dumbfounded Douglas by calling for creation of the Agricultural Adjustment Administration,* Federal Emergency Relief Administration,* and Civilian Conservation Corps.* Douglas objected on the grounds that further deficits would only worsen the climate for business investment, but Roosevelt would have none of it. In fact, as 1933 progressed, the president found Douglas increasingly doctrinaire. When Roosevelt took the country off the gold standard in the fall of 1933, Douglas termed the step ''the end of western civilization.'' He hated the economic theories of George Warren,* resisted the silver purchase policy, and opposed anything less than sound money. By the end of 1933 Douglas, within administration circles, was continuing his call for an end to relief spending, reduction in the RFC's* programs, and a return to the gold standard. In June 1934, when President Roosevelt called for a new $525 million appropriation for drought relief, Douglas registered a vigorous protest. By then Roosevelt had tired of him, excluded him from important policymaking meetings, and essentially forced his resignation on August 30, 1934, even though always protesting he wanted Douglas to stay on.

After resigning, Douglas became vice-president of the American Cyanamid Corporation (1934-1937), vice-chancellor of McGill University (1937-1940), and president of Mutual Life Insurance Company of New York (1940-1947). He served as ambassador to Great Britain between 1947 and 1950. He was on the board of directors of a number of prominent banks until his death on March 7, 1974. (James E. Sargent, ''FDR and Lewis Douglas: Budget Balancing and the Early New Deal,'' *Prologue* VI:33-44, 1974.)

DOUGLAS, WILLIAM ORVILLE William O. Douglas, one of the most liberal Supreme Court* justices in American history, was born on October 16, 1898, in Maine, Minnesota. Raised in a desperately poor farm family, Douglas retained for his entire life a sensitivity to the plight of low-income people and a suspicion of corporate power. A polio attack in his childhood only intensified his compassion for the weak and suffering. He grew up in Yakima, Washington, and graduated from Whitman College in 1920 and then at the top of his class at the Columbia University Law School. He tried for two years to work at a Wall-Street law firm, but his own suspicions of his corporate clientele left him frustrated and unhappy. Douglas returned for a year to Yakima, then joined the law faculty at Columbia, and in 1929 moved to New Haven to teach at Yale. He soon earned a national reputation as an expert in finance law. In 1936 President Franklin D. Roosevelt* brought Douglas to Washington as a member of the

Securities and Exchange Commission,* and in 1937 Douglas became chairman of the SEC. Douglas was a clear symbol of the "Second New Deal's"* emphasis on corporate regulation, anti-trust action, and progressive taxation. In 1939 Roosevelt named Douglas an associate justice of the Supreme Court to replace the retiring Louis Brandeis.*

On the Roosevelt court, Douglas maintained his reputation as an unabashed liberal. Throughout the 1930s and 1940s, Douglas was a strong advocate of state taxation and regulation laws, clearly recognizing the principle of legislative supremacy and the "right to govern." He also was a general supporter of civil liberties and an opponent of government interference in them, except for wartime freedoms, where he believed that national emergencies sometimes justified extraordinary exercises of national power. Douglas was also a long-time protector of the rights of accused criminals to legal counsel and jury trials. Finally, Douglas was a vigorous supporter of federal anti-trust legislation and pro-labor legislation.

During the 1940s and 1950s, Douglas's lifestyle and liberal views caused him severe political problems. Divorced three times between 1954 and 1966, he remarried quickly after each divorce and raised eyebrows in conservative Washington. Also, his outspoken support of civil and criminal rights on the Warren court raised the ire of conservatives, and in 1953 and 1970 Douglas faced impeachment charges. Special House judiciary subcommittees investigated him each time but found no grounds for impeachment. In January 1975 Douglas suffered a severe stroke. He tried to continue working but his physical ailments weakened him, and he resigned in November 1975 after serving nearly thirty-seven years, longer than any other justice. William O. Douglas died on January 19, 1980. (James C. Duram, *Justice William O. Douglas*, 1981; *New York Times*, January 20, 1980.)

DUBINSKY, DAVID David Dubinsky was born David Dobnievski in Brest Litovsk, Russian Poland, on February 22, 1892. At age eleven he was apprenticed as a baker to his father, who opened a bakery at Lodz. By age fifteen he had achieved the status of master baker. He joined the local bakers' union and led a strike against his own father's bakery, and his activities attracted the attention of the Czarist police. Dubinsky was arrested as a labor agitator and exiled to Siberia. He escaped and evaded capture until 1910, when he received amnesty. In 1911 he immigrated to the United States. After working at menial jobs for a few months, Dubinsky abandoned baking for garment making. He joined Local 10 of the International Ladies Garment Workers Union. Although the industry was still in the sweatshop era, Dubinsky did not involve himself in union organizational work until 1916 during an ILGWU strike. He was elected vice-chairman (1919) and then chairman (1920) of the Local 10. In 1922 he was named vice-president and a member of the ILGWU executive board.

At a time when Communist influence was expanding in other New York locals of the ILGWU, Dubinsky had thwarted such penetration into Local 10. In 1916 the Communists carried the ILGWU into a disastrous strike which lasted twenty-eight weeks and plunged the union $2 million into debt, but Dubinsky's Local 10 emerged from the strike both solvent and strong. In 1929 he was elected secretary-treasurer of the ILGWU and assumed the post of acting president during the illness of President Benjamin Schlesinger. Dubinsky was elected president of the ILGWU in 1932. Section 7(a) of the National Industrial Recovery Act* proved to be a godsend. Within six months, ILGWU membership expanded by about 160,000 and stood at 200,000 in 1935. In 1935 Dubinsky threw in his lot with John L. Lewis* and others to form the Committee for Industrial Organization (it became the Congress of Industrial Organizations* in 1938). But in 1937 he opposed the establishment of the CIO as a permanent and independent organization. After two years without affiliation, the ILGWU rejoined the AFL* in 1940. In 1945 Dubinsky regained his post as AFL vice-president and member of the executive council. During these years, Dubinsky had been active in other affairs as well. He left the Socialist party in 1928, and with Sidney Hillman* and others formed the American Labor party* in 1936. He strongly supported New Deal* policies. In 1935 while vice-president of the AFL executive council, he served with the International Labor office in Geneva. In 1943 Dubinsky quit the labor party because it had fallen under Communist influence. With Adolph A. Berle, Jr.,* and others, he formed the Liberal Party of New York. In 1947 he helped to organize Americans for Democratic Action. Although admitting the problem of abuses in the labor movement, Dubinsky vigorously opposed passage of the Taft-Hartley Act. During the late 1940s and 1950s, he actively fought against Communist influence in unions. He also worked extensively through the ILGWU to help revitalize the labor movement in Western Europe and Israel. He served as president of the ILGWU until his death on September 17, 1982. (Max D. Danish, *The World of David Dubinsky*, 1957.)

JOSEPH M. ROWE, JR.

"DUST BOWL" "Dust bowl" was the term applied to an area of the southern Great Plains comprising western Kansas, eastern Colorado, northeastern New Mexico, and the Texas and Oklahoma panhandles afflicted during the 1930s by a series of calamitous dust storms. Although dust storms also struck the northern plains, the dust bowl suffered the worst effects.

The dust bowl resulted from a combination of causes. The soils of the high plains are historically volatile and liable to blow during periods of drought. During the years 1932-1939 drought was severe throughout the plains, often preventing winter wheat crops from achieving sufficient fall growth to protect the soil. The drought followed a period of agricultural expansion on the plains which lasted from World War I through the 1920s and which converted millions of acres of grassland used for grazing into cropland devoted to wheat. This expansion was characterized by rapid mechanization, by emphasis on wheat as a cash crop, and by techniques of dry farming that preserved little crop residue. Still another contributing factor was the prevalance of absentee ownership and suitcase farming.

The dust storms of the "dirty thirties," as residents referred to the decade, commenced in 1932 and became more serious until 1935, the worst year, when the famous black blizzard of April 14 scarred the recollections of a generation of plains-dwellers. The storms continued to be severe through 1936-1937 but moderated in 1938-1939.

Southwesterly storms marked the summer months, but the northerly black blizzards of winter were considered more destructive. These often brought brief periods of total darkness and extended hours of half-light during which the blowing dirt compelled residents to seek shelter, closing businesses and schools. The wind-borne dirt not only scoured the surface of the ground but also boiled up thousands of feet into the air in menacing clouds. Like snow, the dust piled in drifts around buildings and fences.

The social and economic effects of this environmental disaster were profound. Only a few deaths were directly and immediately attributable to the storms, but the population suffered long-term ill effects from dust pneumonia. Crop failure resulted in commercial stagnation of towns, widespread abandonment of farms, and heavy dependence on federal relief programs. Of chief importance to farmers in the dust bowl were the wheat program and the Emergency Cattle Purchase Program of the Agricultural Adjustment Administration.*

Misfortune inspired some accomplishments, however, including *The Plow That Broke the Plains*, Pare Lorentz's* landmark documentary film, and such songs as "The Great Dust Storm," by Woodrow Wilson "Woody" Guthrie. Agriculturally, the dusters provoked new emphasis on soil conservation on the plains.

Some of the initiative in soil conservation was local—the invention of the chisel plow by Fred Hoeme of Hooker, Oklahoma, for instance, or the requirement by county commissioners of emergency tillage on blowing ground. Federal efforts were more notable. Some of these attempted to alter the basic pattern of land use on the plains. Numerous projects of the Resettlement Administration* aimed to remove dust bowl farmers from erosion-prone acreage and relocate them on model farms. Lands acquired from displaced farmers were reseeded to grass; national grasslands resulted from this process.

Of greater general effect were the development and dissemination of practical techniques of soil conservation on cropland. H. H. Finnell was a key figure in this process from 1934 when he assumed direction of the Soil Erosion Service's wind erosion station at Dalhart, Texas. Early efforts were hampered by a dearth of scientific knowledge about wind erosion or its control. Contouring, stripping, and terracing, effective against water erosion, did little to stop wind erosion. The key to better management, Finnell and others discovered, was to cease such destructive practices as burning stubble and to substitute methods of tillage that retained enough crop residue on the surface to assist in holding the soil. The main reason for the cessation of the dust storms in the 1940s, however, was the opportune return of adequate rainfall.

Although dust storms were to recur on the plains, especially in the 1950s and

1970s, no later series of dust storms was to match those of the 1930s in scope or severity. (Paul Bonnifield, *The Dust Bowl: Men, Dirt, and Depression*, 1979; R. Douglas Hurt, *The Dust Bowl: An Agricultural and Social History*, 1981; Donald Worster, *Dust Bowl. The Southern Plains in the 1930s*, 1979.)

THOMAS D. ISERN

E

EARLE, GEORGE HOWARD George H. Earle was born in Devon, Pennsylvania, on December 5, 1890, to a well-to-do family whose wealth rested in the railroad, sugar, public utility, and banking industries. Earle attended the exclusive DeLancey School in Philadelphia and entered Harvard in 1909. He dropped out of school in 1911, travelled in Europe for two years, returned to work in the family business for a year, and then moved out to Chicago. He joined the army in 1916, completed a tour of duty on the Mexican Border, and gained the rank of second lieutenant. When the United States entered World War I in 1917, Earle joined the navy and used his own yacht as a submarine-chaser. Eventually, President Woodrow Wilson awarded him the Navy Cross for valor.

After World War I, Earle established the Flamingo Sugar Mills in Philadelphia and became active in politics. Although his family had been Republican for generations, he switched to the Democratic party* in 1932 and endorsed Franklin D. Roosevelt's* campaign. He made large contributions to the campaign and in return the new president named him minister to Vienna in 1933. At the urging of Senator Joseph Guffey,* Earle resigned his diplomatic post in 1934 to run for governor of Pennsylvania. Earle enthusiastically endorsed the New Deal* and became only the second Democratic governor in Pennsylvania's post-Civil War history. He modeled his administration after Roosevelt's New Deal, and his programs became known as the "Little New Deal"* after an unfriendly newspaperman used the term as an epithet. He worked hard in his first term to establish that "Little New Deal," but encountered extreme opposition from the Republican-dominated state senate. When the Democratic landslide of 1936 gave his party control of the state senate, Earle then implemented his "Little New Deal." That program included higher utility and corporate taxes, stricter child labor laws, curbs on company police, an anti-injunction law, an occupational disease act, improved workmen's compensation, the "Little Wagner Act," a minimum wage and maximum hours law for women, a teacher tenure law, a "Little AAA" for farmers, and establishment of the Bureau of Civil Liberties. Earle began to be hailed as the "Crown Prince of the New Deal" and the "Heir

Apparent of the Roosevelt Administration.'' Earle had hopes of winning the Democratic presidential nomination in 1940; but in his bid for a U.S. Senate seat in 1938, he lost the election because of serious power struggles inside the Democratic party in Pennsylvania and disillusionment with the New Deal nationwide.

In 1940 President Roosevelt returned Earle to the diplomatic corps, making him ambassador to Bulgaria and then naval attaché to Turkey in 1943. Earle was openly anti-Soviet and became a liability to Roosevelt in the Balkans, so he was transferred to Samoa where he stayed until the end of the war. Eventually, Earle became an intense anti-Communist and returned to the Republican party* in 1952, endorsing Dwight Eisenhower for president and helping to raise funds for the campaign. George Earle died on December 30, 1974. (Richard C. Keller, ''Pennsylvania's Little New Deal,'' in John Braeman, et al., *The New Deal: State and Local Levels*, 1975.)

LENNA HODNETT ALLRED

EARLY, STEPHEN TYREE Stephen T. Early, born August 27, 1889, in Crozet, Virginia, became one of the most well-known and respected public relations specialists of his time. He attended public and private schools in Washington, D.C., and at the age of nineteen joined the Washington staff of United Press International. In 1913 he moved to the Associated Press. During World War I he helped edit the army's *Stars and Stripes*. After the war Early served as press relations officer for the U.S. Chamber of Commerce,* resigning in 1920 to serve as an advance man in Franklin D. Roosevelt's* vice-presidential campaign. After the election he returned to the Associated Press, and in 1927 Early became the Washington representative for the Paramount News and Paramount Public Corporation.

President Franklin D. Roosevelt appointed Early as his assistant press secretary in 1933 and moved him to the position of press secretary four years later. In 1945, at President Harry S Truman's* request, Early agreed to remain in the White House for a few months to assist in the administrative transition. Early retired from public service later in 1945 and became vice-president of Pullman-Standard Car Manufacturing of Chicago with an office in Washington, D. C. The company allowed Early a leave of absence in 1948 to become under secretary of defense and again in 1949 when he served as first deputy secretary of defense. Stephen Early died of a heart attack on August 11, 1951, in Washington, D. C. (*New York Times*, August 12, 1951.)

EASTMAN, JOSEPH BARTLETT Born in Katonah, New York, on June 26, 1882, Joseph Eastman graduated from Amherst College in 1904 and studied law for a year at Boston University. He took the position of secretary to the Public Franchise League in Boston in 1905 and remained there until 1913, when he began assisting Louis Brandeis* in investigations of the Boston Elevated Railway Company and the New York, New Haven & Hartford Railroad. Between 1913 and 1915 he served as adviser to the Electric Street Railway Employees' Union as a wage arbitrator and in 1915 accepted appointment to the Massachusetts Public Service Commission. There he earned a reputation as an independent progressive willing to judge rate cases on their merits and always considering the public welfare. In 1919 President Woodrow Wilson appointed Eastman to the Interstate Commerce Commission,* a position he held for the rest of his life.

By the 1930s Joseph Eastman was known as the most liberal mind in the public utility field as well as a legal expert in transportation. He helped draft the Emergency Railroad Transportation Act of 1933* and accepted appointment under it as the federal coordinator of transportation. Although Eastman believed the only answer to railroad troubles was massive reorganization and consolidation, as well as possible nationalization, he was unable as federal coordinator or later as chairman of the ICC (1939–1942) to bring about these goals. Opposition from railroads, labor unions, and shippers blocked serious attempts to reorganize the ailing industry. When World War II broke out, President Franklin D. Roosevelt* appointed Eastman director of the Office of Defense Transportation to supervise the movement of war materials through the various carrier systems. Joseph Eastman died in Washington, D. C., on March 15, 1944. (Ari Hoogenboom and Olive Hoogenboom, *A History of the ICC. From Panacea to Palliative*, 1976; *New York Times*, March 16, 1944.)

ECCLES, MARRINER STODDARD Born on September 9, 1890, in Logan, Utah, Marriner Stoddard Eccles was raised in a wealthy Utah family whose interests included lumber, sugar, food processing, railroad construction, mining, and cattle. Eccles graduated from the high school section of Brigham Young College in 1909, and after returning from three years service as a Mormon missionary in Scotland in 1912, he began to manage the family's assets through the Eccles Investment Company. From that time through the 1920s, Eccles built the family enterprises into a multimillion-dollar empire, founding the First Security Corporation in 1929. By then the family had controlling interest in thirteen corporations. A respected Utah banker, Marriner followed in the footsteps of his father, maintaining a loyalty to a late nineteenth-century version of McKinley Republicanism. The onset of the Great Depression changed that.

From 1929 through 1933, Eccles re-examined his father's faith in the value of thrifty saving, lean governments, and public leadership by private businessmen. His Mormon and western background meant that Eccles did not have fixed ideas about economics; in that sense his lack of formal education proved an asset. He had no real ideological commitment to balanced budgets or expectations that the business cycle would always fluctuate. Eccles' success in leading the family banks through the banking crisis of 1932–1933 without one bank failure led to an invitation to testify before the Senate Finance Committee in February 1933. Eccles argued that the depression stemmed from underconsumption and lagging private investment. He strongly advocated an increase in consumer purchasing power led by federal government spending as a way to stimulate more private investment. He testified in favor of federal monies for relief, federal loans for self-liquidating public works, the domestic allotment plan,* refinancing of farm mortgages at lower interest rates, and cancellation of World War I debts. In October 1933 Rexford Tugwell* called Eccles back to Washington to meet with Mordecai Ezekiel,* Henry A. Wallace,* Jerome Frank,* and Harry Hopkins.* These people became the core of the spending group.

After Henry Morgenthau, Jr.,* became acting secretary of the treasury, he persuaded Eccles to come to Washington as his special assistant in monetary and credit matters. Eccles helped draft the Federal Housing Act. Though planning to remain in Washington only until June 1934, Eccles stayed on when Morgenthau recommended to Franklin D. Roosevelt* that Eccles be appointed head of the Federal Reserve Board.* Eccles accepted the position on the condition that the board be reorganized to move control away from the New York Reserve Bank toward more centralized control in the Washington Federal Reserve Board. He helped draft the Banking Act of 1935* that led to the reorganization.

From his position as chairman of the new board of governors of the reserve board, Eccles argued the need to increase purchasing power to overcome lagging private investment and consumer spending. Though usually described only as an advocate of increased federal deficit spending, Eccles also advocated use of monetary policy and tax reform as complementary economic policies. He always emphasized that government spending was a compensatory policy aimed at preserving the American economic system based in profit-motivated private enterprise. Once purchasing power had been stimulated through government expenditures, private investment would take over and the federal budget should be balanced.

With the economic downturn in the fall of 1937, Eccles joined in the recovery debate over the need to resume spending which had been cut back in 1937. He advocated a resumption of spending, while his old superior Morgenthau advocated balancing of the federal budget. As a longtime Hyde Park neighbor and old friend to Roosevelt, Morgenthau had the inside track to Roosevelt. Eccles had to work indirectly through the spending group.

In October and November of 1937, Eccles continued discussions with the spenders and sent several memoranda to Roosevelt. He also talked with members of the National Resources Committee* who were developing a moderate spending policy position. By late March 1938 Eccles' ideas had percolated throughout Washington policymaking circles. Harry Hopkins, Beardsley Ruml,* Aubrey Williams,* and Leon Henderson* convinced Roosevelt to resume spending. On April 14, 1938, Roosevelt asked Congress for over 3 billion dollars for the WPA,* the PWA,* the FSA,* and the U.S. Housing Authority.* The policy debate continued throughout 1938 and 1939 in the Fiscal and Monetary Advisory Board in which Eccles, Morgenthau, Budget Director Daniel Bell,* and a representative of the National Resources Committee took part. Massive expenditures for World War II led to final acceptance of compensatory spending policy which Eccles had advocated since 1933. Eccles served as chairman of the board of governors of the Federal Reserve Board until 1948 and remained a member of the board until 1951. After his tenure there ended, Eccles returned to his family enterprises. He died on December 18, 1977. (Marriner Eccles, *Beckoning Frontiers*, 1951; Sidney Hyman, *Marriner S. Eccles*, 1976; Dean May, *From New Deal to New Economics*, 1982.)

PATRICK D. REAGAN

ECONOMY ACT OF 1933 Throughout the presidential campaign of 1932, Democratic candidate Franklin D. Roosevelt* had criticized the Herbert Hoover* administration for letting the federal budget expand too rapidly. Although Roosevelt pledged at the Democratic convention that he would not economize "at the expense of starving people," he was convinced that cuts in federal spending would help improve the country's morale and create a better economic environment for recovery. Close advisers like Lewis Douglas* and Henry Morgenthau, Jr.,* would repeatedly echo that feeling. On March 20, 1933, President Roosevelt signed the Economy Act of 1933 in an attempt to balance the federal budget and keep his campaign promise. The law immediately cut $100 million from the federal payroll by reducing government salaries, departmental budgets, and veterans' allowances. Reductions in federal salaries were based on a percentage decline in the cost-of-living, using the first six months of 1928 as the base figure. Salaries for the vice-president, senators, and congressmen were reduced by a flat 15 percent. Although Congress had no power to reduce the president's salary while he was in office, the president could voluntarily submit to the cut. He also had the authority to reduce or eliminate certain veterans' benefits. Grenville Clark,* a private lawyer and adviser to the president, was responsible for drafting major portions of the law.

The irony surrounding the Economy Act of 1933 was the tremendous increases in federal relief spending. A common criticism of President Roosevelt was "how is he going to show real economy if he saves with one hand and spends with the other?" Throughout his administration, Roosevelt tried to separate general expenditures and emergency budgets, hoping to reduce total spending, but he was quick to approve "temporary" emergency measures to alleviate pressing needs. Money spent on programs to alleviate suffering and stimulate the economy was an "investment" not a "waste." By cutting federal salaries, reducing non-service-related disability payments to veterans, consolidating some administrative programs, and standing as a symbol for efficiency in government, the Economy Act succeeded in saving approximately $243 million, short of the president's goal of $500 million.

One year later Congress stepped back from the Economy Act by passing the Independent Offices Appropriations Act increasing the salaries of government employees by $125 million and the allowances of World War I veterans by $228 million. President Franklin D. Roosevelt vetoed the Independent Offices Appropriations Act on March 27, 1934, on the grounds that it would violate his economy goals, but the House and Senate overrode the veto by votes of 310 to

72 and 63 to 27. The election year demands of veterans and government employees were too powerful for Congress to resist. (James E. Sargeant, ''FDR and Lewis Douglas. Budget Balancing in the Early New Deal,'' *Prologue*, VI:33–43, 1974.)

EDMONDSON, ROBERT EDWARD Born in Ohio in 1872, Robert Edward Edmondson was a public relations contractor and economic consultant working out of New York City. During the 1930s, he became a fanatical anti-Semite. He founded the Edmondson Economic Service because he believed he could not live comfortably on an income of $50,000 a year due to a Jewish conspiracy led by Franklin D. Roosevelt* and the New Deal.* He was convinced that by centralizing the banking system and manipulating the currency, they were destroying the American upper- and middle-classes. The Edmondson Economic Service released an enormous volume of anti-Semitic propaganda. Eventually, Edmondson had to move his operation to Pennsylvania after Mayor Fiorello La Guardia* began libel proceedings against him. (George Wolfskill and John A. Hudson, *All but the People. Franklin D. Roosevelt and His Critics, 1933–1939*, 1969.)

EDWARDS V. PEOPLE OF THE STATE OF CALIFORNIA *Edwards v. People of the State of California* struck down a California statute making it a misdemeanor for a person to bring or assist in bringing into California a person known to be an indigent non-resident of the state (the so-called Okie Law). Under this law, Fred F. Edwards of California was convicted in justice court in Marysville, California, for bringing his brother-in-law into California from Texas. The Texas man, Frank Duncan, was unemployed. Edwards filed a demurrer to the complaint contesting the constitutionality of the law. The demurrer was overruled. On appeal, the case went to the Superior Court of Yuba County, California, which held the law valid and affirmed conviction. After some hesitation, the Supreme Court* agreed to accept jurisdiction. The case was reargued before the Court on October 21, 1941, and decided on November 24, 1941. Justice James F. Byrnes* wrote the opinion for the unanimous Court.

In a relatively short brief Justice Byrnes stated that the movement of people across state lines was no less interstate commerce than the movement of goods. In his judgment, therefore, the California statute placed an unconstitutional restriction on interstate commerce. Conceding that in the early nineteenth century the Court had sanctioned state and local regulations against what had historically been called the ''pestilence of paupers,'' Justice Byrnes expressed grave doubts that a man like Duncan was a pauper in the historical meaning of the word. He noted: ''Poverty and immorality are not synonymous.'' He concluded, therefore, that the California law ''is not a valid exercise of the police power of California, that it imposes an unconstitutional burden on interstate commerce, and that the conviction under it cannot be sustained.''

Although concurring in the opinion, Mr. Justice William O. Douglas* argued that the right of persons to move freely from state to state was an aspect of national citizenship protected by the privileges and immunities clause of the Fourteenth Amendment against state interference. (Alfred H. Kelley and Winfred A. Harbison, *The American Constitution*, 1970; *Supreme Court Reporter*, LXII: 164–171, 1941.)

JOSEPH M. ROWE, JR.

ELECTION OF 1932 In the summer of 1932, with perhaps 12 million people unemployed, the Democrats eagerly expected to win the presidency. The overwhelming majority of Republicans sensed their fate. Their job was to go through the motions of a national convention, campaign with chins up, and try to minimize their losses in Congress and the statehouses.

Democratic Governor Franklin D. Roosevelt* of New York formally announced his candidacy in January 1932 after James Farley* and Louis Howe* had conducted an extensive letter-writing campaign in several states and travelled broadly finding Roosevelt supporters for the delegate selection process.

By the time the Democratic Convention opened in Chicago on June 27, Roosevelt had the largest bloc of supporters, although not enough to secure the nomination. Former Senator James A. Reed of Missouri and Maryland Governor Albert Ritchie were two of the hopefuls encouraged by Al Smith.* Favorite son candidates abounded, including Governors George White of Ohio, William "Alfalfa Bill" Murray of Oklahoma, and Senator James H. Lewis of Illinois. Speaker John Nance Garner* of Texas was more than his state's favorite son; publisher William Randolph Hearst,* chairman of the California delegation, dragged him into the contest, giving the crusty old Texan all the votes of two delegations. Garner did not attend the convention and clearly was the least active of the major delegates.

Struggles over the contested delegations, rules of nomination and the convention chairmanship were all won by Roosevelt majorities but not by the two-thirds rule* needed to nominate. At the end of an all-night, three-ballot session, Roosevelt was eighty-nine votes shy of nomination. John Nance Garner's agreement then to release the Texas delegation from its obligation to vote for him also freed the California delegation. California's forty-four vote switch to Roosevelt created the bandwagon effect, putting him over the top. Garner accepted the second spot on the ticket. In a precedent-breaking move, Roosevelt asked the convention to remain in session so that he might fly to Chicago to deliver an acceptance speech. There he pledged a new deal for the American people.

The Roosevelt campaign focused largely on domestic reforms and economic recovery. To get the farmer back on his feet, the Democratic nominee hinted at an agricultural allotment program, elimination of marginal land from production, conversion of land to three crops, barter agreement permitting exchange of American agricultural produce for industrial goods of other nations, and relief measures to permit farmers to keep their land. In the domain of economic reforms, Roosevelt called for correction of price disparities between sectors of the economy, aid to railroads, industrial planning where needed, and government regulation of securities markets, banks, and public utilities. To moderate human suffering and serve to stimulate the economy simultaneously, Roosevelt advocated emergency relief aid and a public works program. Seemingly out of step with the general tone of his campaign was the call for a balanced budget and criticism of Hoover for failing to achieve this goal. If the above position represented an example of Roosevelt's waffling on the issues, Prohibition was the counterpoint. Repeal was the word.

The personality style of the two leading candidates was as different as day and night. Hoover attacked his opponent. Roosevelt ignored the president. Hoover's speeches went "thud-thud-thud." Roosevelt's radiated charisma. He seemed to draw energy from the crowd; his voice was perfect for radio. He conveyed the feeling that he knew what he would do when he took over the reins of government.

When the votes were counted, Roosevelt had carried forty-two states, secured 472 of 531 electoral votes and defeated the president by over 7,000,000 popular votes (22,809,638–15,758,901). The Democratic majority in the House of Representatives increased by 90. The Republican minority in the Senate was reduced to 35. The president-elect clearly had the momentum to govern. (Richard Oulahan, *The Man Who . . . : The Story of the Democratic National Convention of 1932*, 1971; Elliot Rosen, *Hoover, Roosevelt, and the Brains Trust: From Depression to New Deal*, 1977.)

EDWIN S. DAVIS

ELECTION OF 1934 In the election of 1932,* Franklin D. Roosevelt* and the Democratic party* triumphed, handing the Republicans their worst electoral defeat in history. Not only did Roosevelt defeat Herbert Hoover* by a vote of 22,809,683 to 15,758,901, but Democrats won the Senate with 60 members to 35 Republicans and 1 Farmer-Laborite, and the House with 310 members compared to 117 Republicans and 5 Farmer-Laborites. As the off-year elections of 1934 approached, most commentators from both parties expected history to hold true, with the party in power losing a substantial number of seats. But 1934 was an unusual year. The combination of the Great Depression, Republican failure to deal with it successfully between 1929 and 1933, and the New Deal's* whirlwind of activity in 1933 and 1934 had created an overwhelming support for Franklin Roosevelt. Although some conservative columnists and old-line Republicans were bemoaning the demise of tradition and increasing power of the federal government, the general public had few such fears. To them, Roosevelt had replaced the insensitivity of the Republican party* with a whole range of "relief, recovery, and reform" measures. The election was an overwhelming vindication of the president. Instead of losing ground, the Democrats turned history upside down by increasing their control of Congress. When the final results were in, they had 319 seats in the House, to 103 for the GOP and 10 for Farmer-Laborites, and 69 seats in the Senate. Democrats also controlled all but seven governorships in the country. William Allen White* remarked that the president had been "all but crowned by the people." (William F. Leuchtenburg, *Franklin D. Roosevelt and the New Deal, 1932–1940*, 1963.)

ELECTION OF 1936 President Franklin D. Roosevelt* produced a stunning electoral outcome for the Democratic party* in 1936. The outcome of 1936 was not the product of an inept opponent, poor organization by Alf Landon* and the Republicans' confidence resulting from the favorable (and horribly mistaken) *Literary Digest** poll, or a failure to generate issues and go on the attack. Rather, the Republican issues failed to appeal to the common people, and Roosevelt turned the election into a referendum pitting the masses against the elite and the new order against the old. Surrogates for the president attacked the Mellons, Grundys, Pews, Morgans, and the du Ponts. To elect Republicans would be to let the old enemies, "business and financial monopoly, speculation, reckless banking, and class antagonism, back into power," they said.

The Democratic Convention in Philadelphia was like a family reunion. The teamwork between the Democratic National Committee headed by James Farley,* Roosevelt's 1932 and 1936 campaign manager, and state and local efforts was grand. The candidate and surrogates made few mistakes; the outcome was never in doubt. Republicans charged Roosevelt with failure to solve the unemployment problem and balance the budget, destruction of the merit system, and abandonment of the gold standard. Free enterprise was threatened by federal subsidy. Social security taxes would erode the purchasing power of the worker, and there was no guarantee future Congresses would maintain the system. Roosevelt responded by acknowledging that because "humanity came first" the budget could not have been balanced. He claimed that some restoration of economic well-being between the sectors of the economy had taken place and deflation had been arrested. Progress would be furthered by an enactment of fair wage and hour legislation and preservation of social security. Republican opposition to social security, the president intoned, was really based upon the matching 1 percent tax on employers not employees. The free enterprise system, on its way to collapse under the previous Republican administration, had been "saved" by federal aid, by regulation of selective markets, and by public works programs which enabled people to become consumers again. The program of the administration also strengthened democracy. Surely, without a new socio-economic role for government, the Communist menace would threaten the United States, Roosevelt argued.

The coalition which the Roosevelt forces put together in 1936 had many protagonists: southerners, northern big-city machines, radical and moderate labor officials, blacks, Jews, Catholics, farmers, the unemployed, and liberals of every economic class. The first two classifications had been the pre-Roosevelt core of the Democratic party. The other groups were attracted to Roosevelt and the New Deal.* Time would tell whether the coalition was stable and whether it would identify with the party in the future.

Roosevelt was not particularly concerned with the party pe se. He told Rexford Tugwell,* one of his "brain trust,"* that after his administration there might not be a national Democratic party but there would be a Progressive party. In 1937 the coalition would be severely tested. But in 1936 that test was only in the future. In the November elections, the Democrats rolled up the greatest majorities in American history. In the popular vote President Roosevelt defeated Republican candidate Alf Landon by 27,752,869 to 16,674,665 votes, with William Lemke* of the Union party* getting 882,479 votes. In the electoral college, Roosevelt received 523 votes to Landon's 8. The Democratic majorities in Congress were equally overwhelming. When the dust from the election settled, Democrats outnumbered Republicans in the Senate by 76 to 16, with 4 Farmer-Laborites. In the House, Democrats outnumbered Republicans by 331 to 89, with 13 others Socialists, Progressives, and Farmer-Laborites. (Howard F. Gosnell, *Champion Campaigner: Franklin Roosevelt,* 1952.)

EDWIN S. DAVIS

ELECTION OF 1938 After impressive victories in the elections of 1932,* 1934,* and 1936,* the Democratic party* experienced a major setback in the congressional elections of 1938. Franklin D. Roosevelt's* court-packing* scheme in 1937 had raised a storm of protest, from politicians as well as the general public, and the specter of political authoritarianism frightened many people. At the same time, the recession of 1937 and early 1938* had undermined much of the New Deal's* economic credibility. In the farmbelt wheat and corn prices had been devastated by another series of record harvests, and discontent was widespread. Rumors were also rampant that Harry Hopkins* and the Works Progress Administration* were politically corrupt, using relief jobs as a form of patronage to build a national machine behind the president in preparation for his third term. The New Deal had also been weakened by the internecine fighting among the labor movement. Bitterly upset by the defection of the CIO* unions in 1936, William Green* and the American Federation of Labor* took a conservative posture in the election of 1938, opposing liberals like Maury Maverick* in Texas and even endorsing some reactionary Republicans like Senator James Davis* of Pennsylvania. The New Deal appeared to be in disarray.

The election was further complicated by the president's frustration with conservative Democrats who were teaming all too frequently with northern Republicans to stall or stop New Deal legislation. In what would prove to be a political disaster, Roosevelt decided to actively enter the Democratic primaries and campaign against incumbent, conservative Democrats. He was particularly interested in unseating people like Senator Ellison ''Cotton Ed'' Smith* of South Carolina, Senator Guy Gillette* of Iowa, Senator Walter George* of Georgia, Senator Millard Tydings* of Maryland, and Congressman John J. O'Connor* of New York. Roosevelt's intervention in the campaign came quickly to be known as the ''purge of 1938,'' an unfortunately volatile term given political developments in Germany and the Soviet Union. His personal campaigning backfired, and only John J. O'Connor was defeated. Most political commentators felt the public had resented the president's intervention in local elections and that southern Democrats in particular were outraged by what they considered a violation of states' rights.

In the general elections in November, the Republicans gained 75 seats in the House of Representatives, 7 in the Senate, and 13 governorships. Not only was the GOP revived after eight long years of decline, but the conservative coalition in Congress—the association of southern Democrats and northern and western Republicans—was greatly strengthened. (James T. Patterson, *Congressional Conservatism in the New Deal*, 1967.)

ELECTION OF 1940 The election of 1940 tested the Democratic coalition forged by the New Deal,* but Democrats achieved a solid triumph nationwide, though they did not repeat their overwhelming victory of 1936. Franklin D. Roosevelt* defeated Wendell L. Willkie* in every region of the country except the Midwest, amassing a popular vote of 27,307,819 (54.8 percent of the total vote) to 22,321,018 (44.8 percent of the total) for his Republican challenger; the electoral vote was 449 to 82. The parties split the Congressional vote. Democrats gained seven seats in the House, while Republicans picked up five senatorial positions.

Events abroad influenced both parties. Dramatic Nazi victories in Europe, especially France, in the spring and summer of 1940 created a sense of emergency in the United States. German power seemed immense. The public supported large increases in defense spending and hoped that Great Britain could somehow defeat Germany, but Americans were also overwhelmingly opposed to joining the war. Each of the Republican front runners—Thomas E. Dewey, Arthur H. Vandenberg,* and Robert A. Taft*—was a determined opponent of war and of extensive material aid to Britain. Willkie had begun the year as a dark horse with scant public or party support. His standing within the GOP skyrocketed upward during the spring as German successes roused American apprehensions and Willkie made known his strong support of aid to the allies. As late as April, polls suggested that only 10 percent of Republican voters preferred him, but six weeks later Willkie entered the convention as a serious contender along with Taft and Dewey. Taft evoked only a tepid response from rank and file Republicans, while the relative youth and inexperience of Dewey cast doubt upon his ability to handle the foreign affairs crisis. After six ballots the convention settled on a ticket of Wendell Willkie and Senator Charles McNary* of Oregon.

The crisis in Europe helped to solidify Democratic support for an unprecedented third term for Roosevelt. Roosevelt's intentions for 1940 had been enigmatic. In public he had been non-commital and in private had given varying impressions to different people. No other public figure matched Roosevelt's power as a vote-getter, and he had not groomed a successor. Cordell Hull* commanded the strongest support among the public and the party, but the president thought Hull lacked a sufficient commitment to the New Deal* to make an acceptable replacement. By Roosevelt's choice the convention was held in Chicago, where the local machine was intensely loyal to him. But Roosevelt refused to sanction formal efforts to seek renomination and in fact told the convention he wished not to run. Harry Hopkins* attempted to organize Roosevelt forces at the convention, but it was the Chicago machine which precipitated the actual draft. Their effort was clumsy, but it overcame all opposition and took the nomination for Roosevelt. The president insisted on Henry A. Wallace* as his running mate, and the delegates glumly agreed.

Willkie and the Republicans lacked a clear strategy for the remainder of the campaign. The candidate himself had been a registered Democrat until 1938. Willkie was a Wall-Street lawyer who had come to prominence as spokesman for one of the least popular sectors of American business, the utility industry. Moreover, Willkie built his public reputation battling the Tennsessee Valley Authority,* which was among the most popular of all New Deal agencies. Yet Willkie's posture on domestic reform seemed ambivalent. He denounced the New Deal as state socialism but endorsed many of its essential components such as the minimum wage, unemployment insurance, and social security. Willkie's foreign policy stance was similarly clouded. He denounced fascism and supported administration initiatives on preparedness and aid to Britain, while simultaneously insisting that Roosevelt was reckless and would land the nation in war. Throughout the campaign, Willkie was unable to establish clear alternatives to administration programs or to find an issue which struck sparks with the voters.

Willkie's popularity surged, however, in the final weeks before the election. The resurgence was enough to force Roosevelt to modify his strategy. Until then, Roosevelt had emphasized his status as a national leader by visiting various defense plants and installations and refraining from direct campaigning. Democratic leaders became alarmed over Willkie's late gains and convinced Roosevelt to become more active. Believing that Willkie's most effective issue was the public's unwillingness to go to war, Roosevelt emphasized his own commitment to peace in terms which were categorical and misleading. Throughout the campaign, however, Democrats trumpeted the achievements of the New Deal, continued to remind voters of the legacy of Herbert Hoover,* and ignored the third term issue.

The New Deal coalition sustained itself handsomely in 1940. Both the South and labor remained loyal as did most of the big-city ethnic populations. Voter participation, 62.5 percent of those eligible, was the highest since 1908 and was not exceeded again until 1952. Overall, the Democrats lost roughly 7 percent from their record levels of 1936 but still carried every state outside rural New England and the Midwest. Domestic issues were substantially more influential than foreign policy issues for most voters. The election of 1940 was an important factor in establishing the New Deal coalition as an enduring factor in American politics. (Ellsworth Barnard, *Wendell Willkie: Fighter for Freedom*, 1966; James MacGregor Burns, *Roosevelt: The Lion and the Fox*, 1956; Herbert S. Parmet and Marie B. Hecht, *Never Again, A President Runs for a Third Term*, 1968.)

JAMES C. SCHNEIDER

ELECTRIC HOME AND FARM AUTHORITY A major objective of the Tennessee Valley Authority* was to bring the "miracle" of electricity to all

Americans, including those isolated in rural areas. Although the need for electricity was overwhelming in rural areas, there was little market for it in rural homes, even if the TVA constructed transmission lines and connected homes. To assist the TVA in creating a demand for electric power, Congress established the Electric Home and Farm Authority in December 1933. The EHFA was designed to increase domestic consumption of electricity by convincing appliance manufacturers and retail dealers to make the equipment available at reasonable prices to private homes and farms. The EHFA supervised a public relations campaign to persuade farmers and homeowners to purchase the appliances and then provided them with credit through local appliance dealers. In August 1935 a new EHFA replaced the old authority and became an aid to the Rural Electrification Administration* after 1936 in addition to its assistance to the Tennessee Valley Authority. By 1938 the Electric Home and Farm Authority, a subsidiary of the Reconstruction Finance Corporation,* had purchased over 100,000 installment contracts from over 2,500 dealers, spending $15.5 million in thirty-three states. (James S. Olson, "The Reconstruction Finance Corporation, 1932–1940," Ph.D. dissertation, SUNY, at Stony Brook, 1972.)

ELIOT, THOMAS HOPKINSON Thomas H. Eliot was born in Cambridge, Massachusetts, in 1907 and graduated from the Harvard Law School in 1932. Eliot served as counsel to the president's Committee on Economic Security* from 1934 to 1935 and was the principal writer of the Social Security Act of 1935.* After the act passed, Eliot became counsel to the Social Security Board and remained there until 1938. Between private law practice and university teaching, Eliot served one term in Congress from 1947 to 1948, where he became known as a civil liberties advocate and an enemy of the House Un-American Activities Committee. After World War II, Eliot practiced law in Boston and then became a professor of political science at Washington University in St. Louis. He was named chancellor of the university in 1962 and stayed there until his retirement in 1971. (Katie Louchheim, ed., *The Making of the New Deal. The Insiders Speak*, 1983).

EMERGENCY BANKING ACT OF 1933 On Thursday, March 9, 1933, in the midst of the most serious financial crisis in American history, President Franklin D. Roosevelt* convened Congress in special session and introduced an emergency banking bill to deal with the panic. Within a matter of hours, the bill was law. The Emergency Banking Act of 1933 had five titles, three of them especially important. Title I formally legalized Roosevelt's decision to declare a national bank holiday.* Title II permitted the comptroller of the currency to appoint a conservator with powers of receivership over all national banks threatened with suspension, and it permitted the conservator to subordinate certain depositor and stockholder interests to reorganize those banks. Title III authorized the Reconstruction Finance Corporation* to purchase the preferred stock or capital notes of banks and trust companies to provide them with long-term investment funds and relieve them of short-term debts to the RFC. These first three titles were critical for the banking system. Title IV permitted Federal Reserve Banks to discount previously ineligible assets and to issue new Federal Reserve notes on the basis of those assets as a means of ending the currency shortages in certain areas of the country. It proved to be of little use after the bank holiday because of the surprising return of hoarded currency to the banks. Title V appropriated $2 million to implement the act.

Late in 1932 large numbers of depositors, panic-stricken about losing their money in weak banks, began demanding money in Nevada and Idaho, precipitating statewide bank holidays there. Early in 1933 the panic spread to Louisiana and then to Michigan. When the two largest banks in Detroit closed in February, a general panic spread throughout the country, ultimately closing banks everywhere. Each of the three major provisions of the Emergency Banking Act of 1933 originated in Herbert Hoover's* administration during the banking panics of 1931, 1932, and 1933. The idea for a bank holiday had first appeared during World War I when the Trading-With-the-Enemy Act of 1917 authorized President Woodrow Wilson to impose a banking embargo in case of any financial emergencies. In January 1932, during the liquidity crisis preceding establishment of the Reconstruction Finance Corporation, Secretary of the Treasury Ogden Mills and President Herbert Hoover considered declaring a national bank holiday to relieve the crisis. They considered it again during the June 1932 crisis surrounding the collapse of the Central Republic Bank of Chicago. As financial conditions worsened in January and February 1933, Hoover again looked to the idea of a national bank holiday, even approaching President-elect Roosevelt for a cooperative declaration. Hoover had Ogden Mills, Walter Wyatt of the Federal Reserve Board* staff, and attorney General DeWitt Mitchell draft a holiday proclamation. Protecting his political flank, however, Roosevelt refused to issue any joint declaration. Upon his inauguration, he then issued the declaration as Wyatt had written it and included it as Title I of the Emergency Banking Act of 1933.

Title II of the Emergency Banking Act dealt with the problem of reorganizing the thousands of closed banks throughout the United States. Comptroller of the Currency Francis Awalt, along with Ogden Mills and Walter Wyatt, had already written a piece of legislation in early 1933 allowing the comptroller of the currency to evaluate and isolate the free assets of any national bank and forcing depositors and stockholders to subordinate the exact amount of any deficiency. The bank would then have to issue a certificate of deposit to each depositor for his share of the deficiency, guaranteeing that the profits of the bank would be credited and paid to each depositor until losses had been recovered. Known as the Bank Conservation Act, the bill never made it through the Democratic Congress in 1933, but Roosevelt included it as Title II of the Emergency Banking Act.

Title III, providing for RFC investment in troubled banks, had originated in a 1932 proposal by Franklin W. Fort, head of the Federal Home Loan Bank

System. Fort believed that RFC loans were too expensive and too short-term to be of much help to troubled banks, so he urged President Hoover to seek legislation authorizing the RFC to purchase the preferred stock or capital notes of commercial banks. At first Hoover found the proposal too drastic, but as the financial situation deteriorated in 1933 he gradually came around to the idea. In February 1933 he had Franklin Fort, Walter Wyatt, and Francis Awalt draft a bill giving the RFC such powers. But like the proposed Bank Conservation Act, the proposal had no chance of making its way through the Democratic Congress before Roosevelt's inauguration.

After the inauguration of President Franklin D. Roosevelt, Hoover's former advisers—Ogden Mills, Walter Wyatt, Francis Awalt, and Arthur Ballantine, the under secretary of the treasury—met with Roosevelt's new economic staff: William Woodin,* secretary of the treasury; Adolph Berle, Jr.,* and Raymond Moley* of the "brain trust."* Woodin asked Wyatt and Ballantine to draft the Emergency Banking Act of 1933, and they pulled together Hoover's proposals for a bank holiday, the Bank Conservation Act, and the RFC stock-buying plan. That bill then went to Congress on March 9, 1933, and President Roosevelt signed it into law the same day. (James S. Olson, *Herbert Hoover and the Reconstruction Finance Corporation, 1931–1933*, 1977.)

EMERGENCY FARM MORTGAGE ACT OF 1933 The Emergency Farm Mortgage Act was an amendment to the Agricultural Adjustment Act* signed by President Franklin D. Roosevelt* on May 12, 1933. It provided for refinancing farm mortgages to prevent the loss of homes and land by thousands of farmers. World War I had created huge export markets for American produce, and the government had encouraged farmers to increase production as demand swelled. After the war those export markets declined and prices collapsed. Debts which had seemed reasonable during the war became heavy burdens as farm income declined in the 1920s. Thousands of farmers were unable to pay their mortgages and faced the possibility of losing their property. Groups like the National Farmers' Holiday Association* organized to protest the agricultural crisis, and farmers across the country began to demand federal legislation. On April 3, 1933, President Roosevelt sent a message to Congress requesting legislation to help farmers refinance their indebtedness. He urged readjustment of mortgage principal, reduction of interest rates, and a temporary change in amortization schedules to give farmers more time to pay off their mortgages and reduce payments. In response to the president's request, Congress added an amendment to the Agricultural Adjustment Act which authorized Federal Land Banks to issue up to $2 billion worth of tax exempt bonds at 4 percent interest guaranteed by the federal government. Proceeds from the bond sales would be used to make new loans or refinance existing mortgages. The amendment also allowed the direct exchange of bonds for existing mortgages. A loan ceiling of $50,000 per farm or $25,000 per individual was established. Loans issued at 4 1/2 percent could not exceed 50 percent of the appraised value of the land. Borrowers were not required to make payment on the principal for five years. The act also directed the RFC* to allocate $200 million to the Farm Loan commissioner for loans to enable farmers to redeem farm property lost through foreclosure after July 1, 1931, refinance minor debts, and provide farmers with working capital. The maximum loan was not to exceed $5,000 at 5 percent. The total of first and second mortgages could not exceed 75 percent of the appraised value of the property. Payment was to be made in ten annual installments with no payment on the principal for the first three years. (*Congressional Digest*, XII:156–157, 1933).

CATHERINE EGGERS

EMERGENCY RAILROAD TRANSPORTATION ACT OF 1933 By the 1930s the American railroad industry was on the verge of collapse. Since the stock market crash, railroad freight revenue, already devastated by the growth of the trucking industry, had fallen drastically. With revenue down sharply, a substantial number of roads were unable to meet their short- or even long-term obligations. Because of decades of overbuilding, duplication of service, and enormous capital investments, most railroads were burdened with huge debt structures and high fixed payments. The only hope for the railroads was massive reorganization and consolidation as well as federal regulation of the trucking industry to coordinate both of them and keep each profitable. While the Motor Carrier Act of 1935* addressed the problems of the trucking industry, the Emergency Railroad Transportation Act of 1933 was an attempt to restore structural health to the railroad industry.

Signed into law on June 16, 1933, during the first "hundred days,"* the Emergency Railroad Transportation Act was a makeshift law pleasing few people. It created a federal coordinator of transportation who would divide railroads into eastern, southern, and western groups. Each group would select a coordinating committee of railroad managers to eliminate duplication and promote joint use of tracks and terminals, to encourage financial reorganization to cut fixed costs, and to study ways of improving transportation. Although the general philosophy of the law was for the committees to coordinate voluntary action to eliminate waste, the federal transportation coordinator could order uncooperative carriers to participate. Before taking any formal action, the coordinator had to consult with labor leaders, and neither railroad employment nor salaries could be reduced below their May 1933 levels, except for a modest 5 percent reduction to handle resignations, retirements, and deaths. All decisions of the federal coordinator could be appealed to the ICC* or to federal courts. Finally, the act exempted carriers from anti-trust laws.

President Franklin D. Roosevelt* appointed Joseph B. Eastman* of the ICC as federal coordinator of transportation, but no significant consolidation or coordination of facilities occurred. When Eastman tried to force consolidation, he encountered bitter opposition from railroad management afraid of losing corporate independence, railroad workers afraid of losing their jobs, various communities afraid of losing railroad service, and large shippers afraid of losing cheap, competitive fares. Consequently, the reductions in fixed costs so desperately needed by the railroads did not occur. Congress allowed the federal coordinator's office to die in June 1936. (Ari Hoogenboom and Olive Hoogenboom, *A History of the ICC. From Panacea to Palliative*, 1976.)

EMERGENCY RELIEF APPROPRIATION ACT OF 1935 By late 1934 President Franklin D. Roosevelt* and many New Dealers were prepared to establish a large-scale work relief program for the unemployed, "to preserve not only the bodies of the unemployed from destitution, but also their self-respect, their self-reliance and courage and determination." The president wanted a work relief program which would finance useful projects, not compete with private business, and spend funds on labor rather than material and equipment. Early in April 1935, Congress passed the Emergency Relief Appropriation Act providing $4.8 billion for work relief. It was the largest single appropriation ever made in the United States up to that time. The law allowed the president to distribute the money among various existing relief and public works agencies and to establish any new agencies to provide work relief. On May 6, 1935, President Roosevelt established the Works Progress Administration* and assigned it the largest share of the Emergency Relief Appropriation Act funds—$1.4 billion. All of the original $4.8 billion had to be spent within two years, and the president established relief wages below prevailing pay scales, hoping to encourage workers to move to better-paying jobs in the private sector when they became available. (Barbara Blumberg, *The New Deal and the Unemployed: The View from New York City*, 1979.)

EMERGENCY RELIEF APPROPRIATION ACT OF 1937 At the start of President Franklin D. Roosevelt's* second term in office, the question of federal work relief was becoming a political "hot potato." Although some groups like the U.S. Conference of Mayors or people like Congressman Maury Maverick* of Texas wanted increased relief spending, other influential Americans were opposed. Treasury Secretary Henry Morgenthau, Jr.,* desperate to balance the federal budget, wanted to cut relief spending, and Senator Joseph Robinson* of Arkansas saw such cuts as the only way of avoiding tax increases. Republican Congressman Bertrand Snell* of New York worried that continued federal relief spending might create a disastrous inflationary spiral. Early in April 1937, the president took the middle road, asking Congress for only $1.5 billion for relief in fiscal 1937–1938. Reaction to the proposal was predictable. WPA* union workers marched on Washington, D. C., and demonstrated against the proposal as too meager, while conservatives like Senator James Byrnes* of South Carolina and Congressman Clifton Woodrum* of Virginia tried to cut $500 million from the appropriation. The Emergency Relief Appropriation Act of 1937 gave Roosevelt his $1.5 billion, but it also contained a clause insisting that there would be no supplemental appropriations and that aliens not applying for citizenship be dropped from the WPA rolls. The inadequate appropriation led to dismissals of 35,000 WPA workers in 1937 and widespread criticism from labor representatives and the unemployed. (Barbara Blumberg, *The New Deal and the Unemployed: The View from New York City*, 1979.)

EMERGENCY RELIEF APPROPRIATION ACT OF 1939 The debate over federal relief spending continued into 1939, with labor leaders and social workers demanding more money and budget balancers and conservatives insisting on less. In April 1939 Roosevelt proposed a $1.477 billion WPA budget* for fiscal year 1940, a reduction of one-third from the previous year. Clifton Woodrum,* the economy-minded Democrat from Virginia, launched an investigation of the WPA and in June 1939 his House Appropriations Subcommittee introduced a WPA funding bill to Congress which would cut $125 million from Roosevelt's request, prohibit the WPA from constructing any building costing more than $25,000, forbid the agency from keeping any worker longer than eighteen months, reduce the relief work week to thirty hours, eliminate the Federal Theatre Project,* and require local funding for the WPA art, music, writing, and history programs. A few conservatives like Republican Congressman John Taber* wanted to liquidate the WPA altogether, but most conservatives were pleased with the Woodrum bill. Congressional liberals like Samuel Dickstein* of New York City, along with members of the Franklin D. Roosevelt* administration, tried to maneuver to rescind many of the restrictive Woodrum proposals. A compromise measure emerged as the Emergency Relief Appropriation Act of 1939. The law provided $1.477 billion for the WPA, required local governments to supply 25 percent of the cost of WPA projects, limited construction to buildings costing less than $52,000, required automatic lay-offs of all WPA employees after eighteen months on the job, cut the WPA work week to thirty hours, and eliminated the Federal Theatre Project. (Barabara Blumberg, *The New Deal and the Unemployed: The View from New York City*, 1979.)

EMERGENCY RELIEF APPROPRIATION ACT OF 1940 Optimistic about a business revival in 1940 because of the war in Europe, President Franklin D. Roosevelt* proposed a budget of only $985 million for the WPA* in fiscal 1941. By April 1940, however, when the expected recovery had not materialized, the president changed his request, asking for $975 million to be spent in the next eight months. Congressional conservatives like John Taber* and Clifton Woodrum,* disappointed in the WPA and afraid Roosevelt might award jobs to prospective voters for the 1940 election, wanted to contain WPA activities. Still, the president got his way. The Emergency Relief Appropriation Act of 1940 provided $975,650,000 for the WPA, with the money to be used in the first eight months of the fiscal year ending June 30, 1941. The bill resembled the 1939 appropriation act. The rule requiring termination of employees after eighteen months of service was retained, but exceptions could be made for veterans and their wives or widows and for employees over forty-five years of age and with dependents to support. The provision for a 25 percent local contribution remained except for defense-related projects. The ban on WPA construction costing more than $52,000 was raised to $100,000 as a means of stimulating defense projects. Communists and Nazis were barred from WPA employment, and all WPA employees had to take a loyalty oath. Finally, to prevent the administration from increasing the Works Projects Administration* (name changed, 1939) employment force just before the election of 1940*, the act stipulated that WPA rolls were not to exceed 1.7 million in the summer, 1.8 million in the fall, and 2 million in the winter. (Barbara Blumberg, *The New Deal and the Unemployed: The View from New York City*, 1979.)

EMERGENCY RELIEF APPROPRIATION ACT OF 1941 Because unemployment had persisted during 1940, President Franklin D. Roosevelt* had permitted the Works Projects Administration* to spend all of its $975 million budget under the Emergency Relief Appropriation Act of 1940* by January 1941. He then managed to secure from Congress a supplemental appropriation of $375 million. In May 1941 he asked Congress for a WPA budget of $875 million for the next year. Some southern Democrats and conservative Republicans tried but failed to cut that request down to $500 million. The Emergency Relief Appropriation Act of 1941 provided $875 million for the WPA and eliminated the dismissal rule for all WPA employees with more than eighteen months on the job. (Barbara Blumberg, *The New Deal and the Unemployed: The View from New York City*, 1979.)

EMERSON, THOMAS IRWIN Thomas I. Emerson was born in 1907 in Passaic, New Jersey, to a family with roots in American history reaching back to its Puritan beginnings. He graduated from Yale in 1928 and then was first in his class at Yale Law School and editor of the *Yale Law Journal*. Emerson then studied one semester under Felix Frankfurter* when the Harvard professor was in residence in New Haven and then went to work for Walter Pollak, a civil liberties attorney working on the Scottsboro case. On the recommendation of Frankfurter, Emerson went to Washington in 1933 to work with Donald Richberg* and the National Recovery Administration.* Because of his long interest in civil liberties and labor rights, Emerson stayed with the NRA only until 1934 when he switched over to Lloyd Garrison* and Francis Biddle's* National Labor Relations Board.* There Emerson helped develop the NLRB ''master plan'' for pressing for court enforcement of the National Labor Relations Act.* To guarantee favorable federal court review of cases, they selected test cases where they could easily show that interstate commerce was affected by the unfair labor practice. In 1936 Emerson accepted an offer from John Winant* to join the legal staff of the Social Security Board. After the *Jones & Laughlin* case in April 1937, when the Supreme Court* upheld the National Labor Relations Act of 1935,* Emerson went back to the NLRB and remained there until 1940. Emerson resigned in protest from the NLRB in 1940 when President Franklin D. Roosevelt* refused to reappoint Joseph Warren Madden* as head of the NLRB. The AFL* opposed Madden because they felt he was too pro-CIO.* Emerson remained in Washington until 1946, serving as deputy administrator for enforcement at the Office of Price Administration, general counsel for the Office of Economic Stabilization, and general counsel at the Office of War Mobilization and Reconversion. In 1946 Emerson returned to Yale as a professor of law and became Lines Professor in 1955. (Peter H. Irons, *The New Deal Lawyers*, 1982; Katie Louchheim, ed., *The Making of the New Deal. The Insiders Speak*, 1983.)

EPSTEIN, ABRAHAM Abraham Epstein was born in Russia on April 20, 1872, immigrated to the United States in 1910, and settled in Pittsburgh. He graduated from the University of Pittsburgh in 1917, spent a year in graduate school, and then went to work as research director of the Pennsylvania Commission on Old-Age Pensions, which had been established in 1917. He was also a leading figure in the establishment of the American Association for Old-Age Security, which became the American Association for Social Security in 1933. Throughout the 1920s, Epstein worked to create a statewide system of old-age insurance in Pennsylvania but failed to secure legislative funding and became an advocate of a federal program. Only then could a uniform, equitable system of social security be established throughout the country. He was also a firm believer that any social security plan should be financed by government appropriations, not individual and employee contributions, and on those grounds he became an outspoken critic of the Social Security Act of 1935.* He even urged states to refuse to participate in the tax offset unemployment system, and hoped that the Supreme Court* would declare the old-age and unemployment titles unconstitutional. Epstein continued to call for federal government financing of the program so that economic security would be based on income redistribution. Epstein also desperately wanted some form of health insurance, which the Social Security Act of 1935 had ignored. Abraham Epstein died on May 5, 1942. (Roy Lubove, *The Struggle for Social Security, 1900–1935*, 1968; *New York Times*, May 6, 1942.)

EVANS, LUTHER Luther Evans was born in Texas in 1902. After receiving a bachelor's degree in political science at the University of Texas in 1923, Evans did graduate work at Stanford University, completing the Ph.D. in 1927. He taught at New York University (1927–1928), Dartmouth (1928–1930), and Princeton (1930–1935). In June 1935 Raymond Moley* and Harry Hopkins* had been discussing the need for a national records survey, and Moley, acquainted with Evans through a student, invited him to discuss the project in depth with Hopkins. Evans did so, and they contacted leading archivists throughout the country, after which Evans wrote a detailed prospectus for the project. He joined the WPA* as supervisor of historic projects in October 1935, and one month later was named director of the Historical Records Survey* of the WPA. He worked under the direction of Henry Alsberg* of the Federal Writers' Project* until 1936 when the Historical Records Survey became an independent program under Federal Project No. 1 of the WPA. Evans proved to be a strong administrator, earning the respect of archivists, historians, local historical societies, and politicians. The HRS was closely associated with the American Historical Association, American Library Association, and Society of American Archivists as well as groups like the Daughters of the American Revolution and the Daughters of the Confederacy. Evans resigned as director of the HRS in 1939 to accept a position with the Library of Congress. He later served as director of UNESCO (1953–1958). (William F. McDonald, *Federal Relief Administration and the Arts*, 1969.)

EVANS, RUDOLPH MARTIN Rudolph M. Evans was born in Cedar Rapids, Iowa, on November 4, 1890. He graduated with a degree in civil engineering from Iowa State College in 1913, worked for the Allied Machinery Company until 1921, and then farmed and raised livestock in Laurens, Iowa, until 1933. Evans went to work for the Agricultural Adjustment Administration* in 1933 as head of the Iowa state board, campaigned effectively for Franklin D. Roosevelt* in the election of 1936,* and in 1936 became special assistant to Secretary of Agriculture Henry A. Wallace.* A faithful Democrat who had an extraordinary loyalty to Wallace, ''Spike'' Evans inspired confidence in the people around him. A prosperous, gentleman livestock raiser who believed passionately in farmer-run federal programs, Evans rose quickly in reputation among New Deal* insiders. When Howard R. Tolley* became chief of the USDA's Bureau of Agricultural Economics in 1938, Evans became the new administrator of the AAA. As head of the AAA, Evans worked closely with the American Farm Bureau Federation,* which he considered the legitimate voice of the American farmer. Not until 1942, when the new Secretary of Agriculture Claude Wickard* wanted to restrict Farm Bureau influence, did Evans leave the Department of Agriculture to accept a position as governor of the Federal Reserve Board.* He was an unsuccessful candidate for the United States Senate in 1956 and died on November 21, 1956. (Dean Albertson, *Roosevelt's Farmer. Claude R. Wickard in the New Deal*, 1961; *Who Was Who in America*, III:267, 1960.)

EVANS, WALKER Born in St. Louis, Missouri, in 1903, Walker Evans was reared in an environment of cultural and financial privilege and was educated at private eastern schools and at Williams College. In 1926 he lived in Paris, where he was stimulated by the revolutionary movements in literature and painting. By 1928 he had turned to photography, and he confirmed his career by beginning a photographic study of American architecture, a subject that would always be integral to his study of people.

In the mid-1930s, Evans participated in the famous program commissioned by the Farm Security Administration* to record American lives during a unique era of social and economic hardship. The photographic unit, under the direction of Roy Stryker, included such major photographers as Dorothea Lange,* Ben Shahn,* Carl Mydans, Arthur Rothstein, and Russell Lee. Of the 75,000 photographs collected by this effort, Evans' contribution was prodigious. Between June 1935 and summer 1938, he captured the hardship, fragility, and durability of lives in selected terrain of the Southeast and in areas of New York City, West Virginia, and Pennsylvania. Midway into the first year of the assignment, he took a leave from the FSA to join James Agee* in Alabama, where the two began their record of a two-month stay with three sharecropper families. The faces and the essence of environment of Bud Fields, Frank Tengle, and Floyd Burroughs, emerging in *Let Us Now Praise Famous Men*, have become indelible images in the mythology of the depression era. As critic John Szarkowski has said, "Beyond doubt, the accepted myth of our recent past [especially the 1930s] is in some measure the creation of this photographer." Besides his work in rural Alabama, Georgia, and Mississippi, Evans also captured scenes in coal mining and industrial towns, in severely flooded areas of Arkansas and Tennessee, and on 61st Street in New York City, between First and Third Avenues.

In 1943 Evans was employed as contributing editor of *Time*, and in 1945 he moved to *Fortune*, where as associate editor he remained for twenty years, his photo-essays and photographs there enjoying the full expression of his abilities. In 1965 Evans moved to New Haven, Connecticut, where he was a professor of graphic design at Yale throughout the last decade of his career.

Walker Evans was honored as one of America's pre-eminent photographers in 1971 when 200 of his pictures were selected for exhibition at the Museum of Modern Art. He died in New Haven, Connecticut, in April 1975. (John Szarkowski, *Walker Evans*, 1971.)

BARBARA M. TYSON

"EVER-NORMAL GRANARY" The "ever-normal granary" was a concept for creating agricultural stability that gradually evolved in the mind of Henry A. Wallace.* Beginning in 1912, Wallace wrote of using the biblical lesson of Joseph in Egypt for solving the boom and bust cycle of Iowa wheat farming. During good years, wheat surpluses would be kept off the market and stored until production fell below demand. Wallace was seeking a balance in production and consumption rather than mere price supports for a glutted wheat market because both consumer and producer would benefit from stable supplies and stable prices. Wallace found precedent for the plan in an ancient Chinese law that empowered the government to buy grain during good production years and sell during lean years. Only the government had the financial resources to implement an ever-normal granary. The Great Depression and the New Deal* gave Wallace the political climate he needed to create the "ever-normal granary."

Although Henry A. Wallace became secretary of agriculture in 1933, it was not until the passage of the Agricultural Adjustment Act of 1938* that he was able to put his pet theory into practice. The serious crisis situation in American agriculture had precluded any long range planning in the Agricultural Adjustment Act of 1933.* Crop failures in the early 1930s caused by droughts, disease, and insects convinced Wallace of the need to make the granary a major part of federal agricultural policy. Even though the new law continued the soil conservation features of earlier legislation, the Agricultural Adjustment Act of 1938 deeply reflected his sentiment and concern that the very survival of the nation depended upon a consistent food supply. The AAA* shifted the policy away from crop reductions to the systematic storage of surplus agricultural commodities. (Richard S. Kirkendall, *Social Scientists and Farm Politics in the Age of Roosevelt*, 1966; Edward L. Schapsmeier and Frederick H. Schapsmeier, *Henry A. Wallace of Iowa: The Agrarian Years, 1920–1940*, 1968.)

DAVID L. CHAPMAN

EXPORT-IMPORT BANK During the 1930s, the New Deal* experimented with several different approaches to recovery. One of these, inherited from Herbert Hoover's* administration, involved using federal lending agencies to strengthen private credit markets. Only when businessmen could obtain the working capital to increase employment and production would recovery emerge. To increase the volume of bank credit available to private financial institutions, farmers, and businessmen, the New Deal established a number of federal loan agencies, including the Farm Credit Administration,* Commodity Credit Corporation,* and the Home Owners' Loan Corporation.* The Roosevelt administration, interested in stimulating foreign trade and American exports in order to help bring about an economic recovery, also tried to increase the volume of international bank credit. In February 1934 President Franklin D. Roosevelt,* as part of his decision to extend diplomatic recognition to the Soviet Union, established the Export-Import Bank of Washington to finance trade with them. A few weeks later, when Cuba requested a loan for purchasing and minting silver coins, Roosevelt established the Second Export-Import Bank of Washington to handle the transaction. Soon the president decided to expand the Second Export-Import Bank's activities to finance trade with other nations. The Export-Import Bank remained confined to the Soviet trade. Eventually, negotiations with the Soviet Union over her World War I debts disintegrated, and in 1936 the administration liquidated the Second Export-Import Bank and transferred its obligations and responsibilities to the Export-Import Bank of Washington.

At first, the Export-Import Bank wanted to focus on long-term loans to stimulate private lending in the international market. But because private commercial banks were reluctant to make export loans, the Export-Import Bank spent large sums at first granting credit on tobacco and cotton. Commercial banks handled the loans but sold most of them to the Export-Import Bank. The bank also granted some intermediate credit to exporters of capital goods, primarily railway and heavy equipment, and advanced long-term credit to exporters and banks against obligations issued by foreign governments in settlement of claims arising out of blocked exchanges. Despite great hopes, the Export-Import Bank did little to stimulate foreign trade until later in the 1930s. By 1937 it had advanced only $35 million to exporters and bank participations were minimal.

The Export-Import Bank operated as a subsidiary of the Reconstruction Finance

Corporation,* and its first director was George N. Peek,* former head of the Agricultural Adjustment Administration.* Peek was replaced at the Export-Import Bank in 1936 by Warren Lee Pierson,* who had been serving as the bank's general counsel. Export-Import Bank loans did not really begin to increase until large-scale lending to foreign governments began. In 1937 the bank extended a $37 million loan to China, secured by a promise to supply tung oil to the United States. The bank also made loans of $35 million to several Scandinavian countries, $16 million to Spain, and $20 million to Chile—all in 1939 and 1940. In fact, by then the purposes of the Export-Import Bank had changed from economic to diplomatic. Conservatives in Congress like Senator Robert Taft* of Ohio began accusing Roosevelt of using the Export-Import Bank to extend American influence abroad. In 1939 they managed to place a $100 million limit on the bank's outstanding obligations. In March 1940 the president was able to add $100 million to that total, but Congress stipulated that no more than $20 million in credit could be extended to one country and that the Export-Import Bank was subject to the Neutrality Act of 1939. Only the German invasion of Western Europe in the spring of 1940 eased the pressure and enabled Roosevelt to get the loan ceiling up to $700 million. The pace of loans then increased dramatically, and by 1945 the bank had authorized loans totaling nearly $1.2 billion. (Frederick C. Adams, *Economic Diplomacy: The Export-Import Bank and American Foreign Policy, 1934–1939*, 1976.)

EZEKIEL, MORDECAI JOSEPH BRILL Mordecai Ezekiel was born on May 10, 1899, in Richmond, Virginia. He took a bachelor's degree at the University of Maryland in 1918 and a master's degree at the University of Minnesota in 1923, where he met Dr. John D. Black* in the Department of Economics. Black became very influential in American agricultural policy because of his "domestic allotment plan,"* which envisioned raising farm prices by limiting acreage production. Ezekiel went to work in the Bureau of Agricultural Economics in the Department of Agriculture in 1922. By the early 1930s he was advocating the domestic allotment plan as the only way of solving the agriculture problem. In 1932 he wrote agricultural speeches for candidate Franklin D. Roosevelt* and became close to Henry A. Wallace.* When Roosevelt defeated Herbert Hoover* in the presidential election, Ezekiel became the chief economic adviser to the new Secretary of Agriculture Henry A. Wallace. He played a major role in drafting the Agricultural Adjustment Act of 1933,* calling it the "greatest single experiment in economic planning under capitalist conditions ever attempted by a democracy in times of peace."

During 1935 and 1936, Ezekiel gained national attention for his conviction that national economic planning was the only answer to the depression. His faith in planning was so intent and his image so public that Father Charles Coughlin* openly called him a Communist. Ezekiel had come out of the institutional economic school made famous by Thorstein Veblen. He was convinced that the rise of large corporations and their control over prices had eliminated competition as a market mechanism. To replace the old control of prices, Ezekiel began calling for creation of an Industrial Expansion Administration which would set production goals for every industry and guarantee contracts by federal purchases of unsold surpluses. In that sense his proposal resembled some of the New Deal* agricultural programs. Ezekiel published his views in *$2500 a Year: From Scarcity to Abundance* (1936) and *Jobs For All Through Industrial Expansion* (1939). Surplus goods would be stocked in an ''ever-normal warehouse'' and an industrial processing tax would provide funds for benefit payments to cooperating companies.

Ezekiel's idea never gained much support because of fears of a monumental federal bureaucracy to administer it and because by the time he was promoting it, the tone of New Deal policy had shifted away from industrial planning toward anti-trust, social security, and pro-labor legislation. Also, by 1937 Ezekiel was convinced that the spending theories of John Maynard Keynes* were appropriate tools for dealing with the depression, and he advocated their adoption by the administration. Mordecai Ezekiel died on October 31, 1974. (*New York Times*, November 1, 1974; Arthur M. Schlesinger, Jr., *The Age of Roosevelt. Vol. III. The Politics of Upheaval, 1935–1936*, 1960.)

F

FAHEY, JOHN H. John H. Fahey was born in Manchester, New Hampshire, on February 19, 1873. Immediately after graduating from high school, he went to work as a reporter for *The Manchester Mirror*. By 1897 he had risen to become superintendent of the northeastern division of the Associated Press. He left that position in 1903 to become editor and publisher of *The Traveller* in Boston. Fahey stayed there until 1910. In 1910 he joined the staff of the Associated Press again, this time as second vice-president in the national office. Later he served as president and publisher of *The Worcester Post* (1914–1937), publisher of *The Manchester Mirror* (1922–1925), and publisher of the *New York Evening Post* (1923). Early in his career Fahey had become director of the Boston Chamber of Commerce and played a leading role in formation of the United States Chamber of Commerce* in 1912. He was president of the U.S. Chamber of Commerce in 1914–1915. During his publishing career in Boston, Fahey associated closely with Louis Brandeis* and Joseph B. Eastman* and took a progressive position on public regulation of street railways. Franklin D. Roosevelt* named him to the board of the Home Owners' Loan Corporation* in June 1933 and then as chairman of the board in November 1933. Fahey held that position until his retirement in 1948. He died on November 19, 1950. (*New York Times*, November 20, 1950.)

FAHY, CHARLES Charles Fahy was born August 17, 1892, in Rome, Georgia. He was a student at the University of Notre Dame in 1910 and 1911, and then he took a law degree at Georgetown University in 1914. Fahy practiced law in Washington, D. C., for ten years until health problems forced him to move to Santa Fe, New Mexico. He remained in Santa Fe until 1933, serving for one year in 1932 as city attorney and learning much about western politics and resources law. Fahy combined the style of a southern gentleman with an iron will and a narrow, legalistic view of the law. He was appointed first assistant solicitor in the Department of Interior in 1933, and later in the year Harold L. Ickes* made him a member of the Petroleum Administrative Board.* Fahy served as chairman of the board in 1934 and 1935. After the *Panama Refining** decision by the Supreme Court* in January 1935 had destroyed the Petroleum Administrative Board, Fahy moved to the staff of the National Labor Relations Board* as general counsel. Fahy was general counsel to the NLRB for five years. Fahy had little interest in social policy or jurisprudential theory; he simply wanted to enforce the National Labor Relations Act of 1935.* Under Fahy's direction, the NLRB legal staff developed a "master plan" to enforce the law and gain favorable treatment from the federal courts. Fahy methodically selected test cases which showed that labor problems did "obstruct the stream of commerce" and therefore came under the federal right to regulate interstate commerce. Fahy also led the fight against the American Liberty League's* "injunction assault" on the National Labor Relations Act. In 1940 President Franklin D. Roosevelt* appointed Fahy as assistant solicitor general of the United States, and in 1941 he became a member of the president's Naval and Air Base Commission to London. Later that year, Roosevelt appointed him solicitor general of the United States, a post Fahy filled until 1945. After World War II, Fahy served in a number of advisory positions in the State Department and United Nations and in 1947 returned to private law practice in Washington, D. C. In 1949 he served briefly as chairman of the Personal Security Review Board for the Atomic Energy Commission, but later in the year President Harry S Truman* appointed him justice of the United States Court of Appeals for the District of Columbia Circuit. In 1967 Fahy became senior judge there. He died September 17, 1979. (Peter H. Irons, *The New Deal Lawyers*, 1982; *Who Was Who In America*, VII:186, 1981.)

FAIR EMPLOYMENT PRACTICES COMMITTEE In 1941 A. Philip Randolph* of the Brotherhood of Sleeping Car Porters called for a march on Washington, D. C., to protest employment discrimination in defense industries. President Franklin D. Roosevelt* was concerned about the effect a major civil rights demonstration would have on the American image abroad, and he was concerned the march would draw attention away from New Deal* domestic programs. After meeting with the leaders of the March-on-Washington Committee, Roosevelt appointed a special task force, headed by Fiorello La Guardia,* mayor of New York City. La Guardia's committee proposed an executive order on non-discrimination. The march committee approved the plan, cancelled the demonstration, and on June 25, 1941, Roosevelt issued Executive Order 8802 establishing the Fair Employment Practices Commission.

The FEPC was understaffed and underbudgeted. Without enforcement powers, it was not taken seriously by business leaders or government officials. Its main functions were to hold public hearings on complaints and to propose policy. The FEPC was also severely limited by the social climate in the United States at the time. While the committee was conducting hearings on discrimination in employment, racism was clearly evident on the West Coast. In the wake of Pearl Harbor, Japanese-Americans were being driven from their homes to relocation camps. Prejudice in the South also limited the committee's power. At a time when he needed broad-based support for his New Deal programs, Roosevelt could not afford to lend full support to the FEPC for fear it would upset southern congressmen, a substantial legislative bloc. In June 1942 FEPC hearings in Birmingham, Alabama, so angered southern leaders that Roosevelt abandoned plans to increase the effectiveness of order 8802. Instead, he transferred the FEPC to the War Manpower Commission, giving Congress the power to limit the committee's funding. Soon after the transfer, the FEPC was split over opposition to the leadership of the chairman, Paul V. McNutt.* Several members quit, citing differences with McNutt as their reason for termination. By 1943, two years after its inception, the FEPC had ceased to function. Later in 1943 Roosevelt issued Executive Order 9346 to replace the unsuccessful FEPC. His order led to the establishment of a new Committee on Fair Employment Practices with redefined powers, a larger staff, and field offices. Non-discrimination clauses were extended to all government contracts, not just those dealing with defense industries. Funding for the new FEPC was provided by a presidential emergency appropriation. The expenditures were approved twice by Congress, but the second budgetary approval of the fund was for liquidation of the commission. (Ruth P. Morgan, *The President and Civil Rights*, 1970; Joseph Parker Witherspoon, *Administrative Implementation of Civil Rights*, 1968.)

DAN K. UTLEY

FAIR LABOR STANDARDS ACT OF 1938 To appease labor unions about the powers given to the National Recovery Administration* under the National Industrial Recovery Act of 1933,* Congress had specifically written in Section 7 and 7(a) of the law that workers had the right to a minimum wage, bargain collectively, and to be free of "yellow-dog" contracts. When the Supreme Court* invalidated the NIRA in May 1935, the labor standards provisions also died. Facing re-election in 1936 and realizing the need for strong labor support, President Franklin D. Roosevelt* began demanding a restoration of minimum wage and maximum hours legislation. Congress passed the Walsh-Healey Public Contracts Act* on June 30, 1936, which required all federal contractors to agree to a Department of Labor minimum wage and not employ workers more than eight hours a day or forty hours a week without paying them overtime.

The administration introduced a comprehensive wages and hours package into Congress in the summer of 1937, but after extensive hearings the measure was postponed. After calling Congress into special session late in 1937, the president again requested action on the wages and hours bill, and he had the near unanimous support of AFL* and CIO* leaders. Democratic Congressman John O'Connor* of New York, chairman of the House Ways and Means Committee, opposed the measure and bottled it up in committee. Later in the session, the administration managed to retrieve it, and the bill was passed on June 14, 1938. Roosevelt signed it on June 25, 1938.

The Fair Labor Standards Act established a Wage and Hour Division in the Department of Labor to enforce its provisions. The act affected all workers engaged in interstate commerce or producing goods for interstate commerce. It set a minimum wage of 25¢ per hour for 1938 and 30¢ per hour for 1939. It also said that the minimum wage would rise to 40¢ per hour after a period of seven years. The act also fixed a maximum work week of forty-four hours for 1938, forty-two hours for 1939, and forty hours in 1940 and thereafter. Child labor for people under sixteen years was prohibited. The act exempted certain occupations, including agricultural workers, intrastate retail employees, seamen, street railway employees, and fishermen. By 1939 there were nearly 13 million workers covered by the law. (Paul H. Douglas and Joseph Hackman, "The Fair Labor Standards Act of 1938 II," *Political Science Quarterly*, LIV:29–55, 1939.)

FARLEY, JAMES ALOYSIUS James A. Farley was born on May 30, 1888, in Grassy Point, New York, the son of a brick manufacturer and one of a small number of Democrats in Rockland County. The younger Farley showed an early interest in politics. In the election of 1896, he carried a torch in a Bryan parade; and by the time he was in secondary school, he already exhibited the ability to remember the first names of virtually everyone he met. His father was killed in an accident before Farley was ten, so he helped to provide for the family by taking work after school. When his mother bought a small grocery and saloon, Jim helped out in both businesses. He earned a reputation for being hard-working and friendly, a devoted son, a talented baseball player, and a regular church-goer.

After graduating from high school in 1905, Farley moved to New York City to study bookkeeping. He completed the course at Packard Commercial School and went to work as a bookkeeper. He eventually gained a position with Universal Gypsum Company and in fifteen years moved through the ranks from bookkeeper to company correspondent and finally to salesman. During this time he retained his early interest in politics. In 1912 he ran for the position of town clerk for Stony Point, New York. Farley was undaunted by the fact that no Democrat had won in Stony Point since 1894. While on the road making his sales rounds, he kept in touch with the voters by post card. He easily won the election. Farley quickly ingratiated himself with his constituents. He refused fees for his services; he personally delivered marriage licenses; and he knew everyone's name and everyone's problems. And he got to know the power brokers in the New York Democratic party.

Farley was one of the first persons to urge Al Smith* to seek the governorship, and in 1918 he helped Smith get his party's nomination. When Smith won the election, he rewarded Farley by appointing him port warden for New York. By 1919, Farley was chairman of the Rockland County Democratic Committee, and he served as supervisor from 1920 to 1923. In 1922 Farley was elected to the State Assembly. Although Farley was responsible for several reform bills, he was defeated for re-election in 1924 because he had voted against a Prohibition enforcement bill. The next year Governor Smith appointed him to the State Boxing Commission (1925–1933). In 1926 Farley resigned as sales manager for

Universal Gypsum and formed his own company dealing in building materials. In 1929 he merged with five other companies to form the General Building Supply Corporation. He served as president until his appointment as postmaster general in 1933. During these years, Farley was a rising power in the Democratic party.* In 1928 he became secretary of the New York State Democratic Committee and helped manage Franklin D. Roosevelt's* gubernatorial campaign. He had known and admired Roosevelt since 1920. By 1930 Farley was chairman of the State Democratic Committee. When Roosevelt was re-elected governor by a record plurality, Farley hailed him as the next president of the United States.

Farley's political skills and style won many supporters for Roosevelt. Farley had a phenomenal memory for faces and names, was genuinely fond of people, and excelled at "pressing the flesh." Initial meetings were followed up by letters, and he maintained an extensive correspondence. By 1932 Farley and Louis Howe* had laid the ground-work for Roosevelt's nomination, and in 1933 Farley was named postmaster general of the United States and chairman of the Democratic Party National Committee. These positions enabled him to dispense party patronage. He was a firm believer in the spoils system for those jobs not on the merit list, and he also believed in using appointments to maintain party loyalty. He held off making many appointments for months so that he could keep track of how members of Congress voted on New Deal* measures. He kept a card file on each congressman to insure that only the loyal would be rewarded. His policies caused some resentment, but as crusty a curmudgeon as Secretary of the Interior Harold Ickes* praised Farley for playing an honest and fair game.

In the election of 1936,* Farley again managed a flawless campaign for Roosevelt. He correctly forecast that Governor Alf Landon* would carry only Maine and Vermont. Although Farley continued in the positions of postmaster general and chairman of the Democratic National Committee for four more years, his relationship with President Roosevelt cooled after the 1936 election. He found himself at odds with advisers such as Tommy Corcoran.* He was not consulted on the Supreme Court* reorganization plan. He opposed Roosevelt's decision to go after the recalcitrant conservatives within the party in the congressional elections of 1938.* And although he was a major figure in the administration, Farley never really made it into the White House inner circle. Eleanor Roosevelt* told him that the president only felt comfortable relaxing with his social equals. The inference clearly was that Farley was not a social equal. Although estranged, the two men remained on good terms, however.

By 1940 Farley opposed Roosevelt's inclination to seek a third term. He did so both in principle and for personal reasons. Farley himself had ambitions to run for president or perhaps vice-president, and he had informed Roosevelt of his intentions before the president had made up his own mind to run again. When Roosevelt made known his decision to seek the nomination, Farley felt betrayed and never forgave Roosevelt. At the Democratic National Convention, Farley had his name placed in nomination, but Roosevelt easily came away with the prize. Farley soon after resigned from the cabinet and from the Democratic

National Committee. The stated reason was to accept the position of chairman of the board of Coca-Cola Export Corporation, a position he held until 1973. He was not one to bolt the party, however. He supported the Democratic ticket in 1940 and again in 1944, if only perfunctorily. He maintained an active interest in politics until his death on June 9, 1976. (*Current Biography*, 1944, 196–200; *New York Times*, June 10, 1976.)

JOSEPH M. ROWE, JR.

FARM CREDIT ACT OF 1933 As part of the progressive reform movement and the struggle during the 1920s to deal with the farm crisis, the federal government had gradually become more and more involved in the agricultural economy. The Federal Farm Loan Act of 1916, the Agricultural Credits Act of 1923, and the Agricultural Marketing Act of 1929 had all been designed to ease credit and marketing problems. When the Great Depression spread from agriculture to the rest of the economy after 1929, farm problems became even more acute. Commodity prices and farm income dropped, mortgage foreclosures became more common, and many farmers had trouble securing production loans from troubled rural banks. Political insurgency, led by the National Farmers Holiday Association,* was breaking out in the Midwest. Responding to the crisis, Congress passed the Agricultural Adjustment Act* on May 12, 1933 (with its amendment, the Emergency Farm Mortgage Act*), and on June 16 the Farm Credit Act. The Farm Credit Act was drafted by Representative J. Marvin Jones* of Texas and Cornell economist William I. Myers.* Its main purpose was to establish local credit institutions for farmers to ease their working capital and marketing problems. A Central Bank for Cooperatives and twelve regional banks for cooperatives were created to replace the Federal Farm Board and make loans to national farm cooperatives. Those loans had to exceed $500,000 each. The Farm Credit Act also established a Production Credit Corporation with $7.5 million in each Federal Land Bank District. The corporations were designed to promote the formation of Production Credit Associations—groups of ten or more farmers which could borrow from the Federal Intermediate Credit Banks. The programs of the Farm Credit Act were administered by the Farm Credit Administration,* and the Farm Credit Act of 1933 formally institutionalized President Franklin D. Roosevelt's* executive order creating the FCA in March 1933. (W. Gifford Hoag, *The Farm Credit System: A History of Financial Self-Help*, 1976; W. N. Stokes, Jr., *Credit to Farmers. The Story of the Federal Intermediate Credit Banks and Production Credit Associations*, 1973.)

FARM CREDIT ADMINISTRATION To coordinate the federal government's increasingly large agricultural credit complex, President Franklin D. Roosevelt* issued an executive order on March 27, 1933, creating the Farm Credit Administration. Beginning work on May 27, 1933, the Farm Credit Administration assumed control over the Federal Farm Board, Federal Farm Loan Board, Federal Land Banks, Federal Intermediate Credit Banks, RFC* regional agricultural credit corporations, and Department of Agriculture farm loans. The name of the office of the chairman of the Federal Farm Board was changed to the governor of the Farm Credit Administration. Roosevelt appointed Henry Morgenthau, Jr.,* as the first governor of the FCA, with William I. Myers* of Cornell University as deputy governor. When Morgenthau replaced William Woodin* as secretary of the treasury early in 1934, Myers became the new FCA governor. The Farm Credit Administration had four divisions. The Land Bank Division supervised the twelve Federal Land Banks and fifty joint stock land banks. The Intermediate Credit Division headed the twelve Federal Intermediate Credit Banks. The Production Credit Division supervised the operations of the twelve Production Credit Corporations established under the Farm Credit Act.* Finally, the Cooperative Bank Division controlled the Central Bank for Cooperatives and the twelve regional banks for cooperatives.

After only eighteen months of operations, the Farm Credit Administration had refinanced more than 20 percent of all farm mortgages in the United States, saving millions of farms from foreclosures and thousands of rural banks from catastrophic declines in their assets. On a typical day, the FCA would refinance more than 300 mortgages. By 1936 there were a total of 549 Production Credit Associations functioning in the United States and borrowing money from the Federal Intermediate Credit Banks. J. Marvin Jones,* chairman of the House Agriculture Committee, had also sponsored the Crop Loan Act, which became law on February 23, 1934. The Crop Loan Act authorized the FCA to make loans to farmers for crop production and harvesting. Nearly $38 million of the $40 million fund was loaned out. Based on the success of the Home Owners' Loan Corporation,* Congress had also passed the Farm Mortgage Refinancing Act on January 31, 1934, establishing the Federal Farm Mortgage Corporation under the FCA to issue up to $2 billion in bonds and refinance farm debts. By the end of 1940, the agencies directed by the Farm Credit Administration had made loans totaling $6.87 billion. Of that, $3.1 billion was still outstanding on December 31, 1940. A total of $2.55 billion of the outstanding debt consisted of long-term mortgage financing by Federal Land Banks, the Land Bank Commissioner, and joint stock land banks. There was also a total outstanding debt of $381 million in short-term credit extended to farmers for production, emergency relief, and drought loans. William I. Myers returned to Cornell in 1938, and Forrest Frank Hill replaced him as governor of the Farm Credit Administration. In 1939, as part of the federal reorganization effort, the Farm Credit Administration lost its independent status and was transferred to the Department of Agriculture. (W. Gifford Hoag, *The Farm Credit System: A History of Financial Self-Help*, 1976; W. N. Stokes, Jr., *Credit to Farmers. The Story of the Federal Intermediate Credit Banks and Production Credit Associations*, 1973.)

FARMER-LABOR PARTY The Farmer-Labor party was founded in 1919 by John Fitzpatrick, president of the Chicago Federation of Labor. Its first national chairperson was Edward N. Nockels, and its major objective was to create a new third party based on a strong labor movement and socialist economic principles. In 1920 the party nominated Parley P. Christensen of Utah for president. Reflecting its mixed agrarian-industrial background, the Farmer-Labor party advocated free coinage of silver, unemployment and old-age insurance, immigration restriction, massive public works construction, a five-year moratorium on mortgage foreclosures, public ownership of the railroads and public utilities, higher income taxes on the rich, a $1.00 per hour minimum wage and six-hour workday, government regulation of the stock exchanges, and tariff reductions. In the election, which Republican Warren G. Harding won handily, Christensen earned only 189,339 votes, about 1 percent of the total.

Communists took control of the Farmer-Labor party at the national level in 1921, and in the process many socialists, labor leaders, and social welfare advocates defected. The party, which had at least a recognizable following in the upper Midwest, disintegrated in the 1920s, with only the Farmer-Labor party of Minnesota surviving. It specifically had been organized in 1920 from the fusion of organized city workers and remnants of the Nonpartisan League.* The Nonpartisan League, a minor group in the Midwest, appealed to unhappy farmers and provided the nucleus for Minnesota Farmer-Laborites. It also drew substantial support from Minnesota Democrats. In 1922, when its statewide ticket for governor lost by a narrow margin, the Farmer-Labor party elected Henrik Shipstead* to the United States Senate, and in a 1923 special election, it also put Magnus Johnson in the Senate.

Throughout the 1920s, the Minnesota Farmer-Labor party managed to keep its two main factions in line, even though the movement was dominated by agrarian demands. With the coming of the Great Depression, the labor wing of the party became more influential and urban; industrial issues took precedence. Governor Floyd Olson,* elected in 1930 and re-elected in 1932 and 1934, kept a balance between the two factions. Olson generally admired Franklin D. Roosevelt* and the New Deal.* He viewed the NRA* as the only viable plan he had seen to end the depression and accepted the AAA,* even though he would have preferred a more aggressive farm program based on price-fixing and licensing of processors. But he also felt the New Deal was too conservative and not doing enough to solve the depression. So he specifically advocated a state income tax, mortgage moratoriums, unemployment and old-age insurance and publicly-owned electrical power, and generally a move toward more government ownership of the basic means of production and distribution.

The Farmer-Labor party of Minnesota formed an alliance with Roosevelt in 1934. In supporting the Farmer-Labor party, President Roosevelt wrote to his political organizer and Postmaster General James Farley:* "In Minnesota, keep hands off—don't encourage opposition to Shipstead and Olson." Both men were opposed by regular Democrats, but they won easily. Although openly critical of the New Deal, the Farmer-Labor party reciprocated and endorsed Roosevelt in 1936. Throughout the 1930s, the Farmer-Labor party remained the main opposition of the Minnesota Republican party in state elections as the Democratic party declined to third-party status. The Farmer-Labor candidates won each of the gubernatorial elections from 1930 through 1936, but Floyd Olson died in 1936. The Farmer-Labor party decline began in 1938 when Harold Stassen, the Republican "boy-wonder," won the governor's election by defeating Farmer-Laborite Elmer Benson.* By 1944 the party was joined by the Democrats to form the new Democratic-Farmer-Labor party of Minnesota. (Murray S. Stedman and Susan W. Stedman, *Discontent at the Polls: A Study of Farmers and Labor Parties, 1827–1948*, 1967.)

E. LARRY DICKENS

FARM MORTGAGE MORATORIUM ACT OF 1935 (See FEDERAL FARM BANKRUPTCY ACT OF 1934.)

FARM MORTGAGE REFINANCING ACT OF 1934 (See FARM CREDIT ADMINISTRATION.)

FARM SECURITY ADMINISTRATION Because of the political activism of the Southern Tenant Farmers' Union,* the problems of farm poverty became more publicly recognized in the 1930s than ever before. The main effort of the New Deal* to assist poor farmers came in 1935 with the creation of the Resettlement Administration.* Rexford Guy Tugwell,* one of the original "brain trust,"* headed the Resettlement Administration, and he developed programs for land utilization and improvement, resettlement, and rehabilitation for tenant farmers and sharecroppers. Because of Tugwell's vocal sympathy for the plight of poor farmers as well as his public support for national economic planning, he proved too controversial and had to resign in January 1937. President Franklin D. Roosevelt* had already established the president's Special Committee on Farm Tenancy,* and early in 1937 they recommended a comprehensive federal assault on rural poverty through a program of land ownership, rehabilitation, and use of farm cooperatives. The Bankhead-Jones Farm Tenancy Act of 1937* authorized low-interest loans to tenants, farm laborers, and small landowners for the purchase of farms. Still, many people in the administration were convinced that more would have to be done, so later in 1937 Secretary of Agriculture Henry A. Wallace* established the Farm Security Administration to supervise the programs of the Resettlement Administration and the new farm ownership program established by the Bankhead-Jones Act. Will W. Alexander,* head of the Resettlement Administration after Tugwell left, became the first administrator of the Farm Security Administration.

The constituency of the FSA consisted of the rural poor portrayed in Erskine Caldwell's* *Tobacco Road* and John Steinbeck's* *The Grapes of Wrath*. One of the major criticisms liberals had leveled at the Agricultural Adjustment Administration* was that its programs had actually increased the suffering of the rural, landless poor. The Resettlement Administration and Farm Security

Administration had been designed to address that problem by focusing their resources on the chronically poor in rural areas. But because the FSA had been created by executive order with no legislative authority beyond the loan provisions of the Bankhead-Jones Act and because it represented only poor people, it had little political clout in the New Deal and was vulnerable to conservative criticism.

The Farm Security Administration sponsored a number of programs for the rural poor. The Rural Rehabilitation Program was designed to help farm families become self-sustaining. The FSA extended rehabilitation loans to small farmers to increase their productivity through purchases of equipment, fertilizer, livestock, and land. The average loan was $240 per family in 1937 and $600 per family by 1940, and by 1946 the FSA had made 893,000 rehabilitation loans. The Rural Rehabilitation Programs also made grants to poor families suffering through natural disasters. Those averaged about $20 per family. The Farm Debt Adjustment Program helped debt-burdened farmers adjust their cost of operations. By bringing farmers and their creditors together, the FSA helped extend and refinance obligations. Occasionally, the FSA also made loans to assist this process. By early 1944 the Farm Debt Adjustment Program had completed 187,272 cases of debt adjustment. The Farm Security Administration also made loans to help in the formation of farm cooperatives. Also, between 1938 and 1945, the Farm Security Administration gave $292 million in loans under the Bankhead-Jones Act to farm families to help them purchase land. The Resettlement Program, administered by the Resettlement Administration, assisted 15,000 poor farm families by building 164 resettlement projects. The FSA purchased the land and subdivided it among poor families participating in the program. Each participant had the option to purchase the farm given to them on a forty-year mortgage. The resettlement programs accounted for only about 10 percent of the FSA budget. The FSA also operated ninety-five camps for migrant laborers capable of housing 75,000 people. Finally, the FSA's Rehabilitation Division sponsored a series of medical cooperatives for poor people. By 1942 more than 785 of them were operating in forty-one states, and there were 221 dental cooperatives as well.

After the outbreak of World War II, criticism of the Farm Security Administration grew especially bitter. The American Farm Bureau Federation* opposed the FSA's attempt to make tenants and migrant laborers more independent because it would eliminate a cheap labor pool. The American Medical Association opposed the cooperatives because they undermined physician fees, and grain elevators opposed the FSA cooperative program because it undermined their rental fees. Even many of the FSA's clients resented the bureaucratic paternalism of the agency. Finally, congressional conservatives viewed the agency as a liberal attempt to redistribute wealth in the United States. Beginning in 1941, appropriations for the Farm Security Administration declined each year, and in 1946 Congress created the Farmers Home Administration to take over FSA programs, liquidate outstanding loan obligations, and terminate loans to FSA cooperatives. (Sidney Baldwin, *Politics and Poverty: The Rise and Decline of the Farm Security Administration*, 1968; D. Clayton Brown, ''The Farm Security Administration,'' in Donald R. Whitnah, *Government Agencies*, 1983.)

FECHNER, ROBERT Robert Fechner, labor leader and director of the Civilian Conservation Corps,* was born in Chattanooga, Tennessee, on March 22, 1876. He attended public schools at Macon and Griffin, Georgia, until he was fifteen years old, after which he worked as a magazine and candy vender on trains. During those years he managed to fit in a few months of training at the Georgia Institute of Technology. At the age of sixteen he became a machinist's apprentice for the Georgia Central Railroad and four years later was an itinerant machinist (''boomer''), working in mines and in smelters in Mexico and in Central and South America. Late in the 1890s, Fechner returned to Savannah, Georgia, and became active in labor union activities. From 1913 to 1933 he served as an executive officer of the International Association of Machinists.

Franklin D. Roosevelt* and his secretary, Louis Howe,* became acquainted with Fechner during World War I, when Roosevelt was assistant secretary of the navy and Fechner was serving in Washington, D.C., as an adviser on labor policy. Roosevelt was impressed by Fechner's skill and patience in negotiating the settlement of the Boston and Maine Railroad strike during the summer of 1917. In early 1933 Roosevelt and Howe, wanting to offset the opposition of William Green* and the AFL* to the Civilian Conservation Corps, decided that they needed a labor leader to head the agency and that Fechner was the man for the job.

Although Fechner's six years as director of the CCC were generally successful, he had his share of difficulties. In early 1933 he rejected an education plan for the corps submitted by W. Frank Persons,* director of selection, but under continuing pressure from the federal commissioner of education and from state selection agencies, Fechner agreed to a modified plan of voluntary classes which would not conflict with working hours. He never retreated from his insistence that the CCC was chiefly a work relief and conservation agency and that education must be secondary.

Fechner was also harassed by complaints from within the administration and from Congress. Louis Howe created an embarrassment by authorizing the purchase of 200,000 ''toilet kits'' for the corps without competitive bidding. Harry Hopkins,* director of the WPA,* argued that the cost of camp operation was too high and once claimed that if he had the CCC camps, he could operate them for a fraction of the money Fechner was spending. Harold Ickes,* secretary of the interior, complained that Fechner was ''uncooperative,'' that the number of camps allotted to his department was too small, and that, in fact, the director's office ought to be abolished. Attracting wider attention was the issue of military training for the CCC, with some army officers and congressmen strongly advocating a training program, especially after the outbreak of war in Europe. Fechner disagreed, and in December 1939 he told the House Labor Committee that if it became necessary to build up army reserves, it should be done in a program exclusively for military training and not by attempting "to militarize what is essentially a civilian conservation corps."

In 1940, however, Congress approved non-combatant training for the CCC, but by then the organization had a new director, James J. McEntee,* Fechner's friend and labor union associate who had been assistant director of the corps from its beginning. In December 1939 Fechner, whose health had been bad for months, suffered a severe heart attack, and he died on December 31, 1939. (John A. Salmond, *The Civilian Conservation Corps, 1933–1942: A New Deal Case Study*, 1967.)

JOHN PAYNE

FEDERAL ALCOHOL ADMINISTRATION In its special session following the election of 1932,* Congress passed the Twenty-First Amendment* to the Constitution which repealed the Eighteenth Amendment and Prohibition. Utah was the thirty-sixth state to ratify the amendment, and its passage of the Amendment on December 5, 1933, formally ended a controversial issue in American history. By Executive Order No. 6474 on December 5, 1933, President Franklin D. Roosevelt,* using authority granted him by the National Industrial Recovery Act,* established the Federal Alcohol Control Administration, with John H. Choate of the Treasury Department as chairman. The Federal Alcohol Control Administration was used to regulate the alcohol industry through its NRA* code authorities. To guarantee cooperation with the NRA, distillers, importers, and wholesalers had to acquire operating permits from the Federal Alcohol Control Administration. This federal regulation of the alcohol industry came to an end when the Supreme Court* invalidated the NRA in May 1935. So on August 29, 1935, Congress passed the Federal Alcohol Administration Act, abolishing the Federal Alcohol Control Administration and creating in its place the Federal Alcohol Administration. The Federal Alcohol Administration regulated the alcohol industry until 1940, when Reorganization Plan No. 3 abolished it and transferred its functions to the Internal Revenue Service. (*U. S. Government Organizations Manual*, 1973.)

FEDERAL ANTI-LYNCHING BILL During the 1930s the most important goal for civil rights activists was passage of a federal anti-lynching bill. Its roots went back to 1922 when an anti-lynching bill was defeated in Congress by a southern filibuster. Although lynching declined after 1926, there was a resurgence with the Great Depression, with over sixty blacks hanged or shot between 1930 and 1934. Alarmed at the increase in lynchings, the NAACP* drafted a federal anti-lynching bill in 1933. It was sponsored in Congress by Senators Edward Costigan* and Robert Wagner.* President Franklin D. Roosevelt* often denounced lynching, but he did not make the anti-lynching bill a priority. He feared that southern committee chairmen would kill his economic proposals. The anti-lynching bill was also supported by almost a dozen northern governors. Even with this support, it had no chance in 1934.

In 1935 Wagner and Costigan reintroduced it to Congress. By late April the bill had reached the Senate floor with a favorable vote from the Judiciary Committee. Supporters expected a filibuster and got one. Josiah Bailey* of North Carolina denounced the bill as an attack against states' rights. Hugo Black* of Alabama called it an anti-labor bill, and James F. Byrnes* of South Carolina characterized it as unconstitutional. As the filibuster dragged on, Roosevelt worried that the rest of his legislative program might be compromised. He also expressed doubts about its constitutionality. William E. Borah* of Idaho delivered the final blow to the bill in a Senate speech attacking it. The Senate voted to adjourn without considering a motion to bring the bill up. The bill was finally abandoned in February 1938. (Arthur M. Schlesinger, Jr., *The Age of Roosevelt. Vol. III. The Politics of Upheaval, 1935–1936*, 1960.)

MICHAEL DENNIS

FEDERAL ANTI-PRICE DISCRIMINATION ACT OF 1936 Under many of the NRA codes, wholesalers and independent retailers had enjoyed protection against chain store buying power. In order to keep their costs low, chain stores were able to approach manufacturers directly and purchase large volumes of goods at very low prices. Very often the retail prices they sold their products for were lower than the wholesale prices small businessmen and wholesalers had to pay. When the *Schechter** decision overturned the National Industrial Recovery Act* in 1935, the codes protecting wholesalers from chain store buying power were also eliminated. Senator Joseph Robinson* of Arkansas and Representative Wright Patman* of Texas then sponsored legislation to replace that code protection with statutory authority. Signed by President Franklin D. Roosevelt* on June 20, 1936, the Federal Anti-Price Discrimination Act prohibited price discrimination by manufacturers on behalf of large chain stores. It also prohibited discounts, rebates, and excessive selling allowances. The law empowered the Federal Trade Commission* to investigate and abolish any price discrimination tending to reduce competition.

Although the Federal Anti-Price Discrimination Act spoke in Brandeisian terms of the importance of protecting competition and small businessmen, it also had the support of the United States Wholesale Grocers Association, a group threatened by direct chain buying from manufacturers. In one sense, the act was the culmination of a struggle between chain stores and large wholesalers. Nor was the act an integral part of the "Little NRA".* Although it was passed in the wake of the *Schechter* decision, it really had little active support from the Roosevelt administration beyond the political advantages accruing from rhetorical support of small businessmen and lip-service to the idea of competition. (Arthur M. Schlesinger, Jr., *The Age of Roosevelt. Vol. III. The Politics of Upheaval, 1935–1936*, 1960.)

FEDERAL ART PROJECT Like the other artistic and professional programs of "Federal One,"* the Federal Art Project was an integral part of the Works Progress Administration.* And like the other projects, the FAP was a symbol of the New Deal's* commitment to cultural democracy. As the depression grew more serious in 1930 and 1931, museums and artists' organizations began sponsoring "unemployed exhibitions" for destitute artists. Also, some states sponsored relief programs for unemployed artists. While head of the New York Temporary Emergency Relief Administration, Harry Hopkins* organized evening art classes and paid the teachers out of relief funds. The Federal Emergency Relief Administration,* Civil Works Administration,* Public Works of Art Project,* and the Treasury Relief Art Project* were all early New Deal experiments in work relief for artists, and all of them enjoyed the enthusiastic support of Franklin D. Roosevelt* and Eleanor Roosevelt.* When the Works Progress Administration was established in 1935, the Federal Art Project began as part of Federal One, and Holger Cahill* was named director.

With regional field offices throughout the country, the Federal Art Project proved to be an enduring success. By November 1935 the Federal Art Project employed 1,893 persons, and that increased to 3,190 in December and over 6,000 in March 1936. The number of employees fluctuated periodically between those ranges depending on federal appropriations. Because of its ability to accommodate itself to local tastes and needs, the Federal Art Project enjoyed almost immediate success and public acceptance. More than 50 percent of Federal Art Project employees were directly engaged in producing works of art; 10 to 25 percent worked in art education projects throughout the country; and perhaps 10 percent worked in art research, of which the Index of American Design was the most important result. By 1938 the Federal Art Project had produced more than 42,000 easel paintings and, influenced by the Mexican mural style of Diego Rivera and Jose Orozco, more than 1,100 murals on public buildings. There were also large numbers of sculptures, silk-screenings, posters, and graphic arts works. The Index of American Design was a research project which eventually produced 20,000 photographic reproductions and classifications of a wide variety of American art, paintings, sculptures, handicrafts, and folk art. The index recorded the country's "usable past" and helped popularize American folk art. As part of its art education work, the Federal Art Project established hundreds of community art centers serving tens of thousands of Americans; sponsored hundreds of individual and group exhibitions; and provided hundreds of communities with original works of art. It was a great success.

When the Emergency Relief Appropriation Act of 1939* eliminated much support for the Federal One projects and required 25 percent local sponsorship on all programs, the Federal Art Project was better able than any of the others to secure local funding. Its reputation in local communities was that good. Cahill stayed with the FAP until 1943, and even throughout World War II the project managed to stay busily employed, producing a wide range of poster and propaganda art for the armed services. (Richard D. McKinzie, *The New Deal for Artists*, 1973.)

FEDERAL BUREAU OF INVESTIGATION Until 1933 the Federal Bureau of Investigation was a small and rather obscure agency within the Department of Justice. Attorney General Homer Cummings,* however, maintained a close working relationship with FBI director J. Edgar Hoover. Hoover was also close to White House aide Edwin "Pa" Watson* and press secretary Stephen Early.* Under the auspices of the New Deal,* the FBI became a powerful federal bureaucracy with excellent media connections. To deal with the problem of inept local law enforcement officials and the sensational and sometimes popular crimes of people like Kate "Ma" Barker and Charles "Pretty Boy" Floyd, President Franklin D. Roosevelt* implemented a major expansion in FBI power. In May 1934 Congress approved an administration anti-crime package. The Fugitive Felon Act prohibited suspected criminals from crossing state lines to escape prosecution; the Anti-Racketeering Act prohibited extortion through the telephone or mail; and the National Firearms Act gave the FBI the right to collect taxes on weapons, require registration of firearms, and restrict the importation of weapons. At the same time, the attorney general promoted a vigorous public relations campaign to glorify the "G-men" and demythologize the most popular criminals of the 1930s. Finally, the FBI budget increased from $2.9 million in 1933 to more than $6 million in 1936. By the late 1930s, as the fascist threat abroad appeared more real, the major focus of the FBI came to be on internal subversion. That orientation increased dramatically during World War II. (Kenneth O'Reilly, "A New Deal for the FBI: The Roosevelt Administration, Crime Control, and National Security," *Journal of American History*, LXIX:638–658, 1982.)

FEDERAL COMMUNICATIONS COMMISSION In 1933 President Franklin D. Roosevelt* created a government commission, which included Senator Clarence Dill of Washington and Representative Sam Rayburn* of Texas, to study the problem of regulating communications services in the United States. He was concerned about competition within the industry, lack of service to rural areas, and the technical advances underway. The commission reported in January 1934 and recommended creation of a federal regulatory commission to reduce rates by regulating profits, overhead charges, and inter-company charges; prevent discrimination; control exclusive contracts; regulate annual depreciation charges; prevent the watering of stocks; extend services into rural areas; and regulate mergers between communications companies. President Roosevelt forwarded the recommendations to Congress in February 1934, and under the leadership of Senator Dill and Congressman Rayburn, Congress passed them as the Communications Act of 1934 on May 31. Roosevelt signed the measure on June 19, 1934, creating the Federal Communications Commission.

The Federal Communications Commission replaced the Federal Radio Commission, which had been established in 1927, and consolidated the relevant duties of the Interstate Commerce Commission,* the post office, and the Department of Commerce into one federal agency. The FCC was responsible for regulating interstate and foreign communications by radio, telegraph, wire, or cable. The commission was also charged with the orderly development and operation of broadcast services, promotion of efficient national telephone and telegraph services at reasonable rates, and coordination of all licensed communications services for national defense through the Emergency Broadcast System. The FCC was composed of seven members appointed by the president and confirmed by the Senate. Its principal operating sections were the Common Carrier Bureau, to regulate foreign and interstate communications services and rates; the Broadcast Bureau, to license and regulate radio stations; the Safety and Special Radio Services Bureau, to license and regulate aviation, police, fire, taxi, National Guard, and amateur facilities; and the Field Engineering Bureau to carry out monitoring and investigation, as well as licensing examinations for operators. The FCC began with a budget of $1,146,885 and 442 employees, and they were supervising a communications network in the United States consisting of more than 800 commercial and educational broadcast stations as well as approximately 51,000 special broadcast facilities. (Erik Barnouw, *The Golden Web: A History of Broadcasting in the United States, 1933 to 1953*, 1968; *Dictionary of American History*, III:1–2, 1976.)

CHARLES E. DARBY, JR.

FEDERAL CROP INSURANCE ACT OF 1938 The idea of private crop insurance had surfaced in the late nineteenth century when a number of private companies tried to protect farmers against losses caused by natural disasters. Well into the 1920s all of the experiments in private crop insurance were shortlived. In the 1920s Senator Charles McNary* began promoting the idea of federal crop insurance and held a special investigation on the question in 1923. In the early 1930s, after creation of the Commodity Credit Corporation* and the drought of 1934, the idea of federal crop insurance gained ground, especially when Secretary of Agriculture Henry Wallace* linked it to his "ever-normal granary."* More drought in 1936 gave it added momentum, and in the election of 1936,* both Franklin D. Roosevelt* and Alf Landon* endorsed the idea. Early in 1937 the President's Committee on Crop Insurance, headed by Wallace, called for a federal crop insurance program covering only wheat. Senator James Pope* of Idaho introduced a crop insurance bill drafted along the lines of the committee's recommendations, and one year later the Federal Crop Insurance Act was passed as Title V of the Agricultural Adjustment Act of 1938.*

The act established a Federal Crop Insurance Corporation within the Department of Agriculture. The FCIC had a capital stock of $100 million, with an annual treasury appropriation of $6 million for operating costs. Insurance was authorized for wheat in 1939, with growers insured for 50 to 75 percent of their recorded average yield against losses from natural phenomena. Local committees of the AAA* administered the program. Participation in the program increased steadily from 165,775 in 1939 to 371,392 in 1941. Because of poor yield records on many farms, the program proved expensive, with indemnities exceeding premiums by a rate of 1.52 to 1.68. Although President Roosevelt vetoed a bill in 1940 adding cotton to the crop insurance program, he signed an identical bill in 1941. (Randall A. Kramer, "Federal Crop Insurance, 1938–1982," *Agricultural History*, LVII:181–200, 1983.)

FEDERAL CROP INSURANCE CORPORATION (See FEDERAL CROP INSURANCE ACT OF 1938.)

FEDERAL DANCE PROJECT Hallie Flanagan,* director of the Federal Theatre Project,* recognized the symbiotic relationship between the theater and the dance and was committed to creating a dance unit in the FTP. Modern dance pioneer Helen Tamiris, inspired by the idea of exposing the masses to modern dance in concert halls or theaters, travelled to Washington, D.C., to discuss the necessity of a dance unit with Harry Hopkins,* director of the WPA.* Don Oscar Becque, the first director of the Dance Project, and Fanya Geltman, a dancer in New York, were also claimed as important figures in the beginning of the unit. Through the joint efforts of Flanagan, Becque, Tamiris, and Geltman, the FTP authorized the creation of three dance units in January 1936. With a budget of $150,000, the dance units were to hire 185 dancers at weekly salaries of $23.86 each and were to produce eight works in six months. Because relations were strained between dancers and theater officials in the FTP, Helen Tamiris, president of the Dance Association, requested that Hallie Flanagan create an independent Federal Dance Project, and the WPA complied in March 1936, naming Don Oscar Becque as director and Helen Tamiris, Doris Humphrey, Charles Weidman, Felecia Sorel, and Gluck-Sandor as staff choreographers.

Problems soon developed. Cuts in personnel, discrimination charges against the Audition Board, and questions of professional status of board members were a few of the problems that resulted in production delays and demonstrations by dancers. On April 5, 1936, eleven dancers were arrested for disturbing the peace while picketing outside the Dance Project's office demanding the original quota be met by hiring 185 dancers. Dancers were successful in stirring public sympathy as audiences joined the performers in an all-night sit-down strike following the performances of "Candide," choreographed by Charles Weidman, and "How Long Brethren," choreographed by Helen Tamiris. Most of the turmoil in administrative rulings fell on the shoulders of director Don Oscar Becque. His orders to re-audition dancers previously hired ignited the dancers again; and though they submitted to his request, the dancers began working on plans for Becque's dismissal.

Throughout 1936 pressures mounted on Becque. Critics charged that the Dance Project staff was not professionally trained and that modern dance received preferential treatment over ballet. In December 1936 the Audition Board of the the Dance Project resigned, accusing Becque of dictating orders to pass over any dancer not representing the modern or interpretive schools of dance. On December 24, 1936, Don Oscar Becque resigned from office. The administrator of the New York Theater Project became production manager in his place.

One problem encountered by the Federal Dance Project developed through the availability of free dance classes offered by the government. Private studio teachers violently opposed the program as a threat to their business. Although the Works Progress Administration released a statement expressing their intention of not wanting to harm private enterprise and promising to abort all competitive programs, private dance teachers remained quite threatened with the work of the FDP.

Despite the problems, the Federal Dance Project made an enormous contribution to the development of the arts in the United States. Low admission prices allowed thousands of people to experience dance as a new medium of enjoyment. Free dance lessons actually allowed many people to experience dance themselves. The FDP was also instrumental in the development of modern dance, permitting it to prosper during very difficult years. Large audiences gathered to view modern productions, proving its existence to be a force in the dance world. Choreographic output instilled in many a sense of national pride as audiences viewed productions reflecting themes of Americana. Myra Kinch's "American Exodus" depicted the pioneers crossing the plains, and Helen Tamiris' "How Long Brethren" was based on Lawrence Gelherdt's "Negro Songs of Protest." Ruth Page and Bentley Stone, coordinators of the Chicago unit, produced "Frankie and Johnny" in 1938, and Katherine Dunham's choreography "L'Ag 'ya" depicted Caribbean ethnic and folk themes. Political problems eventually spelled the end of the Federal Dance Project. Dancers and dances alike came under political scrutiny as Martin Dies* of Texas (chairman of the House Committee on Un-American Activities) and Clifton Woodrum* of Virginia (chairman of the House Appropriations Committee) charged them with being pro-Communist. In order to alleviate any ammunition that might discredit Franklin D. Roosevelt's* administration in 1940, the Emergency Relief Appropriation Act of 1939* completely cut funding for the Federal Theatre Project, and hence the Federal Dance Project. (Richard Kraus, *History of the Dance*, 1969; Kathleen Ann Lally, "History of the Federal Dance Theater," Ph.D. Thesis, Texas Women's University, 1978.)

PATTY L. HASELBARTH

FEDERAL DEPOSIT INSURANCE CORPORATION Of all the agencies to emerge from the New Deal,* none has been as enduring or as universally accepted as the Federal Deposit Insurance Corporation. During the 1920s, because of the problems of undercapitalization, overextension, conflicting federal and state supervision, and the prevailing depression in American agriculture, more than 5,600 banks failed, tying up more than $2 billion in assets and imposing financial ruin on large numbers of depositors. When the stock market crashed in 1929 and securities values began their long descent, the value of bank assets dropped precipitously, triggering public panic in 1931 and 1932. Several thousand more banks closed. By then, the problem of closed banks had become a political as well as an economic issue, and public demand for some solution grew intense. Even when closed banks had some assets left, the process of receivership was long and complicated, sequestering people's money for years. Because private bankers vehemently opposed any federal deposit guarantee and state banking departments did not have the resources to implement any meaningful program, people began turning to the federal government for relief. By 1932 a number of deposit guarantee proposals had been introduced to Congress.

The two most meaningful bills came from Senator Carter Glass* of Virginia and Congressman Henry Steagall* of Alabama. Glass basically opposed the idea of deposit guarantees but did call for the establishment of a liquidation corporation, a federal agency to expedite receiverships so that depositors would be able to get some of their funds quickly from closed banks. Contributions from the Federal Reserve System and member banks would finance the liquidation corporation. Steagall, on the other hand, wanted a government corporation to do more than just expedite receiverships. Sensing the political atmosphere, he proposed creation of a government corporation which would actually guarantee an individual account up to a predetermined maximum. It would be an insurance program. Member banks would pay a premium based on the value of their total deposits and those funds, along with some federal money, would then be available to pay off the claims of depositors against a closed bank. In Steagall's view, such a corporation would not only prevent tens of thousands of individual financial tragedies each year but would also protect the money supply and banking system against public panic and "runs" on private institutions. Assured of getting their money even if a bank closed, depositors would not be so inclined to demand their funds simultaneously and destroy the bank in a liquidity crisis. Because of the opposition of President Herbert Hoover,* the reluctance of Carter Glass, and the outright hatred of most bankers for the idea, the deposit guarantee of Henry Steagall did not get off the ground. Even the more moderate proposal for a liquidation corporation stalled. The bill became entangled in the partisan politics of the months preceding Franklin D. Roosevelt's* inauguration.

But the banking panic of 1932–1933, the bank holiday,* the overwhelmingly Democratic Congress, and the enormous public demand for some kind of deposit guarantee to protect people immediately resurrected the idea. Both Glass and Steagall introduced banking measures to the Democratic Congress. Glass' bill did not provide for deposit guarantees but did contain much of what would become the Banking Act of 1933.* Steagall's bill called for creation of a Federal Deposit Insurance Corporation. A Senate-House conference committee joined both bills, and Roosevelt signed the Banking Act of 1933 into law on June 16,

1933. The Federal Deposit Insurance Corporation was one of the most significant features of the bill.

Under provisions of the Banking Act of 1933, a Temporary Deposit Insurance Fund, with $150 million from the federal government, would begin operations on January 1, 1934. Only banks certified as sound would be eligible to join, and individual accounts would be insured up to a maximum of $2,500. All national banks had to join the program, and all state banks joining the program would have to become part of the Federal Reserve System by July 1, 1936. On July 1, 1934, the permanent Federal Deposit Insurance Corporation would replace the Temporary Deposit Insurance Fund. Subsequent legislation in 1934 extended the life of the Temporary Deposit Insurance Fund by one year, raised the insurance on individual accounts to $5,000, and postponed compulsory Federal Reserve membership for insured state banks until July 1, 1937. President Roosevelt appointed Leo Crowley* to head the FDIC, and after a crash program of RFC* loans and investments to approximately 2,000 weak banks in 1933, the insurance program went into effect on January 1, 1934. The FDIC itself started up on July 1, 1935.

The Federal Deposit Insurance Corporation was an unparalleled success. By 1935 more than 14,400 banks had joined the corporation, and bank failures had dropped to sixty-one in 1934 and thirty-two in 1935. Never again would they exceed eighty-five in a year. Although the requirement that all FDIC banks join the Federal Reserve System was postponed several times and finally eliminated in 1939, the FDIC had imposed a measure of unity on the dual banking system, helped eliminate depositor panic and the rash of bank failures, and protected the money supply from catastrophic fluctuations. (Helen M. Burns, *The American Banking Community and New Deal Banking Reforms: 1933–1935*, 1974; James S. Olson, *The Reconstruction Finance Corporation, 1932–1940*, Ph.D. dissertation, SUNY, at Stony Brook, 1972.)

FEDERAL EMERGENCY RELIEF ACT OF 1933 In July 1932 the Herbert Hoover* administration and Congressional Democrats passed the Emergency Relief and Construction Act authorizing the Reconstruction Finance Corporation* to loan up to $300 million at 3 percent interest to states and their political subdivisions for relief payments to the poor and unemployed. Although controversy surrounded the program, the $300 million fund was exhausted by March 1933. When President Franklin D. Roosevelt* took over the White House, his first weeks in office were consumed with the banking and agricultural crises. But with nearly 15 millon people out of work, demands for more federal relief spending could not long be ignored. Prominent United States senators like Edward Costigan* of Colorado, Robert Wagner* of New York, and Robert La Follette, Jr.,* of Wisconsin were demanding a new relief program, as were leading social workers throughout the country. Harry Hopkins,* head of the New York Temporary Emergency Relief Administration, and William Hodson, head of the New York City Welfare Council, met with Secretary of Labor Frances Perkins,* and she arranged a meeting for them with President Roosevelt. The president agreed with the request for a national relief system, and La Follette, Wagner, and Costigan introduced an administration-backed measure to Congress. The Federal Emergency Relief Act was passed on May 12, 1933. The law created a Federal Emergency Relief Administration* with $500 million to make grants, not loans, to states, which would then distribute the money. (Barabara Blumberg, *The New Deal and the Unemployed: The View from New York City*, 1979.)

FEDERAL EMERGENCY RELIEF ADMINISTRATION On May 12, 1933, Congress created the Federal Emergency Relief Administration. The act empowered President Franklin D. Roosevelt* to spend $500 million, with $1.00 of federal assistance for every $3.00 of local money. The FERA gave direct cash grants to city and state work relief projects. The RFC* funded the program.

Roosevelt appointed Harry L. Hopkins* to direct the FERA. At the time of Hopkins' appointment, there were approximately 15 million unemployed people in the United States, about 25 percent of the work force. Roosevelt urged Hopkins to relieve suffering as quickly as possible and to ignore local and state politicians who attempted to control relief patronage.

Hopkins succeeded brilliantly in adhering to Roosevelt's first command, appointing people of great ability to help him. Such assistants as Aubrey Williams,* Jacob Baker, Corrington Gill, and Pierce Williams stayed with Hopkins throughout much of his career as a relief administrator. In the field, people like Howard O. Hunter, Allan Johnstone, and Lorena Hickok* served Hopkins well. They divided the FERA into four principal divisions. The Works Division initiated federal projects and supplemented existing state or local projects. After Roosevelt ended the Civil Works Administration,* the Works Division began paving the way for the Works Progress Administration.* The Division of Relations with the States handled daily operations. Supervised by Aubrey Williams, it made policy decisions affecting the states. The Division of Research, Statistics, and Finance collected information and handled the money, while the Division of Rural Rehabilitation removed desperate farm families from sub-marginal land and helped rebuild their agricultural operations on relatively fertile soil.

In addition to helping destitute farmers, the FERA became the first federal relief program to assist transients. Since vagrants infrequently found employment on locally-funded and directed projects and since most states naturally wanted to assist their citizens first, the FERA created a special bureau for transients. Millions of migrants found refuge in this special program. As with the Civil Works Administration, the FERA's greatest and most tangible contribution was its work program. It finished over 235,000 projects and at its peak employed nearly 2.5 million workers and aided millions of farmers. Despite some severe criticisms, the FERA succeeded in relieving economic, psychological, and political distress throughout the country.

For Hopkins relieving the distress caused by economic deprivation proved easier than avoiding politics in the dispensation of relief. Although several states required federal attention, the primary example of political interference involved Governor Martin L. Davey* of Ohio. Davey came into office armed with the intention of rewarding his numerous supporters with positions in the Ohio Emergency Relief Administration. After Hopkins ordered a thorough examination of relief in Ohio, the FERA investigators uncovered conclusive evidence proving Davey's aides had been demanding kickbacks from companies with contracts with the Ohio Relief Administration. When Hopkins attempted to stop the corruption and ordered the FERA to initiate federal control over Ohio relief, the governor fought back by threatening to have the Federal Relief administrator jailed when he visited Cleveland. However, when Hopkins came to Ohio, the threat never materialized.

National press coverage given to Hopkins' struggles with Davey, Colorado's Ed Johnson and North Dakota's William Langer enhanced his reputation as an honest, able minister of relief. However, critics disparaged the FERA as an encouragement to laziness and a wasteful use of government funds and resources. By January 1, 1935, the agency had spent over 2 billion dollars on relief and President Franklin D. Roosevelt felt it had become a political liability. Eventually, he proposed to "substitute work for relief" and initiated a massive public employment program (the Works Progress Administration) that offered jobs to 3.5 million destitute workers. But until the WPA became an effective alternative, the FERA kept millions fed and hopes alive during those first, dark days of the New Deal's* experience with the depression. (Edward A. Williams, *Federal Aid for Relief*, 1939.)

J. CHRISTOPHER SCHNELL

FEDERAL FARM BANKRUPTCY ACT OF 1934 The Federal Farm Bankruptcy Act of 1934, also known as the Frazier-Lemke Farm Bankruptcy Act, was the single most important legislative accomplishment of William Lemke,* Republican congressman from North Dakota. Long concerned about the plight of farmers, especially declining commodity prices and land values along with increasing debt burdens, Lemke was determined to bring relief after his election to the House of Representatives as a Republican in 1932. Prominent in the National Farmers' Holiday Association* and supported by the Non-Partisan League,* Lemke marshaled overwhelming support for a farm bankruptcy bill in the Midwest, even though Franklin D. Roosevelt's* administration initially opposed it. The bill Lemke introduced and successfully promoted in Congress involved a modification in bankruptcy laws for farmers whose debts so exceeded the value of their property that their financial outlook was hopeless. It provided for legal machinery in each county to permit an appraisal of the property of a debt-ridden farmer. The federal courts could then scale down the farmer's debts until they compared favorably with the value of his property. He would then be able to continue farming on the same land with the same equipment and chattels. If he succeeded in retiring his debts at the scaled-down figure, the property would be his and all encumbrances against it would be removed. In its final form, the

Federal Farm Bankruptcy Act permitted farmers to repurchase their properties at a newly appraised value with small annual payments, at an interest rate of 1 percent, distributed over a six-year period. If creditors opposed such a settlement, the farmer could retain possession of the land for five years and no foreclosure could occur. The Supreme Court* held the law unconstitutional in 1935 in the *Louisville Joint Stock Land Bank v. Radford** on grounds that it deprived creditors of property without due process of law. Lemke and Lynn J. Frazier* then came back in August 1935 with the Farm Mortgage Moratorium Act of 1935 (Frazier-Lemke Act of 1935). The law provided for a three-year moratorium against seizure for farmers who secured court permission. Debt-ridden farmers were then able to keep possession of their land by paying a fair rental rate determined by the court. (Edward B. Blackorby, *Prairie Rebel. The Public Life of William Lemke*, 1963.)

FEDERAL FARM MORTGAGE CORPORATION (See FARM CREDIT ADMINISTRATION.)

FEDERAL HOUSING ADMINISTRATION The Federal Housing Administration was established under the provisions of the National Housing Act* passed in June 1934. Because nearly one-third of the unemployed had formerly worked in the building trades, President Franklin D. Roosevelt* placed special emphasis on reviving the housing industry. The act was intended to encourage investments in housing construction, provide employment, and increase demand for manufacturing for the housing industry.

The president wanted a federal program to help revive the industry—but without large expenditures and without involving government directly in construction and financing. He appointed a President's Emergency Commission on Housing to investigate ways of stimulating building by private enterprise. Members of the commission included Frank Walker* (chair), Winfield Riefler, John Fahey,* Harry Hopkins,* Frances Perkins,* Averell Harriman, Rexford Tugwell,* Henry Wallace,* and Marriner Eccles.* The group accepted Eccles' and Riefler's draft of a bill setting up the FHA to insure loans made by private institutions to middle-income families that wanted to repair their homes or build new ones. Despite opposition by building and loan associations, which had held a favorable position in the mortgage market, Congress passed the measure.

In addition to insuring financial institutions against losses on improvement and mortgage loans, the act included provisions authorizing the Federal Housing administrator to establish national mortgage associations to buy up mortgages by issuing notes or other obligations. Savings and loan associations and federal home loan banks were insured through the Federal Savings and Loan Insurance Corporation* established under the new law.

By greatly reducing the risks in financing housing, the FHA helped stimulate modernization of existing structures, but new home construction did not increase to the hoped-for extent, and the private sector generally ignored the invitation to establish mortgage associations. Roosevelt appointed businessman James Moffett* to head the FHA, which during his tenure did more to encourage modernization than new home construction. From the beginning, the agency was reluctant to insure mortgages in blighted neighborhoods, especially in the inner city, and to insure rental housing ventures. Its conservative policies, critics charged, helped encourage the exodus from central cities and led to the restrictive covenants that assisted residential segregation. Also, James Moffett was an opponent of public housing projects, fearing they would undermine the construction industry and mortgage markets. His opposition frequently brought him into conflict with such public housing advocates as Senator Robert Wagner* of New York and Secretary of the Interior Harold Ickes.* Not until the late 1930s did the FHA move aggressively into new home construction. Amendments in 1938 to the National Housing Act of 1934 substantially eased down payment requirements on new home financing and increased the FHA financing limit to $3 billion. That number became $4 billion in 1939. Between 1934 and 1940, the FHA helped homeowners repair or modernize 1,544,217 houses. While only 111,474 new homes were financed by the FHA between 1935–1937, more than 383,000 were financed between 1938 and 1940. These were considered small homes. The FHA also specialized in single family home construction, increasing its volume from 220,000 in 1937 to 394,000 in 1940, an amount greater than the construction in 1929. Between June 1934 and December 1940, the FHA extended $4.076 billion in insured loans. Its effect was to reduce the need for second and third mortgages on homes and to make owning a home more affordable to larger numbers of people. (Gertrude S. Fish, *The Story of Housing*, 1979; Mark I. Gelfand, *A Nation of Cities*; Samuel I. Rosenman, ed., *The Public Papers and Addresses of Franklin D. Roosevelt*, VI:530–532, 1941.)

JANE A. ROSENBERG

FEDERAL INTERMEDIATE CREDIT BANK (See FARM CREDIT ACT OF 1933 and FARM CREDIT ADMINISTRATION.)

FEDERAL LAND BANKS (See FARM CREDIT ACT OF 1933 and FARM CREDIT ADMINISTRATION.)

FEDERAL LOAN AGENCY Because of the collapse of the money markets in 1932 and 1933, along with the subsequent reluctance of many banks, savings banks, building and loan associations, and insurance companies to make loans, the federal government was forced to fill the credit void if any economic recovery was to occur and if the poor and unemployed were to find any relief from their mortgage problems. During the Hoover administration the Reconstruction Finance Corporation* and Federal Home Loan Bank System had initiated the large-scale government move into private credit markets, and the programs mushroomed into a multitude of agencies and billions of dollars during the New Deal.* Between 1933 and 1937, the Roosevelt administration approached all of these agencies as temporary measures necessary only until the economic recovery materialized. But when the recession of 1937 and 1938* helped push the administration toward Keynesian spending policies, it also confirmed the suspicions of many that federal government lending programs would be permanent. Ever since 1934 President Franklin D. Roosevelt* had coordinated government lending operations through a loan committee composed of the heads of the major lending agencies. In 1939, after deciding that federal lending activities would be indefinite and that efforts to reorganize and streamline the government programs should be continued, Roosevelt replaced the temporary loan committee with the Federal Loan Agency, naming Jesse H. Jones,* head of the Reconstruction Finance Corporation, as Federal Loan Administrator, and Stewart McDonald,* Federal Housing Administrator, as Deputy Federal Loan Administrator. The Federal Loan Agency supervised the activities of the Reconstruction Finance Corporation, Export-Import Bank,* Federal Housing Administration,* Home Owners' Loan Corporation,* RFC Mortgage Company, Disaster Loan Corporation, Federal National Mortgage Association,* and the Electric Home and Farm Authority.* When Germany invaded and defeated France in 1940, triggering a preparedness campaign in the United States, the domestic lending programs of the Federal Loan Agency were transformed into a new series of government agencies designed to prepare the economy for war. (Jesse H. Jones, *Fifty Billion Dollars*, 1951.)

FEDERAL MUSIC PROJECT The Federal Music Project of the Works Progress Administration* was formed in 1935 to employ, retrain, and rehabilitate unemployed musicians. The music industry was hard-hit by the depression; as many as two-thirds of the nation's professional musicians were unemployed. Pre-depression technological developments in phonographs, radio, and sound motion pictures created an employment crisis in the industry which was intensified by the depression. Music and entertainment were considered luxuries. Attendance at concerts and dances declined; public school music programs faced budgetary cuts; and the demand for private classes almost disappeared. Theater owners introduced sound equipment to reduce overhead, putting additional musicians out of work, while symphonies cut rosters.

The Federal Music Project was an outgrowth of programs developed during the first years of the New Deal* under the Federal Emergency Relief Administration* and the Civil Works Administration.* These agencies were unable to develop effective programs for the sustained, meaningful employment of musicians. The creation of the WPA in 1935 united all emergency public work programs under a single agency. Federal One,* announced in August 1935, included the Federal Music Project. Its primary goal was to provide employment for professional musicians on relief using their training and skills; a secondary goal was to serve the community.

The Federal Music Project was organized into educational and performing units. Project teachers directed choruses, bands, and orchestras, conducted group classes in vocal and instrumental music, and served as directors of amateur community productions and group sings. By March of 1940, these teachers had conducted 1.5 million classes attended by 17.7 million individuals. The performing groups—symphonies, orchestras, concert bands, dance bands, and ensembles—gave public performances in schools, community centers, settlement houses, orphanages, prisons, hospitals, public parks, Civilian Conservation Corps* camps, and rented halls in urban and rural areas. From January 1936 to March 1940, 250,000 performances were heard by an aggregate audience of 159 million. Additional millions heard 14,000 Federal Music Project radio broadcasts. Works by American composers were emphasized in performances, and young directors and composers were encouraged by project programs. Units in several states collected and recorded folk music, and the project provided copying, research, and other services for performing units.

The project was successful. At its peak in 1936, it employed 15,000 musicians; 10,000 musicians were still on the rolls at the beginning of World War II. The services they provided reached millions of Americans and stimulated a nationwide growth in music appreciation as seen by the increased audiences for musical performances, the growth of community orchestras, and the expansion of interest in both public and private music instruction. (Cornelius B. Canon, "The Federal Music Project of the Works Progress Administration: Music in a Democracy," Ph.D. dissertation, University of Minnesota, 1963; William F. McDonald, *Federal Relief Administration and the Arts*, 1969.)

VIRGINIA F. HAUGHTON

FEDERAL NATIONAL MORTGAGE ASSOCIATION Throughout the 1930s, New Dealers had struggled to stimulate the housing industry by liquidating frozen real estate financial markets. Lending institutions were reluctant to make housing loans because the secondary mortgage market was all but dead. To stimulate the construction industry by expanding mortgage credit, President Franklin D. Roosevelt* asked Jesse Jones* of the Reconstruction Finance Corporation* to organize a federal national mortgage association. The National Housing Act of 1934* had provided for the establishment of National Mortgage Associations, and the Federal Housing Administration* had offered to match private capital in buying the preferred stock of the associations. Private bankers wanted nothing to do, however, with the program. They were still too cautious and frightened of another liquidity crisis. So in 1938, at the president's request, Jones established the Federal National Mortgage Association ("Fannie Mae") as a subsidiary of the Reconstruction Finance Corporation. By 1939 Fannie Mae had purchased 26,276 mortgages totaling more than $100 million. Eight years later, those totals had risen to 66,966 FHA-insured mortgages totaling $271,716,894. (Jesse Jones, *Fifty-Billion Dollars*, 1951.)

FEDERAL ONE "Federal One" was a term used to describe Federal Project No. 1 of the Works Progress Administration*—the artistic and professional work relief programs of the Federal Art Project,* Federal Music Project,* Federal Writers' Project,* Federal Theatre Project,* and the Historical Records Survey.* (William F. McDonald, *Federal Relief Administration and the Arts*, 1969.)

FEDERAL POWER ACT (See FEDERAL POWER COMMISSION.)

FEDERAL POWER COMMISSION On June 10, 1920, Congress passed the Federal Water Power Act creating the Federal Power Commission. Its original purpose was to exercise general administrative management of water-power sites and similar installations on navigable rivers, public land, and reservations. It issued licenses and permits for the construction of dams, power facilities, reservoirs, transmission lines, and generators. The Federal Power Commission in the 1920s also regulated the operations of power projects. In 1930 Congress strengthened the FPC, giving it more authority over rates, services, and operations; but until 1935 the commission never made use of its new authority.

During the New Deal,* the FPC acquired new administrative teeth. Title II of the Public Utility Holding Company Act of 1935* amended the Federal Water Power Act of 1920 and renamed it the Federal Power Act. The law gave the Federal Power Commission supervisory power over all electric energy transmitted in interstate commerce regardless of whether the power came from water or fuel sources. The FPC gained major regulatory authority over rates, securities, accounting systems, property, physical operations, and service. The Federal Power Commission was also authorized to assist state power regulatory agencies by providing them with necessary information. Through regional offices, the Federal Power Commission also promoted power pooling projects, conducted surveys on power rates and services, and published comparative rates, helping consumers to discover if the rates of their local public utilities were in line with those of the industry in general. On June 21, 1938, Congress passed the National Gas Act,* giving the FPC regulatory control over natural gas companies engaged in interstate commerce. Before natural gas could be exported or imported, FPC authorization was required. Finally, during the late 1930s, as President Franklin D. Roosevelt* and the Congress became increasingly worried about the outbreak of war and the need to guarantee adequate energy supplies, the authority of the Federal Power Commission increased through executive orders. (Richard Lowitt, "The Federal Power Commission," in Donald R. Whitnah, ed., *Government Agencies*, 1983.)

FEDERAL PRISON INDUSTRIES, INC. For years prisoners in federal penitentiaries had produced a variety of products for use by federal agencies. As the economy declined in the early 1930s, however, many private manufacturers began to protest the prison industries. At the same time, the federal government needed to keep inmates working. After a White House conference in March 1934 to discuss the question, the administration pushed a bill through Congress to create Federal Prison Industries, Inc. The bill passed late in June 1934. On

January 1, 1935, the incorporated federal agency took over all prison manufacturing and greatly diversified it so that no single private industry would suffer. Federal Prison Industries, Inc., concentrated on cotton textiles, shoes, clothing, belts, rubber mats, laundry, printing, dry cleaning, mattresses, and clerical supplies; and much of the private criticism of federal production dissipated. (Samuel I. Rosenman, ed., *The Public Papers and Addresses of Franklin D. Roosevelt*, II:495–498, 1938.)

FEDERAL PROJECT NO. 4 (See SURVEY OF FEDERAL ARCHIVES.)

FEDERAL REAL ESTATE BOARD By the mid-1930s, because of terrible drought conditions in many parts of the country, the federal government found itself taking over large amounts of property, thereby removing it from local tax rolls. Secretary of the Treasury Henry Morgenthau, Jr.,* conducted a study of the problem between 1935 and 1938. By executive order in January 1939, President Franklin D. Roosevelt* established the Federal Real Estate Board. The board's major duties were to survey and carefully monitor all federal property and to consult with all other federal agencies considering any new property acquisitions. The Federal Real Estate Board would inform federal agencies of any suitable, alternative sites already owned by the government and would provide economic impact statements on the tax effects of federal property purchases on local communities. (Samuel I. Rosenman, ed., *The Public Papers and Addresses of Franklin D. Roosevelt*, VIII:87–88, 1941.)

FEDERAL RESERVE BOARD The Federal Reserve Act of 1913 established the Federal Reserve Board and what eventually became twelve regional Federal Reserve Banks to provide some general coordination of monetary policy throughout the country. It was a compromise between the complete centralization of financial power exercised by European central banks and the state of laissez-faire and extreme decentralization existing before 1913. Congress intended the Federal Reserve Board to exercise minimum controls over the money supply by making it "elastic" through discounting eligible securities when presented to the Federal Reserve Banks. Each bank could set the interest rate on discounted securities, subject to the Federal Reserve Board's approval. The law, however, was very vague as to exactly what power the Federal Reserve Board had to change those locally-established rates.

Until 1933 the Federal Reserve Board had not exercized much real influence on the monetary supply. Since its chairman was the secretary of the treasury, the FRB often felt the need to keep interest rates low as a means of making government bond issues more attractive. At the same time, it had to face the conservative interests of the Federal Reserve Bank of New York, which usually wanted higher rates as a means of limiting inflation, speculation, and uncontrolled growth. The collapse of the stock market in 1929 and then the collapse of the banking system in 1933 illustrated clearly how more central control was needed over the money supply. The Banking Act of 1935* provided that centralized control. It centered power in the renamed board of governors of the Federal Reserve System. The secretary of the treasury and comptroller of the currency were eliminated as members of the board. The board also had power over the newly-established Federal Open Market Committee, which formerly had been dominated by the chairmen of the regional Federal Reserve Banks. Open market operations, now coordinated centrally, quickly replaced manipulation of the discount rate as the primary tool of monetary policy. Marriner Eccles* of Utah was appointed first chairman of the new board of governors. He was a strong supporter of Franklin D. Roosevelt* and a believer in deficit spending as a means of stimulating the economy. His ideas anticipated those of John Maynard Keynes.* Under Eccles' direction, the Federal Reserve Board became the major monetary institution in the United States, eclipsing the influence Wall Street used to have. During the years of the New Deal,* the Federal Reserve Board assumed the modern role it has played ever since in monetary and economic policy. (Lester V. Chandler, *American Monetary Policy, 1928–1941*, 1971.)

FEDERAL SAVINGS AND LOAN INSURANCE CORPORATION As Title IV of the National Housing Act of 1934,* Congress established a Federal Savings and Loan Insurance Corporation to insure the deposits of federal savings and loan associations and to offer the services of insuring the accounts of other savings and loan associations, building and loan associations, homestead associations, and cooperative banks. During the 1920s, the assets of building and loan and savings and loan institutions had grown by over $6 billion, but most of those assets were invested in the booming real estate market. When that market collapsed in the late 1920s and early 1930s, hundreds of those institutions found themselves with frozen portfolios and had to close. By 1934, when the public and Congress had already approved the idea of a Federal Deposit Insurance Corporation* for banks and seen it go into operation, people were ready to do the same for building and loan associations. Roosevelt signed the National Housing Act on June 28, 1934. Under its provisions, the Federal Savings and Loan Insurance Corporation was to insure individual accounts up to $5,000, provided the participating institution submitted to a thorough examination, paid an annual insurance premium, and agreed to issue securities only with the approval of the FSLIC. When any institution defaulted, each depositor was to receive an amount not in excess of 10 percent in cash and 50 percent of the balance within one year and the balance within three years from the date of the default. The Federal Home Loan Bank System supervised the operations of the FSLIC. By 1940 the Federal Savings and Loan Insurance Corporation had insured 2,189 institutions and had paid off depositors in seven defaulted associations. Like the Federal Deposit Insurance Corporation, it proved to be a permanent addition to the federal government's economic "safety net." (*Monthly Labor Review*, XXXIX:369–370, 1934.)

FEDERAL SECURITY AGENCY Established by Reorganization Plan No. 1 of 1939, the Federal Security Agency consolidated into one organization the Social Security Board, Public Health Service, U.S. Office of Education, National Youth Administration,* Civilian Conservation Corps,* Food and Drug Administration, Columbia Institution for the Deaf, Federal Advisory Board for Vocational Education, Freedmen's Hospital, St. Elizabeth's Hospital, Howard University, and the U. S. Employment Service.* Paul V. McNutt* was named the first administrator of the Federal Security Agency. In 1953 the responsibilities of the Federal Security Agency were assumed by the newly created Department of Health, Education, and Welfare. (*Congressional Digest*, XXI:101, 1942.)

FEDERAL SURPLUS COMMODITIES CORPORATION (See FEDERAL SURPLUS RELIEF CORPORATION.)

FEDERAL SURPLUS RELIEF CORPORATION As in previous depressions, Americans in 1933 witnessed the paradox of poverty in a land of plenty. American farmers produced abundant surpluses of crops and livestock, yet, during the Great Depression, many individuals experienced unemployment, poverty, and hunger. Some destitute ate their meals from garbage cans. Meanwhile farmers, burdened with heavy mortgages and prices below their costs of production, faced the cruel dilemma of whether or not to shoot their livestock or see them starve to death. The nation faced a problem of efficient utilization of food that could not be solved by private charitable organizations nor local governmental agencies. These organizations lacked the funds and the management to solve a national crisis. Equally important, by 1933 many Americans had concluded that the federal government should undertake a program of direct aid to the poverty-stricken.

During "the hundred days"* of the New Deal,* the Federal Emergency Relief Corporation and the Agricultural Adjustment Administration* were created to deal with the crisis. The AAA implemented production controls and crop reduction programs in cotton and swine. These activities preceded the creation of the Federal Surplus Relief Corporation that was part of the New Deal's war on poverty.

Federal officials faced the unpleasant task of destroying sows and little pigs in an attempt to increase farm income while at the same time many individuals could not pay for the food. In September 1933 President Franklin D. Roosevelt* provided 75 million dollars to purchase surplus food. A month later, Jerome Frank,* counsel for the AAA, created the Federal Surplus Relief Corporation to administer the procurement and distribution of agricultural surpluses to the needy. Frank gave the non-profit corporation broad powers for direct and work relief. Harry Hopkins,* head of the Federal Emergency Relief Administration,* agreed to serve as president, assisted by Henry A. Wallace.* The FSRC would be a liaison between the FERA and the Department of Agriculture. In achieving its primary aid of direct relief, the FSRC received financial support from both administrations.

From 1933 until 1935, the FSRC operated as a subsidiary of the FERA. It procured agricultural surpluses—pork, butter, flour, syrup, cotton, and other commodities—and transported them to the state emergency relief administrations, who then distributed them to the needy. Yet, in their dealings with the AAA, FSRC officials found food relief a low priority item, and the union between relief and agriculture was very difficult. Naturally, the federal government and agriculture had a tenuous relationship; nor did the federal government provide welfare recipients with all the ingredients necessary for healthy nutrition. On the other hand, some of the food surpluses went unwasted and into the mouths of poverty-stricken Americans.

The FSRC also participated in work relief programs in conjunction with the FERA. The FSRC served as a liaison between the Emergency Work Relief Program of 1934–1935 which aided the unemployed, and the Emergency Cattle Purchase Program of 1934 which benefited the producers. Limited FSRC activities dealt mainly with canning of beef and manufacture of mattresses. These activities produced criticism from business and resulted in the FSRC abandoning additional work relief proposals. Often extravagant and inefficient, the work relief was for Americans who could not be absorbed into industrial employment at the time. On the positive side, the programs preserved morale, provided meaningful employment, and processed agricultural products for distribution during an emergency.

In November 1935 the FSRC was permitted to die, but agricultural and relief officials arranged to continue the program of food distribution by establishing the Federal Surplus Commodities Corporation. The FSRC's principal importance was that it established a pattern of federal food distribution that was later expanded. These programs would lead to aid for school lunches, food stamps,* and other federal efforts to supply food to those who otherwise could not afford it. In this way, the FSRC manifested New Deal humanitarianism and served as a good early example of cooperative federalism. Without the FSRC many workers, farmers, and destitute individuals would have been unable to obtain food during the Great Depression. (C. Roger Lambert, ''Want and Plenty: The Federal Surplus Relief Corporation and the AAA,'' *Agricultural History*, XLVI:390–400 [July, 1972]; Irvin M. May, Jr., ''The Paradox of Agricultural Abundance and Poverty: The Federal Surplus Relief Corporation, 1933–1935,'' Ph.D. dissertation, University of Oklahoma, 1970.)

IRVIN M. MAY, JR.

FEDERAL TENDER BOARD As part of the National Recovery Administration's* program to raise wholesale prices, the administration cooperated with Oklahoma, Texas, and Louisiana officials in cutting oil production. But by May 1934 the production of illegal ''hot oil'' (oil produced in excess of state quotas) has reached nearly 200,000 barrels a day, and in October 1934 Secretary of the

Interior Harold Ickes* created a Federal Tender Board. The board issued certificates to all legal oil shipped across state lines and had a staff of examiners making physical checks of the oil. The board functioned until January 7, 1935, when the Supreme Court* destroyed it in its *Panama Refining Company v. Ryan.** The decision invalidated Section 9(c) of the National Industrial Recovery Act* on the grounds that it gave the president legislative authority. On February 22, 1935, Congress responded by passing the Connally Act,* giving the administration the power to control "hot oil." (Samuel I. Rosenman, ed., *The Public Papers and Addresses of Franklin D. Roosevelt*, II:257–259, 1938.)

FEDERAL THEATRE PROJECT At the National Theatre Conference in Iowa City Iowa, Harry Hopkins* called for a "free, adult, uncensored theatre" and swore in Hallie Flanagan* as head of the Federal Theatre Project. Locating theater people in New York, Chicago, and Los Angeles, however, was no problem. In New York, for instance, thousands of people swarmed into Federal Theatre offices, and by December 28, 1935, 3,350 people were at work, 60 percent actors, 15 percent stagehands and technicians, and 10 percent newspapermen and playwrights and 15 clerical and administrative workers. Out of the early confusion and conflicts, five units emerged in New York City: the Living Newspaper, sponsored by the New York Newspaper Guild and supervised by Morris Watson; the Popular Price Theatre under Edward Goodman, designed to present original plays by new authors; the Experimental Theatre for new plays under Virgil Geddes and James Light; the Negro Theatre under Rose McClendon and John Houseman; and the Tryout Theatre under Otto Metzer. Soon there was also a one-act play unit, a classical repertory unit, a poetic drama unit, a children's unit, a Negro youth theatre, a Yiddish vaudeville unit, a German unit, and an Anglo-Jewish theater.

The earliest New York productions, such as *Comedy of Errors* and *American Holiday*, were nervous and faltering efforts. But three productions in March 1936 (*Chalk Dust*, an attack on the educational system; *Triple A Plowed Under*, the first living newspaper, and *Murder in the Cathedral* by T. S. Eliot) needed no apologies. Later that month a "supernatural" adventure, the production of the voodoo *Macbeth*, meant that the Federal Theatre had four big productions in operation by the end of March. Produced by John Houseman and directed by Orson Welles, *Macbeth* won almost universal acclaim. In May three new productions opened: a second living newspaper, *1935*; Michael Gold and Michael Blandfort's *Battle Hymn*; and *Class of '29* about the economic difficulties of four college graduates. In addition, two dance productions, Charles Weidman's *Candide* and Helen Tamiris' *Salut au Monde*, opened in Brooklyn.

After nearly a year of having to concentrate on problems peculiar to New York City, Flanagan initiated plans for a national exchange of plays, directors and ideas; but in late 1936 the Federal Theatre needed national recognition, so she opened simultaneous productions of *It Can't Happen Here* across the country.

The anti-fascist play had great appeal, and before it was over nearly 500,000 people saw the show.

But the first year had taken its toll: E. C. Mabie, Elmer Rice, Frederick Koch, Gilmore Brown, Frederick McConnell, Thomas Wood Stevens, Jasper Deeter, Rosamond Gilden and Eddie Dowling had all left the project. The Living Newspaper unit had proved irksome and hard to control, a case in point being *Injunction Granted*, where Mrs. Flanagan came into direct conflict with Joseph Losey and Morris Watson.

Trying to put into effect the hard-won lessons of the first year, Hallie Flanagan met in Birmingham, Alabama, with leaders from the South. She suggested simultaneous productions of plays about contemporary problems, anti-war plays, ''living newspapers'' on regional themes, children's plays, and plays on religion. At the same meeting, John Temple Graves, lawyer and newspaperman on the *Birmingham Age Herald*, called for a play on steel, since steel and cotton were dictating the new political economy of the South. The Federal Theatre readily complied, producing *Altars of Steel* by Thomas Hall-Rogers, a Birmingham author. Produced in Atlanta, the play stressed the need for economic freedom in the South and the development of its great resources. Praised and blamed, the play and the furor it created made it clear that playwrights and audiences were keenly interested in plays with social and economic themes. 60,000 people in New York bought tickets for *Power*, a living newspaper on the TVA,* before it opened. But *Power* and *Sweet Land*, produced at the Lafayette, were still the only social plays of the early 1937 season.

But by May 1937 a congressional order to cut was again rumored, and all the unions began protesting even before the cut materialized. On June 10 an order to cut the New York project by 30 percent was received, clearly signaling the growing opposition in Washington. Subsequently, *The Cradle Will Rock* was prevented from opening, and just as importantly the publication of *Federal Theatre Magazine* was stopped. Despite the cuts, protests, picketing, and bitter disappointment over the cancellation of *Cradle*, the Federal Theatre went on with its plans for the summer caravan season. Five trucks from Broadway theaters went rolling out to the boroughs of Richmond, Brooklyn, Queens, the Bronx, and Manhattan. Plans for the first Federal Summer Theatre, to be held at Vassar, also continued, but by the end of the summer over a thousand people had been cut from the Federal Theatre rolls.

By September 1937 a battered Federal Theatre began its third season and was ousted from the McLean mansion in Washington, D. C. In December 1937 the future not only of the theater project but of the entire WPA* hung in the balance.

Ironically the national aspect of the Federal Theatre seemed to grow stronger in this climate of distrust and embattlement. Directors from the Federal Theatre Summer Theatre returned to their communities and began a nationwide program. A nationwide Shaw and O'Neill cycle and a nationwide program of children's and religious plays proved immensely successful. A program of dance reached new audiences in New York City, Los Angeles, Chicago, and Philadelphia.

Chicago sent *Swing Mikado* to New York; New York sent *Haiti* to Boston and *Prologue to Glory* to Chicago and Philadelphia. Federal Theatre was clearly a producing organization and reviewers talked increasingly of a permanent government-sponsored theater.

But in spite of the obvious vitality and caliber of the project, members of the theatrical world from all over the country found it necessary in 1939 to join in a campaign to try to save the FTP. It was in mortal danger. The cut in funds was not an economy move, a human issue, or even a cultural issue; the Federal Theatre had become a political issue. The House Committee to Investigate Un-American Activities, under Chairman Martin Dies,* and the House Committee on Appropriations, under Chairman Clifton A. Woodrum,* went after the project. The Federal Theatre had become a microcosm of all the New Deal* represented to Franklin D. Roosevelt's* enemies, notably in its spending policy and its liberal attitude toward labor, aliens, and minorities. It was, Mrs. Flanagan reflected, "perhaps the triumph as well as the tragedy of our actors that they became indeed the abstract and brief chronicle of the time." The Federal Theatre was ended by an Act of Congress on June 30, 1939. (William F. McDonald, *Federal Relief Administration and the Arts*, 1969.)

LORRAINE A. BROWN

FEDERAL TRADE COMMISSION In September 1914 Congress passed the Federal Trade Commission Act to establish federal regulation of business practices. At first, President Woodrow Wilson had conceived of the FTC as a fact-finding group designed to assist businessmen in avoiding unfair trade practices. But the law also gave the Federal Trade Commission broad powers to investigate, publicize, and prohibit all unfair "methods of competition." Although the FTC did investigate thousands of cases of unfair competition during the Progressive era, its effectiveness was hampered by conservatives in Congress, suspicious federal courts unwilling to allow it to define "unfair competition," and its case-by-case approach to regulation. During the 1920s, especially during the Coolidge administration, the FTC changed dramatically into a pro-business organization, under its new chairman, William E. Humphrey.* The Wilsonian ideal of strict regulation had given way to "normalcy" and the belief in industrial self-regulation.

The New Deal* brought more changes to the Federal Trade Commission. William Humphrey had to resign, but the passage of the National Industrial Recovery Act* and creation of the National Recovery Administration* sent the entire anti-trust movement into an eclipse between 1933 and 1935. Franklin D. Roosevelt* allowed the FTC to drift into near oblivion, using it as a patronage device to reward the "Tennessee gang" of Memphis political boss Ed Crump and Senator Kenneth M. McKellar. But when the Supreme Court* declared the NRA unconstitutional in 1935 and as Roosevelt's patience with the business community waned, interest in anti-trust activity revived, as did the Federal Trade Commission. The Robinson-Patman Act of 1936* gave the FTC authority to prevent price concessions given by manufacturers to large chain stores, and the federal courts began allowing the FTC to prohibit deceptive advertising policies. Economists from the Federal Trade Commission worked for the Temporary National Economic Committee,* which Congress had created in 1938 to investigate concentrations of economic power. Congress passed the Wheeler-Lea Act in 1938, broadening FTC powers to prohibit unfair trade practices. The Wool Products Labeling Act of 1939 gave the Federal Trade Commission power to draft substantive rules governing trade practices in the industry. It was the increases in FTC power in the late 1930s which paved the way for subsequent expansions which created the modern Federal Trade Commission. (Susan Wagner, *The Federal Trade Commission*, 1971.)

FEDERAL WORKS AGENCY Established by Reorganization Plan No. 1 of 1939, effective July 1, 1939, the Federal Works Agency consolidated several public works agencies. President Franklin D. Roosevelt* named John M. Carmody,* the administrator of the Rural Electrification Administration,* to be head of the Federal Works Agency and transferred to him control over the Works Progress Administration* (renamed Works Projects Administration),* Public Works Administration,* Bureau of Public Roads, and the United States Housing Agency.* The Federal Works Agency also set up a Public Buildings Administration composed of the Public Buildings Branch of the Treasury Department and the Branch of Public Buildings Management and Space Control Division of the National Park Service. Congress abolished the Federal Works Agency in 1949 and transferred its duties to the General Services Administration. (*American City*, LIV:5, 1939.)

FEDERAL WRITERS' PROJECT By the early 1930s unemployment among teachers and writers was serious. The Federal Writers' Project was part of the Works Progress Administration,* from 1935 until June 30, 1943, when the WPA expired. The FWP distributed $27,189,370 in seven years and completed over seven twelve-foot bookcases of printed works including 378 commercially published books. The FWP was organized to provide work-relief for writers and publication-experienced, unemployed white collar workers. Most FWP workers were neither writers nor professional authors but were simply willing workers in need; many were lawyers, ministers, newspapermen, librarians, and teachers. Total employment during FWP's existence was small, between 6,000 and 7,000 employees. Under the direction of Henry Alsberg,* the FWP completed an amazing breadth of articles, pamphlets, books, and monographs on all aspects of American life, including history, folklore, nature studies, children's educational materials, and the first black studies to reach the general American public. Many FWP publications were forerunners of evolving trends (such as *These Are Our Lives, The Negro In Virginia, American Stuff*) and reflected a contemporary focus on "the common hero" and "the forgotten American." They presaged such commercial literary favorites of the period as *Let Us Now Praise Famous Men, You Have Seen Their Faces, An American Exodus*, and John Dos Passos' documentary masterpiece—*U.S.A.* FWP's publications contributed greatly to the

New Deal's* emphasis on portraying cultural heritage in American democracy and regional social consciousness. The FWP was a major contributor to WPA* special projects which gained the most acclaim and suffered the least criticism, such as the Historical American Building Survey, the Historical Records Survey,* and the Index of American Design.*

Almost from its inception FWP became a storm center of political concern about Communist infiltration and influence. While many FWP personnel admitted to or were identified as being Communist party* members or members of organizations affiliated with or sympathetic to Party goals, no evidence ever surfaced to prove that their influence had any ideological effect on FWP publications. Communist party influence resulted primarily in union activity and the hiring of personnel not possessing competent occupational skills. Censorship, in the form of control-of-copy at the Washington level, was the greatest danger faced by the Writers' Project. Criticism limited appropriations and personnel authorizations and usually became the subject of embarrassing debate in the Congress, increasing pressure on the FWP to exercise censorship.

Originally directed from the WPA level by Washington-appointed state directors, the FWP came under state control in 1939 when directors became appointed by governors. FWP publications were required to have a 25 percent contribution or sponsorship from non-federal sources. The major and most famous project was then accelerated. The American Guide Series consisted of a separate guide for each state, for principal cities, for counties and their towns, for major highways, and for the territories of Alaska and Puerto Rico. The American Guide Series were compendiums of the history, geography, and culture of the United States and each state, and received wide acclaim even from some major opponents of the New Deal. The American Guide Series is considered to be the most significant and most important FWP contribution to the New Deal and its emphasis on preserving the cultural heritage of the American past while thrusting society into the future. In 1962, two decades after its demise, John Steinbeck* summed up his opinion of FWP publications in his book *Travels With Charley*, "The complete set comprises the most comprehensive account of the United States ever got together, and nothing since has ever approached it."

In its waning years, FWP publications were subject more and more to private and local control due to the sponsorship requirement. Local political and ideological squabbles ensued, especially whenever political party control changed in a state, county, or municipality. After Pearl Harbor the Writers' Program was again retitled, *The Writers' Unit of the War Services Division of WPA*, and produced as its last effort a series of sixty-four "Serviceman's Recreational Guides" for areas surrounding the nation's principal military training sites. (Jerre Mangione, *The Dream and The Deal: The Federal Writer's Project 1935–1943*, 1972; Monty Naom Penkower, *The Federal Writers' Project: A Study in Government Patronage of the Arts*, 1977.)

AUSTIN N. LEIBY

FESS, SIMEON DAVISON Simeon D. Fess was born on a farm in Allen County, Ohio, on December 11, 1861. He graduated from Ohio Northern

University in 1889 and then received a master's degree and a law degree from Wilberforce University in 1891 and 1897. Between 1889 and 1902, Fess worked at Ohio Northern University, first as a professor of history, then as head of the college of law, and finally as vice-president of the university. He was a graduate student and lecturer at the University of Chicago between 1902 and 1907 and in 1907 became president of Antioch College. Fess served as president of Antioch until 1917 and resigned then to devote all of his energies to his congressional career, which had begun in 1913 as a Republican in the House of Representatives. Fess won a seat in the United States Senate in 1922 and served two terms. During the closing stage of his political career, Fess was recognized as one of the Republican "Old Guard" who hated the New Deal.* Fess died on December 23, 1936. (*New York Times*, December 24, 1936.)

FINANCE COMMITTEE OF WOMEN Organized in 1936 by conservative Republican women, the Finance Committee of Women campaigned against the New Deal* because they viewed it as a "forerunner of socialism and communism." Led by Grace H. Brosseau, the Finance Committee numbered several thousand women scattered through approximately twenty states. They opposed Franklin D. Roosevelt's* re-election in both 1936 and 1940. (George Wolfskill and John A. Hudson, *All but the People. Franklin D. Roosevelt and His Critics, 1933–1939*, 1969.)

"FIRESIDE CHATS" The origins of the famous "fireside chats" exist in Franklin D. Roosevelt's* unpretentious conversations with friends and acquaintances at Hyde Park and Warm Springs. He translated these chats to the new medium of radio during his first term as governor of New York. Despite technical problems which sometimes impeded reception, he used radio successfully for his engagingly personal talks with constituents. Roosevelt continued the talks during his presidency. Seeking an apt term to advertise the president's second radio message, Harry C. Butcher, head of the Washington office of CBS, decided on a "fireside chat." Roosevelt accepted the label, and in his fireside chat of June 24, 1933, he quipped that the members of the press are "creatures of habit. It is the warmest night I have ever seen in Washington and yet this talk will be referred to as a fireside talk."

Roosevelt delivered twenty-eight fireside chats. M. H. Aylesworth, president of NBC, had suggested to the president-elect during the interregnum that he give a weekly speech to the nation, and he had offered NBC facilities for the broadcasts. Roosevelt felt that a weekly speech would amount to an overkill, but he declared his intention to present "personal talks from time to time." His advisers concurred and wanted to use the talks only to achieve a maximum dramatic effect. The first "fireside chats" were early examples of managed news.

The president delivered his first fireside chat at 10:00 PM, March 12, 1933, only eight days after his inauguration, to reassure the public about the reopening of the banks. Like all the fireside chats, it was broadcast from the basement of the White House, with seating for an audience of thirty. The president seemed intuitively to understand how to address a mass audience as if he were addressing an individual or a family. He was animated and natural as he spoke, gesturing and smiling as though his radio audience were seated before him. More than 17 million families listened to the first fireside chat. In 1939 the Elmo Roper organization reported that 24.1 percent of the population usually listened to the fireside chats, while 38.6 percent sometimes did and 37.3 percent never did. By any standard, Roosevelt had a substantial audience, and the fireside chats, in addition to solidifying his political base, set a standard for political communication in the United States. (Waldo W. Braden and Earnest Brandenburg, ''Roosevelt's Fireside Chats,'' *Speech Monographs*, XXII:290–302, 1955.)

BERNARD K. DUFFY

''FIRST NEW DEAL'' Although historians have debated the extent and nature of the ''First New Deal'' and ''Second New Deal,''* the term ''First New Deal'' emerged in the mid-1930s when a shift began to occur in the philosophy and policies of the Roosevelt administration. The ''First New Deal'' has been used to describe the legislation passed by Congress in 1933 and 1934. Between March 9 and June 16, 1933, and during the regular session of the 73rd Congress, Franklin D. Roosevelt's* New Deal* emerged. This ''First New Deal'' was primarily concerned with relief and recovery, basically accepted the industrial concentration of the modern economy, and worked to coordinate various interest groups to stimulate production and employment. Led by people like Raymond Moley,* Rexford Tugwell,* Adolph Berle,* Donald Richberg,* and Hugh Johnson,* the ''First New Deal'' was responsible for the NRA,* AAA,* TVA,* and the major relief bills. The central premise of the ''First New Deal'' was national planning. Early New Dealers no longer trusted the capacity of the private market to allocate resources and dictate production and prices. More reminiscent of Theodore Roosevelt's ''New Nationalism'' than Woodrow Wilson's ''New Freedom,'' the ''First New Deal'' was dedicated to major structural reform in the American economy which would replace older market values with new institutions of coordinated planning by government, business, and labor. The purpose of the relief laws during the ''First New Deal'' was primarily to buy time until the more fundamental recovery measures had stimulated production and employment. In that sense, the CCC,* CWA,* and FERA* were not so much economic measures as political and humanitarian devices.

Historians generally have concluded that the ''First New Deal'' disintegrated in late 1934 and 1935 when business criticism of the administration mounted, large corporations and wealthy farmers came to dominate the NRA and AAA, and the Supreme Court's* *Schechter** decision declared the National Industrial Recovery Act* unconstitutional. By 1935 the Roosevelt administration had shifted gears to a greater emphasis on social reform, anti-trust activities, and later to Keynesian spending. These would come to be known as the ''Second New Deal.'' (Raymond Moley and Elliott Rosen, *The First New Deal*, 1966; Arthur M. Schlesinger, Jr., *The Age of Roosevelt. Vol. III. The Politics of Upheaval, 1935–1936*, 1960.)

FISH AND WILDLIFE SERVICE Before the New Deal,* two government agencies were specifically designed to deal with wildlife preservation and control: the Bureau of Biological Survey in the Department of Agriculture and the Bureau of Fisheries in the Department of Commerce. Both of them focused most of their resources on research and administration of game and bird refuges and fish hatcheries. Because of President Franklin D. Roosevelt's* interest in wildlife and conservation, both programs enjoyed major support from the Civilian Conservation Corps* and the Public Works Administration.* The New Deal's wildlife programs also received a boost when Roosevelt appointed Jay N. Darling, nationally recognized conservationist and cartoonist, as head of the Bureau of Biological Survey. Darling immediately spent money to restore water levels in many exhausted reservoirs in government reclamation projects to protect birds and wildlife. Darling's sudden death in 1935 brought Ira N. Gabrielson to the Bureau of Biological Survey, and by July 1, 1937, they had increased the number of game and bird refuges in the United States from 109 to 245 and the number of protected acres from 5,639,000 to 11,379,000. The Pittman-Robertson Act of 1937 then applied the 10 percent federal excise tax on arms and ammunition to state wildlife conservation projects on a matching funds basis. (Richard Lowitt, *The New Deal in the West*, 1984.)

FISHER, IRVING A leading economist at Yale University, Irving Fisher wrote prolifically on a variety of subjects. Born February 27, 1867, at Saugerties, New York, Fisher earned an undergraduate degree and a Ph.D. in economics at Yale. His dissertation became a landmark in the development of mathematical economics. Fisher took a position at Yale in 1890 and became full professor in 1898. Between 1894 and 1898 he published widely in scholarly journals on bimetallism, theory of utility and prices, interest, and capital. A serious bout with tuberculosis left Fisher with an extraordinary interest in health; and he became a crusader for exercise, proper diet, relaxation therapy, and avoidance of tobacco and alcohol. He played an important role in ratification of the Eighteenth Amendment and campaigned vigorously for the League of Nations. In 1928 Fisher published *The Money Illusion* to educate laymen about prices and money. The stock market crash of 1929 caught him by surprise, wiping out his personal fortune and eventually destroying much of his reputation as a leading economist. In February 1930 he wrote an optimistic book about the crash, *The Stock Market Crash and After*, in which he argued that recovery was just around the corner. Two years later he had to revise his point of view, arguing in *Booms and Depressions* that devastating shifts in the business cycle could be controlled by the Federal Reserve System. The depression could be stopped if the federal government pursued a policy of "reflating the price level up to the average level at which outstanding debts were contracted, and maintaining that level unchanged." Supported by the leading silver monetarists, Fisher urged President Franklin D. Roosevelt* to abandon the gold standard and try to stabilize currency at the 1926 level. The president's ill-fated gold-buying* scheme in 1933–1934 was one consequence of Fisher's arguments about manipulating price levels through purchases of hard metal. At the same time, Fisher disagreed with prevailing New Deal* schemes to raise farm prices by restricting acreage and production. Instead, prices should be raised by "restoring" the monetary unit to "normal" rather than creating artificial shortages. Although Fisher was an early supporter of Franklin D. Roosevelt, he eventually became quite critical of the AAA,* NRA,* and many of the relief programs; and by 1944 he was claiming that Herbert Hoover* could have handled the depression with more success. Perhaps the most vivid symbol of the "old economics" in the United States, Irving Fisher died on April 29, 1947. (W. Fellner, et al., *Ten Economic Studies in the Tradition of Irving Fisher,* 1967; Irving N. Fisher, *My Father Irving Fisher*, 1956.)

FISH, HAMILTON, JR. Hamilton Fish, Jr., was born on December 7, 1888, in Garrison, New York, to one of the state's most distinguished Republican families. He graduated from Harvard University in 1910 and served in the New York State Assembly between 1914 and 1916. After leaving the army in 1919, Fish entered the oil development business and in 1920 was elected to Congress, a position he held until 1945. During the 1930s, Fish was an articulate spokesman for the Republican "Old Guard" in the House of Representatives. In his view, the New Deal* symbolized a radical change in public policy, one which was creating huge bureaucracies, massive deficits, labor unrest, and business fear. "The New Deal," he said, "was like a merry-go-round with its gaudy trimmings and painted horses which gave the people a good time while the music lasted, but it got nowhere." Fish was also convinced that the "court-packing"* scheme and the executive reorganization plans were sure signs of Franklin D. Roosevelt's* authoritarianism and willingness to lead the country down the road to dictatorship. His tax policies and deficits had only prolonged the depression. Finally, Fish was always suspicious of Roosevelt's foreign policies as too aggressive and too likely to lead the country down the road to war. Hamilton Fish, Jr., was defeated for re-election in 1944 and re-entered private business. He died in 1983. (George Wolfskill and John A. Hudson, *All but the People. Franklin D. Roosevelt and His Critics, 1933–1939*, 1969.)

FLANAGAN, HALLIE Born in Redfield, South Dakota, on August 27, 1890, and raised in Grinnell, Iowa, Hallie Ferguson graduated from Grinnell College, taught school for a year, and married Murray Flanagan. They had two sons. Murray died in 1919, and Flanagan found a teaching position in the English Department at Grinnell. She won a $100 prize in 1922 given by the Des Moines Little Theater Society for *The Curtain*; a performance of the play was scheduled for the following season. This success and her innovative productions at Grinnell brought her to the attention of George Pierce Baker, who invited her to become his production assistant in 1923 at the Baker 47 Workshop at Harvard. She accepted and also took an M.A. at Radcliffe in 1924. Flanagan began as Baker's production assistant and ended as his only assistant director. When he moved his workshop to Yale because of better facilities, he took with him *Incense* by Hallie Flanagan, the opening play of his new season. Flanagan returned to Grinnell as head of dramatic production, where she implemented the Grinnell Experimental Theatre. After becoming the first woman to receive a Guggenheim Fellowship, Flanagan went to Vassar College. With her Guggenheim Fellowship, she travelled to Europe, recording her impressions of contemporary theatrical personages and theaters. An extremely valuable experience, the journey acquainted her with the innovations of Craig, Meyerhold, Reinhardt, and Stanislavski; Meyerhold especially was influential on her subsequent work at Vassar and the Federal Theatre Project.*

In the next years at Vassar her Experimental Theatre attracted the attention of scholars and critics. Her production of Chekhov's *The Marriage Proposal* in three separate styles in one evening was well received by critics. Three other Vassar productions reflected how open she was to all theatrical forms and how well she had mastered her craft. In 1935 Hallie Flanagan (now Hallie Flanagan Davis, for she had married Philip Davis, professor of Greek at Vassar) was invited by Harry Hopkins,* another Grinnell graduate, to head the Federal Theatre Project. Whatever her misgivings, she accepted the challenge, hopeful of implementing her idea on a national level. What she set about creating was a theatre—national in scope, regional in emphasis, and experimental in form—which would put unemployed people to work and serve the community. It was the greatest single experiment ever undertaken in the American theater; and when the project got fully under way, it employed 12,464 people working in 153 actively producing theaters in twenty-eight states.

A constant source of difficulty was the uneasy alliance between the WPA* bureaucracy and the needs of the theater. Requisition forms filled out in triplicate and innumerable regulations slowed the development of a truly regional theater, not to mention the desire of government officials to choose the plays for production. But her courage and indefatigability under unrelenting pressure, administrative entanglements, and constant budget cuts are a tribute to this brave woman who stayed on when others quit and fought long and hard when others had given up. During the first two years, the success of the Living Newspapers, the simultaneous openings in twenty-one theaters across the country of *It Can't Happen Here*, and the success of the "voodoo" *Macbeth* in Harlem ranked as the greatest achievements of the Federal Theatre.

But in spite of her endless tours and vigilance, criticisms were rampant about the Federal Theatre Project; and Harry Hopkins, once her staunch supporter, abandoned her. The power of two congressional committees, the Dies Committee* and the Appropriations Committee headed by Clifton A. Woodrum,* spelled the demise of the Federal Theatre. Cries of "boondoggle,"* "red-menace," and "extravagance" filled the air. Testifying before the Dies Committee, Flanagan held her own and never backed down; but she was not allowed to make a final statement nor have her brief read into the record. On June 30,

1939, the Federal Theatre Project ended; and by this action 7,900 people operating in twenty states, a plant worth roughly a million dollars, and some ten thousand volumes of records of the first government-sponsored theater in the United States were abandoned.

Flanagan took her defeat in stride, making plans to write a book about the history of the FTP, but again tragedy struck when her husband, Philip Davis, died of a heart attack—a bitter blow since it was his unfailing encouragement that had made it possible for her to bear the burdens of her Federal Theatre Project.

When her book *Arena*, history of the FTP, was completed, Flanagan resumed directing and experimenting with plays at Vassar. In 1942 she joined the faculty of Smith College, serving at various times as dean of the college, professor of drama, and director of the college theatre until she retired in 1955. Flanagan died of Parkinson's disease on July 23, 1969. (William F. McDonald, *Federal Relief Administration and the Arts*, 1969; *New York Times*, July 24, 1969.)

LORRAINE A. BROWN

FLETCHER, DUNCAN UPSHAW Duncan Fletcher was born in Sumter County, Georgia, on January 6, 1859. Raised in the era of Reconstruction, he assumed the loyalty to religion, property, and the Democratic party* so characteristic of the postwar South. Fletcher graduated from Vanderbilt University in 1880 and then entered the law school, studying there and entering the Tennessee bar in 1881. He later opened a law practice in Jacksonville, Florida. Practicing law quickly involved him in local politics, and he adopted a reform-progressive posture. With strong backing from blacks, Fletcher won a spot on the city council in 1887. In the 1890s he too was caught up in the agrarian radicalism sweeping through the South, and he won a seat in the state legislature, where he sponsored bills for a state board of medical examiners, regulation of party primary elections, and abolition of the convict lease system. Fletcher also recommended regulation of the railroads through a state commission. In 1893 he became mayor of Jacksonville and continuously campaigned for free silver, a federal income tax, direct election of U.S. senators, and city ownership of public utilities. In 1909 Fletcher took a seat in the United States Senate.

A moderate Democrat, Fletcher became active on the Senate Banking and Currency Committee. When the Democrats took over Congress in 1932, Fletcher became chairman of the committee. He had endorsed Franklin D. Roosevelt* for president, and throughout the 1930s he remained a faithful supporter. Fletcher directed the "Pecora investigations" of the banking community, defended New Deal* measures against Senator Carter Glass'* opposition, and sponsored legislation which became the Securities Exchange Act of 1934* and the Banking Act of 1935.* A loyal New Deal Democrat, Duncan Upshaw Fletcher died on June 17, 1936. (Wayne Flynt, *Duncan Upshaw Fletcher. Dixie's Reluctant Progressive*, 1971.)

FLETCHER-RAYBURN BILL (See SECURITIES ACT OF 1933.)

FLOOD CONTROL ACT OF 1936 Because of serious flooding, erosion, and drought problems affecting the country in the early and mid-1930s, President Franklin D. Roosevelt* had initiated Department of the Interior studies of hydrology, conservation, erosion, and flood control. On January 30, 1936, he submitted his ''Little Waters'' report to Congress, and on May 12, 1937, he forwarded the ''Headwaters Control and Use'' report. The result was a series of legislation to deal with the problem. The Flood Control Act of 1936 authorized studies of small stream watersheds on how to retard water run-off and soil erosion. Amendments in 1937 required state and local flood control laws, and further amendments in 1938 permitted the secretary of agriculture to begin operations to control water run-off in areas where the War Department had authorized dam construction and flood control work. Local officials were to establish soil conservation districts with programs to protect forest cover, improve small stream channels, construct minor basins for debris, and assist farmers in controlling erosion with contour cultivation, terraces, cover crops, and tree planting. (Samuel I. Rosenman, ed., *The Public Papers and Addresses of Franklin D. Roosevelt*, VI:193–196, 1941.)

FLYNN, EDWARD JOSEPH Edward ''Boss'' Flynn, head of the powerful Bronx, New York, political machine, was born on September 22, 1891, in New York City. Coming from Irish Catholic stock, Flynn was a gifted politician. He graduated from the Fordham University Law School in 1912 and was admitted to the New York bar the next year. After practicing law for five years and being active in local Democratic politics, Flynn won a seat as a Bronx County representative in the New York state assembly. He served in the state legislature until 1921, when he resigned after winning election as sheriff of Bronx County. At that time, Flynn also became chairman of the Bronx County Democratic Committee, a position he held throughout the 1920s and 1930s. He joined the law firm of Goldwater & Flynn in 1924 and remained with the firm for the rest of his life. In 1926 Flynn won election as chamberlain of the city of New York and in 1929 became secretary of the State of New York. Along with people like Edward Crump of Memphis and Frank Hague* of New Jersey, Edward ''Boss'' Flynn was one of the major urban political leaders in the United States.

During the 1930s, Ed Flynn played an influential role in the New Deal.* On a political level, he represented a major strength of the Democratic party*—its machine base in the northern cities. Ever since the late nineteenth century, the power of the urban bosses had been rising in the party as more and more people moved to the cities; and Franklin D. Roosevelt* had carefully cultivated them politically with respect, deference, support, and patronage. Ed Flynn was one of the most powerful of those urban bosses and a key figure in New York and New York City politics. On a personal level, Flynn was also a personal friend of the president, able and willing to argue with Roosevelt over political and policy matters without fear of injuring their relationship. With easy access to the president, Flynn was part of the White House inner circle and argued articulately on behalf of urban and labor interests. Although independent enough to oppose the president on some matters, such as the "court-packing"* proposal in 1937, Flynn was nevertheless a loyal New Deal supporter in New York City. In 1940 the president named him head of the Democratic National Committee, a position Flynn held until 1942. Flynn was considered one of the "old-time" bosses whose concerns were completely non-ideological; his interests were in the maintenance of power. But by the mid-1930s, Flynn too had changed, becoming more overtly liberal in his pro-labor, pro-social welfare interests and his willingness to espouse a clear New Deal perspective in return for sizeable allocations of WPA* relief funds. Edward "Boss" Flynn died on August 18, 1953. (Lyle W. Dorsett, *Franklin D. Roosevelt and the City Bosses*, 1977; *New York Times*, August 19, 1953.)

FOOD, DRUG, AND COSMETIC ACT OF 1938 The Food, Drug, and Cosmetic Act of 1938 was, along with the Fair Labor Standards Act of 1938,* the last major legislation of the New Deal.* By the mid-1920s, many reformers had felt the Pure Food and Drug Act of 1906 needed refining; and in 1933 Rexford G. Tugwell,* with the help of Professors Milton Handler* of Columbia and David Cavers of Duke, drafted new legislation. The bill greatly expanded government control over the drug and food processing industry. It specified that drugs making any therapeutic claims contrary to general medical opinion were illegal; that palliatives must be clearly labelled as such and not as cures; that all medical ingredients must be disclosed; food labels must list all ingredients in order of predominance by weight; that the government could establish identity standards for quality and fill of containers; and that the government could inspect factories to make sure the law was being obeyed. The food, cosmetic, and pharmaceutical industries opposed the bill and lobbied against it successfully. Senator Royal Copeland* of New York then became a major sponsor of the measure.

For the next five years Copeland fought for the measure, and two events gradually gave the legislation more and more support. Over the years, the industries concerned had become frightened over increasing volumes of state regulatory laws, which they found diverse and often contradictory. They began favoring some type of federal legislation as a means of rationalizing the problem. Also, late in October 1937, more than 100 people died after taking the drug sulfanilamide for venereal disease and strep infections. Produced by S. E. Massengill Company, a veterinary medicine manufacturer, the drug did extensive kidney and liver damage in many patients. Under the leadership of Senator Copeland and Representative Clarence Lea* of California and with the constant assistance of Walter Campbell, head of the Food and Drug Administration, the Food, Drug, and Cosmetic Act moved through Congress in 1938. President Franklin D. Roosevelt* signed it into law on June 24, 1938. The law, which is still the country's basic governing statute, greatly expanded consumer protection. It increased the minimal penalties of the 1906 law and added the power of injunction to the law's seizure and criminal sanctions. The Food and Drug Administration could establish food standards that had the effect of law, and cosmetics and therapeutic devices came under government control for the first time. Nor did the government any longer have to prove fraudulent intent on the part of manufacturers or advertisers of false claims. The law also required all drug manufacturers to convince the FDA of a new drug's safety before it could be marketed. Finally, the law insisted that trade as well as generic products had to live up to the new legislation. (Charles O. Jackson, *Food and Drug Legislation in the New Deal*, 1970.)

FOOD STAMP PLAN The Food Stamp Plan was established on May 16, 1939, in Rochester, New York, by the Federal Surplus Commodities Corporation* to help dispose of surplus agricultural products. The successor to the Federal Surplus Relief Corporation, the FSCC managed to coordinate the distribution of a wide variety of surplus products to poor people during the late 1930s. The Food Stamp Plan was one mechanism for disposing of surpluses. People participating in the program had to be on work relief and could purchase between $1.00 and $1.50 worth of ''orange stamps'' for each member of the family each week. For each $1.00 of ''orange stamps' they possessed, a family received $.50 worth of ''blue stamps'' which they then could use to purchase surplus commodities from the Federal Surplus Commodities Corporation. By 1940 the plan was operating in 100 cities and came to an end only when World War II eliminated the need for relief programs. In 1959 the food stamp program was revived. (C. Roger Lambert, ''Want and Plenty: The Federal Surplus Relief Corporation and the AAA,'' *Agricultural History*, XLVI:401–413, 1972; Richard B. Morris, *The Encyclopedia of American History*, 1976.)

FORD, HENRY Henry Ford was born near Dearborn, Michigan, on July 30, 1863. He attended school until 1878 when he moved to Detroit and worked for several years as a machine-shop apprentice and farm machinery repairman. In the mid-1880s Ford operated a sawmill and in 1887 became the chief engineer for Edison Illuminating Company in Detroit. Ford's personal interests rested on the ''horseless carriage,'' and by 1896 he had constructed his first automobile. He built the ''999'' racing car in 1903 and then organized the Ford Motor Company that same year. Ford developed the ''Model T'' later in the decade and in 1909 began producing it on a mass scale, using factory assembly methods which brought international acclaim. In 1914 Ford became a pioneer in labor relations by introducing the eight-hour day and $5 per day minimum wage as well as a profit-sharing program. Hoping to stave off World War I Ford chartered the ship *Oscar II* and carried a large group of pacifists, feminists, and reformers to Scandinavia. Ford made an unsuccessful bid for a U.S. Senate seat in 1918 and in 1919 resigned as president of Ford Motor Company, naming his son Edsel B. Ford as his successor.

Ford's reputation as an enlightened entrepreneur did not survive the 1920s and 1930s. He became widely known for reactionary, anti-Semitic attitudes, and during the 1930s was a bitter opponent of the New Deal. Harboring pro-fascist views, Ford saw the New Deal and the Congress of Industrial Organizations* as the symbols of radicalism and Communism. He saw the "sit-down" strikes of 1937 by the United Automobile Workers as the beginning of a revolution, and unlike General Motors he refused to sign a contract with them. He resorted to violence-prone, strike-breaking hoodlums to cajole workers. Ford also actively provided money to black churches in Detroit if they would condemn the CIO and urge their parishioners to work as strikebreakers. Not until 1941, when global war was on the horizon and huge production orders were mounting, did Henry Ford acquiesce and recognize the United Automobile Workers. When Edsel B. Ford died in 1943, Henry Ford resumed the presidency of Ford Motor Company, and he remained there until his death on April 7, 1947. (Allan Nevins, *Ford*, 1954.)

FORTAS, ABE Abe Fortas was born in Memphis, Tennessee, in 1910 and worked his way through school playing the violin. He secured scholarships to Southwestern College in Memphis, graduated from there in 1930, and then went on to the Yale Law School, where he became the prize student of Professor William O. Douglas.* After graduating from Yale in 1933, Fortas remained on the Yale law faculty for four years while commuting to Washington where he served as an assistant chief in the AAA* legal division. At Douglas' request, Fortas went to work for the Securities and Exchange Commission* in 1934, and in 1939 he transferred over to the Department of Interior. There Fortas served as under secretary between 1942 and 1946. Fortas practiced law in Washington with his own firm—Arnold, Fortas, and Porter—after leaving the Interior Department in 1946, and in 1965 President Lyndon B. Johnson appointed him an associate justice of the Supreme Court.* Fortas remained on the court until 1969 when he had to resign in a storm of controversy over alleged financial improprieties. Fortas then returned to private law practice. He died on April 6, 1982. (Katie Louchheim, ed., *The Making of the New Deal. The Insiders Speak*, 1983.)

FOSTER, WILLIAM ZEBULAN William Z. Foster was born in Taunton, Massachusetts, on Februray 25, 1881. When he was still a child, his family moved to Philadelphia, where he grew up amidst the poverty of the immigrant slums. Between 1887 and 1917, Foster worked at a variety of jobs, including a paperboy, deep-water sailor, lumberjack, fruit picker, streetcar motorman, sweeper in a chemical rendering plant, miner, and circus canvas man. Usually, he lost his jobs when company spies discovered him trying to organize workers into labor unions. Originally a Socialist, Foster joined the International Workers of the World in 1909, worked as an AFL* organizer during World War I, and became notorious for his work in the great steel strike of 1919. After that, Foster was widely recognized for his radicalism. By the early 1920s he had emerged as a leading American Communist and ran for president in 1924, 1928, and 1932 on the American Communist party* ticket. In the election of 1932,* Foster criticized both Herbert Hoover* and Franklin D. Roosevelt* as "different sides of the same capitalist coin," and he only polled 102,785 votes. Throughout the 1930s, Foster viewed Franklin D. Roosevelt and the New Deal* as a subtly-veiled and enormously successful attempt by the business community to salvage American capitalism and perpetuate its exploitation of industrial workers. In 1945 Foster helped oust Earl Browder* as leader of the Communist party, and he took over the post until 1957. William Z. Foster died in Moscow on September 1, 1961. (*New York Times*, September 2, 1961.)

FOWLER, HENRY HAMILL Henry H. Fowler was born in Roanoke, Virginia, in 1908. After graduating from Roanoke College in 1929, he attended the Yale Law School and graudated there in 1933. He practiced law briefly with the firm of Covington, Burling, and Rublee, but he then went to work for the Tennessee Valley Authority* as head of its legal staff. Between 1934 and 1939, Fowler supervised TVA* litigation and defended the agency before the Supreme Court.* Fowler was appointed chief counsel of the Senate Civil Liberties Subcommittee in 1939, where he concentrated on the problems of migrant workers. During World War II, Fowler worked with the Office of Production Management, and at the end of the war he served with the Allied Control Council. Fowler returned to private practice until the Korean War when President Harry S Truman* appointed him head of the Office of Defense Mobilization and the Defense Production Administration. After Korea he returned to private practice until 1961, when President John F. Kennedy appointed him as under secretary of the treasury. In 1965 Lyndon Johson named him secretary of the treasury. Fowler returned to private law practice in 1969. (Katie Louchheim, ed., *The Making of the New Deal. The Insiders Speak*, 1983.)

FRANK, JEROME Jerome Frank was born in New York City on September 10, 1889, to the descendents of German-Jewish immigrants. He attended the University of Chicago for both his undergraduate and legal education, impressing his professors with his outstanding academic record. Upon graduation, Frank entered private practice, and by the time he was thirty he was admitted to full partnership in the Chicago law firm of Levinson, Cleveland, and Schwartz. In 1927 he left Chicago to continue his private practice in New York with the firm of Chadbourne, Stanchfield, and Levy, one of the biggest and most important corporate firms in the nation. But Frank disliked Wall Street, and when Franklin D. Roosevelt* was elected to the presidency, he took advantage of his acquaintance with Felix Frankfurter* to obtain a post in the new administration.

Frank was named general counsel to the Agricultural Adjustment Administration* and quickly established his office as a leading force for liberal reform with the Agriculture Department and the administration. He assembled a talented staff of lawyers, all with a dedication to reform, and some, it was alleged, with a penchant for communism. Among Frank's subordinates at the AAA were Alger Hiss,* Abe Fortas,* Adlai Stevenson, and Thurman Arnold.* Frank and his men soon fell into factional infighting with George Peek,* the administrator of the AAA, who favored a conservative approach to the nation's problems in general and to the farmers' problems in particular. Peek was soon replaced by Chester Davis,* but the tension within the AAA continued. In early 1935 it reached a peak, and Roosevelt found it necessary to dismiss Frank.

Frank left Washington and returned to his private law practice in New York but continued an active association with the Roosevelt administration. In 1937 he was recalled to Washington and named a commissioner of the Securities and Exchange Commission,* at the suggestion of commission chairman William O. Douglas.* When Douglas left the SEC to take his seat on the Supreme Court,* Frank was named his replacement as chairman. As the top man at the SEC, Frank clashed with conservative Wall-Street businessmen, who resented his conviction that the SEC existed to protect the investing public. Nevertheless, he pursued a vigorous enforcement of the Public Utility Holding Company Act* in an effort to rationalize the arcane organization of Wall-Street holding companies.

Frank's service to the Roosevelt administration throughout the 1930s extended far beyond his formal duties. He participated in the discussions that led to the drafting of the National Industrial Recovery Act of 1933;* his major contribution was the inclusion of a provision in the act guaranteeing the right of labor to bargain collectively. He also developed a plan to distribute surplus farm products to the unemployed and needy, a proposal implemented through the Federal Surplus Relief Corporation.* He was, briefly, special counsel to the Reconstruction Finance Corporation* but made no lasting contribution. During his return to private practice in 1936 and 1937 he served on a per diem basis as a litigator for the Public Works Administration* in an important suit against the Alabama Power Company.

The pinnacle of Frank's legal career came with his appointment to the United States Court of Appeals for the Second Circuit. Because of Frank's liberal views and because his court handled many important business cases arising out of New York City, his appointment generated some opposition. On the bench, Frank was known for his opinions advancing civil liberties and the rights of criminal defendants. His opinions drew often from extra-legal sources and dealt with legal problems in the light of broad political, social, and moral considerations. They reveal the depth of Frank's mind and the breadth of his education.

Frank was the author of several important books dealing with politics and jurisprudence and was known for his incisive speeches and articles. Perhaps his most important contribution to legal scholarship was the influential *Law and the Modern Mind* (1930), in which he argued that it was necessary for lawyers and judges "to look at, not away from, the non-rational and non-idealistic elements at play" in the mind of the judge. Later, he wrote several important pieces on "fact-skepticism," challenging the ability of the modern legal system to reach unambiguous and unbiased decisions on matters of fact. After a distinguished career on the bench, Frank died suddenly on January 13, 1957. (J. Mitchell Rosenberg, *Jerome Frank: Jurist and Philosopher*, 1970; Walter E. Volkomer, *The Passionate Liberal: The Political and Legal Ideas of Jerome Frank*, 1970.)

WILLIAM LASSER

FRANKFURTER, FELIX Felix Frankfurter was born to Jewish parents in Vienna on November 15, 1882. The family immigrated to New York City in 1894, and the brilliant, ambitious young immigrant graduated from the City College of New York in 1901. He consistently led his class at Harvard Law School. He regarded religion as an accident of birth and was determined to become a part of the Brahmin establishment. Frankfurter returned to New York in 1904 and went to work for Hornblower, Byrne, Miller and Potter, a distinguished Harvard bastion. In the fall of 1906 he went to work for Henry L. Stimson,* the new United States attorney for the Southern District of New York.

Stimson became his mentor. When President William Howard Taft appointed Stimson secretary of war, Frankfurter was appointed law officer in the Bureau of Insular Affairs in the War Department. In 1914 Frankfurter began his remarkable career at Harvard. He supplemented the traditional Langdellian case method of instruction with large doses of history, economics, political science and sociology in order to demonstrate the importance of the law's social context. He hoped students would come to realize that the law constituted more than judge-made rules and that legislation could become a positive force in the resolution of social problems. When he reentered government service in 1917 he became a one man employment agency, staffing the burgeoning network of government agencies with his competent young law students. He travelled throughout the western states mediating labor disputes as a member of the President's Mediation Commission. Wilson then appointed him chairman of the newly created War Labor Policies Board in the Labor Department.

During the 1920s, the Supreme Court's* aggressive use of the due process clause to destroy social experimentation in the states dramatized for Frankfurter the dangers of centralization that existed in every exercise of federal judicial power. Justice Louis Brandeis'* robust defense of decentralization made more sense to Frankfurter as the federal judicial veto continued to thwart social reformers. His liberal politics brought him into sharp conflict with Harvard President A. Lawrence Lowell. The dean of Harvard Law School, Roscoe Pound, promised him free time for outside activities. Frankfurter helped defend liberal academic colleagues at Harvard and other institutions, and Sacco and Vanzetti, and such groups as the NAACP* and the ACLU.

After Franklin D. Roosevelt's* election as governor of New York in 1928, Frankfurter reopened a relationship that had flourished briefly during the last years of the Wilson administration and continued off and on in the postwar decade. In visits to Albany he shared with Roosevelt many key ideas of his political and economic philosophy: the importance of fostering federalism, the management of contemporary economic life through government spending, and the crucial role that could be played in modern government by university trained experts.

Frankfurter never held an official position in Roosevelt's administration. Roosevelt asked him to become solicitor general, but he was already committed to becoming the Visiting Eastman Professor at Oxford in 1933. His primary contribution to the New Deal* was his ability to measure and allocate the talents of the gifted young lawyers who had studied under him at Harvard. Before sailing for England he helped to draft the Securities Act of 1933,* expressed apprehension about NRA* code arrangements, and cautiously supported the AAA.* He felt both programs emphasized centralized planning and promoted monopolies. He also felt both laws had been poorly drafted.

At Oxford, Frankfurter cultivated a friendship with John Maynard Keynes* and arranged for Roosevelt to meet Keynes later. When he returned to New York in 1934, Frankfurter agreed that Roosevelt should begin a bold spending program, especially for housing and large public works. At first Roosevelt expressed annoyance at his friend's grandiose fiscal ideas but was eventually convinced. Roosevelt had little choice but to join the liberals in 1935, and Frankfurter played a critical role in this shift. He became a source of almost constant intellectual stimulation while pushing the president leftward, and he placed his personal mark upon more pieces of legislation in 1935 than any other adviser. The Wealth Tax of 1935,* showed both Frankfurter's commitment to localism and his hostility to concentrated economic power, positions that infuriated both big businessmen and national planners. The momentum of reform, generated with Frankfurter's assistance, continued into the election of 1936.* The New Deal placed more emphasis on social justice, income redistribution, and reducing the power of big business. Frankfurter urged an all-out war upon concentrated economic power represented by "interlocking directors, interlocking bankers, and interlocking lawyers." He felt it "necessary to destroy the roots of economic fascism in this country, if we wish to remove the dangers of political fascism, which engulf freedom in other lands."

Frankfurter hoped to delay as long as possible a final confrontation between the Roosevelt administration and the Supreme Court. He advised the administration's lawyers to avoid litigation at all costs and specifically warned Stanley Reed,* the solicitor general, not to appeal adverse rulings on the NRA's lumber code and the AAA's live poultry code. After the government's humiliating defeat on both issues, Associate Justice Brandeis urged Frankfurter to explain to the president that the Court was determined to put an end to centralization. The president became more defiant than ever. Frankfurter warned Roosevelt against a general attack on the Court and suggested he seek broad political support for his programs and then propose a constitutional amendment giving the federal government adequate power to cope with national economic and industrial problems. Roosevelt opted for the "court-packing"* scheme, and Frankfurter urged him to be more candid with the American people by deemphasizing the issues of judicial efficiency and stressing the Court's abuse of power. He never endorsed the president's plan openly, but Frankfurter was pleased that a chastised court began to be more responsive to New Deal legislation.

American liberals, scarred by the court-packing battle, were encouraged by Frankfurter's appointment to the Supreme Court in 1939. The fact that he was a Jew, a liberal, and an internationalist almost kept him off the Court, but his friends convinced Roosevelt that Frankfurter was the most qualified candidate by virtue of intellect and experience, and the one appointment most likely to bring stability as well as luster to the Court. As a loyal New Dealer, Frankfurter could be expected to defend the social and economic gains of the decade. Public reaction to his appointment was generally favorable, and he was confirmed without a dissenting vote. Although his overt activities as adviser to the president were curtailed after he took his place on the Supreme Court, Roosevelt still called upon him for advice, particularly in reviewing speeches and making government appointments.

By the end of his second term, Roosevelt had appointed five justices to the Supreme Court. For a brief period, Frankfurter led his liberal colleagues, but he began to isolate himself as he became a more persistent and strident spokesman for austere judicial self-restraint. The other members of the Court were forging more innovative judicial philosophies that involved civil liberties and human rights. With Roosevelt's death in 1945, Frankfurter's behind-the-scenes intervention in government affairs ceased. At the end of 1958 he began to have the first indications of the coronary affliction that finally felled him. Upon his retirement in August 1962, President John F. Kennedy appointed Arthur Goldberg to his seat. Two days before his death in 1965, Frankfurter instructed his biographer Max Freedman to "tell the whole story. Let people see how much I loved Roosevelt, how much I loved my country, and let them see how great a man Roosevelt really was." (H. N. Hirsch, *The Enigma of Felix Frankfurter*, 1981; Michael E. Parrish, *Felix Frankfurter and His Times*, 1982; Max Freedman, *Roosevelt and Frankfurter*, 1967.)

ANITA PILLING

FRAZIER-LEMKE FARM BANKRUPTCY ACT OF 1934 (See FEDERAL FARM BANKRUPTCY ACT OF 1934.)

FRAZIER, LYNN JOSEPH Lynn J. Frazier was born near Medford, Minnesota, on December 21, 1874. He moved with his parents to the Dakota Territory in 1881 when they decided to homestead a tract of land in Pembina County. Frazier graduated from the Mayville State Normal School in 1895 and from the University of North Dakota in 1901. He farmed in Pembina County for several years and became active in the politics of the new Nonpartisan League.* Representing the league in the election of 1916, Frazier surprised himself and everyone else by winning the governorship. He was re-elected in 1918 and 1920, but the postwar backlash caught up with his progressive politics, and he was ''recalled'' from the governor's mansion in 1921. Frazier than affiliated himself with the Republican party* and won election to the United States Senate in 1922. He was temporarily read out of the Republican party in 1924 for endorsing the Progressive presidential candidacy of Robert M. La Follette, but was nonetheless re-elected to the Senate in 1928 and 1934. During the New Deal,* Frazier allied himself with the Progressive Republican coalition in the Senate and worked with people like Senators Charles McNary* of Oregon and Robert La Follette, Jr.,* of Wisconsin in promoting federal legislation to assist the unemployed and underprivileged and to regulate the power of the major corporations. Along with Congressman William Lemke* of North Dakota, Frazier sponsored the two Frazier-Lemke bills to address the problem of farm debt. His intense foreign policy isolationism was as strong as anyone's in the Senate, and he failed to be renominated in 1940 when William Langer won the Republican primary. Frazier returned to farming in Pembina County and died on January 11, 1947. (*New York Times*, January 12, 1947.)

FREUND, PAUL ABRAHAM Paul A. Freund was born February 16, 1908, in St. Louis, Missouri. He graduated from Washington University in 1928, took a law degree at Harvard in 1931, and then spent a year of postgraduate work as a research assistant to Professor Felix Frankfurter.* In 1932 Freund went to Washington for a year as clerk to Supreme Court* Justice Louis Brandeis,* and at the end of the term he went to work in the legal division of the Department of the Treasury. Freund spent most of his time on special assignments from Under Secretary of the Treasury Dean Acheson.* But in November 1933, when Acheson had to resign because of his opposition to Franklin D. Roosevelt's gold-buying program,* Freund left the Justice Department for Stanley Reed's* legal staff in the Reconstruction Finance Corporation.* Freund did much of the work in preparing the government's case defending gold-buying and the abrogation of gold clauses in private and public bonds. When Stanley Reed became solicitor general of the United States in 1935, Freund moved with him back to the Department of Justice and worked on most of the government's cases before the Supreme Court between 1935 and 1939. In 1939 Freund left Washington to teach law at Harvard. He returned to the Justice Department in 1942 to work as an assistant to Solicitor General Charles Fahy,* and then went back to Harvard in 1946. During his two stints with the Office of Solicitor General, Freund argued thirty cases before the Supreme Court. He turned down an offer to become solicitor general under John F. Kennedy, eventually becoming Carl M. Loeb University Professor Emeritus at Harvard. (Katie Louchheim, ed., *The Making of the New Deal. The Insiders Speak*, 1983.)

G

GANNETT, FRANK ERNEST Frank E. Gannett was born on September 15, 1876, on Gannett Hill, forty-eight miles southeast of Rochester, New York. He graduated from Cornell in 1898 and then worked for a year as secretary to Jacob Gould Schurman, chairman of the First Philippine Commission. In 1900 Gannett became city editor of *The Ithaca News* in Ithaca, New York, and bought the paper three years later. He bought half-interest in *The Elmira Gazette* in 1906 and in 1918 moved to Rochester and purchased the *Rochester Union and Advertiser* and *The Rochester Times*. Later he combined them into *The Rochester Times-Union*. Through his Gannett Company as the parent organization supervising his interests, Gannett eventually built a media empire which included twenty-two newspapers, five radio stations, and three television stations. As an old guard Republican, Gannett was an outspoken opponent of Franklin D. Roosevelt* and the New Deal.* He organized the National Committee to Uphold Constitutional Government in 1937 to "help mobilize and coordinate individual and mass protests against the proposed undermining of our independent judiciary." After the "court-packing"* scheme, Gannett's national committee fought against the Reorganization Act of 1939* as an attempt "to undermine democratic government and substitute centralized one-man power—inevitable forerunner of dictatorship." In March 1938 the committee claimed that Franklin D. Roosevelt was "deliberately trying to liquidate our democratic institutions, and set up in their place . . . a political and economic dictatorship." Over the years the national committee continued to resist a wide range of New Deal reform and relief legislation. Gannett tried to secure the Republican presidential nomination in 1940 but could not outmaneuver Wendell Willkie.* Between 1940 and 1942 he served as assistant chairman of the Republican National Committee. As for the National Committee to Uphold Constitutional Government, it did not really survive Franklin D. Roosevelt's re-election in 1940. The committee's contribution-base began to erode rapidly early in 1941. It disbanded in April 1941 and was replaced by a corporation titled the Committee for Constitutional Government. Frank Gannett died on December 3, 1957. (*New York Times*, December 4, 1957; Richard Polenberg, "The National Committee to Uphold Constitutional Government, 1937–1941," *Journal of American History*, LII:582–598, 1965.)

GARNER, JOHN NANCE Born on November 22, 1868, in Red River County, Texas, John Nance Garner had few opportunities for advanced education. He read law privately and entered the Texas bar in 1890. Garner practiced law privately until 1898, when he won election to the Texas House of Representatives. In 1902, he was elected to Congress, and he maintained his seat for the next thirty years. During the Republican ascendancy of the 1920s, Garner emerged as a leader of the Democratic party,* and in 1931 he was elected Speaker of the House by the narrow margin of three votes. As leader of the opposition, Garner steered a delicate course, favoring such Herbert Hoover* policies as the RFC* but offering Democratic alternatives in order to assure the party's success in 1932. He became a favorite-son candidate for the presidency at the Democratic convention in Chicago. Governor Franklin D. Roosevelt* of New York emerged as the front-runner but lacked the two-thirds* vote necessary for nomination. On the fourth ballot Garner released his delegates, principally from Texas and California, in order to avoid the divisive results of the deadlocked 1924 convention. His move created a stampede to Roosevelt, and in turn, the party faithful nominated Garner for the vice-presidency by acclamation. During the election campaign, Garner offered his Southwestern colloquialisms and blunt opinions when asked but generally adopted a low profile and let Roosevelt do most of the public appearances.

As vice-president, Garner shunned the social amenities of the office and in matters of policy deferred to Roosevelt. During the first three months of the New Deal,* Garner teamed with Roosevelt in the experimental approach to relief and recovery. Only on two issues did he differ with the president: the need to guarantee bank deposits following the period of bank holidays* and the rush to grant diplomatic recognition to Russia. On the former Roosevelt became a convert but on the latter Garner's cautionary notes failed to prevail. The tandem of Roosevelt and Garner worked so well that the 1936 Democratic convention renominated them by acclamation. Their Republican opponents, Governor Alf Landon* and Colonel Frank Knox, carried only the states of Maine and Vermont.

As a result of the adoption of the Twentieth Amendment to the constitution, their second inauguration took place on January 20, 1937. During this second term, a number of issues divided the pair. Although there was no open disruption, the channels of communication were interrupted and the executive-legislative cooperation broken. From Garner's perspective, the most divisive issues were the following: Roosevelt's failure to oppose the sit-down strike in the labor-management struggles, the continuance of an unbalanced budget, the "court-packing"* scheme, the interference in the Senate leadership contest between Alben Barkley* of Kentucky and Pat Harrison* of Mississippi, the "leftish" reform inclinations evidenced in the desire to "purge" Democratic conservatives, and ultimately the decision to violate the unwritten constitutional prohibition against a third term. This disenchantment led Garner to seek the party nomination in 1940 against Roosevelt, but the primary results were crushing to his hopes and the convention unsympathetic to his conservative stances. Henry A. Wallace* replaced him as the vice-presidential running mate. Roosevelt and Wallace then defeated Wendell L. Willkie* and Senator Charles McNary* of Oregon. Garner retired to the Texas homestead, where he died on November 7, 1967. (Ovie C. Fisher, *Cactus Jack*, 1978; Bascom N. Timmons, *Garner of Texas*, 1948.)

ROBERT A. WALLER

GARRISON, LLOYD KIRKHAM Lloyd K. Garrison was born in New York City on November 19, 1897. He graduated from Harvard in 1919 and took a law degree there in 1922. Garrison then practiced law in New York with Root, Clark, Buckner, and Howland between 1922 and 1926 and with Parker and Garrison between 1926 and 1932. In 1932 Garrison was selected as the dean of the University of Wisconsin Law School, a position he held until 1945. At President Franklin D. Roosevelt's* request, he agreed to accept the chairmanship of the National Labor Relations Board* in the summer of 1934, but he insisted on limiting his stay to only four months, since he wanted to return to the University of Wisconsin. At the NLRB, he appointed Harry A. Millis,* a labor economist, and Edwin Smith, formerly commissioner of labor in Massachusetts, to serve with him on the board. From the outset, Garrison treated the National Labor Relations Board as a legal agency rather than a mediating instrument between management and labor. Because of that philosophy, the NLRB began to accumulate a body of labor common law, which continued under the chairmanship of Francis Biddle.* During his four months in office, Garrison constantly pushed the National Recovery Administration* and the Justice Department to enforce Section 7(a) of the National Industrial Recovery Act* to make sure that businesses were allowing labor to bargain collectively. He grew extremely frustrated with the NRA and the Justice Department for their reluctance to file lawsuits in NLRB cases. The board had responsibility but no power, and Garrison publicly demanded more cooperation. He returned to Wisconsin in the fall of 1934, but his demands helped spark labor criticism of the administration and led to passage of the National Labor Relations Act in 1935.* During World War II he was general counsel and then director of the National War Labor Board; and during the 1950s and 1960s, while maintaining his private law practice, Garrison was active in the American Civil Liberties Union, the National Urban League (which he served as president from 1947 to 1952), and as legal counsel to various civil rights organizations. (Peter H. Irons, *The New Deal Lawyers*, 1982.)

GEORGE, WALTER FRANKLIN Walter F. George, conservative Democrat and opponent of the New Deal,* was born on January 29, 1878, on a farm near Preston, Georgia. The son of tenant farmers, George nevertheless triumphed academically, graduating in 1900 from Mercer University and from the law school there in 1901. He began practicing law in Vienna, Georgia, and served as solicitor general of the Cordele judicial court between 1907 and 1912 and judge of the superior court between 1912 and 1917. From 1917 to 1922 George was an associate justice of the state supreme court, but he resigned after being elected to the United States Senate to fill the seat vacated by the death of Thomas E. Watson. George was re-elected in 1926 and 1932 and became a political institution in Georgia.

During the first two years of the New Deal, George did not assume any significant public profile as an opponent of Franklin D. Roosevelt.* Blessed with a judicial mind which searched for precedents, he became increasingly concerned about the drift of New Deal legislation after 1935. He maintained close ties with the Georgia business community, particularly the Coca-Cola Company and the Georgia Power Company, and hated the Wealth Tax Act of 1935* and the Public Utility Holding Company Act of 1935.* When Roosevelt proposed the "court-packing"* plan in 1937, George saw only a conspiracy to increase the power of the executive branch as well as the federal government. He viewed executive reorganization in 1939 in the same light. George also resented the New Deal support for labor rights and the consistent deficit spending. He became close to Frank Gannett* and his National Committee to Uphold Constitutional Government* and in the process earned the enmity of President Roosevelt. In the Democratic primaries of 1938, Roosevelt openly favored George's opponent, Lawrence Camp, funneled campaign money into the campaign, and engaged in local political rhetoric as no president had in American history. The attempt to "purge" George, however, backfired when Georgia Democrats renominated him handily. George was later re-elected in 1938, 1944, and 1950 and served as president pro tempore of the Senate between 1955 and 1957. He did not run for re-election in 1956, and served as President Dwight D. Eisenhower's special ambassador to NATO. George died on August 4, 1957. (James T. Patterson, *Congressional Conservatism and the New Deal*, 1967.)

GERARD, LEONA B. Leona B. Gerard was born in 1899 and educated at the University of Chicago, where she graduated Phi Beta Kappa in 1920. Gerard was very active in the League of Women Voters, and there she became a friend of Harold L. Ickes.* Ickes invited her to Washington, D.C., in October 1933, and Gerard became a political aide to the secretary of interior and an assistant division chief in the Department of Labor. She worked for the federal government until the late 1950s and began a writing career, which resulted in *Poems Mostly about Love and Other Benchmarks* (1977) and *Benchmarks* II (1980). (Katie Louchheim, ed., *The Making of the New Deal. The Insiders Speak*, 1983.)

GERRY, PETER GOELET Peter G. Gerry was born in New York City on September 18, 1879. He attended and graduated from Harvard University in 1901, then studied law privately, and was admitted to the Rhode Island bar in 1906. A conservative Democrat, Gerry served one term in Congress between 1913 and 1915, was elected to the Senate in 1922, defeated in 1928, and then re-elected to the Senate in 1934 and served until 1947. Gerry was not a candidate for re-election in 1946. During the years of the New Deal,* Gerry was known widely as an opponent of Franklin D. Roosevelt.* He opposed the Agricultural Adjustment Administration* because he believed its processing taxes were hurting Rhode Island textile mills. The president's "court-packing"* scheme enraged him as an example of executive authoritarianism, as did the administrative reorganization plan. Gerry regularly allied himself with a coalition of conservative Republicans and anti-New Deal Democrats during the 1930s. After his retirement from the Senate, Gerry resumed his law practice and died on October 31, 1957. (*New York Times*, November 1, 1957.)

GIANNINI, AMADEO PETER Amadeo Peter Giannini was born on May 6, 1870, in San Jose, California. He quit school in 1883 to go to work in the family produce business, and by 1891 he owned half-interest in the firm. Giannini retired in 1901 with a small fortune. When his father-in-law died in 1902, family members asked Giannini to manage the estate, including shares in Columbus Savings and Loan Society. Giannini encouraged the institution to cultivate the favor of small borrowers and depositors. When they refused, Giannini resigned and organized the Bank of Italy in 1904 with assets totaling $300,000. The bank's clientele consisted almost exclusively of Italian merchants, laborers, and small businesses. When the California legislature passed a statute in 1909 permitting branch banking, Giannini quickly expanded, and by 1918 had twenty-four branches in addition to headquarters in San Francisco. In 1927 Giannini merged his banking interests into the Bank of Italy National Trust and Savings Association, eventually to be known as the Bank of America, part of the Transamerica Corporation.

Through careful management, cutting costs, and campaigning for accounts, Giannini guided his network of banks through the Great Depression, but in 1932 he had to accept a loan for $15 million from the RFC.* During the 1930s, Giannini was a fervent supporter of Franklin D. Roosevelt's* New Deal.* Unlike most bankers, he had only praise for the Emergency Banking Act of 1933,* the Banking Act of 1933,* and the Banking Act of 1935.* He frequently told the president not to worry about deficit spending for relief measures, since it was "money well spent." He viewed the federal government as a stabilizing influence in an economy gone awry, since there was "something wrong with a system that lets 14,000,000 men get out of work." In 1934 Giannini retired as chairman of the board of the Bank of America. He died of a heart attack on June 3, 1949. (Marquis James and Bessie R. James, *Biography of a Bank. The Story of Bank of America, NT & SA*, 1954.)

GILLETTE, GUY MARK Guy Mark Gillette was an independent New Dealer from Iowa. Born on February 3, 1879, in Cherokee, Iowa, he served as a sergeant in the army during the Spanish-American War, graduated from Drake University, and was admitted to the Iowa bar in 1900. He was city attorney of Cherokee from 1906 to 1907, Cherokee County district attorney until 1909, and won a seat in the Iowa state legislature in 1912. After a tour in the army during World War I, Gillette returned to Iowa and worked as a farmer and dairyman for fourteen years. He won a seat in Congress in 1932 and was re-elected in 1934. In 1936 Gillette won the special election to the United States Senate seat vacated by the death of Richard Louis Murphy. Gillette's primary interests were exposing semi-monopolies in the food industry, eliminating middleman profiteering, and opposing the National Recovery Administration* and the Agricultural Adjustment Act.* President Franklin D. Roosevelt* wanted Gillette defeated in the Democratic primaries of 1938, but he was returned to the Senate with the support of the AFL,* Iowa Catholics, and the Democratic political machine of Iowa. Part of the midwestern isolationist tradition, Gillette opposed the drift of American foreign policy in the 1930s, speaking out against lend-lease, extension of the draft, and any modifications of the Neutrality Acts. He did not support Roosevelt's bid for a fourth term in 1944 and lost his own re-election campaign to Republican Bourke B. Hickenlooper. Roosevelt then appointed Gillette to head the Surplus Property Disposal Board, a position he held for only five months before resigning. In August 1945 Gillette became president of the American League for a Free Palestine, a group lobbying for an independent Jewish state. He served one more term in the Senate between 1948 and 1954, and after losing the election of 1954 he retired, serving as legal counsel for several Senate committees until 1961. Guy Gillette died on March 3, 1973. (*New York Times*, March 4, 1973.)

CHARLES E. DARBY, JR.

GIRDLER, TOM MERCER Tom M. Girdler, steel executive and foe of the New Deal,* was born in Clark County, Indiana, on May 19, 1877. His father operated a farm and a cement mill, but family income was limited. Only with financial help from a rich aunt could Girdler afford to send his son to college. Tom graduated from Lehigh University in 1901 with a degree in mechanical engineering and went to work as a sales engineer in the London office of the Buffalo Forge Company. After a year in England Girdler returned to Pittsburgh to take a job with the Oliver Iron and Steel Company. He later worked for short periods with the Colorado Fuel and Iron Company in Pueblo and for Atlantic Steel Company in Atlanta. In 1914 Girdler was hired by Jones and Laughlin Steel Corporation, where he stayed until 1930, having risen to the presidency of the company. That year Cyrus Eaton, the Cleveland financier, hired Girdler to take charge of the newly-organized Republic Steel Corporation. The company operated at a loss until 1935, when it earned $4.5 million. By 1937 it was showing annual earnings of around $9 million and had plants and mines in seventy-seven cities.

By this time John L. Lewis* and his Committee for Industrial Organizations* had won a contract with United States Steel and were moving for a pact with "little steel" (Republic, Bethlehem, and smaller companies). Girdler and his associates, he later wrote, "were determined to fight." During the six-week strike that followed, nearly a million men were made idle and there were over

500 instances of violence. Despite union picketing, Republic Steel officials tried to keep the plants in operation, sending food and supplies to workers inside the plants. On May 30, 1937, Memorial Day, some 2,000 people gathered a half mile from Republic's South Chicago plant for a picnic and protest march. As the marchers started moving across a marshy prairie toward the plant, they were confronted by several hundred armed policemen, nervous and uncomfortable in their heavy winter uniforms. When the marchers were about 250 yards from the plant, with some of them taunting the police and throwing a few rocks, the police began to throw gas shells into the crowd. There followed a few gunshots, after which the marchers turned and ran. The police began firing volleys at the retreating mass. Ten marchers were killed and over ninety wounded, the majority of them shot or clubbed from behind. Girdler blamed John L. Lewis and associates for the "Memorial Day massacre." President Franklin D. Roosevelt,* shocked and angered, blamed both Girdler and Lewis. ("A plague on both your houses," he said, thus insuring that neither man would support him in the election of 1940.) The strike was broken, and the workers went back to their jobs without a contract. But Girdler's victory was only temporary: in 1941 "little steel" signed contracts after the National Labor Relations Board* ordered the reinstatement of workers who had been discharged for involvement in the 1937 strike.

During World War II Girdler served as chairman of Republic Steel and of Consolidated Vultee Aircraft Corporation, commuting regularly by plane between Republic's headquarters in Cleveland and Convair's in San Diego. Under his direction both companies set remarkable production records. In the postwar years, Republic Steel spent heavily on new plants and expanded its work force to nearly 70,000. In 1956, when Girdler retired, the company's net income was $90.4 million, its highest profit to that date. Girdler retired to Harleigh, his thirteen-acre estate near Easton, Maryland. He died on February 4, 1965. (Tom M. Girdler, *Boot Straps*, 1943; Nathan Miller, *F. D. R.: An Intimate History*, 1983; *New York Times*, February 5, 1965; Studs Terkel, *Hard Times*, 1970.)

JOHN PAYNE

GLASS, CARTER Born in Lynchburg, Virginia, on January 4, 1858, Carter Glass was the son of Robert Henry Glass and Augusta Christian. His father was a newspaper editor, so Glass grew up in a political atmosphere. He attended school until he was fourteen; then he went to work as a printer's apprentice for the *Lynchburg Daily Republican*. Glass also worked for several years as an auditor for the Atlantic, Mississippi, and Ohio Railroad but in 1880 became a reporter and writer for the *Lynchburg Daily News*, a paper he purchased later in his life. Between 1881 and 1901 Glass was clerk for the Lynchburg city council, held a seat in the state senate between 1899 and 1903, and served in the United States House of Representatives from 1902 until 1918. As chairman of the House Committee on Banking and Currency, Glass was the sponsor and acknowledged "father" of the Federal Reserve Bank Act in 1913. For the rest of his life, Glass treated the Federal Reserve System as one of his own family, tenaciously guarding its independence. Between 1918 and 1920 Glass served as secretary of the treasury under Woodrow Wilson. He resigned that position in 1920 to accept appointment to the United States Senate, filling the seat vacated by the death of Thomas S. Martin of Virginia. Glass was re-elected to the Senate in 1924, 1930, 1936, and 1942 and served as president pro tempore of the Senate between 1941 and 1945.

In 1933 President Franklin D. Roosevelt* offered Glass the cabinet position of secretary of the treasury, but he declined it, preferring the power he had as an experienced Democratic senator and chairman of the Senate Appropriations Committee. He was also worried about Roosevelt's monetary views, concerned that the president might turn to inflationary tinkering if prices continued to fall. Glass became particularly disturbed with the gold-buying* program of late 1933, and even by the late summer of 1933 already believed that the New Deal* was a "dangerous effort of the federal government to transplant Hitlerism to every corner of the nation." Glass opposed massive government spending, feared the growth of the federal bureaucracy, and worried about the prerogatives of the state governments. As a conservative Democrat, Glass was frequently disturbed by bureaucracy, so much so that he opposed many New Deal programs on those grounds. He also chastised Roosevelt for the supply of lawyers and social workers who seemed to be "taking over the Democratic party."* Glass bitterly attacked the "court-packing"* scheme as proof of his worst fears. As a states' rights Democrat, protector of the Federal Reserve System, and spokesman for the banking community, Glass had also opposed the Federal Deposit Insurance Corporation* and the centralizing tendencies of the Banking Act of 1935,* finally acquiescing only when further resistance was pointless. From 1933 on, Carter Glass opposed most of the New Deal, even when it helped Virginia. Stubborn, exceedingly independent, and rigidly committed to his own point-of-view, Glass was a thorn in Roosevelt's side, but one which could not be politically removed because of the senator's popularity in Virginia. Glass never made the transition from what he called the progressivism of Woodrow Wilson to the "radicalism" of Franklin D. Roosevelt. Carter Glass died on May 28, 1946. (Norman Beasley, *Carter Glass: A Biography*, 1939; James T. Patterson, *Congressional Conservatism and the New Deal*, 1967.)

GLASS-STEAGALL BANKING ACT OF 1933 (See BANKING ACT OF 1933.)

GLAVIS, LOUIS RUSSELL Louis Glavis was born in Eastern Shore, Maryland, on June 10, 1883, the son of George O. Glavis and Lucette Smith. He graduated from the Lawrenceville (N. Y.) School in 1899 and in 1904 got a job as a special agent in the General Land Office of the Department of the Interior. In 1909 Glavis sided with Gifford Pinchot, chief of the U.S. Forest Service, in his dispute with Secretary of the Interior Richard A. Ballinger over Ballinger's decision to reopen several water power sites in Wyoming and Montana to public development. Glavis was dismissed, and on November 13, 1909, he published an article in *Collier's* charging that Ballinger had sided with Guggenheim interests in privately patenting claims to Alaskan coal fields. After leaving the Department of the Interior, Glavis studied law and was admitted to the California bar in 1914. He practiced law in San Francisco and Washington, D.C., and in 1933 Secretary of the Interior Harold Ickes* appointed Glavis to his staff. President Franklin D. Roosevelt* also signed an order restoring Glavis' civil service status. Glavis served as Ickes' special investigator and sometimes tapped the phones of Interior Department employees to provide information to his chief. Between July 1936 and January 1937 Glavis was the chief investigator for the Senate Campaign Expenditures Committee. He left government service for private law practice in 1937. Louis Glavis died on November 20, 1971. (*Who Was Who in America*, V:272, 1973.)

GOLD-BUYING PROGRAM (See GOLD RESERVE ACT OF 1934.)

"GOLD CASES" "Gold cases" was a collective name given to four cases which had the common characteristic of challenging the constitutionality of the Emergency Banking Act* of March 9, 1933, and the Joint Resolution of June 5, 1933, which repudiated the gold clause in all private and government obligations. The common charge was that these measures abrogated the obligations of contract without due process, in violation of the Constitution. Chief Justice Charles Evans Hughes* wrote the majority decisions in all four cases which were argued before the Court between January 8 and 11, 1935, and decided on February 18, 1935. These cases were: *Norman v. Baltimore & Ohio Railroad Company; United States et al. v. Bankers' Trust Company* (294 U.S. 240); *Nortz v. United States* (294 U.S. 317); and *Perry v. United States* (294 U.S. 330).

The first two cases originated in lower federal courts. Both involved suits by bondholders who complained that the obligations due them were originally stated in gold coin rather then in depreciated paper dollars. They insisted on payment in currency equal in value to the gold content as of May 1, 1903 (i.e., at 25.8 grains of gold .9 fine). That would have meant a 69 percent mark-up in the dollar value of the obligation. In *Nortz v. U.S.*, a case which originated in the court of claims, the plaintiff had been required to surrender $10,000 in gold certificates by changes in national monetary policy. He claimed the difference between the value in gold of the gold certificates he had given up and the currency he received in place of these certificates. In *Perry v. United States*, which also arose in the court of claims, the plaintiff held a $10,000 Liberty Loan Gold Bond issued during World War I. He too insisted that he had a right to recover the difference between the original gold value of the bond and the mature value in "new" dollars.

In the first two cases, Chief Justice Hughes upheld the validity of congressional action on monetary policy. He asserted that it was clearly within the power of

Congress to establish a uniform currency, to set the relative value between different kinds of currency, and to make the currency legal tender for the payment of debts. Concerning the gold clauses in private contracts, he asserted: "It is clearly shown that these clauses interfere with the exertion of the power granted to the Congress, and certainly it is not established that the Congress arbitrarily or capriciously decided that such an interference existed."

In *Nortz v. United States*, Chief Justice Hughes rejected the contentions of the petitioner in a very short brief. The petitioner claimed a right to be paid in gold coin when he surrendered his gold certificates to the treasury on January 17, 1934, in accordance with the Emergency Banking Act.* But in lieu of being paid in gold, he demanded "just compensation." Justice Hughes noted that gold certificates were currency and did not involve any contractual obligations. As far as claims for compensation, Hughes responded: "It is plain that he cannot claim any better position than that in which he would have been placed had the gold coin then been paid to him." That is, had Nortz been paid in gold, he would have had to turn the gold in to the treasury and would have received currency for it. The dollar had not yet been devalued, so the petitioner had not sustained any loss. He was not entitled, therefore, to any compensation.

Perry v. United States was a more difficult matter because it did involve contractual obligations of the United States government which were abrogated by the Joint Resolution of June 5, 1933. Chief Justice Hughes concluded: "the Joint Resolution . . . in so far as it attempted to override the obligation created by the bond in suit, went beyond the congressional power." But that proved to be little comfort to Perry. Hughes found untenable the petitioner's claim that he was entitled to $1.69 in currency for every dollar promised on the bond, i.e., the difference in the gold content between the "old" and "new" dollar. The chief justice contended that such a formula was without merit, and the petitioner had been unable to show any loss in buying power. Thus, said Hughes, compensation would not constitute recoupment of losses, but unjustified enrichment. The chief justice denied to Perry any right to sue in the court of claims. (*Supreme Court Reporter*, LV:407–439, 1935; Alfred H. Kelly and Winfred A. Harbison, *The American Constitution*, 1970.)

JOSEPH M. ROWE, JR.

GOLD RESERVE ACT OF 1934 Most historians have agreed that Franklin D. Roosevelt,* if anything, was a pragmatist willing to employ a variety of programs to stimulate recovery. His gold-buying program* of late 1933 and early 1934 was a perfect illustration. Along with large numbers of Americans, President Roosevelt had been especially concerned about the deflationary spiral and the demands of western farmers and mining interests to inflate the currency. On April 19, 1933, to help create a proper atmosphere for some domestic price-raising ventures, Roosevelt abandoned the gold-standard, much to the consternation of conservative advisers like Lewis Douglas* and Henry Morgenthau, Jr.* A few months later, fascinated by the "commodity dollar"* theories of economists

Irving Fisher,* George Warren,* and Frank Pearson, Roosevelt inaugurated his gold-buying program. The major theory behind the "commodity dollar" was the belief that if the government purchased gold at steadily increasing prices, the United States would deflate the value of the dollar, trigger a rise in wholesale prices, and capture an increased share of world trade. Business confidence would revive as would employment and production. The dollar devaluation, they argued, would restore the connection between the prices of consumer goods and raw materials. This was the "commodity dollar"—fixed purchasing power for all commodities because the gold content of the dollar would be tied to the price index.

Late in October 1933 the president began meeting daily with George Warren, Jesse Jones,* and Henry Morgenthau, Jr., to set the price at which the government would purchase gold. They set a price above the world price for gold and altered it each day to keep speculators off guard. Wall-Street bankers were horrified by the program but inflation-devoted agrarian and business entrepreneurs in the South and West loved it. Close economic advisers like James Warburg* and Oliver M. W. Sprague* resigned from the administration over the program. Their doubts were well-founded. Commodity prices and farm prices continued to drop late in 1933, and the "commodity dollar" proved to be a short-term panacea. Roosevelt stopped buying gold in January 1934, and on January 30, 1934, he signed the Gold Reserve Act, giving him the power to fix the price of gold in the United States and concentrate more credit and currency power in the treasury. On January 31, 1934, the president set the price of gold at $35 an ounce, an amount fixing the value of the dollar at 59 percent of its pre-1933 level. The end of the gold manipulation program satisfied conservatives, but the monetary inflationists still wanted more. Their demands led to the Silver Purchase Act* later in the year. (William E. Leuchtenburg, *Franklin D. Roosevelt and the New Deal, 1932–1940*, 1963.)

GOLDSCHMIDT, ARTHUR Arthur Goldschmidt was born in San Antonio, Texas, in 1910. He graduated from Columbia University in 1932 and went to work as an aide to Harry Hopkins* in the Federal Emergency Relief Administration* in 1933. Because of his association with Hopkins, Goldschmidt played an important role in the establishment and early operation of the FERA, the Civil Works Administration,* National Youth Administration,* and the Works Progress Administration.* Later in the 1930s, Goldschmidt went to work in the Department of the Interior, first in the power division of the Public Works Administration* and then in the division of power for the entire department. After World War II, Goldschmidt was the Department of Interior's representative on the State Department's interdepartmental committees, and he helped in the development of the Marshall Plan and the Point Four program. Goldschmidt joined the United Nations in 1950 to help establish its technical assistance programs, and in 1966 President Lyndon B. Johnson appointed him as the U.S. representative to the UN Economic and Social Council. After 1969 Goldschmidt served as consultant for the United Nations Development Program. (Katie Louchheim, ed., *The Making of the New Deal. The Insiders Speak*, 1983.)

GOOD NEIGHBOR LEAGUE Just before his death, Louis Howe* suggested the creation of a Good Neighbor League to attract ministers, editors, social workers, and college professors into the Roosevelt camp for the election of 1936.* White House speechwriter Stanley High* formally organized the league in April 1936, and social worker Lillian Wald and philanthropist George Peabody agreed to serve as co-chairpersons. By the time of the election, the Good Neighbor League had been established in more than twenty states, and large numbers of its members were Republicans. Along with other groups like the Progressive National Committee* and the American Labor Party,* the Good Neighbor League helped Franklin D. Roosevelt* appeal to groups which might not normally have voted Democrat in 1936. (Arthur M. Schlesinger, Jr., *The Age of Roosevelt. Vol. III. The Politics of Upheaval, 1935–1936*, 1960.)

GORE, THOMAS PRYOR Thomas Pryor Gore was born on December 10, 1870, in Webster County, Mississippi. Blinded at the age of eleven by an accident, he went on to achieve excellent grades in high school and normal school. He taught school for three years to obtain the money needed to study law, and his interest in politics developed while serving as a page in the Mississippi legislature. Gore entered Mississippi politics in the 1890s as an outspoken Populist and continued as a Populist after moving to Texas. An ardent supporter of William Jennings Bryan, Gore stumped the Dakotas and Nebraska in Bryan's behalf during the presidential election of 1900. He moved to Lawton, Oklahoma, in 1901, and Lawton remained his permanent residence until his death. Gore served three years as a territorial commissioner; and when Oklahoma achieved statehood in 1907, he was elected as one of its two United States senators. He won re-election in 1908 and 1914 but lost the nomination in 1920. Gore was re-elected to the Senate during the Democratic congressional landslide of 1930, and during his third term sponsored legislation dealing with Indian affairs (especially tribal rights to oil royalties in Oklahoma), farm credits, banking, income tax reform, war debts, veterans' relief, fiscal reform in government, and tariff reform. He opposed President Franklin D. Roosevelt* on the National Recovery Act,* Social Security,* and work relief programs. Labor leaders warned Gore that his opposition to federal work relief might cost him his Senate seat in the 1936 elections,* but he remained an outspoken critic. As expected, he lost the Democratic primary in 1936. Gore then retired to practice law. He died in Washington, D.C., on March 16, 1949. (Monroe Billington, *Thomas P. Gore: The Blind Senator from Oklahoma*, 1967.)

GREAT PLAINS DROUGHT AREA COMMITTEE Because of severe droughts in the Midwest in 1934 and then another series of droughts in the

Midwest and Southeast in 1936, President Franklin D. Roosevelt* established the Great Plains Drought Area Committee on July 22, 1936. Morris L. Cooke* of the REA,* formerly head of the Mississippi Valley Committee, was designated chairman of the committee, and other members included John C. Page of the Bureau of Reclamation,* Frederick H. Fowler of the National Resources Committee,* Col. Richard C. Moore of the U.S. Army Corps of Engineers, Rexford Tugwell* of the Resettlement Administration,* and Harry Hopkins* of the Works Progress Administration.* The committee surveyed drought conditions, identified 1,194 counties in twenty-five states as drought areas, adjusted the soil conservation program to provide for increased grain production, created a Federal Livestock Feed Agency in Kansas City to coordinate feed distribution and stabilize prices, provided work relief to the needy, helped resettle hundreds of families, and generally coordinated federal relief activities. The committee's report, published as *The Future of the Great Plains*, recommended an intensive survey of Great Plains land and resources, acquisition of range lands for controlled sale or lease, encouragement of family-size farms large enough to give people an adequate living, development of small-scale irrigation projects, and permanent establishment of a government agency to coordinate economic and social activities on the Great Plains. (Richard Lowitt, *The New Deal and the West*, 1984.)

"GREENBELT TOWNS" In April 1935 President Franklin D. Roosevelt* united several different programs in the Resettlement Administration.* Assistant Secretary of Agriculture Rexford G. Tugwell* headed the new agency, which included rural rehabilitation and land programs and the subsistence homestead* projects. Tugwell successfully argued for additional funding from the Emergency Relief Appropriation Act of 1935* for a new program. He established a Suburban Resettlement Division within the RA to plan and construct new towns named "greenbelt towns" because each was to be surrounded by unoccupied land. Although twenty-five greenbelt towns were planned, financial and legal obstacles reduced the number to three. They were constructed between 1935 and 1938 and named Greenbelt, Maryland (near Washington, D.C.); Green Hills, Ohio (near Cincinnati); and Greendale, Wisconsin (near Milwaukee).

Major reasons for building the towns were to provide work for the unemployed, to build low-rent housing in pleasant surroundings for low-income families, and to demonstrate the utility of planning towns on principles that had been applied in the English "garden city" movement and in the planned community of Radburn, New Jersey. Each town was built on rural land, surrounded by fields and woods. Plans for the communities emphasized light, air, space, playgrounds, parks, gardens, and walkways, with highways relegated to the periphery. Services, retail establishments, and government offices were built in a single location known as the town center. The government appointed a resident community manager for each town.

Frequently called "Tugwell towns" in honor of their controversial sponsor, the greenbelt towns were plagued with troubles from the outset. In order to put men back to work quickly, the Resettlement Administration had to hurry both land acquisition and planning. Ultimately, the projects provided jobs for over 20,000 men for the three-year period, but costs were high. Over $36 million was spent on the three towns. The agency was forced to scale down its plans as expenses mounted, and fewer homes were constructed than originally planned. Only two-fifths of the funding could be used for family housing; the rest was spent on utilities and other expenses involved in constructing entire towns from the ground up. No industries were located in the towns, which meant that residents had to commute to jobs. Although some relocation of industry was planned for at least one community, Greendale, no funding was available to help businesses move.

Ignoring the heavy expenditures for community facilities, critics calculated the average unit cost for housing at $15,968—a figure that confirmed their allegations that the RA had failed to provide the promised low-cost housing. Among the critics were urban interests and private real estate and building firms. They maintained that the government had unnecessarily entered into competition with private enterprise. In the absence of widespread recognition of the intensity of housing problems, many agreed and added to their criticisms the charge that planned communities were the harbingers of socialistic regimentation.

The administration had planned to divest the government of ownership of the towns after construction, but action was delayed. Officials were concerned about preserving the original character of the communities and feared that rents might rise above prices tenants were able to afford. Consequently, the government continued to administer the towns until the early 1950s, when they were broken up into tracts and sold. (Joseph Arnold, *The New Deal in the Suburbs: A History of the Greenbelt Town Program, 1935–1954*, 1971.)

JANE A. ROSENBERG

GREEN, WILLIAM William Green guided the American Federation of Labor* from 1924 until 1952. Born in Coshocton, Ohio, on March 3, 1870, he quit school at the age of sixteen to work in the coal mines. He joined the United Mine Workers of America and became active in local leadership, serving as secretary, treasurer, and president of the local chapter. Green became the AFL statistician in 1911 and served as national secretary-treasurer from 1912 to 1924. He was elected vice-president and a member of the AFL executive council in 1913 and succeeded Samuel Gompers as president in 1924. A devoted Baptist and bitter anti-Communist, Green felt labor must be disciplined and responsible for winning management confidence. Strikes were always a last resort when peaceful negotiations and collective bargaining had failed. During the 1930s, Green became an ardent supporter of government legislation to protect workers and provide jobs. In 1933 he even threatened to call a general strike unless Senator Hugo Black's* thirty-hour work week bill was passed. Green had been instrumental in creating Ohio's workmen's compensation program, and in the

1930s he put the weight of the AFL behind the Social Security Act* and the National Labor Relations Act,* which guaranteed the right of labor to bargain collectively. During the 1930s and 1940s he served on the president's Committee on Economic Security,* National Recovery Administration,* Management-Labor Policy Committee of the War Production Board, the Economic Stabilization Board of the Office of Economic Stabilization, the Management Labor Council of the War Production Board, and the advisory council to the Office of War Mobilization and Reconversion. Throughout World War II he supported a no-strike pledge from labor to keep production lines operating at full speed. He opposed the Taft-Hartley Act of 1946 as a slave labor law, and in 1949 organized the International Confederation of Free Trade Unions. His last official act as president of the AFL was to endorse the presidential candidacy of Governor Adlai Stevenson of Illinois in September 1952 at the AFL convention in New York. Green died on November 21, 1952. (*New York Times*, November 22, 1952.)

GUFFEY, JOSEPH F. Joseph F. Guffey was born at Guffey's Station, Pennsylvania, on December 29, 1870. He attended the Princeton Preparatory School and Princeton University and went to work for the U.S. Postal Service in Pittsburgh in 1894. Between 1899 and 1918 he served as secretary and then general manager of a public utilities company and in 1918 was a member of the Petroleum Service Division of the War Industries Board and director of the Bureau of Sales of the Alien Property Custodian Office. A liberal Democrat, Guffey was a member of the Democratic National Committee between 1920 and 1932, and he won a seat in the United States Senate in 1934, where he quickly accumulated a record as an unabashed supporter of New Deal* labor, spending, and social welfare legislation. After the Supreme Court* nullified the National Recovery Administration* in 1935, Guffey sponsored the Guffey-Snyder Bituminous Coal Stabilization Act of 1935* to maintain federal coordination of the coal industry. When the Supreme Court declared it unconstitutional in 1936, Guffey sponsored the Guffey-Vinson Act of 1937* to replace it. He was also among the first northern Democrats to accept the growing power of urban blacks in the party, and he openly solicited their support, much to the anger of southern Democrats. Guffey was re-elected to the Senate in 1940 but lost his seat in the election of 1946. He then retired, and he died in Washington, D.C., on March 6, 1959. (*New York Times*, March 7, 1959.)

GUFFEY-SNYDER BITUMINOUS COAL STABILIZATION ACT OF 1935 By the spring of 1934, John L. Lewis* of the United Mine Workers and a number of northern coal operators were pushing for a coal stabilization act. Unemployment and corporate losses were severe, not only because of the depression but because non-union coal from the southern and western fields was increasing its market share. The National Industrial Recovery Act was scheduled to expire on June 16, 1935, and both the UMW and northern operators wanted new legislation, more centralized and more specific than the NRA* codes had been and better able to stop the growth of the southern and western coal companies. They envisioned rigid controls on production, prices, and wages. A strong coalition existed between the United Mine Workers and the northern coal operators, both of whom were threatened by the southern and western fields, and they enjoyed much support from the New Deal.* A major objective of the coal stabilization plan, beyond improving profits and employment, was to give northern coal operators and UMW workers a competitive edge over the non-union coal from the South and West. Lewis asked Senator Joseph Guffey* of Pennsylvania to submit the bill to Congress. The Guffey bill went well beyond the National Industrial Recovery Act.* It called for the creation of a National Bituminous Coal Commission to create a code of fair competition, fix minimum prices, and regionally allocate production. A National Coal Producers Board and a National Bituminous Coal Labor Board* would work under the National Bituminous Coal Commission in protecting the interests of labor and management. To encourage participation, an industry-wide tax of 25 percent on all coal would be rebated to participating companies. Any wage contract negotiated with operators producing two-thirds of the tonnage in a particular district would be binding on all code members in that area. The proposal received President Franklin D. Roosevelt's* approval as well as the wrath of the National Association of Manufacturers,* the U.S. Chamber of Commerce,* southern and western operators, and the railroads.

When the Supreme Court* outlawed the NIRA with its *Schechter** decision in May 1935, Lewis pressed harder for the Guffey bill, even threatening a coal strike unless Congress acted. Roosevelt pushed the bill, but intense opposition brought a number of significant amendments. The original labor provisions of the Guffey bill remained intact, with its Bituminous Coal Labor Board, but the provisions for regional allocation of production and the National Coal Producers Board were eliminated. Districts rather than a central agency would determine prices, and the tax rebate was dropped to 15 percent on all coal produced. It narrowly passed Congress, and President Roosevelt signed it on August 30, 1935.

The Guffey-Snyder Act had little effect on the soft coal industry. Roosevelt established the National Bituminous Coal Commission; and it began soliciting operators to join, but most refused. No sooner had the act been signed than lawsuits began being filed against it in the federal courts. Most people did not expect it to survive the Supreme Court, so the commission only collected $800,000 of the $10 million it assessed the operators. The Supreme Court decided to hear the *Carter v. Carter Coal Company** case, which claimed that the production tax was a government-imposed penalty and therefore a violation of Fifth and Tenth Amendment property rights. The Supreme Court agreed with the general principle of Fifth and Tenth Amendment violations but in May 1936 specifically declared the Guffey-Snyder Act unconstitutional because of its wages-and-hours provisions. The federal government, the Court argued, did not have the authority to intervene in intrastate commerce for the local fixing of wages and hours. The Supreme Court had destroyed a central provision of the New Deal's "Little NRA."* (James P. Johnson, *The Politics of Soft Coal: The Bituminous Industry from World War I through the New Deal*, 1979.)

GUFFEY-VINSON BITUMINOUS COAL ACT OF 1937 After the Supreme Court's* *Carter** decision in 1936 striking down the Guffey-Snyder Act,* President Franklin D. Roosevelt,* John L. Lewis,* and some northern coal operators, still interested in coal stabilization, prepared another bill. Following Roosevelt's labor-supported victory in the election of 1936,* Congress acted quickly and passed the Guffey-Vinson Act. Roosevelt signed it on April 26, 1937. The act established another National Bituminous Coal Commission. Twenty-three operator-dominated district boards would propose minimum coal prices, which the NBCC would then establish. A 1¢ per ton tax on all coal sold in the United States, with a 19 1/2¢ per ton penalty on all non-code coal, replaced the tax and rebate system of the Guffey-Snyder Act. A new Consumers' Counsel was also established. District board members were exempt from anti-trust laws in administering the code. Essentially, the Guffey-Vinson Act reenacted all of the major provisions of the earlier Guffey act except the outlawed wages and hours provisions. The whole theory behind the Guffey acts was misguided in its hope of bringing recovery to the soft coal industry. It only encouraged retention of high-cost mines and the operation of marginal facilities and exaggerated the industry's basic problem—excess capacity. (James P. Johnson, *The Politics of Soft Coal: The Bituminous Industry from World War I through the New Deal*, 1979.)

GULICK, LUTHER HALSEY Luther Gulick was born in Osaka, Japan, on January 17, 1892. He graduated from Oberlin College in 1914, took a master's degree there in 1915, and received a Ph.D. in public administration from Columbia University in 1920. Gulick then worked as a staff member for the Bureau of Municipal Research in New York City and for a number of other state government bodies in the 1920s. Gulick taught as Eaton Professor of Municipal Science and Administration at Columbia University between 1931 and 1942, and while there President Franklin D. Roosevelt* appointed him to the President's Committee on Administrative Management* (Brownlow Committee)* in 1936. Gulick stayed on the committee until 1939, when the Reorganization Act of 1939* was passed. Gulick served on the staff of the War Production Board between 1940 and 1944 and was assistant to the director of the Smaller War Plants Corporation in 1943 and 1944. After the war he continued to teach and to serve as a consultant with a wide variety of government agencies. Luther Gulick is the author of *Notes on the Theory of Organization* (1937), *Administrative Reflections* (1947), *American Forest Policy* (1952), and *Metropolitan Problems and America Ideas* (1962). (Barry D. Karl, *Executive Reorganization* *and Reform in the New Deal: The Genesis of Administrative Management, 1900–1939*, 1963; *Who's Who in America*, I:1378, 1972.)

H

HAGUE, FRANK Frank Hague, "boss" of Jersey City and kingpin of the New Jersey Democratic party, was born on "the wrong side of the tracks" in 1876 to immigrant parents in the Jersey City area called the "Horseshoe." From a meager start as ward constable in the "Horseshoe," Hague worked his way up the Democratic ladder, becoming a city commissioner in 1911 and mayor in 1917, an office he held until he retired in 1947. As mayor, Hague first pleased reformers by calling for efficiency and honesty in government and modernizing the city's police and fire departments. He also created social clubs in some neighborhoods, provided tax breaks for local businessmen, gave the Roman Catholic church huge sums of money, and generally built a large, loyal machine to control and command. The machine served Franklin D. Roosevelt* well during four presidential elections. Despite revelations regarding the machine's corruption, Roosevelt did not allow the Justice Department to prosecute Hague or his lieutenants.

Throughout the depression Roosevelt and Hague cultivated a relationship through New Deal* agencies which allowed the New Jersey boss to exploit New Deal patronage. Roosevelt appreciated the fact that Hague placed New Jersey's delegates and electoral votes in his domain during Democratic National Conventions and presidential elections. Unlike most states where federal appointments went to the governor or United States senators, New Jersey's spoils system belonged to Frank Hague.

From the New Deal's turbulent beginnings in 1933 until its slow decline when the United States entered World War II, Franklin D. Roosevelt funnelled most federal patronage in New Jersey through Hague's machine. Hague controlled patronage in the Civil Works Administration.* Working hand-in-glove with Hague, Harry L. Hopkins* allowed the machine to control 18,000 CWA jobs in 1934, and 76,000 to 97,000 WPA* jobs from 1935–1941. Despite immense corruption and crime, Roosevelt and his advisers felt Hague was too much of a political asset to warrant federal prosecution. In 1938 Postmaster General James Farley* discovered that Hague ordered New Jersey officials to scrutinize all mail moving to and from one of his political enemies. But when Farley demanded that the federal government arrest and prosecute the New Jersey boss, Roosevelt refused.

Hague delivered his support time and time again—on crucial relief bills and other New Deal legislation. Together with Harry L. Hopkins and Edward J. Kelly,* Hague managed Roosevelt's unprecedented third term nomination during the 1940 Democratic national convention in Chicago. Finally, Hague delivered New Jersey's electoral votes to Roosevelt on four occasions: 1932, 1936, 1940, and 1944. The relationship between Hague and Roosevelt was representative of the changing nature of American federalism during the 1930s. The New Deal tolerated corruption when the bosses served its chief executive and did not become expendable. Frank Hague died on January 1, 1956. (Lyle W. Dorsett, *Franklin D. Roosevelt and the City Bosses,* 1977.)

J. CHRISTOPHER SCHNELL

HAGUE, MAYOR, ET AL., V. COMMITTEE FOR INDUSTRIAL ORGANIZATION This case involved the constitutionality of a municipal ordinance in Jersey City, New Jersey, which required a permit from the chief of police in order to hold public meetings in the city. The Committee for Industrial Organization filed suit in federal district court against the mayor and other officials charging that they conspired to deny the CIO* permission to hold meetings in Jersey City on the ground that the CIO was a Communist organization; that acting under the ordinance, police seized and destroyed union leaflets and pamphlets; and that union leaders were arrested by police and forcibly ejected from the city. The CIO complained that it had consistently been denied permits to hold meetings even though its activities were legal and peaceful, i.e., to explain to workers the provisions of the National Labor Relations Act.* The suit charged that city officials had entered into a conspiracy to deny plaintiff's "free exercise and enjoyment of the rights and privileges secured to them by the Constitution and laws of the United States." Alleging that the ordinance was unconstitutional, the CIO requested an injunction against Mayor Frank Hague* and others prohibiting enforcement of the law.

The federal district court accepted jurisdiction and found in favor of the CIO; that the actions of city officials were in violation of the Fourteenth Amendment. The circuit court of appeals affirmed the decree but modified one provision of the decree pertaining to the question of jurisdiction. Mayor Hague appealed to the Supreme Court,* which granted certiorari.

The case was argued on February 27 and 28, 1939, and decided on June 5, 1939. The majority affirmed the decision of the appeals court but arrived at their judgment by different routes. Justices Hugo Black* and Owen Roberts* argued that the ordinance of Jersey City violated the privileges and immunities guaranteed to citizens of the United States by the Fourteenth Amendment, viz., the right to peaceably assemble. Justices Harlan Stone* and Stanley Reed* thought that the Court should confine itself to ruling that the ordinance violated the due process clause of the Fourteenth Amendment. Chief Justice Charles Evans Hughes* concurred but based his agreement on the contention that the right to discuss the National Labor Relations Act was a privilege guaranteed by United States citizenship. Justices Felix Frankfurter* and William O. Douglas* took no part in the case, and Justices James McReynolds* and Pierce Butler* dissented. This decision struck down the arbitrary use of police power by local and state governments to interfere with the right of labor "peaceably to assemble." (Alfred H. Kelly and Winfred A. Harbison, *The American Constitution*, 1970; *Supreme Court Reporter*, LIX:954–972, 1939.)

JOSEPH M. ROWE, JR.

HAMILTON, JOHN DANIEL MILLER John Hamilton was born in Ft. Madison, Iowa, on March 2, 1892. He graduated from Phillips Academy in Andover, Massachusetts, in 1913 and from the Northwestern University Law School in 1916. Hamilton practiced law in Kansas City between 1916 and 1918 and then moved to Topeka, Kansas, where he practiced from 1918 to 1940. He served in the state legislature from 1925 to 1928 and during the last year was speaker of the house. Hamilton worked as chairman of the Republican State Central Committee from 1930 to 1932 and in 1932 became a member of the Republican National Committee. Between 1936 and 1940 he was chairman of the committee. During his tenure as chairman in the late 1930s, Hamilton maintained an intense criticism of Franklin D. Roosevelt* and the New Deal,* but he also rejected all attempts by Republicans to forge political coalitions with conservative Democrats. He recognized that Roosevelt's prestige was dwindling, but he preferred to change the Republican party* internally rather than to try to accommodate with conservative Democrats. After his term as chairman of the Republican National Committee, Hamilton returned to private law practice. He died on September 24, 1973. (James T. Patterson, *Congressional Conservatism and the New Deal*, 1967; *Who Was Who in America*, VI:178, 1976.)

HANDLER, MILTON Milton Handler was born in New York City on October 8, 1903. He graduated from Columbia University in 1924 and took a law degree there in 1926. Handler began private practice in 1927 and joined the law faculty at Columbia, a position he held until 1972. In 1933 Rexford G. Tugwell* had Handler assist him in drafting new food and drug legislation, and although the proposed measure did not succeed at the time, much of it was later enacted as the Food, Drug, and Cosmetic Act of 1938.* Handler was appointed general counsel of the National Labor Board* in 1933 and served until the board's demise in 1934. During those two years, Handler fought desperately for the principle of employee majority rule in selecting bargaining agents, but his efforts were largely destroyed by the agreement of the Automobile Labor Board* settling the automobile strike in 1934. Handler then returned to Columbia and later came back to the federal government in 1938 as an assistant to the general counsel of the Treasury Department. After leaving the treasury in 1940, Handler taught at Columbia and then served as an assistant general counsel to the Lend-Lease

Administration (1942–1943), special counsel to the Foreign Economic Administration (1943–1944), and a member of the National War Labor Board (1944). After the war, Handler continued to teach at Columbia, and wrote a number of books, including *Antitrust in Perspective* (1957) and *Twenty-Five Years of Antitrust* (1973); (Peter H. Irons, *The New Deal Lawyers*, 1982; *Who's Who In America*, I:1427, 1982.)

HANSEN, ALVIN Known as the "American Keynes," Alvin Hansen was born on August 23, 1887, into a Danish immigrant family in Viborg, South Dakota. He graduated from Yankton College in 1910, worked as a school principal for a few years, and then entered graduate school at the University of Wisconsin to study economics. He studied under John R. Commons* and Richard T. Ely and earned his Ph.D. in 1918. Hansen taught at the University of Wisconsin and Brown University before his appointment at the University of Minnesota in 1919. He wrote *Business Cycle Theory* in 1927 and then broadened his research into unemployment. During the early 1930s, Hansen worked for the Social Science Research Council's Commission of Inquiry into National Policy in International Economic Relations, Columbia University's Commission on Economic Recovery, and as an economic adviser to Secretary of State Cordell Hull* on reciprocal trade agreements.

Between 1936 and 1939 Hansen moved away from neo-classical economics to Keynesian assumptions on compensatory spending. In September 1937 he moved to Harvard University and, along with Dean John H. Williams, began jointly teaching the Fiscal Policy Seminar where a younger generation of economists discussed the implications of Keynesian economics. Many of the seminar's students and faculty participants, including Paul Samuelson and John Kenneth Galbraith, would go on to important policy positions in government agencies and corporations during the 1940s, 1950s, and 1960s.

Scholars often credit Hansen with leading the "Keynesian revolution" in America and providing the theoretical foundation for the economic policymaking of the late New Deal.* Actually, Hansen combined the work of pre-Keynesian economists such as Knut Wicksell, Arthur Spiethoff, Joseph Schumpeter, Gustav Cassel, and D. H. Robertson; his own interest in business cycle theory; and his modification of Keynesian theory to point the way toward a mixed economy. Hansen argued that the recession of 1937* stemmed from declining investment opportunities, lagging consumer credit, and the deflationary effects of the withdrawal of federal net expenditures in that year. In his presidential address to the American Economic Association in December 1938, Hansen extended this analysis more broadly in the most clearly set forth version of his famous "secular stagnation theory." Economic changes since the nineteenth century meant the American economy was undergoing fundamental structural change. Declining population growth, declining availability of new land and natural resources, and lagging technological innovations left the economy without emerging new industries. Lack of private investment opportunities in the twentieth century now had to be supplemented with increased consumer expenditures and careful consideration of increased federal expenditures through deficit spending policies. Only this way, Hansen argued, would national income increase, making possible increased production, consumption, and a full employment economy. Hansen recommended these policies in carefully worded testimony before the Temporary National Economic Committee* on May 16, 1939.

Throughout the early New Deal, Hansen had criticized government public works spending as a "salvaging operation" that failed to address the real issue of how to increase national income in a time of lagging private investment and a downturn in consumer spending after 1936. Hansen's work paved the way for consideration of Keynesian economic policymaking in the United States. Hansen's personal influence remained indirect through his published work and the Fiscal Policy Seminar at Harvard. Hansen expanded his own advisory work during the New Deal-World War II period, serving as economic adviser to the Committee on Economic Security* which drafted the Social Security Act of 1935,* adviser on Prairie Provinces to the Canadian Royal Commission on Dominion-Provincial Relations (1937–1938), member of the Advisory Council to the Social Security Board (1937–1938), chairman of the Economic Advisory Council of the National Industrial Conference Board (1938–1939), economic adviser to the Federal Reserve Board* (1940–1945), chairman of the U.S.-Canadian Joint Economic Committee (1941–1943), and consultant to the National Resources Planning Board.* The acknowledged dean of American Keynesians, Hansen helped educate a generation of emerging Keynesian economic policy advisers who staffed the war mobilization agencies of World War II and the postwar Council of Economic Advisers. Alvin Hansen wrote *A Guide to Keynes* in 1953, retired from Harvard in 1958, and died on June 6, 1975. (J. Ronnie Davis, *The New Economics and the Old Economists*, 1971; Robert Lekachman, *The Age of Keynes*, 1966; Herbert Stein, *The Fiscal Revolution in America*, 1969.)

PATRICK D. REAGAN

"HAPPY DAYS ARE HERE AGAIN" Lyricist Jack Yellen and composer Milton Alger wrote "Happy Days Are Here Again" in 1929 for an MGM movie, "Forever Rainbows." Lacking confidence in the film, MGM stored it until 1930, but Yellen and Alger arranged that the song be performed in October 1929 at the Pennsylvania Theater in New York on what became known as "Black Friday," the day of the stock market crash. The song was so successful that MGM reshot the scene in which it was performed so that choruses could be added and promptly released the film. It became Franklin D. Roosevelt's* theme song at the 1932 Democratic National Convention in Chicago. Roosevelt preferred the song "Anchors Aweigh," but Louis Howe* could not abide the pipe organ rendition of it which he heard on the radio from his room at the Congress Hotel. Lela Stiles, a reporter who worked for Howe, suggested "Happy Days Are Here Again," and Howe telephoned the organist at the convention and told him to play it after Roosevelt was nominated. New Dealer Raymond Moley* remembers that after the nomination the exhausted Howe ''groaned out between coughs: 'Tell them to repeat ''Happy Days Are Here Again.'' ' '' At first the ironic ''theme song of ruined stock speculators,'' the song became a symbol of hope during the Great Depression. Its use by Harry S Truman,* John F. Kennedy, and Jimmy Carter suggests that this legacy of the New Deal* is an enduring tradition in the Democratic party.* (David Ewen, ed., *American Popular Songs*, 1966; Raymond Moley, *After Seven Years*, 1939.)

BERNARD K. DUFFY

HARRIMAN, HENRY INGRAHAM Henry I. Harriman was born in Brooklyn, New York, on December 26, 1871. He graduated from Wesleyan University in 1895 and took a law degree at the New York Law School in 1897. Harriman's business career took him first to a number of New England textile manufacturing firms and then to the organization of the New England Power Company where he was the company's first president. During the 1920s, Harriman was active in the trade association movement, primarily in his own New England Power Association, and an advocate of national economic planning through industrial self-regulation. He worked closely with Secretary of Commerce Herbert Hoover* in forming codes of fair competition in the power industry during the 1920s and became a major supporter of the National Recovery Administration* during the New Deal.* During the early 1930s, Harriman was serving as president of the United States Chamber of Commerce,* whose endorsement of the National Industrial Recovery Act* was a major impetus to the bill's success. In 1933 and 1934 Harriman served as a member of the Business Advisory Council* in the Department of Commerce where he continually supported the philosophy behind the NRA as the only way of eliminating destructive competition, improving productivity, strengthening business profits, and ending the Great Depression. But business support of the New Deal was quickly evaporating at the same time, and in 1935 the U.S. Chamber of Commerce replaced Harriman with Harper Sibley and formally censured Franklin D. Roosevelt* and the New Deal. Harriman remained on the board of directors of the chamber and continued to speak out for business-government cooperation, but business alienation from the New Deal lead directly to the Chamber's criticism of the National Labor Relations Act,* Social Security Act,* Walsh-Healey Act,* Robinson-Patman Act,* Guffey coal acts,* the Banking Act of 1935,* anti-trust policy, and all forms of labor standards legislation. Harriman's hopes for a new era of national economic planning through government-approved codes of industrial self-regulation were never realized. He died on July 4, 1950. (Robert M. Collins, ''Positive Business Response to the New Deal: The Roots of the Committee for Economic Development, 1933–1942,'' *Business History Review*, LII:369–391, 1978; *Who Was Who in America*, III:372, 1961.)

HARRINGTON, FRANCIS CLARK Born in 1887 in Bristol, Virginia, Francis C. Harrington graduated from West Point with a degree in engineering and began a career as an army officer. In 1933 he helped design the Civilian Conservation Corps,* providing it with a philosophy of military discipline and a set of work project objectives. Harrington spent a two-year tour of duty abroad in France between 1933 and 1935 and upon his return was selected to conduct a survey of Works Progress Administration* procedures and projects. Later in the year, he joined the WPA staff as chief engineer and late in 1936 was promoted to assistant administrator for operations and project control. He held that position until December 1938 when, after being commissioned an army colonel, he was appointed federal administrator of the WPA. When the Reorganization Act of 1939* changed the Works Progress Administration to the Works Projects Administration,* under the new Federal Works Agency,* Harrington became commissioner of the new WPA. An able administrator with an impeccable sense of honesty, he brought to the WPA a reputation for continuity, stability, and respect. Francis C. Harrington died on September 30, 1940. (*New York Times*, October 1, 1940.)

HARRISON, BYRON PATTON Pat Harrison was born in Crystal Springs, Mississippi, on August 29, 1881, and was educated in the public schools of that town. He attended what is today Louisiana State University, never graduating. After a brief tenure as a public school teacher and a lawyer, he entered Mississippi politics, rising from the post of district attorney to serve four terms in the United States House of Representatives (1911–1919), where he was an ardent Wilsonian. In 1918 he defeated James K. Vardaman for a United States Senate seat, remaining in the Senate until his death in 1941. As a leader of the Democratic minority in the 1920s, he gained a reputation as a zestful and effective ''gadfly'' and a ranking position on the Committee on Finance, becoming its chairman when the Democrats gained power in March 1933.

Under Harrison's tutelage the Finance Committee handled many of the measures of the New Deal:* the National Industrial Recovery Act,* the Social Security Act* and successive amendments, the Reciprocal Trade Agreements Acts* of 1934 and 1940, and fourteen distinct revenue acts including the Wealth Tax Act of 1935* and the undistributed profits act of 1936. He brought to his post enormous influence based not only upon congressional longevity but also a happy combination of personal qualities that made him one of the most popular men in the Senate. Although never the author of any major legislation, Harrison was a master tactician and broker for the ideas of others. Defeated by one vote in 1937 in a contest with Alben W. Barkley* for the position of majority leader, Harrison was named president pro tempore in January 1941.

Senator Harrison was a devoted supporter of Franklin D. Roosevelt* during the first years of the New Deal, but his basic conservatism, subdued by the exigencies of total depression, became manifest during the latter years of the decade. His reservations, which appeared in the open during deliberations over the Wealth Tax Act of 1935, grew out of his basic belief that revenue bills should be written for revenue only. After he became disenchanted with the later

New Deal's emphasis upon deficit spending and social engineering, disillusioned by the president's refusal to support him against Barkley in 1937, and convinced that the emergency was over, Harrison became less of a champion of Roosevelt and the New Deal. Subsequently his refusal to support the administration, particularly in wage and hour legislation and continued relief appropriations, his open leadership of the Finance Committee in diminishing the effect of administration measures, and his affection for senators, such as Walter George* of Georgia, who were cast off by the president, all indicated that Harrison was ready to challenge the chief executive. The Harrison-Roosevelt estrangement, which was clear by 1938, did not end until the two agreed upon the need for defense revenue and preparedness in 1940. His final success was the passage of the Lend-Lease bill which the administration channeled to the Finance Committee rather than to Foreign Relations.

Harrison embodied a curious blend of conservatism and liberalism. He was an important New Deal figure by reason of both his ability to "horse-trade" through the Senate key Roosevelt measures and the influence he exerted along with other southerners, such as James F. Byrnes* and John Nance Garner,* in curbing liberal measures unpopular in their region. Architects of social reform and racial justice were frustrated by the influence the southerners had in restraining the president from championing anti-lynching or poll tax repeal. On the other hand, Harrison and Alabama Senator Hugo Black* combined efforts to pass successive large-scale federal aid to education bills but never succeeded. In 1939 Washington correspondents named him the most influential of all senators. Two years later, on June 22, 1941, Harrison died of cancer. (Martha H. Swain, *Pat Harrison: The New Deal Years*, 1978.)

MARTHA H. SWAIN

HARRISON, GEORGE George Harrison was born in San Francisco, California, on January 26, 1887. He took his A.B. degree from Yale in 1910 and a law degree from Harvard in 1913. Harrison then served as a legal secretary to Supreme Court* Justice Oliver Wendell Holmes, Jr. in 1913–1914. When he left his appointment with the Supreme Court, Harrison became assistant general counsel to the Federal Reserve Board* in Washington, D.C., (1914–1918) and then general counsel (1919–1920). He was appointed deputy governor of the Federal Reserve Bank of New York in 1920, governor in 1928, and president in 1936. Harrison played a central role in the banking crisis of 1933, and in the formulation of the Banking Acts of 1933* and 1935.* He retired from the Federal Reserve Bank of New York in 1941 to become president of the New York Life Insurance Company. He was named chairman of the board in 1948 and retired from that position in 1954. George Harrison died on March 6, 1958. (*New York Times*, March 6, 1958.)

HASTIE, WILLIAM HENRY William Henry Hastie was born in 1904 in Knoxville, Tennessee, and was educated at Amherst College (B.A., 1925) and

Harvard (LL.B., 1930; S.J.D., 1933). After receiving his law degree from Harvard, Hastie joined the law faculty at Howard University in Washington, D.C., where he remained for seven years. He also joined the law firm of Houston and Houston. Hastie was brought into the New Deal* as a member of the "black cabinet,"* serving as assistant solicitor in the Department of the Interior from 1933 to 1937. Southern Democrats protested his appointment because of his close association with the NAACP.* Hastie became the first black appointed to the federal bench in 1937 when President Franklin D. Roosevelt* named him judge of the U.S. District Court for the Virgin Islands. Hastie stayed on the bench for two years, returning in 1939 as dean of the School of Law at Howard University. Between 1940 and 1943 he was on leave of absence from Howard to serve as a civilian aide to Secretary of War Henry L. Stimson,* but he resigned that position in protest over continued segregation of the armed services. In 1946 President Harry S Truman* appointed him governor of the Virgin Islands and in 1949 made him judge of the U.S. Court of Appeals, Third Circuit. Hastie retired in 1971 and died in 1976. (W. A. Low and Virgil A. Clift, *Encyclopedia of Black America*, 1981.)

HATCH ACTS The modern civil service system of the federal government began in 1883 with the Pendleton or Civil Service Act. The statute created a bipartisan Civil Service Commission, selection for "classified service" positions by competitive examination, and allocation of civil service appointments to states and territories in proportion to population. Job categories assigned to the "classified service" were determined by the president in executive orders. Over time, succeeding presidents increased the proportion of classified jobs from 10 to 70 percent of executive department positions. The Pendleton Act, passed in response to the assassination of President James Garfield by an unsuccessful job seeker, effectively ended the traditional spoils system. It also addressed political contributions by and solicitation of federal classified employees. The law specifically protected such employees against coercion or solicitation of funds or assistance by political parties or private individuals. Classified employees could not contribute to any candidate for elective federal office; but they could make contributions to non-federal candidates so long as the solicitation did not occur in a public building. In 1912 the Lloyd-La Follette Act guaranteed the right of union membership and provided for procedural rights in dismissal cases.

The first of two Hatch Acts was passed in 1939 (PL 76–252). It had partially originated in the suspicions of Republicans that President Franklin D. Roosevelt* was manipulating WPA* work rolls to generate votes for himself. He signed the act reluctantly, suspecting it was actually aimed at reducing his own patronage opportunities. The Hatch Act was an anti-New Deal measure rather than a further effort to improve "purity in politics." Its main support in Congress came from administration critics on the heels of the Reorganization Act* and "court-packing"* controversies. Given the civil service reform aspects of the bill, President Roosevelt had to approve the measure despite his misgivings.

The Hatch Act of 1939 covered three dimensions of the political activity of classified employees. First, it reiterated the political contribution and solicitation provisions of the Pendleton Act. Second, classified employees were prohibited from holding elective office at any level of government. Third, they were prohibited from interfering in elections; and certain other restrictions were placed on their political activities in general. Basically, these restrictions had previously been stipulated by Civil Service Commission administrative rules. Classified employees were guaranteed the right to vote, belong to political clubs and labor organizations, disseminate factual information, and campaign or render services in strictly non-partisan (generally local) elections. They also were permitted to hold other appointed positions. The Hatch Act of 1939 was enforced by the Civil Service Commission, with dismissal specified for infractions.

A second Hatch Act was passed in 1940 (PL 76–753). It had two purposes. First, it extended the provisions of the original 1939 law to state and local government employees financed wholly or in part by federal funds. For such employees, any nomination, election, or campaign was stipulated to be illegal. Second, the Hatch Act of 1940 exempted politics in local jurisdictions where the majority of voters were employed by the federal government. Exemption had to be obtained by petition to the Civil Service Commission. This exemption was explicitly directed to local politics in Maryland and Virginia surrounding the District of Columbia.

While a body of federal and state case law had already supported the constitutionality of such legislation, the Hatch Acts were challenged in federal court after World War II. Grounds for the challenges were cited in the First, Fifth, Ninth, and Tenth Amendments. Both the 1939 and 1940 acts were upheld by the United States Supreme Court in *United Public Workers v. Mitchell*, 67 S. Ct. 556 (1947) and *Oklahoma v. U.S. Civil Service Commission*, 67 S. Ct. 544 (1947). The Supreme Court* concluded that there was a constitutional basis for the reasonable protection of the public service against employee partisanship, where the participation rights of employees were restricted only as positive necessity required. (Ferrel Heady, "The Hatch Act Decisions," *American Political Science Review*, [August 1947]; L. V. Howard, "Federal Restrictions on the Political Activity of Government Employees," *American Political Science Review*, [June 1941].)

DUANE WINDSOR

HATFIELD, HENRY DRURY Henry D. Hatfield was born in Logan County, West Virginia, on September 15, 1875. After receiving a medical degree from the University of Louisville in 1895, Hatfield became commissioner of health in Mingo County, West Virginia, and served there until 1900, when he became commissioner of district roads for McDowell County. In 1895 the Norfolk and Western Railway named Hatfield its surgeon, and he worked for the railroad until 1913. Between 1908 and 1912 Hatfield was a Republican member of the state senate, and he served as governor of West Virginia between 1913 and

1917. Hatfield entered the army medical corps in 1917 and after World War I remained active in Republican politics in West Virginia. He won a seat in the United States Senate in 1928, and during 1933 and 1934 was a critic of the New Deal,* seeing in the NRA,* AAA,* and relief programs a burgeoning bureaucracy which was consistent with the teachings of "Norman Thomas,* Stalin, Mussolini, and Hitler." Defeated for re-election in 1934, Hatfield joined the American Liberty League* in 1934 and continued his attacks on Franklin D. Roosevelt* and the New Deal. Hatfield practiced medicine after the end of his political career, and he died on October 23, 1962. (*Biographical Directory of American Congresses, 1776–1971*, 1971; George Wolfskill and John A. Hudson, *All but the People. Franklin D. Roosevelt and His Critics, 1933–1939*, 1969.)

HEARST, WILLIAM RANDOLPH William Randolph Hearst was born in San Francisco, California, on April 29, 1863. He studied at Harvard from 1882 to 1885, and was awarded an LL.D. degree from Oglethorpe in 1927. His interest in politics was deep, if erratic, and he served two terms in Congress (1903–1907) as a Democrat from New York. Although he ran for mayor of New York City and later for governor of New York, his influence was primarily the result of his ownership of such important newspapers and magazines as the San Francisco *Examiner*, Los Angeles *Examiner*, Los Angeles *Herald and Express*, Chicago *Herald-American*, Boston *American*, Boston *Record*, New York *Journal-American*, New York *Mirror*, Baltimore *News-Post*, Pittsburgh *Sun-Telegram*, Detroit *Times*, and Milwaukee *Sentinel*.

Hearst's political career started on the left and moved dramatically and continually to the right. By the time of Franklin D. Roosevelt's* election in 1932,* he had comfortably settled on the right, and he became a vocal critic of the New Deal.* In 1934 he visited Germany, was impressed by Adolf Hitler, and predicted that a fascist movement would emerge in America to combat the inroads being made by communism in the United States. On his return to America, Hearst began a crusade to warn his countrymen about the threat of communism. During 1935 many people rallied to Hearst's side, but the lack of any substantial proof of a serious Communist threat eventually ended the crusade. Like Hearst's attempts to keep America out of World War I, prevent the Democratic party* from nominating Al Smith* in 1928, and make Marion Davies a popular movie star, the crusade against communism ended in failure.

Failing to convince the majority of Americans that the Roosevelt administration was Communist-influenced, Hearst attempted to aid Republican opponents of the president. He was particularly captivated by the unique charm of Alf Landon.* In 1936 he believed Landon was "a man of destiny," and his newspapers strongly backed the midwesterner's presidential hopes. Once again Hearst's desires were frustrated. However, by the time of the election, he had become resigned to a Roosevelt victory. After 1936 Hearst drifted away from the political spotlight. Out of touch with the ambitions and beliefs of most Americans, he held opinions increasingly regarded as extreme. Hearst died on August 14, 1951. (Rodney P. Carlisle, *Hearst and the New Deal: The Progressive as Reactionary*, 1982.)

RANDY ROBERTS

HENDERSON, LEON Leon Henderson, influential New Deal* economist, was born in Millville, New Jersey, on May 26, 1895. Henderson graduated from Swarthmore College in 1920 with a degree in economics and then did post-graduate work at the University of Pennsylvania between 1920 and 1922. Henderson had an impressive mind and became an instructor at the Wharton School of the University of Pennsylvania between 1919 and 1922 and an assistant professor of economics at the Carnegie Institute of Technology from 1922 to 1923. He served for nearly two years, 1924–1925, as the deputy secretary for the Commonwealth of Pennsylvania and then became director of consumer credit research for the Russell Sage Foundation in 1925. Henderson stayed there until 1934 when he became director of the Research and Planning Division of the National Recovery Administration.*

During his more than a year's service with the NRA, Henderson became an important economic figure in the New Deal. Although he had been willing to accept the philosophical rationale of the NRA—that price increases were necessary to sustain business confidence and trigger an economic recovery—he had always been skeptical. By 1934 Henderson was convinced that the NRA codes were only magnifying the problem of business concentration, squeezing small businesses into an increasingly isolated part of the economy, and retarding recovery by permitting price rises and reductions in production. His internal criticisms of the NRA coincided well with the external criticism rendered by the National Recovery Review Board* in 1934. By 1935, when the *Schechter** decision of the Supreme Court* destroyed the National Recovery Administration, Henderson's own economic philosophies were demanding a major shift in the direction of New Deal economic policy. He was no longer as interested in national planning through business self-regulation as he was in a restoration of competition and the use of deficit spending to stimulate the economy.

Those views were expressed after 1935 in the variety of New Deal posts Henderson held. After the *Schechter* decision ended the National Recovery Administration, Henderson took a job as economic adviser to the Senate Committee on Manufacturers, and during 1936 he served as economic adviser to the Democratic National Committee. There his views on deficit spending and anti-trust activity represented the shift from the First New Deal* to the Second New Deal.* While advising the Democratic National Committee in 1936, Henderson also became economic consultant to Harry Hopkins* in the Works Progress Administration.* A convert to Keynesian economics, Henderson was a major advocate of using relief spending as a means of stimulating consumer demand, production, and employment. Inside the administration, Henderson became closely associated with people like Lauchlin Currie,* Harry Hopkins,* William Douglas,* and Marriner Eccles* in opposing budget balancers like Secretary of the Treasury

Henry Morgenthau, Jr.* In 1938 Henderson became executive secretary to the Temporary National Economic Committee* and there continued to push his belief in competition and his opposition to monopoly. Henderson was outspoken and aggressive in his convictions and a major force behind the TNEC. Unlike earlier progressives who approached anti-trust activities as moral crusades, Henderson was rationally committed to competition, and in a very broad context. In addition to anti-trust laws, he wanted the federal government to deal with the related problems of obsolescent technology, rigid wage-and-freight structures, high tariffs, and weak capital structures.

In 1939 Henderson accepted appointment as a commissioner on the Securities and Exchange Commission,* and he stayed on the SEC until 1941, when he became administrator of the Office of Price Administration. He resigned from the OPA in 1942 to become head of the Civilian Supply Division of the War Production Board. After World War II, Henderson served as president of the International Hudson Corporation, chairman of the Americans for Democratic Action, and chief economist for the Research Institute of America. (''Leon Henderson,'' *The National Cyclopedia of American Biography*, F:43, 1942; William E. Leuchtenburg, *Franklin D. Roosevelt and the New Deal, 1932–1940*, 1963; Arthur M. Schlesinger, Jr., *The Age of Roosevelt. Vol. III. The Politics of Upheaval, 1935–1936*, 1960.)

HICKOK, LORENA Lorena Hickok was born in East Troy, Wisconsin, on March 7, 1893, and in 1913 began a long career in journalism. Becoming an Associated Press reporter, she covered the 1928 political campaign of Alfred E. Smith,* various state party conventions, and the New Deal* years of Franklin D. Roosevelt.* She became acquainted with Eleanor Roosevelt* while doing a series of articles on her during the 1932 presidential campaign, and a deep friendship developed between the two women which lasted a lifetime. In 1933 Hickok left the Associated Press to be the eyes and ears of the New Deal on the local and state level. New Dealers desperately wanted to know how the hundred days* legislation was perceived by the public, how it affected them, and how it was administered on the state and local levels, so they selected Hickok to travel quietly throughout the country investigating the three issues. Her secret reports to Harry Hopkins,* head of the FERA,* were read by a select group in the administration, who found the candid information essential to formulate new anti-depression policies. The reports helped generate an evangelical support for more public relief in 1933, which influenced the creation of the Civil Works Administration,* a stopgap measure to provide work and relief in the winter of 1933–1934 until the PWA* could become fully operational.

Her letters were witty, angry, and direct. They told of poor tubercular citizens declared undesirables and refused admission to Arizona, children in West Virginia emaciated by diphtheria and typhoid, starving people whose sunken and lifeless eyes still haunt the present day, and breadlines and soup kitchens barely keeping people alive. Bureaucratic inefficiency received hammer blows. Memorable descriptions of "wicked" politicians manipulating New Deal programs to benefit themselves and cronies contrasted with moving accounts of resourceful Americans trying to care for themselves without much help. How the depression and New Deal programs upset racial and class relationships reached Hopkins and Roosevelt through Hickok. Men fighting over CWA shovels in order to work convinced many New Dealers that every able-bodied man had a right to a job; and if private enterprise failed to provide it, the government should. The conviction found partial fulfillment in the Emergency Relief Appropriation Act of 1935.*

Hickok left New Deal service after the 1936 election for a public relations job and spent several quiet years living on Long Island. But in 1940 she agreed to live at the White House with the Roosevelts and to return to New Deal activities by joining the Democratic National Committee. She served for four years as executive secretary in the Women's Division. In 1945 ill-health prevented regular employment and also forced Hickok to resign from political office. Until her death on May 1, 1968, she wrote a great deal, including *Reluctant First Lady* (1962), *The Story of Franklin D. Roosevelt* (1956), *The Story of Eleanor Roosevelt* (1959), and *The Road to the White House* (1962). (Doris Faber, *The Life of Lorena Hickok*, 1980; Richard Lowitt and Maurine Beasley, *One Third of a Nation: Lorena Hickok, Reports on the Great Depression*, 1983.)

H. CARLETON MARLOW

HIGH, STANLEY Stanley High, a journalist and speechwriter for Franklin D. Roosevelt* during the 1930s, was born in Chicago, Illinois, on December 30, 1895. He graduated from Nebraska Wesleyan University in 1917 and from the Boston University School of Theology in 1923. High served with the Methodist Mission to China in 1919 and 1920 and was European correspondent for *The Christian Science Monitor* between 1921 and 1924. He worked for the Board of Foreign Missions of the Methodist Church and as a lecturer on international affairs between 1924 and 1929 and in 1928 became editor of the *Christian Herald*. During the early 1930s High joined the staff of the National Broadcasting Company as a current events radio lecturer. Although a Republican, High had been discouraged by what he considered the hopeless conservatism of Herbert Hoover's* administration, and in 1936 Samuel Rosenman* recruited him to Roosevelt's speechwriting staff. The president also occasionally used High to communicate messages to other members of the administration. High organized and served as president of the Good Neighbor League,* a 1936 Roosevelt election vehicle used to bring Republican educators, intellectuals, and social workers into the Democratic camp as well as to rally the black vote for the president. After leaving the administration, High served as a correspondent for *The Saturday Evening Post* and after 1952 as senior editor of the *Reader's Digest*. High was the author of a number of books, including *China's Place in the Sun* (1922), *The Revolt of Youth* (1923), and *Roosevelt—And Then* (1937). High died on February 3, 1961. (Arthur M. Schlesinger, Jr., *The Age of Roosevelt. Vol. III. The Politics of Upheaval, 1935–1936*, 1960; *Who Was Who in America*, IV-438, 1968.)

HILLMAN, SIDNEY Sidney Hillman was born on March 23, 1887, in Zagare, Lithuania. Educated at the Slobodka Rabbinical Seminary in Lithuania, Hillman fled to the United States in 1907 after being arrested and jailed for labor agitation in favor of the ten-hour working day. He settled in Chicago and went to work as an apprentice cutter at the Hart, Schaffner, and Marx factory. In September 1910, when women workers went on strike, Hillman joined them; and he negotiated an agreement with the firm which established the foundation for the impartial chairman plan. His prominence in the strike gave him a public profile among fellow workers, and Hillman became a trade union officer for the Chicago local of the United Garment Workers of America. He then joined the Amalgamated Clothing Workers of America. Hillman became the first president of the ACWA in 1914. He played a critical role in ACWA, organizing victories in New York, Philadelphia, and Chicago; established the union's unemployment insurance, cooperative housing, and worker bank programs; and built it into one of the most powerful industrial unions in the country. When the depression hit, Hillman called for limiting the work week as a way of preserving jobs, helped draft the public works section of the National Industrial Recovery Act,* and sat as a member of the NRA* board. Hillman served as vice-president of the CIO* from 1935 to 1940, was a founder of Labor's Non Partisan League* to re-elect Franklin D. Roosevelt* in 1936, and was co-director of the Office of Production Management between 1940 and 1942. Hillman was also founder and chairman of the American Labor Party.* He died of a heart attack on July 10, 1946. (Matthew Josephson, *Sidney Hillman, Statesman of American Labor*, 1952.)

HISS, ALGER Alger Hiss was born in Baltimore in 1904 and educated at Johns Hopkins University and the Harvard Law School. Hiss served on the *Harvard Law Review* in 1928 and 1929, was a protégé of Felix Frankfurter,* and clerked with Supreme Court* Justice Oliver Wendell Holmes, Jr., in 1929. Although he had come from a conservative background, Hiss developed a strong social liberalism at Harvard. Following his year with Holmes, Hiss returned to Boston and spent two years in private practice. In 1931 he joined the Wall-Street firm of Cotton and Franklin, where he specialized in corporate reorganization. On Frankfurter's recommendation, Jerome Frank* recruited Hiss to become assistant general counsel and legislative draftsman at the Agricultural Adjustment Administration.* As head of the Benefit Contract Section of the Legal Division, Hiss helped draft the master cotton contract on which individual farmer contracts for acreage reduction would be based. Deeply concerned about the plight of tenant farmers and the impact AAA acreage reductions was having on them, Hiss sympathized with the urban liberals in the Agricultural Adjustment Administration intent upon assisting them. Although not directly involved in the "purge of 1935" in the Department of Agriculture, Hiss resigned in protest of the firing of Jerome Frank, Lee Pressman,* Francis Shea, and Victor Rotnem. Hiss then moved on to the Senate Munitions Committee investigating the munitions industry, and then he moved to the office of the solicitor general. Under Stanley

Reed's* direction, Hiss worked with Paul Freund* in preparing the government's position in the *Butler* case defending the constitutionality of the Agricultural Adjustment Act.* After the Supreme Court declared the AAA unconstitutional, Hiss became an assistant to Assistant Secretary of State Francis B. Sayre, and later he became responsible for Far Eastern affairs for the State Department. Hiss's influence in the State Department increased rapidly, and in 1944 he participated in the Dumbarton Oaks conference preparing for the United Nations. He was also secretary general at the conference in San Francisco which drafted the United Nations charter. With that assignment completed, Hiss became president of the Carnegie Endowment for International Peace. His legal and political career was destroyed in 1949 and 1950 when the federal government accused him of being a Communist and jailed him for perjury. He spent the next thirty years of his life claiming and trying to prove his innocence. He eventually again became a member of the Massachusetts Bar Association. (Peter H. Irons, *The New Deal Lawyers*, 1982; Katie Louchheim, ed., *The Making of the New Deal. The Insiders Speak*, 1983.)

HISTORICAL RECORDS SURVEY Designated in 1936 as an independent program of Federal One* of the Works Progress Administration,* the Historical Records Survey had its origins in the early work of the Federal Emergency Relief Administration* and the Civil Works Administration.* Archival work relief projects were ideally suited for white collar workers and often had influential support from conservatives and local historical and genealogical societies. With grants from the RFC,* FERA, and CWA, the Alabama Department of Archives and History in 1933 began employing white collar workers to survey, classify, and collect public and private documents from Alabama history. In Pennsylvania a CWA grant in 1933 helped fund a survey of manuscript materials throughout the state. At the same time, private groups like the Russell Sage Foundation, American Historical Association, and the American Council of Learned Societies began calling for a national records survey as a work relief project. By 1935 Raymond Moley* and Harry Hopkins* were discussing the idea, and they had Luther Evans* appointed in 1935 as the supervisor of historic records for the Works Progress Administration. In 1936 Luther Evans was appointed director of the Historical Records Survey, formerly a branch of the Federal Writers' Project* but now an independent agency of the WPA's Federal One.

Using unemployed clerks, teachers, writers, librarians, and archivists, the HRS concentrated its energies on state and county records, cataloging and analyzing public records and providing inventories of materials. Each county inventory, for example, included a historic and legal description of the county and the value of its various records. The HRS did the same for many state archival materials, manuscript collections, and church archives. The HRS also compiled an inventory of early American imprints, supplements to the union list of newspapers, and surveys of portraits in public buildings; initiated microfilming projects across the country; compiled bibliographies of American history and literature, as well as an historical index of American musicians; constructed an atlas of congressional roll call votes; published a list and index of unnumbered executive orders; and worked to collate various collections of presidential papers and messages.

The HRS was financially the most efficient of the WPA professional programs. Between 1936 and 1938 the HRS averaged between 2,000–3,000 employees, with an average cost of $73 per employee per month. The number of employees was increased to more than 6,000 in 1938. In 1939 Congress abolished Federal One, turning all projects over to state and local direction. Luther Evans resigned as director and was succeeded by Sargent Child, who tried to complete the survey projects already underway. The Emergency Relief Appropriation Act of 1939* abolished the Federal Theatre Project and limited other Federal One* programs to the local level and called for dismissal of all employees with more than eighteen months seniority and local sponsorship of 25 percent of the cost of survey projects, both of which limited the work of the HRS. When Federal One was abolished, the HRS became part of the Community Service Programs, which became the Service Division in 1942. By January 1941 the HRS central staff was down to only twelve people, and without national supervision the local projects had come to an end. (William F. McDonald, *Federal Relief Administration and the Arts*, 1969; Burl Noggle, *Working With History: The Historical Records Survey in Louisiana and the Nation, 1936–1942*, 1981.)

HOEY, JANE MARGUERETTA Born in 1892 to a large Irish Catholic family, Jane Hoey was raised in New York City after spending several years in Nebraska. Her early life had been a steady diet of Democratic politics in the Tammany Hall tradition, and Hoey developed a strong commitment to the social welfare obligations of modern government. She attended Hunter and Trinity Colleges, graduated in 1914, and then took a master's degree in political science at Columbia. She also studied social work under Mary Richmond at the New York School of Philanthropy and then went to work under Harry Hopkins* in 1916 with the Board of Child Welfare in New York City. Between 1926 and 1936 Hoey was assistant director of the Health Division of the Welfare Council of New York, and then she established and directed the Bureau of Public Assistance for the Social Security Board in Washington, D.C. Hoey remained with the Social Security Administration until 1953, when she left after the Eisenhower administration had come to power. Between 1953 and 1957 Hoey was director of social research for the National Tuberculosis Association. She died in 1968. (Susan Ware, *Beyond Suffrage: Women in the New Deal*, 1981.)

HOME OWNERS' LOAN ACT OF 1934 (See HOME OWNERS' LOAN CORPORATION.)

HOME OWNERS' LOAN CORPORATION By early 1933 more than 40 percent of the $20 billion in home mortgages in the United States were in default, and mortgage lending institutions throughout the country were in serious trouble. Herbert Hoover's* administration had tried to deal with the problem through Reconstruction Finance Corporation* loans and creation of the Federal Home Loan Bank system in 1932, but those loans were repayable with interest by the savings and loan associations and did little to help people maintain their mortgage payments. The default situation was also undermining housing values and the asset portfolios of thousands of lending institutions. During the first ''hundred days''* of the New Deal,* Senator Joseph Robinson* of Arkansas sponsored legislation to deal with the problem, and on June 13, 1933, President Franklin D. Roosevelt* signed the Home Owners' Refinancing Act. The law authorized the Federal Home Loan Bank Board to establish a Home Owners' Loan Corporation with $200 million in capital from the RFC and the right to issue up to $2 billion in bonds. The bond total was increased to $3 billion in June 1934 and to $4.75 billion in May 1935. The Home Owners' Loan Act of April 1934 guaranteed the principal and interest of HOLC bonds. Under the program, HOLC bonds would be exchanged for mortgages (up to a maximum of $14,000) and changed into a single first mortgage. The corporation could also issue cash advances for payment of taxes and repairs up to 50 percent of the value of the property. The HOLC also could redeem properties lost by foreclosure after January 1, 1930. Mortgagees would then pay back the HOLC over the course of fifteen years at 5 percent interest.

Under the direction of John H. Fahey,* the Home Owners' Loan Corporation had made 992,531 loans totaling $3,005,408,000 by February 29, 1936. The corporation stopped accepting loan applications in June 1935 and stopped making loans in June 1936. By that time the HOLC had financed perhaps 20 percent of mortgaged urban homes in the United States, and one sixth of the total urban home mortgage debt. Under the National Housing Act of 1934,* the Home Owners' Loan Corporation also extended $100 million in its bonds to finance the Federal Savings and Loan Insurance Corporation* and $300 million for purchasing stock in federal savings and loan associations. After 1936 the HOLC spent fifteen years collecting its payments and terminated operations in 1951. (*Congressional Digest*, XV:107–108, 1937.)

HOME OWNERS' REFINANCING ACT OF 1933 (See HOME OWNERS' LOAN CORPORATION.)

HOOVER, HERBERT CLARK Born on August 10, 1874, in West Branch, Iowa, Herbert Hoover was orphaned as a child and raised in Iowa and Oregon by relatives. He graduated from Stanford University in 1895 and began a career as a mining engineer. By 1914 he had established an excellent reputation as a mining engineer and businessman and had accumulated a personal fortune. After heading the successful Commission for Relief in Belgium during the years of American neutrality in World War I, Hoover served as U.S. food administrator under President Woodrow Wilson and then as secretary of commerce under Presidents Warren G. Harding and Calvin Coolidge. His reputation as a humanitarian and as an administrator started a ''Hoover for President'' boom in 1920, but he announced his Republican party* affiliation and later accepted a cabinet position. In 1928 he was a natural choice for the Republican presidential nomination, and he defeated Democrat Al Smith* in the general election.

Hoover had barely embarked upon his presidency when the depression struck the United States in 1929. Far more active than any of his predecessors in responding to such an economic crisis, Hoover's efforts to stimulate recovery did not begin to show results until the summer of 1932, when the country began a slow and very gradual recovery. In the United States, however, the recovery was aborted by the presidential election of 1932,* which found Hoover defeated by Franklin D. Roosevelt.* During the four months of the ensuing ''interregnum,'' the American economy drifted gradually downward, culminating in the banking collapse of February and March 1933. When Hoover left office on March 4, 1933, the banking system of the nation was prostrate.

For two years after he left the White House, Hoover maintained silence in public concerning the New Deal.* He felt that Roosevelt deserved a chance, free from partisan criticism, to produce recovery if he could, and he doubted that there was an audience for anything he might have to say. His sole contribution during these two years to the dialogue over the New Deal was a book, *The Challenge to Liberty*, published late in 1934, that reaffirmed his basic philosophy. Early in 1935, however, Hoover went public with his misgivings about the New Deal, and thereafter he was one of the leading and most articulate of the New Deal's opponents. Anxious that the Republican party should offer a genuine alternative to the New Deal, Hoover covertly sought the 1936 Republican presidential nomination, but saw it go instead to Governor Alf Landon* of Kansas. Disturbed by what he regarded as a willingness to compromise with the New Deal on Landon's part, Hoover battled him for leadership of the GOP during 1937 and 1938 and took a prominent role in the congressional elections of the latter year—elections that resulted in substantial gains for the Republicans. In 1940 Hoover tried again for the Republican nomination but lost out to Wendell Willkie.*

The 1940 effort was Hoover's last quest for the Republican nomination. The losing efforts of 1936 and 1940 had shown that his personal popularity and the support which his attacks on the New Deal received were not enough to overcome the loser's image which dogged him as a result of the 1932 defeat. During the remaining years of his life, Hoover remained a dedicated opponent of much of the New Deal, and as head of two Hoover Commissions, under Presidents Harry S Truman* and Dwight Eisenhower, he continued to seek, successfully in some cases, to weaken the New Deal influence on American life. Herbert Clark Hoover died on October 20, 1964. (Gary Dean Best, *Herbert Hoover: The Postpresi-*

dential Years, 1983; David Burner, *Herbert Hoover: A Public Life*, 1979; Joan Hoff-Wilson, *Herbert Hoover: Forgotten Progressive*, 1975.)

GARY DEAN BEST

''HOOVERVILLES'' A pejorative term clearly reflecting public convictions that Herbert Hoover* was responsible for the Great Depression, ''Hoovervilles'' described the shanty towns sprouting throughout the United States in the early 1930s. By 1932 the communities of the homeless and unemployed had increased in size and number. With unemployment rates exceeding 25 percent and the number of business failures and farm and home foreclosures increasing, thousands of Americans were migrants and tens of thousands were homeless. In empty lots, city outskirts, beaches, river banks, municipal parks, and garbage dumps, these families erected makeshift shacks of cardboard, scrap metal, and cloth. The largest of the ''Hoovervilles'' was in St. Louis, where more than 1,000 people lived in makeshift housing. In New York City, hundreds of people lived along the Hudson River between 72nd St. and 110th St. In California groups of migrant families lived out of their cars while they searched for farm labor. Like ''Hoover blankets'' (newspapers), ''Hoover heaters'' (campfires), and ''Hoover hogs'' (armadillos), the term ''Hooverville'' was a symbol of the suffering wrought by the depression and the implication that President Hoover and the Republicans were responsible. (Martin G. Towey, ''Hooverville: St. Louis Had the Largest,'' *Gateway Heritage*, I:4–11 [Fall, 1980].)

HOPKINS, HARRY LLOYD After Franklin D. Roosevelt* signed the act creating the Federal Emergency Relief Administration,* he appointed Harry L. Hopkins as its chief administrator on May 19, 1933. Born on August 17, 1890, in Sioux City, Iowa, Hopkins became one of Franklin D. Roosevelt's best appointments. Prior to meeting Roosevelt, he held several social work positions in New York City following his graduation from Grinnell College. At the most important of these institutions, Christadora House and the Association for Improving the Condition of the Poor, Hopkins witnessed abysmal poverty and misery considered uncommon in his native state. Unlike most of his colleagues, Hopkins crossed social lines and counted several millionaires among his friends. His ability to mix successfully with rich and poor alike served him well throughout his career. In 1931 Roosevelt appointed him deputy director of New York's Temporary Emergency Relief Administration where he became proficient at dealing with the problems of massive poverty. In addition to acting as Federal Emergency Relief Administrator, Hopkins directed the Civil Works Administration* (1933–1934), the Works Progress Administration* (1935–1938), and served as secretary of commerce (1938–1940).

Throughout the New Deal* years, Harry Hopkins formed a close friendship with and admiration for Franklin D. Roosevelt. By 1940 he was perhaps the most influential adviser within the president's inner circle. As the nation's number-one relief and public works administrator, Hopkins emphasized the necessity of maintaining the American public's self-respect and reliance. Although direct cash relief (the dole) would have been less expensive, Hopkins stressed work relief, including controversial programs for actors, artists, and historians. These programs, especially the Works Progress Administration with its average monthly payroll of 2,122,000 from 1935–1941, proved immensely popular with the American people. Basic criticisms leveled against Roosevelt and Hopkins included the charge, to which there was considerable merit, that the New Dealers manipulated federal work-relief programs through the cash-disbursement, pump-priming process in order to attain immediate political rewards and, ultimately, the development of a self-perpetuating New Deal machine. In fact, noted columnist Arthur Krock* once quoted Hopkins (despite the latter's heated and vigorous denials) as stating that the New Deal would last indefinitely because he and other Roosevelt loyalists had found a magic political formula of taxing, spending, and electing. Despite this controversy, most historians agree that Hopkins' administration of federal public works programs generally reflected honesty and efficiency in setting a positive example for John F. Kennedy's New Frontier, Lyndon B. Johnson's Great Society, and Richard M. Nixon's New Federalism. On the other hand, in the process Roosevelt and Hopkins also established the precedent of presidents spending for election or to influence public opinion.

Such political controversies, including Hopkins' own presidential aspirations and failing health, led Roosevelt to remove him from the Works Progress Administration and appoint him secretary of commerce during the final two years of Roosevelt's second term. When that position became politically uncomfortable, the president moved Hopkins into the White House where he served as Roosevelt's special adviser on all affairs—foreign and domestic. During World War II, Hopkins acted as Roosevelt's personal emissary, travelling to the Soviet Union and Great Britain and meeting with Joseph Stalin and Winston Churchill. In this capacity Hopkins represented the United States at all the major military and diplomatic planning conferences including the "Four Freedoms" Atlantic session between Roosevelt and Churchill in 1941, the Arcadia Conference in 1942 which planned the United Nations, and the Yalta discussions in 1945 which arranged the post-war European configuration and the Soviet Union's military offensive against Japan during the final stages of the war.

All of this must have been pretty heady business for the son of an Iowa harnessmaker. But Hopkins rarely became flustered under any conditions. His chief consideration was loyalty to Roosevelt and the United States—which he considered as one and the same goal. When the war ended, Hopkins returned to New York, serving briefly as chairman of the garment industry arbitration board before his death on January 29, 1946. (Searle F. Charles, *Minister of Relief: Harry Hopkins and the Depression*, 1963.)

J. CHRISTOPHER SCHNELL

HORNER, HENRY Born in 1878, Henry Horner became the first Democratic governor elected in Illinois since World War I and the first Jew to occupy the executive office in Springfield. As governor, he served as an important middleman between the New Deal* and the people of Illinois. When he took office in 1933, one of every two workers in Chicago was unemployed; public school teachers had been paid in scrip and tax anticipation warrants for a year; corn farmers were seething with unrest from foreclosures, evictions, low prices, and high taxes; and rival coal mines in southern Illinois were battling one another to organize the industry. Surrounding himself with academicians and politicians, Horner tried to address the state's problems, but when an assassin's bullet, aimed at President-elect Franklin D. Roosevelt,* accidentally killed Chicago mayor Anton J. Cermak, Horner lost a friend and political ally. Horner would not yield when Cermak's successor, Edward J. Kelly,* tried to dominate state politics, but the political struggle hurt his administration.

To deal with the crisis in the state economy, Horner proposed a retail sales tax, which proved to be quite unpopular. After months of wrangling, "High Tax Henry" got his two-cent sales tax through the Illinois General Assembly. Later, the legislature reluctantly approved a $30 million bond issue in order to supplement federal relief funds supplied by the Federal Emergency Relief Administration.* Following the relief and recovery legislation of the New Deal's "one hundred days,"* the Illinois legislature was in almost constant session working on its own "Little New Deal."* Actions were taken, for example, to avoid farm and home mortgage foreclosures, reinforce public school aid, and implement the industrial codes of the National Recovery Administration.*

The battle between Horner and Kelly proved to be the nemesis of the governor, complicating the implementation of New Deal programs at the state level. Roosevelt, awed by the Democratic political machine led in Chicago by Mayor Kelly and his partner, Patrick A. Nash, gave control over federal patronage in Illinois to the Kelly-Nash machine rather than Horner. In the 1936 primary, the White House acquiesced in the endorsement by the Democratic organization of Dr. Herman Bundesen, Chicago's popular city health commissioner, to replace Horner. The governor fought back, however, and was renominated in the April primary, carrying every county except Cook County. Horner and his unwelcome running mate, John Stelle, who defeated Horner's choice for lieutenant governor in the primary, won in November. They received 53.1 percent of the vote over Republicans C. Wayland Brooks and William Hale Thompson, while Franklin D. Roosevelt carried the state with a landslide 57.7 percent over Alf Landon.*

Plagued with continuing patronage disputes, sit-down strikes, severe flooding in southern Illinois, violence in the coal mines, and partisan regional feuding in the legislature, Horner knew no peace. He had so expended his energies that he was stricken with a stroke two days before the election. A long recovery period necessitated government by a bedside cabinet and constant bickering with Lt. Governor Stelle. The status quo prevailed. After a lingering illness, Horner died on October 6, 1940, ninety-nine days short of completing his second term. As an articulate spokesman for such early New Deal measures as emergency relief, NRA, social security, and unemployment insurance, Horner labored tirelessly for a state New Deal. In the end, Roosevelt's attraction to big-city machines undercut the governor's effectiveness in Illinois and created party fissures that not only disrupted reform but created a succession of political problems for the national administration. (Thomas B. Littlewood, *Horner of Illinois*, 1969.)

ROBERT A. WALLER

HOWE, FREDERIC CLEMSON Frederic C. Howe was born in Meadville, Pennsylvania, on November 21, 1867. He graduated from Allegheny College in 1889 then took a master's and doctorate at Johns Hopkins University in 1890 and 1892. Howe also studied law at the Maryland Law School and the New York Law School and was admitted to the bar in 1894. Howe practiced law in Cleveland until 1909, served in the city council between 1901 and 1903, and was a member of the Ohio state legislature between 1906 and 1909. As director of the People's Institute of New York between 1911 and 1914 and commissioner of immigration for the port of New York between 1914 and 1919, Howe acquired a sensitivity to the needs of poor, working class immigrants. During the New Deal,* Jerome Frank* of the Agricultural Adjustment Administration* recruited Howe to serve as head of the AAA's Consumer Council. There Howe tried to make sure that the AAA's processing taxes were not simply passed on to consumers. Along with other lawyers in the AAA, Howe sympathized with the plight of southern tenant farmers being displaced from their land by acreage reductions. He was "purged" in 1935 along with Frank, Gardner Jackson,* and several others. Between 1935 and 1940 Howe served as a special adviser to Secretary of Agriculture Henry Wallace,* but his effective power in the New Deal was over. Frederic Howe died on August 3, 1940. (*Who Was Who In America*, I:595, 1942.)

HOWE, LOUIS McHENRY Louis McHenry Howe, adviser and secretary to Franklin D. Roosevelt,* was born on January 14, 1871, in Indianapolis, Indiana, the only child of Edward Howe and Eliza (Ray) Howe. For a time Louis' father prospered as a real estate speculator, but his business was ruined by the panic of 1873. When Louis was five, the family moved to Saratoga Springs, New York, where the father became a printer and owner of a weekly newspaper, the *Saratoga Sun*. To prepare for Yale, Louis entered Saratoga Institute, a private day school, but lack of money and poor health forced him to give up plans for college. When he was seventeen, he was hired by his father as a printing salesman and part-time reporter. At the age of twenty-one he became a partner in the family firm.

In Saratoga, a resort town, Howe mingled with society people, Tammany politicians, race track gamblers, actors from the New York stage, and the town's middle-class permanent residents—an ideal preparation for journalism and politics. Saratoga's summer theater also stimulated his lifelong interest in dramatics. Sharing this interest was a young summer visitor to Saratoga, Grace Hartley of Fall River, Massachusetts. They were married in 1898 and had three children, one of whom died in infancy.

When the family business declined, Howe had to work as a freelance journalist, but with little success. In 1906 he was hired as assistant to the *New York Herald* correspondent in Albany. The job gave him additional insight into the hard-boiled world of politics and, more important, led in 1911 to his acquaintance with Franklin D. Roosevelt, a young state senator about whom Howe had written favorably in the *Herald.* When Roosevelt was confined to his New York City home with typhoid fever in 1912, he hired Howe to take charge of his re-election campaign. Howe's work brought an impressive victory for Roosevelt and marked the beginning of a political partnership that lasted for a quarter of a century.

When Roosevelt became assistant secretary of the navy in 1913, Howe went to Washington as his secretary. He was active during part of Roosevelt's unsuccessful campaign for the vice-presidency in 1920. Later, when Roosevelt was stricken with polio, Howe, more than anyone else except Eleanor Roosevelt,* kept alive Roosevelt's hopes for a political future. During Roosevelt's four years as governor of New York, Howe, with Jim Farley,* devised much of the strategy that won Roosevelt the Democratic nomination for president and the election in 1932.*

On the day after the election, Howe learned that he was to be chief secretary to the president, a title that pleased him, though he referred to himself as "the dirty-job man." He was given his own quarters in the White House and had a hand in some of the early New Deal* decisions, but failing health limited his role. He successfully backed William Woodin* for secretary of the treasury over Senator Carter Glass,* who had strong conservative support. Howe advised the president in planning the Civilian Conservation Corps* and was instrumental in the selection of Robert Fechner,* an AFL* official, as its head. A more newsworthy assignment, which Howe handled successfully with Eleanor Roosevelt's help, was to persuade the "bonus army" veterans to go back home in exchange for his promise that some 1,200 of them could join the CCC. Less successful was Howe's and Mrs. Roosevelt's collaboration on a project called Arthurdale, a New Deal subsistence homestead in West Virginia which turned out to be a failure. Howe also supervised the newspaper digest, facetiously known as "Howe's *Daily Bugle*," which gave the president a broad view of national opinion. Although Howe became critically ill in 1935 and in mid-August was moved to the Naval Hospital, he kept in close touch with the president by special phone and continued to plot strategy for the approaching re-election campaign. On April 18, 1936, Howe died quietly in his sleep from chest and heart complications. (Alfred B. Rollins, *Roosevelt and Howe*, 1962; Lela Stiles, *The Man Behind Roosevelt: The Story of Louis McHenry Howe*, 1954.)

JOHN PAYNE

HUDDLESTON, GEORGE George Huddleston was born in Wilson County, Tennessee, on November 11, 1869. He studied law at Cumberland University and was admitted to the Alabama bar in 1891. Huddleston practiced law in Birmingham between 1891 and 1912 and was elected to Congress as a Democrat in 1914. He served in Congress until 1937. A conservative Democrat, Huddleston resented the bureaucratic complexities of the New Deal* and spoke out frequently against relief spending, excessive taxation, deficit spending, and the public utilities regulation bill. He led the fight against the "death sentence clause" of the Public Utility Holding Company Act of 1935.* Huddleston was not re-elected in 1936 and resumed his law practice. He died on February 29, 1960. (*Who Was Who In America*, III:425, 1960.)

HUGHES, CHARLES EVANS Charles Evans Hughes, one of the great figures in American government during the first half of the twentieth century, was born April 11, 1862, in Glen Falls, New York. His father was an itinerant Baptist preacher; and, as was appropriate, the child was brought up in the atmosphere of a strict Christian household. In 1876 he was sent to Colgate University (then called Madison). He found the work there not very challenging, and in 1878 he transferred to Brown University. Blessed with a quick and retentive mind, Hughes graduated third in his class, then he taught school for a year while reading law on the side. In 1882 he entered Columbia Law School. He completed his law degree in 1884 and passed the bar examination with a near perfect score. Taken into the law firm of Walter S. Carter, Hughes became a partner and son-in-law to the senior partner within three years, marrying Antoinette Carter in 1888.

Hughes specialized in commercial law and quickly acquired an outstanding reputation. But he worked himself to exhaustion and to recover his health, he took leave of the firm in 1891 to teach law at Cornell Law School. He returned to his law practice in 1893. In 1905 Hughes was asked to serve as legal counsel on two separate investigative committees of the New York legislature. One looked into the New York City utilities industry; the other examined the scandal-ridden insurance industry of the state. Hughes performed brilliantly in both investigations, and he attracted the attention of New York progressives, who in 1906 asked him to run for governor against Democratic candidate William Randolph Hearst.* In a tight race, Hughes defeated Hearst by a margin of about 58,000 votes.

During his first term, Hughes was a very able administrator and helped secure passage of important progressive reform legislation, especially in the areas of utilities regulation and workmen's compensation. Never popular with minor party bosses, he alienated many Republicans when he fought to maintain the state ban on racetrack betting. Moreover, he offended President Theodore Roosevelt when he rebuffed the president's friendly attempts to intervene in a bitter fight to oust Hughes' superintendent of insurance. The split between the two men was permanent. In 1908 Hughes was re-elected as governor, but he ran well behind his party. Clearly, he had lost popularity in the state. His fight for further reform legislation was rebuffed by his own party in the legislature. In 1910, when President Taft offered Hughes a seat on the Supreme Court,* the governor accepted almost with a sigh of relief.

Hughes brought youth and vigor to the Court. In his six years of service, he wrote 151 opinions, dissented only thirty-two times, and encountered dissent to his opinions in only nine cases. In the context of the times, he was regarded as an activist and a liberal. In such decisions as the *Minnesota Rates Cases* (1913) and the *Shreveport Case* (1914) Hughes wrote the majority opinion for the Court, asserting the exclusive power of Congress over interstate commerce and even over areas of intrastate commerce where it was intertwined with interstate commerce. He also staunchly defended the rights of labor and minorities. In the critical election of 1916, Hughes was persuaded to leave the Court and challenge Woodrow Wilson's bid for re-election. But the campaign did not go well. Under the influence of the Roosevelt wing of the party, Hughes supported positions on foreign policy which seemed bellicose to many voters. Unable to challenge Wilson's domestic reform program, Hughes seemed to back traditional Republican attitudes toward labor, business, and the tariff. And he failed to court Republican progressives in the Midwest and California, a failure which cost him the election.

Out of politics, Hughes returned to his law practice in New York and continued to speak out on the issues. On the question of the League of Nations, Hughes was a moderate reservationist and supported that position in the election campaign of 1920. With Harding and the Republican party* victorious, Hughes was given the State Department. Despite his continued support for the league he had to accept the reality of Senate opposition to United States membership. But he was able to pursue a policy of cooperation in many of the non-political activities of the league, especially in such matters as reparations and fiscal policy. In 1923 he was instrumental in the formulation of the Dawes Plan for the Restructuring of the German Economy. His most successful venture in foreign policy was the Washington Conference of 1921–1922, which resulted in a series of treaties which checked the danger of a naval arms race and reduced tensions between the former Allies in the Far East.

Hughes resigned as secretary of state in 1925 to return to his law practice. In 1930 President Herbert Hoover* nominated him to succeed Chief Justice William Howard Taft. The vote in the Senate to confirm him, 52 to 26, both surprised and embarrassed Hughes. Some senators disliked his Wall-Street associations, and others never forgave him for quitting the Court in 1916 to run for president. But at age sixty-eight, he was confirmed as chief justice of the United States. To meet the tragic conditions of national depression, the New Deal* of Franklin D. Roosevelt* embraced programs which transformed public policy in the United States. In the early period of the New Deal (1933–1935), the Supreme Court seemed to stand in the way of that transformation, striking down legislation which conflicted with the conservative interpretation of the Constitution. Chief Justice Hughes was often and unjustly assailed by the Court's critics. Actually, Hughes was far more flexible than his critics would admit. In several major cases which pained the administration (*Louisville Bank v. Radford*,* and *Schechter v. U.S.*,* for example), the Court ruled unanimously against constitutionality. And in many decisions after 1935, Hughes took sides against the conservative faction on the Court. In what could be considered a lecture to the conservative justices, he expressed his judicial philosophy in his opinion upholding the constitutionality of the National Labor Relations Act* (*NLRB v. Jones & Laughlin Steel*,* 1937):

> The cardinal principle of statutory construction is to save not to destroy. We have repeatedly held that as between two possible interpretations of a statute, by one of which it would be unconstitutional and by the other valid, our plain duty is to adopt that which will save the act. Even to avoid a serious doubt the rule is the same.

And during the 1930s, Hughes defense of the rights of labor and minorities was as staunch as it had been during his earlier service. On June 2, 1941, at age seventy-nine, Chief Justice Hughes submitted a letter of resignation to President Roosevelt, citing reasons of age and health. He continued to live in Washington, D.C., busy with his autobiographical notes and papers until his death on August 29, 1948. (Merl J. Pusey, *Charles Evans Hughes*, 1951.)

JOSEPH M. ROWE, JR.

HULL, CORDELL Cordell Hull was born on October 2, 1871, in Overton County, Tennessee. He graduated from Cumberland University Law School in 1891 and began practicing law. Entering the political arena in 1893, he was elected to the Tennessee House and served there until 1897. Hull returned to private law practice until 1903, when he was appointed to fill a judgeship in the 5th Judicial Circuit of Tennessee. In 1907 he was elected to the U.S. House of Representatives, where he served continuously (except for 1921–1922) until his election to the Senate in 1931. In Congress, Hull was a leading progressive, authoring the Federal Income Tax Act (1913), the Revised Federal Income Tax Act (1916), and the Federal Inheritance Tax Act (1916). In 1933 Cordell Hull became Franklin D. Roosevelt's* secretary of state.

Although Hull had no previous diplomatic experience, the president was aware of Hull's support of reciprocal trade agreements. Throughout the 1920s Hull had supported such schemes to rebuild the international economy, believing it was the only rational way to restore America's foreign trade. Hull pursued reciprocal trade doggedly, and in 1934 Congress passed the Reciprocal Trade Agreements Act,* cornerstone of New Deal* foreign economic policy. Hull was its architect. The Reciprocal Trade Agreements Act granted the executive branch broad powers to negotiate mutually beneficial trade agreements with corresponding reductions in American and foreign tariffs. Between 1934 and 1935 Hull negotiated with the European powers, namely Great Britain and France, for drastic reductions in tariffs. Here too Hull was successful. In the arena of Latin American diplomacy, Hull enlisted the talents of Sumner Welles to negotiate reciprocal agreements with the nations of the Western Hemisphere. Anti-American sentiments within Latin America lessened. Roosevelt and Hull agreed to withdraw troops from Central America and to disavow the Platt Amendment with regard to Cuba.

Hull became a key advocate of New Deal policies and he demonstrated his loyalty to the New Deal in the election campaign of 1936,* travelling across the United States promoting Franklin Roosevelt. Next to Roosevelt, Hull was one of the most popular Democrats in the country, and some party leaders wanted the president to support Hull's nomination as vice-president. Hull's tenacity and popularity, however, denied him this opportunity. Harry Hopkins* feared such a candidacy because it might increase Hull's power to the point of surpassing Roosevelt's popularity. More importantly, Hull was denied any large role in the formulation of foreign policy with regard to the European continent and dealings with Fascist Germany. After the election of 1936, discord surfaced within the State Department between Hull and the Under Secretary of State Sumner Welles. Welles' return to the State Department in 1937 allowed Hull to slacken his workload. Hull, however, believed this action by Roosevelt was an affront, and the media began to assume that Welles played a much greater role in directing foreign affairs than formerly thought. Hull consequently became angered at these news leaks which he attributed to Welles. Hull became particularly embittered with Welles when Roosevelt dispatched him as his special emissary to the European continent in 1940. Hull then determined that Welles had to leave the State Department, and in 1943 he was successful in forcing Welles' departure. During World War II, Hull concentrated his efforts on creating the United Nations, for which he received the Nobel Prize in 1945. He also participated in preparations for the Dumbarton Oaks Conference in 1944. Hull retired from the State Department in 1944 and died on July 23, 1955. (*New York Times*, July 24, 1955; Julius W. Pratt, *Cordell Hull, 1933–1944*, 1964.)

JOHN S. LEIBY

HUMPHREY, WILLIAM EWART William E. Humphrey was born near Alamo, Indiana, on March 31, 1862. He graduated from Wabash College in 1887 and practiced law at Crawfordsville, Indiana, between 1888 and 1893. Humphrey moved to Seattle, Washington, in 1893 to practice corporate law, and there he specialized in the timber industry. A conservative Republican, Humphrey was a member of Congress between 1903 and 1917, and in 1924 he was campaign manager for President Calvin Coolidge's successful re-election bid. Because the Federal Trade Commission* had repeatedly investigated the northwestern timber industry, Humphrey was a bitter opponent of the FTC; and in 1925, with the clear hope he would transform the agency into a pro-business institution, Coolidge appointed him to a six-year term as a commissioner. There Humphrey dominated the conservative majority and essentially changed the FTC from a progressive body working to guarantee free competition into a pro-business, conservative body. President Herbert Hoover* reappointed him in 1931.

During the early New Deal,* however, President Franklin D. Roosevelt,* James M. Landis,* and Felix Frankfurter* saw Humphrey as a hopeless reactionary. Roosevelt fired Humphrey in 1933 in a decision which the commissioner fought in the courts. Two years later, after Humphrey's death in 1934, the Supreme Court* handed down its decision in *Humphrey's Executor (Rathbun) v. United States*, overturning the firing on the grounds that the president did not have the authority to remove officials of regulatory agencies for political reasons before their scheduled reappointment. (G. Cullom Davis, "The Transformation of the Federal Trade Commission, 1914–1929," *Mississippi Valley Historical Review*, XIL:437–455, 1962; Donald A. Ritchie, *James M. Landis: Dean of the Regulators*, 1980.)

"HUNDRED DAYS" Shortly after his inauguration, President Franklin D. Roosevelt* called the 73rd Congress into special session to deal with the banking crisis. That session lasted until June 16, 1933, when the Congress adjourned. Known as the "hundred days" of the New Deal,* the special session quickly went beyond the banking crisis to enact a broad series of relief and recovery measures, including the Emergency Banking Act,* Economy Act,* Beer Tax Act,* Civilian Conservation Corps* Reforestation Relief Act, Federal Emergency Relief Act,* Agricultural Adjustment Act,* Tennessee Valley Authority,* Securities Act,* National Employment System Act,* Home Owners' Refinancing Act,* Banking Act of 1933,* Farm Credit Act,* Emergency Railroad Transportation Act,* and the National Industrial Recovery Act.* Ever since the spring of 1933, the "hundred days" has been recognized as one of the most dramatic periods in the history of public policy in the United States. (James E. Sargent, *Roosevelt and the Hundred Days: Struggle for the Early New Deal*, 1981.)

HUNT, HENRY ALEXANDER Henry A. Hunt was born on October 10, 1866, near Sparta, Georgia. He was the youngest of eight children. Abandoned by their white father, the family survived by eking out an existence chopping cotton, dropping corn, and shelling peanuts. In 1882 Hunt went to Atlanta University and, while working part-time, learned the construction trade in a vocational program. He graduated from Atlanta University in 1890 and became a public school principal in Charlotte, North Carolina. Hunt was appointed business manager of Biddle University in 1891 and also served as proctor of boys. After more than thirteen years at Biddle, Hunt accepted the position of principal of the Fort Valley High and Industrial School in Georgia. Hunt headed the school until 1938, building it by then into Fort Valley State College. At Fort Valley, Hunt concentrated his energies on building a fine academic program and using the school as a benefit for the rural black community through extension services, community programs, health care campaigns, and literacy drives. In the process he became an expert in the problem of rural black poverty. The Julius Rosenwald Fund awarded him a fellowship in 1931 to study rural cooperatives in Denmark, and in November 1933 President Franklin D. Roosevelt* appointed him as assistant to the head of the Farm Credit Administration* and an adviser on black problems. Hunt informed blacks of their opportunities for government credit and jobs and helped adjudicate disputes concerning discrimination in local federal programs. Henry A. Hunt died in October 1938. (Donnie D. Bellamy, ''Henry A. Hunt and Black Agricultural Leadership in the New South,'' *Journal of Negro History*, LX:464–479, 1975.)

HUTSON, JOHN B. John B. Hutson, an important agricultural administrator during the New Deal,* was born on September 7, 1890, in Murray, Kentucky. He had a strong interest in agricultural economics, graduated from the University of Kentucky in 1917, then received an M.S. from the University of Wisconsin (1925) and a Ph.D. from Columbia University (1930). Hutson's special research interest was tobacco farming, and in 1933 Secretary of Agriculture Henry Wallace* named him chief of the tobacco section of the AAA.* He stayed in that post until 1936, when he became assistant administrator of the AAA after the Supreme Court* had declared unconstitutional the enabling legislation of 1933. Wallace had Hutson supervise the drafting of the Agricultural Adjustment Act of 1938,* and in 1941 President Franklin D. Roosevelt* named him head of the Commodity Credit Corporation.* Hutson remained there until 1944 when he became deputy director of the Office of War Mobilization and Reconversion. Hutson closed out his public career by serving as under secretary of agriculture in 1945 and 1946. He then retired after working briefly as an assistant secretary general for administrative and financial services with the United Nations. John B. Hutson died on May 5, 1964. (Dean Albertson, *Roosevelt's Farmer. Claude Wickard in the New Deal*, 1961; *Who Was Who In America*, IV:479, 1968.)

I

ICKES, HAROLD LeCLAIR Harold L. Ickes, secretary of the interior and head of the Public Works Administration* during the New Deal,* was born on March 15, 1874, in Frankstown, Pennsylvania. Ickes attended the University of Chicago and graduated in 1897. He then went into journalism as a reporter for the *Chicago Tribune* and the *Chicago Record* and developed strong progressive political views as well as a hatred for the business domination of municipal government. An independent Republican, Ickes supported C. E. Merriam* for mayor of Chicago in 1911, campaigning for good government and an end to graft and corruption. Ickes bolted the party in 1912 to support Theodore Roosevelt and the Bull Moose campaign and remained leader of the Progressive party in Illinois until 1916. That year he came back into the fold and endorsed Republican candidate Charles Evans Hughes* for president, but he defected again in 1920, unable to countenance the Warren Harding-Calvin Coolidge ticket. Ickes openly endorsed the Democratic ticket of James Cox and Franklin D. Roosevelt.* During the 1920s, Ickes practiced law with Donald Richberg* in Chicago and together they waged war against the influence of the Samuel Insull* utilities empire and the political power of ''Big Bill'' Thompson. Ickes also served a term as president of the Chicago chapter of the NAACP* and promoted black civil rights. By the end of the decade, he was widely known in progressive political circles for his impeccable honesty and unwavering commitment to conservation and good government.

In February 1933 President-elect Franklin D. Roosevelt named Ickes as secretary of the interior. When the National Industrial Recovery Act of 1933* was passed four months later and established the Public Works Administration, Roosevelt doubled up on Ickes and named him head of the PWA as well. Ickes proved to be one of the most influential figures in the New Deal. As secretary of the interior, he was a consistent advocate of conservation and national planning for the orderly development of natural resources. During the 1930s, he worked closely with the National Resources Planning Board* and wanted rigid controls placed on private power companies. Ickes was very close to Eleanor Roosevelt* and the civil rights cause, and he played a critical role in extending New Deal benefits to blacks. Not only did he lobby widely across administrative lines to encourage the hiring of blacks in the Department of the Interior, Ickes made sure blacks got a fair share of jobs on interior construction projects. He also integrated the cafeteria of the Department of the Interior and saw to it that Marian Anderson* could sing at the Lincoln Memorial after the Daughters of the American Revolution denied her access to Constitution Hall. As director of the Public Works Administration, Ickes was indefatigable in his control of the agency. Obsessed with the need to maintain PWA integrity, Ickes carefully analyzed each project; decided if it was economically sound, useful, and capable of producing employment; scrutinized each proposal's potential for graft, corruption, and ''pork-barrel'' rewards; and examined architectural drawings and engineering requirements. Because of his concern, the PWA was almost incorruptible and immune from political criticism, at least by conservatives worried about waste and inefficiency.

Ickes did not inspire much public devotion because of his tough and aggressive rhetoric as well as his stubborn tenacity. But he was privately a nervous, insecure, and sensitive man. He trusted few people but desperately needed affection; he was as competent as any official in Washington, yet constantly afraid that others were conspiring against him, either to reduce the power of the Department of the Interior or to squeeze him out of the administration. Impatient and unable to accept criticism, Ickes was forever seeking audiences with Roosevelt to complain about someone in the administration, and the president listened to him with a bemused patience. For years, Ickes battled Henry A. Wallace* and the Department of Agriculture for control of the Forest Service. Ickes wanted to change the name of the Department of the Interior to the Department of Conservation and Works and bring all federal conservation programs under his control. He never succeeded, but the struggle revealed more than anything else his commitment to a national conservation policy. Enraged at conservative Democrats unwilling to support the New Deal, Ickes helped talk Roosevelt into embarking on the ''purge of 1938,''* when the president unsuccessfully tried to defeat his recalcitrant colleagues in the Democratic primaries.

During World War II, Ickes also served as head of the Solid Fuels Conservation program, and he denounced the incarceration of Japanese Americans in War Relocation Authority camps. Ickes finally resigned from the Department of the Interior in 1946 when he developed political problems with President Harry S Truman.* Dedicated, egotistical, and self-righteous in his certitude, Harold L. Ickes was one of the New Deal elite who so dramatically influenced public policy in the 1930s and 1940s. He died on February 3, 1952. (Linda J. Lear, *Harold L. Ickes: The Aggressive Progressive, 1874–1933*, 1981; *New York Times*, February 4, 1952; Arthur M. Schlesinger, Jr., *The Age of Roosevelt. Vol. II. The Coming of the New Deal*, 1959, *Vol. III. The Politics of Upheaval, 1935–1936*, 1960.)

INDEPENDENT OFFICES APPROPRIATIONS ACT OF 1934 (See ECONOMY ACT OF 1933.)

INDEX OF AMERICAN DESIGN (See FEDERAL ART PROJECT.)

INDIAN ARTS AND CRAFTS BOARD On August 27, 1935, President Franklin D. Roosevelt* signed into law the Indian Arts and Crafts Board Act, a component of Indian Commissioner John Collier's* "Indian New Deal"* program. The act created the Indian Arts and Crafts Board. Earlier attempts to create such a body had failed until Secretary of the Interior Harold Ickes* appointed a prominent committee to study the matter in 1934. The committee's findings and recommendations played a key role in securing passage of the act creating the Indian Arts and Crafts Board the following year. Five commissioners appointed for four-year terms comprised the Indian Arts and Crafts Board. The board sought to improve the quality and expand the distribution of Indian arts and crafts. The board established government trademarks for Indian-made products to ensure their authenticity. Those attempting to misrepresent Indian products or counterfeit government trademarks faced possible imprisonment not exceeding six months, or a fine up to $2,000, or both.

Rene d'Harnoncourt, a European-born artist who helped revive Mexican arts and crafts, served ably as the board's first general manager. One of the major challenges the board overcame was establishing standards for affixing the government trademark on Indian-made products. Other successful board activities included creating craft guilds on reservations to help Indian artists and craftsmen and serve as marketing outlets; organizing art classes in federal schools; providing weaving, silverwork, leatherwork, and beadwork projects; exhibiting Indian-made objects at the 1939 San Francisco World's Fair; and publishing *Indian Art of the United States* (1941) in cooperation with the Museum of Modern Art in New York.

Congressional cuts of appropriations to the board and attacks on d'Harnoncourt's foreign birth crippled the board's effectiveness. Nevertheless, the Indian Arts and Crafts Board improved the quality and marketing of Indian-made products, preserved the Indians' artistic heritage, promoted an appreciation of Indians' artistic abilities by non-Indians, and supplied needed income to many destitute Indians. (Robert Fay Schrader, *The Indian Arts and Crafts Board: An Aspect of New Deal Indian Policy*, 1983.)

RAYMOND WILSON

"INDIAN NEW DEAL" (See INDIAN REORGANIZATION ACT OF 1934.)

INDIAN REORGANIZATION ACT OF 1934 When John Collier* became commissioner of Indian Affairs in April 1933, he promised an "Indian New Deal" for native Americans. The cornerstone of this new direction in federal Indian policy was the Indian Reorganization Act of 1934. Collier, Assistant Commissioner of Indian Affairs William Zimmerman, and members of the Department of Interior's legal staff, particularly Nathan Margold* and Felix Cohen, wrote the original draft of the Indian Reorganization Act. Representative

Edgar Howard of Nebraska introduced the bill in the House, and Senator Burton K. Wheeler* of Montana sponsored it in the Senate. The Wheeler-Howard bill was forty-eight pages long and contained four titles regarding Indian self-government, education, lands, and a special court for Indian affairs.

Although Collier held several meetings with Indian tribes throughout the West to explain the benefits of the legislation and subsequently reported that most of the tribes embraced the bill, congressional critics and others remained unconvinced. They charged that the Wheeler-Howard bill severely retarded the process of assimilation by segregating Indians from the dominant society and perpetuating federal guardianship over them, promoted communism among Indians, and threatened individual Indian land ownership and heirship lands. In order to overcome these criticisms and others, Collier accepted several major revisions of the original draft. For example, the special Indian court was eliminated and the powers of the tribal self-governments reduced. Receiving congressional approval, the bill was signed into law by President Franklin D. Roosevelt* on June 18, 1934.

In its amended form, the Indian Reorganization Act (sometimes called the Wheeler-Howard Act) repealed the allotment in severalty laws, restored to tribes surplus reservation lands that the Dawes Severalty Act of 1887 had created, and allowed for voluntary exchanges of restricted trust lands for shares in tribal corporations. Congressional appropriations of $2 million annually to the secretary of the interior were authorized for the acquisition of additional lands for tribes. A $10 million revolving credit fund was created to provide loans to tribal corporations, while an annual appropriation of $250,000 was provided to aid Indians in organizing tribal governments. Additional appropriations of $250,000 a year established a fund to help Indian students attend colleges and vocational schools. Finally, the act relaxed civil service requirements for Indians seeking employment in the Indian Service. Because of various circumstances, Indians in Alaska and Oklahoma were excluded from certain provisions of the Indian Reorganization Act. In 1936 Congress addressed these matters and passed both the Alaska Reorganization Act and the Oklahoma Indian Welfare Act, allowing Alaskan Indians to establish tribal corporations and Oklahoma Indians to create tribal governments and corporations.

Indian tribes had the right to accept or reject the Indian reorganization through tribal referenda. Those accepting the act could hold additional elections to establish self-governments and charters of incorporation. Although the figures vary, approximately 181 tribes with a population of 129,750 accepted the act, and seventy-seven tribes numbering 86,365, including the Navajos, rejected it. Moreover, only ninety-three tribes adopted constitutions, while only seventy-three established charters of incorporation. Of the over 100,000 Indians living in Oklahoma, only eighteen tribes numbering 13,241 wrote constitutions, while thirteen tribes with a population of 5,741 drew up charters of incorporation under the Oklahoma Indian Welfare Act. In Alaska, forty-nine villages with a total population of 10,899 established constitutions and incorporation charters under the Alaska Reorganization Act.

Although the Indian Reorganization Act did not achieve the Indian millenium that Collier desired, it ended the policy of land allotments, increased the land base of reservations, allowed tribes to have a larger degree of control over their political and economic destinies, and promoted Indian culture. Reasons for the failure of the act to achieve its objectives include lack of support from Indians, members of Congress, and Bureau of Indian Affairs officials; the Bureau of the Budget* and the House slashing annual appropriations; the recurring fear that the act retarded assimilation; and Collier's inability to recognize the complexities of native American tribalism. (Kenneth R. Philp, *John Collier's Crusade for Indian Reform, 1920–1954*, 1977; Graham D. Taylor, *The New Deal and American Indian Tribalism: The Administration of the Indian Reorganization Act, 1934–1945*, 1980.)

RAYMOND WILSON

INDUSTRIAL EMERGENCY COMMITTEE By executive order on June 30, 1934, President Franklin D. Roosevelt* established the Industrial Emergency Committee as part of the National Emergency Council.* The purpose of the committee was to coordinate government relief and unemployment programs under the National Recovery Administration.* Donald R. Richberg,* general counsel of the NRA, was named director of the Industrial Executive Committee; and other committee members were Harold Ickes,* Frances Perkins,* Harry Hopkins,* and Hugh Johnson.* The Industrial Emergency Committee continued functioning until Roosevelt dissolved it on October 29, 1934. (Samuel I. Rosenman, ed., *The Public Papers and Addresses of Franklin D. Roosevelt*, II:333–334, 1938.)

INSULL, SAMUEL Born in London on November 11, 1859, Samuel Insull attended fine private schools and in 1874 went to work for an auctioneering company. In 1879 he went to work as a secretary to Colonel George E. Gouraud, the European representative for Thomas A. Edison's electric power industry. Several of Insull's reports to the United States impressed Edison, and in 1881 he brought Insull to the United States as his secretary. Edison soon put Insull in charge of the Thomas A. Edison Construction Company. In 1892 Insull became president of Chicago Edison. By 1929 Insull had built an unparalleled utility empire in the Midwest by corporate combinations and use of holding companies. The Insull empire consisted of five great corporate systems with more than 150 subsidiaries, 4.5 million customers, and $2.5 billion in assets. At the top of the holding company empire were two companies, the Insull Utility Investments, Inc., and Corporation Securities Company of Chicago. Revenue from the operating companies sustained the holding companies, but any interruption in those revenues immediately would threaten the corporate superstructure. When the stock market crashed in 1929, Insull was unable to keep the empire liquid. By December 1931 Insull Utilities Investment was in the hands of creditors; and in 1932, when Middle West Utilities failed to secure refinancing credit, the company and its 111 subsidiaries went into receivership. Insull resigned from sixty corporations and fled to Europe. In September 1932 Franklin D. Roosevelt,* then Democratic nominee for president, attacked Insull publicly; and politicians used the collapse of Insull's empire to illustrate business corruption and the evil forces at work causing the Great Depression. Insull was indicted, tried, and acquitted of charges of embezzlement, mail fraud, and violation of the Bankruptcy Act, and died in France on July 16, 1938. The publicity surrounding his career, the spectacular collapse of his corporate empire, and public outrage over the suffering caused by the Great Depression led to unprecedented demands for reform. Those demands eventually led to significant portions of the Banking Act of 1933,* the Corporate Bankruptcy Act,* and the Wagner-Connery Act,* as well as the Public Utility Holding Company Act of 1935,* the Securities and Exchange Commission,* the Tennessee Valley Authority,* and the Rural Electrification Administration.* (Forrest McDonald, *Insull*, 1962.)

CHARLES E. DARBY, JR.

INTERDEPARTMENTAL COMMITTEE TO COORDINATE HEALTH AND WELFARE ACTIVITIES As part of its deliberations in 1934 and 1935, the Committee on Economic Security* looked into the idea of national health insurance while it was considering the need for unemployment insurance and federal old-age pensions. For political reasons, they decided not to include health provisions in the Social Security Act of 1935,* but in August 1935 President Franklin D. Roosevelt* appointed the Interdepartmental Committee to Coordinate Health and Welfare Activities. In 1938 the committee recommended a comprehensive program of national health insurance, and the president convened a special White House conference on health needs in July of that year. The National Health Conference adopted the proposal, and Senator Robert Wagner* introduced the National Health Act of 1939 to Congress. The bill encountered the immediate and intense opposition of the American Medical Association as well as private insurance carriers, particularly to the federal grant-in-aid and federal health insurance provisions. Congress failed to act on the measure. The Interdepartmental Committee to Coordinate Health and Welfare Activities continued to meet sporadically, but generally lost most of its administrative energy after creation of the Federal Security Agency* in 1939, which assumed control over a wide variety of health and welfare programs. (Samuel I. Rosenman, ed., *The Public Papers and Addresses of Franklin D. Roosevelt*, VIII:99–100, 1941.)

INTERDEPARTMENTAL LOAN COMMITTEE Because of the tremendous number of federal lending agencies within the early New Deal,* President Franklin

D. Roosevelt* established the Interdepartmental Loan Committee on November 4, 1934. With Secretary of the Treasury Henry Morgenthau, Jr.,* as chairman, the committee was composed of Secretary of the Interior Harold L. Ickes;* Governor W. I. Myers* of the Farm Credit Administration;* Chairman John H. Fahey* of the Home Owners Loan Corporation; Chester C. Davis,* administrator of the Agricultural Adjustment Administration;* President George N. Peek* of the Export-Import Bank;* President Lynn P. Talley* of the Commodity Credit Corporation;* Chairman Leo T. Crowley* of the Federal Deposit Insurance Corporation;* Chairman Jesse H. Jones* of the Reconstruction Finance Corporation;* Governor Marriner S. Eccles* of the Federal Reserve Board;* and James A. Moffett* of the Federal Housing Administration.* The committee was especially active in 1934 and 1935 in coordinating the activities of the various lending agencies, eliminating duplication, and assisting in the sale of government securities directly to investment markets. (Samuel I. Rosenman, ed., *The Public Papers and Addresses of Franklin D. Roosevelt*, III:450–451, 1938.)

INTERSTATE COMMERCE COMMISSION Established in 1887 as the first independent regulatory agency, the Interstate Commerce Commission had been designed to stabilize the railroad industry by preventing destructive competition and unfair freight rates. Congress hoped to protect shippers and consumers as well as provide the country with a functional, profitable transportation system. Despite a series of laws over the years (the Elkins Act of 1903, the Hepburn Act of 1906, and the Mann-Elkins Act of 1910) and increasing ICC regulatory authority, the nation's railroad system was a shambles by the 1930s. Burdened with enormous debt structures and fixed costs, plagued by increased competition from the burgeoning trucking industry, and devastated by the economic collapse of the Great Depression, the railroad system desperately needed consolidation and a competitive edge against the trucking industry. At the same time, the trucking industry was marked by cutthroat competition between common, contract, and private carriers. Transportation experts like Joseph Eastman* of the ICC wanted comprehensive federal legislation to coordinate the entire transportation system. In 1932 the private Railroad Credit Corporation and later the Reconstruction Finance Corporation* had provided millions of dollars in loans to the railroads, but loans were only temporary answers. Only massive consolidation of individual railroads into larger regional systems as well as government regulation of other modes of transportation could solve the crisis.

Three major New Deal* measures achieved the latter goal but not the former. The Emergency Railroad Transportation Act of 1933* created a federal coordinator of transportation to consolidate the railroads into three regional groups with coordinating committees to effect cuts in cost by ending duplication and promoting joint use of tracks and terminals, financial reorganization, and ICC approval of all combinations. But no significant consolidations occurred because of opposition from railroads, labor unions, and shippers afraid that consolidation would eliminate jobs and harm service quality while raising rates. To deal with the chaotic trucking industry and limit its competition with the railroads, Congress passed the Motor Carrier Act of 1935,* giving the ICC power to set maximum and minimum rates for common motor carriers and minimum rates for contract carriers. Although the ICC, under authority of the Motor Carrier Act, raised the minimum freight rates of common and contract motor carriers to a parity level with railroad rates, its decisions were based on the value-of-service rate structure. That too, of course, was only a short-term solution. On a parity basis, railroads could not compete with motor carriers using a value-of-service rate structure, but the ICC employed that method rather than a cost-of-service parity, which could have allowed railroads to compete. So while the Motor Carrier Act of 1935 increased ICC power over the modes of transportation, it did not really address basic problems in the railroad industry. Finally, the Transportation Act of 1940* extended ICC authority over coastwise, intercoastal, inland, and Great Lakes common and contract water carriers while relieving the ICC of its twenty-year old obligation to create a consolidation for railroads. By 1940 the ICC had secured power over the rail, motor, and water carriers of the national transportation system. Apart from air transportation, controlled by the Civil Aeronautics Authority* after 1938, the ICC regulated all significant modes of interstate transportation. But no consolidation of the railroad system had occurred, nor had the problem of trucking competition been eliminated. Only World War II and its unprecedented increase in freight traffic saved the railroads from certain collapse. (Ari Hoogenboom and Olive Hoogenboom, *A History of the ICC. From Panacea to Palliative*, 1976.)

INVESTMENT ADVISERS ACT OF 1940 A companion to the Investment Company Act of 1940,* the Investment Advisers Act required all individuals and companies profiting from the sale of securities to register with the Securities and Exchange Commission.* After November 1, 1940, unregistered individuals or companies were prohibited from using the federal mail, interstate commerce, or national securities exchanges in their investment advice business. Newspapers, banks, accountants, and lawyers whose securities advice was incidental to their regular business were exempted from the law. President Franklin D. Roosevelt* considered the Investment Advisers Act a major improvement in federal regulatory power over the securities markets and a natural follow-up to the Securities Act of 1933,* the Securities Exchange Act of 1934,* the Public Utility Holding Company Act of 1935,* the Chandler Act of 1938,* and the Investment Company Act of 1940. (*New York Times*, August 2, 9, and 24, 1940.)

INVESTMENT COMPANY ACT OF 1940 During the 1930s, because of the tremendous liquidation of stock values as well as the sensational revelations of the Pecora Committee in 1932 and 1933, the public reputation of the investment banking and trust industry had plummeted. Their resistance to the Securities Act of 1933,* the Securities Exchange Act of 1934,* and the Public Utility Holding Company Act of 1935* had only added to public hostility. Late in the 1930s, a number of trade associations, but especially the Investment Bankers' Association, began developing their own regulatory legislation to standardize and stabilize industry-wide practices and eliminate corruption and fraud. Drafted by the Securities and Exchange Commission* with the assistance of the Investment Bankers' Association, the legislation was sponsored by Congressman William P. Cole of Maryland and became law as the Investment Company Act in June 1940. The law prohibited "self-dealing" between companies and their affiliates, required proportion of independent directorships, and prohibited basic changes in investment policies without consent of stockholders. The law also forced investment trust companies to register with the SEC, provide full information to stockholders, and allowed the SEC to oversee their operations. Along with the Investment Advisers Act of 1940,* President Franklin D. Roosevelt* considered the Investment Company Act of 1940 a major addition to federal securities regulation. (*New York Times*, August 2, 9, and 24, 1940.)

J

JACKSON, GARDNER Gardner (Pat) Jackson was born in 1897. His father, William S. Jackson, had made a fortune building the Denver & Rio Grande Railroad and was one of the largest landowners in Colorado and New Mexico. Gardner Jackson graduated from Harvard in 1921 and immediately entered the newspaper business as a reporter with the *Boston Globe*. Between 1921 and 1927, as he worked with the *Globe*, Jackson became increasingly involved in liberal social and political causes, first inspired by the Sacco and Vanzetti case. He took a leave of absence from the *Globe* just prior to Sacco and Vanzetti's execution to serve as chairman of their defense fund. Jackson became Washington correspondent for the *Montreal Star* in 1927 and in 1933 joined the staff of the Agricultural Adjustment Administration,* where he promoted the interests of tenant farmers and sharecroppers. Jackson became associated in the AAA with the urban lawyers like Jerome Frank* and Alger Hiss* who were concerned with the displacement of tenant farmers from their land because of AAA production quotas. He too was a victim of the "purge of 1935" which drove Frank and Hiss from the Department of Agriculture. After that Jackson became a major financial supporter of the Southern Tenant Farmers' Union* through his Committee to Aid Agricultural Workers. In 1936 Jackson brought H. L. Mitchell, head of the STFU, to Washington, D.C., to meet Rexford Tugwell* and Will Alexander* of the Resettlement Administration* and Aubrey Williams* of the NYA.* Jackson also played an influential role in Senator Robert M. La Follette, Jr.'s* decision to hold a special investigation into violations of labor rights and in President Franklin D. Roosevelt's* decision to establish the Special Committee on Farm Tenancy,* which led to the Bankhead-Jones Farm Tenancy Act of 1937* and establishment of the Farm Security Administration.* Throughout the rest of the 1930s and into World War II, Jackson kept up his defense of the economic and political rights of farm tenants, and after 1945 his interests led him into support for the civil rights movement. Gardner Jackson died on April 17, 1965. (Donald H. Grubbs, "Gardner Jackson, That 'Socialist' Tenant Farmers' Union, and the New Deal," *Agricultural History*, 42:125–137, 1968.)

JACKSON, ROBERT HOUGHWOUT Robert H. Jackson was born in Spring Creek Township, Pennsylvania, on February 13, 1892. After Robert completed grammar school, the family moved to Jamestown, New York, where the elder Jackson bred horses and operated a livery stable. Upon completing high school, Robert Jackson enrolled in a two year law course at Albany Law School (Union University). He completed the course in one year and returned home to practice law. Jackson was admitted to the New York bar in 1913. By the time Franklin D. Roosevelt* became governor of New York, Jackson had already made his reputation defending local transportation and telephone companies against the threat of takeover by monopolies. He attracted Roosevelt's attention when he served on a state commission investigating the courts. When Roosevelt became president, Jackson joined the administration, serving in a variety of posts: general counsel for the Bureau of Internal Revenue (1934); special counsel for the Securities and Exchange Commission* (1935); then to the Tax Division of the Department of Justice (1936); and assistant attorney general in charge of the Anti-Trust Division.

In 1937 Jackson aspired to become governor of New York, but he could not get the backing of the state party leaders. Back in Washington, Roosevelt appointed Jackson solicitor general of the United States (1938–1939). During his tenure, Jackson won wide recognition and praise for his skill in defending New Deal* measures before the Supreme Court.* In January 1940 Jackson was appointed attorney general of the United States. One of the more difficult problems which confronted him was that of dealing with aliens and investigating alleged fifth columnists in the charged atmosphere of the time. Then in June 1941 President Roosevelt named Jackson to the Supreme Court as an associate justice. On the Supreme Court, Jackson gained a reputation as a maverick who became increasingly critical of his colleagues for their judicial activism. Jackson justified restraints on individual liberties in the interest of maintaining public order, and in one dissent he accused the majority of converting the Bill of Rights into a suicide pact. In other opinions, Jackson approved the constitutionality of placing restrictions on the Communist party.* But although he defended the power of Congress, under the Taft-Hartley Act, to require union officers to swear that they had never belonged to the Communist party, Jackson insisted that such oaths could not be used merely to extract disclosures of political beliefs. Jackson's service on the Supreme Court was briefly interrupted when President Harry S Truman* appointed him to the War Crimes Commission in May 1945. Jackson helped draft the provisions which created the International Military Tribunal, and he then served as chief United States prosecutor at the war crimes trials held at Nuremberg, Germany. Although in later years the trials became somewhat controversial, Jackson was widely praised at the time for his performance and received the Medal of Merit for his "outstanding service to the United States."

In the 1950s, Jackson was generally considered to have moved right of center on many issues before the Court. But he remained a staunch advocate of civil liberties as he perceived them. During the last two years of his life, he suffered from recurring ill health which often kept him away from the Court. On March 30, 1954, Justice Jackson suffered a mild heart attack. He seemed to recover after several weeks' rest and insisted on returning to the Court on May 17, 1954, to participate in the decision in *Brown vs. the Board of Education of Topeka*. He considered it important that the Court's decision should be unanimous in that historic case. During the summer of 1954, Jackson took an extended vacation in California. When the Supreme Court began its term in October 1954, Jackson was on the bench. But on October 9, while driving to Washington from his home in McLean, Virginia, he suffered a stroke. He was able to make it to his secretary's house but died there of coronary thrombosis shortly after his arrival, ending his long career in the law and public service. (Eugene C. Gerhart, *America's Advocate: Robert H. Jackson*, 1958.)

JOSPEH M. ROWE, JR.

JAMES TRUE ASSOCIATES Headquartered in Washington, D.C., the James True Associates was an anti-Semitic, anti-New Deal organization led by James True. Through the weekly newsletter *Industrial Control Report*, James True called Franklin D. Roosevelt* and the New Dealers every epithet in the book, describing them as "that 'Karl Marx' Professor, Frankfurter, and his legal kikes." True frequently talked of the need to "kill kikes" and stop the Roosevelt-based, Jewish takeover of the United States. (George Wolfskill and John A. Hudson, *All but the People. Franklin D. Roosevelt and his Critics, 1933–1939*, 1969.)

JOBLESS PARTY Founded in 1932 in St. Louis by Father James R. Cox, the Jobless party was committed to drastic action by the federal government to ease the effects of the Great Depression. At a national political convention in 1932, they nominated Father Cox for president and V. C. Tisdal for vice-president. The Jobless party called for nationalization of banks, government seizure of private wealth and fortunes, and a massive program of public works construction for the unemployed. Although Cox got less than 1,000 votes in the national election, President Franklin D. Roosevelt* later appointed him to the National Recovery Administration's* state board in Pennsylvania. (Edward L. Schapsmeier and Frederick H. Schapsmeier, *Political Parties and Civic Action Groups*, 1981.)

JOHNSON, HIRAM WARREN Hiram Warren Johnson was born September 2, 1866, in Sacramento, California. His father, Grove Johnson, was an attorney in Sacramento who handled a large number of cases for the Southern Pacific Railroad, the dominant force in California politics. He was a conservative Republican who was elected to the state legislature in 1877 and the United States Congress in 1894. Hiram attended public schools in Sacramento and began reading law after three years at the University of California at Berkeley. In 1894 Hiram managed his father's congressional campaign, but while working in the family law firm, he became estranged, both personally and politically, from his father. Hiram gained a reputation as a progressive Republican. In 1901 he supported the reform candidate for mayor of Sacramento, and in 1906 he worked to oust Abraham Ruef, the machine mayor of San Francisco. In 1910 Hiram Johnson ran for governor of California and won the election. He quickly established his reputation as a progressive by establishing a civil service system, regulating railroads and public utilities, workmen's compensation, and an eight-hour day for women and children workers. He ran in 1912 as Theodore Roosevelt's vice-presidential running mate with the Bull Moose party. Though defeated, he was re-elected governor of California in 1914. Two years later the people of California sent Johnson to the United States Senate.

In the Senate, Johnson earned a reputation as a progressive in domestic affairs and an isolationist in foreign affairs. His alienation from the Republican party* intensified during the Great Depression, and in 1932 he openly endorsed the candidacy of Governor Franklin D. Roosevelt* for president. Johnson was a strong supporter of the New Deal* during Roosevelt's first term, but he broke with the president later in the 1930s over foreign policy questions. Johnson came to see Roosevelt as an internationalist leading the country down the path to war; so while supporting the neutrality legislation of the 1930s, Johnson openly opposed naval expansion, selective service, and lend-lease. In July 1945 he cast one of the two dissenting votes against the United Nations charter. Hiram Johnson died on August 6, 1945. (Ronald L. Feinman, *Twilight of Progressivism: The Western Republican Senators and the New Deal*, 1981; George Mowry, *California Progressives*, 1951.)

JOHNSON, HUGH SAMUEL Hugh S. Johnson was born in Ft. Scott, Kansas, on August 5, 1882, and was raised in the Cherokee Strip of Oklahoma. He graduated from Northwestern Teachers' College in 1901 and then took a B.S. at the U.S. Military Academy at West Point in 1903. Between 1903 and 1918 he rose from the rank of second lieutenant to brigadier general and received a law degree from the University of California in 1916. During World War I, Johnson served as chief of the Bureau of Purchase and Supply for the army general staff and as a member of the War Industries Board, where he worked on liaison matters with the army and came to know Bernard Baruch.* Johnson retired from the military in 1919 to become vice-president and general counsel of the Moline Plow Company, and by 1925 he was chairman of the board of the Moline Implement Company. Because of his business experience, work in the War Industries Board, experience in the development of the selective service system in World War I, and his relationship with Bernard Baruch, Hugh S. Johnson became President Franklin D. Roosevelt's* nominee to head the National Recovery Administration* in 1933.

Not the most genteel or politically effective individual, Johnson charged into the code-making program with abandon and quickly began alienating people. Although the economy appeared to be recovering by the summer of 1933, it was only short-lived. Johnson, angered by the refusal of most major industries to cooperate with the NRA, decided on a national "Liberty Loan" type of campaign to sign up businesses into the government program, especially to pledge to maintain the NRA's wages and hours standards. The "blue eagle"* symbol which he designed became the national symbol of the NRA, and its legend "We Do Our Part" indicated a business's willingness to cooperate in the recovery program. Throughout the summer of 1933 Johnson travelled throughout the country in an army plane trying to convince major industries to adopt the "Blue Eagle" and join the National Recovery Administration. The cotton textile industry was the first major manufacturing sector to join the campaign; and during the summer he managed to secure the cooperation of the shipbuilding, electrical, wool textile, garment, oil, steel, and lumber industries to make their pledges to the National Recovery Administration. Late in August 1933 the automobile industry, except for Ford Motor Company, agreed; and three weeks later the bituminous coal operators joined as well. By September 1933 Hugh S. Johnson reached the peak of his popularity, both within the country and within the New Deal.*

After the completion of the major code-making campaigns, however, Johnson became the symbol of the controversy over the National Recovery Administration. By the spring of 1934 the NRA was being assaulted from all sides: southern Democrats hated the bureaucratic power it represented; progressive Republicans viewed it as a monopolistic opportunity for big business to exploit small businesses; labor leaders resented its inability to enforce Section 7(a); and many economists thought its production controls were actually retarding recovery. Things went from bad to worse when the National Recovery Review Board,* headed by Clarence Darrow,* concluded that the NRA really was dominated by giant corporations and helped exploit labor and small business. The criticism of the National Recovery Administration made Johnson expendable, as did his drinking problem, temper, and political insensitivity. In September Johnson resigned at the president's request and left the NRA on October 15, 1934. He worked as WPA* administrator for New York City in 1935 but then left the New Deal altogether. Johnson became a columnist for the Scripps-Howard newspaper chain, and by the late 1930s his relationship with Roosevelt and the New Deal had deteriorated completely. In fact, he blamed the president for the recession of 1937–1938,* accused him of dictatorial ambitions in the court packing* issue and government reorganization plan, and came to view the New Deal as "semi-Socialist and anti-business." Hugh S. Johnson died on April 15, 1942. (Bernard Bellush, *The Failure of the NRA*, 1975; George Wolfskill and John A. Hudson, *All but the People. Franklin D. Roosevelt and His Critics, 1933–1939*, 1969.)

JOHNSON-O'MALLEY ACT OF 1934 On April 16, 1934, Congress passed the Johnson-O'Malley Act as part of Commissioner of Indian Affairs John Collier's* "Indian New Deal."* The act was similar to earlier proposed legislation that had failed to gain congressional approval. The Johnson-O'Malley Act authorized the secretary of the interior to enter into contracts with states and territories to provide monetary assistance for Indian educational, medical, agricultural, and social welfare services. Although federal funds had been provided to public schools for over forty years, this act finally compromised on a federal and state arrangement to overcome the previously complicated contracting method between individual school districts and the federal government.

Collier had high expectations for the act. Several problems soon arose. The act was passed on the belief that state and federal officials could work harmoniously together to help Indians. Such was not the case, however. State administrators viewed Bureau of Indian Affairs people as threats to their authority and guarded jealously their independence from federal interference. BIA officials, on the other hand, tended to have a ''superior-than-thou'' attitude toward the state people, causing strained relations. Moreover, the BIA educators predicted correctly that the public schools would not use the federal funds properly. Indeed, in most cases, the states channeled Johnson-O'Malley money, which was supposed to be earmarked for special Indian programs, into their general operating budgets.

Between 1934 and 1941 the states of California (1934), Washington (1935), Minnesota (1937), and Arizona (1938) contracted for Johnson-O'Malley funds. All of these states except Minnesota, which had an extremely efficient Department of Education already interested in Indian programs, encountered some of the above-mentioned difficulties. There were other problems as well. For example, racism on the part of local communities, school teachers, and non-Indian students' attitude toward Indian children hampered the act's effectiveness. And some BIA officials believed that Indian students were better off in federally-run schools than in public ones.

Thus, the Johnson-O'Malley Act fell short, in most cases, of providing better opportunities for Indian children in public schools. Later legislation improved the act substantially: providing for tribal control over the funds and more accountability on the part of the states to have special Indian educational programs. In 1981–1982, twenty-six states with approximately 165,988 Indian students received Johnson-O'Malley funds. (Margaret Szasz, *Education and the American Indian: The Road to Self-Determination Since 1928,* 1977.)

RAYMOND WILSON

JONES-CONNALLY FARM RELIEF ACT OF 1934 Many ranchers had been opposed to cattle being included as a basic agricultural commodity; however, the drought of 1933–1934 caused Dolph Briscoe, president of the Texas and Southwestern Cattle Raisers Association, to appeal for federal aid. As a result, Secretary of Agriculture Henry Wallace* invited representatives of the American National Livestock Association, the Texas and Southwestern Cattle Raisers Association, and the Panhandle Livestock Association to meet in Denver to discuss ways of increasing cattle prices. They were joined by Representative Marvin Jones* of Texas, chairman of the House Agriculture Committee.

As a result, Jones introduced a bill making cattle a basic commodity and persuaded Senator Tom Connally,* also from Texas, to introduce a companion measure in the United States Senate. Hearings revealed that many cattlemen wanted government aid, but most of them opposed a processing tax and many ranchers feared competition with dairy cattle, should the latter be included as a basic commodity. Assisted by conservative Representative Richard Kleberg, of Texas and the King Ranch, Jones led the House in passing a bill that included cattle as a basic commodity and $200 million for production adjustments for beef and dairy cattle. Franklin D. Roosevelt* supported the bill.

In the Senate, opposition to cattle as a basic commodity was far stronger than in the House. Faced with pressure from the House and president, the senators broadened the bill—to gain support—by increasing the bill's scope to include barley, rye, peanuts, flax, and grain sorghum. For these reasons senators also accepted an amendment introduced by Senator Robert La Follette, Jr.,* for appropriations to the Federal Surplus Relief Corporation* and for the eradication of tubercular cattle. The House agreed to these provisions; and the bill became law on April 7, 1934.

The act had immediate and long-range results. For example, the act provided funds that contributed to extensive purchases during the drought of cattle that were distributed as beef to the needy through the Federal Surplus Relief Corporation. However, the most important result was long-range: the beginning of federal control measures against brucellosis. (Irvin M. May, Jr., *Marvin Jones: The Public Life of an Agrarian Advocate*, 1980; John T. Schlebecker, *Cattle Raising on the Plains, 1900–1961*, 1963.)

IRVIN M. MAY, JR.

JONES-COSTIGAN SUGAR ACT OF 1934 In February 1934 President Franklin D. Roosevelt* called for legislation to increase sugar producers' prices, stabilize production, stop the decline of Cuban sugar imports, and maintain existing acreages of sugar cane and sugar beets. Such measures had been unsuccessfully proposed as an amendment to the Jones-Connally Farm Relief Act.*

Roosevelt asked House Agriculture Chairman Marvin Jones* to sponsor a House bill making sugar beets and sugar cane basic agricultural commodities. Jones agreed to do so with reluctance. Senator Edward Costigan* of Colorado introduced a similar measure in the Senate. Led by Representative Fred Cummings of Colorado, the House Agriculture Committee reported a bill increasing the quota for domestic sugar beet producers and providing for benefit payments from a processing tax on sugar and a minimum wage for workers. Child labor was prohibited.

The House bill went, not to the Senate Committee on Agriculture and Forestry, but to the Senate Finance Committee, chaired by Pat Harrison* of Mississippi. Sugar beet producers favored the bill; Puerto Rican and Hawaiian sugar cane producers opposed it. Senator Arthur Vandenberg* of Michigan modified the child labor provision to allow regulations, but not abolition, of child labor. Senators eliminated the minimum wage, and the House accepted these changes. Yet, this was the first, and perhaps only case, of a child labor feature in any New Deal* agricultural aid legislation. (Murray R. Benedict, *Farm Policies of* *the United States, 1790–1950*, 1953; Irvin M. May, Jr., *Marvin Jones: The Public Life of an Agrarian Advocate*, 1980.)

IRVIN M. MAY, JR.

JONES, JESSE HOLMAN Jesse H. Jones, "czar" of the New Deal* credit establishment, was born April 22, 1874, in Robertson County, Tennessee. His family moved to Dallas, Texas, and he graduated from Hill's Business College there in 1891. A self-made man, by 1929 he had become known as "Mr. Houston." After rising in his uncle's lumber company to general manager, Jones had purchased his own firm. He entered real estate and construction in 1903, banking in 1905, and newspaper publishing in 1908. Eventually he became one of the largest real estate developers in the country, constructing and operating some fifty major buildings in Houston, together with properties in other major cities. In 1912 he became president (subsequently chairman) of what developed into the Texas Commerce Bank. In 1917 he was briefly an original stockholder in the newly organized Humble Oil and Refining Company, later Exxon Corporation. By 1926 he was sole owner of the *Houston Chronicle*. In 1931 he briefly owned the *Houston Post* and a radio station which he sold to former Texas governor William P. Hobby.

Jesse Jones had also become a prominent figure in the Democratic party.* During 1913–1917, he served as chairman of the Houston Harbor Board which developed a ship channel (opened in 1914) that ultimately made the city a major seaport. In 1917–1919 he was appointed by President Woodrow Wilson as director general of Military Relief in the American Red Cross and a member of the Red Cross War Council. At the end of World War I, he helped form the League of Red Cross Societies of the World. Jones developed a close relationship with President Wilson. He served in 1945 as president and treasurer of the Woodrow Wilson Foundation; he also established a Woodrow Wilson School of Foreign Affairs at the University of Virginia in the president's honor. In 1928 Jones brought the Democratic National Convention (at which Al Smith* was nominated for the presidency) to Houston, building a 25,000-seat convention center for the meeting. Texas made Jones a "favorite son" candidate for the Democratic presidential nomination. Earlier in 1926 he had been appointed director general of the Texas State Centennial (held in 1936 with Jones as chairman), for which he designed and built the San Jacinto Monument.

In 1929 a banking crisis in Houston following the onset of the Great Depression was averted by Jones's quick action. President Herbert Hoover* appointed him in January 1932 as one of the seven directors of the newly created Reconstruction Finance Corporation.* It was with the RFC that Jones' New Deal fame was established. During 1932 Jones was instrumental in averting a banking crisis in Chicago through the use of RFC funds. President Franklin D. Roosevelt* quickly made Jones chairman of the RFC in 1933, a position he held until his resignation from the federal government in 1945. The RFC, which in 1953 under the Eisenhower administration was reorganized into the Small Business

Administration, made $50 billion in loans under Jones' chairmanship. It was Jones' proudest accomplishment that these loans were largely repaid to the government with interest. The RFC became known as "The Fourth Branch of Government," due to its importance as a New Deal emergency agency. Jones' wide business and banking experience was of incalculable value at the RFC.

In 1939 President Roosevelt further appointed Jones to be head of the newly created Federal Loan Agency,* a position he occupied until 1945. During 1940–1945, when he also served as secretary of commerce, special legislation was passed to permit Jones to serve simultaneously as an agency administrator and a member of the cabinet. In 1940, as war approached and France surrendered to Germany, the RFC was given broad powers related to national defense; it subsequently played an important role in war procurement. Roosevelt was quoted as saying that, "Jesse Jones is the only man in Washington who can say 'yes' or 'no' intelligently twenty-four hours a day." In 1944 Roosevelt replaced Henry A. Wallace* as vice-president with Harry S Truman.* At Roosevelt's request, Jones resigned as secretary of commerce to provide Wallace with a consolation cabinet post. Jones resigned his other federal offices as well and returned to private life in Houston.

He devoted much of his time to philanthropy in the post-war era until his death on June 1, 1956. In 1937 Jones and his wife had established Houston Endowment, Inc., then the largest philanthropic foundation in Texas and the fifteenth largest in the U.S. Over the years the foundation has built many community facilities, endowed academic chairs, and provided thousands of scholarships. The Jesse H. Jones Graduate School of Administration was established at Rice University in Houston in his memory. (Jesse H. Jones, *Fifty Billion Dollars: My Thirteen Years with the RFC, 1932–1945,* 1951; Bascom Timmons, *Jesse H. Jones: The Man and the Statesman*, 1956.)

DUANE WINDSOR

JONES, JOHN MARVIN J. Marvin Jones, congressman, administrator, and jurist, served in all three branches of the federal government. During the New Deal,* he was the most powerful and influential person in the United States House of Representatives about agricultural legislation and policies. Jones was born on February 26, 1882, in Valley View, Texas, and graduated from Southwestern University in 1905 and the University of Texas Law School in 1908. He practiced law briefly in Amarillo before winning election to Congress where he served until 1940.

A close friend of Sam Rayburn,* Jones learned his political lessons from John Nance Garner.* Failing to receive an appointment to the judiciary committee in 1921, Jones accepted an assignment to the Agriculture Committee where he crusaded in support of the export debenture plan. In 1930 Jones became chairman and remained in this post until he voluntarily resigned ten years later. As chairman of the House Agriculture Committee, Jones generally specialized in farm finance rather than identify with commodity groups. He wanted low interest loans and mortgages for farmers, soil conservation, farm subsidies, agricultural research, and new markets for farm products. As a result, he helped create the Farm Credit Administration* and the Federal Farm Mortgage Corporation. Additionally, he played important roles in the Jones-Connally Act,* Soil Conservation and Domestic Allotment Act,* Section 32 of the Agricultural Adjustment Act of 1933* (the first guaranteed annual appropriation for agriculture in United States history), Bankhead-Jones Farm Tenancy Act,* and the Agricultural Adjustment Act of 1938.*

After 1940 Jones became a member of the United States Court of Claims but took a leave of absence in 1942 to head the War Food Administration during World War II. In this capacity, he used his knowledge of agriculture and congressional relations to bring stability to that strife-torn administration. Returning to the court in 1945, he became chief judge two years later. From 1947 until 1964, Jones received respect from attorneys for his just, but compassionate, opinions that were written in everyday language. John Marvin Jones died on March 4, 1976, in Amarillo. (Irvin M. May, Jr., *Marvin Jones: The Public Life of an Agrarian Advocate*, 1980.)

IRVIN M. MAY, JR.

JONES V. S.E.C. *Jones v. S.E.C.* was decided in 1936, when the Supreme Court* denied the Securities and Exchange Commission* access to the business papers of J. Edward Jones, a Wall-Street promoter. A six–three majority argued it was a violation of his right to personal liberty. Chief Justice Charles Evans Hughes* and Justices Willis Van Devanter,* Pierce Butler,* James McReynolds,* George Sutherland,* and Owen J. Roberts* were in the majority; and Justices Louis Brandeis,* Benjamin Cardozo,* and Harlan Fiske Stone* were in the minority. The minority was outraged at the court's decision, claiming that the SEC "rule now assailed was wisely conceived and carefully adopted to foil the plans of knaves intent upon obscuring or suppressing the knowledge of their knavery." (Alpheus Thomas Mason, *Harlan Fiske Stone. Pillar of the Law*, 1956.)

JUDICIAL PROCEDURES REFORM ACT OF 1937 (See "COURT-PACKING" BILL.)

K

KELLY, EDWARD JOSEPH Born in a Chicago slum on May 5, 1876, Edward J. Kelly worked his way up through the city Sanitary District and political machine. Although Franklin D. Roosevelt* worked well with most urban bosses, his earliest and closest alliance was with Mayor Edward J. Kelly of Chicago. Prior to becoming mayor, Kelly served as chief engineer of the Chicago Sanitary District in Anton Cermak's administration. Behind the scenes, however, Kelly and Pat Nash, a former superintendent of sewers, ran the Cermak machine. Kelly's golden opportunity appeared in 1933 when the city council appointed him mayor after a deranged gunman assassinated Cermak.

Kelly built an even more powerful machine than the one he inherited from Cermak. He promoted the migration of blacks and the immigration of Italians, who previously had supported "Big Bill" Thompson's Republican organization. These groups joined Poles, Jews, Swedes, Lithuanians, Germans, Irish, and Slavs who formed the bulwark of the Cook County Democratic party. Kelly's machine, which supported 30,000 workers, served Chicago well by effectively providing vitally-needed services for the metropolitan area's huge population.

Running for his own term of office in 1935, Kelly scored one of the greatest victories in Chicago's history, capturing over 75 percent of the vote. This victory convinced Roosevelt, Harry L. Hopkins,* James A. Farley,* and even Harold L. Ickes* of the need to funnel federal money and patronage into the Chicago machine. Before the Works Progress Administration* began pumping its billions into the national economy, the "Windy City" already received millions of dollars through the Federal Emergency Relief Administration* and the Civil Works Administration.* But Kelly also wanted to dominate downstate Illinois' share of state patronage and had to wrest control from his chief competitor, Governor Henry Horner.* Until Kelly's election in 1935, Harry Hopkins divided Illinois' relief patronage between the Chicago machine and Horner's coalition. By the summer of 1935, Hopkins was cooperating completely with Kelly and urging Roosevelt to fund every project requested by the mayor.

Not only did Roosevelt and Hopkins support Kelly's original funding requests, they looked for additional money to fuel the machine. Despite numerous complaints from various Illinois citizens and even a warning from Interior Secretary Harold Ickes that 20 percent of the federal money to Kelly would be converted to graft, Roosevelt formed a close political friendship with the Chicago boss. Kelly returned the friendship, saying "Roosevelt is my religion." In December of 1936 Hopkins informed Robert Dunham, Kelly's WPA director in Illinois, that he had found an additional $750,000 and wanted to give it to the Chicago machine. From 1935 to 1940, the New Deal* allowed Kelly to control approximately 180,000 to 200,000 Illinois WPA jobs per month. Consequently, the machine spread its influence throughout the state.

Ed Kelly and Harry Hopkins formed a close political relationship. They managed to arrange secretly for Roosevelt's unprecedented third term nomination at the 1940 Democratic Convention in Chicago. With Hopkins planning the strategy in Roosevelt's behalf, Kelly engineered the tactics that produced the draft that Roosevelt demanded. Kelly handled all the details from determining the convention site (Chicago Stadium) to packing the galleries with machine workers prompted to demonstrate on cue. Kelly and Hopkins also arranged for other bosses (Edward Crump of Memphis, Frank Hague* of Jersey City, Ed Flynn* of New York and Tom Pendergast* of Kansas City) to concentrate their support behind the president. The 1940 Democratic convention became a classic example of machine politics operating at the national level in a democratic environment. Although some critics questioned the "democracy" of the moment Roosevelt received his "bossed nomination," none denied its efficiency. Certainly it was a highlight in Edward Kelly's career. He died on October 20, 1950. (Gene De Lon Jones, "The Local Political Significance of New Deal Legislation in Chicago, 1933–1940," Ph.D. dissertation, Northwestern University, 1970.)

J. CHRISTOPHER SCHNELL

KENNEDY, JOSEPH PATRICK Born in 1888, Joseph Patrick Kennedy married Rose Fitzgerald in 1914; their children include President John F. Kennedy, Senator and Attorney General Robert F. Kennedy, and Senator Edward M. Kennedy. Joseph Kennedy graduated from Boston Latin School and Harvard College and subsequently earned a fortune in banking, moviemaking, real estate, and the stock market. He was an early financial backer of New York's Governor Franklin D. Roosevelt* for the presidency. During the 1932 campaign Kennedy claimed credit for persuading William Randolph Hearst,* the newspaper tycoon, to support Roosevelt. The awarding of American franchises on Gordon's gin and several Scotch whiskies to Kennedy may have been a reward for his help.

In 1932 Roosevelt delivered a speech prepared by Kennedy that laid the blueprint for what would become the Securities and Exchange Commission.* Wishing to retain Wall-Street's confidence, the president appointed the conservative Kennedy to head the SEC when it was created in 1934. Kennedy's most famous innovation was to prohibit short sales from being consummated at a price lower than the last one on the stock market ticker. He worked hard on the commission, resigning in 1935. The following year Kennedy published *I'm For Roosevelt*, arguing that businessmen should be grateful for the president's rescue of capitalism. Kennedy returned to government service for nearly a year beginning in March of 1937. As chairman of the U.S. Maritime Commission, he helped to revive the ailing shipbuilding industry.

Kennedy had his thirst for achievement quenched in 1938 when Roosevelt appointed him ambassador to Great Britain. The office made him the social superior of Boston's best people and was an accomplishment by which one generation of Kennedys could extend the reach of the next. In London Joseph Kennedy adopted an informal style that pleased the British press and the people. But his stubborn isolationism soon clashed with Roosevelt's growing internationalism. It irritated the president that Kennedy brought Charles Lindbergh's oral reports of Nazi air superiority to the attention of Prime Minister Neville Chamberlain, and in a Trafalgar Day address before the Navy League Kennedy remarked that the "democracies and dictators should cooperate for the common good." Kennedy's rhetorical anti-Semitism alienated Jewish Democrats in the era of Adolf Hitler's rise. And Kennedy's references to the king of England's stuttering, the queen's manner as resembling that of a dowdy housewife, and to Winston Churchill's heavy drinking were small indiscretions compared to his prediction of the "death of democracy" in Britain. Nonetheless, the ambassador wondered whether the presidency itself might be within his reach: a political poll listed him fifth among likely candidates should the president not seek a third term. Certainly Kennedy had attained great political prominence among Irish Catholics. When Roosevelt died in 1945 after having kept Kennedy at arm's length during the war, the former ambassador remarked that while there was "real sorrow" for two or three days, "there is also no doubt that it was a great thing for the country." Kennedy spent the 1950s watching his son John Fitzgerald become politically successful, and seek the presidency of the United States. Joseph P. Kennedy died on November 8, 1969. (David E. Koskoff, *Joseph P. Kennedy. A Life and Times*, 1974.)

DAVID BURNER

KENT, FRANK RICHARDSON Frank R. Kent, conservative columnist during the 1930s, was born in Baltimore, Maryland, on May 1, 1877, and educated in public and private schools. He went to work as a reporter for the *Baltimore Reporter* in 1898 and the next year joined the staff of the *Baltimore Sun*. Kent was a political reporter for ten years and Washington correspondent for the *Sun* for two years before being named managing editor in 1911. After serving as managing editor for ten years Kent became the paper's London correspondent between 1922 and 1923. After returning to the United States, Kent became a syndicated political columnist whose articles were regularly published in more than 100 daily newspapers. Kent was the author of a number of books, including *The Story of Maryland Politics* (1911), *The Great Game of Politics* (1923), *History of the Democratic Party* (1925), and *Political Behavior* (1928).

Frank Kent looked on the New Deal* as the most significant political watershed in modern American history but one which he personally questioned because of its great emphasis on bureaucracy and executive power. He especially resented the New Deal's tendency to use government work relief projects as political patronage, and he accused Franklin D. Roosevelt* and Harry Hopkins* of doing just that. Kent also feared the centralizing tendencies of the New Deal. Frank Kent died on April 14, 1958. (Eugene W. Goll, "Frank R. Kent's Opposition to Franklin D. Roosevelt and the New Deal," *Maryland Historical Magazine*, LXIII:158–171, 1968; *New York Times*, April 15, 1958.)

KERR, FLORENCE STEWART Born on June 30, 1890, in Harriman, Tennessee, Florence Stewart moved as an infant with her parents to her mother's home in Iowa. She spent most of her childhood in Marshalltown. From 1908 to 1912 she attended Grinnell College, where she formed a lifelong friendship with a classmate, Harry L. Hopkins.* On September 1, 1915, she married Robert Y. Kerr and made her home with him in Grinnell, where she taught English from 1921–1926 and 1931–1932 at Grinnell College. In 1930 Mrs. Kerr was named a member of the Unemployment Relief Council in Iowa; and in July 1935 Hopkins recommended her appointment as one of the five regional directors of the Division of Women's and Professional Projects within the new Works Progress Administration.* From her office in Chicago she supervised the work relief activities of the division in thirteen midwestern states. Much of her time was spent on the road consulting with the state WPA administrators and the women directors of the projects within her jurisdiction. The largest among the relief activities for unskilled women that she supervised were numerous sewing and library projects; for white-collar women she oversaw the Federal Art,* Writers',* and Theatre Projects.* When Ellen S. Woodward* resigned as assistant administrator of the WPA and director of the Women's and Professional Projects in December 1938, Kerr, generally viewed as the strongest of the regional directors, was named to the post. Soon after she assumed her Washington duties in early 1939, executive reorganization reconstituted the WPA as the Works Projects Administration* within the new Federal Works Agency.* Kerr's division became the Division of Professional and Service projects. During her administration, the WPA work projects experienced successive budget cuts, but she managed to retain the institutional and community service aspects of the women's programs. In May 1940 her division staged a massive nationwide, week-long "This Work Pays Your Community" promotion and exhibition. As national defense became an administration goal, the women's clothing and food production, health, library, and all other remaining projects shifted in focus as well. WPA daycare centers, which Kerr defended vigorously before congressional committees, assumed a vital role within the defense effort until their functions were transferred to communities under the Lanham Act in 1942. Most of the women's projects remained in force until the final liquidation of the WPA in 1943.

In 1944 Kerr became director of the war public services of the Federal Works

Agency. She resigned from the government to become an executive with Northwest Airlines based in Minneapolis. After retirement from the post she returned to Washington in the mid-1950s and lived there until her death on July 6, 1975. (Florence Kerr interview 29 July 1974, transcript, Columbia University Oral History Collection; *Washington Post*, July 10, 1975.)

MARTHA H. SWAIN

KERR-SMITH TOBACCO CONTROL ACT OF 1934 To counter the problem of overproduction and falling prices, the New Deal's* Agricultural Adjustment Act of 1933* had taken the approach of offering subsidies to farmers who would leave some acreage fallow. Reduction of the surpluses would then stimulate a rise in commodity prices. The administration wanted to reduce 1934 production of flue-cured tobacco down to about 500 million pounds, so growers contracting to participate in the AAA* program agreed to reduce acreage and production by 30 percent of their previous three-year average. In return, the farmer would receive a rental payment of $17.50 for every acre taken out of production and a benefit payment of 12 percent of the selling price of his tobacco. The AAA program was originally designed to be voluntary. If a grower chose not to sign an AAA contract, he was free to plant as much tobacco as he wanted. He would not receive any rental or benefit payments but would certainly enjoy higher profits from higher tobacco prices.

Almost immediately after signing their participation contracts, cooperating farmers began worrying that those not participating might plant so much tobacco as to defeat the program, leaving prices chronically low. In January 1934 the North Carolina Tobacco Growers Association called on the AAA to make the program compulsory. Potato and cotton farmers were making similar demands, which resulted in the Bankhead Cotton Control Act of 1934* and the Warren Potato Control Act of 1935.* Although the Department of Agriculture opposed compulsory programs, Congressman John Kerr of North Carolina and Senator Ellison "Cotton Ed" Smith* of South Carolina agreed to introduce the necessary legislation. After overcoming the opposition of Marvin Jones,* chairman of the House Agriculture Committee, and Senator Josiah Bailey,* the Kerr-Smith Tobacco Control Act passed through Congress in June 1934. The act provided for a 25 to 33 percent tax on the sale price of all tobacco, with tax exemption warrants issued to all growers contracting to reduce production. Additional warrants could be issued to non-contracting farmers unable to get an equitable allotment from the AAA. These could total up to 6 percent of a county's allotment if at least 67 percent of the total allotment in any county was allocated to growers raising less than 1,500 pounds. The act was in effect only for 1934 and 1935, but for the tax to be levied in 1935 it would have to be approved by farmers owning or working 75 percent of tobacco land. The tax in 1934 applied to all types of tobacco except Maryland and Virginia sun-cured and cigar-leaf. Secretary of Agriculture Henry Wallace* placed the tax at 25 percent. The results of the law were quite positive. The AAA production under contract was 534 million pounds and total production ended up at only 557 million pounds, so very little tax had to be collected. The average price for flue-cured tobacco went up to 27.3¢ a pound, and total crop receipts were $151.7 million, 350 percent higher than in 1932. But after the Supreme Court* declared the AAA unconstitutional in 1936, Congress had to repeal the Kerr-Smith Act. (Anthony J. Badger, *Prosperity Road. The New Deal, Tobacco, and North Carolina*, 1980.)

KEYNES, JOHN MAYNARD Although not an American and never a member of any New Deal* agency, John Maynard Keynes had enormous influence on United States public policy. He was born in 1883 in Cambridge, England, attended Eton and went on to a brilliant career at King's College, Cambridge. After graduation he spent some time in the civil service with the India Office, but quit after two years, returned to Cambridge, and wrote *Indian Currency and Finance* (1913). The book was considered a triumph, and Keynes was given the editorship of the *Economic Journal*, Britain's most prestigious economic publication. In 1918 Keynes went to Versailles as deputy for the chancellor of the exchequer on the Supreme Economic Council. He protested the imposition of reparations on Germany because he fervently believed they would destroy the German economy and trigger a new round of military authoritarianism. Keynes resigned in protest and wrote *The Economic Consequences of the Peace* (1919), a book which gave him an international reputation.

During the 1920s, he accumulated a fortune speculating in the international securities markets, taught classes at Cambridge, and wrote the *Tract on Monetary Reform* (1923) and the *Treatise on Money* (1930), both of which criticized the world's preoccupation with gold and currency. Keynes then turned the economic world upside down with *The General Theory of Employment, Interest, and Money* (1936). *The General Theory* argued that contrary to the classical theory, which assumed in the long run the economy would also balance itself into a position of equilibrium, modern industrial economies were capable of declining indefinitely. Declines in production, employment, and income could be mutually reinforcing, depleting private savings and creating a miserable depression. Instead of waiting, as the classical economists advocated, for the economy to find its equilibrium, Keynes insisted that government investment, income, and spending would have to temporarily supplement private investment, income, and spending. The technique to provide that supplement was deficit spending. Keynes visited Washington, D.C., in 1934 and urged New Dealers to do more of the same—more relief, more work relief, more spending. He wrote several letters to President Franklin D. Roosevelt* during the 1930s explaining the need for government spending to pick up the slack from the private sector. For Keynes, the New Deal relief programs were not to be considered temporary political expedients but good medicine for a sick economy—indeed, the only way private investment and income could be stimulated. It was not until World War II, with its massive government spending and deficit financing, that the "Keynesian Revolution" was complete, and not until the 1970s, when unemployment and inflation occurred together, did Keynes' theories come into question again. John Maynard Keynes suffered a heart attack in 1937 and had to curtail some of his activities, but during World War II he served as an economic adviser to the British government and travelled to the United States several times working on international economic concerns. His last visit came in 1945 to attend the Bretton Woods Conference. Keynes died on April 21, 1946. (Robert Lekachman, *The Age of Keynes*, 1966.)

KEYSERLING, LEON H. Leon H. Keyserling was born in Charleston, South Carolina, in 1908. He graduated from Columbia University in 1928 and three years later received a law degree from Harvard. At Columbia, Keyserling had come to know his professor, Rexford Tugwell,* and in 1933 Tugwell invited him to Washington, D.C., to go to work for the government. He urged Keyserling to join the legal staff of the AAA.* When Jerome Frank* heard that Keyserling's father was a close friend of Senator Ellison ''Cotton Ed'' Smith* of South Carolina, chairman of the Senate Agricultural Committee, Frank hired him on the spot. He worked with the AAA, however, for only two weeks. Late in March 1933 Keyserling visited the office of Senator Robert Wagner* of New York along with several other New Deal* lawyers where they discussed the evolving National Industrial Recovery Act and the inflationary theories of Professor George Warren.* Keyserling vigorously denied the efficacy of monetary inflation and instead argued for an underconsumption theory of the depression, urging Wagner to insert into the NIRA* the $3.3 billion public works program which he and Senators Robert La Follette, Jr.* and Edward Costigan* had been urging for years. Impressed with Keyserling, Wagner hired him as a legislative assistant. As Wagner's assistant, Keyserling played a major role in drafting Section 7(a) of the NIRA, the Home Owners' Refinancing Act of 1933,* the National Housing Act of 1934,* the National Labor Relations Act of 1935,* and the Wagner-Steagall Housing Act of 1937.* He joined the staff of the U.S. Housing Authority* in 1937, wrote the Democratic party's* platform in 1936, 1940, and 1944, composed Roosevelt's executive order in 1942 creating the National Housing Agency, drafted the Employment Act of 1946 and the Housing Act of 1949. Keyserling served as a member and chairman of the Council of Economic Advisers under President Harry S Truman.* After leaving government service, he continued to work as a private economic and political consultant. (Katie Louchheim, ed., *The Making of the New Deal. The Insiders Speak*, 1983.)

KHAKI SHIRTS When the ''bonus army'' disbanded from Washington, D.C., in the summer of 1932, a small remnant of politically-conscious veterans stayed behind under the leadership of Art J. Smith. Known as the Khaki Shirts, they began demanding payment of the bonus, abolition of Congress, revaluation of silver at the Populist rate of sixteen to one, and massive increases in the army and navy budgets. They were also bitter anti-Semites. From his headquarters in Philadelphia, Smith tried to organize a veterans march on Washington, D.C., for Columbus Day in 1933, but his dreams of 1.5 million brown-shirted soldiers descending on the White House never materialized. When a Khaki Shirt rally in New York in July ended in a riot with one dead and twenty-four people injured, Smith was arrested and eventually convicted of perjury. He received a six-year sentence, and the Khaki Shirts declined rapidly. (Arthur M. Schlesinger, Jr., *The Age of Roosevelt. Vol. III. The Politics of Upheaval, 1935–1936*, 1960.)

KING, WILLIAM HENRY William H. King was born in Fillmore, Utah, on June 3, 1863. He served a mission to Great Britain for the Mormon Church between 1880 and 1883 and then returned home where he attended Brigham Young University and the University of Utah. King served two terms in the territorial legislature and received a law degree from the University of Michigan. He was admitted to the Utah bar in 1890, began a private law practice, and was elected to the territorial council in 1891, where he served as president. Between 1894 and 1896, King was associate justice of the Utah Supreme Court, and when Utah was admitted as a state, he was elected as a Democrat to Congress. King was not a candidate for renomination in 1898 but was elected in 1900 to fill the vacancy caused by the unseating of Brigham H. Roberts. King was unsuccessful in his bid for re-election in 1900 and 1902, so he then returned to private law practice. He was elected as a Democrat to the United States Senate in 1916 and re-elected in 1922, 1928, and 1934.

During the New Deal,* King was known as a conservative Democrat whose states' rights political philosophy rivaled that of many southerners. He was strongly committed to a balanced budget, looked askance at the rising deficits, hated Franklin D. Roosevelt's* "coddling" of labor activists and "sit-down" strikers, and broke with the president on executive reorganization and the court-packing plan.* In the Democratic primaries of 1938, when the president was trying to "purge"* a number of conservative Democrats, King actually endorsed several of them, including Senator Guy Gillette* of Iowa. King was an unsuccessful candidate for renomination in 1940, engaged in private law practice in Washington, D.C., until 1947, and died in Salt Lake City on November 27, 1949. (*New York Times*, November 28, 1949.)

KNIGHTS OF THE WHITE CAMELIA Headed by George Deatherage, the Knights of the White Camelia was a fascist, anti-Semitic group of the 1930s. Using a swastika as its insignia, the Knights openly campaigned against Franklin D. Roosevelt* and the New Deal* as the "Jew Deal" because of their convictions that the president was of Jewish descent. The Knights of the White Camelia were also openly anti-black and accused Harold L. Ickes* and Eleanor Roosevelt* of conspiring to replace white power in the United States with Jewish and "Negro power." (George Wolfskill and John A. Hudson, *All but the People. Franklin D. Roosevelt and His Critics, 1933–1939*, 1969.)

KROCK, ARTHUR Arthur Krock, one of the most renowned American journalists of the twentieth century, was born on November 16, 1887, in Glasgow,

Kentucky. He studied at Princeton University for a year in 1904 but had to drop out because of financial problems and instead took an associate of arts degree at the Lewis Institute in Chicago in 1906. Krock then went to work as a reporter for the *Louisville Herald*. He became Washington correspondent for the *Louisville Times* in 1910, where his perceptive political commentaries earned him the reputation as the paper's most valuable reporter. In 1919 Krock was appointed editor-in-chief of the *Times*. Krock's only direct experience in politics came during the 1920 election campaign, when he served briefly as an aide to George White, chairman of the Democratic National Committee. Krock left the *Louisville Times* in 1923 and went to work as a public relations assistant to Will Hays, head of the Motion Pictures Producers and Distributors of America. But he desperately missed journalism and later in 1923 joined the staff of the *New York World*. For the next four years Adolph S. Ochs of the *New York Times* watched Krock's reputation rise and in 1927 invited him to join staff. Krock agreed, and four years later was assigned as the Washington correspondent for the *Times*.

Krock proved to be somewhat of an anomaly in Washington. Although he represented one of the more liberal daily newspapers in the United States, his own politics were quite conservative. Krock distrusted executive power and was afraid of the growth of the federal bureaucracy during the New Deal.* At the same time, he earned an unparalleled reputation for objectivity and journalistic observation. Krock's own expertise in the workings of Washington, D.C., politics was unmatched. In 1937 President Franklin D. Roosevelt* granted Krock an exclusive interview in which he tried to explain his goals for the next administration and his reasons for trying to propose reform of the Supreme Court.* After that interview, Krock never lost his reputation as the premier, and most powerful, journalist in the United States. Arthur Krock died on April 12, 1974. (*New York Times*, April 13, 1974.)

L

LABOR ADVISORY BOARD The Labor Advisory Board was an agency of the National Recovery Administration;* its major function was to protect labor interests in the NRA code-making process. The members of the Labor Advisory Board were appointed by Secretary of Labor Frances Perkins* and included William Green* of the AFL,* John L. Lewis* of the United Mine Workers, John P. Frey of the AFL's Metal Trade Department, Rose Schneiderman* of the Women's Trade Union League, Sidney Hillman* of the Amalgamated Clothing Workers, and Rev. Francis J. Haas of the National Catholic Welfare Conference. Although most of the NRA codes were written by lawyers and technicians from management on loan to government and therefore represented the interests of business rather than those of labor, the Labor Advisory Board did have some success between 1933 and 1935 in protecting collective bargaining, limits on homework, and safety and health provisions. Over the years, it consistently pressed for concessions to labor in code-making issues. The Labor Advisory Board also urged the president to establish a National Labor Board* to mediate labor-management disputes. (Bernard Bellush, *The Failure of the NRA*, 1975.)

LABOR'S NON-PARTISAN LEAGUE By the mid-1930s, because of the rise of the Committee for Industrial Organization and later the Congress of Industrial Organizations* as well as the pro-labor atmosphere created by the National Labor Relations Act of 1935,* Franklin D. Roosevelt* had secured overwhelming labor support. With the election of 1936* approaching, the president wanted an unprecedented victory and mandate, and he began to solicit formal labor support. In April 1936 Labor's Non-Partisan League was organized by John L. Lewis* of the CIO and United Mine Workers, Sidney Hillman* of the Amalgamated Clothing Workers, and George L. Berry* of the Printing Pressmen. The sole purpose of the league was to re-elect Roosevelt, whom Lewis described as the "greatest statesman of modern times." They had added the term "Non-Partisan" to make sure that the league was not seen as an entity of the Democratic party.* The Labor's Non-Partisan League brought both AFL* and CIO unions behind Roosevelt, spent nearly $1 million on the campaign, and formed the American

Labor party* in New York to give Socialists and other leftists a way to vote for Roosevelt without voting on the Democratic ticket. Roosevelt swamped Alf Landon* with 61 percent of the vote, and the league took credit for helping Roosevelt carry Ohio, Illinois, and Indiana. By 1940 factional squabbles within the labor movement compromised the power of Labor's Non-Partisan League. John L. Lewis, president of the CIO, endorsed the presidential candidacy of Republican Wendell Willkie,* and several members of the league, like Gardner Jackson,* resigned in protest. Roosevelt still defeated Willkie by 4.9 million votes, but the effectiveness of the league had been called into question. In 1944 the CIO formed its nationwide Political Action Committee to support pro-labor candidates. (Irving Bernstein, *Turbulent Years. A History of the American Worker, 1933–1941*, 1970.)

LA DAME, MARY Mary La Dame, longtime assistant to Secretary of Labor Frances Perkins,* was born in 1885 and graduated from Pembroke (later Brown University) in 1906. After doing graduate work at Harvard, Columbia, and Carnegie Tech, she went to work for the Russell Sage Foundation doing industrial research. La Dame spent nearly a decade there before becoming an associate director for the Clearing House for Public Employment for New York City early in the 1920s. In 1933 Secretary of Labor Frances Perkins brought La Dame into the federal government to become associate director of the U.S. Employment Service* in New York, and in 1938 she promoted her to special assistant to the secretary of labor. La Dame served as Perkins's special assistant until 1945. (Susan Ware, *Beyond Suffrage: Women in the New Deal*, 1981.)

LA FOLLETTE COMMITTEE (See LA FOLLETTE, ROBERT MARION, JR.)

LA FOLLETTE, PHILIP FOX Philip La Follette was born on May 8, 1897, in Madison, Wisconsin. He graduated from the University of Wisconsin in 1919 and took a law degree there in 1922. After graduation he joined his father's law firm, but like the rest of the family, his heart was in progressive politics. La Follette served as the district attorney of Dane County from 1924 to 1927 and then as a professor at the University of Wisconsin Law School from 1926 to 1931. In 1930 he entered the Republican primary for governor and upset Walter J. Kohler. He went on to win the general election. Two years later, however, Kohler defeated him, and La Follette had to reconsider his political career. As the incumbent governor in a state with an unemployment rate near the national average in 1932, he had been a target of much criticism and could not overcome the Franklin D. Roosevelt* landslide. By 1934 he had another problem, as the New Deal* had usurped much of his progressive political philosophy. Progressive Republicans found themselves without a political home, because their own party was increasingly the voice of conservatism while the Democratic party* was representing liberalism. So in 1934 Philip La Follette bolted the GOP, established the Wisconsin Progressive party,* endorsed much of the New Deal, and won back the governorship. During the next four years he established a "Little New Deal"* thereby advocating a guaranteed farm income, protection of the collective bargaining rights of labor, unemployment insurance, old-age pensions, public works projects, tax reform, aid to homeowners, public ownership of utilities, and nationalization of the munitions industry. Friendly with Franklin D. Roosevelt and many leading Democratic liberals, La Follette even hoped that his Progressive party could lead to a national political realignment.

But in 1938 La Follette took a political gamble and lost. With the recession of 1937–1938* deepening, he thought Roosevelt was politically vulnerable and suspected the country might be ready for a new progressive leader, so he launched the National Progressives of America.* La Follette blamed Roosevelt for the depression and adopted a position much to the left of the New Deal. But in the 1938 elections,* Republican Julius Heil handily defeated him for governor, ending La Follette's political career. He joined the America First Committee in 1939 and campaigned against United States involvement with World War II in Europe. After that he had little to do with politics for the rest of his life. He continued to practice law privately, and died on August 18, 1965. (John E. Miller, "Governor Philip F. La Follette, the Wisconsin Progressives, and the New Deal, 1930–1939," Ph.D. dissertation, University of Wisconsin, 1973.)

LA FOLLETTE, ROBERT MARION, JR. Born on February 6, 1895, in Madison, Wisconsin, Robert Marion La Follette, Jr., was raised in one of the most politically prominent families in America. His father, Robert M. La Follette, served as a congressman, governor, and United States senator, and his name became synonymous with early twentieth century progressivism—a political philosophy committed to good government, regulation of monopolies, conservation, and popular control of political institutions. Robert M. La Follette, Jr., who entered the Senate in 1925 and served until 1949, was a transitional figure linking progressivism with the urban liberalism of the New Deal.* He entered the University of Wisconsin in 1913 but never graduated, quitting school in 1916 and going to work as a clerk in his father's senatorial office. He became his father's personal secretary in 1919; and when Robert M. La Follette died in 1925, Robert, Jr., won the special election to fill the vacant seat.

La Follette did not emerge from his father's shadow until after the stock market crash of 1929. Until then he had been preoccupied with the traditional issues of progressivism. But after 1929 La Follette became an outspoken critic of Herbert Hoover,* despite their shared Republican party affiliation. He demanded direct relief to the unemployed, a massive expansion of public works, and national economic planning. Along with Democratic Senator Robert Wagner* of New York, La Follette became recognized as one of the most liberal members of the Senate. During the early years of the New Deal, La Follette played a key role in the formulation and passage of important relief, public works, and taxation legislation, but he also became a major administration critic.

In his view, the New Deal was not moving fast enough or far enough in restoring mass purchasing power or protecting the collective bargaining rights of labor. La Follette was also appalled at the contradictions of New Deal economic policy—especially at Franklin D. Roosevelt's* willingness to implement diverse programs to satisfy various interest groups. La Follette took a position well to the left of the New Deal. He found Roosevelt too conservative and too cautious about changing the economic order. Although the personal relationship between the two men remained cordial, La Follette felt the president was squandering an unprecedented opportunity to reform America. On virtually every labor, relief, public works, and taxation issue of the 1930s, La Follette tried to push the president farther to the left. In 1934 La Follette reluctantly followed the lead of his brother Philip in forming the Wisconsin Progressive party* and running on the third-party ticket. He won re-election that year. During 1936 and throughout much of the rest of the decade, La Follette headed the subcommittee of the Senate Committee on Education and Labor, known popularly as the La Follette Civil Liberties Committee. He conducted the most extensive investigation of civil liberties violations in American history, concentrating on management violations of labor rights under the National Industrial Recovery Act* and the National Labor Relations Act.* The committee was overwhelming pro-labor, and many staff members were active participants in the CIO* organizing campaigns in the steel, automobile, and coal industries. Robert M. La Follette, Jr., was defeated for the Senate in 1946 by Joseph McCarthy, and he committed suicide on February 24, 1953. (Jerold S. Auerbach, *Labor and Liberty: The La Follette Committee and the New Deal*, 1966; Patrick J. Maney, *''Young Bob'' La Follette. A Biography of Robert M. La Follette, Jr., 1895–1953*, 1978.)

LA GUARDIA, FIORELLO HENRY Fiorello H. La Guardia, dynamic mayor of New York City and the only man in the country whose popularity rivaled that of Franklin D. Roosevelt* during the 1930s, was born in New York City on December 11, 1882. He received his early education in Arizona and wrote articles for the Phoenix *Morning Courier*. La Guardia was a war correspondent for the St. Louis *Post-Dispatch* during the Spanish-American War. Master of seven languages, he had travelled widely as a young man, serving with the American consulate in Hungary and Austria between 1901 and 1906 and working as an interpreter at Ellis Island for incoming immigrants between 1907 and 1910 while studying for his law degree at New York University. La Guardia received his law degree in 1910 and began practicing law. A progressive Republican, La Guardia opposed Tammany Hall in New York City and served as deputy attorney general of New York between 1915 and 1917. La Guardia was elected to the 65th and 66th Congresses as a Republican but resigned in 1918 to serve with the army air corps during World War I. When he returned from the war, La Guardia won election as the president of the Board of Aldermen of New York City for 1920 and 1921 but then was re-elected to Congress, where he served until 1933. In Congress, he consistently fought for legislation protecting the rights of labor and co-authored the Norris-La Guardia anti-injunction bill in 1932. La Guardia was elected mayor of New York City on a fusion ticket in 1933 and re-elected in 1937 and 1941.

During the 1930s, he proved to be an aggressive, popular, and incorruptible mayor. Blessed with boundless energy and an uncanny sense of humor and showmanship, La Guardia became famous for his public spectacles, like running to fires with the fire department, reading comic strips over the radio, or guest conducting the New York Philharmonic Orchestra. His election as mayor inaugurated a period of close cooperation between the government of New York City and the New Deal* administration in Washington. La Guardia regularly conferred with Harold L. Ickes* and Harry Hopkins* on New York City's relief problems, and consistently demanded more projects, more money, and more jobs. He frankly acknowledged in 1936 that without the assistance of such federal agencies as the Civil Works Administration,* Federal Emergency Relief Administration,* Public Works Administration,* and Works Progress Administration,* "there would have been no cities left at this time." Later in the 1930s, La Guardia fought just as consistently against any cuts in WPA funds. During the years 1936–1945, La Guardia was also the president of the United States Conference of Mayors. After World War II, La Guardia served briefly as director general of the UNRRA. He died on September 20, 1947. (Barbara Blumberg, *The New Deal and the Unemployed: The View from New York City*, 1979; *New York Times*, September 21, 1947.)

LAMONT, THOMAS WILLIAM Thomas William Lamont was born on September 30, 1870, near Albany, New York. He obtained his preparatory education at Phillips Exeter Academy and graduated from Harvard in 1892. He obtained a position as secretary to the Cushman Brothers, a food distributing firm; and when they approached bankruptcy in 1898, they asked Lamont to reorganize and manage the business. His success was immediate, and in 1903 he joined the Bankers' Trust Company, becoming vice-president in 1905. In 1911 Lamont became a partner with J. P. Morgan and Company. During World War I Lamont coordinated wartime finances among the Allied countries for President Woodrow Wilson, helped assist with the Dawes and Young plans for payment of German reparations during the 1920s, and served as President Herbert Hoover's* secretary of commerce. When the stock market crashed in 1929, Lamont unsuccessfully attempted to stabilize the market by establishing a banking consortium. He consistently believed the depression was a crisis of confidence and would be short-lived; and during the 1930s, although supporting Cordell Hull's* liberal trade policy, Lamont was an open critic of the New Deal,* primarily because of its bureaucratic invasion of the private economy. When J. P. Morgan* died in 1943, Lamont succeeded him as chairman of the board. He died on February 2, 1948, in Boca Grande, Florida. (*New York Times*, February 3, 1948.)

LAND, EMORY SCOTT Emory Scott Land was born on January 9, 1879. He graduated with a B.S. and M.A. from the University of Wyoming in 1898 and then went to the United States Naval Academy, where he graduated in 1902. With his engineering background, Land worked in naval construction after an initial sea tour in 1902–1904. He served as assistant chief of the Bureau of Aeronautics in the Navy Department between 1926 and 1928; chief of the Bureau of Construction and Repair between 1932 and 1937; and as a commissioner on the U.S. Maritime Commission* in 1937 and 1938. When President Franklin D. Roosevelt* named Joseph P. Kennedy* as ambassador to Great Britain, vacating his chairmanship of the U.S. Maritime Commission, he named Land to fill the position. Land served as chairman of the Maritime Commission until 1946. During all those years he worked diligently to improve the merchant marine and make it more competitive with foreign carriers. In 1942 the president asked Land to also serve as administrator of the War Shipping Board, a position he was eminently qualified for after years of supervisory experience in naval construction and repair as well as with the U.S. Maritime Commission's vigorous shipbuilding program in the late 1930s. Land rose to the rank of vice-admiral before his retirement in 1946. After retiring from government service, Land served for years as president of the Air Transport Association of America. He died on November 27, 1971. (Samuel A. Lawrence, *United States Merchant Shipping Policies and Politics*, 1966.)

LANDIS, JAMES McCAULEY James M. Landis was born on September 25, 1899, to Presbyterian missionary parents in Japan. Brilliant and desperate to live up to his parents' expectations, Landis attended the Tokyo Foreign School and in 1912 returned to the United States to finish his education. He enrolled at Princeton in 1916, volunteered with the YMCA relief program during World War I, and graduated from Princeton in 1921. Landis entered the Harvard Law School and quickly impressed Professor Felix Frankfurter.* He graduated from Harvard Law in 1924 and took a doctoral fellowship under Frankfurter, and the two of them formed a warm friendship. In 1925 Frankfurter awarded him the highest accolade by successfully recommending Landis for a clerkship with the Supreme Court* Justice Louis Brandeis.* From Brandeis, Landis developed a suspicion of concentrated economic power and a faith in the marketplace and competition. In 1926 he returned to Harvard to join the law faculty. Landis rose quickly through the academic ranks, specializing in the legislative process and becoming a full professor in 1928.

When Franklin D. Roosevelt* became president in 1933, Landis had an open door in Washington because of the influence of Frankfurter. They both came to Washington in April 1933 to work on the administration's proposed securities legislation. Landis labored closely with Benjamin Cohen* and Congressman Sam Rayburn* in producing the bill which became the Securities Act of 1933.* Late in 1933, Roosevelt appointed Landis to a commissionership on the Federal Trade Commission,* where he expected the young law professor to defend the new securities legislation and work for its enforcement. From his position on the FTC, Landis in 1934 helped Cohen, Rayburn, and Thomas Corcoran* prepare the Securities Exchange Act of 1934.* When the bill passed in June, Roosevelt named Landis, along with Ferdinand Pecora* and Joseph Kennedy,* as chairman, to head the new Securities and Exchange Commission.* Kennedy resigned in 1935 because he did not want to be on the SEC when it had to enforce the Public Utility Holding Company Act of 1935,* and Landis replaced him as chairman. Landis labored diligently to enforce the new securities legislation, but court tests of its constitutionality as well as concerted opposition from private industry limited his effectiveness. In 1938 Landis resigned from the SEC to become dean of the Harvard Law School.

When World War II erupted for the United States in 1941, President Roosevelt again turned to Landis, naming him to head the Office of Civil Defense early in 1942. Landis stayed there until 1943, spent some time in the Middle East as a special minister on economic affairs, and in 1945 returned to Harvard. In 1946 President Harry S Truman* asked Landis to head the Civil Aeronautics Board, and he accepted; but in the air safety investigations of 1947, he sided with the airline pilots rather than the industry. In the anti-labor atmosphere of 1947, he became a political liability and Truman did not reappoint him. Landis then went to work for Joseph Kennedy, concentrating on legal problems as well as John F. Kennedy's political career, but he never really recovered from Truman's treatment. President John Kennedy had Landis undertake a study of the regulatory commissions, but by then Landis' alcoholism was becoming an increasing problem. He completed the study, but in 1963 was brought to trial and convicted of income tax evasion. After a brief jail sentence in 1963 and disbarment in 1964, Landis retired. He died on July 30, 1964. Brilliant and pragmatic, Landis was without ideological concerns. In a pluralistic society, he believed, regulatory commmissions were to be mediators rather than advocates, working diligently to decide which large, monopolistic institutions in the economy were in the public interest. (Donald A. Ritchie, *James M. Landis. Dean of the Regulators*, 1980.)

LANDON, ALFRED MOSSMAN Alfred Mossman Landon was born on September 9, 1887, in West Middlesex, Pennsylvania; grew up in Marietta, Ohio; and moved with his family to Independence, Kansas, in 1904. He attended the University of Kansas, graduating and winning admission to the bar in 1908. After brief experience in banking in Independence, he began a successful career as an independent oil driller. His business soon sprawled beyond the mid-continent field of Kansas and Oklahoma to scattered interests across both states.

Landon began his political career as a Progressive and was closely allied with Kansas Governor Henry Allen. Not until 1928, when he managed the gubernatorial campaign of Clyde Reed and became chairman of the state Republican party,* did he seek conciliation with party conservatives and assume the middle-of-the-road posture that would characterize his later career.

After losing the state chairmanship in 1930, Landon devoted his time to dealing with the depression in the oil business, especially as it affected small, independent oilmen. During a time of chaotic markets, he feared the fostering of oligopoly. He led the independents in their efforts to retain a share of markets, to gain access to interstate pipelines, and to reserve a place in the conservation-proration laws passed by various states.

In 1932 Landon won the Republican nomination for governor with an easy primary victory. In a close general election he defeated the Democratic incumbent, Harry Woodring, soon to become secretary of war under President Franklin D. Roosevelt,* and Independent John Brinkley, popularly known as the "goat gland doctor."

Landon built a praiseworthy record as governor. He cut taxes and tightened administration. Prior to the national bank holiday,* he placed restrictions on withdrawals to stop runs on banks. He secured a moratorium on farm mortgage foreclosures. He dealt forthrightly with the revelations of the Finney bond scandal, the greatest financial scandal in the state's history. Except in the case of farm programs, he worked well with federal efforts to combat the depression. He labored to shape an equitable oil code in the National Recovery Administration* and organized the expenditure of federal work-relief funds in Kansas.

Landon's dovetailing with federal programs was effective enough that he made it an issue in his campaign for re-election in 1934.* He was the only Republican governor in the United States re-elected in that year.

In 1936 Landon eased into the Republican presidential nomination with a stay-at-home campaign. As his running mate, the Republicans chose Frank Knox of Chicago. Landon's nomination marked the ascendancy of a new generation of young, western, Main-Street (as opposed to Wall-Street) Republicans in the party.

In the ensuing campaign, Landon attacked the New Deal* vigorously but ineffectively. He criticized the incumbent president for failing to achieve recovery and restoration of full employment, for pursuing an economy of scarcity instead of an economy of plenty. Landon maintained that recovery would come only when the federal government ceased efforts to manage business and established a sound monetary policy. Although he pledged to continue relief efforts, Landon railed against deficit spending: "We must drive the spenders out," he declared.

More basically, Landon accused the president of exploiting the national economic emergency in order to usurp the powers of the Congress, the states, and the people. He warned of dangerous concentration of power in the executive office—his campaign song, to the theme of "Oh Susanna," calling for return to the "dear old Constitution."

Landon attempted to stake out a moderate position of opposition to the New Deal without becoming a mouthpiece for his party's Old Guard, but his stance of moderation was frequently eroded by statements from such spokesmen of the right as the American Liberty League* or his own national party chairman, John D. M. Hamilton.* Moreover, as the economy recovered a bit in 1936, the public grew less receptive to criticism of the New Deal.

The election proved disastrous for Landon. He carried only two states with but eight electoral votes. The election clearly showed the strength of the new Democratic coalition built by Roosevelt during his first term. Although his defeat obscured it at the time, Landon's candidacy was nevertheless important to the evolution of the Republican party during the New Deal. He kept alive such ideas as an economy of plenty, limited government, fiscal restraint, and governmental regulation rather than management of business, pointing the way for eventual reconstruction of the party.

Landon remained prominent in Republican affairs for a few years after his defeat in 1936. He urged his party to keep alive the idea of a spirited, loyal opposition during World War II. Meanwhile, in Kansas he looked after his oil interests and invested in commercial broadcasting. By the late 1940s his political influence was negligible, although he remained well-known, well-liked, and often quoted in his home state. (Donald R. McCoy, *Landon of Kansas*, 1966; Francis W. Schruben, *Kansas in Turmoil, 1930–1936*, 1969.)

THOMAS D. ISERN

LANGE, DOROTHEA The world renowned photographer Dorothea Lange was born May 26, 1895, in Hoboken, New Jersey. She graduated from the New York Training School for Teachers determined to be a photographer rather than an educator. Lange then went to San Francisco where her studio on Sutter Street attracted wealthy merchant families, and for over a decade, it was the focus of her attention. But the Great Depression changed Lange's life. Deeply disturbed by the contrast between her wealthy clients and the unemployed that she observed on walks, Lange vowed to use photography to bring the tragedy of the depression home to the American people. Pictures, she concluded, were a better medium for that than the written word in newspapers or the spoken word on radio. After several long, arduous trips, Lange's first exhibition on the depression was held at the Oakland Studio of Willard Van Dyke. Among the viewers was Paul S. Taylor, professor at the University of California, who had successfully used photography to illustrate the impact of the depression on society. Greatly impressed with each other's abilities, the two struck up a lifelong friendship which eventually turned to marriage. They did an outstanding report on the sordid situation of migrant farmers for the California State Emergency Relief Administration which led to federal grants for the first sanitary facilities for such people.

Lange and Taylor's next activities were for the Resettlement Administration* of the New Deal.* The agency sought to rehabilitate close to one million farmers in or near poverty and to resettle about 500,000 farm families from submarginal land. During the summers of 1936 to 1938, Lange and Taylor documented the mechanization and unseasonable weather driving people off the land in the South and Midwest. The photographs proved the desperate plight of those people and stirred Congress to enlarge the agency in 1937 and rename it the Farm Security Administration.* Their photographs for the FSA appeared in magazines, exhibits, newspapers, and books, and in 1939 came out in book form as *An American*

Exodus: A Record of Human Erosion. Other photographers commissioned by the Farm Security Administration imitated their approach.

During the first half of the 1940s, Lange continued to use her photographic skills for the New Deal. After a brief period with the Bureau of Agricultural Economics, the War Relocation Authority employed her to record in photographs the forced movement of Japanese aliens and Japanese-Americans to relocation camps. Because officials feared her photographs would arouse great sympathy for such persons, the pictures were filed and many of them not released until a third of a century later. Shifting to the Office of War Information in 1943, Lange took pictures for the magazine *Victory* until, at the end of World War II, the State Department hired her to pictorially document the historic writing of the Charter of the United Nations. Although declining health forced Lange into retirement for the rest of her life, she did a few commercial projects and accompanied her husband on several overseas assignments. Finally, overcome by cancer, Dorothea Lange died on October 11, 1965. (Therese T. Heyman, *Celebrating a Collection: The Work of Dorothea Lange*, 1978; Milton Meltzer, *Dorothea Lange: A Photographer's Life*, 1978; Karin B. Ohrn, *Dorothea Lange and the Documentary Tradition*, 1980.)

H. CARLETON MARLOW

LEA, CLARENCE FREDERICK Clarence F. Lea was born near Highland Springs, California, on July 11, 1874. He attended Stanford University and then graduated from the law department of the University of Denver in 1898. Lea practiced law in Santa Rosa, California, and in 1907 became district attorney of Sonoma County, where he served until his election to Congress in 1916 as a Democrat. Lea was re-elected as a candidate of the Democratic* and Republican parties* to the next fourteen Congresses, serving from 1917 to 1949. He did not run for re-election in 1948. During the 1930s, Lea was a powerful figure in Congress, chairing the House Interstate Commerce Committee and generally playing a conservative role on New Deal* legislation. Because of his unique bipartisan political constituency at home, Lea supported the Democratic administration whenever possible, but he could not alienate his Republican support. Consequently, he was considered by President Franklin D. Roosevelt* to be one of the more ''unreliable'' committee chairmen in the House. Lea decided not to run for re-election in 1948 and returned to California where he worked in public relations until 1954, when he retired. Clarence F. Lea died on June 20, 1964. (*New York Times*, June 21, 1964.)

LEAGUE FOR INDEPENDENT POLITICAL ACTION The League for Independent Political Action was founded in 1929 by educator John Dewey, labor leader James H. Maurer, journalist Oswald Garrison Villard, and economist Paul H. Douglas of the University of Chicago. Dismayed at the conservatism of both the Democratic* and Republican parties,* they wanted to start a new political organization to fulfill their liberal and socialist hopes. At first, the league endorsed non-Communist liberals and Socialists, hoping to create a new unity among Americans committed to national economic planning, social welfare legislation, and nationalization of major industries. During the election of 1932,* they endorsed Norman Thomas* of the Socialist Party of America* and called for massive relief and public works spending, nationalization of major industries, higher inheritance taxes and higher income taxes on corporations and the wealthy, guarantees for collective bargaining, unemployment and old-age insurance, an anti-lynching law, disarmament, and cancellation of World War I debts. In the elections of 1932,* two League candidates—Elbert Thomas of Utah for the U. S. Senate and Marion Zionchek of Washington for the House of Representatives—won their campaigns.

During the first two years of the New Deal,* the league remained quite critical of President Franklin D. Roosevelt* for not doing enough to end the depression and formed the Farmer-Labor Political Federation in hopes of creating the new third party. But the shift of the New Deal to the left after 1934 undermined the league's rationale. After Roosevelt's unprecedented re-election of 1936,* the league dissolved and many of its members, like Paul H. Douglas, became active New Dealers. (Donald R. McCoy, *Angry Voices, Left-of-Center Politics in the New Deal Era*, 1958.)

LE HAND, MARGUERITE ALICE Marguerite (Missy) Le Hand was born in 1898 in Potsdam, New York. She graduated from Somerville High School in 1917, passed the federal civil service exam, and went to work as a typist in the Emergency Fleet Corporation. She stayed there until 1922. Franklin D. Roosevelt,* then just beginning his recovery from polio, had decided to resume his political correspondence and was looking for a secretary to handle his mail. Charles McCarthy, a former Roosevelt aide during his tenure as assistant secretary of the navy during World War I, recommended Le Hand. Roosevelt hired her, and Le Hand moved into the family compound at Hyde Park, taking over his correspondence and managing the household. She became a close friend of the president and Eleanor Roosevelt* as well as the Roosevelt children. Le Hand joined the White House staff in 1933 and continued to supervise the president's correspondence until her retirement early in 1943 because of ill health. Marguerite Le Hand died on July 31, 1944. (*New York Times*, August 1, 1944.)

LEMKE, WILLIAM William Lemke was born at Albany, Minnesota, on August 13, 1878. The family moved to Grand Forks, Dakota Territory, in 1881 and eventually to Towner County in 1883 where they had accumulated 2,700 acres of land. The Lemke children spoke German at home. William Lemke entered the University of North Dakota in 1898. He graduated in 1902 and then attended the Yale Law School, where he graduated in 1905. He returned to practice law in North Dakota and at the same time became publisher of a monthly magazine called *The Common Good*. The Equity Cooperative Exchange, a business storing and selling grain, hired Lemke as its attorney in 1911, as did the Nonpartisan

League* a few years later. Basically a farmers' group promoting agricultural interests, the Nonpartisan League helped shape Lemke's political ideas. He became state chairman of the Republican party* in 1916 and worked hard to create a Republican-Non-Partisan League fusion platform. His interest in the welfare of farmers grew steadily. In 1920 he was elected attorney general and vigorously prosecuted lawsuits against railroads and public utilities, even though he was defeated in a 1921 recall election. After that defeat Lemke devoted much of his time to expanding league programs for home-building, guaranteeing bank deposits, and operating the mill and elevator. Lemke also remained interested in consumer protection and protecting farmers against the banks and insurance companies holding their notes. Lemke won a seat in Congress in 1932, where he served until 1941. During those years he sponsored a series of laws to protect farm prices and provide lower interest rates along with mortgage protection. The only major piece of legislation he successfully pushed through Congress was the Federal Farm Bankruptcy Act (Frazier-Lemke Farm Bankruptcy Act) of 1934,* which established a new bankruptcy law for debt-ridden farmers. By declaring bankruptcy under the law, the farmer could have a federal court scale down the level of his debts until they matched the value of his property. If the farmer then succeeded in paying off the reduced debts, he would regain title to his farm. During the entire process, the farmer would be able to continue farming the land. The Federal Farm Bankruptcy Act* was quite an accomplishment given the initial opposition of Franklin D. Roosevelt's* administration and Lemke's Republican party membership.

During 1934 and 1935 Lemke became increasingly agitated about the New Deal,* primarily because he viewed it as too conservative. Lemke tried to push a refinance bill which would provide for reducing interest rates to farmers, refinancing farm mortgages by a government credit agency, and issuing $3 billion in notes by the Federal Reserve Board* to finance the measure. The Roosevelt administration opposed the bill as inflationary, and Lemke became a bitter enemy of the New Deal. He turned to the left-wing critics of the Roosevelt administration: Father Charles Coughlin* and his National Union for Social Justice; Senator Huey Long* and "Share Our Wealth"* schemes; and Dr. Francis E. Townsend* and his Old-Age Revolving Pensions, Ltd. When Huey Long was assassinated, Gerald L. K. Smith* assumed temporary leadership of his constituency. All three groups believed strongly that the New Deal was not going far enough in meeting the needs of the poor and unemployed, so in 1936 they merged politically, forming the Union party* and seeking out Lemke as their presidential candidate. Embittered by the fate of his refinance bill, Lemke was responsive and accepted the nomination. The Union party endorsed an inflated currency, the Lemke refinance bill, and the Townsend pension plan, but it had little support nationwide. Lemke received fewer than a million votes and only 12.8 percent of the North Dakota vote. He retained his House seat, however, and won again in 1938 even though the Nonpartisan League refused to support him. His bid for a Senate seat in 1940 failed. Lemke continued to believe in the transfer of credit control from banks to the government, states' rights, foreign policy isolationism, and sympathy for the underprivileged. He died in Fargo, North Dakota, on May 30, 1950. (Edward C. Blackorby, *Prairie Rebel. The Public Life of William Lemke*, 1963.)

LENROOT, KATHERINE FREDRICA Katherine Lenroot was born in 1891, daughter of Republican Senator Irvine Lenroot of Wisconsin. She graduated from the University of Wisconsin in 1912 and immediately went to work for the Industrial Commission of Wisconsin. Lenroot came to the Children's Bureau of the Department of Labor in 1914 as a special investigator, and she was promoted to assistant chief of the bureau in 1922. When Grace Abbott* resigned as head of the Children's Bureau in 1934, Lenroot got the job; and the next year, while serving as president of the National Conference of Social Work, she also helped draft the Social Security Act of 1935.* Lenroot worked as head of the Children's Bureau until 1949. (Susan Ware, *Beyond Suffrage: Women in the New Deal*, 1981.)

LEWIS, JOHN LLEWELLYN As the leader of the United Mine Workers and founder of the CIO,* John L. Lewis, with his fearsome eyebrows and thundering voice, dominated the American labor scene during the New Deal.* The son of a Welsh immigrant miner, Lewis was born on February 12, 1880, in Cleveland, Lucas County, Iowa. Lewis almost finished high school; and between 1897 and 1901, he had a variety of jobs, working as a farm laborer, manager of a small-town theater, and as a miner in the bituminous coalfields of southern Iowa. He left Iowa in 1901 to work in the mines of the western states but returned to Lucas County and in 1907 married Myrta Bell, a schoolteacher. In 1908 Lewis and his entire family moved to Panama, Illinois, a company town in the central Illinois coalfields, where he began his union career. He quickly won election as president of the UMW local in Panama and soon rose to become a lobbyist for the UMW in Illinois. In 1911 he attracted the attention of Samuel Gompers, head of the AFL,* and he became an AFL field agent. By means of patronage appointments, Lewis rose to vice-president of the UMW in 1917 and president in 1920, a position he did not surrender for forty years.

Lewis ruled the UMW in grand autocratic style, but his authority did not rest unchallenged. During the 1920s, he struggled almost ceaselessly to establish and keep absolute control over his union, the usual problems of cutthroat labor politics being exacerbated by a growing depression in the coal industry, unsuccessful strikes, and sharp declines in UMW membership. As a prominent Republican labor leader, Lewis backed Herbert Hoover* in 1928; but in the four years that followed, neither he nor the troubled UMW garnered any advantage from the Hoover administration in return for that support. In 1932 Lewis again publicly endorsed Hoover. This time, however, he covered all bases, privately indicating to the Roosevelt camp that he would work behind the scenes for the election of Franklin D. Roosevelt.*

The New Deal signaled a change of fortune for Lewis and the UMW. Lewis lobbied successfully for the inclusion of Section 7a, guaranteeing workers the right to organize and bargain collectively, in the National Industrial Recovery Act of 1933,* and he later influenced the enactment of other laws favorably affecting the welfare of miners and the strength of their union—notably, the Guffey-Snyder Act* (1935) and its successor, Guffey-Vinson* (1937). In addition, Lewis launched an intensive organizing drive in the coalfields during the summer of 1933, taking full advantage of the opening provided by the NIRA and invoking the name of Roosevelt to draw miners into the ranks of the UMW.

Although the membership of the UMW climbed to 500,000 within a year, Lewis became increasingly frustrated and angered by the failure of the leadership of the craft-oriented AFL to pursue vigorously the organization of semi-skilled and unskilled workers in other big industries. Recognizing that the unionization of the mass-production industries—especially steel—was of vital importance to the UMW and to his own ambitions within the labor movement, Lewis began a campaign to promote the organization of the less skilled into single unions for each major industry (industrial unions). Since the idea of industrial unionism violated the jurisdictional claims of existing AFL affiliates, Lewis encountered considerable opposition to his efforts within the hierarchy of the AFL, labor's old guard. The conflict between the champions of industrial unionism and the defenders of the traditional craft trades approach to organization boiled over during the tumultuous AFL convention at Atlantic City in October 1935 when, in an exchange of blows, Lewis literally bloodied the face of "Big Bill" Hutcheson, the president of the carpenters' union. Soon after that incident, Lewis and other like-minded labor leaders (Sidney Hillman,* David Dubinsky,* and Philip Murray*) established the Committee for Industrial Organization (ostensibly within the framework of the AFL) to facilitate the unionization of the labor force in the mass-production industries. In the summer of 1936, following repeated warnings and a prolonged period of maneuvering and confrontation, chiefly between Lewis and AFL President William Green,* who denounced the CIO as a schismatic organization, the CIO leaders and their unions were suspended by the AFL Executive Council on such charges as "dual unionism" and jurisdictional infringements. The split became formal and complete in 1938 when the CIO, abandoning all pretense of being anything other than a rival labor movement, designated itself the Congress of Industrial Organizations and elected John L. Lewis as its first president.

Even before this final break, however, Lewis had embarked on a CIO crusade to organize the automotive and steel industries. General Motors, holding the key to the unionization of much of the rest of the auto industry, capitulated to the CIO on February 11, 1937, after a bitter and often violent struggle in which Lewis gained the upper hand using the novel tactic of the "sit-down' strike. Less than three weeks later, U. S. Steel, to the astonishment of many, backed down without a fight and signed a contract with the Steel Workers Organizing Committee of the CIO. With such victories, by 1938 the CIO outstripped the

AFL in size (CIO: 3.7 million members; AFL: 3.4 million members) and rivaled it in influence.

On the political front, Lewis supported Roosevelt in 1936 and joined with Sidney Hillman of the Amalgamated Clothing Workers and George L. Berry* of the AFL's Printing Pressmen's Union in creating Labor's Non-Partisan League* to rally the labor vote for the re-election of the president. In addition, the CIO unions dumped nearly $800,000 into the Roosevelt campaign chest. The UMW alone contributed almost $500,000—in return for which Lewis clearly anticipated a substantial satisfaction of the needs of the labor movement.

Not surprisingly, the Roosevelt-Lewis alliance soon began to show signs of strain. On May 30, 1937, during the little steel strike, police fired into a crowd demonstrating against Tom Girdler's* Republic Steel plant in South Chicago, killing ten and wounding dozens more. When Roosevelt responded to the terrible carnage of the so-called Memorial Day massacre* with a pronouncement of "a plague on both your houses," the outraged Lewis, who certainly had expected more for the UMW's $500,000 than that, scathingly censured the President. By 1940 various factors (including setbacks suffered by the CIO* as a result of the "Roosevelt depression" of 1937–38,* serious disagreement with Roosevelt regarding foreign policy, and a clash of massive egos) caused Lewis to oppose Roosevelt's third-term bid for the presidency. Seeking to rally the vote of organized labor in support of Wendell Willkie,* Lewis vowed to resign as president of the CIO if Roosevelt won re-election. He kept his promise, turning over control of the CIO to Philip Murray, his longtime lieutenant, in November 1940. Two years later, he broke with Murray and pulled the UMW out of the CIO.

Lewis' prestige and influence declined after his departure from the CIO, but as leader of the UMW, he remained a powerful figure in the labor movement. During the 1940s, he conducted a crucial series of coal strikes (1941, 1943, 1946), winning wage increases and other benefits for miners; but these strikes alienated public opinion and probably contributed to the passage of the Smith-Connally (1943) and Taft-Hartley (1947) anti-labor legislation. Lewis retired as UMW president in 1960 and died in Washington, D. C., on June 11, 1969, at the age of eighty-nine. (Melvyn Dubofsky and Warren Van Tine, *John L. Lewis*, 1977.)

ROBERT L. SHADLE

LIBERTY PARTY Founded in 1932 by Frank E. Webb, the Liberty party advocated socialism as the answer to the Great Depression. At a national convention that year, the Liberty party nominated William H. Harvey, former Populist and author of *Coin's Financial School* (1894), as their presidential candidate with Frank F. Hemenway for vice-president. Harvey immediately tried to merge the Liberty party with the Jobless party,* but the effort failed over whether Harvey or Jobless party candidate James Cox should be the coalition's nominee. The Liberty party called for massive relief and public works spending as well as nationalization of all industry. Although the Liberty party ticket was on the ballot in nine states, they managed to secure only 53,425 votes and disintegrated once the New Deal* was underway. (Donald R. McCoy, *Angry Voices, Left-of-Center Politics in the New Deal Era*, 1971.)

LILIENTHAL, DAVID ELI David E. Lilienthal was born in Morton, Illinois, on July 8, 1899, to Czechoslovakian immigrant parents. He graduated from DePauw University in 1920 and then entered the Harvard Law School, where he became close to Professor Felix Frankfurter.* Lilienthal left Harvard with a law degree in 1923 and a passionate interest in conservation and controlled development of natural resources. He moved to Chicago and joined the law firm of Donald Richberg.* His handling of a difficult telephone rate case before the Supreme Court* impressed a number of liberals throughout the country, particularly Governor Philip La Follette* of Wisconsin, who appointed Lilienthal to the State Utility Commission in 1931. In 1933 President Franklin D. Roosevelt,* hearing of Lilienthal from Frankfurter, appointed the young lawyer to the board of the new Tennesssee Valley Authority.* There he joined Arthur Morgan,* TVA chairman, and Harcourt Morgan* as an administrative triumvirate.

Lilienthal soon found himself at odds with Arthur Morgan. The TVA chairman was primarily interested in national economic planning through business-government cooperation, so he wanted very badly to maintain a close relationship with the utility companies. To achieve that, he set TVA power rates at levels comparable to those of private industry. Lilienthal, however, was filled with a Brandesian suspicion of concentrated economic power, particularly the utility empire, and he urged the sale of cheap TVA power throughout the region. In 1938, with the battle between Morgan and Lilienthal becoming increasingly public, Roosevelt intervened and fired Morgan. By that time the New Deal* had already shifted its emphasis from the national planning vision of people like Arthur Morgan to the more anti-trust and competition vision of people like Louis Brandeis.* Lilienthal was clearly the victor. Harcourt Morgan succeeded Arthur Morgan as head of the TVA. After that, Lilienthal became embroiled in a controversy with Wendell Willkie,* president of the huge Commonwealth and Southern Corporation, the major utility in the Tennessee Valley. Willkie accused Lilienthal of trying to force Commonwealth out of business through unfair rate competition, a charge which Lilienthal publicly denied but privately acknowledged, at least in his more wishful thinking. In 1939 TVA purchased more than $78 million of Commonwealth properties, and in 1941 the president named Lilienthal head of the Tennessee Valley Authority.

Lilienthal headed the TVA throughout World War II, building it into the country's largest producer of electric power. President Harry S Truman* reappointed Lilienthal to a nine-year term in May 1945. He did not finish the term, however, because in January 1946 Truman asked Lilienthal to join Secretary of State Dean Acheson* in developing a plan for ''controlling atomic energy production and safeguarding peaceful nations'' against atomic aggression. It became known as the Acheson-Lilienthal Report. When Congress created the

Atomic Energy Commission in 1946 to provide civilian control of the army's vast atomic energy programs, Truman named Lilienthal as its first chairman. Despite charges from Senator Kenneth McKellar that Lilienthal's Czech heritage made him a Communist suspect, the Senate confirmed his appointment by fifty to thirty-one. As head of the AEC, Lilienthal worked to build the American nuclear arsenal and stimulate the nuclear energy industry. He resigned from the Atomic Energy Commission in 1950 and spent the rest of his career in private business and consultation on atomic energy projects. David E. Lilienthal died on January 14, 1981. (David E. Lilienthal, *The Journals of David E. Lilienthal*, Vols. 1–7, 1964–1983; Wilson Whitman, *David Lilienthal. Public Servant in a Power Age*, 1948.)

LIPPMANN, WALTER Walter Lippmann was born September 23, 1889, in New York City. He graduated from Harvard in 1909 and began a career in journalism. Two years before Franklin D. Roosevelt's* inauguration, Walter Lippmann began writing his syndicated column "Today and Tomorrow." Through this vehicle Lippmann reached millions of readers and became the most authoritative and respected journalist in America. He wrote with clarity and grace, revealing an intellect both analytical in bent and wide ranging in interest. Towards so diverse, evolving, and even contradictory an enterprise as the New Deal,* Lippmann formed not so much an attitude as a complex of attitudes. Though after 1935 Lippmann and Roosevelt were often at odds over specifics, they agreed on the need to reform economic practices by the use of governmental action in order to preserve capitalism and republican government and on the need for the national state to assume responsibility for providing a decent standard of living.

Lippmann's response to the New Deal was affected in important ways by three factors: an optimistic faith in human nature and the power of reason, an awareness of the spread of totalitarian states in the contemporary world and a loathing for that form of government, and an acceptance of the economic thought of John Maynard Keynes.*

Hallmarks of Lippmann's thought were his belief that most humans were fundamentally decent and honorable and his abiding confidence in the ability of informed intelligence to solve problems. Lippmann drew these beliefs from the Enlightenment and was convinced that the United States reflected the ideals in its political and economic system. That system was therefore fundamentally sound and ought to be preserved. It did contain important flaws, however, such as a continuing ideology of individualism—a concept that the rise of large corporations had long since undercut. The depression revealed many of these flaws unmercifully, and it required modification of the system if they were to be corrected. The severity of the early depression years prompted Lippmann to abandon his initial emphasis on the need for thrift in government and to emphasize prompt action over careful procedure and exacting analysis. Thus he endorsed the flurry of legislation during the hundred days.* Lippman admired Roosevelt's strong leadership in tackling the depression, and he applauded the sense of a common purpose among all elements of society which much early New Deal legislation attempted to evoke. One of his columns helped to precipitate the president's decision to abandon the gold standard, and he endorsed the Emergency Banking Act,* the TVA,* and the AAA.*

Lippmann was one of the first Americans to become converted to the theory of countercyclical spending being propounded by John Maynard Keynes. The two had long been friends and discussed the theory in detail while Lippmann was in England covering the London Economic Conference.* Keynes supported most of the early New Deal, and his influence further inclined Lippmann to view Roosevelt's program favorably. Throughout the president's first two years, as the economy stayed mired in its slump, Lippmann praised the overall thrust of the New Deal and most of its particulars.

By 1935, as the economy stabilized and the sense of crisis eased, certain flaws in the early New Deal became obvious and Lippmann's reservations increased. He continued to endorse specific measures, including social security and creation of the SEC,* but he was becoming alarmed by what he perceived as excessive collectivization of the economy and centralization of government power in the executive. Roosevelt's domination of Congress led him to fear that the two branches were becoming seriously imbalanced. He objected also to the often indirect and guileful style of leadership the president employed. At the center of Lippmann's written attack was his condemnation of "personal government by devious methods." Unlike many other New Deal critics, he never feared that Roosevelt wanted to make himself a dictator; rather he was concerned that the presidential high-handedness would provoke a reaction against progressive reform.

Lippmann first broke with Roosevelt over his handling of the tax bill and then, with uncharacteristic bitterness, fought the administration during the court-packing* struggle. The New Deal was already at odds with most of the business community, and Lippmann deplored divisions of this sort as antithetical to the unified national effort which he insisted was essential if prosperity were to be regained. Furthermore, the sloppiness of many New Deal experimental programs upset Lippmann, and he came to believe that New Deal economic planning would lead to collectivism.

Lippmann was especially sensitive to this danger because he had become gravely concerned by the mid-1930s over the trend towards totalitarianism abroad. A determination to prevent domestic dictatorship gradually supplanted his emphasis on the urgency of domestic economic problems as the guiding element in Lippmann's thinking about the New Deal. He never abandoned his belief in the need for reform, but by 1936 he was most interested in establishing a balance between economic security and individual freedom and self-reliance. The *Good Society*, published in 1939, represented his most elaborate effort to propound an answer. In it he attacked authoritarianism and attempted to reconstruct liberalism. Lippmann contended that totalitarian political systems developed from collectivist economics, rather than the reverse. In other words, he continued to believe that political democracy could only exist in a society where the economy was based on private enterprise. But Lippmann was not proposing laissez-faire, instead he called for a "compensated economy." The term and most of the concepts came from Keynes. Government should intervene in the economy in order to smooth its performance and to provide for needy citizens. Deficit spending and manipulation of tax and interest rates were the means to influence the overall economy, while public works projects, social insurance and the minimum wage were ways to aid the victims of modern life. It all sounded very much like the New Deal itself, but Lippmann insisted that his program differed in that it would be carried out systematically through legislation.

In retrospect, it seems clear that Lippmann agreed with most of the fundamentals of the New Deal as they are generally understood today. Both he and Roosevelt wished to preserve the essential nature of the American political economy by altering individual components and methods of operation. A great increase in federal government activity and a significant widening of its responsibilities were the chief means by which this would be done. That Lippmann so often criticized the New Deal after 1935 should not mask his basic agreement with Roosevelt's goals. In large measure, Lippmann's attacks were prompted by his aversion to inconsistency and sloppiness of design, both of which plagued the New Deal. His criticisms stemmed too from his mistaken belief that a unifying philosophy of collectivism underlay the New Deal, when in fact the program was one of *ad hoc* experimentation. And if Lippmann's fears of totalitarianism became decisive to his thought, this was true because he had lost an appreciation for the desperate plight which faced millions of Americans throughout the depression. The long-range implications of the New Deal which came to trouble Lippmann mattered little to citizens with more pressing problems. To Lippmann's credit, however, he remained always a constructive critic whose goal was to improve the performance of government in order to promote the general welfare. Walter Lippmann died on December 14, 1974. (Walter Lippmann, *The Good Society*, 1939; Ronald Steele, *Walter Lippmann and the American Century*, 1980.)

JAMES C. SCHNEIDER

LITERARY DIGEST The *Literary Digest*, a weekly magazine founded in 1890 by Isaac K. Funk and Adam Wagnalls, was designed as "a repository of contemporaneous thought and research as presented in the periodical literature of the world." Funk and Wagnalls, former Lutheran ministers, intended to provide information on a wide variety of subjects for a readership which had the time, interest, and desire to investigate and analyze major issues of the day. In its early years, the magazine appealed primarily to theologians and educators by condensing articles from North American and European journals. Other features included book reviews, a summary of the week's events, lists of current periodical literature and books, and news clippings.

The magazine grew slowly until 1905 when William S. Woods replaced Edward J. Wheeler as editor. Circulation increased steadily through the 1910s and early 1920s, passing 1.5 million in 1927. The magazine's excellent coverage of World War I, with colored maps by its own cartographers and annual résumés of events, and its collection of $10 million for wartime and postwar relief for Belgium and the Middle East attracted public attention and support. The introduction of the straw poll also contributed to increased circulation. The *Digest* conducted these informal, unofficial polls among select groups to indicate trends in public opinion. In 1920 the magazine ran its first national poll on presidential nominations and in 1924 its first national presidential election poll. These were followed by national political polls in 1928, 1932, and 1936, and with polls on special issues such as Prohibition, the veteran's bonus, and Andrew Mellon's tax reduction plan. The polls, based on subscription lists, telephone directories, and automobile registrations, were not accurate by modern standards; the 1924 and 1928 polls averaged a 12 percent plurality error per state. The polls served a threefold purpose: they interested *Digest* readers, resulted in newspaper publicity, and solicited subscriptions.

In 1936 the *Literary Digest* predicted victory for Alfred M. Landon.* Landon's landslide defeat to Franklin D. Roosevelt* damaged the credibility and prestige of the magazine, and the erroneous prediction was considered a cause of the *Digest*'s eventual failure. Other factors also contributed to its demise. Circulation had begun to slide in the late 1920s and early 1930s, a result of the competition of newer magazines such as *Time* and *Newsweek* which provided a single, easily read overview of the news. Efforts to encourage subscriptions through insurance plans and gift premiums proved ineffective. Decline in circulation, combined with the depression, discouraged advertisers, leading to reduction in the size of the magazine and then further decline. Editors changed its format several times, but it suspended publication in February 1938. *Time* absorbed the *Literary Digest* in May of that year. (Frank L. Mott, *A History of American Magazines, 1885–1905*, 1957; Theodore Peterson, *Magazines in the Twentieth Century*, 1964.)

VIRGINIA F. HAUGHTON

"LITTLE NEW DEAL" The term "Little New Deal" emerged in the mid-1930s to describe efforts at the state level to implement and then to strengthen New Deal* programs. In strongly Democratic states with powerful urban machines, the New Deal received overwhelming support, and many state leaders even tried to magnify its impact by passing supportive legislation, including laws outlawing child labor, providing unemployment insurance and workmen's compensation, increasing corporate taxes, improving work relief programs, and enforcing labor standards and union rights. Similar legislation was also passed in states where progressive Republicans were dominant. The most prominent "Little New Deals" developed under Governors George Earle* (Pennsylvania), Herbert Lehman (New York), Frank Murphy* (Michigan), Philip La Follette* (Wisconsin), and Culbert Olson* (California). (James T. Patterson, *The New Deal in the States: Federalism in Transition*, 1969.)

"LITTLE NRA" By the early 1930s, a number of economists like Rexford Tugwell* were advocating national economic planning while prominent businessmen like Gerard Swope* of General Electric and Henry I. Harriman* of the United States Chamber of Commerce* were arguing that an economic recovery would not materialize until a national plan to coordinate growth was developed. In their view, the highly individualistic, competitive, laissez-faire characteristics of the American economy had fostered a serious economic decline. While wholesale and retail prices were so depressed, business confidence and business investment would remain low, as would production and employment. They advocated an economic philosophy which eventually became one of the New Deal's* many approaches to recovery. Only by suspending the anti-trust laws and permitting trade associations to participate in industry-wide planning could destructive competition and deflation be stopped. Cooperation and planning, they believed, would help raise prices, business confidence, production, and employment. The National Industrial Recovery Act of 1933* implemented their point of view.

When the Supreme Court* declared the National Industrial Recovery Act unconstitutional in 1935, destroying the National Recovery Administration,* the political philosophy behind the NRA still survived. Desperate to salvage their program, the planners called for a "Little NRA," a series of laws designed to preserve some semblance of industry-wide cooperation. Threatening a national strike of coal miners, John L. Lewis* of the United Mine Workers managed to push the Guffey-Snyder Act of 1935* through Congress. The bill protected collective bargaining, established uniform wage and hour scales, created a bituminous coal commission to set prices and control production, permitted the closing of marginally profitable mines, and imposed a tax on coal production to help retrain unemployed miners. Because of the wages and hours provisions, the Supreme Court outlawed the Guffey-Snyder Act in 1936, so Congress passed the Guffey-Vinson Act* in 1937, resurrecting all but the wages and hours titles of the earlier law. There were several other measures also associated with the "Little NRA." The Connally Act of 1935* outlawed the shipment of "hot oil" across state lines; the Robinson-Patman Act of 1936* prohibited manufacturers from giving discounts or rebates to large-volume buyers; the Walsh-Healey Public Contracts Act of 1936* required the federal government to insist on minimum labor standards in its contracts; and the Miller-Tydings Act of 1937* amended the Sherman Anti-trust Act of 1890 to permit "fair trade" laws. (William E. Leuchtenburg, *Franklin D. Roosevelt and the New Deal, 1932–1940*, 1963.)

LONDON ECONOMIC CONFERENCE OF 1933 Because of the troubled economies throughout the western world in 1931 and 1932, political leaders in the United States and Europe decided to convene a world economic conference in London in the late spring of 1933, where they hoped the United States, France, and England could stabilize their currencies and relieve pressure on the money markets. By March 1933 President Franklin D. Roosevelt* had tentatively accepted the proposal put forward by his adviser James Warburg:* France would accept inflationary open market operations; England would stabilize the pound; and the United States would restore a full gold standard. But the hopes were never realized, and the conference broke up in a storm of controversy. Late in March and early in April 1933, the inflationary bloc of western farming and mining interests in Congress began demanding inflation by expansion of the currency. The Thomas amendment to the Agricultural Adjustment Act* on April 20 did just that by providing for increased use of silver in the currency, and Roosevelt, to satisfy silver interests and to stop foreign attacks on the dollar, halted gold exports, which essentially was an abandonment of the gold standard.

When the world economic conference convened in London on June 12, 1933, a major battle erupted between the gold-bloc countries headed by France and those like England and the United States which had gone off the gold standard. As more and more world leaders talked of currency stabilization, Roosevelt began to fear the agreement would only retard his efforts to raise commodity prices. When commodity and securities prices dropped in mid-June, his fears were confirmed, and he vetoed the stabilization idea. With the conference in trouble, Roosevelt sent his adviser Raymond Moley* to London with a statement that the United States would do its best to cooperate with the other gold-bloc countries in working out a stabilization agreement. But on July 3, after Moley had released the statement, the president announced to the world that the United States would not cooperate in any "premature stabilization" agreements and accused European nations of trying to hurt his attempts to raise prices in the United States. The president's message was a "bombshell" and destroyed the conference, enraging European political leaders. Economic internationalism had given way to economic nationalism. (James R. Moore, "Sources of New Deal Economic Policy: The International Dimension," *Journal of American History*, LXI:728–744, 1974.)

LONG, HUEY PIERCE Huey Long was born on August 30, 1893, near Winnfield, Winn Parish, in northern Louisiana. His father was a modestly successful farmer who sent six of his ten children to college. The Long family had a reputation for being pious Baptists and political mavericks, which was hardly uncommon in Winn Parish. Opposed to the traditional Louisiana ruling class which resided in New Orleans, Winn Parish had supported Populist "radicals" and Eugene Debs. Huey Long loved to talk, serving on the Winnfield High School debate team and working as a travelling salesman before enrolling in the University of Oklahoma School of Law. He only spent a semester there but in 1915 passed a special bar examination after attending the Tulane University Law School for eight months. In 1914 Huey Long returned to Winnfield to practice law.

His ambition was boundless, and he was soon dissatisfied with the life of a smalltown, southern lawyer. In 1918 Long was elected to the state office of railroad commissioner. Although the title was changed in 1921 to public service commissioner, Huey was re-elected in 1924, and from 1921 to 1926 he served as chairman with considerable distinction. He earned a reputation as a defender of the common folk. It was also during these years that Long started to attack Standard Oil, insisting on the enactment of higher severance taxes. Long ran for governor for the first time in 1924, but his strength in the country districts was offset by his weakness in New Orleans. He ran again in 1928, and this time he won. Once governor, Long proceeded to consolidate his power. This was no easy task, for he was opposed by the Old Regular machine of New Orleans and by those who resisted his attempts to increase taxes on the oil interests. In 1929 these groups brought the governor up before the Louisiana House of Representatives on impeachment charges, but he escaped conviction. Thereafter his power in Louisiana was nearly absolute. Between 1930 and 1934 he made peace with the Old Regulars and dominated state politics. He built highways and bridges, started construction on a new capitol building, improved Louisiana State University, and strengthened elementary and secondary education.

In 1930 Long was elected to the United States Senate, but he refused to give up the governor's office and postponed taking the oath of office as a senator until 1932. He advocated the redistribution of wealth, but his fellow senators were frustrated by his efforts. In the national election of that year he supported the nomination of Franklin D. Roosevelt* and campaigned actively for the New York politician. His courting of Roosevelt was short and disappointing. Roosevelt rejected Long's redistribution ideas and failed to fund much patronage in his direction. By the late summer of 1933 Huey started his criticism of the president. In addition, around the same time Long split with the Old Regulars. In an effort to maintain his power base, Long reorganized the governmental structure of Louisiana. The legislature passed laws giving him control over the appointment of everything from policemen to school teachers. It was during this period that his critics claimed he was a dictator, and his power was virtually unchecked.

On the national level, he continued his attack on Roosevelt. In early 1934 he organized a Share-Our-Wealth* Society, advocating a minimum income and a decent standard of living for every American family. Using this program as a springboard, he announced in November 1935 his intention to run for president in 1936. Although few gave him any chance for success, his candidacy posed a serious threat to Roosevelt. In September 1935 he returned to Louisiana for a special session of the legislature. At the capitol on September 8, Dr. Carl Austin Weiss shot Long. Two days later the senator died. Gerald L. K. Smith,* a Long associate in the Share-Our-Wealth Society, tried to take over the organization; but he had no political base in Louisiana, and the group rapidly declined. By the summer of 1936 most of the Share-Our-Wealth clubs across the country had disbanded. Long's death ended the life of one of the most controversial figures in American politics in the 1930s. To call Long a fascist ignores his essential lack of ideology, just as to call him a buffoon fails to take into consideration his political genius. If he was occasionally dishonest and corrupt, he was also undoubtedly sincere in his championing of underdogs and his support of the state of Louisiana. (T. Harry Williams, *Huey Long*, 1969.)

RANDY ROBERTS

LORENTZ, PARE Born in 1905 in Clarkburg, West Virginia, Pare Lorentz began his career as a journalist and film critic, first in his native state, then in New York. His film criticism was nationally known, with articles appearing in such magazines as *Fortune* and *Harper's*. His belief in the potential of movies to treat American problems seriously, yet show some promise, is evident in his two books, *Censored: The Private Life of the Movies* (a collaboration with Morris Ernst, 1930), and *The Roosevelt Year: 1933* (1934), a survey of significant people, places, and problems, a book Lorentz hoped would forward the spirit of the New Deal.*

In 1935 Lorentz was hired by the Resettlement Administration* to produce a film on the Dust Bowl.* It was to be a "film of merit," of a quality that could compete with commercial Hollywood films. The result was "The Plow That Broke the Plains," written, directed, and edited by Lorentz. Shot on location across the Great Plains and into the Texas Panhandle, supported and advised by King Vidor and Dorothea Lange,* and improvised from a thin script, Lorentz captured the awful realities of drought, dust storms, and migrant poverty. The musical score by Virgil Thomson, beautifully counterpointing the narration read by Thomas Chalmers, largely accounts for the film's power. Although "The Plow" was sometimes labelled as propaganda for the New Deal, it was clearly an education for the public in the fragility of the plains ecology and the crushing effects of land abuse. To complete the film Lorentz surmounted enormous obstacles, including a small budget, a hostile commercial film industry, and bureaucratic snares. But from its first public showing in May 1936, it was acclaimed by reviewers and an enthusiastic public, and it has remained his best known film.

The two subsequent films and a radio broadcast filmscript Lorentz produced in the late 1930s were as meritorious as "The Plow" and, like the first film, they received a major endorsement from President Franklin D. Roosevelt.* "The River" was a compelling education in flood control. Its subject was the Mississippi River and its tributaries; its drama, the exploitation of the river valley by agriculture and industry and the resultant flooding, soil erosion, and cost to human life and welfare. The film's epilogue showed the beginning work of the TVA,* a glimpse of new horizons in government aid and engineering. During the filming, in January 1937, the unforeseen major flooding of the Ohio River devastated whole communities, a shocking but fortuitous event that gave Lorentz access to a realism in motion pictures that had no precedent. Virgil Thomson was again hired to compose the score. His blend of folksongs, hymns, and original composition was even more significant in establishing a film's mood and theme than was his score for "The Plow." Lorentz changed his own script to a lyrical narrative, using repetitions, lists, and other poetic devices to compliment the music. "The

River'' won many awards, was shown widely in Great Britain and Europe, and won first prize at the prestigious Venice Film Festival. When Roosevelt saw it at a private screening, he immediately acted to form the United States Film Service,* an agency designed to produce documentaries for both federal employees and the public, the goal being to focus on urgent social problems and to generate support for relief and planning agencies.

''The Fight for Life'' was a study of childbirth mortality and its relation to unemployment and slum conditions. First proposed to Lorentz by the president as part of his larger health care initiative and financed by the U. S. Film Service, it was photographed in the Chicago Maternity Center. Using monologues, death scenes, and long sequences in which the innovative score of Louis Gruensberg was the only comment on the action, the feature length movie was another triumph in social realism for Lorentz and his photographer Floyd Crosby. At the same time, Lorentz was trying to secure financing to complete ''Ecce Homo,'' a documentary on the displacement of men by machines. But in 1939 the U. S. Film Service was suddenly reorganized under the Federal Security Agency* and the Office of Education, after bi-partisan politics had prompted a congressional investigation into the agency's budget. Without film service funding and with the nation's attention increasingly diverted to the war in Europe, ''Ecce Homo'' was never completed.

Other achievements of Lorentz's include his initial work on ''The Power and the Land'' (1940), a film on rural electrification, and his production of ''The Nuremberg Trials'' (1946), made while he was chief of Motion Pictures, Music, and Theatre in the occupied areas of Germany, under the Civil Affairs Division of the War Department. In 1963 the secretary of agriculture awarded him a gold medal for ''The River.'' (Robert L. Snyder, *Pare Lorentz and the Documentary Film*, 1968.)

BARBARA M. TYSON

LOUISVILLE JOINT STOCK LAND BANK V. RADFORD In the early 1920s, William W. Radford, Sr., had twice mortgaged his farm in Kentucky to the Louisville Joint Stock Land Bank, the property serving as surety for the loans. In 1933 Radford defaulted on his payments and other obligations to the bank. When Radford failed to effect a composition of his debts, a state court entered judgment against him in June 1934, ordering foreclosure sale of his farm.

That same month, the Frazier-Lemke Act* was passed by Congress, amending the Federal Bankruptcy Act to protect bankrupt farmers from loss of their land by providing several alternative options with regard to the mortgaged property. One effect would have been to allow the bankrupt farmer to retain possession of his land for five years while provisions were made to satisfy his obligations. The bank, however, protested that the Frazier-Lemke Act was unconstitutional and refused to abide by its provisions. The federal district court overruled the bank's objections and upheld the validity of the Frazier-Lemke Act. When a referee appointed by the court ordered a course of action under the Frazier-

Lemke Act, the bank refused to comply. The case was appealed to the 6th Circuit Court in February 1935. The Circuit Court affirmed the decree of the district court, and upon petition by the bank, the Supreme Court* granted certiorari.

The case was argued on May 6, 1935, and decided on May 27, 1935, with Mr. Justice Louis Brandeis* writing for a unanimous Court. Justice Brandeis presented a detailed analysis of the effect which the Frazier-Lemke Act had on federal bankruptcy laws. He concluded that as applied in the Radford case, the Frazier-Lemke Act had indeed deprived the bank of its rights in specific property without compensation. Therefore, the Court ruled that the act was in violation of the Fifth Amendment and invalid. In response, Congress passed the Farm Mortgage Moratorium Act on August 29, 1935. (Alfred H. Kelly and Winfred A. Harbison, *The American Constitution*, 1970; *Supreme Court Reporter*, LV:854–869.)

JOSEPH M. ROWE, JR.

LUDLOW, LOUIS Louis Ludlow, prominent author and congressman, was born in southeastern Indiana on June 24, 1873. He began his career as an Indianapolis reporter in 1891 and in 1901 became a Washington correspondent for the *Indianapolis Sentinel*. Highly regarded by his fellow correspondents, he became president of the national press club in 1927. In the 1920s he wrote *From Cornfield to Press Gallery* (his autobiography), *In the Heart of Hoosierland*, and *Senator Soloman Spiffledink*. Elected as a Democrat to Congress in 1928, Ludlow represented Indianapolis for the next twenty years. In the 1930s he urged an isolationist policy abroad and at home deplored the growth of the executive branch of the government as evidenced by his book, *America Go Bust: An Exposé of the Federal Bureaucracy and Its Wasteful and Evil Tendencies* (1933).

During his first six years in Congress, Ludlow supported such liberal measures as a constitutional amendment for equal rights for women, anti-lynching legislation, and the establishment of a federal industrial commission to stabilize employment; but he opposed the repeal of Prohibition. In 1935 he attracted national attention for the first time with his war referendum amendment. The proposed amendment called for a nationwide vote prior to the declaration of war except in the event of an attack on or invasion of the United States. As soon as war was declared, the president should conscript all private and public war properties, supplies, and employees necessary for their operation. Wartime compensation for their use was not to exceed 4 percent of their pre-war tax valuation. Although hearings on the amendment were held before the House Judiciary Committee in June 1935, the amendment was not reported from committee. Ludlow solicited support through letters, radio addresses, congressional orations, newspaper and magazine articles, and a book, *Hell or Heaven* (1937), stressing the importance of the decision for war, the excessive influence exercised by the president over the foreign policy, and the lack of means to determine the popular will on the issue of war.

Although the Ludlow proposal received overwhelming popular support (in the mid-1930s, opinion polls showed as high as 75 percent of the public supported the referendum), newspapers and the administration argued that it would hamstring the conduct of foreign policy. Opposition increased in December 1937 when Ludlow received the signatures necessary to force consideration of the discharge petition.

Prior to consideration of the discharge petition, the amendment was redrafted to exclude the property confiscation provision and to make the war referendum unnecessary if an attack appeared imminent or if a non-American nation threatened to invade the western hemisphere. However, it was never considered by Congress; the discharge petition failed on January 10, 1938, by a vote of 188 to 209. Popular interest in the measure then declined rapidly as the threat of war in Europe increased. Ludlow took the lead in other measures to limit the chance of war, including arms limitation, a referendum on peacetime conscription, and a resolution to mediate the European conflict. After the war he urged an international war referendum, the ban of atomic weapons, and creation of a cabinet-level Department of Peace and Good Will. Ludlow died in Washington, D. C., on November 28, 1950, a year and a half after his retirement from Congress. (Walter R. Griffin, "Louis Ludlow and the War Referendum Crusade, 1935–1941," *Indiana Magazine of History*, LXIV:267–288, 1968.)

VIRGINIA F. HAUGHTON

LUNDEEN, ERNEST Ernest Lundeen was born near Beresford, South Dakota, on August 4, 1878. His undergraduate studies at Carleton College were interrupted by the Spanish-American War, when he served with the Twelfth Minnesota Volunteers. Lundeen returned to Carleton and graduated in 1901 and then took a law degree at the University of Minnesota. After practicing law in Minneapolis for several years, Lundeen won a seat in the state house of representatives and served as a Republican between 1910 and 1914. He won a seat in Congress in 1916 but failed his re-election bid in 1918 and returned to private law practice. Lundeen's progressive views on social welfare, corporate wealth, and the power of the federal government left him increasingly uncomfortable in the Republican party,* and early in the 1930s he found a home in the Farmer-Labor party* in Minnesota. Lundeen regained his congressional seat as a Farmer-Laborite in the election of 1932* and served two terms, during which he allied himself with the radical bloc of congressmen led by Thomas Amlie,* Vito Marcantonio,* and Maury Maverick.* Unlike the others, however, Lundeen had no real fears of the impact of Communist sympathies on American liberals and even respected some of their views about the confiscation of wealth. In 1936 Lundeen won a seat in the United States Senate on the Farmer-Labor ticket and continued to be a liberal and progressive force supporting and demanding more and more of the New Deal.* He died in an airplane crash on August 31, 1940. (*New York Times*, September 1, 1940.)

M

MACLEISH, ARCHIBALD Born in 1892 in Glencoe, Illinois, to a wealthy family (his father had amassed a fortune as a Chicago merchant), Archibald MacLeish attended Hotchkiss Preparatory School and then took his A. B. at Yale. After active duty with the U. S. Army in France during World War I, MacLeish earned a law degree from Harvard (with highest honors) and taught there for a year before accepting a position with a distinguished Boston law firm. In 1923 he and his family moved to France, where he spent the next six years studying and writing poetry. The verse he published during this period includes a pessimistic work, *The Hamlet of A. MacLeish* (1928) and a frequently anthologized statement of the art-for-art's sake credo, the short poem ''Ars Poetica'' (1926).

Returning to America in 1928, MacLeish moved to the Berkshire farm in Conway, Massachusetts, that he would call home for the rest of his life. While serving on the editorial board of *Fortune* Magazine, a position he accepted in 1930, he won his first Pulitzer Prize for *Conquistador* (1932), a long poem about Cortez's subjugation of Mexico. *Frescoes for Mr. Rockefeller's City* (1933) celebrates vigorous working Americans while satirizing both capitalists and doctrinaire radicals.

MacLeish's enthusiastic support of Franklin D. Roosevelt* and the New Deal* brought him into public life when he became librarian of Congress in 1939. During the five years he held that position he also wrote speeches for Roosevelt and served as director of the Office of Facts and Figures and assistant director of the Office of War Information. He also argued eloquently in *America Was Promises* (1939) and *The Irresponsibles* (1940) for artists and intellectuals to descend from their ivory towers and defend democracy against the encroachments of fascism. From 1944 to 1945 MacLeish was assistant secretary of state, charged with the task of helping establish the United Nations Educational, Scientific, and Cultural Organization.

After 1949, when he left government service to become Boylston Professor at Harvard—an appointment he retained until 1962—MacLeish continued to write poetry and verse drama and to collect literary awards and other honors.

His *Collected Poems 1917–1952* (1952) brought him a second Pulitzer Prize for Poetry, a Bollingen Prize, and a National Book Award. He became president of the American Academy of Arts and Letters in 1953 and was awarded honorary degrees by Columbia and Harvard Universities in 1954 and 1955, respectively. But MacLeish also continued to address contemporary problems. In *The Trojan Horse* (1952) he warned against the main danger of the witch-hunting tactics of Senator Joseph McCarthy: bringing about our own destruction by adopting the tactics of the enemy. In the poetic drama *J. B.* (1958), a modern rendition of the biblical story of Job, he explores the conundrum of pointless suffering in an absurd world. *J. B.* ran on Broadway and brought MacLeish his third Pulitzer Prize. Among his last works were *An Evening's Journey to Conway, Massachusetts*, a play he wrote in 1967 for the bicentennial of the town he had lived in for many years, and *Scratch* (1971), a play based on the tale of the devil and Daniel Webster. MacLeish died on April 20, 1982, two and one-half weeks shy of his ninetieth birthday.

Early in his literary career, Archibald MacLeish decided that men of letters should bring their learning into the arena of public affairs. Always a realist mindful of the dangers threatening freedom in the twentieth century, he nonetheless maintained the optimistic conviction that an intellectual activist could make a significant contribution to the defense of liberty and the humanitarian tradition. His myriad of literary expressions attest to his persistent faith in liberal democracy and make him indeed deserving of the title occasionally bestowed informally upon him: ''Poet Laureate of the New Deal.'' (Signi L. Falk, *Archibald MacLeish*, 1965; William MacLeish, ''The Silver Whistler,'' *Smithsonian*, XIV:54–65, 1983.)

DONALD V. COERS

MADDEN, JOSEPH WARREN Joseph Warren Madden was born in Damascus, Illinois, on January 17, 1890. He graduated from the University of Illinois in 1911 and then took a law degree at the University of Chicago in 1914. Madden spent the next two years as a professor of law at the University of Oklahoma, practiced law privately in Rockford, Illinois, between 1916 and 1917, and then joined the law faculty at Ohio State University. He became dean of the law college at West Virginia University in 1921 and then professor of law at the University of Pittsburgh in 1927. Madden went on leave from the University of Pittsburgh in 1935 to become chairman of the National Labor Relations Board.* He stayed with the NLRB until 1940, and under his leadership the board vigorously attacked unfair labor practices. Madden also successfully defended the board against bitter attack from manufacturers' trade groups, the conservative press, and the American Federation of Labor,* which viewed the NLRB as a tool of the newly-established CIO.* In 1941 President Franklin D. Roosevelt* named Madden to the U. S. Court of Claims in Washington, D. C., a position he held until 1961. Madden then served on the Ninth Circuit Court of Appeals until his retirement in 1972. He died on February 17, 1972. (James A. Gross, *The Making of the NLRB: A Study in Economics, Politics, and the Law*, 1974; *Who Was Who in America*, V:452, 1973.)

MARCANTONIO, VITO Vito Marcantonio was born on December 10, 1902, in New York City. He graduated from the NYU Law School in 1925 and began practicing law in the city. Marcantonio became assistant United States district attorney in 1930 and 1931. He was elected as a Republican to Congress in 1934, lost his seat in 1936, and then won another congressional seat in 1938 on the American Labor party* ticket. Marcantonio then stayed in Congress for six terms, losing his seat again in the election of 1950. A protégé of Fiorello La Guardia,* Marcantonio allied himself in the House of Representatives with the small group of perhaps thirty congressmen who desperately wanted the New Deal* to use the federal government to reshape the American social and economic order. Along with people like Maury Maverick* of Texas and Ernest Lundeen* of Minnesota, Marcantonio advocated a radical approach to the Great Depression—one involving large-scale social welfare legislation, massive regulation of corporate power, and confiscation of "excess" wealth. To Marcantonio and his associates, the New Deal was "too little, too late," and he constantly called for a more drastic approach to the economy. In July 1935, at a Chicago meeting of the Farmer-Labor Political Confederation, Marcantonio left the meeting when his associates tried to exclude Communists from a proposed new political party. His unwillingness to denounce and exclude Communists made his existence in the Republican party* tenuous. He lost the general election of 1936.* Only by affiliating himself with the American Labor party in New York did he regain that seat. After his defeat in the election of 1950, Marcantonio practiced law privately until his death on August 9, 1954. (Salvatore J. LaGumina, *Vito Marcantonio: The People's Politician*, 1969.)

MARGOLD, NATHAN Nathan Margold was born on July 21, 1899, in Jassi, Romania, and immigrated to the United States with his parents in 1901. He graduated from the City College of New York in 1919 and from the Harvard Law School in 1923. Margold began practicing law in New York City in 1923 and in 1925 became an assistant United States attorney for the Southern District of New York. He taught law at Harvard in 1927 and 1928, was special counsel for the New York Transit Commission in 1928 and 1929, was legal adviser on Indian affairs with the Institute for Government Research in 1930, and from 1930 to 1933 was special counsel for the NAACP.* Margold was Harold L. Ickes'* choice for solicitor in the Department of Interior, a position Margold accepted in 1933. After the National Recovery Administration* had developed the code for the petroleum industry, Ickes established a Petroleum Administrative Board* and later a Petroleum Labor Policy Board* to administer the code. He named Margold chairman of both agencies. Margold served on the Petroleum Administrative Board until January 1935 when the Supreme Court,* in the

*Panama Refining Company v. Ryan** case, declared Section 9(c) of the National Industrial Recovery Act,* which delegated petroleum code-making authority to the president, unconstitutional. Margold then remained a solicitor for the Department of Interior until 1942, when he became judge of the Municipal Court of the District of Columbia. Nathan Margold died on December 16, 1947. (Peter H. Irons, *The New Deal Lawyers*, 1982; *Who Was Who In America*, II:345, 1950.)

MARITIME LABOR BOARD (See U. S. MARITIME COMMISSION.)

MARTIN, JOSEPH WILLIAM, JR. Joseph William Martin, Jr., was born on November 3, 1884, in North Attleboro, Massachusetts. He graduated from high school in 1902 and went to work for the *North Attleboro Sun* and the *Providence Journal*. In 1908 Martin joined nine businessmen, each contributing $1,000, to buy the *North Attleboro Evening Chronicle*. He became manager of the paper and eventually purchased controlling interest in it. Newspaper work frequently drew him into local politics, and in 1911 he won a seat in the state legislature. He returned to private life in 1917 but remained chairman of the Massachusetts Republican Legislative Campaign Committee. Martin ran for Congress in 1924 against incumbent William S. Greene and lost. But six months later Greene died, and Martin won the special election by over 9,000 votes. He supported Nicholas Longworth for Speaker of the House in 1925 and also became friends with John Nance Garner,* the Democrat who became Speaker in 1931. Although he personally liked President Franklin D. Roosevelt,* Martin opposed many New Deal* programs. He supported most relief measures, but fought the Agricultural Adjustment Act,* Reciprocal Trade Agreements Act,* wages-and-hours bills, the Tennessee Valley Authority,* and several government tax measures. In Martin's view, the huge federal expenditures of the New Deal undermined local political sovereignty and centralized too much power in Washington, D. C. He became Speaker of the House in 1947, a position he held periodically whenever Republicans controlled the House until 1959 when his congressional colleagues relieved him of the position. Martin died on March 7, 1968. (Joe William Martin, *My First Fifty Years in Politics*, 1960.)

MAVERICK, FONTAINE MAURY Maury Maverick, a radical Texas congressman during the 1930s, was born in San Antonio, Texas, on October 23, 1895. He attended the Virginia Military Institute and the University of Texas Law School and was admitted to the Texas bar in 1916. Maverick's budding legal career was postponed by World War I; he served in the American Expeditionary Force in Europe and was wounded in action. When he returned to Texas in 1919, Maverick entered the housing, real estate, and mortgage business; and in 1929 he became tax collector for Bexar County, Texas. In 1934 Maverick ran for Congress on a progressive, neo-populist platform, and he served in the House of Representatives for two terms. Raised on a diet of left-wing politics and a familiarity with socialism, Maverick had a powerful sympathy for the poverty and suffering of Mexican workers in the valley of south Texas. At the same time, his liberalism and radicalism had a pragmatic tone, and he greatly admired the work of Robert La Follette, Jr.* and George Norris.* In the Congress, Maverick became allied with the small group of liberal Democrats and progressive Republicans—people like Thomas Amlie* of Wisconsin and Ernest Lundeen* of Minnesota—who supported the New Deal* even while demanding more social welfare, higher labor standards, increased work relief, and national economic planning. Maverick's brand of liberal politics was well-defined, for he loathed and ridiculed doctrinaire Communists as hopelessly ill-suited to American life. Maverick lost his seat in Congress in the election of 1938* and returned to San Antonio, where he was elected mayor in 1939. His term as mayor of San Antonio came to an end in 1941, and he returned to Washington, D. C., when President Franklin D. Roosevelt* appointed him vice-chairman of the War Production Board. Eventually he served as chairman of the Smaller War Plants Corporation. In 1946 Maverick returned to San Antonio to practice law, and he died there on June 7, 1954. (Richard B. Henderson, *Maury Maverick, A Political Biography*, 1970.)

McADOO, WILLIAM GIBBS William Gibbs McAdoo, Democratic party* leader and Woodrow Wilson's secretary of the treasury, was born near Marietta, Georgia, on October 31, 1863. He was the son of William Gibbs and Mary Faith (Floyd) McAdoo. The father, a lawyer who was ruined financially by the Civil War, moved the family to Tennessee, where in 1877 he became adjunct professor of english and history at the University of Tennessee. Young McAdoo attended the university from 1879 to 1882 but withdrew in his junior year to take a deputy clerkship in the federal circuit court at Chattanooga. After studying law at night, he was admitted to the bar in 1885. In November of that year he married Sara Houstoun Fleming. In 1892 he moved to New York, where his law practice did not thrive. It was as a tunnel builder rather than as a lawyer that McAdoo gained fame and prosperity. He organized the Hudson and Manhattan Railroad Company, enlisted the aid of New York bankers, and in March 1904 completed the first tunnel under the Hudson River.

A few years later, McAdoo became active in the Democratic party and in 1912 was a delegate to the party convention in Baltimore, where he worked energetically for Woodrow Wilson's nomination. During the 1912 campaign, he assumed the duties of William F. McCombs, Wilson's ailing campaign manager. Thus, McAdoo, with financial experience but no close ties with Wall Street, was a logical choice as Wilson's secretary of the treasury. He quickly became known as one of the most influential members of the cabinet. In May 1914 McAdoo, a widower since 1912, married Eleanor Randolph Wilson, the president's daughter. During his six years in the cabinet, McAdoo helped plan the Federal Reserve Act of 1913, served as chairman of the Federal Reserve Board,* the Federal Farm Loan Board, the War Finance Corporation, and as director of the nation's railroads during the war. By 1919, when he resigned to take a much-needed rest, he had raised for the government $43 billion—more than all previous administrations combined.

At the Democratic convention in 1920, McAdoo, as Woodrow Wilson's son-in-law (the "Crown Prince"), was considered by many as the president's rightful political heir; but Wilson refused to endorse him, and McAdoo did not seek the nomination with his customary vigor. In 1924, however, he made a strong bid for the nomination, only to become deadlocked with Governor Al Smith* at the Democratic convention in New York. John W. Davis* was chosen as the compromise candidate. McAdoo, now sixty-one, realized that his presidential hopes were gone and returned to Los Angeles, where he had resided since 1922.

His influence within the party remained strong, however, and in 1932, as head of the California delegation at the Democratic convention in Chicago, he helped make the momentous decision to switch California's support from John N. Garner* to Franklin D. Roosevelt,* in exchange for a Roosevelt-Garner ticket. That same year he benefitted from the Roosevelt landslide by winning election as senator from California. McAdoo became a loyal supporter of President Roosevelt. He favored federal insurance of bank deposits and, ironically for a former "dry," voted for repeal of Prohibition; but illness frequently kept him away from the Senate during votes on important New Deal* measures. He was defeated for re-nomination in 1938 by Sheridan Downey, who ran on an old-age pension ("Thirty Dollars Every Thursday") slogan. McAdoo died of a heart attack at his apartment at the Shoreham Hotel in Washington, D.C., on February 1, 1941; and as a member of Woodrow Wilson's War Cabinet, he qualified for burial at Arlington National Cemetery. (Otis L. Graham, Jr., "William Gibbs McAdoo," in *Dictionary of American Biography*; *New York Times*, February 2, 1941; *Who Was Who in America*, Vo. 21, 1940.)

JOHN PAYNE

McCARRAN, PATRICK ANTHONY Patrick A. McCarran was a four-term Democratic senator from Nevada. The only child of Irish immigrants, McCarran was born near Reno on August 8, 1876, and spent his entire career, prior to election to the Senate, in Nevada. McCarran attended the University of Nevada in Reno for three years but had to quit to help his father on the family ranch. He married a school teacher, Martha H. Weeks, in 1903 and they had five children. Although he continued farming and sheep ranching, McCarran studied law on his own and was admitted to the Nevada bar in 1905.

According to McCarran, his parents instilled in him a love of politics, and he began his political career by being elected to the Nevada legislature in 1902. McCarran was elected to the Nevada Supreme Court and served from 1913–1918. As a justice, he made significant decisions on mining and irrigation law and supported social legislation. McCarran wanted to serve in the United States Senate and tried unsuccessfully in both in 1916 and 1926. However, in 1932, he made it on Franklin D. Roosevelt's* landslide. In reality, McCarran was only a nominal Democrat. He never wore the party harness comfortably and broke with the president on numerous issues. Indeed, by 1935 McCarran was part of the bi-partisan conservative coalition that opposed much New Deal* legislation. An opponent of "court-packing",* the NRA,* the TVA,* and the NYA,* McCarran was at odds with administrative supporters continually. Although neither Roosevelt nor Harry S Truman* ever endorsed him, McCarran won re-election in 1938, 1944, and 1950.

McCarran gained considerable notoriety as an American nativist. During the years immediately following World War II, McCarran's virulent anti-communism came to the fore. As a member of the "China Lobby," McCarran fought for additional aid for National China in 1949. When Mao Tse-tung and the Communists won control of the mainland, McCarran charged Truman with abandoning the Chinese. In 1950 he sponsored the Internal Security Act, a repressive law aimed at Communists and their organizations. All Communists had to register, and persons could be detained if it was believed that they might commit espionage or sabotage. Consequently, McCarran generally supported Senator Joseph McCarthy's attacks upon alleged Communists and was opposed to the move to censure the Wisconsin senator. McCarran also battled Truman over immigration laws, and the Nevada senator was successful in obtaining passage of the Immigration and Nationality Act of 1952, which retained the pro-northern and western European bias. McCarran died on September 28, 1954. (Jerome E. Edwards, *Pat McCarran: Political Boss of Nevada*, 1982.)

F. ROSS PETERSON

McCORMACK-DICKSTEIN COMMITTEE Because of a rising fear of American fascist organizations, the House of Representatives launched a special investigation into "un-American" activities in March 1934. Lead by John W. McCormack* of Massachusetts and Samuel Dickstein* of New York, the committee investigated a wide range of radical organizations, including the Silver Shirts,* Khaki Shirts,* Sentinels of the Republic,* American Communist party,* and Crusaders for Economic Liberty.* Although the Committee studiously took pains to respect civil rights and avoid hearsay, it eventually became the House Un-American Activities Committee in 1938 under the chairmanship of Martin Dies* of Texas. By then the menace of fascism seemed even more real and the committee's tactics deteriorated. By the 1950s many liberals viewed HUAC as the symbol of government indifference to civil liberties. (August R. Ogden, *The Dies Committee*, 1945.)

McCORMACK, JOHN WILLIAM John W. McCormack was born in Boston, Massachusetts, on December 21, 1891. He studied law in a private office and was admitted to the bar in 1913. McCormack served in the army during World War I, returned home to his law practice, and then won a seat in the state legislature in 1920. In 1922 he won election to the state senate, where he served as Democratic floor leader in 1925 and 1926. Carrying the Irish Democratic background of his ancestors, McCormack was elected to the House of Representatives in 1928 to fill the seat vacated by the death of James A. Gallivan. He served continuously between 1928 and 1971, becoming one of the most senior and experienced congressmen in United States history. During the 1930s, McCormack headed the special House committee investigating "un-American" activities. He managed to conduct the investigations of the McCormack-Dickstein Committee* efficiently without violating civil liberties. Although generally supportive of New Deal* legislation, McCormack resisted and successfully led the House movement to eliminate the "third-basket" tax from revenue legislation in 1938. By 1940 McCormack was rising rapidly through the ranks of House leadership. He served as majority floor leader from 1940 to 1947, 1949 to 1953, and 1955 to 1961; minority whip from 1947 to 1949 and 1953 to 1955; and Speaker of the House from 1962 to 1970. He retired from the House in 1970 and died on November 22, 1980. (*New York Times*, November 23, 1980.)

McDONALD, STEWART Steward McDonald, head of the Federal Housing Administration* between 1935 and 1940, was born in Owatonna, Minnesota, in 1879. He attended the University of Notre Dame and then graduated with a master's degree in engineering from Cornell University in 1901. McDonald moved to St. Louis, Missouri, and with an investment of $17,000 established the Moon Motor Company, a manufacturer of automobiles, farm implements, and electrical systems. He was known as a conservative Democrat, served briefly as police commissioner of St. Louis, and worked on the boards of directors of several banks and building and loan associations. When James Moffett* left the FHA in 1935, President Franklin D. Roosevelt* asked McDonald to replace him. The president was also interested in going beyond Moffett's distaste for federal housing projects; and McDonald led the FHA in a new direction, one which emphasized home improvements, new home financing, and some low-cost housing. After the administrative Reorganization Act of 1939* had created a new Federal Loan Agency* and President Roosevelt had named Jesse Jones* to head it, Jones picked McDonald to serve as deputy federal loan administrator. After the war, McDonald returned to private life, continuing to serve on the boards of a number of banks, railroads, and insurance companies. He died on January 4, 1957. (*New York Times*, January 5, 1957.)

McENTEE, JAMES JOSEPH James Joseph McEntee was born September 19, 1884, in Jersey City, New Jersey. He began work as a machinist in 1902 and rose through the ranks of the International Association of Machinists in New Jersey. During World War I, President Woodrow Wilson appointed McEntee to a New York arbitration board designed to resolve maritime disputes. While serving there, McEntee met Franklin D. Roosevelt,* then assistant secretary of the navy. In 1933 President Roosevelt named McEntee executive assistant to Robert Fechner,* director of the Civilian Conservation Corps.* After Fechner's death, McEntee became acting director of the CCC and then director in 1940.

He served there until the CCC was dissolved in 1942. As director, McEntee viewed the CCC as an employment agency and resisted all attempts to transform it into a military training program for young men. When he died on October 15, 1957, McEntee was serving as vice-president of the New Jersey Council of Machinists and a delegate to the New Jersey Federation of Labor. (*New York Times*, October 16, 1957.)

McINTIRE, ROSS T. Ross T. McIntire was born in Salem, Oregon, in 1889 and received his medical degree from Willamette University in 1912. He practiced medicine privately in Salem until 1917, when he entered the U. S. Navy Medical Corps. In the summer of 1921, McIntire became head of the eye, ear, nose, and throat department at the San Diego Naval Hospital. He was promoted to lieutenant commander in 1924 and began temporary White House duty in March 1933. He accompanied President Franklin D. Roosevelt* on a trip to Panama and Hawaii in June 1934 and quickly gained the president's confidence. McIntire became Roosevelt's personal physician in February 1935 and kept that position until the president's death in 1945. Roosevelt appointed him surgeon general of the navy in December 1938, where he remained until 1947, attaining the rank of vice-admiral. After his retirement, McIntire headed up the American Red Cross's annual blood donor drive and in 1955 became head of the International College of Surgeons. Ross McIntire died on December 8, 1959. (*New York Times*, December 9, 1959.)

McINTYRE, MARVIN HUNTER Marvin H. McIntyre was born November 27, 1878, in La Grange, Kentucky. He attended Vanderbilt University for a short time then went to work for several railroads in the public relations field between 1901 and 1908. He left public relations with the railroads in 1908 and began to work for several newspapers; and in 1918 he became special assistant to the secretary of the navy. While with the Navy Department McIntyre specialized in public relations work and met Franklin D. Roosevelt,* then the assistant secretary of the navy. He left the federal government in 1922 to become the east coast representative for several motion picture newsreel companies. McIntyre had been impressed with Roosevelt from their first meeting, and during the 1932 presidential campaign, he served as business manager and publicity representative. The president-elect then made McIntyre his personal secretary. McIntyre stayed in that position until his death on December 13, 1943. (*Who Was Who in America*, II:361, 1963.)

McMILLIN, LUCILLE FOSTER Born in Tennessee in 1870, Lucille Foster married Congressman Benton McMillin and supported his political career by serving as his hostess during his years in Congress and between 1899 and 1903 when he served as governor of Tennessee. In 1913 President Woodrow Wilson appointed Benton McMillin ambassador to Peru, and they lived there until 1922. After their return, Lucille McMillin began her political career, serving as the national committeewoman from Tennessee for the Democratic National Committee and as regional director of women in the southern states. She was also active in the League of Women Voters. Her husband died in 1933, and she then was appointed to the United States Civil Service Commission, where she served until her death in 1949. (Susan Ware, *Beyond Suffrage: Women in the New Deal*, 1981.)

McNARY, CHARLES LINZA Born on June 12, 1874, near Salem, Oregon, Charles Linza McNary was raised in a large, farm family until his parents died during his early teens and he left to live with an older sister. He attended Stanford University from 1896 to 1898. Too poor to finish, McNary returned to Salem in 1898, studied law privately, and served a two-year term on the state supreme court between 1913 and 1915. He became chairman of the Oregon Republican State Committee in 1916, and in 1917 he was appointed to complete the unexpired term of Senator Harry Lane. McNary was re-elected to full terms in 1918, 1924, 1930, 1936, and 1942. In 1926 he became chairman of the Senate Agriculture Committee and during the 1920s sponsored the unsuccessful McNary-Haugen Bill to dump American farm surpluses abroad after the federal government had purchased them from farmers. A leading liberal Republican in the Senate, McNary was still not perceived as an insurgent progressive. He was considered a pragmatic Republican, supporting the National Industrial Recovery Act* and the Agricultural Adjustment Act* but opposing the Reciprocal Tráde Agreements Act,* Franklin D. Roosevelt's* gold-buying* scheme, and wages-and-hours legislation for labor. He occupied a middle-of-the-road position among Senate Republicans, negotiating compromises between the old guard and the progressives. In 1940 Wendell Willkie* selected McNary to run as vice-president on the Republican ticket. Charles McNary died on February 25, 1944. (Ronald L. Feinman, *Twilight of Progressivism: The Western Republican Senators and the New Deal*, 1981; Ronald A. Mulder, *The Insurgent Progressives in the United States Senate and New Deal*, 1979; *New York Times*, February 26, 1944.)

McNUTT, PAUL VORIES Born on July 19, 1891, in Franklin, Indiana, Paul V. McNutt graduated from Indiana University in 1913 and the Harvard Law School in 1916. He taught at the Indiana University Law School from 1917 to 1925, except for service in the army during World War I, and became dean of the law school in 1925. An active Democrat, he became national commander of the American Legion in 1928 and was elected governor of Indiana in the election of 1932.* McNutt was governor of Indiana from 1933 to 1937 and accumulated a reputation as a reformer, particularly in government reorganization after he reduced state government from 169 to eight departments. Between 1937 and 1939 McNutt served as U. S. High Commissioner to the Philippines, and in 1939 President Franklin D. Roosevelt* named him to head the newly-created Federal Security Agency.* He served there until 1942 when Roosevelt put him in charge of the War Manpower Commission. McNutt had serious presidential ambitions, especially in 1940 when he anticipated Roosevelt's retirement. ''McNutt for President'' clubs sprang up early in 1940 but quickly died out after the president announced his intentions to serve a third term. Paul McNutt returned to the Philippines as high commissioner in 1945 and became the first ambassador to the Philippines in 1946. He died March 24, 1955. (I. George Blake, *Paul V. McNutt: Portrait of a Hooiser Statesman*, 1966.)

McREYNOLDS, JAMES CLARK James C. McReynolds, conservative justice of the Supreme Court* during the New Deal,* was born in Elkton, Kentucky, on February 3, 1862. The son of Dr. John O. McReynolds and Ellen Reeves, he was raised in the highly individualistic tradition of his Scots-Irish forebearers. McReynolds also carried throughout his life the suspicions of external institutions—economic or political—so common to southern Democracy. He graduated from Vanderbilt University in 1882 and from the law department of the University of Virginia in 1884. McReynolds practiced law in Nashville, Tennessee, for many years, serving for a while as secretary to United States Senator Howell E. Jackson, who later ascended to the Supreme Court. In 1903 Attorney General Philander C. Knox appointed McReynolds as an assistant attorney general of the United States, and for four years he vigorously prosecuted anti-trust cases under the Sherman Act. McReynolds returned to private law practice for a short time until President William Howard Taft recalled him to the Justice Department to preside over the dissolution of the tobacco and anthracite trusts. President Woodrow Wilson then named McReynolds to his cabinet as attorney general in 1913, where he continued to earn his reputation as a trustbuster. At that point in his career, McReynolds was considered by many to be an extreme progressive, even a radical. Wilson had great confidence in him, and appointed him an associate justice of the Supreme Court in 1914.

By the time of the 1930s, despite his early reputation as a progressive trustbuster, James McReynolds had become one of the most conservative justices on the Supreme Court. But times had changed, not the justice. Ever since his young adulthood he had believed passionately in states' rights, and he therefore approached the Tenth Amendment from the position of a southerner. The amendment specifically reserved to states all powers not clearly designated for the central government. McReynolds was suspicious of any distant, concentrated forms of power—political or economic—which limited individual and local freedom. Given that perspective, he looked at a powerful central government with the same distrust with which he had earlier viewed corporate trusts. McReynolds also believed strongly in his concept of a ''written constitution'' which did not change with the social and political wind. Sociological jurisprudence, for him, was simply a rationale for accepting unconstitutional changes in American life.

During the early years of the New Deal, McReynolds often found himself in the conservative majority along with Chief Justice Charles Evans Hughes* and Justices Owen Roberts,* George Sutherland,* Pierce Butler,* and Willis Van Devanter.* And McReynolds was the most conservative of the conservatives.

In *Norman v. Baltimore & Ohio Railroad* (Gold Cases), when the court upheld the government's decision not to enforce gold payments of private bond contracts, McReynolds dissented, arguing that the decision violated the contract clause and was the "end of the Constitution." He similarly opposed the TVA,* AAA,* NRA,* Social Security Act,* and NIRA* as actions clearly out of line with the constitutional powers of the federal government.

During the "court-packing"* controversy of 1937, McReynolds spoke out publicly against President Franklin D. Roosevelt,* and he was furious when Chief Justice Charles Evans Hughes and Justice Owen Roberts began switching their votes to line up with Justices Louis Brandeis,* Benjamin Cardozo,* and Harlan Fiske Stone* during the controversy. In his view, they were simply pandering to political pressure and destroying the independence of the Court in the process. McReynolds grew increasingly bitter in his later years as he was isolated, by Roosevelt's later appointments, into a minority of one on the Supreme Court. He would hardly speak to Brandeis, whom he considered a hopeless radical, and refused to participate in the Washington social circle. He retired from the Supreme Court on February 1, 1941, and died on August 24, 1946. (Alpheus Thomas Mason, *The Supreme Court from Taft to Warren*, 1958; *New York Times*, August 26, 1946.)

MEANS, GARDINER COIT Gardiner C. Means was born in Windham, Connecticut, on June 8, 1896. Means was passionately interested in economics, and he took all of his degrees at Harvard— A. B., 1918; A. M., 1927; Ph.D., 1933. He served in the infantry during 1917 and then as an army aviator in 1918 and 1919. During graduate school, Means focused his attention on the corporate economy, and published *The Holding Company* in 1932. He made his intellectual mark, however, in a book he co-authored in 1932 with Adolph Berle*—*The Modern Corporation and Private Property*—in which he argued that American economic life was controlled by about 2,000 people actively directing the largest 600 corporations. Rather than an economic aberration, monopoly had become the rule, and the market system of classical economics no longer existed. Competition was gone, so prices did not have to respond to market conditions. Means and Berle, therefore, advocated increased cooperation between government and business, marked by federal spending to supplement consumer demand; regulation of the stock markets; centralization of the banking system; federal regulation of concentrated industries, not in any anti-trust crusade but only to guarantee social and economic responsibility; and health, old-age, and unemployment insurance. The book was one of the most influential of the 1930s. Because of his work at Columbia University in the 1920s, Means became an economic adviser to Secretary of Agriculture Henry A. Wallace* between 1933 and 1935 as well as a member of the Consumer's Advisory Board* of the National Recovery Administration.* Between 1935 and 1939 Means served as director of the Industrial Section of the National Resources Committee* and from 1939 to 1940 as an economic adviser to the National Resources Planning Board.* Means also continued his prolific writing career, including *The Modern Economy in Action* (1936), *The Structure of the Modern Economy* (1939), *Jobs and Markets* (1946), *Pricing Power and the Public Interest* (1962), and *The Corporate Revolution in America* (1962). (*Who's Who In America,* II:2142, 1976–1977.)

"MEMORIAL DAY MASSACRE" (See GIRDLER, TOM MERCER.)

MENCKEN, HENRY LOUIS H. L. Mencken, the iconoclast journalist and social critic, was born in Baltimore, Maryland, on September 12, 1880. He graduated from the Polytechnic Institute and immediately went into newspaper work, serving as police reporter and then city editor of the *Baltimore Morning Herald* until 1906 and then joining the staff of the *Baltimore Sun*. During the 1920s, Mencken's cynicism about American materialism made him enormously popular in literary circles, and he played an important role in boosting the careers of people like Theodore Dreiser, D. H. Lawrence, and Sherwood Anderson. Mencken served as the editor of the *American Mercury* between 1925 and 1933. During the 1930s and World War II, when his debunking cynicism no longer seemed appropriate, Mencken lost some of his popularity. He became particularly critical of Franklin D. Roosevelt* and the New Deal,* describing them as "the sorriest mob of mountebanks ever gathered together at one time, even in Washington . . . vapid young pedagogues, out-of-work YMCA secretaries, third-rate journalists, briefless lawyers, and soaring chicken farmers." In return, the president was quite critical of Mencken, even satirically roasting him publicly on a number of occasions. H. L. Mencken died on January 29, 1956. (William Manchester, *Disturber of the Peace*, 1951.)

MERCHANT MARINE ACT OF 1936 Ever since the Civil War, the United States merchant marine had declined as trade fled to cheaper foreign vessels. World War I helped the service as it forged a firm link between national defense, trade, and the merchant marine. After the war, however, the older trend reasserted itself, and despite the Jones Act of 1920 and the Merchant Marine Act of 1928, the service continued to lose volume to foreign shippers. When Franklin D. Roosevelt* took office, he made it clear that he favored a strong American merchant marine and a policy which would protect United States foreign commerce from the peacetime ravages of foreign-dominated shipping combines; permit the continuance of trade in the event of foreign wars, and provide the necessary national defense tonnage if the United States became involved in a war. Congress then determined the significant needs of shippers, shipowners, shipbuilders, and manufacturers as well as questions concerning the ownership, operation, and size of government-assisted vessels. Debate raged for fifteen months before Congress passed the Merchant Marine Act of 1936.

The Merchant Marine Act of 1936 recognized that there was a discrepancy between foreign-flag operating and shipbuilding costs and American-flag operating and shipbuilding costs and provided for "parity" in the form of direct subsidies for United States shipbuilding and United States flag vessels on essential foreign trade routes. The subsidies would cover the differentials between foreign and domestic costs and make the United States merchant marine competitive. The act also authorized the government to build ships and charter them to shipping concerns for use on essential trade routes; required subsidized lines to establish special funds for ship replacement; provided subsidy support through guaranteed mortgage loans; gave the government new responsibilities to oversee living and working conditions, manning levels, and citizenship requirements on subsidized ships; authorized a training program for American seamen; encouraged American shippers to patronize domestically-chartered vessels; and established the U. S. Maritime Commission* as a quasi-judicial, independent regulatory agency to implement the act.

The Merchant Marine Act of 1936 was basically designed to enable American shipowners and shipbuilders to compete on an equal basis with the foreign industry and to provide for national defense shipping needs. It was landmark legislation which had a fundamental impact on all subsequent maritime programs. Critics pointed out that the act failed to reconcile the debate over whether to have public or private ownership of the merchant fleet. Instead, the act was a compromise which provided a measure of protection to the privately-owned shipping lines through the parity approach. Although committed to the welfare of the shipping companies, the government did not guarantee return on investments nor exclusivity of routes to shipping companies. Other critics also argued that the parity payments excused inefficiency in the United States merchant fleet and destroyed incentives to be more competitive. (Samuel A. Lawrence, *United States Merchant Shipping Policies and Politics,* 1966; Gerard J. Mangione, *Marine Policy for America*, 1977.)

DONALD H. DYAL

MERRIAM, CHARLES EDWARD A prominent social scientist of the 1920s and 1930s, Charles E. Merriam was born on November 15, 1874, in Hopkinton, Iowa. He graduated from Lennox College in 1893, studied law for a year at Iowa State University, and then took a doctorate in political science at Columbia University in 1900. Merriam became the first political scientist at the new University of Chicago and stayed there until 1941. Between 1904 and 1919, he was a progressive Republican alderman in Chicago and he served as a city councilman between 1909–1911 and 1913–1917. He concentrated on promoting business-like efficiency in city government. In 1923, with the help of Beardsley Ruml* of the Laura Spelman Rockefeller Memorial, Merriam proved instrumental in founding the Social Science Research Council, an umbrella organization of academics, government officials, and philanthropic managers. He headed the SSRC between 1923 and 1927 and worked to create what became the President's Research Committee on Social Trends (1929–1933). Conducting the most comprehensive review of the nation's resources to that time, the committee served as the link between Herbert Hoover's* promotion of cooperation between social scientists and the executive branch and creation of the New Deal* planning board.

On July 7, 1933, Public Works Administrator Harold Ickes* appointed Merriam to the advisory committee of the newly-formed National Planning Board* under the authority of Title II of the National Industrial Recovery Act.* The board grew out of ideas raised in the 1920s to plan public works projects as an economic balancing wheel in a recession. Merriam worked with fellow planners Wesley Clair Mitchell* and Frederic Delano.* Merriam served as the philosopher of New Deal planning, explaining in reports, speeches, articles, and books what he meant by the idea of advisory national planning.

Merriam had concluded that urbanization and industrialization had made organized interest groups, not self-reliant individuals, the center of political and economic activity. Political parties should function as mediators between competing interest groups to promote social cooperation, political harmony, and economic stability. Distinguishing between ''administration'' and ''politics,'' Merriam saw the proper role of American planners as administrators responsible for conducting research and presenting broad alternative policy options to the president and the Congress.

During his first year on the planning board, Merriam expanded the narrow definition of public works planning to include broader planning in a variety of areas done by both private and public sectors. He saw national planning as a continuously changing process of interaction among research-oriented social scientists, politicians, and representatives of business, labor, and agriculture.

Between 1933 and 1935, Merriam advocated executive branch reorganization; he played a key role in convincing Franklin D. Roosevelt* to establish the President's Committee on Administrative Management* (1936). Merriam served with public administration experts Luther Gulick* and Louis Brownlow* on the committee which helped draft a reorganization bill.* After a heated fight in Congress from 1937 to 1939, the bill passed in compromise form in the spring of 1939. The reorganization bill created the Executive Office of the President, shifted the Bureau of the Budget* from the Department of the Treasury to the Executive Office, replaced a Cabinet-dominated planning board with the National Resources Planning Board* as a staff agency within the Executive Office, and authorized the president to appoint six new administrative assistants.

Merriam continued to serve on the planning agency until its abolition in the spring of 1943. Despite his efforts to clarify the idea of American advisory national planning, conservative Democrats and Republicans attacked the board increasingly after 1939. Angry with the growth of executive power during the New Deal and war years, Congress struck at Roosevelt by abolishing the planning board in 1943. As the philosopher of New Deal planning, Merriam had failed to convince Congress that the effort was worth continuing, but his work was definitely a link between Hooverian associationalism and New Deal planning.

Charles E. Merriam died on January 8, 1953. (Barry Karl, *Charles E. Merriam and the Study of Politics*, 1974.)

PATRICK D. REAGAN

MILLER, EMMA GUFFEY Emma Guffey was born in 1874 in Pennsylvania and graduated from Bryn Mawr in 1899, where she had majored in history and political science. A committed suffragette who was also somewhat suspicious of the value of social welfare legislation, Guffey married Carroll Miller and had four children. During the 1920s, she was an active member of the National Women's party and an articulate supporter of the Equal Rights Amendment. She was also active in Democratic politics, working with the Democratic National Committee and chairing the Advisory Board of the Pennsyvlania National Youth Administration* between 1935 and 1943. Her influence on the New Deal* came from three sources: her own position as vice-chairman of the Democratic National Committee after 1936; her husband's position as a member of the Interstate Commerce Commission* and her close relationship with her brother, Senator Joseph Guffey* of Pennsylvania, with whom her family shared a home in Washington. Emma Guffey Miller died in 1970. (Susan Ware, *Beyond Suffrage: Women in the New Deal*, 1981.)

MILLER-TYDINGS ACT OF 1937 After the Supreme Court's* decision in the *Schechter** case had destroyed the National Recovery Administration,* Congress and the New Dealers wanted to salvage something from the National Industrial Recovery Act.* Congress then proceeded to create the ''Little NRA''* with a series of laws, including the Guffey-Snyder Act,* Guffey-Vinson Act,* Connally Act,* Walsh-Healey Act,* Robinson-Patman Act,* and the Miller-Tydings Act of 1937. The Miller-Tydings Act amended the Sherman Anti-trust Act of 1890 to uphold fair-trade laws. The first portion of the act stated that manufacturers and producers could establish a minimum resale price for their goods. The clause held that the establishment of such minimum resale prices did not constitute a restraint on trade or competition, for similar commodities produced by opposing manufacturers were engaged in free and open competition. The second proviso of the Miller-Tydings Act provided clarification of the amendment, stating that any collusion between competing enterprises to create a minimum resale price would indeed be illegal. The establishment of such agreements between competing businesses would be a misdemeanor punishable by a fine of $5,000 or one-year imprisonment or both. Similar statutes had been passed by state legislatures in the 1930s; and in 1936 the Supreme Court, in *Old Dearborn Distributing Company v. Seagram Distillers Corporation*, decided that fair-trade laws were not a restraint on trade and, in fact, served to protect the manufacturer's goodwill. By allowing fair-trade laws to exist, the Miller-Tydings Act of 1937 tried to foster the planning and efficiency originally promoted by the National Industrial Recovery Act, all on the assumption that the elimination of destructive competition would help raise prices, improve business profits, and lead to increased employment and production. (*Dictionary of American History*, II:482–484, 1976.)

MILLIS, HARRY ALVIN Harry Alvin Millis was born on May 14, 1873, in Paoli, Indiana. Very early in his life he exhibited an interest in economics, and he received A. B. and A. M. degrees from the University of Indiana (1895 and 1896) and then took a Ph.D. at the University of Chicago in 1899. Millis quickly climbed the academic ladder, teaching at the University of Arkansas (1902–1903), Stanford University (1903–1912), University of Kansas (1912–1916), and then he returned as a full professor to the University of Chicago. While at the University of Chicago, he published *Sickness and Insurance* (1926) and the multi-volume Labor Economics (1945). Millis served briefly on the National Labor Relations Board* in 1934 and 1935 and then returned to the NLRB in 1940 as chairman, a position he held until 1945. Millis had a passionate commitment to the right of labor to bargain collectively, and he enthusiastically endorsed the National Labor Relations Act of 1935* and constantly worked to strengthen it. At the end of World War II Millis retired from the NRLB. He died on June 25, 1948. (James A. Gross, *The Making of the NLRB: A Study in Economics, Politics, and the Law*, 1974; *New York Times*, June 26, 1948.)

MITCHELL, CHARLES EDWIN Charles E. Mitchell was born on October 6, 1877, in Chelsea, Massachusetts, and educated at Amherst, where he graduated in 1899. Mitchell began work with the Western Electric Company in 1899, became assistant manager in 1904, and went into banking as president of the Trust Company of America in New York in 1907. In 1911 he founded Charles E. Mitchell & Company Investments and became president of the National City Bank in 1921. Between 1929 and 1933, Mitchell was chairman of the board of the National City Bank. In 1932 and 1933 the investigations of the Pecora committee put Mitchell in the national spotlight as a series of bank frauds and shady loan deals to bank officers were exposed at National City Bank. A conservative Republican, Mitchell tried to defend the bank's practices and laissez-faire values by praising private property and individual liberty; but Pecora was relentless in his questioning, and Mitchell's reputation was seriously tarnished. He resigned from the National City Bank in 1933 and joined the firm of Blyth & Company, an investment banking concern, in 1935. Charles Mitchell died December 14, 1955. (*New York Times*, December 15, 1955.)

MITCHELL, WESLEY CLAIR Wesley C. Mitchell was born in Rushville, Illinois, on August 5, 1874. He attended the University of Chicago, receiving an A. B. degree in economics in 1896 and a Ph.D. in 1899. Mitchell then entered academia, teaching at the University of Chicago (1900–1902), the University of California (1902–1912), Columbia University (1913–1919), the New School for Social Research (1919–1922), and then finished his academic career at Columbia

(1922–1944). During those years, Mitchell took several leaves of absence from Columbia to serve in the federal government. In 1918 and 1919 Mitchell was head of the price section of the War Industries Board, and there he acquired his lifetime commitment to national economic planning based on long-term research and government coordination. During the 1920s, Mitchell was a member of Professor Irving Fisher's* Stable Money Association and became an advocate of the idea of the "commodity dollar."* President Herbert Hoover* asked Mitchell to chair his President's Research Commission on Social Trends, and he worked on the project between 1929 and 1933. With the coming of the New Deal,* Mitchell joined the Public Works Administration* as a member of its National Planning Board,* and in 1934 and 1935 he served on the National Resources Board.* Mitchell was committed to long-range rather than short-term planning and was convinced that national economic planning was here to stay—the only question was whether it would be effective or haphazard in nature. The author of a number of books—including *Gold Prices and Wages Under the Greenback Standard* (1908), *Business Cycles* (1913), and *The Art of Spending Money* (1927)—Wesley C. Mitchell died on October 29, 1948. (Philip Warken, *A History of the National Planning Board, 1933–1943*, 1979.)

MOFFETT, JAMES ANDREW James Andrew Moffett was born in Parkersburg, West Virginia, on June 30, 1886. He attended Princeton for a while but did not graduate and in 1906 became a clerk for the Vacuum Oil Company. Blessed with fine administrative and marketing skills, Moffett rose quickly in the oil business. By 1909 he had become director of sales and assistant to the president of the Standard Oil Company of Louisiana, and in 1919 he was elected to the board of directors of Standard Oil Company of New Jersey. Between 1924 and 1933 he served as vice-president and senior vice-president of Standard Oil. In 1933 President Franklin D. Roosevelt* asked Moffett to serve as a member of the Industrial Advisory Board of the National Recovery Administration.* Moffett stayed there through 1933, accepted the vice-presidency of Standard Oil Company of California in 1934, and then, in a surprise appointment, agreed to the president's nomination of him as administrator of the new Federal Housing Administration.* Moffett was quite conservative politically and rather unsympathetic to many federal programs. He opposed low-cost public housing programs and even restricted the FHA's new home construction efforts. Moffett left the FHA in 1935 to become chairman of the board of the California-Texas Oil Company. James Moffett died on March 25, 1953. (Pearl Janet Davies, *Real Estate in American History*, 1958; *Who Was Who in America*, III:608, 1963.)

MOLEY, RAYMOND Raymond Moley, a major figure in the formation of the early New Deal,* was born in Berea, Ohio, on September 27, 1886. Moley graduated from Baldwin-Wallace College in 1906 and then entered public education as superintendent of schools in Olmsted Falls, Ohio, between 1907 and 1910. Moley began graduate work at Oberlin College while teaching high school at

West High School in Cleveland. He received his master's degree from Oberlin in 1913. Moley then entered higher education as an instructor and then assistant professor of politics at Western Reserve University between 1916 and 1919, and he earned his Ph.D. at Columbia in 1918. He served as director of the Cleveland Foundation between 1919 and 1923 and returned to Columbia as an associate professor of government in 1923. He wrote prolifically during his early academic career, including: *Lessons in American Citizenship* (ten editions between 1917 and 1930), *The State Movement for Efficiency and Economy* (1918), *Lessons in Democracy* (1919), *Commercial Recreation* (1919), and *Parties, Politics, and People* (1921). Moley was promoted to professor of public law in 1928, and he remained at Columbia with that rank until his retirement in 1954.

During the election campaign of 1932,* Samuel I. Rosenman* suggested to Democratic presidential candidate Franklin D. Roosevelt* that he continue consulting major academic figures to assist in the development of campaign issues. Rosenman turned to Raymond Moley for assistance because of Moley's academic reputation and for his work as research director of the New York State Crime Commission in 1926 and 1927 and of the New York State Commission on the Administration of Justice in 1931–1933. Moley then assembled the "Brain Trust"* and served as its unofficial leader. During the campaign they argued and discussed economic policy, politics, and administrative concerns and assisted Roosevelt with his speeches. After the election, the "Brain Trust" disbanded, but Moley remained as a close adviser to the president-elect, interviewing potential administrative officials and developing a legislative program which reached fulfillment during the "first hundred days."* In 1933 President Roosevelt appointed Moley an assistant secretary of state, but Moley really continued to serve as the president's adviser and legislative assistant. His influence with the president and impact on the New Deal peaked during 1933.

Raymond Moley made four major contributions to the New Deal. Between 1932 and 1935, he helped draft most of the president's speeches and fireside chats.* Second, Moley had an enormous impact on the early New Deal's emphasis on business-government planning and reform. A progressive Democrat, Moley tended to be conservative but hardly reactionary on economic matters, believed that the days of laissez-faire were over forever, and that together business and government could plan an economy which would provide growth and equity. Moley supported most of the legislation of the "first hundred days" and maintained a neutrality only about the Tennessee Valley Authority* and the Public Works Administration.* As editor of the magazine *Today*, which many people considered a New Deal organ in 1934 and 1935, Moley supported every administration measure except the corporate surplus profits section of the Wealth Tax Act of 1935. He openly supported the Securities Exchange Act of 1934,* the Gold Reserve Act of 1934,* the deficit spending necessary to fund the Works Progress Administration,* the Public Utility Holding Company Act of 1935,* the Banking Act of 1935,* and the National Labor Relations Act of 1935.* Although he disagreed with the Wealth Tax Act of 1935,* he did not publicly criticize it in

Today. Third, Moley played a similar role to Felix Frankfurter* in recommending dozens of talented people to join administrative positions. Finally, through his writings in *Today* and books like *After Seven Years* (1939) and *The First New Deal* (1966), Moley played a critical role in publicizing and interpreting the meaning of the New Deal.

After 1935, however, Moley broke his connection with the New Deal. During 1932 and 1933, his relationship with Roosevelt had been close and intimate, but when the president announced in July 1933 to the London Economic Conference* that the United States would not cooperate in any currency stabilization arrangements, just after Moley had publicly promised the conference that the United States would provide such support, their relationship began to deteriorate. Moley was hurt and humiliated, and he never really recovered from the incident. After 1935 he became somewhat uncomfortable about the New Deal's more anti-business sentiments, but his formal break with the administration came with the ''court-packing''* proposal in 1937. Moley bitterly denounced the move, became much more critical of deficit spending in 1938, and joined the Republican party* in 1939. He had warned that Roosevelt would seek a third term in 1940, and he worked for Wendell Willkie's* election. Moley then continued his academic and writing career at Columbia and published a number of books after leaving the administration, including *Twenty Seven Masters of Politics* (1949), *How to Keep Our Liberty* (1952), *Political Responsibility* (1958), and *The Republican Opportunity* (1962). Raymond Moley died on February 18, 1975. (Raymond Moley and Elliott A. Rosen, *The First New Deal*, 1966; James E. Sargent, ''Raymond Moley and the New Deal: An Appraisal,'' *Ball State University Forum*, XVIII:62–72, 1977; *Who Was Who In America*, VI:288, 1976.)

MONETARY ACT OF 1939 With the Thomas amendment to the Agricultural Adjustment Act of 1933,* the president had acquired authority to devalue the dollar, and early in 1934 he had set the value of the dollar at 59¢. Because Congress had renewed that power over the years, Franklin D. Roosevelt* still had the right to devalue the dollar by another 9¢ in 1939. In the past Congress had willingly renewed the president's authority, but in 1939 Republicans in the House almost unilaterally opposed the move. By April the bill had been approved by a 225 to 158 vote in the House, and in mid-June the Senate Banking and Currency Committee reported it out favorably. But the Senate silver bloc then came out against the measure unless Roosevelt would raise the price the government paid for silver, end purchases of foreign silver, and issue another $2 billion in new currency. Since the government was already paying nearly 65¢ an ounce for silver, about 21¢ above the world price, Roosevelt refused to agree since it would only mean a windfall to silver producers. Silverites joined with southern Democrats and conservative Republicans and defeated the devaluation bill by a 47 to 31 vote. Conservatives then voted with the silverites and raised the government price for silver to more than 77¢ an ounce and prohibited foreign silver buying. In the compromise which Roosevelt engineered, the Senate restored his devaluation power, eliminated the prohibition on foreign buying, and set the domestic silver price at 71¢. The silverites then agreed to the measure in the conference committee hearings, and the bill passed early in July 1939. (James T. Patterson, *Congressional Conservatism and the New Deal*, 1967.)

MOREHEAD V. TIPALDO In June 1936's *Morehead v. Tipaldo* decision, the Supreme Court* overturned a New York minimum wage law for women. Chief Justice Charles Evans Hughes* and Justices Owen J. Roberts,* George Sutherland,* James McReynolds,* Pierce Butler,* and Willis Van Devanter* were in the majority, arguing that no state legislation could violate the Fourteenth Amendment right of an employee and employer to bargain privately with each other for the best terms possible. Justices Benjamin Cardozo,* Louis Brandeis,* and Harlan Fiske Stone* dissented, arguing that the Fourteenth amendment did not protect individuals from every law that a reasonable legislature passed. They claimed that if the majority's decision prevailed generally throughout the society, government would lose the capacity to govern. (Alpheus Thomas Mason, *The Supreme Court from Taft to Warren*, 1958.)

MORGAN, ARTHUR ERNEST Arthur Ernest Morgan was born in Cincinnati, Ohio, on June 20, 1878. Although he graduated from high school, his engineering skills were learned by working for his father and by individual study. By 1909 he had become president of the Morgan Engineering Company and in 1915 of the Dayton-Morgan Engineering Company. Morgan specialized in flood control, land reclamation, and dam construction. He was appointed chief engineer of the Miami (Ohio) Conservancy District in 1913 to control flooding on the Miami River and of the Pueblo (Colorado) Conservancy District in 1921. Throughout the early 1900s, Morgan also assisted a number of state legislatures in drafting drainage codes. In 1920 Morgan became president of Antioch College, a position he held until 1936. During the last three years of his tenure at Antioch, he was on leave because President Franklin D. Roosevelt* had selected him to become chairman of the Tennessee Valley Authority.*

Morgan had ambitious plans for the TVA. A strong believer in engineering and technology, he wanted the TVA to become an agency for regional planning, a vehicle for transforming the social, political, and economic institutions of the Tennessee Valley. For Morgan, the ideas of regional planning and the elimination of poverty were more important than cheap power and better technology. Morgan recommended and Roosevelt accepted Harcourt Morgan* and David Lilienthal* as the other directors of the TVA. Almost from the beginning, the TVA board became a center of acrimony. Harcourt Morgan,* a long-time advocate of commercial farming interests, was far more conservative than Arthur Morgan and extremely suspicious of bureaucratic planning, especially from Washington, D. C. He was quite convinced that the TVA should cooperate with state agencies, universities, agriculture experimental stations, and local farm organizations. Arthur Morgan, of course, saw Harcourt as stubborn and obdurate, a lobbyist for large commercial farmers in the Tennessee Valley. If Harcourt Morgan had his way, Arthur Morgan thought, there would be no real reform of social and economic life in the valley. David Lilienthal, who specialized in public power issues on the board, was basically an anti-trust Brandesian who viewed the utility companies as exploitive and reactionary. Because Arthur Morgan believed passionately in cooperative business-government planning, Lilienthal came to see him as a tool of the utility companies. Morgan, of course, saw Lilienthal as a youthful but archaic progressive unwilling to accept the reality of the modern economy.

By 1936 Arthur Morgan began publicly criticizing both Harcourt Morgan and David Lilienthal. He tried to block Lilienthal's reappointment to the board and to revise board policy to centralize more power in his hands. But Arthur Morgan's political philosophy was by then out of step with the evolution of the New Deal.* His faith in national planning and reform was more a part of the pre-1936, NRA* New Deal, where the influence of people like Rexford Tugwell* and Daniel Richberg* had been great. After 1935, the New Deal shifted to its Brandesian-Keynesian stage, emphasizing anti-trust and compensatory spending policies rather than planning as the cure for the economy. By 1938 Roosevelt had tired of Arthur Morgan's public criticism of his TVA associates and his unwillingness or temperamental inability to be more politically circumspect. After private hearings at the White House in 1938, where Morgan refused to substantiate his criticisms or apologize for them, Roosevelt fired him. Morgan unsuccessfully sought redress in the federal courts. Harcourt Morgan replaced him as chairman of the TVA.

Arthur Morgan became president of Community Service, Inc., in 1941, as well as of the Yellow Springs (Ohio) Housing Corporation. In 1950 he was temporary chairman of the Conciliation and Arbitration Board for U. S. Steel and the CIO.* He also authored a number of books after his departure from the TVA,* including *The Small Community* (1942), *Small Community Economics* (1943), *Edward Bellamy* (1945), *Industries for Small Communities* (1953), *The Search for Purpose* (1955), *The Community of the Future* (1956), and *The Making of the T. V. A.* (1974). Arthur Morgan died on November 12, 1975. (Thomas K. McGraw, *Morgan versus Lilienthal: A Feud within the TVA*, 1970; Arthur E. Morgan, *The Making of the T. V. A.*, 1974; Roy Talbert, Jr., "Beyond Pragmatism: A Biography of Arthur Morgan," Ph.D. dissertation, Vanderbilt University, 1972.)

MORGAN, HARCOURT ALEXANDER Born in Strathroy, Ontario, Canada, on August 31, 1867, Harcourt Morgan exhibited an early interest in science and became an entomologist after graduating from the University of Toronto in 1889 and doing graduate work at Cornell between 1891 and 1898. He was an entomologist and horticulturist for Louisiana State University between 1889 and 1894 and during those years worked closely with county extension agents and USDA experimental stations. Morgan became director of the University of Tennessee

Agricultural Experiment Station in 1905, dean of the College of Agriculture in 1913, and president of the university in 1919. By that time he had become an extremely articulate spokesman for commercial farmers. When President Franklin D. Roosevelt* was looking for directors of the new Tennessee Valley Authority* in 1933, farm interest groups promoted Morgan. Along with Arthur E. Morgan* and David Lilienthal,* Morgan became one of the first directors of the Tennessee Valley Authority. The three men immediately divided up their responsibilities, with Arthur Morgan overseeing dam construction, education, and rural life; David Lilienthal directing public power policy; and Harcourt Morgan supervising fertilization production and agricultural policy.

The meetings of the TVA board of directors soon become tempestuous, primarily because Lilienthal and Harcourt Morgan disagreed with the philosophy of Arthur Morgan. Convinced that only centralized social and economic planning could transform the Tennessee Valley into a region of production and prosperity, Arthur Morgan was suspicious of local prerogatives. He was afraid that TVA fertilizer, electricity, and resettlement might only play into the hands of rich landowners and perpetuate the poverty of the region. Only large-scale planning could reform the basic social, political, and economic institutions of the Tennessee Valley. But Harcourt Morgan, as a long time resident of the area, was suspicious of bureaucratic planning and preferred a slow, deliberate approach to change. While Arthur Morgan was extremely suspicious of large, commercial farmers, Harcourt Morgan trusted them and wanted to do nothing to lose their support. Instead, he promoted the idea of "grassroots democracy" in which federal planning would not move faster than local communities could tolerate. On the TVA board, Harcourt Morgan and David Lilienthal teamed up to oppose Arthur Morgan's regional planning schemes.

When Arthur Morgan tried to oppose David Lilienthal's reappointment to the board in 1936, the internal struggles of the TVA burst into public. Harcourt Morgan sided with Lilienthal, and gradually between 1936 and 1938 Arthur Morgan became increasingly intemperate in his public criticisms of his colleagues, accusing them of gross improprieties, obstructionism, and narrow-mindedness. After Morgan refused to substantiate his allegations during a private hearing with the president in 1938, Roosevelt fired him and named Harcourt Morgan as the new chairman of the TVA. Morgan's appointment clearly symbolized how the enthusiasm for planning in the early New Deal* had given way to a concern for competition and local prerogatives. Harcourt Morgan stayed on as chairman until 1941 and remained on the board until 1948. In 1941 the president named David Lilienthal as the new chairman. Harcourt Morgan died on August 25, 1950. (Michael J. McDonald and John Muldowny, *TVA and the Dispossessed: The Resettlement of Population in the Norris Dam Area*, 1982; Marguerite Owen, *The Tennessee Valley Authority*, 1973.)

MORGAN, JOHN PIERPONT, JR. The third generation of America's most prominent banking dynasty, John Pierpont Morgan, Jr., was born on September

7, 1867, at Irvington-on-Hudson, New York. He attended St. Paul's School in Concord, New Hampshire, and graduated from Harvard in 1889. He immediately entered the banking business with Jacob C. Rogers and Company in Boston and in 1891 joined his father's firm—Drexel, Morgan & Company in New York. Between 1898 and 1905, his banking apprenticeship continued in London as a partner in J. S. Morgan & Company. When his father died in 1913, Morgan became senior partner of J. P. Morgan & Company. For the next two decades he was a leading figure in the international banking community. By the time of the New Deal,* J. P. Morgan, Jr., was the leading symbol of private capitalism in the United States. He at first welcomed President Franklin D. Roosevelt's* activism and initiative, especially in closing down the banking system, but his enthusiasm was short-lived. The Pecora investigations embarassed and made a spectacle of Morgan, and he had opposed the Banking Act of 1933* because it had forced him to separate his banking and securities-underwriting affiliates. J. P. Morgan & Company remained a bank, while a new company—Morgan, Stanley & Company—took over the underwriting business. Morgan came to view the New Deal as hopelessly anti-business and narrow-minded, the tool of reform-minded lawyers and economists. In addition, the higher taxes and regulatory legislation cut into his personal income, a fact which did little to endear the New Deal to him. Morgan gradually withdrew from his business affairs in the 1930s, liquidating large volumes of assets, and died on March 13, 1943. (John D. Forbes, *J. P. Morgan, Jr., 1867–1943*, 1981.)

MORGENTHAU, HENRY, JR. Henry Morgenthau,. Jr., secretary of the treasury under President Franklin D. Roosevelt* for eleven years, was born on May 11, 1891, in an apartment at Central Park West and 81st Street in New York City. He was the son of Henry and Josephine (Sykes) Morgenthau. His father was a lawyer and investor who made a fortune in real estate in Harlem and the Bronx and later served as ambassador to Turkey during Woodrow Wilson's presidency. Young Morgenthau attended Phillips Exeter Academy for three years, then returned home to finish preparing for college at Sachs Collegiate Institute. In 1909 he enrolled at Cornell University to study architecture, but having no real interest in the subject, left after three semesters, apparently with no other plans for a career. In 1911, on a visit to a Texas ranch while recuperating from an attack of typhoid fever, he became interested in farming and ranching and returned to New York determined to become a farmer. Morgenthau went back to Cornell to study agriculture but left in 1913 without taking a degree. With his father's help, he purchased several hundred acres of farmland in Dutchess County, about fifteen miles from the Roosevelt estate. A short time afterward, he met Franklin Roosevelt. The social acquaintance of the two young Hudson River squires soon ripened into a friendship and political association that lasted until Roosevelt's death thirty years later.

During Roosevelt's long convalescence from poliomyelitis in the 1920s, the two men met frequently and spent long hours talking, planning, and playing game after game of Parcheesi. When Roosevelt began his political comeback, Morgenthau often acted as his driver, advance man, and canvasser. After his election as governor of New York in 1928, Roosevelt appointed Morgenthau chairman of the Agricultural Advisory Commission, and, following his re-election in 1930, named him commissioner of conservation, an office that gave Morgenthau a leading role in the state's $2 billion reforestation program. Morgenthau also had the unofficial job of winning support of the upstate farmers, who were already being reached by his *American Agriculturalist*, a farm journal he had published since 1922.

With the coming of the New Deal* in 1933, Morgenthau, who had hoped to become secretary of agriculture, was made instead chairman of the Federal Farm Board and assigned the job of consolidating nine conflicting farm loan agencies into the Farm Credit Administration.* As governor of the new organization, he was lending an average of one million dollars a day to mortgage-burdened farmers by the end of 1933. By this time, William H. Woodin,* the ailing secretary of the treasury, had tendered his resignation, which Roosevelt did not accept until late December. Meanwhile, Morgenthau had been appointed acting secretary. On New Year's Day, 1934, the appointment became permanent.

Morgenthau, a gentleman-farmer with little knowledge of law of finance, was an unusual choice to head the most complex department of the federal government. The treasury was in charge of the Coast Guard, the Bureau of Narcotics, the Secret Service, the Bureau of Engraving and Printing, the Public Health Service, the Alcohol Tax Unit, and Procurement Division (which built post offices and courthouses and bought supplies of almost every description), and, most important, the Bureau of Internal Revenue. His first major responsibility was defending the U. S. dollar, which President Roosevelt had devalued, against competitive devaluation by other countries. Operating with a large stabilization fund, Morgenthau bought and sold foreign currencies, gold, and dollars until 1938, when a stabilization agreement was reached. By the next year the dollar had become the world's strongest currency. During the eleven years that Morgenthau held his cabinet post, the government intervened more actively in financial markets of the world and spent more money than all previous administrations combined. In 1934, when he took office, national expenditures were about $5 billion a year; when he resigned in 1945 they had risen to a wartime high of $98 billion.

In the early years of the war, when England stood alone against Hitler, Morgenthau, according to *Time* magazine, "helped procure everything from SPAM to destroyers for Britain, and drafted the Lend-Lease Act." After American entry into the war, he had the tasks of financing the war effort and helping plan for a post-war international monetary system. At the forty-four nation conference at Bretton Woods, New Hampshire, in July 1944, Morgenthau and Assistant Secretary of the Treasury Harry D. White took the lead in winning a plan which led to the establishment of the International Monetary Fund to stabilize national currencies and the World Bank to supply capital to underdeveloped nations.

Other plans that Morgenthau offered during the war were controversial, especially the one that came to bear his name. The so-called Morgenthau Plan for post-war Germany would have dismantled that nation's industry and made it an agricultural state, but Roosevelt, who had favored the plan at the second Quebec conference in 1944, had turned against it by the time of the Yalta meeting in early 1945. The plan for Germany, in fact, was partly responsible for Morgenthau's resignation three months after Roosevelt's death. He had hoped to stay in the cabinet until the defeat of Japan, but President Harry S Truman,* who had a low opinion of the Morgenthau Plan, turned down the secretary's request to go with him to the Potsdam conference. Morgenthau resigned in July 1945.

After his resignation, Morgenthau devoted much time to Jewish causes, serving as general chairman of the United Jewish Appeal from 1947 to 1955 and as chairman of the board of governors of the American Financial and Development Corporation for Israel from 1951 to 1954. His first wife, the former Elinor Fatman whom he married in 1916, died in 1949. In November 1951 he married Mrs. Marcelle Puthon Hirsch. Morgenthau died of a heart and kidney condition at Poughkeepsie, New York, on February 6, 1967, at the age of seventy-five.

Morgenthau, a large, neat, bald-pated man whose eyes squinted behind pince-nez, often appeared shy and withdrawn in public, and usually came off badly at press conferences. (Roosevelt jokingly called him "Henry the Morgue.") Although Morgenthau's training and experience had not ideally fitted him for the treasury post, he brought to it, said the *New York Times*, "a rigid honesty, a capacity for grinding work and detail, a willingness to learn and a deep concern for the plight of his fellow citizens." (John Morton Blum, *From the Morgenthau Diaries*, 3 vols., 1959, 1965, 1967; Frank Freidel, *Franklin D. Roosevelt: Launching the New Deal*, 1973; *New York Times*, February 8, 1967.)

JOHN PAYNE

MOTOR CARRIER ACT OF 1935 By 1935 a state of confusion and near-anarchy reigned in the trucking industry. The development and widespread use of the internal combustion engine had changed the social and economic landscape of America. Trucking rates, because of cutthroat competition and depression-level prices, had fallen dangerously. Common carriers, contract carriers, and private operators had all undermined rates and brought tremendous competition to the railroads. Joseph Eastman* of the Interstate Commerce Commission* proposed to rationalize the trucking industry by extensive regulation of common carriers, partial regulation of contract carriers, and no regulation of private carriers. Not only would such a program bring order and stability to the trucking industry, it would help the railroad industry by making it more competitive. Eastman's proposal got support from railroads, motor common carriers, big truckers, buses, and organized labor; but small truckers, truck manufacturers, farmers, and shippers opposed it because it would probably raise freight rates. When Eastman agreed to exemptions for the haulers of livestock, newspapers, and unprocessed farm products, he received support from the American National

Livestock Association, National Grange, and the American Newspaper Publishers Association. The Eastman bill became the Motor Carrier Act on August 9, 1935.

The Motor Carrier Act gave the ICC power to prescribe employee qualifications, maximum hours they could work, and motor carrier equipment standards; to issue certificates of public convenience and necessity, assuring certificates for common carriers in operation on June 1, 1935; to control maximum and minimum rates, service, accounting, finances, organization, and management of common carriers; and to issue permits to contract carriers. For contract carriers, the Motor Carrier Act regulated only minimum rates and accounting procedures. Except for hours and safety regulations, the act ignored private carriers. The Motor Carrier Act established a Bureau of Motor Carriers in the ICC to regulate the trucking industry. By the end of 1936, the bureau had received 85,836 certificate and permit applications, 52,979 tariff publications, 16,897 schedules, and 1,867 contracts. With only 110 employees, it was understaffed and unable to enforce many of its regulations, especially since many truckers simply ignored the rules. Rates were already depressed so there were not many complaints from shippers and relatively few cases. Although the Motor Carrier Act increased trucking rates and gave railroads a chance to be more competitive, the ICC approach was to base rates on the value-of-service method rather than the cost-of-service method, leaving the railroads chronically unable to compete with trucks. The Motor Carrier Act of 1935 dramatically increased the scope of ICC power. (Ari Hoogenboom and Olive Hoogenboom, *A History of the ICC. From Panacea to Palliative*, 1976.)

MUNICIPAL BANKRUPTCY ACT OF 1934 Because of declining tax revenues associated with depression unemployment levels in the early 1930s, hundreds of towns and cities across the country were unable to meet current expenses as well as the fixed costs of their own bonds. As a result, the municipal bond market in the United States was in a state of shambles, and such industry groups as the Investment Bankers' Association as well as urban machines were demanding some type of federal action. Early in 1934 President Franklin D. Roosevelt,* seeing widespread support for the measure in the banking and municipal government communities, sponsored legislation which reached the floor of the House and Senate in May 1934. It encountered a good deal of opposition from some conservatives convinced that cities had wasted their resources through mismanagement, and Senator Carter Glass* of Virginia was convinced it would destroy the municipal bond government. In mid-May Senator Patrick McCarran* of Nevada offered up a compromise which provided cities with the opportunity of scaling down their debts with federal court approval. With the consent of 51 percent of the holders of its outstanding obligations, a city hovering on bankruptcy could take a refinancing plan to the federal courts. If the court found it equitable and 75 percent of its debt holders agreed, the plan could go into effect. Cities had an application period of two years in which they could apply for reorganization.

President Franklin Roosevelt signed the measure on May 24, 1934, and in the next several years it contributed greatly to the revival of the municipal bond market. (*New York Times*, May 25, 1934.)

MURPHY, FRANCIS WILLIAM Born on April 13, 1890, in Harbor Beach, Michigan, Frank Murphy graduated from the University of Michigan in 1912 and received his law degree there in 1914. After graduate studies at Trinity College in Dublin, he went into private law practice. During World War I, Murphy went into the army and served as a captain with the American Expeditionary Force in Europe. After the war, he was appointed first assistant U. S. attorney for the eastern district of Michigan, a position he held until 1920. He returned to private practice and in 1923 became judge of the recorder's court in Detroit. In that position he built a political base for himself in the Democratic machine and in 1930 was elected mayor of Detroit. At that time, nearly 500,000 people were out of work in Detroit, and Murphy vigorously tried to meet their needs, inaugurating a work-relief program which spent the unprecedented sum of $14 million. He was reelected in 1932, but resigned in May 1933 to accept Franklin D. Roosevelt's* offer to become governor-general of the Philippines. Again at the president's suggestion, he left that post in 1936 to run for the governorship of Michigan.

He won the election and then quickly implemented a "Little New Deal"* in Michigan. Legislation passed during his term in office included liberalized old-age assistance, workmen's compensation, and increased appropriations for education and mental health. Murphy approved a civil service law, and supported a referendum to end the township system of distributing relief. During the "sit-down strikes" in the automobile industry in January and February 1937, Murphy vehemently refused to call out state troops to break the strikes. It proved to be a politically unpopular decision, and along with the recession of 1938,* Murphy could not keep hold of the governor's office. The "Little New Deal" in Michigan ended with his defeat.

In 1939 President Roosevelt named Murphy to the cabinet position of attorney general, and during his administration, Murphy instigated an investigation and reorganization of the district attorney and federal marshall's office which led to the ousting of the Pendergast machine in Kansas City and the removal of Martin T. Manton of the U. S. Circuit Court of Appeals in New York. Both Thomas J. Pendergast* and Manton were convicted and served time in the federal penitentiary for crimes Murphy's investigation had uncovered.

In 1940 Roosevelt appointed Murphy to fill a vacancy on the Supreme Court,* and during the next nine years Murphy wrote 132 majority opinions, earning a reputation as a champion of civil liberties. "It is our proud achievement," he wrote, "to have demonstrated that unity and strength are best accomplished, not by enforced orthodoxy of views, but by diversity of opinion through the fullest possible measure of freedom of conscience and of thought." He protested the incarceration of Japanese Americans during World War II and always upheld the rights of labor unions to picket, demonstrate, and strike. Never a man of means, Murphy died penniless on July 19, 1949. (Sidney Fine, *Frank Murphy: The New Deal Years*, 1979.)

LENNA HODNETT ALLRED

MURRAY, PHILIP Born on May 25, 1886, in Blantyre, Scotland, Philip Murray came to the United States in 1902. He had already been working as a coal miner for six years, and he went to work near Pittsburgh, Pennsylvania. Murray finished his education through correspondence courses and became active in the United Mine Workers. He was elected president of District 5 of the UMW in 1916. During World War I Murray served as a member of the War Labor Board and the National Coal Production Committee, and by 1920 he had obtained the vice-presidency of the UMW, a position he held for twenty-two years. During the New Deal* years, while serving under John L. Lewis* in the UMW, Murray was also a member of the board of the National Recovery Administration* and helped draft the Guffey-Snyder Act of 1935.* In 1935 Murray played a major role, along with John L. Lewis and Sidney Hillman* of the Amalgamated Clothing Workers, in forming the Committee for Industrial Organization (CIO).* When the National Labor Relations Act of 1935* guaranteed the right of workers to organize, the CIO made a massive organization assault on the heavy industries. Murray served as chairman of the Steel Workers' Organizing Committee in its campaign against ''Big Steel'' and the United States Steel Corporation. He was also a president of the Congress of Industrial Organizations, a founder of the United Steelworkers of America, and a close adviser to Presidents Franklin D. Roosevelt* and Harry S Truman* on labor affairs. He died on November 9, 1952. (*New York Times*, November 10, 1952.)

MUSCLE SHOALS (See NORRIS, GEORGE WILLIAM and TENNESSEE VALLEY AUTHORITY.)

MYERS, WILLIAM IRVING Born in Lowman, New York, on December 18, 1891, William Myers attended Cornell University, receiving his B. S. degree in 1914 and a Ph.D. in agricultural economics and farm management in 1918. He immediately joined the Cornell faculty in 1918, becoming a full professor in 1920 and keeping that position until 1959. In 1933 President Franklin D. Roosevelt* created the Farm Credit Administration* as a consolidation of many federal farm agencies, and named Henry Morgenthau, Jr.,* as governor. Morgenthau selected Myers as his deputy governor, and Myers took a leave of absence from Cornell. After the death of William Woodin* in 1934, Morgenthau became the new secretary of the treasury, and Myers was appointed head of the Farm Credit Administration, where he presided over the refinancing of farm debt in the 1930s. Myers resigned from the FCA in 1938 and returned to Cornell where he became head of the department of agricultural economics from 1938 to 1943 and then dean of the college of agriculture until 1959. He resigned from the faculty to become professor emeritus in 1959. Over the years, Myers also played a leading role in a number of federal farm commissions, including the President's Commission on Farm Tenancy (1937), President's Famine Emergency Commission (1947), Commission on Foreign Aid (1947), and chairman of the National Agricultural Advisory Commission (1952–1959). (W. Gifford Hoag, *The Farm Credit System: A History of Financial Self-Help*, 1976.)

N

NATIONAL ASSOCIATION FOR THE ADVANCEMENT OF COLORED PEOPLE Black people were the most impoverished group in America because of the Great Depression, and because they lacked political power they benefitted very little from New Deal* programs. Even though blacks served in the New Deal, their role was largely advisory, and they were not in a position to put much pressure on Franklin D. Roosevelt's* administration. Early New Deal programs elicited a great deal of criticism from black leaders. They complained that the National Industrial Recovery Act* displaced many black industrial workers. The policies of the Agricultural Adjustment Administration* also had the effect of driving black tenant farmers and sharecroppers from the land. Discrimination was so pervasive that black people were not allowed to live in the model town of Norris, Tennessee, nor the subsistance homestead community of Arthurdale, West Virginia. The economic depression of the early 1930s only served to worsen the poverty already suffered by black people, but without compensating relief.

Before the depression the National Association for the Advancement of Colored People was primarily concerned with achieving civil rights through the legal system. The NAACP had never before concerned itself with economic problems. These problems had been relegated to the National Urban League. Therefore, with the onset of the Great Depression the NAACP did not have the experience to deal with economic problems nor did it have the money because of acute financial difficulties as a result of the depression.

The AAA was of most concern to the NAACP because over half of the black labor force was employed in agriculture. Besides lobbying efforts, the NAACP gave financial support to the Southern Tenant Farmers' Union.* The NAACP also attempted to end discrimination in organized labor. At the 1934 national American Federation of Labor* conference, a resolution to cease discrimination in that organization failed to pass. The NAACP further made efforts to keep wages in Works Progress Administration* programs from falling to the level of regional wages and to stop the practice of firing WPA workers around harvest time, forcing them to work in the fields for lower wages. The NAACP was successful in getting a rule that Public Works Administration* contracts must carry a non-discrimination clause, but this was easily avoided by contractors.

The NAACP met with only limited success in obtaining government support for blacks. Most of their victories were gained within the executive branch, where they could find a sympathetic ear. The NAACP was not satisfied. Their failure to gain passage of a long sought after federal anti-lynching bill,* or any other civil rights legislation, and the reticence of Roosevelt to actively support civil rights legislation, forced the NAACP to break with the president in April 1935.

The NAACP itself was coming under increasing criticism, especially among young black activists and intellectuals who felt that the organization was not properly addressing the economic needs of black people, nor did it have a program to do so. The NAACP was further weakened in the 1930s by a feud between W. E. B. Du Bois and Walter White,* the NAACP secretary, over economic policies. After the resignation of Du Bois, White spent the later half of the 1930s fighting the decentralizing Harris Plan. White was able to create a highly centralized organization which brought financial solvency and increased membership to the NAACP. (William E. Leuchtenburg, *Franklin D. Roosevelt and the New Deal, 1932-1940*, 1963; W. Augustus Low and Virgil A. Clift, ed., *Encyclopedia of Black America*, 1981.)

MICHAEL G. DENNIS

NATIONAL ASSOCIATION OF MANUFACTURERS As it had been throughout its history, the National Association of Manufacturers was a symbol of business conservatism during the New Deal.* Because of the depression, the NAM had a difficult time in the 1930s. By 1933 membership was down from a high of 5,350 businesses in 1922 to less than 1,500, and resignations were running an average of sixty-five per month. Although the membership climbed back to almost 3,000 by the mid-1930s, the NAM felt its position in American society was threatened by the New Deal and by the rise of the labor movement. Robert L. Lund had assumed the presidency of the NAM in 1931, and he was determined to make sure that "radicals" and "demagogues" did not take over the country. Worried about the pro-labor provisions of the National Industrial Recovery Act's* Section 7(a) and the National Labor Relations Act of 1935,* as well as the prevailing public hostility toward the business community, Lund and the association set out to educate them. Throughout the 1930s, they opposed anti-business legislation of the New Deal and tried to show that industry's managers were the "true leaders of America." The public and labor interest, they argued, were best served in the protective hands of business management because a basic harmony existed between the classes in the United States. They opposed the candidacy of Franklin D. Roosevelt* in 1932, 1936, 1940, and 1944 and constantly called for fiscal responsibility and balanced budgets. (Richard S. Tedlow, "The National Association of Manufacturers and Public Relations during the New Deal," *Business History Review*, L:25-45, 1976.)

NATIONAL BITUMINOUS COAL LABOR BOARD Established by Congress on July 12, 1921, the National Bituminous Coal Labor Board was part of the Department of Labor. It consisted of eighteen members, three of whom served on one of six divisional boards across the country working to maintain contractual arrangements between the coal operators and the United Mine Workers. The NBCLB was simply an appeals board for decisions which could not be settled on the local level. On September 18, 1933, when the NRA* code for the bituminous coal industry was announced, the NBCLB was given the authority to mediate labor-management disputes and work to implement Section 7(a) of the National Industrial Recovery Act of 1933.* Many disputes were held on the local level, so the NBCLB met only twice during 1933 and 1934. The *Schechter** decision of the Supreme Court* in May 1935 destroyed the National Recovery Administration, and the Guffey-Snyder Bituminous Coal Conservation Act* of August 30, 1935, transferred the NBCLB to the Department of Labor. On May 18, 1936, in *Carter v. Carter Coal Company*,* the Supreme Court declared the Guffey-Synder Act unconstitutional and abolished the NBCLB. (Lewis L. Lorwin and Arthur Wubnig, *Labor Relations Boards*, 1935.)

NATIONAL COMMITTEE TO UPHOLD CONSTITUTIONAL GOVERNMENT (See GANNETT, FRANK E.)

NATIONAL ECONOMIC AND SOCIAL PLANNING ASSOCIATION Founded in 1934, the National Economic and Social Planning Association represented a wide variety of business, labor, farming, and professional groups which believed in the idea of economic planning rather than laissez-faire. Beardsley Ruml,* the economist and tax planner, was head of the association. They helped promote the Reorganization Act of 1939* as well as the New Deal's* efforts at national planning through the National Recovery Administration* and the National Resources Planning Board.* The National Economic and Social Planning Association changed its name to the National Planning Association in 1941. (J. D. Millett, *The Process and Organization of Government Planning*, 1947.)

NATIONAL EMERGENCY COUNCIL By the end of the "first hundred days,"* the New Deal* had created an unprecedented array of new agencies, and President Franklin D. Roosevelt* felt the need for some general administrative coordination of the growing bureaucracy. To promote more effective management, he created the Executive Council in July 1933, with Frank Walker* serving as executive secretary. On November 17, 1933, the president reorganized the Executive Council and created the National Emergency Council. The council was composed of the Secretaries of Labor, Interior, Agriculture, and Commerce, as well as the heads of the PWA, FERA,* AAA,* HOLC,* and FCA.* In December 1933, to assert more control over General Hugh Johnson* and the National Recovery Administration,* Roosevelt transferred the Special Industrial Recovery Board, a kind of board of directors for the NRA, to the National

Emergency Council. Almost a year later, after the Industrial Emergency Committee had been put in charge of the NRA, Roosevelt transferred it to the National Emergency Council. In October 1934 the president then merged the IEC, Executive Council, and the old National Emergency Council into a new National Emergency Council headed by Donald Richberg.* Richberg served until April 1935, when Frank C. Walker returned to head the council. He resigned in December 1935, and by that time the NEC had lost much of its power. It was formally abolished in July 1939 when Reorganization Plan Number 1 went into effect.

The National Emergency Council never fulfilled the president's expectations for policy formation and administrative coordination. Since many New Deal programs, like TVA* reclamation and AAA crop reduction, were contradictory, it was difficult to coordinate policy. Also, cabinet officials and agency heads resisted any coordination which threatened their own prerogatives, and at the same time Roosevelt was receiving policy advice from a number of sources besides the National Emergency Council. Neither Richberg nor Walker was a close Roosevelt intimate, at least in terms of public policy, and when the president stopped attending the meetings, so did the cabinet members and agency heads. They sent subordinates instead. The NEC then declined rapidly in influence. When the *Schechter** decision destroyed the NIRA,* the National Emergency Council had already been eclipsed by a new emphasis in the New Deal on anti-trust, social security, and pro-labor legislation. (Lester G. Seligman and Elmer E. Cornwell, Jr., eds., *New Deal Mosaic. Roosevelt Confers with his National Emergency Council, 1933-1936*, 1965.)

NATIONAL EMPLOYMENT SYSTEM ACT OF 1933 (See WAGNER-PEYSER ACT OF 1933.)

NATIONAL FARMERS' HOLIDAY ASSOCIATION (See RENO, MILO.)

NATIONAL FARMERS' UNION The National Farmers' Union, considered one of the "big three" farm organizations of the New Deal* era, was more strictly oriented toward the family farm and somewhat more militant than the American Farm Bureau Federation* or the National Grange.

The National Farmers' Union, technically (but uncommonly) known as the Farmers' Educational and Cooperative Union of America, originated in Texas, where the first local was organized by Isaac Newton Gresham in 1902. Gresham, a veteran of the Farmers' Alliance, infused the new organization with alliance principles. It grew rapidly in Texas and expanded into other southern states, its membership reported at 200,000 by the time of its annual meeting in 1905. The purposes of the organization were economic cooperation and non-partisan political action.

Although the early strength of the National Farmers' Union was in the South, where it promoted cooperative purchasing by farmers and cooperative marketing of cotton, the organization soon declined there. At the same time it prospered in the north-central grain-growing region, where its principal activities were cooperative terminal marketing of livestock and grain.

During the 1920s the Farmers' Union both expanded its cooperative base, especially in the north-central states, and intensified its political lobbying. It joined other farm organizations in support of the Capper-Volstead Act and of the successive McNary-Haugen bills. With passage of the Agricultural Marketing Act in 1929, the NFU quickly demonstrated support of the Federal Farm Board, joining with the Grange and the Farm Bureau to establish the Farmers National Grain Corporation, the first national marketing cooperative under the Federal Farm Board.

By 1931, when John A. Simpson* of Oklahoma was elected president of the NFU, its disaffection from the Federal Farm Board was obvious. Radical elements of the organization followed Milo Reno* into the direct and sometimes violent action of the Farm Holiday movement. Simpson meanwhile led the main stream of the NFU into a still greater emphasis on political action, beginning with the shaping of the Agricultural Adjustment Act of 1933.*

Ideologists in the NFU were disappointed with the AAA.* By this time they had articulated what was to become known as the NFU's characteristic statement on farm income—that it should guarantee the farmer his "cost of production" and a "fair profit." This differed from the AAA's announced goal of "parity."* Most grain-growers in the organization, however, appreciated the practical benefits of the AAA. Simpson continued to work for monetary reform and mortgage relief, goals also espoused by his 1934 successor, E. E. Everson of South Dakota.

In the later 1930s the influence of the Farmers' Union with the Franklin D. Roosevelt* administration waxed as that of the Farm Bureau waned. Unlike the more conservative Farm Bureau, the NFU supported efforts of the administration to reform the economic structure of farming through such agencies as the Resettlement Administration* (later the Farm Security Administration),* viewing these as attempts to strengthen the family-size farm. Largely content with the New Deal's programs for control of production, maintenance of farm income, and extension of farm credit, the NFU backed off from political activism after electing Kansas's John Vesecky to its presidency in 1937. Cooperative activities received renewed emphasis. Through World War II and the immediate postwar years President John Patton maintained good relations with the Roosevelt and Harry S Truman* administrations.

During the era of the New Deal and thereafter, the NFU, although often cooperative with other farm organizations, maintained principles and means that set it apart from them. The basic tenets of the NFU were advocacy of the family farm and opposition to the industrialization of agriculture. These and a more militant tone of rhetoric particularly distinguished the NFU from the Farm Bureau. The NFU cultivated more cordial relations with organized labor than did most farm organizations. Its emphasis on cooperative organization and its grass-roots democracy in organizational operations also were notable features. In 1983 the approximate membership of the NFU was 275,000 farm families. (David Edgar

Lindstrom, *American Farmers and Rural Organizations*, 1948; William P. Tucker, "Populism Up-To-Date: The Story of the Farmers' Union," *Agricultural History*, XXI:198-208, 1947.)

THOMAS D. ISERN

NATIONAL GAS ACT OF 1938 (See FEDERAL POWER COMMISSION.)

NATIONAL HOUSING ACT OF 1934 The late 1920s bust in the real estate bubble and the crash of the stock market in 1929 devastated the construction industry and building trades. Major financial institutions—banks, savings banks, building and loan associations, and insurance companies—were frightened by the liquidity crisis in the money markets and increasingly reluctant to make construction and mortgage loans. At the same time, as unemployment increased and delinquent mortgages became more common, public demand for housing money also declined. Most economists and political officials were convinced that any recovery would have to include the construction industry. On July 22, 1932, under the direction of the Herbert Hoover* administration, Congress established the Federal Home Loan Bank System to discount the home mortgages of building and loan associations. The administration assumed with more liquidity, lending institutions would start extending more money and stimulate a recovery in the construction industry.

In addition to the concern about unemployment in the construction industry, there was also concern (especially among urban liberals like Senator Robert Wagner* of New York, social workers like Mary Simkhovitch, and housing experts like Catherine Bauer) about the state of housing for the poor in America. They were calling for a federal agency to construct low-cost housing on a permanent basis. They were opposed, of course, by landlord and real estate interests afraid of having rental markets undercut by low-cost housing.

President Franklin D. Roosevelt* was more inclined to worry about unemployment in the construction industry than about slum housing conditions in the cities. In his view, the federal housing program should be directed at reviving the construction industry, not at undertaking a massive slum renewal project. The Roosevelt administration created the Home Owners' Loan Corporation* in 1933 to assist people about to lose their homes but in 1934 also developed a comprehensive housing program embodied in the National Housing Act, which the president signed into law on June 28, 1934. Designed to make more private credit available for the repair and construction of homes and stimulate the building trades and heavy industry, the National Housing Act established the Federal Housing Administration* to insure banks, mortgage companies, and building and loan associations against losses they might sustain as a result of home improvement and new construction loans. The Reconstruction Finance Corporation* provided the FHA with $200 million in capital. Insured loans on home improvement were not to exceed $2,000, and the FHA would not insure loans totaling more than 20 percent of the institution's assets. The FHA could also insure first mortgages not exceeding $16,000 and 80 percent of the appraised value. The FHA had the power to insure low-cost housing project loans up to $10 million. Under the law, the FHA could also create national mortgage associations to buy first mortgages from banks and building and loan associations. The law also raised HOLC* borrowing power to $3 billion. Finally, the National Housing Act created the Federal Savings and Loan Insurance Corporation* to insure the deposits in building and loan associations, savings and loan associations, homestead associations, and cooperative banks. Although the FHA met important needs of middle-class families and home owners, it did not really address the needs of the poor, so Senator Robert Wagner and the social work profession continued to lobby for a more comprehensive federal housing program. That was not achieved until the Wagner-Steagall Housing Act of 1937.* (*Monthly Labor Review*, XXXIX:369-370, 1934; Pearl Janet Davies, *Real Estate in American History*, 1958.)

NATIONAL INDUSTRIAL RECOVERY ACT OF 1933 On June 16, 1933, President Franklin D. Roosevelt* signed the National Industrial Recovery Act into law, calling it one of the most important pieces of legislation in American history. Ever since the crash of the stock market in 1929 and onset of the Great Depression, large numbers of Americans had speculated about the origins and solutions to the crisis. Some, like Lewis Douglas,* advocated severe government economies to restore business confidence. Neo-Brandesians remained committed to trust-busting and competition as the only way of saving the country from the misery of monopolies. Another group, led by financier and industrialist Bernard Baruch,* Henry I. Harriman* of the U.S. Chamber of Commerce,* and Gerard Swope* of General Electric, believed the depression was the result of overproduction and too much competition and urged Roosevelt to have the federal government use a policy of industrial self-regulation. By relying on and strengthening the fair trade laws of existing trade associations, the federal government could eliminate destructive competition, encourage national economic planning, and improve business confidence and profits. Corporate leaders from the oil, coal, textile, and retail trade industries were also calling on Roosevelt to suspend anti-trust laws and establish industrial codes regulating prices and production. Labor leaders like John L. Lewis* of the United Mine Workers and Sidney Hillman* of the Amalgamated Clothing Workers were making similar demands for some type of federal stabilization of their industries through national planning and industrial self-government. As early as January 1932, Senator James J. Davis* and Congressman Melville Kelly, both Pennsylvania Republicans, had introduced a coal stabilization bill to relax anti-trust laws, establish a licensing commission, and encourage licensed producers to associate in order to control production and prices. The major philosophical foundation for the NIRA came from industrial and pro-business planners who had experienced the War Industries Board during World War I and believed in national planning by enlightened business leaders through trade associations. New Dealers Raymond Moley* and Hugh S. Johnson* vigorously supported the idea.

At the same time business leaders were advocating national planning and industrial self-regulation, Senator Hugo Black* of Alabama was pushing his thirty-hour workweek bill to spread jobs, protect labor standards, and increase worker purchasing power by outlawing the interstate shipment of goods produced in factories employing people more than thirty hours a week. The AFL* had endorsed the bill and William Connery* of the House Labor Committee supported it. The Black-Connery Bill* was moving through Congress even though Roosevelt opposed it as rigid and unconstitutional. Finally, Senator Robert Wagner* of New York, brain truster* Rexford Tugwell,* and Secretary of Labor Frances Perkins* had met and drafted a proposal for industrial self-regulation through trade associations, for a massive public works program for the unemployed, and for a guarantee of collective bargaining for organized labor.

Early in May, a drafting committee composed of Senator Robert Wagner, Lewis Douglas of the Bureau of the Budget,* Hugh S. Johnson, and labor expert Donald R. Richberg* put together an omnibus measure designed to satisfy without alienating a variety of interests—advocates of social reform, public works, labor, trust-busting, self-regulation, and economic planning. Senator Robert Wagner introduced the measure to Congress in mid-May, and the bill was supported by the AFL as well as by the Chamber of Commerce and the National Association of Manufacturers.* Labor liked the bill because it guaranteed collective bargaining while business accepted it because it would permit price-fixing. Old anti-trusters like Senator William Borah* hated the bill, but they could not exert enough pressure to stop it; and the National Industrial Recovery Act became law on June 16, 1933.

Title I of the NIRA described the steps the government would take to bring about industrial self-regulation. Section 1 of Title I was a broad description of policy—how the National Recovery Administration* would promote cooperative action, eliminate unfair practices, increase purchasing power, expand production, reduce unemployment, and conserve national resources. Section 2 imposed a two-year limit on the measure but extended great authority to the president to create administrative agencies, appoint employees without regard to civil service laws, and delegate power to his appointees. Section 3 gave the president authority to approve equitable, representative codes for various trades and industries and to add or delete segments of codes and establish entirely new codes. Under Section 4, the president could assist businesses to enter into voluntary agreements to help achieve the purpose of the law and to license cooperating concerns. Section 5 exempted all of the codes from anti-trust laws. Section 7 established basic labor standards, including provisions for a minimum wage, and Section 7(a) outlawed yellow-dog contracts and guaranteed the right of employees to organize and bargain collectively. Section 8 guaranteed that none of the codes could conflict with provisions of the Agricultural Adjustment Act of 1933.* Section 9, among other things, gave the president the right to regulate the shipment of petroleum across state lines. Section 10 authorized the president to remake any of the codes at any time during the life of the National Industrial Recovery Act. Title II established an emergency Public Works Administration* with $3.3 billion to construct highways, dams, federal buildings, naval construction, and other projects. Title III provided for excess-profits taxes to help finance the Public Works Administration.* (Bernard Bellush, *The Failure of the NRA*, 1975.)

NATIONAL INDUSTRIAL RECOVERY BOARD (See NATIONAL RECOVERY ADMINISTRATION.)

NATIONAL INSTITUTE OF HEALTH Established in 1901 as the Hygienic Laboratory with a $35,000 grant, the National Institute of Health received its new name in 1930 when congressional legislation authorized the secretary of the treasury to acquire property and construct buildings which became centered in Bethesda, Maryland. The surgeon general was also authorized to make appointments of distinguished scientists and physicians to staff the National Institute of Health. During the 1930s, the National Institute of Health conducted studies dealing with pneumonia, tetanus, leprosy, heart disease, meningitis, nutrition, and mental health. Under the sponsorship of Senator Royal Copeland,* Congress passed the National Cancer Institute Act of 1937, creating a new branch of the National Institute of Health at Bethesda. In addition to conducting widespread research on the causes and prevention of cancer, the National Cancer Institute purchased and distributed radium for the diagnosis and treatment of cancer. (Samuel I. Rosenman, ed., *The Public Papers and Addresses of Franklin D. Roosevelt*, IX:527-529, 1941.)

NATIONAL LABOR BOARD Early in August 1933, President Franklin D. Roosevelt* accepted the recommendation of the Industrial Advisory Board and the Labor Advisory Board* that he create a National Labor Board to mediate labor disputes and make sure that the program of the National Recovery Administration* went forward. Senator Robert Wagner* of New York was named head of the board; and it included: as its labor representatives, William Green* of the AFL,* economics professor Leo Wolman* of Columbia University, and John L. Lewis* of the United Mine Workers; and, as its business representatives, Walter C. Teagle, president of the Standard Oil Company of New Jersey, Gerard Swope,* president of General Electric, and Louis E. Kirstein, general manager of Filene's in Boston. But because of the vagueness of Section 7(a) of the NIRA* and its own lack of power, the National Labor Board could at first do little more than ask recalcitrant employers unwilling to accept collective bargaining to obey the law.

During its first three months, however, the National Labor Board made several important accomplishments because of the willingness of employers to cooperate with the still new NRA. In September, the board managed to get the Berkshire

Knitting Mills to agree to negotiate labor questions with the American Federation of Full-Fashioned Hosiery Workers. It also settled the silk strike in Paterson, New Jersey; several auto strikes in Detroit; and the steel strike at the Weirton Steel Company in West Virginia and Ohio. In the process, the National Labor Board established a ''common law'' understanding of Section 7(a): that the principle of majority rule was to prevail in elections and negotiations; that union membership was not to be a cause for discharge or demotion; that workers could reject company-dominated unions; that elections were secret; and that both strikers and non-strikers could vote in elections, but not workers hired during the strike.

But late in 1933, the National Labor Board entered a period of decline from which it never recovered. It lacked clear statutory power to mediate labor disputes, and as the business crisis began to ease in 1933, major business groups like the National Association of Manufacturers* launched a campaign against the National Labor Board. In December the Weirton Steel Company decided to defy the board by conducting elections only for company-union representatives, and the Edward G. Budd Manufacturing Company of Philadelphia refused to abide a NLB order to end a strike and hold new employee elections. The board protested to the National Recovery Administration, but no action was taken against the companies. In the process the NLB lost much credibility. President Roosevelt issued an executive order on December 15, 1933, retroactively approving the board's activities, but it could not recover from its own lack of power. During its first three months, the board had settled 104 of 155 cases, but in the next three months it successfully negotiated only twenty-eight of eighty-six cases. Business was in a state of defiance. Also, a split had developed between General Hugh S. Johnson* of the National Recovery Administration and Senator Robert Wagner of the NLB because Johnson tended to side with management in the labor disputes. As a result, the federal government was divided and business simply used delaying tactics and outright defiance without fear of reprisal.

The final blow to the National Labor Board came in March 1934 when the AFL threatened to strike General Motors unless the company recognized the union, reinstated men discharged for union activity, and agreed to a 20 percent wage increase. The union presented its demands to the National Labor Board, and General Motors announced its decision that Section 7(a) was a mistake and that it would not cooperate with the NLB. President Roosevelt, pleased that auto producton was increasing and employment in the industry was reviving, feared the strike and negotiated a settlement which hurt the AFL and all but destroyed the NLB. He created a tripartite Automobile Labor Board* within the NRA but separate from the National Labor Board. The Automobile Labor Board then undermined the NLB and Section 7(a) by giving legal sanction to company-dominated unions and endorsing proportional representation rather than majority rule in elections. Two months later, on June 29, 1934, President Roosevelt abolished the National Labor Board by executive order and created a three-person National Labor Relations Board* under the jurisdiction of the Department of Labor. (Bernard Bellush, *The Failure of the NRA*, 1975; Peter H. Irons, *The New Deal Lawyers*, 1982.)

NATIONAL LABOR RELATIONS ACT OF 1935 Described by William Green* of the American Federation of Labor* as ''the Magna Carta of Labor of the United States,'' the National Labor Relations Act of 1935 was the most significant piece of labor legislation, up to its time, in American history. Although Section 7(a) of the National Industrial Recovery Act* had guaranteed labor's right to bargain collectively, the National Labor Board* and its successor the National Labor Relations Board,* had no real power to enforce the law. Under the direction of Lloyd Garrison* and then Francis Biddle,* the NLRB had enjoyed only a quasi-judicial function, investigating violations of Section 7(a) and creating a body of common law referring to labor, but the board had no real authority to punish violators. Although the board had referred thirty-three cases of noncompliance with Section 7(a) to the Department of Justice by March 1, 1935, judgments were received in none of the cases. The board had responsibility without power. The overwhelmingly Democratic congress, elected in November 1934, was determined to give teeth to the National Labor Relations Board, and Senator Robert Wagner* of New York led the way.

Late in 1934 Wagner had his secretary, Leon Keyserling,* resurrect his unsuccessful earlier labor law and redraft it with the assistance of the NLRB legal staff. They were determined to institutionalize the right of labor to organize and bargain effectively with employers. The bill upheld the right of collective bargaining as the only way workers could hope to deal effectively with concentrated industrial power; insisted that employers bargain in good faith with the full intention of reaching amicable settlements; prohibited employers from engaging in anti-union espionage, blacklisting, strikebreaking, yellow-dog contracts, or discriminating on wages and promotions against union members or leaders; forbade employers from dominating or even interfering with the cperations of company unions; specifically stated that the union elected by a majority of workers in free elections would be the sole bargaining agent for all the workers in a company; and established the new National Labor Relations Board as an independent agency to act as a ''Supreme Court'' in labor disputes. With the power to subpoena witnesses and order federal court action, the National Labor Relations Board now had the power to enforce its decisions.

Senator Wagner introduced the measure to the Senate in late February 1935, and William P. Connery, Jr.,* sponsored it in the House. Proponents of the measure viewed it as a recovery measure as well as a labor measure. They argued that the law would promote higher wages, a more equitable distribution of income, and greater mass purchasing power. All of those would stimulate production and employment. The business community, which overwhelmingly opposed the law, viewed it as an unconstitutional, totalitarian scheme to destroy free enterprise. Although President Franklin D. Roosevelt* took a neutral stand on the bill, as did most of his cabinet, the bill moved through the Democratic Congress in the spring and summer of 1935. He signed it into law on July 5, 1935. Because of the National Labor Relations Act, the political and legal atmosphere for union organization was overwhelmingly favorable in the late 1930s, despite the economic effects of the depression. By 1940 there were nearly 9 million union members in the United States. (Irving Bernstein, *Turbulent Years. A History of the American Worker, 1933-1941*, 1970; Cletus E. Daniel, *The ACLU and the Wagner Act: An Inquiry into the Depression-Era Crisis of American Liberalism*, 1980.)

NATIONAL LABOR RELATIONS BOARD The National Labor Relations Board was an independent agency created by the National Labor Relations Act of 1935.* It had two major functions under its original legislative mandate: to conduct secret-ballot representation elections among employees to determine whether or not they wanted to be represented by a particular union and to remedy certain unlawful labor practices by employers or unions. The National Labor Relations Board had two predecessors: the National Labor Board,* which existed from August 1933 to June 1934, and the old National Labor Relations Board, which had functioned between June 1934 and July 1935. President Franklin D. Roosevelt* had created both of them by executive order to help prevent major industrial strikes which would seriously impede the recovery program. They had no decision-making authority, only the right to attempt to amicably settle labor disputes through mediation and voluntary cooperation. The National Labor Board had been headed by Senator Robert Wagner,* and the old National Labor Relations Board, by Lloyd Garrison* and later Francis Biddle.* It quickly became clear, however, that the two goals of the NLB and the old NLRB were not compatible. It was impossible to settle strikes to the satisfaction of both employers and unions while upholding Section 7(a) of the National Industrial Recovery Act* guaranteeing the right of workers to organize and bargain collectively through representatives of their own choosing without interference from employers. Non-compliance with NLB and NLRB efforts became more and more widespread in 1933 and 1934. Voluntarism was not working. Gradually, both bodies moved away from settling disputes to quasi-judicial roles, formulating a set of principles, a common law, of labor relations. They set forth principles of law, conducted formal hearings, issued rules, and insisted on legalistic conformity in all their procedures. But they possessed no statutory authority to enforce their regulations. Not until 1935, when the Supreme Court* declared the National Industrial Recovery Act unconstitutional, did the opportunity appear to pass such statutory authority. The National Labor Relations Act of 1935 gave the new National Labor Relations Board the power it needed to enforce its legal and judicial regulations.

The major provisions of the National Labor Relations Act amounted to legislative embodiments of the previous experiences of the National Labor Board and the National Labor Relations Board. It guaranteed majority rule and exclusive representation; specified unfair labor practices; guaranteed the right of employees to organize and the obligation of employers to bargain with the representatives of their employees; created a new NLRB as an independent agency authorized to enforce its rulings through the federal courts. It also enjoyed wideranging administrative discretion to identify new forms of unfair labor practices and the right to subpoena witnesses and documents.

To serve on the new National Labor Relations Board, President Franklin D. Roosevelt selected J. Warren Madden* of the University of Pittsburgh, Edwin S. Smith, and John M. Carmody.* They selected Charles Fahy* as general counsel, and Fahy then began preparing the NLRB's legal agenda. Interested in neither social policy nor in politics, Fahy approached his task legalistically, committed to enforcing the National Labor Relations Act of 1935 through carefully selected test cases. During much of 1935 and 1936, they were preoccupied with defending the National Labor Relations Act of 1935 against a hostile Supreme Court. Fahy and a brilliant staff of attorneys developed a master plan of cases which clearly demonstrated the commerce clause criterion. In particular, they chose cases which argued that strikes and labor problems unquestionably disrupted the flow of commerce and therefore were subject to Congressional regulation. The National Labor Relations Board was subjected to unrelenting attack from the National Association of Manufacturers* and the U.S. Chamber of Commerce.* It also faced a deluge of injunction suits in district courts. Between November 1935 and June 1936 the board had to deal with eighty-three such suits, most of which put off board hearings by having individuals refuse subpoenas to testify. The American Liberty League* led the assault. Not until 1937, when the Supreme Court upheld the constitutionality of the National Labor Relations Act of 1935 in its *National Labor Relations Board v. Jones & Laughlin Steel Corporation*,* was the NLRB able to concentrate its efforts on violations of labor rights. Even then, they were hurt by accusations from the American Federation of Labor.* Wounded by the defection of the Committee for Industrial Organization* in 1936, the AFL resented the NLRB's willingness to handle CIO cases and adopted a so-called "pro-CIO" stance. After the Democrats suffered serious losses in the congressional elections of 1938,* conservatives in Congress turned on the NLRB as a symbol of the "leftist domination" of the New Deal.* Supported by the AFL, conservative Congressman Howard Smith* of Virginia launched a special investigation of the board in 1939. Although the Smith Committee's recommendations to all but destroy the board never passed, they did force administrative changes and limited the board's effectiveness. The anti-NLRB coalition of the AFL, businessmen, and southern Democrats which formed in the late 1930s ultimately triumphed with the Taft-Hartley Act of 1946. (James A. Gross, *The Making of the N.L.R.B.: A Study in Economics, Politics and the Law*, 1974; Peter H. Irons, *The New Deal Lawyers*, 1982.)

NATIONAL LABOR RELATIONS BOARD V. JONES & LAUGHLIN STEEL CORPORATION Pursuant to a complaint by the Beaver Valley (Pennsylvania)

Lodge No. 200, Amalgamated Association of Iron, Steel, and Tin Workers of America, the National Labor Relations Board* charged Jones & Laughlin Steel Corporation with unfair labor practices in violation of the National Labor Relations Act.* The corporation was accused of discriminating against union members in its hiring and tenure policies, of using coercion and intimidation to discourage union membership, and of firing a number of employees who were union leaders or active in union affairs.

In board hearings on the charges, counsel for Jones & Laughlin insisted that employees had been discharged for reasons other than union membership. Beyond that, counsel challenged the constitutionality of the National Labor Relations Act and its applicability to the case. Upon presentation of evidence, Jones & Laughlin moved for dismissal for lack of jurisdiction. When that motion was denied, counsel for Jones & Laughlin walked out of the hearings.

Upon investigation, the board sustained the charges, and in accordance with the National Labor Relations Act, ordered the corporation to cease and desist from such practices, to reinstate discharged employees with compensation for lost wages, and to post notices for thirty days that the corporation would not discharge or discriminate against union members or against workers wishing to join the union. When Jones & Laughlin refused to comply, the board petitioned the 5th Circuit Court of Appeals to enforce the order under provisions of the National Labor Relations Act. But the court denied the petition, ruling that the order was beyond the scope of federal power. The United States appealed to the Supreme Court,* which granted certiorari. The case was argued on February 10 and 11, 1937, and decided on April 12, 1937. Chief Justice Charles Evans Hughes* wrote the majority opinion upholding the constitutionality of the National Labor Relations Act.

After reviewing the major provisions of the act, Justice Hughes discussed the complex and extensive operations of Jones & Laughlin Steel Corporation, leaving no doubt that the corporation was involved in interstate commerce on a massive scale. He then turned to those questions of law on which Jones & Laughlin had contested the validity of the act. He concluded: (1) that the act was clearly within the sphere of constitutional authority; (2) that employees had a fundamental right to organize and select their representatives for collective bargaining; (3) that Jones & Laughlin's activities constituted a "stream" or "flow" of commerce with the Pennsylvania manufacturing plant as the focal point. Labor strife there, he asserted, would cripple the whole process. "The fundamental principle is that the power to regulate commerce is the power to enact 'all appropriate legislation' for its' protection or advancement." (4) Furthermore he concluded that the effect of labor strife on interstate commerce would be direct and catastrophic. Justice Hughes asked: "When industries organize themselves on a national scale, making their relation to interstate commerce the dominant factor in their activities, how can it be maintained that their industrial labor relations constitute a forbidden field into which Congress may not enter when it is necessary to protect interstate commerce from the paralyzing consequences of industrial war?'' Thus, labor matters were clearly subject to federal regulation.

Finally, Chief Justice Hughes stated that the procedures of the National Labor Relations Board did not violate due process as charged by Jones & Laughlin. He concluded, therefore, that ''the order of the Board was within its competency and . . . the act is valid as here applied.'' The judgment of the circuit court was reversed in a five to four decision by the Supreme Court. (Gerald Dykstra and L. G. Dykstra, *Selected Cases on Government and Business*, 1937; Alfred Kelly and Winfred Harbison, *The American Constitution*, 1970; *Supreme Court Reporter*, LVII:615-641, 1937.)

JOSEPH M. ROWE, JR.

NATIONAL LONGSHOREMEN'S BOARD Under the leadership of Harry Bridges, the International Longshoremen's Association called a strike for March 23, 1934, unless management agreed to wage increases, a six-hour day and a thirty-hour week, and replacement of the ''shape-up'' with a union hiring hall. At President Franklin D. Roosevelt's* request, the ILA postponed the strike on March 22 pending a government investigation of the issues at stake. On June 26, 1934, the president established the National Longshoremen's Board to investigate the causes of the strike and to arbitrate a settlement if both parties agreed. Catholic Archbishop Edward J. Hanna of San Francisco chaired the board; and he was joined by D. K. Cushing, a prominent local attorney, and Assistant Labor Secretary Edward F. McGrady. While the board was investigating, a violent general strike spread throughout San Francisco. After two weeks both the ILA and shipping interests agreed to allow the National Longshoremen's Board to arbitrate the dispute, and on October 12, 1934, the board handed down its decision. It was a great victory for Bridges and the ILA. Although management gained the right to introduce labor-saving devices, the ILA was able to replace the ''shape-up'' with a union hiring hall, raise wages, reduce the work week to thirty hours, and receive overtime pay. The National Longshoremen's Board then went out of existence early in 1935. (Bernard Bellush, *The Failure of the NRA*, 1975.)

NATIONAL PLANNING BOARD (See NATIONAL RESOURCES PLANNING BOARD.)

NATIONAL POWER POLICY COMMITTEE Because of overlapping authority in the area of public power between such agencies as the Public Works Administration,* Tennessee Valley Authority,* Bureau of Reclamation,* Federal Power Commission,* and the Federal Trade Commission,* President Franklin D. Roosevelt* created the National Power Policy Committee on July 5, 1934, and placed it under Secretary of the Interior Harold Ickes'* authority in the Public Works Administration. The committee's purpose was to coordinate federal power policy, and its studies and deliberations in 1934 and 1935 led to the Public

Utility Holding Company Act of 1935* and the creation of the Rural Electrification Administration.* In 1938, after a Federal Power Commission report on the problem of electric power in a national emergency, the president created the National Defense Power Committee to help coordinate federal power policy and prepare for any national emergencies. The primary accomplishments of the committee were to help electric utilities serving major industrial areas to increase generating capacity and to standardize generator specifications to facilitate production and repair. On October 13, 1939, the president consolidated the National Defense Power Committee into the National Power Policy Committee, which then consisted of Harold L. Ickes, Assistant Secretary of War Louis Johnson, Leland Olds* of the Federal Power Commission, Jerome Frank* of the SEC,* John Carmody* of the Federal Works Agency,* Harry Slattery* of the REA, and David Lilienthal* of the TVA. (Samuel I. Rosenman, ed., *The Public Papers and Addresses of Franklin D. Roosevelt*, VIII:544-545, 1941.)

NATIONAL PROGRESSIVES OF AMERICA Following his defeat on the Progressive ticket in the presidential election of 1924, Robert M. La Follette hoped to rebuild the party on a national level, but his death in 1925 destroyed the movement. Robert M. La Follette, Jr.,* was too busy trying to build a power base in the Senate to worry about a Progressive party. But the 1932 elections in Wisconsin helped revive the old progressive spirit. Philip La Follette* and Senator John J. Blaine lost in the Republican primary because of the defection of progressive voters to Democratic primary campaigns. With the liberal vote divided between Democratic and Republican primaries, they had almost an impossible time winning the nominations. Philip La Follette decided that leaving the Republican party* was the only way of salvaging his political career. Robert La Follette, Jr., was much more hesitant, afraid of losing his seniority in Senate committee assignments. So Philip La Follette, along with Thomas Amlie,* led the way in establishing the Wisconsin Progressive party* in 1934. Their platform called for more federal relief appropriations, unemployment insurance, old-age pensions, tax reform, public ownership of utilities, and a public referendum before the United States could enter another war. The Progressives nominated Philip La Follette for governor and Robert La Follette, Jr., for the Senate. Both won their elections, Robert by a landslide and Philip by a narrow margin. Otherwise, the Democratic party* triumphed throughout the state.

Philip La Follette wanted to expand the party to the national level, and he was encouraged in 1936 when Wisconsin Progressives swept the state. The recession of 1937 and 1938* exposed, in Philip La Follette's mind, the failure of the New Deal.* Late in April 1938 he formally launched the National Progressives of America. The new party's platform attacked Wall Street's concentrated financial power, advocated an isolationist foreign policy, opposed all recovery programs involving cuts in production, and insisted on government ownership of all utilities and control of banking and credit. Although the formation of the National Progressives of America at first worried President Franklin D.

Roosevelt,* his fears did not last long. In Iowa and California, the NPA candidates suffered embarrassing defeats, and in Wisconsin, Republican Julius Heil handed Philip La Follette a humiliating defeat in the gubernatorial elections. The Republicans also captured the state legislature in Wisconsin and eight of the ten House seats. The National Progressives of America was dead. (Roger T. Johnson, *Robert M. La Follette, Jr., and the Decline of the Progressive Party in Wisconsin*, 1964.)

NATIONAL RECOVERY ADMINISTRATION The National Recovery Administration was a federal agency created under the National Industrial Recovery Act* of June 16, 1933, and abolished on January 1, 1936, after the law's major provisions were held unconstitutional. Its function was to develop and administer an industrial code system, which through appropriate controls over industrial pricing, production, trade practices, and labor relations was supposed to end destructive competition and bring recovery from the Great Depression.

In part the establishment of the NRA was a response to the crisis conditions of 1933. But the roots of the experiment can be traced back to the system of industrial self-government utilized by the federal war agencies during World War I. After the war there was agitation for a similar peacetime system, and after 1929 this was urged as a way to deal with depression conditions. With governmental support, it was argued, organized industries could stabilize their markets and reemploy the jobless; and with this argument a number of the early new New Dealers, including President Franklin D. Roosevelt* himself, were in sympathy. In their "war on depression," they turned to mechanisms resembling those of 1918, and the result was legislation suspending the anti-trust laws for two years and authorizing industrial organizations to formulate codes that could secure the fair competitive behavior and enlightened labor practices thought necessary to restore economic prosperity. Such codes, when approved by the president, would have the force of law, and in cases where no approvable code was forthcoming the president might devise and impose one.

To head the program, Roosevelt chose General Hugh S. Johnson,* a former member of the War Industries Board; and under Johnson's leadership, the NRA set out to identify codification with national patriotism, all patriots being urged to boycott businesses operating without the NRA's official blue eagle emblem. In all, some 541 industrial codes were eventually written and approved, each combining the regulation of business practices with a required section guaranteeing labor's rights to organize and bargain collectively—Section 7(a) in the act. And despite widespread non-compliance, the results were reduced competition and enhanced business and labor organization. These, however, failed to bring recovery. On the contrary, they are generally thought to have contributed to a further downturn in late 1933, and by early 1934 the code structures were becoming the subject of mounting criticism. Labor leaders saw them as thwarting genuine unionization; small business and consumer spokesmen were concerned about the growth of "monopoly;" political leftists saw the emergence of a "corporate state;" and organized industries involved were becoming increasingly fearful of "government control" and increasingly dubious about the "partnership" they had formed with federal authorities.

Such criticism became particularly pronounced in the spring and summer of 1934. It was articulated in a series of official hearings, in congressional debates, and in the reports of a National Recovery Review Board headed by the criminal trial lawyer Clarence Darrow.* It also strengthened the hands of the NRA's Consumers' Advisory Board* and Research Planning Division, both of which began challenging Johnson's industrial orientation and calling for changes in the codes. And it helped to produce a growing rift between code administrators and the special labor boards to which unions were taking their complaints.

As the criticism continued and the internal quarrels intensified, Johnson became increasingly unstable, behaving in ways that eventually led Roosevelt to make a major reorganization of the agency. In September 1934 Johnson was replaced by a National Industrial Recovery Board; and under its auspices efforts were made to revise the codes so as to reduce their "monopolistic" aspects, prevent further abuses by code authorities, and strengthen their labor provisions. Such efforts, however, met with minimal success, chiefly because they encountered strong opposition from code administrators and their business constituencies. And as these conflicts continued, political support for the program kept eroding. In early 1935, as the date for its expiration approached, Roosevelt recommended that it be extended in a modified form. But by this time it had few friends left, and in Congress there was much reluctance to carry out the president's recommendations.

As it turned out, Congress never got to decide the matter. On May 27, 1935, in the case of *Schechter v. United States*,* the Supreme Court* held that the code system involved both an unconstitutional delegation of legislative power and an unconstitutional attempt to expand the federal power to regulate interstate commerce. It had to be abandoned; and under the temporary extension of the National Industrial Recovery Act that was finally passed, the NRA was reduced to a skeleton of its former self, engaged chiefly now in correlating and summarizing the information that it had gathered. In late 1935 it also attempted to develop voluntary codes, but its efforts to do this failed to produce anything upon which the interested industries and the anti-trust authorities could agree.

Historians have generally regarded the NRA's code system as one of the New Deal's* greatest failures and most egregious mistakes. The underlying economic theory, they argue, was badly flawed; and in operation, the system tended to hamper recovery, foster restrictive cartelization, and create obstacles to effective forms of public regulation. Some, however, have credited the program with giving an initial psychological lift to the nation's depressed spirits. Others have held that it did help to improve business ethics, promote labor unionization, and put an end to child labor. And still others have seen it as a forerunner of the cooperative planning toward which advanced capitalist economies have moved. Parts of it, moreover, were resurrected in the post-*Schechter* period. "Little

NRA's''* were established through special legislation in a number of natural resource, transportation, and service industries; and the labor provisions required of NRA codes were, in strengthened form, incorporated in the National Labor Relations Act of 1935.* (Bernard Bellush, *The Failure of the NRA*, 1975; Ellis W. Hawley, *The New Deal and the Problem of Monopoly: A Study in Economic Ambivalence*, 1966; Robert F. Himmelberg, *The Origins of the National Recovery Administration: Business, Government, and the Trade Association Issue, 1921–1933*, 1976; Leverett S. Lyon et al., *The National Recovery Administration*, 1935.)

ELLIS W. HAWLEY

NATIONAL RESOURCES BOARD (See NATIONAL RESOURCES PLANNING BOARD.)

NATIONAL RESOURCES COMMITTEE (See NATIONAL RESOURCES PLANNING BOARD.)

NATIONAL RESOURCES PLANNING BOARD Title II of the National Industrial Recovery Act of 1933* established the National Planning Board under the direction of the PWA* administrator, and in July 1933 Frederick A. Delano,* Charles E. Merriam,* and Wesley Clair Mitchell* became members of the Advisory Committee of the National Planning Board. America's first experiment in peacetime national planning began under the aegis of the New Deal.* Precedents for the program existed in the War Industries Board of World War I and the associational ideas of Secretary of Commerce Herbert Hoover* during the 1920s. In 1931 Congress created the Federal Employment Stabilization Board to plan public works projects for use in the economic downturn of the Great Depression. Moribund for most of its existence, the board was replaced by the National Planning Board. Personnel manning the board remained remarkably continuous, though the agency changed names several times: National Planning Board (1933-1934), National Resources Board (1932-1935), National Resources Committee (1935-1939), and the National Resources Planning Board (1939-1943).

The New Deal planners came from distinguished backgrounds. Frederic Delano, President Franklin D. Roosevelt's* uncle had moved up the corporate ladder of the Chicago, Burlington, and Quincy Railroad from 1885 to 1905. He moved into the city and regional planning as promoter of the Burnham City Plan of Chicago (1908), director of the Regional Plan of New York and Its Environs (1923-1932), and founder and director of Washington, D.C.,'s National Capital Park and Planning Commission (1924-1943). Chairman of the Political Science Department at the University of Chicago, Charles E. Merriam became a manager of social science research as founder and head of the Social Science Research Council (1923-1927). Institutional economist Wesley Clair Mitchell of Columbia University served as research director of the influential National Bureau of Economic Research (1920) and had written on fluctuations in the business cycle. Mitchell resigned from the planning board in late 1935 to devote his time to work for the NBER.

From 1936 through 1943 an advisory committee of two representatives of the business community replaced Mitchell's position. Delano and Merriam chose Boston businessman Henry S. Dennison and R. H. Macy's Treasurer Beardsley Ruml* for the positions. Dennison had won a considerable reputation as a welfare capitalist at the Dennison Manufacturing Company, instituting such ideas as profit sharing, unemployment insurance, and other welfare reforms. He believed in the idea of intrafirm business planning through the use of socioeconomic research both by individual companies and trade associations. Ruml served as director of the Laura Spelman Rockefeller Memorial (1921-1929), which he used as a philanthropic vehicle for building a national social science network of private research institutes, private and public universities, and cooperative governmental agencies. He worked extensively with Merriam through the 1920s and 1930s, while his organization provided financial support for many of the Hooverian studies between 1921 and 1933.

The idea of advisory national planning united the planners. They argued that skilled researchers working as consultants to the planning board could provide the president and the Congress with alternative plans for future policies. Each of the planners recognized that the rise of urban-industrial America had made organized groups the center of American life. Their purpose as planners involved promoting cooperation between interest groups, social scientists, and politicians on the national level through the work of the planning board. Over the course of the period from 1933 to 1943, the planners expanded their definition of planning to include broader social and economic research that went beyond preparing a shelf of public works projects.

By 1939 the New Deal planning board had established committees to study land-use planning, multi-use water planning, mineral policy, population changes, industrial resources, transportation, energy, the impact of changes in science and technology, and the structure of the economy. Many of these studies remain the only one of their kind even today. The board also established regional planning agencies in New England and the Pacific Northwest, sponsored state planning agencies in a majority of the states, and stimulated numerous city planning groups.

New Deal planning encountered resistance from various quarters. Between 1933 and 1939 the board remained divided by conflict among cabinet members protecting their own turf and the advisory committee of the planners who hoped for cross-departmental coordination. Staff members of government agencies often resented the work of the planners as meddling, duplication of effort, and of little practical use. After the Supreme Court* declared the NIRA unconstitutional in May 1935, the planning agency lacked legislative authority from Congress. Roosevelt temporized through use of executive orders and appropriations from the emergency relief acts, while efforts to make the board a permanent agency were defeated in Congress as southern Democrats, Republicans, and old-line Progressives hit the planning group hard during the 1937-1939 debates over passage of the executive reorganization bill. The provisions in the bill creating a permanent planning board failed to pass, so Roosevelt had to continue the board through executive action between 1939 and 1943.

From late 1937 through the spring of 1943, the planners turned increasingly toward more controversial social and economic research that put them in the political arena facing stiff opposition. Delano, Ruml, and Dennison played important behind-the-scene roles in persuading Roosevelt to resume compensatory spending in the spring of 1938. Merriam helped to establish and served on the President's Committee of Administrative Management* that prepared the initial drafts of the reorganization bill in early 1937. From 1939 through 1943, the planners engaged in war and postwar planning. Early during the World War II mobilization the planning board conducted industrial plant location studies, created the Roster of Specialized and Scientific Personnel, and established the Economic Stabilization Unit which prepared quarterly economic trends reports for Roosevelt. In March 1943 the board released its postwar planning report which called for compensatory spending over the course of the business cycle, the adoption of an Economic Bill of Rights for education, work, health care, and social insurance, and revision of the social security laws to extend coverage to those left out in the Social Security Act of 1935.*

In the spring of 1943, the planning agency came under fierce attack in Congressional appropriations hearings that led to a heated ideological debate over national planning. Congressional critics did not reject the ideas of planning for the postwar era, but they thought that extension of executive power during the New Deal and World War II years had gone too far. Despite the planners' careful explanations on a number of key issues, the critics won out. Conservatives branded the planners with advocating permanent deficit-spending measures after the war on the basis of several pamphlets written by consultant Alvin Hansen.* Tactical errors in legislative maneuvering, lukewarm support from Roosevelt, and critics' misplaced equation of American planning with Soviet and Nazi planning led to abolition of the board effective August 31, 1943.

Historians of the New Deal have tended to emphasize the debate over national planning during the 1930s from the perspective of public commentators rather than the New Deal planners. They envisioned planning as a continuously changing process rather than as a rigid blueprint for the future. In the context of the New Deal, they sought to use social scientific expertise as a way to stimulate economic stabilization, social cooperation between organized interest groups, and political support for a revivified liberalism. Ultimately their vision remained conservative in intent and limited by their faith in the equality of contenders within the pluralistic system of American politics and economics. Their own backgrounds indicated a blindness to flaws within the American political economy that later critics would note. Rather than constituting a cutting edge for New Deal reform, the planners hoped to carry the tradition of voluntary cooperation forward into the corporate-oriented organizational society. They disliked governmental coercion and hoped to avoid the extremes of violent revolution from either the right or the left. They sought to transform nineteenth-century liberalism into twentieth-century cooperation between the private and public sectors. Refusing to see the obstacles in their path revealed by the strength of private interest groups and public sector bureaucratic defensiveness, the planners lost the battle of 1943.

In the post-1943 period planning continued, but in a fragmented way indicative of the confusions of the broker state system created by the New Deal. Jurisdictional disputes among government agencies, party politics, and the rise of private sector organizations such as the National Planning Association and the Committee for Economic Development left planning partial and piecemeal. Yet the New Deal planning legacy remained for those willing to look. The planning board was responsible for drafting the GI Bill of 1944. The spirit of New Deal planning carried on in the Employment Act of 1946 which created the Council of Economic Advisers, the Joint Committee on the Economic Report, and the interplay of presidents and the Congress in economic policymaking. But after 1943, no one formal administrative agency within the federal government held an exclusive brief for national planning. (Philip Warken, *A History of the National Resources Planning Board, 1933-1943*, 1979; Marion Clawson, *New Deal Planning: The National Resources Planning Board*, 1981.)

PATRICK D. REAGAN

NATIONAL SMALL BUSINESS MEN'S ASSOCIATION The National Small Business Men's Association was founded in 1938 by Secretary of Commerce Daniel C. Roper.* As part of the New Deal's* growing concern after 1935 with the problems of monopoly, competition, and small business, the Department of Commerce sponsored a special conference in February 1938 attended by nearly 1,000 small businessmen. They complained loudly and bitterly about the dictatorial power of big business, big banking, and big government. The bad publicity of the conference and the manifest frustration of small businessmen throughout the country prompted the administration to action on two fronts. Daniel C. Roper founded the National Small Business Men's Association to serve as the collective voice of small businessmen, advise them of government services, and lobby for favorable legislation; and President Franklin D. Roosevelt* had the Reconstruction Finance Corporation* increase its small loan program. During World War II, the National Small Business Men's Association helped win war contracts for small businesses, and after the war the association helped secure favorable tax legislation and right-to-work laws. In 1962 the National Small Business Men's Association and the Association for Small Business merged to form the National Small Business Association. (Harmon Zeigler, *The Politics of Small Business*, 1961.)

NATIONAL STEEL LABOR RELATIONS BOARD The National Steel Labor Relations Board was established by Public Resolution No. 44 and implemented by Executive Order No. 6751 on June 28, 1934. The board was specifically designed to deal with problems affecting Section 7(a) in the steel industry, especially the issue of trade or company unions. The Amalgamated Association of Iron, Steel, and Tin Workers was reviving under the impact of the National Industrial Recovery Act,* and in May 1934 it demanded recognition from the major steel firms. Employers rejected or ignored the demand, and the Iron and Steel Institute announced that the vast majority of the industry's 430,000 workers preferred company unions. The union then threatened a strike, and the National Steel Labor Relations Board was created. Members of the board were Judge Walter Stacy of North Carolina, chairman; Rear Admiral (ret.) Henry A. Wiley; and Dr. James Mullenbach, a labor mediator. The union called off the strike when the board promised to respect majority rule. In 1934 and 1935 the NSLRB issued election orders to a number of steel companies, but the companies resisted in the courts. By May 1935, when the *Schechter** decision destroyed the NRA,* the NSLRB had achieved very little in implementing Section 7(a) in the iron and steel industry nor had it made any contribution to resolving the issue of trade or company unions. (Lewis L. Lorwin and Arthur Wubnig, *Labor Relations Boards*, 1935.)

NATIONAL UNION FOR SOCIAL JUSTICE (See COUGHLIN, CHARLES EDWARD.)

NATIONAL YOUTH ADMINISTRATION The National Youth Administration was the only New Deal* agency primarily designed to meet the employment and educational needs of American youth. Signed into law by President Franklin D. Roosevelt* through an executive order of June 26, 1935, the NYA was a recognition that prior federal programs had dealt inadequately with these problems. While the Civilian Conservation Corps* and the Federal Emergency Relief Administration* had employed hundreds of thousands of youths, millions more were unreached by the early New Deal. In addition to enabling 620,000 college students to continue their education, the NYA provided part-time jobs to 1,514,000 high school students and 2,677,000 out-of-school youths. Through 1943 it had assisted many more youths than the CCC at a fraction of the cost. In 1937 alone, when the CCC spent $245 million on 284,000 enrollees, the NYA employed 440,000—for under $57 million.

The NYA had a diverse and somewhat contradictory set of mandates. With an estimated 5 million youths unemployed in 1935, it was obvious that one of the agency's primary tasks would be to put the young to work. Yet, the NYA was intended to be more than a "junior WPA."* The fear that jobless youth might become a reservoir for radicalism animated both Eleanor Roosevelt* and Massachusetts NRA Administrator Edward A. Filene. After visiting Hitler's Germany, Filene urged the president to organize youth "on a national basis" to prevent the diversion of "the youth movement . . . to partisan political ends."

It was the conviction of NYA executive director Aubrey Williams* and National

Advisory Committee Chairman Charles W. Taussig that youth must be educated to gain an understanding of and an appreciation for the principles of democracy. Their objectives was to strengthen the democratic character of the nation internally, while shielding the NYA from charges that it was attempting to "regiment" American youth.

Democratization of the New Deal for youth brought special benefits for rural youths, black Americans, and students. By December 1940, 595 "resident training centers" had been established to bring together dispersed rural youths and the industrial equipment usually found only in cities. Regarded as "communities within themselves," each of these centers had a "Citizenship Instructor" who helped youth "practice the business of self-government."

In 1935 two out of five black young people (as opposed to 20 percent of white youth) were jobless. Under the FERA student aid program, blacks had been allotted part-time jobs in proportion to their percentage in the population, a pattern consistent with CCC policy. Responding to the argument of black leaders that these young people were peculiarly hard-pressed to stay in school and had a dismal future without continued education, NYA officials set up a special fund for black students. At the same time, a Division of Negro Affairs was established under the direction of the noted black educator, Mary McLeod Bethune.*

Administrative authority over the student work program was invested in high school and college authorities. Beginning in 1940 (when NYA student enrollment reached a peak of 449,000), Student Work Councils were formed, giving student leaders and community officials a greater voice in the program. Significantly, the young people's chief complaint concerned the small scope of the program, not its execution.

Equally important to NYA officials was the relief of unemployment and the provision of industry-related skills. Through NYA work, 1,500 miles of roads were paved, 6,000 public buildings erected, 1,429 schools and libraries constructed, and 2,000 bridges built. After 1939, while CCC youths labored in the woods, most NYA workers received experience in arc welding, machine tool work, and other urban-industrial fields.

The coming of World War II ironically accelerated the achievement of all the NYA objectives, while rendering the agency's continued existence untenable. After 1941 more than half of all NYA workers were women. Meanwhile, the resident centers were fully functioning industrial training schools, ideal places to establish near war plants and train young workers. In 1943 alone 31,000 youths "graduated" from these NYA centers and were placed immediately in war industry jobs.

Although its accomplishments were all the more impressive after the war began, an agency created to meet an unemployment problem which no longer existed and which was by then primarily benefiting young women, could not long survive. As armed forces enlistments drained the pool of young labor, the CCC and NYA engaged in a sometimes bitter competition for enrollees. Meanwhile, the National Education Association, which had always regarded the

NYA as a dangerous threat to local control of education, began attacking the agency as its training role increased. Moreover, after Pearl Harbor, Congress favored reductions in non-essential expenditures. Efforts to save the NYA, led by Congressman Lyndon B. Johnson and Senator Harry S Truman,* fell short in 1943. It was ironic indeed that an agency administered to preserve democracy and achieve "freedom from want" was a casualty of a war fought for these same ends. (Richard A. Reiman, "Apprenticeship in Democracy: The Evolution of New Deal Youth Policies Through the Federal Emergency Relief Administration and National Youth Administration, 1933-1943," Ph.D. dissertation, University of Cincinnati, 1984; John A. Salmond, *A Southern Rebel: The Life and Times of Aubrey Willis Williams, 1890-1965*, 1983.)

RICHARD A. REIMAN

"NEW DEAL" No political slogan or campaign theme has been more familiar to more people in the United States and abroad than the "New Deal." The term has been synonymous with the origins of big government—the massive intervention of federal power into the private economy. Conservatives have treated the term with contempt, associating it with the rise of impersonal, inefficient political bureaucracies and the demise of personal property and individual rights. And for each disgruntled conservative bemoaning modern society, there has been an enthusiastic liberal convinced that the New Deal redeemed capitalism and preserved the social order by relieving the suffering of millions of people. More recently, a small group of New Left historians have vilified the New Deal for what it did not do—lead the country down the road to socialism and a planned economy.

The term "New Deal" became public property in June 1932 when Governor Franklin D. Roosevelt* of New York accepted the Democratic presidential nomination in Chicago. In his speech to the convention, he said: "I pledge you, I pledge myself, to a new deal for the American people. Let us all here assembled constitute ourselves prophets of a new order of competence and courage." Samuel I. Rosenman,* a close political adviser and speechwriter for the governor, had drafted that portion of the address, perhaps drawing on a series of articles by Stuart Chase in *The New Republic* entitled "A New Deal for America." One article had already appeared in the June issue. A political cartoonist picked up on the phrase, and Stuart Chase published his essays as *The New Deal* in August 1932, seeing the book go through seven printings by the time of the election in November. Throughout Roosevelt's presidency, politicians and the press used the term to describe his political and economic policies. During World War II, the president even became occasionally frustrated, insisting that the time had come for "Dr. New Deal" to give way to "Dr. Win-the-War." For American historians, the "New Deal" has come to symbolize Roosevelt's political philosophy as well as the role of the Democratic party* and the federal government in dealing with the Great Depression of the 1930s. (Arthur M. Schlesinger, Jr., *The Age of Roosevelt. Vol. I. The Crisis of the Old Order, 1919-1933*, 1957.)

NONPARTISAN LEAGUE Founded in 1915 at Bismarck, North Dakota, by Arthur C. Townley, A. F. Bowen, and Fred B. Wood, the Nonpartisan League was committed to organizing the farm vote to resist the Republican party* in North Dakota. The Nonpartisan League was socialist in its philosophy, advocating government ownership of grain elevators, processing mills, storage facilities, and major meat-packing companies; government crop insurance; state-run banks and government financed rural credit; and tax breaks for farm improvements. The Nonpartisan League succeeded at the polls in 1916 when Lynn J. Frazier* was elected governor of North Dakota. It also captured 81 of 113 North Dakota house seats and 19 of 49 senate seats. The Nonpartisan League also enjoyed great support in Minnesota, where it helped form the Farmer-Labor party,* and in Montana and South Dakota. Because so many Nonpartisan League leaders were isolationist in foreign policy views, the group lost ground during World War I and continued to lose support during the conservative 1920s. The Great Depression, however, revived their political strength when the league began demanding federal assistance to farmers and a moratorium on farm foreclosures. Senator Lynn J. Frazier and Congressman William Lemke* of North Dakota represented the Nonpartisan League in the 1930s and succeeded in passing the Federal Farm Bankruptcy Act of 1934.* When World War II broke out, the Nonpartisan League again lost ground because of its isolationist views, and in 1956 the league merged with the Democratic party.* (Charles E. Russell, *The Story of the Nonpartisan League: A Chapter in American Evolution*, 1974.)

NORBECK, PETER Peter Norbeck, a Progressive Republican from South Dakota, was born on August 27, 1870, near Vermillion. He attended the University of South Dakota and then moved several times throughout the state between 1900 and 1909 working as a farmer, contractor, and driller of oil and gas wells. Norbeck won a seat in the state legislature in 1909, served as lieutenant governor in 1915 and 1916, and was governor of South Dakota between 1917 and 1921. Norbeck was elected to the United States Senate in 1920, and won re-election in 1926 and 1932. During his nearly sixteen years in the Senate, Norbeck adopted a consistently progressive stand on many issues, promoting the McNary-Haugen plan in the 1920s and in the 1930s playing an important role in the coalition of liberal Democrats and progressive Republicans responsible for so much New Deal* legislation. In the election of 1936,* Norbeck could not bear endorsing Alf Landon,* so he gave his support to President Franklin D. Roosevelt.* Six weeks after the election on December 20, 1936, he died in Redfield, South Dakota, (*New York Times*, December 21, 1936.)

NORRIS, GEORGE WILLIAM George W. Norris was born in Sandusky County, Ohio, on July 11, 1861, the son of Chauncey and Mary Magdalene Mook Norris. Tragedy struck the family in 1864. Chauncey Norris died of pneumonia, and the elder son was killed in the Civil War. As soon as he was old enough, George had to help support the family. After completing his education in the local schools, Norris attended Baldwin University (Baldwin-Wallace College, 1877-1878). He taught school for one year to help finance his continued education at Northern Indiana Normal School and Business Institute (Valparaiso University). In 1883 he received hs law degree and was admitted to the Indiana bar. For the next two years, however, Norris taught school in Ohio and Washington. He then moved to Nebraska (1885) to start his law practice.

Times were good in Nebraska during the 1880s. The agricultural economy was booming, and Norris shared in the prosperity. He was retained as counsel for the Burlington and Missouri Railroad, and he also went into the milling and mortgage loan businesses. In the 1890s drought swept the Great Plains, bringing collapse and ruin to the agricultural economy. In the depression Norris' businesses suffered severely. In 1891 he decided to start a new career in public service. Over the next several years Norris served in two local posts: prosecuting attorney for Furnas County (1890-1895) and state judge for the 14th Judicial District (1896-1902). In 1902 he won the Republican congressional nomination for his district and went on narrowly to defeat his Democratic opponent by 181 votes.

In his first term in Congress, Norris was a loyal and partisan Republican. But in his second term, he became more sensitive to the needs of his constituents, many of whom still leaned in the direction of Populism. He backed railroad reform, broke his ties with his railroad clients, and returned his free pass. In 1908 he openly sided with the insurgents in their losing bid to check the power of Speaker Joseph Cannon. But he paid the price in his own race for re-election that year. Although he supported the national ticket, he got almost no help from the Republican party.* It nearly cost him his seat in Congress—he won by the razor-thin margin of twenty-two votes. If this experience was intended to teach Norris a lesson in party loyalty, he drew the wrong conclusion. He was now determined to pursue a more independent course so that he would never again be put in such a position by his party. By 1910 Norris was indelibly identified as an insurgent and a champion of progressive reform. That same year, he was easily re-elected to a fifth term in the House. In the 1912 primary election campaign, Norris at first supported the nomination of Robert M. La Follette as candidate for the Republican party. But when La Follette's bid for the nomination faltered, Norris endorsed former President Theodore Roosevelt. When Roosevelt and the Insurgents bolted the party, Norris dropped his support of Roosevelt. He did not wish to endanger his own position in the Nebraska party organization or jeopardize his own plans to run for the Senate. Norris not only won the Republican nomination, but he bucked the Democratic tide in Nebraska to win the election in November.

In 1913 Norris began his thirty years of service in the Senate. In domestic policy, he supported most of Wilson's progressive reform program. But he strongly opposed what he regarded as Wilson's adventurism in foreign policy, especially in Mexico. In 1917 he voted against arming American merchant ships and against the declaration of war with the Central Powers. He shared the view later advanced by the Nye Committee, that bankers and businessmen had unnecessarily led the nation into war. Once war was declared, however, Norris wholeheartedly supported the military effort. Re-elected to the Senate in 1918, Norris soon found himself numbered among the Irreconcilables. He was not an isolationist. He supported United States cooperation in ensuring peace, but he felt that Wilson's handiwork at Versailles was hopelessly flawed.

The 1920s marked the most frustrating period of Norris' public life. He was constantly at odds with the business-dominated, conservative Republican administrations of the decade. He was increasingly disillusioned with his own party. He was perturbed by the lack of ethical standards and ability among many Republican officials, both elected and appointed. He was dismayed by the revelations of scandal. And he felt that all three Republican administrations (those of Warren Harding, Calvin Coolidge, and Herbert Hoover*) were too much under the influence of corporate wealth. In foreign policy, he opposed the continued interventions in the Caribbean and Central America, supported the objectives of the Mexican Revolution, and called for the recognition of the Soviet Union.

In domestic policy, Norris was in almost constant conflict with administration policy. No issue was more emotionally charged than that concerning the future of facilities built at Muscle Shoals,* Alabama, during World War I. Norris stood like granite against administration attempts to dispose of the facilities to private interests at virtual give-away prices. Rather, he demanded that Muscle Shoals' hydroelectric facilities be operated by the government for the welfare of the people of the great Tennessee River Valley. By 1928 he succeeded in gaining congressional approval for government operation of Muscle Shoals, only to have the bill vetoed by President Coolidge. A similar bill passed in 1931 was vetoed by President Hoover.

As the 1920s progressed, Norris' attachment to the Republican party continued to erode. In 1920 he endorsed Hiram Johnson* rather than Harding. In 1924 he privately supported Robert M. La Follette in an election in which he himself won a third term. In 1925 he succeeded to the leadership of the congressional progressives after the death of La Follette. He spoke out boldly in defense of the farmer and the worker and for conserving national resources at a time when such causes were not popular. He sponsored such measures as the Norris-Sinclair Farm Bill (1924) and the Norris-La Guardia Anti-Injunction Act (1932). He was almost solely responsible for initiating and pushing through to ratification of the Twentieth Amendment to the Constitution eliminating the lame-duck period (1932).

In 1928 he openly broke with the policies of his own party and refused to support Herbert Hoover. Shortly before the election, Norris publicly endorsed Al Smith.* After the onslaught of the depression, he became sharply critical of the Hoover administration. Norris felt that Hoover was excessively generous in bailing out banks and corporations while he ignored the desperation of the poor. In 1930 Republican regulars resorted to trickery in an attempt to deny Norris renomination. They ran an obscure grocery clerk also named George W. Norris in an attempt to confuse voters. But the scheme failed. In a later investigation, officials of the Republican National Committee were accused of helping finance the ruse, and the hapless grocery clerk spent time in jail for his part in the scheme.

In the election of 1932,* Norris denounced the policies and the platform of the Hoover campaign and publicly endorsed Franklin D. Roosevelt* for president. He became a close political ally and personal friend of Roosevelt. After thirty years in public service, Norris finally achieved success and recognition as a major public figure in the United States. And his long crusade for Muscle Shoals finally came to fruition. He was the principal author of the bill creating the Tennessee Valley Authority* in May 1933. In tribute to his contribution, the first dam built by TVA as well as a model community were named in his honor. Norris sponsored the Rural Electrification Act of 1936* and the Farm Forestry Act of 1937. He also pushed through Congress a ''little TVA'' program for Nebraska but failed to secure passage of similar public power projects for other states.

In 1936 Norris ended his long if loose association with the Republican party.* He was re-elected to a fifth term in the Senate as an independent with the endorsement of President Roosevelt. As the world situation deteriorated in the late 1930s, Norris supported Roosevelt's position on such measures as the ''cash and carry'' revision of the Neutrality Act, Lend-Lease, and trade restrictions with Japan. When the Japanese attacked Pearl Harbor, he voted for the declaration of war. But he was critical of administration policies toward Japanese-Americans and aliens. His last great crusade in the Senate was in behalf of civil rights. He sponsored an anti-poll tax bill, but it fell victim to a filibuster by southern Democrats.

In 1940 Senator Norris had announced his intention to retire upon completion of the fifth term in 1943. But in 1942 he changed his mind and decided to run again. He faced a three-man race, however, since the Democrats and Republicans also fielded candidates. And because of pressing business in the Senate, Norris barely took time to campaign. He was defeated by Kenneth S. Wherry, the Republican candidate. Norris found it difficult to accept defeat. Living at McCook in retirement, he harbored the feeling that he and his principles had been repudiated by the voters he had served so long and so faithfully. He survived his forced retirement by less than two years. On September 2, 1944, he died at his home after suffering a cerebral hemorrhage. (Richard Lowitt, *George W. Norris: The Making of a Progressive, 1861 to 1912*, 1963; *George W. Norris: The Persistence of a Progressive, 1913-1933*, 1971; *George W. Norris: The Triumph of a Progressive, 1933-1944*, 1978; ''George W. Norris and the New Deal in Nebraska, 1933-1936,'' *Agricultural History*, LI:396-405, 1977.)

JOSEPH M. ROWE, JR.

NORTON, MARY TERESA Mary Norton was born in Jersey City, New Jersey, on March 7, 1875. She attended parochial schools and then the Jersey

City High School and graduated from the Packard Business College in New York City in 1896. Norton was appointed to represent Hudson County for the State Democratic committee in 1920 and served as vice-chairman from 1921 to 1931 and chairman from 1932 to 1935. In 1924 she was elected on the Democratic ticket to Congress, and she served in Congress until her retirement from political life in 1950. During the New Deal,* Norton was chairman of the House Labor Committee and a loyal Franklin D. Roosevelt* supporter. She enthusiastically supported Section 7(a) of the National Industrial Recovery Act,* the National Labor Relations Act of 1935,* and the Fair Labor Standards Act of 1938.* Norton was also an advocate of pump-priming the economy through federal spending as a means of creating jobs and stimulating demand. Considered one of labor's most consistent friends in Congress, she continued to serve until 1950, when she decided not to run for re-election. In 1951 and 1952 Norton served as a consultant to the Women's Advisory Committee on Defense Manpower in the Department of Labor. She died on August 2, 1959. (*New York Times*, August 3, 1959; James T. Patterson, *Congressional Conservatism and the New Deal*, 1967; Susan Ware, *Beyond Suffrage: Women in the New Deal*, 1981.)

NYE, GERALD PRENTICE Gerald P. Nye was born in Hortonville, Wisconsin, on December 19, 1892. He graduated from high school in 1911 and moved to Iowa to a career in journalism. Later he moved to North Dakota and bought the *Fryburg Pioneer* in 1919 and the *Griggs County Sentinel-Courier* in 1920. In November 1925 Senator Edwin F. Ladd died, and Nye was appointed to fill the unexpired term. In an extremely close election, he won his own seat in 1926. Nye was quite critical of the Coolidge administration, seeing the president as the tool of big bankers and industrialists. During Herbert Hoover's* administration he pushed hard for farm relief, and after 1933 Nye was known as a New Deal* critic. He became especially vocal in his opposition to the National Recovery Administration.* As a progressive Republican, Nye saw the NRA as a hindrance to consumers and a boon to big business intent on increasing their monopolistic powers.

Nye's attack on the New Deal was not limited to the domestic economy and NRA. He also lobbied against the military armaments industry, insisting that a special Senate committee convene to investigate its practices. With the out-break of the Spanish Civil War in 1936, concern mounted about the role the United States would play in European affairs. Nye became a vocal, ardent isolationist and in 1936 succeeded in securing passage in Congress of a Neutrality Act. During the election campaign of 1936,* Senator Nye trekked across the country calling attention to the failure of New Deal policies.

After Franklin D. Roosevelt's* landslide victory Nye became even more convinced of the need to criticize the New Deal. Along with Senator William Borah* of Idaho, Nye planned to reform the Republican party.* In July 1937 Nye claimed that the National Labor Relations Board* was showing favoritism toward the organizing efforts of the CIO.* In August 1937 he called for stricter enforcement of the Neutrality Act with regard to the Chinese-Japanese conflict. When the Japanese bombed the gunboat USS *Panay* in 1937, Nye claimed Roosevelt had provoked the incident. Throughout 1938 the senator continued to avow isolationism and to condemn the president for his attempts to rearm the United States. Beginning in 1939 his attack on the Roosevelt administration became even more vehement. In June 1939 he led a move in the Senate to substantially cut the WPA,* and in the election of 1940,* Nye assailed Roosevelt's domestic and foreign record. He insisted and believed that the sale of munitions to belligerents in Europe would inevitably bring America into war. But the public trusted President Franklin D. Roosevelt and elected him to an unprecedented third term. Shortly thereafter the United States entered another world war.

Isolationist sentiment evaporated quickly, and Nye found himself leader of a tiny minority. During the election of 1944 he suffered a stunning defeat and abandoned his political career. Gerald P. Nye died on July 17, 1971. (Richard S. Kirkendall, *The United States, 1929-1945: Years of Crisis and Change*, 1974; *New York Times*, July 18, 1971; *Who's Who in America, 1934-1935*, 1934.)

JOHN S. LEIBY

O

O'CONNOR, DANIEL BASIL Daniel Basil O'Connor was born January 8, 1892, in Taunton, Massachusetts, the son of a tinsmith. He graduated from Dartmouth College and the Harvard Law School and went into private practice in New York. During the presidential election campaign of 1920, O'Connor was active in Democratic politics and struck up a friendship with vice-presidential candidate Franklin D. Roosevelt.* That friendship lasted a lifetime. In 1925 O'Connor and Roosevelt formed a law partnership, and in 1927 they both helped found the Warm Springs Foundation to raise money for polio victims. For the rest of his life, O'Connor was active in the fight against polio, serving as president of the American Red Cross and the National Foundation-March of Dimes. During the 1932 presidential campaign, O'Connor acted as a close personal adviser to Roosevelt and served as a member of the "brain trust,"* developing issues and policy statements. Until the president's death in 1945, O'Connor maintained his trust. Between 1945 and his death on March 10, 1972, O'Connor continued his law career and vigorous philanthropic interests. (*New York Times*, March 10, 1972.)

O'CONNOR, JAMES FRANCIS THADDEUS Born in North Dakota in 1885, James O'Connor graduated from the University of North Dakota in 1907. He took a law degree there in 1908 and then studied law at Yale, taking a degree in 1909 and teaching there until 1912. He moved to Grand Rapids, North Dakota, to practice law in 1912, served in the state House of Representatives, and ran unsuccessfully as a Democrat for governor in 1920 and United States senator in 1922. O'Connor was a vigorous supporter of William G. McAdoo's* presidential candidacy in 1924, and joined McAdoo's California law firm in 1925. In 1933 President Franklin D. Roosevelt* appointed O'Connor comptroller of the currency, and he served there until 1938, presiding over the examination and reopening of thousands of banks closed during the bank holiday* of 1933. O'Connor resigned as comptroller in 1938 to run for governor of California, but he lost to Culbert Olson.* Roosevelt then appointed him to a federal judgeship for the southern district of California in 1940. James F. T. O'Connor died in Los Angeles on September 29, 1949. (J. F. T. O'Connor, *The Banking Crisis and Recovery Under the Roosevelt Administration*, 1938; *Who Was Who In America*, II:403, 1963.)

O'CONNOR, JOHN JOSEPH John Joseph O'Connor, one of President Franklin D. Roosevelt's* most vociferous Democratic opponents during the 1930s, was born on November 23, 1885, in Raynham, Massachusetts. He graduated from Brown University in 1908 and from the Harvard Law School in 1911, practiced law in Massachusetts briefly, and then moved to New York City. O'Connor became active in Tammany politics, serving as secretary to the Democratic members of the state constitutional convention in 1915. He won a seat in the state legislature in 1920 and in 1923 was elected to fill the congressional seat vacated by the death of W. Bourke Cockran. Before 1935 O'Connor had generally been an administrative supporter, but in 1935 he became head of the House Rules Committee and began causing President Roosevelt a long string of problems. He opposed the "death sentence" clause of the proposed Wheeler-Rayburn Bill* concerning public utilities and played a key role in the elimination of the strict clause from the eventual legislation. O'Connor decried the administration's refusal to use sanctions against the "sit-down strikers," intensely opposed executive reorganization of the federal government, and repeatedly spoke out against pump-priming and deficit spending. Roosevelt grew so frustrated with O'Connor that he personally worked against his re-election in 1938* by refusing to endorse him and allowing administration employees to work for his opponent. The defeat of O'Connor in the New York Democratic primary was one of the few bright spots in Roosevelt's "purge of 1938."* Highly resentful of the president's tactics, O'Connor bolted to the Republican party,* won the GOP congressional nomination, but then lost the general election. He returned to private law practice and died on January 26, 1960. (*New York Times*, January 27, 1960; James T. Patterson, *Congressional Conservatism and the New Deal*, 1976.)

O'DAY, CAROLINE LOVE GOODWIN Caroline (Goodwin) O'Day was born on June 22, 1875, in Perry, Georgia. She graduated from the Lucy Cobb Institute in Athens, Georgia, and then studied art widely throughout Europe. O'Day relocated to New York and became active in politics, paticularly in the drive for political equality for women. She became close to Belle Moskowitz and Eleanor Roosevelt* in promoting women's rights in the Democratic state committee and served as vice-chairman of the Democratic State Committee from 1916 to 1920 and associate chairman from 1923 to 1942. O'Day also served as a commissioner on the state board of social welfare and acquired a strong sensitivity to the needs of poor farmers and workers and their families. She was elected to Congress in the election of 1934* and served there until her death on January 4, 1943. Because of her friendship with Eleanor Roosevelt and her liberal political sympathies, O'Day became an important advocate of the needs of poor southern farmers, unemployed industrial workers, and exploited women and children. (*New York Times*, January 5, 1943; Susan Ware, *Beyond Suffrage: Women in the New Deal*, 1981.)

"OKIES" "Okie" was a term of derogation applied by Californians to hundreds of thousands of migrants from the Southwestern states who entered California during the 1930s. The Okie migration began during the 1920s, but it multiplied during the 1930s, when the Great Depression prompted a general increase in migration throughout the country.

The word "Okie" was used indiscriminately for some 300,000 to 400,000 migrants originating not only from Oklahoma but also from such states as Texas, Arkansas, and Missouri. Perhaps 100,000 of them truly came from Oklahoma. Designations such as "Texie" or "Arkie," although used, were less common. The migrants came to California mainly by automobile, the most common route to the west being Highway 66.

The causes of the Okie migration lay in the agricultural conditions of the Southwestern states. Agriculture in general suffered from economic stagnation due to surplus production. For share-cropping cotton farmers, this problem was compounded by mechanization. With the advent of gasoline tractors, landlords evicted tenants and consolidated their holdings, actions encouraged rather than discouraged by the crop curtailment programs of the Agricultural Adjustment Administration.* At the same time, broad areas of the cotton-producing states showed the effects of soil depletion by intensive cropping over generations.

Finally, during the mid-1930s the Southwest and the Mississippi Valley suffered severe drought, a condition not confined to the much-publicized dust bowl* of the southern plains. Indeed, although popular belief attributed the Okie migration to the dust bowl, most of the Okies came from share-cropping, cotton-farming areas farther east.

Reaction by Californians to the influx of impoverished Okies was ambivalent at best and hostile at worst. The Okies provided cheap agricultural labor to replace repatriated Mexicans, but they also posed social problems. The Okies arrived expecting to obtain temporary jobs in the fruit farms, truck farms, and expanding cotton farms of California and eventually to acquire farms of their own. Disappointed on both counts, they crowded into "ditch bank settlements" along irrigation ditches, into urban slums, and where possible, into government camps. They placed a heavy burden on existing hospitals, schools, and other social services.

Alarm about the Okies increased in the late 1930s. Most of them arrived during the years 1935-1937. Floods left many without shelter early in 1938. The state election of 1938* dwelt much on the migrant question. In mid-1939 came publication of John Steinbeck's* novel, *The Grapes of Wrath*, a sympathetic portrayal of the migrant Joad family.

Californians' sympathies for the Okies also declined to the extent that the newcomers supported the United Cannery, Agricultural, Packing and Allied

Workers of America, organized as an arm of the Committee for Industrial Organization* in 1937. Agricultural growers, united in an organization called the Associated Farmers, met the organizational efforts of UCAPAWA with antipicketing ordinances, vigilante actions, and charges of communism.

The federal government already had extended some aid to the migrants, first through the Federal Transient Service and after 1935 through the Resettlement Administration,* (absorbed by the Farm Security Administration* in 1937). After visiting several migrant settlements, Rexford Tugwell,* director of the Resettlement Administration, ordered construction of a chain of camps for the migrants. The camps, although often unsuccessful as experiments in democratic cooperation, were generally well-run and sanitary.

In 1940, responding to pressure from the California delegation, Congress passed a resolution creating the Select Committee to Investigate Interstate Migration of Destitute Citizens (the Tolan Committee), which travelled extensively and interviewed more than 500 witnesses. Its recommendations were of little significance to the Okies, however, for by the time of the committee's report, defense industries had absorbed most of the unemployed, conferring upon the Okies an enduring place in the economy and society of California. (Walter J. Stein, *California and the Dust Bowl Migration*, 1973.)

THOMAS D. ISERN

OLD-AGE REVOLVING PENSIONS, LTD. (See TOWNSEND, FRANCIS E.)

OLDS, LELAND Leland Olds was born in Rochester, New York, on December 31, 1890. After graduating from Amherst in 1912, Olds studied at Harvard and Columbia before going to work for the Council of National Defense in 1917. In 1918 Olds worked as a statistician for the Shipbuilding Labor Adjustment Board and for the National War Labor Board and then headed the research bureau of the Railroad Employees Department of the AFL.* In 1922 Olds became an editorial writer and economic consultant for Federated Press, a position he held until 1931. Between 1931 and 1939 Olds was assistant to the chairman of the New York State Power Authority, where he gained a strong faith in the value of national economic planning. In 1937 President Franklin D. Roosevelt* appointed Olds to the Commission to study Cooperative Enterprise Abroad, and Olds authored the commission's 1937 report "Inquiry on Cooperative Enterprise in Europe." On June 22, 1939, Roosevelt appointed him to a five-year term on the Federal Power Commission,* and in 1940 Olds became chairman of the FPC. He remained in that position until 1949. During his first term with the FPC, Olds was also a member of the Water and Energy Resources Committee of the National Resources Planning Board.* After his retirement from the FPC, Olds remained active as a consultant in water and energy resource management and died in August 1960. (*Who Was Who In America*, IV:718, 1968.)

OLSON, CULBERT Born on November 7, 1876 in Millard County, Utah, Culbert Olson became the first Democratic governor in California in the twentieth century when he defeated Republican Governor Frank Merriam in the election of 1938.* He was an enthusiastic supporter of Franklin D. Roosevelt's* New Deal* and attempted to create a "Little New Deal"* in California. After attending Brigham Young University, Olson became a reporter and city editor for the *Ogden Standard*. He was an enthusiastic supporter of William Jennings Bryan, and in 1897 went to Washington, D.C., as the secretary to his cousin William H. King,* a newly elected member of the House of Representatives. While in Washington, D.C., he took a law degree at Columbian University (later George Washington University), then he returned to Utah in 1901 to practice law. Olson became an active progressive Democrat, winning a seat in the Utah state legislature in 1916 and sponsoring bills to regulate public utilities, establish the initiative and referendum, limit the use of injunctions in labor disputes, protect collective bargaining, and provide workmen's compensation.

Discouraged by the conservative political climate in Utah, Olson moved his family and law practice to Los Angeles, California, in 1920. He campaigned widely throughout southern California for Robert M. La Follette and the Progressive party in 1924. Olson became president of the Los Angeles Democratic Club and also campaigned for Franklin D. Roosevelt* in 1932. He became interested in Upton Sinclair's* "End Poverty in California" program in 1934 and won a seat in the state senate. The party named him state Democratic chairman in 1934, and Olson managed the 1934 Democratic campaign in California. He proved to be the only avid supporter of Upton Sinclair to retain public office in the election, and he was embittered about the conservatism of the William McAdoo* machine. In the Republican-dominated state senate, Olson worked hard to pass progressive legislation, and he secured a major victory when the governor accepted his proposed bills establishing a state income tax and increasing inheritance, bank, and corporation franchise taxes as administration measures. Olson also successfully sponsored legislation to repeal sales taxes on food sold for home consumption.

In 1938 Olson won the governorship on a platform of public ownership of utilities, taxation by "ability to pay," a welfare system based on "production for use," federal financing and administration of old-age pensions, low-cost housing and slum clearance, creation of a state consumer protection agency, and elimination of usurious interest rates. He also advocated passage of a "California Wagner Act." As governor, although he struggled with Republican conservatism in the state legislature he managed to reform the state's penal and parole systems, to improve treatment of the mentally ill, and to appoint distinguished liberals to state courts. By the time he was elected the reform era was already over in California, however, and he was unable to achieve all his objectives. He left office in 1942 after being decisively defeated by Republican candidate Earl

Warren. Olson never again ran for public office. He died on April 13, 1962. (Robert E. Burke, *Olson's New Deal for California*, 1953.)

LENNA HODNETT ALLRED

OLSON, FLOYD BJORNSTJERNE Floyd B. Olson was born in Minneapolis, Minnesota, on November 13, 1891, to Scandinavian immigrant parents. Olson attended the University of Minnesota and received a law degree from the Northwestern College of Law in 1915. After practicing law privately for four years, he became special prosecutor for Hennepin County. One year later Olson became county attorney after his predecessor was impeached. He remained county attorney until 1930. But it was in 1924 that he gained statewide attention by accusing Senator Thomas D. Schall* with violation of the Corrupt Practices Act. That same year he ran unsuccessfully for governor. In 1930 Olson again tried for the governorship on the Farmer-Labor party* ticket and became the first Farmer-Labor governor in Minnesota history. During his first term Olson consolidated all state conservation functions into a single department, passed a highway appropriation bill to provide jobs for the unemployed, and passed a measure authorizing farmers to issue warehouse receipts on grains stored on their farms as collateral for loans.

Olson supported Franklin D. Roosevelt* in 1932 and won re-election for governor. In his second term in office, he was hampered by a hostile majority in the state senate. Nevertheless, he was successful in implementing a ''little New Deal''* by sponsoring measures for a state income tax, old-age pensions, and regulations on the sales of securities. His relief program included unemployment compensation financed by employers, state-centered unemployment relief, increases in corporate income taxes, and public ownership of utilities. In 1933 he attracted national attention by threatening to declare martial law and confiscate private wealth if his relief measures were not enacted. That same year, he declared a three-month mortgage moratorium to halt foreclosures.

In 1934 Olson took a decided turn to the left in his political philosophy, urging the Farmer-Labor convention to adopt a radical platform calling for the immediate abolition of capitalism with state ownership of mines, utilities, transportation, and all other means of production. As the Farmer-Labor candidate, he defeated both Republican and Democratic candidates in the 1934 election* to win a third term. He also declared martial law at the request of striking truck drivers in Minneapolis after employers rejected federal mediation. After his reelection in 1934, Olson steadily declined in strength because of cancer. He died on August 22, 1936. (*New York Times*, August 23, 1936; James T. Patterson, *The New Deal in the States: Federalism in Transition*, 1969.)

LENNA HODNETT ALLRED

O'MAHONEY, JOSEPH CHRISTOPHER Joseph C. O'Mahoney was a United States senator from Wyoming from 1933-1953 and from 1955-1961. He was born on November 5, 1884, in Massachusetts. After studying journalism at

Columbia, O'Mahoney moved west to Colorado in 1908. In 1913 he married Agnes O'Leary, and they raised three nephews. Originally a Theodore Roosevelt Republican, O'Mahoney switched to the Democratic party* in 1916, the year he became a city editor of the *Cheyenne State Leader*. He went to Washington the next year as executive secretary to Senator John M. Kendrick. While in the nation's capital, he studied law and graduated from Georgetown in 1920. Active in Democratic politics throughout the 1920s, O'Mahoney served as a member of the Democratic National Committee and was on the 1932 platform committee. Franklin D. Roosevelt* rewarded O'Mahoney by naming him to the position of first assistant postmaster general to the U.S.

Upon Senator Kendrick's death in 1933, O'Mahoney was appointed to the U.S. Senate. O'Mahoney served Roosevelt and Wyoming well during the New Deal.* He supported the proposed legislation of the first Roosevelt term with vigor, enthusiasm, and dedication. The Wyoming senator made sure that his state received its share of New Deal largesse. His main disagreement with Roosevelt was over the proposal to reform the Supreme Court* in 1937. He also opposed the creation of a Missouri Valley Authority and the anti-poll tax bill. O'Mahoney was a crusader against monopoly. He chaired the Temporary National Economic Committee* that investigated concentration of wealth and its effect on employment, technology, and the economy. In fact, much of the philosophy of the TNEC was O'Mahoney's own conviction that small business and consumers must be protected. Harry Truman* gave O'Mahoney considerable credit for laying the economic groundwork for the Fair Deal. Joseph C. O'Mahoney was re-elected in 1934, 1940, and 1946; however, he was defeated in 1952 in a McCarthyite campaign which attempted to associate O'Mahoney with liberal causes. O'Mahoney bounced back in 1954 when the voters returned him to the Senate. Following a stroke, he retired from the Senate in 1961 and died on December 1, 1962. (Frank Alan Coombs, "Joseph C. O'Mahoney: The New Deal Years," Ph.D. dissertation, University of Illinois, 1968.)

F. ROSS PETERSON

O'NEAL, EDWARD ASBURY Edward A. O'Neal, a major American farm leader during the 1930s and 1940s, was born near Florence, Alabama, on October 26, 1875. After studying agriculture at the State Normal College at Florence, Alabama, O'Neal went on and graduated from Washington and Lee University in 1898. He then returned to the family farm near Florence and began farming, but he also became active in local farm politics and in the farm bureau and extension movements. He worked as president of the Lauderdale County Farm Bureau in 1921 and 1922 and then became vice-president of the Alabama Farm Bureau Federation. O'Neal became president of the Alabama Farm Bureau in 1923, vice-president of the American Farm Bureau Federation* in 1924, and president of the national federation in 1931, where he remained until 1947. From that vantage point, O'Neal played an important role in the development of New Deal* agricultural policy.

During the 1930s, O'Neal and his associate Earl Smith faithfully represented the interests of large commercial farmers, the main constituency of the American Farm Bureau Federation. They loyally supported the Agricultural Adjustment Acts of 1933* and 1938,* demanded parity* for farmers, and supported the concept of the "ever-normal granary."* O'Neal had little interest in the plight of small farmers and tenants, and actually opposed the Resettlement Administration* and Farm Security Administration* because he feared they would raise wage levels and make it more difficult for large farmers to find the labor they needed. O'Neal was also a consistent proponent of the idea of a National Farm Authority to administer all federal farm programs through the extension service, a piece of legislation which would have given the Farm Bureau almost complete control of New Deal farm policy. During World War II, O'Neal remained head of the Farm Bureau and served on a number of federal agencies, including the Social Security Board, President's Economic Stabilization Board, and the War Manpower Commission. He died on February 26, 1958. (Dean Albertson, *Roosevelt's Farmer. Claude R. Wickard in the New Deal*, 1961; *New York Times*, February 27, 1958.)

P

PANAMA REFINING COMPANY V. RYAN The first major Supreme Court* assault on the New Deal* came on January 7, 1935, in the *Panama Refining Company v. Ryan* case. Section 9(c) of the National Industrial Recovery Act of 1933* had given the president power to regulate petroleum shipments. Franklin D. Roosevelt* had established the Petroleum Administrative Board* to administer the NRA's* petroleum code. Executive orders from the president then prohibited shipment of ''hot oil'' (oil exceeding quota production limits) across state lines. The PAB hoped to stabilize and then gradually increase oil prices by limiting production. The Panama Refining Company argued that the executive orders had failed to mention any criminal penalties and that one of their employees had been arrested and jailed for violating the rule—which was not a law. By an eight to one majority, with only Justice Benjamin Cardozo* dissenting, the court declared Section 9(c) of the NIRA unconstitutional because it delegated essentially legislative power to the executive branch. It was a bad omen for the entire National Recovery Administration, whose constitutionality would soon be tested in the *Schechter** case. Late in 1935, as part of the ''Little NRA,''* Congress responded to the *Panama* decision by passing the Connally Act,* which did prohibit the interstate shipment of ''hot oil.'' (Peter H. Irons, *The New Deal Lawyers*, 1982; Alpheus Thomas Mason, *Harlan Fiske Stone. Pillar of the Law, 1956.)*

''PARITY'' Parity has been a central issue for American farmers. Parity, defined in its simplest terms during the New Deal,* was a ratio between the price brought by an agricultural commodity and the price index of non-farm products that insured a fair price for the product of a farmer's labor. Parity was more than a concept, it was instead the battle cry, watchword, and prescription for farmers during the agricultural depression of the 1920s and 1930s. Since the agricultural depression began a full decade before the stock market crash, farm prices fell faster than non-farm prices. For example, a ready made suit of clothing in 1926 cost the farmer nearly twice as much in bushels of wheat as it had in 1914. Bumper crops and high prices produced during World War I encouraged the farmer to invest in mechanized equipment and to place more acreage into production. When postwar demand failed to keep pace, increases in production created surpluses which flooded the markets and depressed prices. To cover the decrease in prices, farmers planted even more in hopes of recovering their investment. Increased production only created a greater surplus which further depressed prices.

There were numerous attempts during the 1920s to enact corrective federal legislation. The most noteworthy of these attempts to establish parity were the four McNary-Haugen bills introduced between 1924-1928. George N. Peek* of the Moline Plow Company led the fight for this legislation that would have protected farm prices in the domestic market and dumped the surplus abroad. Although unsuccessful, Peek's long flight for farm parity laid the foundation for the passage of the Agricultural Adjustment Act of 1933.* While this act sought to control agricultural prices by restricting production, the goal of the act was to establish and maintain a balance of price between farm and non-farm products. (Gilbert C. Fite, *George N. Peek and the Fight for Farm Parity*, 1954; Van L. Perkins, *Crisis in Agriculture: The Agricultural Adjustment Administration and the New Deal, 1933*, 1969.)

DAVID L. CHAPMAN

PATMAN BONUS BILL OF 1935 (See ADJUSTED COMPENSATION ACT OF 1936.)

PATMAN, WRIGHT Wright Patman, the twentieth-century populist congressman from east Texas, was born on August 6, 1893, in Patman's Switch, Texas. After graduating from high school, Patman went to Cumberland University and left there in 1916 with a law degree. While studying law, Patman had also been a cotton farmer. He was admitted to the Texas bar in 1916 and began practicing law at Hughes Springs. He became assistant county attorney for Cass County in 1916 but left when World War I broke out. Patman was a machine gun officer during the war and stayed in the army until 1919. For the rest of his life, he had a powerful sympathy for the interests of dirt farmers and veterans. He resumed his law practice after the war and served in the Texas state legislature between 1921 and 1924 and then as district attorney for the 5th Judicial District in Texas between 1924 and 1929. Patman was elected to Congress as a Democrat in the election of 1928, and he remained there for the next forty-six years. During the New Deal* era, Patman consistently promoted federal legislation offering assistance to veterans and farmers in the form of bonuses, mortgage moratoriums, and credit assistance. Suspicious of banks, railroads, and large corporations, Patman was also a consistent supporter of anti-trust action. Although generally loyal to the New Deal, he was still independent enough on matters affecting veterans and poor farmers to occasionally frustrate the White House. Wright Patman died on March 8, 1976. (*New York Times*, March 9, 1976.)

PATTERSON, ELEANOR MEDILL Eleanor Medill Patterson, nicknamed "Cissy," was born in Chicago on November 7, 1884. She was the granddaughter of Joseph Medill, owner of the *Chicago Tribune*. Educated at private schools in Connecticut, she wrote two books, *Glass Houses* (1926) and *Fall Flight* (1926) before persuading William Randolph Hearst* to let her edit the *Washington Herald*. In 1939 Patterson purchased the *Washington Herald* and the *Washington Times* from Hearst and combined them into the *Washington Times-Herald*. By 1943 the *Times-Herald* had the largest circulation in the city. At first an enthusiastic supporter of Franklin D. Roosevelt* and the New Deal* because of her own sympathies for the poor, Patterson later broke with the president over the "court-packing"* scheme and his activist foreign policies. By the time of World War II, Eleanor Patterson was known throughout the country as one of the president's most bitter critics. She died on July 24, 1948, of a heart attack. (Ralph G. Martin, *Cissy. The Extraordinary Eleanor Medill Patterson*, 1979.)

PAUL REVERES Founded by Elizabeth Dilling and led during the mid- and late 1930s by Colonel Edwin Marshall Hadley, the Paul Reveres was another anti-Semitic, fascist group bent on purging America of Franklin D. Roosevelt* and the New Deal.* The Paul Reveres were few in number but a noisy addition to the fascist cacaphony of the 1930s. (George Wolfskill and John A. Hudson, *All but the People. Franklin D. Roosevelt and His Critics, 1933-1939*, 1969.)

PECORA, FERDINAND Ferdinand Pecora, who gained a national reputation as legal counsel to the Senate Banking and Currency Committee in 1933 and 1934, was born in Nicosia, Sicily, on January 6, 1882. His family immigrated to the United States in 1887. Pecora graduated from the City College of New York and then took a law degree from the New York Law School in 1906. After practicing law for several years, Pecora became assistant district attorney in New York County between 1918 and 1922 and chief assistant district attorney between 1922 and 1930. A Theodore Roosevelt Progressive who converted to the Democratic party* in the 1920s, Pecora was hired by Senator Peter Norbeck* of the Senate Banking and Currency in January 1933 to serve as legal counsel for its investigation into banking and securities fraud. When the new Democratic Senate took over in March 1933, Senator Duncan Fletcher* of Florida took over the chairmanship of the committee and gave Pecora a free hand. During 1933 and 1934 Pecora worked tirelessly exposing tax and securities fraud, rigged stock market pools, complicated holding company networks, and unethical as well as criminal business practices by such people as J. P. Morgan,* A. H. Wiggin, Clarence Dillon, Winthrop Aldrich,* Thomas W. Lamont,* and George and Richard Whitney.* The hearings led directly to the Securities Exchange Act of 1934,* which Pecora helped draft; and President Franklin D. Roosevelt* named him to serve as one of the original members of the Securities and Exchange Commission.* Pecora resigned from the SEC in January 1935 to accept Governor Herbert Lehman's appointment as justice of the Supreme Court of New York, and he served there until 1950. Ferdinand Pecora died on December 7, 1971. (Arthur M. Schlesinger, Jr., *The Age of Roosevelt. Vol. II. The Coming of the New Deal*, 1959; *Who Was Who In America*, V:561, 1973.)

PEEK, GEORGE NELSON George N. Peek was born in Polo, Illinois, on November 19, 1873. In 1885 the family moved to a farm near Oregon, Illinois. His early years, spent working on the family farm, gave him just enough firsthand experience to decide that he did not like farming. Peek graduated from high school in 1891 and attended one year at Northwestern University. In 1893 he went to work for Deere and Company in Minneapolis as a salesman and collection agent. Peek rose rapidly in the business world and in 1901 was named general manager of the John Deere Plow Company in Omaha. Within a few years, Peek had reorganized the company and turned a mediocre firm into a highly profitable operation.

In 1911 Peek moved to Moline, Illinois, to become vice-president in charge of sales for Deere and Company. These were prosperous times in the farm implement business, and Peek amassed a small fortune that would support him and his cause in the coming years. His growing reputation brought him to the attention of the nation's leading businessmen. When the United States entered World War I, Alexander Legg, an executive of International Harvester Company, recommended Peek as the industrial representative to the War Industries Board. Peek resigned from Deere and served with distinction on the WIB. He gained both national attention and the close friendship of WIB chairman Bernard M. Baruch.* At the end of World War I, Baruch had Peek appointed chairman of the post-war Industrial Board. The IB, charged with lowering prices and stimulating industrial growth, was a dismal failure. Politics and an overall lack of authority doomed the IB from the beginning. Peek resigned and returned to Illinois to accept the presidency of the Moline Plow Company. In his haste to accept the job, however, Peek failed to investigate the sad state of the company's finances. The agricultural depression of the early 1920s made it all but impossible to sell farm implements. He realized that if his business was to prosper, American agriculture must again be profitable.

In 1922 Peek and Hugh S. Johnson,* Moline Plow Company vice-president, developed a comprehensive farm relief plan utilizing protective tariffs, marketing cooperatives, government loans, and a domestic price support scheme. In a pamphlet entitled "Equality for Agriculture," they proposed a government purchase of surplus crops at a fair market value or "parity."* These commodities would then be exported at the world price and an equalization fee for each unit of a commodity sold by the farmer would be collected to make up the difference when the domestic price was higher than the export price. The five McNary-Haugen bills introduced between 1924 and 1928 were a direct outgrowth of Peek and Johnson's ideas. Peek resigned from the Moline Plow Company in 1924 after a bitter reorganization struggle. Although offered numerous business opportunities, he turned them down to devote all his energies to the fight for farm parity. Peek used both his organizational talents and his own personal finances to unite various agricultural factions in the support of McNary-Haugenism. In January 1925 Peek moved to Washington where his apartment in the Roosevelt Hotel became the unofficial headquarters of the movement. Opposition and disappointment faced Peek at every turn. Agricultural processors, middlemen, and urban politicians joined forces to fight the farm bill. Not until 1927 did the first bill clear Congress, only to be vetoed by President Calvin Coolidge. A second passage of the bill in 1928 met a similar fate. The election of Herbert Hoover,* a longtime critic of McNary-Haugenism, all but ended any chance of success.

Although Peek had been a lifelong Republican, constant GOP opposition to his plan gradually forced him into the Democratic camp. He supported unsuccessful candidate Al Smith* in 1928 and Franklin D. Roosevelt* in 1932. Peek believed Roosevelt was the last hope for agriculture. Roosevelt enthusiastically accepted Peek's political support and advice. After the election, Peek undoubtedly believed that he should have a large role in shaping New Deal* farm relief legislation. Roosevelt's staff, fearing a clash with Peek over basic differences in philosophy, prevented him from being appointed secretary of agriculture. Instead, Peek was named as the first administrator of the Agricultural Adjustment Administsration.* His attempts to inject the two-price systems of McNary-Haugenism into the AAA and his hatred of the domestic allotment provisions of the act soon brought him into direct conflict with Secretary of Agriculture Henry A. Wallace.* Peek, whose objective was farm relief and preservation of American agriculture, found himself at cross purposes with his own staff, who were more interested in social reform. After seven short months, Peek resigned from the AAA. Roosevelt attempted to placate him with a job as special adviser to the president on foreign trade and later as president of the Export-Import Bank.* Differences between Peek and the Roosevelt administration were simply too great to be overcome, and he resigned on November 26, 1935. The New Deal had made a bitter enemy, and he now took every opportunity to strike back. In a book entitled *Why Quit Our Own*, Peek presented a blistering attack on New Deal farm policies.

In the 1936 election,* Peek supported Republican presidential candidate Alfred M. Landon.* Increasingly isolationist in his sentiments, Peek became one of the principal speakers of the America First movement. He died quietly at his home at Rancho Santa Fe, California, on December 17, 1943. Although he was unable to see his plan for American agriculture fulfilled during his lifetime, the long crusade for McNary-Haugen focused public attention on the plight of agriculture and laid the foundation for the agricultural programs of the New Deal. Indeed, Peek's two price program would later become an accepted part of American agricultural policy. (Gilbert C. Fite, *George N. Peek and the Fight for Farm Parity*, 1954; Richard S. Kirkendall, *Social Scientists and Farm Politics in the Age of Roosevelt*, 1966.)

DAVID L. CHAPMAN

PENDERGAST, THOMAS JOSEPH Thomas J. Pendergast was born July 22, 1872, in St. Joseph, Missouri. When Franklin D. Roosevelt* secured the 1932

Democratic presidential nomination, he attempted but failed to win support from many powerful urban machines, most of whom supported his adversary, Alfred E. Smith.* One of these leaders, Thomas J. Pendergast of Kansas City, Missouri, claimed later to have supported Roosevelt throughout the convention. Following Roosevelt's election in 1932,* the New Deal* began facilitating Pendergast's control over federal patronage in Missouri—beginning with the replacement of a Republican as state director of Federal Re-employment for Missouri with machine backed Judge Harry Truman* of Independence.

Roosevelt allowed Pendergast to spread his influence over other agencies dispensing federal patronage, including the Federal Emergency Relief Administration* and the Civil Works Administration.* Acting through Postmaster General James Farley* and national relief director Harry L. Hopkins,* Roosevelt permitted Pendergast to expand his power beyond Kansas City in 1935 by appointing a loyal member of the machine, Matthew S. Murray, as state director of the Works Progress Administration.* Murray's appointment proved very profitable to Pendergast's organization because control of WPA jobs throughout the state called for the expenditure of millions of dollars. The WPA strengthened the Pendergast machine's already considerable voting powers. Armed with federal contracts, Pendergast's Ready-Mixed Concrete Company helped construct Kansas City's Municipal Auditorium, Brush Creek, a new city hall, a police station, and a court house. In addition to working through Murray with Hopkins, Pendergast also utilized the machine to send Truman to the Senate in 1934, widening his control over federal patronage.

In 1936 the machine helped secure the election of Guy B. Park as governor of Missouri. Park appointed Pendergast's choice, R. Emmett O'Malley, as state superintendent of insurance. Together with A. L. McCormick, the president of the Missouri Association of Insurance Agents, Pendergast and O'Malley worked out a deal whereby the Kansas City boss received $750,000 (a considerable sum in 1937) for arranging a compromise settlement between the state of Missouri and several insurance companies. This payoff led to an investigation that resulted in the indictment, conviction, and imprisonment of Pendergast, O'Malley, Murray, and numerous other leaders in the Kansas City organization.

Roosevelt displayed an interesting reaction to the machine and the corruption it generated. Despite frequent complaints about vice in Kansas City, voting irregularities, misuse of government agencies, and scandals involving high local and state officials, Roosevelt preferred to leave Pendergast alone since the boss virtually controlled Missouri's electoral votes. Roosevelt avoided intrastate political squabbles and worked with the prevailing political powers. Thus the Pendergast machine, no matter how corrupt, represented political reality to Roosevelt and had to be accepted. Only when the machine's source of power diminished did Roosevelt attack it.

This occurred in 1937 when Lloyd C. Stark, who had succeeded Guy Park as governor in 1936, decided to build his own power base and satisfy Missouri reformers by seeking Pendergast's political demise. Stark persuaded the United

States Treasury Department to investigate crime in Kansas City and the Pendergast-O'Malley insurance deal. Perhaps more important in Roosevelt's eyes, Stark successfully challenged Pendergast's role as political kingmaker by securing the election of Judge James M. Douglas over the machine's choice, Judge James V. Billings, to the Missouri Supreme Court in 1938. Following a bitter and ruthless fight between the two contestants, Roosevelt interpreted Douglas' victory as a signal that Stark was the new power broker in Missouri. Over Truman's objection, Roosevelt allowed the federal investigation of Pendergast to proceed, resulting in the boss' plea of guilty to two counts of income tax evasion. Thomas J. Pendergast served fifteen months in prison and died January 26, 1945, while waiting for a presidential pardon that never arrived. (Lyle W. Dorsett, *The Pendergast Machine*, 1968.)

J. CHRISTOPHER SCHNELL

PEPPER, CLAUDE DENSON Claude D. Pepper, loyal New Deal* senator and later the nation's most prominent spokesman for the rights of the elderly, was born on September 8, 1900, on a farm near Dudleyville, Alabama. Pepper worked in a steel mill before attending college but graduated from the University of Alabama in 1921 and thc Harvard Law School in 1924. Hc taught law at thc University of Arkansas in 1924 and 1925 and then opened a private practice in Perry, Florida. He moved to Tallahassee in 1930 while a member of the state house of representatives and served on the state board of public welfare in 1931 and 1932 and as a member of the state board of law examiners in 1933. Pepper was active in Democratic politics and was elected to the United States Senate in 1936 to fill the seat vacated by the death of Duncan U. Fletcher.* He was re-elected in 1938 and again in 1944.

During the New Deal, Pepper was an outspoken supporter of President Franklin D. Roosevelt* and a frequent critic of the attitudes of conservative Democrats in the South. An opponent of the power of "big business" and such agents as the U.S. Chamber of Commerce* and the National Association of Manufacturers,* Pepper viewed the New Deal as the nation's only hope to achieve an industrial democracy and economic freedom for the working classes. Pepper consistently advocated pro-labor legislation, increased relief spending, and improvements in social security. Pepper was an unsuccessful candidate for re-election in 1950, returned to private law practice, but resumed his public service career when he was elected to the House of Representatives in 1962. (James T. Patterson, *Congressional Conservatism and the New Deal*, 1967.)

PERKINS, FRANCES Frances Perkins was born in Boston, Massachusetts, on April 10, 1880. Years before the New Deal,* she volunteered vigorously for social justice activities in Massachusetts, Chicago, and New York where the squalor and exploitation of the poor by higher income groups angered her. In the 1910s and 1920s, she learned that specific solutions for specific problems were much better than visionary socialism or the unrealistic demands of labor unions. She publicized the horrible sweatshops of New York, lobbied for protective labor laws for women and children, and got a fifty-four-hour work week. The friendship of progressive Democrats like Franklin D. Roosevelt* and Robert F. Wagner* lasted a lifetime and helped her in social justice causes. In 1928 Governor Alfred E. Smith* made her New York's industrial commissioner, a position she also held for four years under the next governor, Franklin D. Roosevelt. The emphasis went to special protective labor laws for children and women, an eight-hour workday, stricter inspections of factories, and a six-day workweek. Being in the circle of Roosevelt's trusted advisers, Perkins helped convince Governor Roosevelt to actively fight the Great Depression in New York by supporting state unemployment insurance, providing relief, and seeking a solution to unemployment on a regional basis. When Roosevelt challenged Herbert Hoover* for the presidency in 1932, Perkins gave him her avid support from the day he announced his candidacy.

On March 4, 1933, Roosevelt appointed Perkins secretary of labor, and she became the first woman cabinet member in American history. Her acceptance was conditioned on the president agreeing to back extensive programs for social justice, which included old-age and unemployment insurance, public work relief, fair labor standards legislation, health insuranace, and aid to the poor. As one of Roosevelt's most trusted New Deal advisers, Perkins helped shape the famous ''hundred days''* legislation in the special congressional session of 1933 as well as the second burst of New Deal legislation in 1935. Her experience went into the Civilian Conservation Corps,* National Industrial Recovery Act,* and Federal Emergency Relief Administration.* The NIRA was important to her in its attempt to implement her dreams of a reasonable workweek, a living wage, improved working conditions, and more job security. It was a step away from economic theory and practices of scarcity in a land of abundance.

During 1933 and 1934 she spent long hours making the Labor Department an effective arm of government. The expansion of the Bureau's Labor Standards furnished the secretary with up-to-date data; an enlarged Bureau of Women and Children pushed for protective labor laws for those two groups; a more efficient Mediation and Conciliation Service came in time to help with the severe labor troubles between 1933 and 1937; and the establishment of the Division of Labor Standards worked for minimum wages and maximum hours.

The second great series of New Deal legislation came from 1935 to 1938. Roosevelt made Perkins chairman of the Committee on Economic Security* which helped write the Social Security Act* to provide pensions for retired persons, unemployment compensation, and public assistance for the blind, lame, and dependent children. The National Labor Relations Act* fulfilled a number of her desires as well. When the Supreme Court* nullified the National Industrial Recovery Act in 1935, Perkins' wages-and-hours provisions were destroyed. Unable to get a modified National Recovery Administration* restored, Perkins participated in the creation of the ''Little NRA''* by pushing for the Walsh-Healey Public Contracts Act of 1936* which required most contractors with the government to agree to an eight-hour day and a forty-hour week and a minimum wage to be set by Secretary Perkins. In 1938 the Fair Labor Standards Act* made her dream of national minimum wages and maximum hours come true.

During World War II, Secretary Perkins stood fast against management's attempt to nullify most of the gains for labor by claiming the exigencies of war made them luxuries. Shortly after the death of President Roosevelt in April 1945, Perkins resigned as secretary of labor. From 1945 until her death, Perkins served on the Civil Service Commission (1945-1952), wrote about her New Deal years, gave public lectures, and taught at Cornell's School of Industrial and Labor Relations (1956–1965). Her death in 1965 brought to a close the life of a woman dedicated to social justice; she had helped create a more just industrial society through practical means of wages-and-hours laws, pensions, public assistance, collective bargaining, an effective Department of Labor, and a compassionate feeling for unfortunate people. (George W. Martin, *Madam Secretary: Frances Perkins*, 1976; Frances Perkins, *The Roosevelt I Knew*, 1946.)

H. CARLETON MARLOW

PERSONS, WILLIAM FRANK W. Frank Persons was born in Brandon, Iowa, in 1877. He attended Cornell College in Iowa and then received a law degree from Harvard in 1900. After practicing law in Sioux Falls, Iowa, Persons became director of the Charity Organization of New York. Between 1917 and 1922, he worked for the American Red Cross, and then he went into industrial relations with the North American Company. Briefly serving as director of enrollment for the Civilian Conservation Corps* in 1933, Persons accepted President Franklin D. Roosevelt's* nomination as head of the United States Employment Service* in 1933. Persons remained with the service until 1939. Following his departure from the federal government, he worked for several major aeronautical firms. W. Frank Persons died on May 28, 1955. (*New York Times*, May 29, 1955.)

PETROLEUM ADMINISTRATIVE BOARD A major problem facing the oil industry in 1933 was overproduction and falling prices, and the Independent Petroleum Association of America endorsed the National Recovery Administration* as a way of enforcing state-imposed quotas on oil production. They were therefore quite hopeful when the NRA completed the petroleum code and when on August 28, 1933, President Franklin D. Roosevelt* issued Executive Order No. 6260A naming Secretary of the Interior Harold Ickes* as administrator of the code. Roosevelt also established the Petroleum Administrative Board to administer the NRA code for the petroleum industry. Nathan Margold,* solicitor of the Interior Department, was named chairman of the board, and Charles Fahy,* associate solicitor of the Interior Department, was vice-chairman. The board estimated the production of oil and the demand for it, established production quotas nationwide, and then allocated production in the oil-producing states. It also worked to limit oil imports, regulate the relationship between crude oil and gasoline prices, and planned the development of new pools. Roosevelt established a Petroleum Labor Policy Board* on December 19, 1933, to help enforce compliance with the wage-and-hour provisions and Section 7(a) of the National Industrial Recovery Act of 1933.* The Petroleum Labor Policy Board also tried to mediate labor disputes and strikes. The NRA petroleum code and the Petroleum Administrative Board were declared unconstitutional in January 1935 by the Supreme Court* in the *Panama Refining Company v. Ryan** case, which said the code was an unconstitutional delegation of legislative powers to the executive branch. (Peter H. Irons, *The New Deal Lawyers*, 1982; Katie Louchheim, ed., *The Making of the New Deal. The Insiders Speak*, 1983; Samuel I. Rosenman, *The Public Papers and Addresses of Franklin D. Roosevelt*, II:282–284, 1938.)

PETROLEUM LABOR POLICY BOARD Unlike most of the early labor boards, the Petroleum Labor Policy Board was independent of the National Recovery Administration,* residing instead under Harold Ickes'* control in the Petroleum Administrative Board.* Formed in November 1933, the board was designed to mediate labor-management disputes in the oil industry. The board consisted of a chairman, Dr. William Leiserson, professor of economics at Antioch College; Dr. George Stocking, professor of economics at the University of Texas; and Dr. James Mullenbach, a labor mediator from Chicago. Leiserson resigned in July 1934 and was replaced as chairman by Stocking; and Dr. John Lapp, former president of the National Conference on Social Work, filled the vacancy. With only vague powers, the PLPB tried to mediate disputes and guarantee collective bargaining, and it also worked to enforce wage-and-hours provisions of the NRA petroleum code. But the board encountered the same non-compliance with Section 7(a) from employers as did the other labor boards. Still, the PLPB assisted the growth of the International Association of Oil Field, Gas Well, and Refinery Workers' Union in 1933 and 1934. Although the PLPB continued until June 16, 1935, its power was effectively ended by the *Panama** decision in January 1935 and completely ended by the *Schechter** decision in May 1935. (Lewis L. Lorwin and Arthur Wubnig, *Labor Relations Boards*, 1935.)

PIERSON, WARREN LEE Warren Lee Pierson was born in Princeton, Minnesota, on August 29, 1896. He graduated from the University of California in 1917 and from the Harvard Law School in 1922. Pierson then returned to California and practiced law in Los Angeles until 1933 when he joined the staff of the Reconstruction Finance Corporation* as special counsel. After two years with the RFC, he went to work for the Export-Import Bank* as general counsel. In 1936 Pierson became president and general counsel of the Export-Import Bank, a position he held until 1944. Under Pierson's direction, the Export-Import Bank extended more than $1 billion in loans and became an important institution in United States foreign policy. Pierson resigned from the bank in 1944 to return to private business and became president of the American Cable

& Radio Corporation and later of Trans World Airlines. In 1951 and 1952 Pierson was a member of the United States delegation to the Tripartite Commission on German Debts, where he enjoyed the rank of ambassador. Between 1953 and 1955, he served as chairman of the United States Council. After retiring, Pierson lived in East Hampton, Long Island, and he died on January 12, 1978. (Frederick C. Adams, *Economic Diplomacy: The Export-Import Bank and American Foreign Policy, 1934-1939*, 1976; *Who Was Who In America*, VII:455, 1981.)

PITTMAN, KEY Key Pittman was born on September 19, 1872, in Vicksburg, Mississippi. He was orphaned at the age of twelve and went to live with his maternal grandmother in Louisiana. Pittman attended Southwestern Presbyterian University in Tennessee for three years but dropped out without graduating in 1890. He moved to Seattle, Washington, in 1890, read law privately, and was admitted to the bar in 1892. Pittman practiced law there until 1897 when he followed the gold rush to Alaska. For two years he labored as a common miner but then began practicing law again, becoming well-known as an excellent mining lawyer. When the Nevada gold fields were discovered in 1901, Pittman moved again, settling in Tonopah and opening his law practice. He flourished there, spent some time in the Silver party, and then became a Democrat in 1908. Pittman ran for the United States Senate in 1910, campaigning against the "power and corruption" of the Southern Pacific Railroad, but he lost to incumbent George Nixon. When Nixon died in 1912, the Nevada state legislature selected Pittman to fill the seat. He served in the Senate for twenty-seven years, winning re-election in 1916, 1922, 1928, 1934, and 1940.

During the 1930s, Pittman was an open advocate of inflationary recovery theories, supporting President Franklin D. Roosevelt's* gold-buying* scheme and pushing the Silver Purchase Act of 1934.* He also played an important role in the World Monetary and Economic Conference's 1933 decision to have the major western powers purchase large volumes of silver to replace low-valued paper currency. Pittman, however, was not known as one of the radical silverites in the United States Senate. Unlike such people as Senator Elmer Thomas* of Oklahoma, Pittman's interest in inflationary schemes and government silver purchases was not a function of theoretical conviction but a desire to make sure that the silver mining industry in Nevada was protected and unemployment eased. When the international price of silver reached 64.5¢ an ounce in April 1935, Pittman was satisfied and remained relatively content with the New Deal's* rather conservative silver-buying program. During the 1930s Pittman also served as chairman of the Senate Foreign Relations Committee, where he played a moderately isolationist role. Key Pittman died on November 10, 1940. (Fred Israel, *Nevada's Key Pittman*, 1963.)

POPE, JAMES PINCKNEY James P. Pope, the liberal New Deal* senator from Idaho, was born on a farm near Jonesboro, Louisiana, on March 31, 1884. He graduated from Louisiana Polytechnic Institute in 1906 and then took a law degree from the University of Chicago in 1909. Pope then moved to Boise, Idaho, and opened a law practice. Soon he found himself active in Democratic politics. He became deputy collector of internal revenue in Boise in 1916 and served as city attorney in 1916 and 1917. Pope served as assistant attorney general of Idaho in 1918 and 1919 and then returned to private law practice in Boise. He was elected to the school board there and served between 1924 and 1929, and between 1929 and 1933 he was mayor of Boise. In the Democratic landslide of 1932, Pope was elected to the United States Senate, where he served one term and was a loyal New Dealer. Pope supported the "death sentence" clause for public utilities, executive reorganization, fair labor standards, and was a prominent internationalist in foreign policy. He was also one of the moving forces behind the Agricultural Adjustment Act of 1938.* But when he came up for re-election in 1938,* his pro-New Deal and internationalist foreign policies proved handicaps, and he lost the Democratic primary to D. Worth Clark. In return for his loyalty, President Franklin D. Roosevelt* appointed him a director of the TVA* in 1939, and he remained there until he resigned in 1951. James P. Pope died on January 23, 1966. (*Biographical Directory of American Congresses*, 1556, 1971; James T. Patterson, *Congressional Conservatism and the New Deal*, 1967.)

PRESIDENT'S COMMITTEE ON ADMINISTRATIVE MANAGEMENT (See REORGANIZATION ACT OF 1939.)

PRESIDENT'S COMMITTEE ON CROP INSURANCE (See FEDERAL CROP INSURANCE ACT OF 1938.)

PRESIDENT'S EMERGENCY COMMISSION ON HOUSING (See FEDERAL HOUSING ADMINISTRATION.)

PRESSMAN, LEE Lee Pressman was born July 1, 1906, and attended Cornell University. He graduated from Cornell in 1926 and then went to the Harvard Law School, where he became a prize student of Felix Frankfurter.* Pressman helped edit the *Harvard Law Review* in 1928 and 1929, and between 1929 and 1933 he worked for the Wall-Street firm of Chadbourne, Stanchfield, and Levy, where he specialized in corporate reorganizations. Brilliant and keenly analytical, Pressman was recruited to the Agricultural Adjustment Administration* legal staff in 1933 by Jerome Frank.* Pressman worked closely with Frank, and when his boss was fired by Secretary of Agriculture Henry Wallace* in 1935 for attempting to shape AAA policy to benefit tenant farmers, Pressman was fired too. He then went to work as general counsel for the Works Progress Administration* and also served with the Resettlement Administration* during 1935 and 1936. Pressman left the federal government in 1936 to work for the new Committee for Industrial Organization* and rose to become the CIO's general counsel. Lee Pressman died on November 19, 1968. (Peter H. Irons, *The New Deal Lawyers*, 1982.)

PRODUCTION CREDIT ASSOCIATIONS (See FARM CREDIT ACT OF 1933 and FARM CREDIT ADMINISTRATION.)

PROGRESSIVE NATIONAL COMMITTEE During the election campaign of 1936,* many Democrats saw an unprecedented opportunity to attract progressive Republicans into the Franklin D. Roosevelt* camp, especially after the Republicans nominated Alfred M. Landon* for president and attacked the New Deal.* In September 1936 a coalition of New Deal Democrats and progressive Republicans—including Robert La Follette, Jr.,* George Norris,* Fiorello La Guardia,* Frank P. Walsh,* Adolf Berle,* Elmer Benson,* John L. Lewis,* Sidney Hillman,* Hugo Black,* and Thomas Amlie*—held a meeting in Chicago and formed the Progressive National Committee. The committee endorsed Roosevelt's re-election and worked to bring all pro-New Deal voters, Democrats as well as Republicans, into the administration camp. (Arthur M. Schlesinger, Jr., *The Age of Roosevelt. Vol. III. The Politics of Upheaval, 1935-1936*, 1960.)

PUBLIC UTILITY HOLDING COMPANY ACT OF 1935 Perhaps no legislation was more symbolic of the "Second New Deal"* and its Brandesian faith than the Public Utility Holding Company Act of 1935. With the faith in national planning largely ruined by the bureaucratic entanglements of the NRA* and business criticism of the New Deal,* President Franklin D. Roosevelt* adopted an anti-trust philosophy consistent with the views of Louis Brandeis* and Woodrow Wilson's earlier "New Freedom." In March 1935 the president addressed Congress and called for the dissolution of the electric power holding company structure because the utilities exploited consumers and evaded state regulation. Memories of the Samuel Insull* empire provided the backdrop for the accusation. Roosevelt had Benjamin Cohen* and Thomas Corcoran* draft the legislation, and Senator Burton K. Wheeler* of Montana and Representative Sam Rayburn* of Texas sponsored it in Congress. The key to the bill was the "death sentence" clause requiring the SEC* to dissolve any utility holding company after January 1, 1940, if it could not justify its existence.

Spending more than $1 million, the utility industry launched an intense lobbying campaign against the bill. In June 1935 the Senate approved it by one vote, but the House rejected the mandatory "death sentence" by 216 to 146. The House then approved the rest of the bill by 323 to 81. Although Senator Hugo Black* of Alabama initiated a congressional investigation of the utility industry's lobbying campaign, the House would still have nothing to do with the mandatory "death sentence." Roosevelt had to settle for a scaled-down version, which he signed into law on August 28, 1935. The Public Utility Holding Company Act gave the Federal Power Commission* the authority to regulate interstate shipments of electrical power and the Federal Trade Commission* the same authority over natural gas shipments. The act also eliminated all holding companies more than twice removed from their operating companies. All utility holding companies had to register with the SEC, and the SEC could supervise their financial transactions. Although there was no mandatory "death sentence," the SEC did have the discretionary power to dissolve any holding company which could not, after a term of five years, demonstrate its local usefulness. The burden of proof rested on the government. Under the provisions of the Public Utility Holding Company Act, the SEC* forced or inspired American utilities to divest themselves of 753 holding company affiliates worth more than $10 billion by 1952. (Philip J. Funigiello, *Toward a National Power Policy: The New Deal and the Electric Utility Industry, 1933-1941*, 1973.)

PUBLIC WORKS ADMINISTRATION During the 1930s, the Public Works Administration distributed nearly $6 billion for the construction of roads, tunnels, bridges, dams, hydroelectric power projects, public buildings, municipal water and sewage systems, and railroad equipment and facilities upgrading. The purpose of the PWA was to provide jobs for the unemployed and stimulate an economic recovery, and it was a major source of construction money during the Great Depression. Half of all school buildings and most municipal water and sewage systems built during the 1930s were PWA projects financed at a rate of 30 percent federal funds and 70 percent local funds. In 1933 the PWA accounted for 33 percent of all construction in the United States. It averaged nearly 140,000 workers each year and indirectly created more than 600,000 other jobs. The PWA also allocated approximately $1.8 billion to fund such government agencies as the Bureau of Reclamation,* Bureau of Roads, and the War Department.

The origins of the Public Works Administration reached back into the early 1920s. In 1921 Otto T. Mallery had written *The Long Range Planning of Public Works*, advocating creation of a federal reserve fund for the construction of valuable public works. William T. Foster and Waddill Catchings wrote *Progress and Plenty* in 1930 and called for new construction of highways, public buildings, and other public projects to augment consumer purchasing power. Various construction trade associations during the 1920s also lobbied on behalf of public works programs, as did many social work organizations. In Congress, such liberal Republicans as Robert M. La Follette, Jr.,* of Wisconsin and Bronson Cutting* of New Mexico and Democrats like Edward P. Costigan* of Colorado and Robert Wagner* of New York, demanded federal public works spending as a means of relieving the unemployment problem. In 1932 Congress passed the Emergency Relief and Construction Act which provided $2 billion, to be administered by the Reconstruction Finance Corporation,* for work relief through self-liquidating public works projects. The RFC created a Self-Liquidating Division and began initiating several projects. During the remainder of Herbert Hoover's* administration, however, the Self-Liquidating Division spent much of its time on feasibility studies and actually spent very little of its appropriation.

By the time of the inauguration of Franklin D. Roosevelt* in March 1933, demands for a strong public works program were becoming more and more strong. Three different rationales were behind the demands. Some people wanted public works construction as a means of ''pump-priming,'' stimulating private purchasing power through the rapid expenditure of federal funds. Others saw the projects as a way of relieving the suffering of the unemployed. Finally, some saw public works programs as a way of building useful public projects which might otherwise have difficulty finding funds. Two of Roosevelt's cabinet members—Secretary of Labor Frances Perkins* and Secretary of the Interior Harold L. Ickes*—became the most prominent advocates of the program. They took Senator Robert La Follette's, Jr.'s* proposal for a $5 billion program, reduced the total of $3.3 billion, and compromised with fiscal conservatives by requiring that projects be funded with 30 percent federal grants and the balance in secured loans. The proposal for creation of a Public Works Administration was attached as Title II of the National Industrial Recovery Act* and passed. Harold L. Ickes was named administrator of the Public Works Administration.

In order to provide jobs for large numbers of faithful Democrats, Ickes decentralized the PWA into state and local committees. He also took over all the files of the RFC's Self-Liquidating Division, employed many of the same staff workers and engineers, and picked up on the existing projects. The projects developed slowly because Ickes insisted that all work was carefully planned according to drawn contracts and that all loans be fully secured. The PWA spent only $2.8 billion of its initial $3.3 billion appropriation, and most of it went to other federal agency construction projects. Ickes turned the PWA over to the Federal Works Agency* in 1939 after the Reorganization Act of 1939,* and at that time the agency had over 2,000 employees.

Because its projects were complex and slow too develop, the PWA disappointed those who wanted it to ''prime the pump'' and relieve unemployment. Late in 1933 Roosevelt took $400 million of the PWA's funds and gave it to the new Civil Works Administration* because the CWA was capable of working much more expeditiously. By 1935 disillusionment with the PWA, primarily because of its deliberateness, caused Congress to shift the relief burden to the new Works Progress Administration.* The Emergency Relief Appropriation Act of 1935* allocated only $313 million to the PWA. Not until 1938, when the PWA received another $1.6 billion, was it prepared to spend the money on its projects.

Although the Public Works Administration failed to bring recovery, it did accomplish three things. First, it pioneered the pattern of direct federal allotments to municipal governments. Second, the PWA initiated the federal housing program which was later institutionalized by the Housing Act of 1938. Finally, the PWA's projects—such as the Grand Coulee Dam, Queens Midtown Tunnel, and the All American Canal—were of high quality and are still functional in the United States. During the course of the Great Depression, PWA funds were spent on more than 34,000 projects. (James S. Olson, *Herbert Hoover and the*

Reconstruction Finance Corporation, 1931-1933, 1977; William D. Reeves, "The Politics of Public Works, 1933-1935," Ph.D. dissertation, Tulane University, 1968.)

PUBLIC WORKS OF ART PROJECT A forerunner of the WPA* Federal Art Project,* the Public Works of Art Project was founded in December 1933 under a Civil Works Administration* grant to the Treasury Department. In May 1933 George Biddle, a Groton and Harvard classmate of Franklin D. Roosevelt,* wrote the president suggesting some federal relief program for unemployed artists. Harry Hopkins,* the new head of the CWA, had already organized work relief for unemployed artists back in 1932 when he supervised the New York Temporary Emergency Relief Administration, and he liked the idea. So did Frances Perkins,* the secretary of labor. She discussed the idea with several New Dealers, including Harold Ickes,* Jerome Frank,* Louis Howe,* and Henry A. Hunt.* The Treasury Department decided to administer the program, and Edward Bruce, a treasury lawyer and art lover, was put in charge of the Public Works of Art Project.

The PWAP was geared to work relief and art production, not to art education. In 1934 the PWAP hired more than 3,600 artists and assistants in all forty-eight states, spending $1.3 million on payroll. To produce murals and sculptures for public buildings, each artist received $35 to $45 per week. When the Civil Works Administration was terminated in the spring of 1934, the PWAP came to an end. It was the first art project sponsored by the federal government on a national scale and established a precedent which led to the art, music, theater, and writers' projects of the Works Progress Administration. (William F. McDonald, *Federal Relief Administration and the Arts*, 1969.)

"PURGE OF 1938" (See ELECTION OF 1938.)

R

RADICALS OF THE RIGHT Radicals of the Right was a conservative, anti-New Deal group established by Seward Collins in April 1933 when he began publishing the *American Review*. Collins tried to appeal to conservative intellectuals, hoping they would join his crusade against the "Communist" tendencies of the New Deal.* A genteel anti-Semite, Collins eventually turned to an intellectual fascism which called for a restoration of monarchy, feudalism, and unfettered property rights. By 1940 his ideas had deteriorated into hopelessly pathetic attempts to protect fascist and Nazi agitators in the United States. (Arthur M. Schlesinger, Jr., *The Age of Roosevelt. Vol. III. The Politics of Upheaval, 1935-1936*, 1960.)

RAILROAD RETIREMENT ACT OF 1934 Although many railroads had pension plans by the early 1930s, the retirement programs varied greatly from road to road, with many smaller railways lacking programs altogether. For years the railroad brotherhoods had lobbied in Congress for a federal retirement program, but not until the New Deal* did they find a sympathetic administrative and legislative ear. Senator Robert Wagner* of New York and Senator Henry Hatfield* of West Virginia sponsored the legislation, which became the Railroad Retirement Act on June 27, 1934. A Railroad Retirement Board administered the law, and the pensions were financed by a 2 percent payroll tax on all employees, matched by a 4 percent contribution from the carriers. By requiring railroad employees to retire at age sixty-five, the law hoped to create 150,000 new jobs in a matter of a few years. The Association of Railway Executives bitterly opposed the law, calling it an unconstitutional violation of private property and certain to bankrupt them. They immediately launched test cases in the federal courts, and in 1935, in *Railroad Retirement Board v. Alton R.R. Company*,* the Supreme Court* declared the law unconstitutional, since mandatory pensions did not come under the commerce clause. Congress then had to respond with what became the Wagner-Crosser Railroad Retirement Act of 1935* and later the Railroad Retirement Act of 1937.* ("Railroads and Their Employees," *Monthly Labor Review*, XXXIX:352-355, 1934.)

RAILROAD RETIREMENT ACT OF 1935 When the Supreme Court* declared the Railroad Retirement Act of 1934* unconstitutional in the *Railroad Retirement Board v. Alton** case, Congress immediately moved to fill the void. On August 29, 1935, after several months of deliberation, Congress passed a new Railroad Retirement Act, one sponsored by Senator Robert Wagner* of New York and Congressman Robert Crosser of Ohio. The law established a Railroad Retirement Board of three members to administer the law. It also exempted railroad employees from the old-age pension provisions of the Social Security Act.* To avoid the Supreme Court ruling that pensions were not included in the commerce clause, Congress passed separate legislation (49 U.S. Stat. 977) to fund the Wagner-Crosser bill. Employees would pay an excise tax of 3.5 percent of payrolls; and employers, an equal percentage in the form of an income tax. The Association of Railway Executives contested both laws, and on June 26, 1936, a United States District Court declared the financing measure unconstitutional, forcing Congress to pass the Railroad Retirement Act of 1937.* (''Railroad Retirement Act of 1937,'' *Monthly Labor Review*, XLV:377-379, 1937.)

RAILROAD RETIREMENT ACT OF 1937 When the U.S. District Court for the District of Columbia invalidated the financing provisions of the 1935 congressional retirement program for railroads, President Franklin D. Roosevelt* asked management and the railway brotherhoods to work out a new pension program. On March 16, 1937, they jointly released a proposal which Congress enacted on June 29, 1937, as the Railroad Retirement Act. A finance measure known as the Carriers' Taxing Act was approved the same day. A Railroad Retirement Board was created to administer the law, with one member from labor, one from management, and an independent chairman. Funds for the program came from the Carrier Taxing Act, which provided for an income tax levied on carriers and employees. (''Railroad Retirement Act of 1937,'' *Monthly Labor Review*, XLV:377-379, 1937.)

RAILROAD RETIREMENT BOARD ET AL. V. ALTON RAILROAD COMPANY ET AL. On June 27, 1934, Congress passed the Railroad Retirement Act,* commonly called the Railroad Pension Act. The law provided a retirement and pension plan for employees of all carriers regulated by the Interstate Commerce Act. Compulsory contributions were levied on all such carriers and their employees to create a retirement fund. A pension would be provided not only for current and future employees, but for those as well who had worked for the carriers within one year before enactment of the law.

The respondents in the case (134 Class I railroads, two express companies, and the Pullman Company) brought suit challenging the law. Constitutionality was questioned on two major points: that the provision granting pensions to former employees violated the due process guarantees of the Constitution by taking property of the respondents and bestowing it on the former employees and that the act itself was not a proper and necessary regulation of interstate commerce.

The Supreme Court of the District of Columbia granted a decree in favor of the plaintiffs, and the government appealed to the court of appeals for the district. But before the case was in the court, the Supreme Court* of the United States granted a writ of certiorari. The case was argued on March 13 and 14, 1935, and decided on May 6, 1935.

A majority of the justices found in favor of the respondents. Writing for the majority, Associate Justice Owen J. Roberts* specifically questioned the provisions of the law granting pensions to former employees, including those who may have been discharged for cause, those whose jobs had been eliminated, and those who had left to take other employment. Mr. Justice Roberts found the law to be "arbitrary in the last degree" for imposing on the carriers the financial burden of supporting such employees with pensions. Since there had been no contractual agreement as to pensions during the period of employment and since such employees had contributed nothing toward the cost of their newly-granted pensions, the Court found that the Retirement Act did in fact violate the due process of law clause of the Fifth Amendment by taking the property of the carriers and giving it to the retirees.

The Court also contended that the act apportioned contributions to the pension fund among the carriers as though they were a single employer without regard to their assets or obligations. This too was declared to be contrary to due process of law.

On the second point, the Court found that the Retirement Act was not a regulation of interstate commerce within the meaning of the Constitution. In the opinion of the majority, arguments adduced by the government to support passage, such as promoting safety and efficiency by improving worker morale, job satisfaction, and retirement security, pertained to the social welfare of the workers and were not a proper exercise by Congress of the power to regulate commerce. By a vote of 5 to 4, the Court held the act to be unconstitutional.

In his dissent, Chief Justice Charles Evans Hughes* objected that the majority decision was too broad in that it denied to Congress any authority to legislate in the area of railroad pensions. Although he agreed that there were deficiencies in the act, he strongly criticized the majority opinion as "a departure from sound principles, [which] places an unwarranted limitation upon the Commerce Clause of the Constitution." (Gerald O. and L. G. Dykstra, *Selected Cases on Government and Business*, 1937; Alfred H. Kelly and Winfred A. Harbison, *The American Constitution*, 1979; *Supreme Court Reporter*, LV:758-780, 1935.)

JOSEPH M. ROWE, JR.

RAILWAY LABOR ACT OF 1934 Because Section 7(a) of the National Industrial Recovery Act* had guaranteed workers in the manufacturing sector the right to bargain collectively, the railroad brotherhoods began demanding similar protection. In June 1934 Senator Clarence Dill of Washington and

Representative Robert Crosser of Ohio sponsored legislation to amend the Railway Labor Act of 1926. The Railway Labor Act of 1934 amended its 1926 counterpart by replacing the Board of Mediation with a National Railroad Adjustment Board with offices in Chicago. With power to penalize either labor or management for refusing to settle mutual disputes, the new board had more power than its predecessor. The act also upheld the right of railroad employees to organize and bargain collectively using representatives of their own choosing. ("Railroads and Their Employees," *Monthly Labor Review*, XXXIX:352-354, 1934.)

RAND, JAMES HENRY James H. Rand was born on November 18, 1886, in North Tonawanda, New York. After working in a variety of business concerns, he established the Remington Rand Corporation to manufacture office supplies and office equipment. Rand served as president of Remington Rand from 1926 to 1955 and vice-chairman of Sperry Rand Corporation after it merged with Remington Rand. During the 1930s, Rand was head of the Committee for the Nation* and an advocate of inflation and revision of the gold standard. In March 1934 Rand testified before Congress that the "brain trust"* was actually a subversive group plotting the overthrow of the United States government. By keeping the country in an economic depression, they were preparing the public for a Communist takeover. Rand's sensational charges, drawn from the writings of William Wirt, caused a brief public stir. Rand then drifted out of the public spotlight. He died on June 3, 1968. (*Who Was Who In America*, V:591, 1973; George Wolfskill and John A. Hudson, *All But the People. Franklin D. Roosevelt and His Critics, 1933-1939*, 1969.)

RANDOLPH, ASA PHILIP Union and civil rights activist Asa Philip Randolph was born in Florida in 1889 and educated at Cookman Institute in Jacksonville. Later, while a student at the City College of New York, he supported himself through a variety of jobs, including porter and elevator operator. In 1917 he organized a union of New York City elevator operators. That same year, with Chandler Owen, he began publishing a weekly journal known as "The Messenger." Promoted as a radical magazine for American blacks, the journal reflected Randolph's interest in the socialist philosophy espoused by such leaders as Eugene V. Debs. An outspoken opponent of segregation and an advocate of minority representation in unions, Randolph became a teacher in New York City's Rand School of Social Science. He also ran, unsuccessfully, as a socialist candidate in several New York political contests.

In 1925 Randolph gained national attention when he founded the Brotherhood of Sleeping Car Porters. Organization of the brotherhood followed action by the Pullman Company, a railroad passenger service corporation, which blocked minority union activities. As the union's first president, Randolph transformed "The Messenger" into the official publication of the brotherhood. Under his leadership, the union overcame setbacks and eventually experienced increased bargaining leverage. In 1937 the union was formally recognized by the Pullman Company with the signing of a collective bargaining agreement.

Through his union work, Randolph became a national civil rights leader. He participated in the organizational work of several trade union groups and also became involved in work on a variety of social issues concerning urban blacks.

Early in 1940, A. Philip Randolph began planning a massive march on Washington, D.C., to protest employment discrimination in the defense industries. He was particularly concerned that blacks would not receive a fair share of new jobs created by the build-up of defense related commerce without the administration's support for equal opportunity programs.

Convinced that the march would be successful and that it would be detrimental to New Deal* programs and to an image of American unity, President Franklin D. Roosevelt* took steps to avoid the planned demonstration. As a result of a meeting with Randolph and other march leaders, Roosevelt appointed a special committee, headed by New York City Mayor Fiorello La Guardia,* to recommend a plan of action. The committee drew up the framework for an executive order on non-discrimination. Randolph agreed with the proposal, and the march was cancelled. On June 25, 1941, Roosevelt issued Executive Order 8802, which set up the Fair Employment Practices Committee* and called for non-discrimination clauses in all defense contracts.

Randolph continued as a civil rights activist through his commitment to such issues as the desegregation of the armed forces and through his leadership in the AFL-CIO. In 1963 he helped organize another march on Washington. Considered the largest demonstration to that date, the event had a significant impact on the development of the civil rights movement. Until his death in 1979, A. Philip Randolph actively continued to support the efforts of black workers. (William H. Harris, *Keeping the Faith: A. Philip Randolph, Milton P. Webster, and the Brotherhood of Sleeping Car Porters*, 1977; W. Augustus Low and Virgil A. Clift, eds., *Encyclopedia of Black America*, 1981.)

DAN K. UTLEY

RANKIN, JOHN ELLIOTT John E. Rankin was born in Itawamba County, Mississippi, on March 29, 1882. He took a law degree at the University of Mississippi in 1910 and began practicing law at Tupelo, Mississippi. Rankin served as prosecuting attorney between 1911 and 1915, and in 1920 he was elected as a Democrat to Congress. He remained there until 1953. Raised on a steady diet of Populism, Rankin was of the same cloth as Sam Rayburn*—suspicious of concentrated economic power, especially that of banks, railroads, and public utilities. Rankin was known as a "roughneck" in Congress, a man passionately committed to workers and farmers. He was chairman of the Public Power Bloc and co-author of the Tennessee Valley Authority Act.* Throughout the 1930s, Rankin was the TVA's most active protector in Congress. He also fought valiantly, and unsuccessfully, to include the "death sentence" clause in the Public Utility Holding Company Act of 1935.* Rankin was also the leader of the struggle in Congress to establish the Rural Electrification Administration* and to keep REA funds out of the hands of private utility companies. John Elliott Rankin died on November 26, 1960. (Arthur M. Schlesinger, Jr., *The Age of Roosevelt. Vol. II. The Coming of the New Deal*, 1959; and *Vol. III. The Politics of Upheaval, 1935-1936*, 1960; *Who Was Who In America*, IV:776, 1968.)

RASKOB, JOHN J. Forced to leave school and go to work upon his father's death, John J. Raskob, born March 17, 1879, in Lockport, New York, went on to become a leading industrialist and a prominent figure in the Democratic party.* At first a stenographer for the Worthington Pump Company, Raskob soon had another job as secretary to Pierre S. du Pont, then president of street railway companies in Ohio. Thus, Raskob's association with the du Pont family began in 1902 and lasted for years. Raskob rose to assistant to Pierre du Pont in Wilmington, Delaware, then treasurer of E. I. du Pont de Nemours & Company, and eventually to director and vice-president. At the same time Raskob was investing in General Motors stock and became a major owner. In the late 1910s and 1920s, as chairman and director of finance at General Motors, Raskob played a major role in restructuring the company and paving the way for the large-scale installment selling of automobiles. A loyal Democrat, Raskob became influential there, rising to the head of the Democratic National Committee in 1928 and helping to engineer the Roosevelt landslide in 1932.

Although Raskob supported Franklin D. Roosevelt* and the New Deal* in 1933, he soon became alienated. Roosevelt had eclipsed everyone else in the Democratic party, including Raskob. Alarmed about the anti-business drift of the New Deal, the personality cult surrounding Roosevelt, and the rise of big government, Raskob became one of the leading figures in the American Liberty League's* campaign against the New Deal. Along with people like Al Smith* and Alfred Sloan,* Raskob accused the president of leading the country down the road to ruin. To eliminate his influence from the party, Democratic officials paid off a $120,000 debt to Raskob in 1934. Late in the 1930s he completely severed his connection with the Democratic party. John J. Raskob died on October 15, 1950. (David Burner, *The Politics of Provincialism*, 1967; *New York Times*, October 16, 1950.)

RAUH, JOSEPH L., JR. Joseph Rauh, Jr., was born in Cincinnati in 1911. He graduated from Harvard in 1932 and received his law degree there in 1935. On the recommendation of Professor Felix Frankfurter* Rauh clerked with Supreme Court* Justice Benjamin Cardozo,* and between 1935 and 1942 he acted as an assistant to Benjamin Cohen* and Thomas Corcoran* in their legislative partnership. Rauh later served for two decades as a lawyer with the firm of Rauh and Silard and as general counsel for the United Automobile Workers. He was also a chief lobbyist for the Civil Rights Act of 1964 and the Voting Rights Act of 1965. He was one of the founders of the Americans for Democratic Action. (Katie Louchheim, ed., *The Making of the New Deal. The Insiders Speak*, 1983.)

RAYBURN, SAMUEL Samuel Rayburn, one of the most powerful people in the history of the United States Congress, was born on January 6, 1882, on a forty-acre farm in Tennessee. Because the farm's worn-out soil would not support the large Rayburn family, they moved in 1887 to another forty-acre farm, this one in Fallin County, Texas. Rayburn's childhood was one of stupefying farm poverty and great family closeness. The entire family, even the little children, had to work in the cotton fields every day, and even then finances were barely at a survival level. During those years, Rayburn developed the intense animosities of the Populist South—a hatred for the railroads, because their freight rates skimmed off most farm profits, and the banks, because their interest rates burdened the farmer for a lifetime. Indeed, Rayburn developed a deep suspicion of big business which never left him. Nor did he trust business's ''political agent''—the Republican party.* As far as he was concerned, the Republican party symbolized all that was wrong with America—big businessmen using the government to enrich themselves at the expense of poor people. He also viewed the GOP with the bitterness of an unreconstructed southerner. Republicans had invaded his homeland, destroyed it militarily during the Civil War, and exploited it economically after the war. Sam Rayburn was a hard-boiled Democrat whose political philosophy was laced for a lifetime with the passions of Populism.

Rayburn left the farm to attend East Texas Normal College, graduated from there four years later, taught school for two years, and in 1906 won a seat in the state legislature. Scrupulously honest and incorruptible in a state whose politics were dominated by the money flowing from land, oil, and railroads, Rayburn quickly earned a reputation for expertise, hard work, and integrity. In 1912 he was elected to Congress, and after a few rebellious years he settled into an apprenticeship which, by the time of the New Deal,* made him one of the most powerful men in the country.

As chairman of the House Interstate Commerce Committee, Rayburn played a key role in a variety of New Deal legislation. He could be counted on as a regular supporter of Franklin D. Roosevelt* and came to look on the president as one of the greatest figures in American history. For years, Rayburn had watched poor farmers lose their life savings by investing in worthless stocks and bonds, and during the Wilson administration he had unsuccessfully sponsored federal ''truth-in-securities'' legislation. When President Roosevelt became an advocate of such a measure, Rayburn enthusiastically took it under his wing. He turned to Raymond Moley;* and Moley had James M. Landis,* a Harvard law professor, and Benjamin V. Cohen* and Thomas G. Corcoran* draft the bill. Rayburn passionately supported the bill and guided it through Congress. When President Roosevelt signed it on May 27, 1933, it was a long-held dream fulfilled for the Texas congressman. The next year, Rayburn played a critical part in maneuvering the Securities Exchange Act of 1934* through Congress. Once enacted, the law created the Securities and Exchange Commission* to regulate the stock markets and ended the century of Wall-Street domination of the major exchanges. In the process, Rayburn was an outspoken critic of the business community and its ''self-serving public rhetoric.'' For Rayburn, federal regulation of Wall Street seemed only a fitting culmination, of decades of reform agitation.

In 1935 Rayburn undertook sponsorship, along with Senator Burton K. Wheeler* of Montana, of the Public Utility Holding Company Act.* Cohen and Corcoran wrote the bill, and Rayburn and Wheeler pushed it through Congress. For Rayburn and Wheeler, the holding companies epitomized business greed gone wild. Not only did they gouge utility consumers, but they refused to extend electric services to poor farmers. The bill at first contained the ''death sentence'' clause, giving the SEC the power to dissolve the holding companies. The utility industry launched an unprecedented lobbying effort against the bill, and Rayburn fought them the entire way. Although Congress eventually amended the bill and softened the clause, the bill passed and was a triumph for Rayburn—he was a major legislative bastion of the New Deal.

In 1940 Rayburn became Speaker of the House, a post he had long aspired to and one which he held for the next seventeen years. During that time he continued to be the leading figure in the House of Representatives, a master of the congressional process because of his capacity of persuasion and his understanding and control of House procedural rules. Above all else, Sam Rayburn was respected for his integrity and dependability. Although he had married in 1927, the relationship did not work out, and he was divorced after only three months; Rayburn remained single the rest of his life. With no family commitments, his life was the House of Representatives, and he became widely known as the most diligent, hard-working member of Congress. During the 1950s, Rayburn played a major role, albeit a private one, in the passage of the Civil Rights Acts of 1957 and 1960. No other person amassed more power or tried to use it more judiciously on behalf of workers and farmers than Sam Rayburn. He died on November 16, 1961, after serving nearly forty-nine years in the House. (Booth Mooney, *Roosevelt and Rayburn: A Political Partnership*, 1971.)

''READING FORMULA'' On July 5, 1933, more than 10,000 workers of the American Federation of Full-Fashioned Hosiery Workers went on strike when the Berkshire Knitting Mills refused to recognize the union. The National Labor Board* brought labor and management together for mediation on August 10 and shortly thereafter announced the ''Reading Formula'' interpretation of Section 7(a) of the National Industrial Recovery Act:* the union would terminate the strike, employees would be rehired without discrimination, and workers would select their own bargaining agent in secret, majority rule elections. In September 1934 the employers agreed to the settlement. (Bernard Bellush, *The Failure of the NRA*, 1975.)

RECESSION OF 1937-1938 Between September 1937 and June 1938 New Deal* efforts at economic relief, recovery, and reform suffered severe setbacks. Industrial production declined by 33 percent, durable goods production by over

50 percent, national income by 13 percent, profits by 78 percent, payrolls by 35 percent, industrial stock averages by over 50 percent, and manufacturing employment by 23 percent. The recession generated new debates about economic recovery and led to a shift from pump-priming to partial adoption of a compensatory government spending policy in the spring of 1938.

During 1936 the federal government employed the policy of deficit spending to provide net contributions of $4.1 billion to national income. Most of the expenditures came from release of the veterans bonus certificates after June 1936. Net governmental contributions in 1937 declined to $800 million because of the deflationary impact of new social security taxes. Changes in monetary policy also created economic disruptions. Between August 1936 and May 1937, the Federal Reserve Board* doubled reserve requirements, leading to a contraction of money and credit out of a misplaced fear of inflation. From December 1936 through April 1938, the treasury's gold stabilization program had similar consequences.

Since the recession came in the wake of New Deal economic recovery measures, many critics renewed their attack on Franklin D. Roosevelt's* administration, saying the recession stemmed from mistaken fiscal and monetary policies that undermined private sector investment and business confidence. The basic analyses of the causes of the depression, underconsumption and underinvestment, were brought out again in political debate during a period of increasing business-government tension. While some businessmen continued to argue for a resumption of industrial self-government under federal sponsorship, most businessmen advocated a return to private sector economic leadership.

The recession brought renewed debate to policymaking circles within the administration. Conservatives such as Reconstruction Finance Corporation* head Jesse Jones,* Secretary of Commerce Daniel C. Roper,* and Secretary of the Treasury Henry Morgenthau, Jr.,* argued that the government must retreat from reform to regain the confidence of the business community. They advocated balancing the federal budget, revising the tax laws, and conciliating business. Anti-monopolists such as Leon Henderson,* Robert Jackson,* Thomas Corcoran,* and Benjamin Cohen* argued that business was engaging in a "sitdown strike" of capital using monopoly power to administer prices and destroy free competition. They joined with members of the spending group such as Chairman Marriner Eccles* of the board of governors of the Federal Reserve, Secretary of the Interior Harold Ickes,* and members of the National Resources Committee* and argued for a resumption of federal spending to increase purchasing power and national income.

The debate over economic policy in 1937 and 1938 led to an internal crisis of faith in the New Deal. If the recession stemmed from mistaken New Deal policies from 1933 through 1936, then the very foundations of the New Deal were in danger of crumbling. Some way had to be found to bring about economic revival. The crisis was reflected in hostile rhetoric on the part of New Deal administrators, Republican politicians, and businessmen which obscured internal confusion within New Deal circles.

Between November 1937 and April 1938 anti-monopolists and spenders conducted a twofold campaign aimed at defending the New Deal in public, while winning over Roosevelt in private. They hoped to convince Roosevelt to adopt the policy of compensatory government spending and begin an extended anti-trust prosecution drive from the Anti-trust Division of the Department of Justice. Roosevelt accepted the need for resumed governmental spending in his message to Congress and the fireside chat* of April 14, 1938. Yet he also brought Thurman Arnold* from the Yale Law School to head the Anti-trust Division in March 1938 and called for an investigation of monopoly power in his anti-monopoly message to Congress on April 29, 1938.

While most scholars attribute the economic revival from June 1938 forward to the resumption of governmental spending, New Deal economic policy actually remained as confused as ever. Roosevelt never wholly accepted the philosophical underpinnings of a compensatory spending policy. His call for creation of the Temporary National Economic Committee* in April 1938 merely translated the competing policy positions of anti-trust, industrial self-government, compensatory spending, and national planning from the executive branch to the congressional investigating committee. Revival did come from a resumption of governmental spending for defense from the spring of 1940 forward, but the economic confusion of the New Deal administrators was solved only by implicit acceptance of spending for prosecution of World War II.

The recession of 1937-1938 brought the debate over industrial recovery to new heights. The debate created increasing tensions between the New Deal and the business community that would not be resolved until World War II. Most importantly, the debate revealed the internal confusion, doubt, and ignorance of New Deal administrators torn between competing economic traditions. While that debate was never completely resolved, the adoption of compensatory spending policy indicated a turning point in New Deal economic policymaking. (Dean May, *From New Deal to New Economics*, 1982; Albert U. Romasco, *The Politics of Recovery: Roosevelt's New Deal*, 1983; Theodore Rosenhof, *Dogma, Depression, and the New Deal: The Debate of Political Leaders over Economic Recovery*, 1975.)

PATRICK D. REAGAN

RECIPROCAL TRADE AGREEMENTS ACT OF 1934 By the early 1930s many economists and New Dealers had become convinced that the restrictive Republican trade policy of the 1920s had precipitated a decline in American exports and contributed to the Great Depression. Secretary of State Cordell Hull* launched a crusade in 1933 to reform American trade policy, not only to stimulate exports and economic recovery but also to improve United States foreign relations. Between 1929 and 1932 American exports had fallen by nearly a third, and Hull's bill called for bilateral trade agreements based on reciprocal reduction of tariff rates. The act passed the House of Representatives in March 1934 by a vote of 274 to 111 and the Senate in June by 57 to 33. It authorized the president to make reciprocal trade agreements with other nations without specific congressional approval and to raise or lower tariff rates in these agreements by up to 50 percent of the levels of the Smoot-Hawley Tariff of 1930. Congress renewed the Reciprocal Trade Agreements Act in 1937, 1940, 1943, and 1945. By that time the United States had negotiated agreements with thirty-seven countries. Although the act did not lead to spectacular increases in American exports, it did help the United States open new markets abroad and improved foreign relations with reciprocity partners. (James C. Pearson, *The Reciprocal Trade Agreements Program: The Policy of the United States and Its Effectiveness*, 1942.)

RECONSTRUCTION FINANCE CORPORATION At President Herbert Hoover's* request, Congress established the Reconstruction Finance Corporation in January 1932 to stabilize the nation's money markets. Hundreds of banks were failing each month, thousands more were in financial trouble, and industrial credit was shrinking rapidly. Endowed with up to $2 billion in working capital, the RFC was to make low-interest loans to banks, savings banks, savings and loan associations, credit unions, railroads, and insurance companies. For Hoover, the Great Depression was largely a crisis of confidence, and employment and production would not increase until private bankers were more willing to make business loans. The RFC would restore banker confidence and stimulate those business loans. Recovery would then ensue.

When Hoover left office fourteen months later, the RFC had loaned $2 billion, but the banking system was in a state of collapse. The first measure of President Franklin D. Roosevelt's* New Deal* was the Emergency Banking Act of 1933* permitting the RFC to purchase preferred stock in commercial banks. Like Hoover, Roosevelt was concerned about declines in business loans; but with repayment of RFC loans always imminent, bankers could hardly afford to be too generous in their lending practices. By permitting the RFC to invest in bank stock and receive dividends, Roosevelt felt that private bankers would have more freedom and time to make long-term commitments. By mid-1935, the RFC had purchased $1.3 billion in preferred stock from more than 6,200 commercial banks. But even that did not increase bank credit and stimulate recovery. From a high of more than $38 billion in 1930, commercial bank loans had dropped to little more than $20 billion in 1935, a precipitous decline which neither Hoover nor Roosevelt had been able to stop.

President Roosevelt then expanded the functions of the Reconstruction Finance Corporation. First, he converted the RFC into a major funding agency, the source of money for the Federal Emergency Relief Administration,* the Home Owners' Loan Corporation,* the Farm Credit Administration,* the Regional Agricultural Credit Corporations, the Federal Home Loan Bank Board, the Federal Farm Mortgage Corporation,* the Federal Housing Administration,* the Rural

Electrification Administration,* and the Resettlement Administration.* To assist the Tennessee Valley Authority* by creating a market for electricity, the RFC established the Electric Home and Farm Authority* which financed the sales of small electrical appliances. Roosevelt also had the RFC set up the Disaster Loan Corporation to extend financial assistance to victims of natural disasters. Second, to liquify bank assets even further, the RFC established and directed the RFC Mortgage Company, the Export-Import Bank,* the Commodity Credit Corporation,* and the Federal National Mortgage Association.* Finally, Roosevelt succeeded in getting the RFC to make direct business loans as a means of stimulating industrial expansion. In 1939, to supervise this vast government credit operation, President Roosevelt created the Federal Loan Agency* and named Jesse Jones,* head of the RFC, to direct its efforts. By 1940, on the eve of its transformation into a war agency, the Reconstruction Finance Corporation had loaned more than $8 billion to a wide variety of financial institutions and private businesses. (Jesse Jones, *Fifty Billion Dollars*, 1951; James S. Olson, *Herbert Hoover and the Reconstruction Finance Corporation, 1931-1933*, 1977.)

REED, DAVID AIKEN David A. Reed, the Republican boss from Pennsylvania, was born December 21, 1880, in Pittsburgh. He graduated from Princeton University in 1900, studied law privately, and was admitted to the bar in 1903. He practiced in Pittsburgh between 1903 and 1917, also serving as chairman of the Pennsylvania Industrial Accidents Commission from 1912 to 1915. Reed joined the army during World War I and then resumed his law practice in 1919. He was appointed to the United States Senate on August 8, 1922, to fill the seat vacated by the death of William E. Crow, and he won election in his own right that November. Reed was re-elected in 1928. A leading figure among Republican conservatives, Reed was a close political associate of Herbert Hoover* and, not surprisingly, an inveterate enemy of Franklin D. Roosevelt* and the New Deal.* He opposed most relief, social welfare, and labor legislation, hated the AAA,* and called for a balanced budget. Because of his conservatism, he lost his Senate seat in 1934 to Democratic challenger Joseph Guffey.* Reed then resumed the practice of law. He died on February 10, 1953. (*New York Times*, February 11, 1953.)

REED, STANLEY FORMAN Stanley Forman Reed was born December 31, 1884, in the tobacco country of Mason County, Kentucky. His family was prosperous and politically active in the local Democratic organization. Reed took undergraduate degrees at Kentucky Wesleyan University (1902) and Yale University (1906) and studied law at the University of Virginia, Columbia University, and at the Sorbonne in Paris. He practiced law in Maysville, Kentucky, from 1910 to 1917 and served two terms in the Kentucky legislature. After a brief stint in the army during World War I, Reed returned to his private law practice, representing such clients as the Chesapeake & Ohio Railroad and the Tobacco Growers Cooperative. His expertise in the financing and marketing of tobacco came to President Herbert Hoover's* attention, and in 1929 he appointed Reed general counsel of the new Federal Farm Board. Early in 1932 Hoover then named Reed general counsel of the Reconstruction Finance Corporation.*

Reed played an important role in the New Deal* throughout the 1930s. In 1933 he helped with the composition of the Agricultural Adjustment Act* and later in the year was instrumental in establishing the Commodity Credit Corporation* as an RFC subsidiary. Although not completely convinced of the economic validity of George Warren's* ''commodity dollar''* theory, Reed was convinced of its legality and urged the president to move forward with the gold-buying program* if he was so inclined in 1933. Working closely with Thomas Corcoran,* Stanley Reed also helped transform the RFC into a fluid, flexible government agency offering expertise, personnel, and money to a wide variety of New Deal agencies. When the ''gold cases''* came before the Supreme Court* in 1935, Roosevelt appointed Reed a special asssitant to Attorney General Homer Cummings* to represent the government. When the Supreme Court decided in favor of the government, Roosevelt appointed Reed to the post of solicitor general of the United States. In that position, Reed not only argued the major government cases before the Supreme Court in 1936, 1937, and 1938, but he built a creative staff of young lawyers in the Department of Justice—people like John Dickinson,* Robert H. Jackson,* Alger Hiss,* Charles Wyzanski,* and Paul Freund.* Together they made major improvements in the drafting of bills and the argumentation of cases before the federal courts. When Justice George Sutherland* retired in 1938, Roosevelt placed Reed on the Supreme Court.

Between 1939 and 1941, he chaired Roosevelt's Commission on Civil Service Improvement and earned a reputation as a politically moderate justice. Although he tended to favor the right of state and federal governments to exercise their taxation and regulatory powers, he was not really sympathetic to civil liberties cases for individuals. While generally pro-labor in his decisions, Reed was not sympathetic to anti-trust activities on the part of the federal government. On the later Roosevelt court of the 1930s and 1940s, Reed was generally on the conservative side. Reed was an associate justice of the Supreme Court until his retirement in 1957. After his resignation from the Court, he served as chairman of President Dwight Eisenhower's U.S. Civil Rights Commission. Stanley Reed died on April 3, 1980. (Peter H. Irons, *The New Deal Lawyers*, 1982; *New York Times*, April 4, 1980.)

RENO, MILO Milo Reno, farm leader and political activist, was born January 5, 1866, on a farm near Agency, Iowa. He attended school in Agency and later in Batavia after his family moved there. Reno attended William Penn College, a Quaker school in Oskaloosa, to train for the ministry but left school during a spiritual crisis. Not until years later, at the age of forty, did he experience a religious re-conversion, becoming a Campbellite minister and popular country preacher. After leaving school, Reno tried selling farm machinery and insurance and later moved to the Black Hills and then to California. A family background of Greenbackism and his former association with Populism led him into the National Farmers' Union* in 1918. By 1921 Reno was president of the Iowa branch of the Farmers' Union. He was to remain the leader of the Iowa Farmers' Union until his death in 1936, though in 1930 he gave up the title of president to take charge of the union's insurance companies at the salary of $9,600.

Reno's guiding principle as he lead the Iowa Farmers' Union was to "secure for the farming industry cost of production plus a reasonable profit." In May 1932 some 3,000 Iowa farmers, hard-hit by the slump in farm prices, gathered in Des Moines and elected Reno head of the National Farmers' Holiday Association, resolving to withhold produce from market until they received cost of production prices. In August milk producers, angry at being forced to sell their product at 2¢ a quart, began stopping trucks outside Sioux City and dumping the milk into ditches. Livestock trucks were also stopped. The strike spread to five states. Violent confrontations were commonplace until Reno called a truce on September 1, 1932.

Believing that Franklin D. Roosevelt's* victory in 1932 would soon bring better farm legislation, Reno and other state holiday presidents met in Omaha soon after the election and declared that strikes and the withholding of products would be suspended until the new administration had a chance to deal with refinancing mortgages and stabilizing farm prices. But when the Senate rejected the Norris-Simpson amendment guaranteeing cost of production prices for farmers on May 12, 1933, Reno announced that the strike would begin on May 13. When Minnesota governor Floyd Olson* wrote Reno expressing his confidence in Roosevelt and following an encouraging statement from Roosevelt himself, Reno sent telegrams to all state leaders calling off the strike.

But by July 1933 Reno was again expressing doubts about the New Deal* farm program. He was concerned about the incorporation of Extension Service agents (county agents) into the program of the AAA,* since he considered county agents to be allies of the American Farm Bureau Federation,* chief rival of the NFU. He argued that the new farm loan program should have been financed by currency expansion rather than through interest-bearing bonds. Reno also attacked the AAA's hog slaughter program as an inexcusable waste when people were going hungry. By autumn 1933 Reno was again calling for a farm strike until currency inflation and cost of production had been implemented. His orders to begin a farm strike met with only scattered response, and within a few days the movement collapsed.

Although Reno continued to make speeches that stirred his rural audiences, he realized that his influence was waning. Frustrated by the defeat of his cost of production plan, he turned to other causes, backing the Townsend old-age pension plan and supporting the third party movements of utopian leaders like Father Charles Coughlin* and Senator Huey Long.* Reno did not live to see the defeat of William Lemke,* the Union party* candidate whom he probably would have supported, in the presidential election of 1936.* Weakened by a bout with influenza, Milo Reno died of a heart attack on May 5, 1936. (John

L. Shover, *Cornbelt Rebellion: The Farmers' Holiday Association*, 1965; Ronald A. White, *Milo Reno: Farmers Union Pioneer*, 1941.)

JOHN PAYNE

REORGANIZATION ACT OF 1939 Prior to his election in 1932,* President Franklin D. Roosevelt* had been well-known for his advocacy of governmental reorganization to improve efficiency and economy. Alfred E. Smith,* governor of New York before Roosevelt's gubernatorial term, had thoroughly reorganized state government in 1927, and Roosevelt had openly praised his program. Most politicians during the Great Depression at least paid lip-service to government reorganization. The Economy Act of 1932 had permitted President Herbert Hoover* to regroup federal agencies, subject to a legislative veto within sixty days by either the House or Senate. The Economy Act of 1933* had given Roosevelt a similarly broad reorganization authority, which he virtually never used because of the priority of relief and recovery measures during his first administration. New Deal* emergency agencies typically bypassed existing organizational arrangements, and many historians attribute this neglect of effective management to Roosevelt's natural proclivity for fostering a competitive approach to administration.

Governmental reorganization for improved management, economy, and efficiency became a major issue in Roosevelt's second administration. The New Deal emergency crisis seemed over, and there was a widely perceived need for better management of the federal government. The image of waste, inefficiency, and "boondoggling"* was widespread. In 1936 Roosevelt appointed a three-man President's Committee on Administrative Management to examine the question. The chairman, after whom the committee was then named, was Louis Brownlow,* director of the Public Administration Clearing House in Chicago and chairman of the Public Administration Committee of the Social Science Research Council. The other members were Charles E. Merriam* and Luther Gulick,* equally distinguished members of the public administration profession. Merriam, a professor of political science at the University of Chicago who had run unsuccessfully for mayor of the city, was founder of the Social Science Research Council and a former president of the American Political Science Association. Gulick was director of the Institute for Public Administration in New York City. All three men were New Deal supporters and proponents of professional administration. The committee established a professional staff under Joseph P. Harris as executive director. Harris subsequently had a distinguished career at the Brookings Institution. The Senate and House also had committees looking into the same question using the Brookings Institution for professional staff.

In January 1937 Roosevelt presented the *Report of the President's Committee on Administrative Management* to Congress with his endorsement. Stating that "the president needs help," the Brownlow Committee recommended major changes in the executive branch explicitly aimed at strengthening the president's managerial capabilities. They proposed that the president be given a White House staff of six executive assistants, together with a permanent National Resources Planning Board* as a central planning agency. They would expand the civil service merit system, raise salaries, and replace the Civil Service Commission with an administrator (a step achieved in the Carter administration). Two new cabinet posts would be created, with all executive branch agencies including the independent regulatory commissions placed under what would then be twelve departments. Other proposals to improve fiscal management, including executive branch control of accounts and budget planning, were made. This set of proposals represented an alliance between President Roosevelt and the leadership of the public administration profession.

The Brownlow Report, however, was challenged by the Brookings Institution. Many congressmen viewed the proposals as a movement toward "presidential dictatorship." There was particular opposition to executive control over accounts. In February 1937 Roosevelt complicated the reorganization debate with his "court-packing"* proposal. It took more than a year for an Executive Reorganization Bill to come before the Congress for a vote. Approved in March 1938 in the Senate by a slim forty-nine to forty-two vote, the bill was narrowly defeated in the House by 204 to 196 after six weeks of debate, even though Democrats controlled 75 percent of both houses. A Republican representative called the defeat "about the biggest political event which has taken place since 1932." Reorganization was particularly opposed by the Veterans Administration, the Forest Service, and the Public Health Service.

President Roosevelt remained committed to executive reorganization, submitting a new bill to Congress in 1939, one that eliminated all of the controversial items debated in 1938. The Reorganization Act of 1939 passed Congress easily in March and was signed by Roosevelt on April 3. The civil service and accounting proposals were dropped; no new departments were created; and many agencies were exempted from coverage. While Roosevelt was authorized six executive assistants, reorganization plans were subject to joint legislative veto by both houses of Congress. An amendment by Senator Harry Byrd* of Virginia made economy in government an explicit objective of the reorganization. The Congress rejected amendments which would have provided for a one-house veto or a two-house approval. On April 25, 1939, Roosevelt submitted Reorganization Plan No. 1 of 1939 which created a Federal Security Agency,* Federal Works Agency,* Federal Loan Agency,* and an Executive Office of the President. Into this office were incorporated a White House staff, the Bureau of the Budget* (from the Treasury Department), and the National Resources Planning Board (from the Interior Department). A Reorganization Plan No. 2 submitted on May 9, 1939, implemented some minor interdepartmental transfers. Both reorganizations were approved by Congress. In July 1939 Roosevelt formally appointed three administrative assistants, one of whom was to work with the Civil Service Commission. (Barry D. Karl, *Executive Reorganization and Reform in the New Deal: The Genesis of Administrative Management, 1900-1939*, 1963; Richard

Polenberg, *Reorganizing Roosevelt's Government: The Controversy Over Executive Reorganization, 1936–1939*, 1966.)

DUANE WINDSOR

REPUBLICAN PARTY On March 4, 1933, when Franklin D. Roosevelt* was inaugurated president, the Republican party entered an unprecedented period of decline and frustration. The Great Depression had destroyed their post-Civil War political hegemony; massive unemployment, the collapse of the farm economy, and the destruction of middle-class savings and prosperity had nearly destroyed the party. The election of 1932* had placed 310 Democrats in the House of Representatives and 60 in the Senate. The Republican minority was further reduced by the liberal sympathies of so many "progressives" like Senators Charles McNary* of Oregon, Hiram Johnson* of California, Robert La Follette, Jr.,* of Wisconsin, William Borah* of Idaho, and Bronson Cutting* of New Mexico, all of whom tended to side with much of the New Deal.* The extraordinary activity of the 73rd Congress (1933-1935) combined with the personal popularity of President Roosevelt to form an overpowering political force in the United States. In the election of 1934,* the Democrats actually increased their membership in the House to 319 and the Senate to 69. To the AAA,* NRA,* HOLC,* and CCC* of the 73rd Congress, the 74th Congress (1935–1937) added the Wealth Tax Act* and Public Utility Holding Company Act of 1935,* the Social Security Act,* and the Works Progress Administration.*

During those first years of the New Deal, the Republican party drifted aimlessly. Ex-president Herbert Hoover* tried to maintain control of the party and managed in 1934 to elect Henry P. Fletcher as the new chairman of the national committee to replace Everett Sanders. Hoover and Fletcher continued to issue blanket anti-New Deal messages, further alienating the party from the public. In 1936 the political culture of America had been dramatically changed by the New Deal, so much so that the anti-big government rhetoric of Hoover and the Republican "Old Guard" was falling on deaf ears. At the national convention in 1936, the party repudiated the Hoover forces because they knew that a renomination of the former president would be a political disaster. Instead, the party turned to Alfred Landon,* governor of Kansas. During the campaign, Landon criticized deficit spending and "runaway bureaucracy," but proved the political power of the New Deal by "in principle" supporting unemployment relief, social security, and federal farm programs. Many prominent Republican progressives bolted the party and endorsed Roosevelt in 1936, leaving Landon and the Republican moderates in an untenable position between the popular New Deal and the repudiated conservative "Old Guard." Landon went down to defeat by an unprecedented 27,752,869 to 16,674,665 votes. He carried only Maine and Vermont. Democrats also controlled Congress with 331 out of 435 House seats and 76 out of 96 Senate seats.

But a revival of Republican fortunes, albeit a modest one, began with the opening of the 75th Congress (1937–1939). When Roosevelt unveiled his "court-packing''* scheme, he lost the support of many Republican progressives and southern Democrats. Indeed, southern Democrats were already alienated by deficit spending, social security, and the National Labor Relations Act,* all of which they viewed likely to improve the social status of blacks and poor whites. Along with most Republicans, they saw the court-packing scheme as a dictatorial move by the president to augment the political power of liberal New Dealers. A coalition of southern Democrats and northern Republicans killed the ''court-packing'' scheme. At the same time, a bitter struggle was waging inside the Republican party between the supporters of Alf Landon and Herbert Hoover. Convinced that Landon's ''liberals'' had destroyed the party's philosophical rationale, Hoover wanted to call a national convention of the party in 1937 where his own anti-New Deal point of view would once again be re-enthroned. Landon and other Republican moderates felt such a convention would only destroy the modest revival the party was experiencing. The convention was not held, and along with the court-packing scheme and national disappointment over the recession of 1937-1938,* the Republicans experienced major gains in the elections of 1938.* The Democratic membership of the House dropped from 331 to 261 and in the Senate from 76 to 69.

In the 76th Congress (1939-1941), the coalition of Republicans and southern Democrats grew more powerful, altering the New Deal's plans for executive reorganization and cutting the appropriations from the Works Progress Administration. Republican isolationists also made political capital out of the threat of war in Europe and the president's internationalist views. Republicans looked to a political triumph in 1940, hoping that the public's fear of war and disappointment with the slow pace of economic recovery would lead to a rejection of Democratic leadership. Events proved otherwise. By the spring of 1940, particularly after the German invasion of France and the Low Countries, public opinion began shifting to a more internationalist position, one which favored increased spending for national defense, while Republicans continued to preach isolationism at all costs. At the same time, increased defense spending in 1940 began creating tens of thousands of new jobs, undermining Republican hopes of using unemployment as a major campaign issue. When the party nominated Wendell Willkie* for president in 1940, they eliminated the other campaign issue because the utilities magnate was an internationalist himself. Roosevelt also disarmed the party by naming Republicans Henry L. Stimson* and Frank Knox to his cabinet as secretary of war and secretary of the navy. In the ensuing election, Roosevelt defeated Willkie with 27,307,819 popular votes and 449 electoral votes to 22,321,018 popular votes and 82 electoral votes. But the vote had been a personal one for Roosevelt; Democrats gained only seven seats in the House and lost three in the Senate. Still, the Republicans had not gained any appreciable ground, and the magnitude of Democratic political supremacy had become overwhelmingly clear. The new coalition of ethnic groups, blacks, blue-collar workers, southerners, northern liberals, and intellectuals had settled in the Democratic party,* and they would dominate American politics for the next generation. (George H. Mayer, *The Republican Party, 1854-1966*, 1967.)

RESETTLEMENT ADMINISTRATION Perhaps the most class-conscious of the New Deal* agencies, the Resettlement Administration had its origins in the ''back-to-the-land'' movement of the early 1930s, which idealized the idea of the rural, communal village and the growing concern with the plight of poor farm families. Not only was rural poverty driving people off their land, but the crop reduction programs of the AAA,* as well as many of the construction projects of the TVA,* were displacing many poor farmers from the land. By 1935 a variety of federal agencies were dealing with the issue, including the Rural Rehabilitation Division of the FERA,* which had spent $85 million for land purchases and rehabilitation; the Subsistence Home Division of the Department of the Interior, which had spent $25 million creating fifty new farm communities; and the Land Policy Section of the AAA. Indeed, the ''purge of 1935'' in the Department of Agriculture had involved the question of farm tenants. When Jerome Frank,* Gardner Jackson,* Victor Rotnem, Francis Shea, Frederic C. Howe,* Lee Pressman,* and Alger Hiss* tried to write a clause into the cotton acreage reduction contracts of 1935 prohibiting displacement of tenants, Chester Davis* of the AAA had them dismissed from the agency. Soon after the ''purge,'' President Franklin D. Roosevelt* decided to consolidate the programs of the FERA, AAA, and Department of the Interior into a new agency—the Resettlement Administration. He named Rexford G. Tugwell* to head the agency, and many former AAA officials, concerned about rural poverty and the plight of farm tenants, joined him.

The Resettlement Administration's goals were quite ambitious, because Tugwell could not render assistance to displaced tenant farmers without interfering with the programs of the Agricultural Adjustment Administration. Although he envisioned a resettlement of perhaps 500,000 farm families, the agency eventually resettled only 4,441 families. Instead, most of the RA assets went into farm rehabilitation, land utilization projects, suburban development, and the establishment of sanitary camps for migratory workers. The Resettlement Administration had inherited nearly 100 rural communities from the FERA and the Subsistence Home Division, and Tugwell had little sympathy for the pre-industrial farming village philosophy dominating them. He felt such villages were idyllic anachronisms, unable to compete economically with technologically advanced farm operations and destined to become simply new pockets of rural poverty. To revitalize them, Tugwell experimented with converting them into commercial farming operations based on community cooperation. The Resettlement Administration organized collective farms at Casa Grande, Arizona; Lake Dick, Arkansas; Walker County, Alabama; and New Madrid, Louisiana—bringing in project managers, building cottages, establishing medical cooperatives, and purchasing heavy farm machinery. The RA also established its own Suburban Resettlement Division, whose goal was to depopulate urban slums and tar-paper tenant farm communities by building new towns in suburban areas. Although he planned to construct twenty-five such towns, a tangle of legal and financial difficulties restricted the program to three towns: Greenbelt, Maryland (near Washington, D.C.); Greendale, Wisconsin (near Milwaukee); and Green Hills, Ohio (near Cincinnati). They were lovely towns, surrounded by encircling belts of farm land and forests yet easily accessible to the major cities. Finally, the Resettlement Administration constructed a series of excellent camps for migrant farm workers and their families, to protect them from the exploitation of growers, and loaned money to small farmers for equipment and necessities, taking a percentage of their crop as repayment.

Eventually, the Resettlement Administration, and particularly its visionary administrator, Rexford Tugwell, infuriated a wide variety of vested interests. Conservatives hated Tugwell's talk of "utopia" and "redistribution of wealth." Large farmers, represented by the American Farm Bureau Federation,* protested the whole idea of collective farming that Tugwell was trying to promote in the RA farming communities. Large farmers in the South also resented the assistance he was giving to farm tenants and sharecroppers because it made their own labor costs higher. Physicians and the American Medical Association protested the medical cooperatives the RA established in its farm communities and migrant camps. Real estate developers complained about the "Greenbelt towns,"* and the idea of federal government management. Even labor unions worried that the Resettlement Administration's programs would undercut their own organizing drives. Criticism of the Resettlement Administration and constant congressional bickering over it became a problem for President Roosevelt.

At the same time, the president was facing some pressure from groups like the Southern Tenant Farmers' Union* to do something about the rising numbers of displaced, poverty-stricken farm tenants. He appointed a Special Committee on Farm Tenancy* in 1936, chaired by Henry A. Wallace,* to study the problem. At Tugwell's request, Wallace made a tour of the rural South and was astounded at the extent of the poverty among poor farmers and tenants. Early in 1937 the committee endorsed the Bankhead-Jones Farm Tenancy Act;* and after Roosevelt signed the measure, he established the Farm Security Administration* to implement it. The Farm Security Administration then absorbed the Resettlement Administration and took over its programs. (Sidney Baldwin, *Politics and Poverty: The Rise and Decline of the Farm Security Administration*, 1968; Donald H. Grubbs, *Cry from the Cotton: The Southern Tenant Farmers' Union and the New Deal*, 1971.)

REVENUE ACT OF 1938 No other New Deal* measure more symbolically illustrated the shift in public policy during the 1930s than the Revenue Act of 1935, or the Wealth Tax Act.* With its steep increases in income tax schedules, estate and gift taxes, and excess corporate profits taxes, the Revenue Act of

1935 demonstrated Franklin D. Roosevelt's* shift away from the cooperative, self-regulating business planning of the early New Deal to the Brandesian and later Keynesian emphasis of the mature New Deal. One year later, the Revenue Act of 1936 included an undistributed profits tax on corporate income which included a new range of tax surcharges. The business community rose up in righteous indignation against the measure, but it passed through Congress nonetheless during the election. In the wake of President Roosevelt's landslide victory in the November 1936 election,* Congress quickly passed the Revenue Act of 1937, closing several loopholes in earlier income tax laws which had permitted widespread evasion.

But the anti-business, anti-corporate tax measures of 1935, 1936, and 1937 received a setback in 1938 from a most unlikely coalition. The Supreme Court* fight and the revival of the conservative forces in Congress, as well as a widely perceived sense that some of the president's magical popularity was slipping, encouraged Democratic and Republican opponents of the New Deal. Also, many people, including anti-New Deal businessmen as well as Keynesian advocates, were arguing that the recent tax increases had triggered the recession of 1937 and 1938.* They were both calling for taxes, although for different reasons. Conservatives were arguing that tax cuts on business and corporate income would revive confidence and stimulate a new wave of investment. The Keynesians believed the cuts would stimulate purchasing power and raise employment. Senators Pat Harrison* of Mississippi and James Byrnes* of South Carolina then sponsored the Revenue Act of 1938. It repealed the undistributed profits tax and progressive normal tax passed in 1936 and greatly reduced capital gains taxes. The president threatened to veto the measure, so the undistributed profits tax was restored in the House, but only in the most superficial way. A 19 percent tax was imposed on corporations whose income exceeded $25,000, but the tax was reduced by 2 1/2 percent of dividends paid out of income subject to the tax. The president still threatened to veto the measure because he viewed it as a step backward in New Deal policy. Eventually, after assessing congressional support for the bill, he let it become law on May 27, 1938, without his signature. (Randolph E. Paul, *Taxation in the United States*, 1954.)

RICHBERG, DONALD RANDALL Donald Randall Richberg was born on July 10, 1881, in Knoxville, Tennessee, to John Richberg, a prosperous Chicago attorney, and Eloise Randall, later a successful physician. Richberg graduated from the University of Chicago in 1901 and from the Harvard Law School in 1904. After leaving Harvard, he joined the family law firm of Richberg and Richberg in Chicago. His experiences with political corruption in Chicago converted him to the idea of municipal reform and to the progressive movement. He endorsed Theodore Roosevelt and the "Bull Moose" campaign in 1912, which led to his chairmanship of the National Legislative Reference Bureau of the Progressive party in 1913 and 1914. Richberg bolted the Progressive party in 1916 when it endorsed Charles Evans Hughes;* instead he campaigned for

Woodrow Wilson's re-election. During World War I and the 1920s, Richberg served as special counsel for the city of Chicago, continued practicing law privately, worked as chief counsel for the railway brotherhoods, and helped write the Railway Labor Act of 1926. He supported Al Smith* in 1928, and in 1932 worked with Senator George Norris* in forming the National Progressive League, which endorsed the campaign of Franklin D. Roosevelt.* During the campaign he also assisted Raymond Moley* in writing speeches about transportation, labor relations, and business recovery.

After the inauguration, Richberg went to work as an assistant to General Hugh Johnson* in planning industrial recovery and government reorganization and helped draft the National Industrial Recovery Act.* Johnson quickly named him as chief counsel for the National Recovery Administration.* When Hugh Johnson resigned from the NRA in 1934, Roosevelt replaced him with a five-member National Industrial Recovery Board.* Richberg remained as chief counsel and head of the Industrial Emergency Committee.* Because of his support of the ''New Nationalism'' of Theodore Roosevelt, Richberg very much believed in the potential of industrial democracy through business-government cooperation. He proved to be a true progressive, with a generally conservative labor philosophy and a faith in the capacity of business to govern itself within larger federal guidelines. As such, he sometimes became the target of criticism from such other progressives as Senator Robert M. La Follette, Jr.,* who felt he was too pro-business.

When the Supreme Court* declared the NIRA unconstitutional in the *Schechter** case in 1935, Richberg resigned. He returned to private law practice and, although disturbed by the rise of the Committee for Industrial Organization* and its power in the New Deal,* remained a supporter of Franklin D. Roosevelt. But after World War II, especially when President Harry S Truman* called for health insurance, a minimum wage law, public housing, increased unemployment compensation, and full employment legislation, Richberg was convinced that the country was headed down the road to the welfare state and socialism. During the last twenty years of his life, Richberg became a celebrated figure in American conservative circles, denouncing the growing power of the labor movement, the size of the federal government, and the rise of the welfare state. Donald R. Richberg died on November 27, 1960. (Frank Annunziata, ''Donald R. Richberg and American Liberalism,'' *Journal of the Illinois State Historical Society*, XLI:531-547, 1975.)

RIVERS, EURITH DICKINSON Born at Center Point, Arkansas, on December 1, 1895, Eurith Dickinson became one of the ''Little New Deal''* governors during the 1930s. He graduated from Young Harris College in Georgia in 1914 and then taught school while studying law through the La Salle University extension division. Rivers received a law degree from La Salle in 1916 and began practicing law in Cairo. He soon became county attorney for Grandy County, Georgia. After moving to Lanier County in 1920, Rivers became county attorney there, and in 1925 he was elected to the state legislature. He served as speaker of the house in Georgia in 1926 and between 1927 and 1928 was a member of the state senate.

Rivers was a staunch supporter of Franklin D. Roosevelt* and the New Deal.* During the first half of the 1930s, Georgia was led by ultraconservative Governor Eugene Talmadge.* Talmadge blocked New Deal programs in Georgia, and finally in 1936 Eurith Rivers defeated him in the Democratic gubernatorial primary. During his term as governor, Rivers enacted legislation providing for free school textbooks, increased aid to education and health, and reorganization of welfare distribution agencies. To deal with the state financial crisis, Rivers called the legislature into special session and passed higher personal and corporate income taxes as well as levies for license plates and chain store operations. He was re-elected in 1938.*

Because of the continuing financial crisis, Rivers diverted $2.5 million from the state highway fund. The state highway commissioner opposed the decision, so Rivers fired him. When state courts ordered him to reinstate the commissioner, Rivers called out the National Guard to thwart the court order. The ensuing court battle ruined Rivers' political career and brought former governor Eugene Talmadge back into office. Rivers spent his last months in office defending himself against a number of fraud charges. After several trials and mistrials, all charges against Rivers were dropped. Rivers continued to practice law and became involved in the banking business. He died on June 11, 1967, in Atlanta, Georgia. (*New York Times*, June 12, 1967; James T. Patterson, *The New Deal in the States: Federalism in Transition*, 1969.)

LENNA HODNETT ALLRED

ROBERTS, OWEN JOSEPHUS Owen J. Roberts was born on May 2, 1875, in Germantown, Pennsylvania. He was educated at the Germantown Academy, the University of Pennsylvania, and the University of Pennsylvania Law School. His academic performance was so superb that he was appointed to the law school faculty as a fellow immediately after receiving his law degree; he taught part-time at Pennsylvania for two decades, eventually reaching the rank of professor. Meanwhile, Roberts pursued a career as a trial lawyer, initially as first assistant district attorney of Philadelphia (1903-1906), then in private practice. In the 1920s he served as special counsel investigating the Teapot Dome and Elk Hills oil scandal. It was his successful prosecution of the Teapot Dome cases that brought Roberts to national prominence and to the attention of President Herbert Hoover,* who appointed him to the United States Supreme Court* in May 1930.

When Roberts assumed office, the Supreme Court was almost evenly divided between liberals and conservatives. On the liberal side were Justices Louis Brandeis,* Harlan Stone,* and Benjamin Cardozo;* on the conservative side were Justices Willis Van Devanter,* James McReynolds,* George Sutherland,* and Pierce Butler.* Chief Justice Charles Evans Hughes* stood in the middle. In his first few terms, Roberts' decisions proved hard to predict; he sided with the liberals in some cases and with the conservatives in others. With the passage of the unprecedented New Deal* legislation in 1933 and 1934, court-watchers were well aware that the fate of Franklin D. Roosevelt's* program rested with the moderate Hughes and the unpredictable Roberts.

Roberts sided with the liberals in two important state cases in 1934, forming a majority of five to uphold emergency economic regulations. In the first, the Court upheld a law placing a moratorium on the foreclosure of home mortgages (*Home Building and Loan Association v. Blaisdell*); in the second, Roberts himself wrote the opinion of the Court, upholding a statute fixing the minimum retail price of milk (*Nebbia v. New York*). Roberts cheered New Dealers with his assertion that "subject to constitutional restraint" private property rights "must yield to the public need," but skeptics pointed out that *Nebbia* was a state case and that the federal programs of the New Deal might well face a different fate.

They were right. When it came time to test the federal programs in court, Roberts joined the four conservatives to form a bare majority against the New Deal. Although he joined Hughes in the gold cases* in February 1935, by May he was decidedly in the conservative camp. He wrote the majority opinion in the *Railroad Retirement Board v. Alton*,* arguing that Congress could not force the roads to establish compulsory pension systems. Roberts also sided with conservatives in several other major anti-New Deal cases, including *Schechter v. United States*,* invalidating the National Industrial Recovery Act;* *Butler v. United States*, invalidating the first Agricultural Adjustment Act;* and *Carter v. Carter Coal Company*,* invalidating the Guffey-Snyder Bituminous Coal Act.* Roberts wrote the majority opinion in *Butler*.

When the Supreme Court came around to accepting the New Deal, beginning in April 1937, it was Roberts who provided the "switch in time that saved nine." His vote created a liberal majority of five justices to uphold the National Labor Relations Act* (*NLRB v. Jones and Laughlin Steel Corporation*)* and state minimum wage legislation (*West Coast Hotel v. Parrish*).* Whether Roberts switched as a result of the 1936 election* or the proposed "court-packing" plan,* or for some other reason, is unclear. The evidence does suggest that Roberts had committed himself to the liberal side in *West Coast Hotel* by December 1936, indicating that the court-packing plan was not a major factor in his decision.

Roberts' judicial career after the New Deal is difficult to summarize. In post-New Deal economic cases, he was generally liberal, but his record on civil rights and civil liberties was mixed. While still a member of the Supreme Court, Roberts headed the government commission that investigated and fixed the blame for the inadequate military precautions against the Japanese raid on Pearl Harbor. Roberts resigned from the court in 1945, the last of the pre-Roosevelt justices to leave the bench. He served for three years as the dean of the University of Pennsylvania Law School; later, he chaired the Fund for the Advancement of Education. He died on May 17, 1955. (Charles A. Leonard, *A Search for a Judicial Philosophy: Mr. Justice Roberts and the Constitutional Revolution of 1937*, 1971.)

WILLIAM LASSER

ROBINSON, ARTHUR RAYMOND Arthur R. Robinson was born in Pickerington, Ohio, on March 12, 1881. He graduated from Ohio Northern University in 1901, the Indiana Law School in 1910, and the University of Chicago in 1913. Robinson began practicing law in Indianapolis, Indiana, in 1910, served in the state legislature between 1914 and 1918, and also was a member of the American Expeditionary Force in France during World War I. He was appointed to the United States Senate to fill the vacancy created by the death of Samuel M. Ralston and was elected in his own right in 1926. He was re-elected in 1928. During the early New Deal,* Robinson was one of the remaining few "Old Guard" Republicans who viewed the New Deal as socialistic and hopelessly bureaucratic, a threat to the Constitution as well as to basic American values. In his view, the New Deal was in a "rush of events carrying us on the road to Moscow." Unsuccessful in his campaign for re-election in 1934,* Robinson returned to his Indianapolis law practice. He died on March 17, 1961. (George Wolfskill and John A. Hudson, *All but the People. Franklin D. Roosevelt and His Critics, 1933-1939*, 1969.)

ROBINSON, JOSEPH TAYLOR Joseph Taylor Robinson, Senate majority leader during the early New Deal,* was born on a farm near Lonoke, Lonoke County, Arkansas, on August 26, 1872. Robinson attended the University of Arkansas and the law department of the University of Virginia and passed the bar exam in 1895. He bagan practicing in Lonoke in 1895, the same year that he won a seat in the state legislature. Robinson won a congressional seat in the election of 1902 and remained in the House of Representatives until 1913, when he resigned after winning the governorship of Arkansas. His tenure as governor was short-lived, however, for he won a seat in the United States Senate on January 28, 1913. He was re-elected in 1918, 1924, 1930, and 1936. Robinson became a prominent figure in the Democratic party,* serving as chairman of the 1920, 1928 and 1936 conventions and running as Al Smith's* vice-presidential candidate in the election of 1928. When Democrats organized the Senate in 1933, Robinson was elected as majority leader.

During the first years of the New Deal, Robinson was faithful to the new administration. Known widely as an aggressive and temperamental leader, Robinson managed to stifle his basic conservatism in order to assist President Franklin D. Roosevelt* in implementing the early New Deal. The president was lucky to have his support. Robinson was one of the most powerful men in the Senate, and during the 1920s he had opposed government development of Muscle Shoals,* called for a balanced budget, and warned about centralization of power in the federal government. He was always worried about the drift of the New

Deal—afraid of deficit spending, concerned that NRA* labor codes would restrict southern industry, and uncertain about the concentration of power in Washington, D.C. But he was also the most loyal of Democrats, who viewed party fidelity as an act of faith. Although his personal relationship with the president was formal rather than friendly, Robinson was determined to keep conservative southern Democrats and liberal northern Democrats united against the Republican party,* under whose thumb he had suffered so long in the 1920s. During the first "hundred days,"* Robinson always stayed with the administration, and even later, although he shared his friend Bernard Baruch's* views that the New Deal was going too far, he always worked for compromise. He also felt that the New Deal was at least doing things that William Jennings Bryan would have favored. Robinson was a leading supporter of most New Deal farm legislation, anti-trust policy, and the revenue proposal of 1935. Although he did not think much of Eleanor Roosevelt's* sympathy for blacks, he was not really threatened by New Deal initiatives in the area of black rights. Robinson saw them for what they were: political necessities to appease the black vote in the North without really changing the basic social and economic structure of the South. Although he became angry with Roosevelt in 1937 when the president did not offer him a Supreme Court* appointment to fill the vacancy created by the resignation of Willis Van Devanter,* Robinson was still prepared to help the president push the "court-packing"* plan through Congress. Robinson's sudden death on July 14, 1937, among other things, helped doom the court reform plan because much of the Senate support it had came simply from the majority leader's personal influence. (Nevin E. Neal, "A Biography of Joseph T. Robinson," Ph.D. dissertation, University of Oklahoma, 1957.)

ROBINSON-PATMAN ACT OF 1936 (See FEDERAL ANTI-PRICE DISCRIMINATION ACT OF 1936.)

ROCHE, JOSEPHINE ASPINWALL Josephine A. Roche was born in Colorado in 1886 and graduated from Vassar in 1908. She attended graduate school at Columbia University between 1908 and 1910 and became a close personal friend of Frances Perkins,* a fellow graduate student. After receiving her master's degree, Roche returned to Colorado and worked for several years in the Denver criminal justice system, specializing in juvenile problems. Between 1924 and 1927, Roche worked for the Children's Bureau of the Department of Labor, but she then returned to Colorado to manage the coal mines she had inherited from her father. She approached labor relations from an enlightened perspective and earned a national reputation. Roche narrowly failed to win the Democratic nomination for governor of Colorado in 1934, and President Franklin D. Roosevelt* then named her assistant secretary of the Treasury Department, where she managed the U.S. Public Health Service. In 1935 he named her chair of the executive committee of the National Youth Administration.* Roche resigned from the Treasury Department in 1937, and in 1938 became president of the National

Consumers' League, a position she kept until 1944. With the strong support of John L. Lewis* of the United Mine Workers, Roche served as director of the UMW Welfare and Retirement Fund from 1947 to 1971. Josephine Roche died in 1976. (Susan Ware, *Beyond Suffrage: Women in the New Deal*, 1981.)

ROOSEVELT, ANNA ELEANOR Anna Eleanor Roosevelt was born October 11, 1884. Public fame seemed an unlikely achievement for the girl born into the Victorian world of New York society, to parents whose distinguished roots stretched back to the colonial period. But the promise of familial security and sheltered privilege quickly evaporated. Roosevelt's beautiful mother first rejected her daughter psychologically and then totally deserted her through an untimely death. Roosevelt's adored, high-spirited father was too unstable and alcoholic to live up to his daughter's adulation or fill the emotional void of her childhood. His death left her a ten-year-old orphan, consigned with her younger brother to the dreary surroundings and detached care of their maternal grandmother.

Unrelieved gloom lifted for three years when Roosevelt attended Allenswood School near London. Under the affectionate, encouraging guidance of Headmistress Marie Souvestre, Roosevelt flourished emotionally and intellectually. She returned to New York at seventeen with self-assurance and a social conscience. A brief foray into settlement house work accompanied the more time-consuming, frivolous activities of her class. Upon her marriage to distant cousin Franklin D. Roosevelt* in 1905, she embraced the conventional routine of a young matron. Her world was quickly and narrowly bounded by five children, a politically ambitious husband, and a domineering mother-in-law.

The family's move to Washington, D.C., in 1913 when Roosevelt was appointed assistant secretary of the navy failed to diminish the importance of domestic and social obligations. The public and private intrusions dramatically shifted the focus of Roosevelt's interests and activities. The nation's entry into World War I created the need for volunteer projects that engaged her organizational skills and social service sensitivities. She staffed canteens, supervised Red Cross activities, and visited the wounded. The war also coincided with her discovery of Franklin's affair with her former social secretary, Lucy Mercer. The heart-breaking sense of personal rejection and betrayal reinforced her determination to create an independent public identity. After her husband's defeat as the Democratic party's* 1920 vice-presidential candidate, she moved the family back to New York and began her apprenticeship as social reformer and political activist.

Roosevelt carefully chose the organizations in which she participated and the people who served as both political teachers and supportive friends. Esther Lape and Elizabeth Read of the League of Women Voters, Rose Schneiderman* and Maud Shawrz of the Women's Trade Union League, Marion Dickerson and Nancy Cook of the newly formed women's division of the Democratic party won her support on behalf of social welfare legislation and female political activism. Her organizational activities began before polio struck her husband

and continued during his convalescence. By 1924 she was awarded a chair of the Democratic women's platform subcommittee. The group recommended that the party endorse the ratification of the Child Labor Amendment, support minimum wage and maximum hour legislation for women, expand services to mothers and infants under the Shepard-Towner Act, and endorse union organizing. The platform committee rejected the recommendations and ignored their spokesperson, actions that taught Roosevelt the difficulties of penetrating the male-dominated bastions of politics.

Although her efforts on behalf of reform organizations and of the New York Democratic party's women's committee remained firm, she officially resigned her membership when Roosevelt was elected governor of New York in 1928. But her support for social reform continued, supplemented by increased efforts on behalf of women's appointment to government posts. She paved the road for party activist Mary Dewson* to convince the new governor to select Frances Perkins* as his state commissioner of labor.

This pattern of influential support for reform and relief legislation and for increased female participation in political affairs continued when Roosevelt became president and launched the New Deal.* Now first lady, Eleanor Roosevelt sat at the hub of a network of social feminists who migrated to the nation's capital with their unfinished agenda of progressive reforms. She worked closely with Dewson to promote appointment of women, encouraging the selection of Frances Perkins as secretary of labor. Perkins, in turn, played a key role, along with other alumnae of the Consumer's League, in drafting and lobbying for the passage of the labor provisions in the National Industrial Recovery Act of 1933,* the Social Security Act of 1935,* and the Fair Labor Standards Act of 1938.* Roosevelt constantly aided the female proponents of New Deal legislation in navigating the corridors of growing bureaucracy and in circumventing internal administrative bickering. In addition, she elicited public support for policies through her newspaper column "My Day," during her travels and lectures, and by providing a forum for women in government to present their positions at her women-only press conference.

Her concern with women's issues extended to the oversights and discriminations that marked many New Deal measures. She joined women in the Department of Labor and women's organizations in protesting the wage differentials between men and women which were approved in many NRA* codes. She voiced her opposition to the dismissal of working wives from public and private employment. She worked tirelessly on behalf of unemployed women, helping to create camps comparable to those established for young men under the CCC and insisting upon increased work relief for women under the FERA,* CWA,* and WPA.* In all instances efforts fell short of goals or failed completely, for in the end Roosevelt, like her social feminist cohort, bowed to the exigencies of legislative and administrative processes, placing the liberal reform and relief agenda ahead of issues focused on equity and equality for women. The issue of female equality centered on a proposed equal rights amendment. Introduced by the National Women's party in 1923, endorsement of a blanket guarantee of legal equality became the litmus test of feminist commitment for several decades. Like other social reformers, Roosevelt firmly opposed the amendment. She was convinced that women's health and conventional familial and social roles required laws that protected women workers and regulated their working conditions. These presumed benefits would be negated by constitutional equality. Unlike other social feminists, however, she indicated that her opposition was not etched in stone. Roosevelt believed that advances made in industrial unionization after the mid-1930s created new opportunities for working-class women to control the terms of their employment through the negotiated contract, thereby alleviating the need for all protective legislation. The New Deal years came to a close twenty years before she decided that time had arrived, and she dropped verbal assaults on the ERA.

As the New Deal progressed, Roosevelt moved beyond the concerns that marked social feminists during the 1930s. Increasingly, she became the spokesperson for the more inarticulate segments of the national community. At a time when New Dealers were dependent on the political goodwill of southern Democrats, Eleanor Roosevelt promoted the cause of civil rights for blacks. She supported federal anti-lynching* laws and helped NAACP* officials make their case at the White House. She became a fervent advocate for fair employment practices and integration of the armed services as the nation increased defense production and moved closer to war. Her intentions far exceeded government action, but blacks—from conservative leaders to dispossessed tenant farmers—appreciated a well-placed friend in Washington.

Roosevelt brought comparable sensitivity to the poor and powerless generally. She supported union organizing of industrial workers and the planned communities of the Resettlement Administration* on behalf of the rural displaced. Although she often encountered more criticism than appreciation, she defended the radical and unpopular views of young people and their organizations, like the American Youth Congress. She exercised considerble weight on behalf of the National Youth Administration* and by pressing for the appointment of Mary McLeod Bethune* to the NYA board, her concerns for blacks, youths, and women in government coincided. She answered the letters of thousands of Americans who had no organizational base with advice and occasionally with donations from her earnings. Often she passed on requests for help to appropriate government officials. All these activities made her a major factor in humanizing the New Deal. Americans believed that their president and first lady formed an incredible partnership. If it was a relationship that had lost its emotional core, it did retain a remarkable congruence of mutual needs and concerns and complementary approaches to addressing them. And when Democrats at the 1940 convention were in revolt against the president's nomination for vice-president, he and party leaders sent Eleanor to the rostrum where she successfully quelled the impending rebellion. She was a seasoned, respected politician who was well prepared to undertake worldwide, humanitarian causes during her widowhood.

Eleanor Roosevelt died on November 7, 1962. (Tamara R. Hareven, *Eleanor Roosevelt: An American Conscience*, 1968; Joseph P. Lash, *Eleanor and Franklin*, 1971; Joan Hoff Wilson and Marjorie Ligniman, eds., *Without Precedent: The Life and Career of Eleanor Roosevelt*, 1984.)

LOIS SCHARF

ROOSEVELT, FRANKLIN DELANO Franklin D. Roosevelt, 32nd president of the United States and one of the most influential political figures in American history, was born in Hyde Park, New York, on January 30, 1882. An only child, Roosevelt was pampered by an elderly, indulgent father (James Roosevelt) and a loving, doting mother (Sarah Delano). His family's wealth on both sides reached back into commercial and maritime businesses of the early nineteenth century, and Roosevelt's chidhood world was one of economic security amidst an atmosphere of gentility common to the ''old rich.'' At the family estate at Hyde Park, he enjoyed servants, pets, limitless toys, money, and family as well as manicured lawns and fields, thick but well-kept forests, and herds of cattle and sheep. The Roosevelts carefully managed their business interests, not as an end in itself but as a means of maintaining the protected, secure world at Hyde Park. So Franklin D. Roosevelt grew up with a personality which was at once competitive but not acquisitive, without a relentless business instinct for constant economic aggrandizement. Extremely self-assured from a life of ego reinforcement, Roosevelt was insensitive to the emotional moods of others and at the same time at ease with large numbers of people. His childhood at Hyde Park proved the perfect breeding ground for political success.

Schooled at Groton, Harvard (1904), and the Columbia University Law School, Roosevelt enjoyed a sense of *noblesse oblige*, characteristic of his economic class. He was rooted in the values of Episcopal Christianity, civic duty, and love of God and country, but thoroughly devoid of ideological commitments. His view of life was conventional and conservative, but Roosevelt was also a man of action rather than ideas, willing to try different things without becoming wedded to abstract concepts or fixed positions. Nor was he a pragmatist, at least in a philosophical sense. Instead, Roosevelt was simply flexible, preferring action to inaction. He was also persuasive and completely comfortable with the political manipulation of others.

The future president began his political career in 1911 when he won a seat in the New York state legislature by opposing Tammany Hall and advocating open and honest government. Eventually, he made peace with the New York City machine, realizing that its support was essential to any statewide Democratic candidate. Exploiting the family name, he followed Theodore Roosevelt by becoming assistant secretary of the navy and served there under President Woodrow Wilson between 1913 and 1920. He ran unsuccessfully for vice-president of the United States, along with presidential candidate James Cox, in 1920 and a polio attack in 1921 confirmed his retreat into private life. The illness brought the first real crisis to Roosevelt, forcing him back to Hyde Park and to evaluate his future, but he emerged emotionally unscathed. At the Democratic national conventions in 1924 and 1928, he nominated Al Smith* for president, and in the election of 1928 he won the governorship of New York. Re-elected in 1930, Roosevelt's administration in Albany was noted for its emphasis on conservation, state regulation of public utilities, prison reform, old-age pensions, and unemployment relief. Because he had remained relatively free of the bitter party fights of 1924 and 1928 and had a national reputation, he was a leading figure for the Democratic nomination in 1932. He secured the nomination and, during the Great Depression, swamped President Herbert Hoover* in the presidential election. His promise of a "new deal"* to end the depression became the theme of his administration.

Roosevelt actually entered the White House with few specific ideas about the "new deal," but he surrounded himself with extraordinary political and intellectual talent and then captured the national imagination with the burst of legislative activity during the "first hundred days."* Enjoying a huge congressional majority, Roosevelt immediately called Congress into special session; and they enacted an unprecedented volume of legislation, which historians have conveniently divided into the categories of "relief, recovery, and reform." Congress immediately enacted the Emergency Banking Act of 1933* to solve the liquidity crisis; addressed the unemployment problem through creation of the Federal Emergency Relief Administration,* Public Works Administration,* and Civilian Conservation Corps;* tried to stimulate the economy by establishing the Agricultural Adjustment Administration,* and the National Recovery Administration;* and tried to deal with structural problems in the economy through amendments to the Reconstruction Finance Corporation* and the Banking Act of 1933.* All of these amounted to the "First New Deal"*—an approach to the depression which emphasized national planning through government-industry-labor cooperation and federal spending to provide relief to the poor and unemployed. In the process, Franklin D. Roosevelt quickly became the most popular figure in American society, worshipped by large numbers of farmers, workers, and the unemployed, and increasingly resented and hated by a small group of businessmen and the well-to-do. In the congressional elections of 1934,* the public confirmed his popularity by actually increasing the Democratic party's* large majorities in the House of Representatives and the Senate. The Republican party* had been reduced to a helpless minority.

In 1935 and 1936 President Roosevelt began to take the New Deal in a different direction, away from the emphasis on government-business planning. Widespread criticism from the business community, which Roosevelt considered premature and unjustified, began to irritate him and undermine his confidence in the ability of businessmen to see anything beyond the narrow constraints of their own corporation's welfare. Also, the bureaucratic nightmare produced by the National Recovery Administration's industrial codes and charges of government-supported monopolies eroded his patience. Finally, the Supreme Court's* conservative decisions destroying the National Recovery Administration in 1935 and the Agricultural Adjustment Administration in 1936 undermined whatever he might have retained for national economic planning. Instead, Franklin D. Roosevelt and the New Deal began resurrecting a more traditional approach to the business community, one emphasizing regulation, taxation, and anti-trust activity. The Securities Exchange Act of 1934* had already created the Securities and Exchange Commission* to regulate the stock markets. The "Second New Deal"* then implemented the Public Utility Holding Company Act of 1935* to break up the utilities' empires; the Wealth Tax Act of 1935,* to increase taxes on the well-to-do; the Social Security Act of 1935,* to provide old-age pensions and unemployment insurance financed by employer and employee contributions; and the Banking Act of 1935,* which increased the authority of the Federal Reserve Board* in Washington. The business community bitterly fought most of the legislation, complaining about socialism and authoritarianism, but the public only reinforced the president's position in the election of 1936* by re-electing him in a landslide over Governor Alf Landon* of Kansas and again increasing the Democratic majorities in Congress. On election night in November 1936, the New Deal had reached its zenith.

Early in 1937, however, Roosevelt's extended "honeymoon" with the country came to an end. Frustrated about what he considered the reactionary conservatism of the Supreme Court, he proposed a court reform to Congress which stirred up a storm of protest. Known as the "court-packing"* scheme, the proposal called for, among other things, expansion of the Supreme Court to a maximum of fifteen members if judges reaching the age of seventy did not retire. Clearly designed to change the philosophical composition of the Supreme Court and guarantee the future of New Deal legislation, the proposal generated enormous opposition from conservative and progressive Republicans, southern Democrats, and the business community and caused great dismay among many of Roosevelt's most devoted supporters. To many Americans, the plan seemed to violate the principle of separation of powers and smacked of authoritarianism. Throughout the spring and summer of 1937, Roosevelt fought for the bill, but congressional opposition was too intense, and he finally gave up the battle. Many historians, however, concede that he had "lost the battle but won the war." Amidst the political crisis, the Supreme Court, aided by the switch of Chief Justice Charles Evans Hughes* and Justice Owen J. Roberts* to the liberal side, had upheld the Farm Mortgage Moratorium Act of 1935,* the Social Security Act, and the National Labor Relations Act.* Roosevelt also managed to fill seven vacancies on the Supreme Court between 1937 and 1941, guaranteeing support of the New Deal. Still, the proposal had split the Democratic party for the first time in his administration and had helped create a coalition of Republicans and conservative Democrats which plagued him politically in 1938 and 1939. That coalition managed to amend drastically his executive reorganization plan in 1938 and severely reduce WPA* appropriations in 1938 and 1939.

The president's political problems increased even more in 1938. After hoping and even suspecting that the economy was responding to New Deal recovery measures, Roosevelt was stunned and disappointed when the recession of 1937-

1938* seemed to wipe out most of his gains. Public skepticism about the effectiveness of the New Deal mounted, as did Roosevelt's frustration. Angry at conservative Democrats who were increasingly independent and negative in their support of the New Deal, the president made an ill-advised decision to enter the primaries of 1938 and try to ''purge''* them from the party. Most of them won renomination, and the president was handed a stinging defeat by a public jealous of local prerogatives and frightened by his willingness to attempt such a power play. In the congressional elections of 1938,* the Democrats took a drubbing, losing eighty-one seats in the House and seven in the Senate.

When Congress convened in 1939, domestic events were rapidly giving way to foreign challenges. The president managed to secure the administrative Reorganization Act of 1939* and a number of amendments to the Social Security Act that year; but the German invasion of Poland and outbreak of World War II in September, followed by the stunning Nazi victories over France and the Low Countries in the spring of 1940, changed ''Dr. New Deal'' to ''Dr. Win-the-War.'' In June 1940 the president began implementing a number of defense measures, including increases in military appropriations, alien registration, the Selective Training and Service Act, and creation of the National Defense Research Committee and the Permanent Joint Board on Defense. Roosevelt decided to seek a third term, was easily renominated despite some opposition from old supporters like James Farley,* and then defeated Republican candidate Wendell Willkie* in a campaign noted for its support of the national defense program, aid to Great Britain, and defense of the Western Hemisphere. Willkie simply found himself caught up in a national crisis where the public preferred to remain loyal to a familiar leader. United States relations with Japan deteriorated throughout 1941, and when the Japanese navy attacked the American fleet at Pearl Harbor, Franklin D. Roosevelt became a beloved wartime leader. Re-elected to a fourth term in 1944 over Republican Thomas Dewey, Franklin D. Roosevelt died in office on April 12, 1945. A charismatic leader capable of inspiring confidence and love among huge majorities and hatred among smaller minorities, Franklin D. Roosevelt was indeed one of the most influential presidents in American history. The Democratic coalition he forged dominated American politics for a generation, and the modern bureaucratic state emerged during his presidency. (James MacGregor Burns, *Roosevelt: The Lion and the Fox*, 1956; Paul Conkin, *The New Deal*, 1967; Frank Freidel, *Franklin D. Roosevelt: Launching the New Deal*, 1973; Arthur M. Schlesinger, Jr., *The Age of Roosevelt. Vol. II. The Coming of the New Deal*, 1958, *Vol. III. The Politics of Upheaval, 1935-1936*, 1960.)

ROPER, DANIEL CALHOUN Daniel C. Roper was born in Marlboro County, South Carolina, on April 1, 1867. He attended Wofford College in Spartansburg, South Carolina, and graduated from Duke University in 1888. For four years he taught school, farmed, and sold life insurance but in 1892 won a seat in the state House of Representatives. He served for three years as a clerk of the United

States Senate Committee on Interstate Commerce, then returned to private business, selling life insurance, and studying law. He received his law degree from the National University Law School in Washington, D.C., in 1901 and later held a number of positions: including clerk of the House Ways and Means Committee in 1911; first assistant postmaster general, 1913-1916; vice-chairman of the United States Tariff Commission, 1917; commissioner of the Internal Revenue Service, 1917-1920; and president of the Marlin-Rockwell Corporation, 1920-1921. Roper returned to private law practice in 1921 and remained there until President Franklin D. Roosevelt* named him secretary of commerce in 1933. During his more than six years as secretary of commerce, Roper worked diligently to generate business support for such New Deal* measures as the Securities Act,* Securities Exchange Act,* National Industrial Recovery Act,* Agricultural Adjustment Act,* and the Public Utility Holding Company Act.* Through the Business Advisory Council* he established in the Department of Commerce, Roper played a critical role in reaching out to a suspicious business community during the 1930s. Roper resigned as secretary of commerce in 1938 and returned to private law practice for the rest of his life, except for a brief stint in 1940 as a temporary minister to Canada. Roper was the author of *The United States Post Office* (1917) and *Fifty Years of Public Life* (1942). Daniel C. Roper died in Washington, D.C., on April 11, 1943. (Barry D. Karl, *Executive Reorganization and Reform in the New Deal: The Genesis of Administrative Management, 1900–1939*, 1963; Daniel C. Roper, *Fifty Years of Public Life*, 1942.)

ROSENMAN, SAMUEL IRVING The youngest of four children, Samuel Rosenman was born on February 13, 1896, in San Antonio, Texas. His parents were Ukrainian Jewish immigrants, and the family moved to New York City in 1905. Rosenman graduated from Columbia in 1915 and received a degree from the Columbia Law School in 1919. Quickly turning to politics as part of the Tammany Hall machine, Rosenman won a seat in the New York State Assembly in 1921 and served there until 1926, building a reputation as an astute legislator, an advocate of social justice, and an expert in housing and labor issues. He retired from the State Assembly in 1926 to accept appointment to the state Legislative Bill Drafting Commission. Rosenman wrote several speeches for Franklin D. Roosevelt* in the New York gubernatorial campaign of 1928, and after the election the governor-elect named him general counsel of his staff. Rosenman also continued to serve Roosevelt as a political adviser, speechwriter, and liaison with Tammany Hall. Governor Roosevelt appointed Rosenman to fill a vacant seat on the New York State Supreme Court in 1932, but because of his Tammany Hall connections, Rosenman failed to get renominated at the next regularly scheduled election. During 1932, however, he continued to draft speeches for Roosevelt's presidential campaign, and was responsible for writing the "new deal"* phrase Roosevelt used when accepting the Democratic presidential nomination at Chicago.

After Roosevelt's landslide victory in 1932, Rosenman's reputation and public profile improved, and in 1933 he finally won that seat on the New York State Supreme Court. As usual, President Roosevelt repeatedly called on him for political advice and speechwriting. By 1936 Rosenman was supervising the White House speechwriting corps while still residing in New York. The president also selected him to begin editing and preparing for publication *The Public Papers and Addresses of Franklin D. Roosevelt*, a thirteen-volume work whose publication between 1938 and 1950 constituted the first and still indispensable scholarly treatment of Roosevelt's career. After Pearl Harbor, Roosevelt's demands on Rosenman became more extensive. His shrewd political skills, intelligence, and winning personality became important in negotiating compromises between various war agencies, and in 1943 he resigned his position on the New York State Supreme Court to become special counsel to the president. After President Roosevelt's death in 1945, Harry S Truman* retained Rosenman as general counsel and speechwriter and even broadened his powers as a political and administrative aide. Samuel I. Rosenman returned to private law practice in 1946. Until his death in 1973, he remained active in public life, serving on a number of commissions, offering political and legal counsel to prominent national and local politicians, and speaking out on important political, social, and economic issues. (Samuel B. Hand, *Counsel and Advice. A Political Biography of Samuel I. Rosenman*, 1979.)

ROSS, CHARLES BENJAMIN A native Idahoan, Charles Benjamin Ross was born in Parma, a small town near the confluence of the Boise and Snake Rivers, on December 27, 1876. His father John Ross was a native of Vermont who had followed a succession of western gold rushes. John Ross was able to expand a homestead into a 1,300-acre sheep ranch and diversified farm. Ben Ross, whose lifelong nickname was "Cowboy" Ben Ross, was literally that—a cowboy. Although he willingly left school after the sixth grade, Ross bemoaned his lack of education. He worked on the Ross ranch and then hired out to several large Oregon ranches as a teen. In 1894 he went to Portland and studied business for three years. In 1900 he married Edna Reavis, a school teacher from Midvale and settled down to ranching. Abandoning the political party of his parents, C. Ben Ross became a Democrat late in the nineteenth century. He was twice elected Democratic county commissioner from Canyon County. In 1921 Ross sold his farm and moved to Bannock County as a pioneer farmer in a new irrigation district. However, he was forced to repossess his Parma ranch and then owned lands in both areas. After only a year in Pocatello, he was elected mayor of the city and served for three terms in that position. Ross was an amazing Populist speaker with an emotional attachment to the agrarian west. The voters identified with his earthiness, his progressivism, and his occasional demagoguery. In 1930 all of his traits assisted by the Great Depression vaulted Ross into the governor's office. He was the New Deal* governor of Idaho and served from 1931-1937.

Ross was a great believer in both public works projects and a loose expandable credit. Ross never worked well with Harry Hopkins,* Henry Wallace,* Harold Ickes,* or other New Dealers. Still Idaho benefitted because of the Idahoans in Washington. Ross fought with the national delegation over patronage and sometimes cooperated more with Senator William Borah,* a Republican, than with Democrat James Pope.* Ross lost some support in his third term by advocating a sales tax and a liquor tax. His detractors attacked him as a power-hungry "boss." In reality, Idaho and Ross did very well during the New Deal. In 1936 Ross attempted to unseat Senator William Borah, Idaho's senior senator. It was a disaster for Ross because Borah defeated him by 54,000 votes. Two years later, Ross attempted to recapture the state house but lost to Republican C. A. Bottolfsen. Ross was a dominant force in Idaho during the New Deal but operated more as an independent and a maverick. He died in 1946. (Michael P. Malone, *C. Ben Ross and the New Deal in Idaho*, 1970.)

F. ROSS PETERSON

ROSS, NELLIE TAYLOR Nellie Taylor was born in Missouri in 1876 and married William Bradford Ross of Wyoming in 1902. Her husband died in office as governor of Wyoming in 1924, and she succeeded him, winning a term in her own right in 1925. She was defeated for re-election in 1927, served as a vice-chairman of the Democratic National Committee in 1928, and vigorously supported Franklin D. Roosevelt's* campaign in 1932. In return, he appointed her director of the mint in 1933, a position she held until 1952. Nellie Ross died in 1977. (Susan Ware, *Beyond Suffrage: Women in the New Deal*, 1981.)

ROWE, JAMES HENRY, JR. James H. Rowe, Jr., was born in Butte, Montana on June 1, 1909 and educated at Harvard and the Harvard Law School. He had a passion for anonymity, worked for the National Emergency Council* in 1934, and was Supreme Court* Justice Oliver Wendell Holmes, Jr.'s last clerk. Rowe worked diligently for Franklin D. Roosevelt's* re-election in 1936* while doing legal work for the RFC* and the SEC.* Between 1938 and 1941, Rowe served as a special White House assistant to the president. During World War II, Rowe saw combat in the Pacific, served as a technical adviser at the Nuremberg War Trials, and in 1946 went into private practice with the law firm of Corcoran, Youngman, and Rowe in Washington, D.C. (Katie Louchheim, ed., *The Making of the New Deal. The Insiders Speak*, 1983.)

RUBINOW, ISAAC MAX Isaac Max Rubinow was born in Grodno, Russia, on April 19, 1875. He immigrated to the United States in 1893 and graduated from Columbia College in 1895 and from the Columbia University Medical College in 1898. But he was always more interested in government insurance systems than in private medicine and worked at the Civil Service Commission, Department of Agriculture, and Bureau of Labor. He was the chief actuary and statistician for the Ocean Accident and Guarantee Company until 1916. Rubinow published a study of workmen's insurance in Europe in 1911 and the first study of social insurance in 1913. In 1914 Rubinow founded the Casualty Actuarial and Statistical Society of America and served as its first president. Convinced that European social welfare institutions should have a place in the United States, Rubinow became a vocal advocate of unemployment, old-age, disability, and medical insurance financed by the federal government.

In 1916 Rubinow became secretary of the Social Insurance Committee of the American Medical Association and published a study of health insurance, and in 1917 he directed the Bureau of Social Statistics in New York City's Department of Public Charities. He spent some time in Palestine in 1919 directing the American Zionist Medical Unit, and upon his return he became director of the Jewish Welfare Society of Philadelphia. He wrote *The Care of the Aged* in 1931 and *The Quest for Social Security* in 1934. When the Social Security Act of 1935* was finally passed, Rubinow supported it but expressed dismay that it was financed through individual and employer contributions, because he felt it would reduce purchasing power, eliminate federal control, and not play any role in redistributing income. Isaac Rubinow died on September 1, 1936. (Roy Lubove, *The Struggle for Social Security, 1900–1935*, 1968; *New York Times*, September 2, 1936.)

RUML, BEARDSLEY Beardsley Ruml was born November 5, 1894, at Cedar Rapids, Iowa. He graduated from Dartmouth in 1915 and received a doctorate in psychometrics from the University of Chicago in 1917. Ruml taught briefly at the Carnegie Institute of Technology before going to Washington, D.C., during World War I to direct the U.S. Army's civilian testing programs. In 1921 Ruml became assistant to the president of the Carnegie Corporation and in 1922 John D. Rockefeller, Jr., recruited him to head the Laura Spelman Rockefeller Memorial, where in seven years he put together the Public Administration Clearing House in Chicago and created a large fellowship program on race relations. During those years Ruml also became a strong advocate of the "domestic allotment plan,"* being promoted by people like John Black* and Milburn Wilson.* He became dean and professor of education at the University of Chicago in 1930 and one year later was appointed treasurer of R. H. Macy & Company in New York City. A believer in government planning and technical expertise, Ruml became a director of the Federal Reserve Bank of New York in 1937 and chairman from 1941 to 1947. He was registered as a Republican but regularly endorsed and voted for Democratic candidates. Beardsley Ruml died on April 19, 1960. (*New York Times*, April 20, 1960.)

RUMSEY, MARY HARRIMAN Mary Harriman, sister of Averill Harriman and one heir to the fortune of railroad magnate E. I. Harriman, was born in New York in 1881. Although raised with immense wealth, she developed a social conscience about poverty and helped found the Junior League in 1901. She graduated from Barnard College in 1905. Mary Harriman married Charles Rumsey in 1910 and she was widowed in 1927. Along with her brother Averill, Mary Rumsey left the Republican party* in the 1920s and became an active Democrat, a close friend of Franklin D. Roosevelt,* Eleanor Roosevelt,* and Frances Perkins.* Rumsey and Perkins had become friends in 1918 while working for the New York Maternity League and for several years during the New Deal* shared a home in Georgetown. In 1933 the president appointed Rumsey to serve as the chairman of the Consumers' Advisory Board* of the National Recovery Administration.* Her wealth, widespread social and political contacts among Democrats and Republicans, and willingness to entertain were real assets in trying to make the Consumers' Advisory Board an influence on the NRA. Mary Rumsey died suddenly in December 1934 after an accident while horseback riding. (Susan Ware, *Beyond Suffrage: Women in the New Deal*, 1981.)

RURAL ELECTRIFICATION ACT OF 1936 Using funds from the Emergency Relief Appropriation Act of 1935,* President Franklin D. Roosevelt* issued Executive Order No. 7037 on May 11, 1935, creating a Rural Electrification Administration.* One year later, in May 1936, Congress passed the Rural Electrification Act giving the REA a ten-year statutory authority. (Samuel I. Rosenman, ed., *The Public Papers and Addresses of Franklin D. Roosevelt,* IV:172-174, 1938.)

RURAL ELECTRIFICATION ADMINISTRATION The creation of the Rural Electrification Administration in 1935 established a partnership between the federal government and local electrical cooperatives to extend the benefits of electrification to rural America.

Prior to 1935 power companies had been slow to extend lines into rural areas. Rural service required long lines to reach few homes. The companies passed high costs on to rural consumers, who consequently curtailed power use, making rural lines still less remunerative. The few rural electrical cooperatives organized during the 1920s and early 1930s, facing not only the same high costs but also the opposition of the power generating companies, enjoyed little success. Many farmers, impatient for electricity, bought gasoline-powered generators.

During the presidential campaign of 1932 Franklin D. Roosevelt* proposed federal aid for rural electrification. In this he was influenced by Morris L. Cooke,* who had studied and promoted public power, including rural public power, during service under the gubernatorial administrations of Gifford Pinchot in Pennsylvania and Roosevelt in New York. Cooke subsequently entered the Roosevelt presidential administration as a consultant in the Public Works Administration.*

Roosevelt, undecided at first how to proceed toward rural electrification, eventually created the REA by executive order on May 11, 1935. By this time the Tennessee Valley Authority* had bolstered confidence in public power; agricultural organizations had pressed for action on the subject; Cooke had continually urged it; and North Carolina and South Carolina had initiated their own programs for rural electrification.

Roosevelt placed the REA within the Department of the Interior and appointed Cooke its first administrator. Cooke made two important decisions that set the course of the agency for subsequent decades. First, after being frustrated in attempts to interest private power companies and municipal power districts in expanding service into the countryside, he decided that the only means by which the purpose of the agency might be accomplished was through aid to local rural electrical cooperatives. Second, he determined that the agency's role in such aid should be that of a lending agency.

The REA reduced the initial cost of rural service by extending low-interest, long-amortization loans to cooperatives. Rural dwellers organized the cooperatives, applied for loans, built the systems, and purchased electricity from power companies.

On May 21, 1936, Roosevelt signed a bill making the REA a permanent agency with statutory authorization. In 1937 John M. Carmody* succeeded Cooke as administrator. In 1939 Congress moved the agency into the Department of Agriculture, where it remained.

The REA worked swiftly: by 1939 it had assisted 417 cooperatives to provide service to 268,000 households. This was accomplished despite resistance from private power companies, some of which built "spite lines" to usurp the more profitable rural areas.

The work slowed when a new administrator, Harry Slattery,* feuded with a new Secretary of Agriculture Claude R. Wickard,* and it stalled under restrictions by the War Production Board in 1942. Advocates of rural power responded by forming the National Rural Electrical Cooperative Association. This organization, after obtaining resumption of rural electrical financing, also persuaded the REA to begin financing its member cooperatives for generation of electricity, not just distribution.

By the mid-1950s, only the most remote and marginal of American farms were without electricity. Surveys showed that electric irons, radios, washing machines, and refrigerators were the first conveniences farm families sought after electrification. The most visible result of electrification, of course, was the appearance of innumerable home and yard lamps in the previously black rural night. (D. Clayton Brown, *Electricity for Rural America: The Fight for the REA*, 1980.)

THOMAS D. ISERN

S

SABATH, ADOLPH, JR. Adolph J. Sabath, Jr., was born in Czechoslovakia on April 4, 1866, and immigrated to the United States in 1881. He graduated from the Chicago College of Law in 1891 and took a law degree at Lake Forest University in 1892. Sabath practiced law in Chicago between 1891 and 1895, became active in the Democratic political organization in Chicago, and served as a municipal judge and police magistrate between 1895 and 1907. The Cook County Democratic Central Committee put Sabath up for Congress in 1906, and he remained there for the next forty-six years. Although a trustworthy supporter of the New Deal* and a spokesman for immigrant problems, Sabath's immigrant accent and ineffectual leadership did not make him a powerful figure in the congress. Still, as chairman of the House Rules Committee after 1938, Sabath could be counted on to support the administration as well as a wide variety of social welfare and labor legislation. Adolph J. Sabath died on November 6, 1952. (*New York Times*, November 7, 1952.)

SCHALL, THOMAS DAVID Thomas D. Schall, implacable enemy of the New Deal,* was born in Reed City, Michigan, on June 4, 1878. He moved with his mother to Campbell, Minnesota, in 1884, graduated from the University of Minnesota in 1902, and received a law degree from the St. Paul College of Law in 1904. Schall was blinded in an electrical shock accident in 1907, but continued practicing law, and was elected to the House of Representatives as a Republican in 1914. He served in the House until 1925, when he assumed his recently-won seat in the United States Senate. Schall was re-elected in 1930, and he became one of Franklin D. Roosevelt's* most bitter political enemies after 1933. Convinced that the New Deal was leading the country down the road to socialism and then to communism, Schall began to publicly vilify President Roosevelt as a radical, drunkard, and conspirator. He claimed that the country was in danger of falling under dictatorial control, and Schall compared Roosevelt and the New Deal to the "Apocalypse." Thomas D. Schall died suddenly in an automobile accident on December 22, 1935. (George Wolfskill and John A. Hudson, *All but the People. Franklin D. Roosevelt and His Critics, 1933–1939*, 1969.)

SCHECHTER POULTRY CORPORATION V. UNITED STATES Section 3 of the National Industrial Recovery Act* authorized the president to promulgate "Codes of Fair Competition" submitted to him upon approval by a trade or industry. Once adopted, violations of the provisions of such codes were deemed a misdemeanor punishable by fine. On April 13, 1934, President Franklin D. Roosevelt* approved the "Live Poultry Code" for the metropolitan area in and around New York City. Among other things, the code established the forty-hour workweek and 50¢ per hour minimum wage for poultry workers, prohibited certain practices termed "unfair methods of competition," and required the submission of weekly reports reflecting the volume of sales and range of daily prices for the produce sold.

ALA Schechter Poultry Corporation and Schechter Live Poultry Market operated wholesale poultry slaughter-house markets in Brooklyn, New York. They purchased live poultry from commission men in New York or occasionally in Philadelphia. Poultry sold by Schechter was slaughtered under the provisions of Jewish law immediately before delivery. Schechter did not sell in interstate commerce.

The Schechters were indicted for conspiracy to violate and on eighteen specific violations of the poultry code. Among other charges, they were accused of violating the hours-and-wages provisions of the code, of ignoring the "straight killing" requirements, and of selling "an unfit chicken," (thus, the common description "The Sick Chicken Case"). Defendants were convicted in the district court, and the Circuit Court of Appeals (2nd Circuit) upheld the conviction on the count of conspiracy and on sixteen counts of violating the code. But the circuit court reversed two counts charging violation of the maximum hours and minimum wage provisions. The court contended that such matters were beyond the regulatory powers of Congress.

Upon application by both the defendants and the government, the Supreme Court* granted writs of certiorari on April 15, 1935. The case was argued May 2 and 3, and decided on May 27, 1935. Before the court, counsel for the Schechter Brothers argued that (1) the Codes for Fair Competition constituted an unconstitutional delegation by Congress of legislative powers; (2) that the poultry code attempted to regulate intrastate commerce; and (3) that the fines imposed for violations of the code were themselves violations of the due process clause of the Fifth Amendment.

Writing for the Court, Chief Justice Charles Evans Hughes* first disposed of the government's contention that the gravity of the national crisis justified "extraordinary remedies." Justice Hughes answered by stating that "extraordinary conditions do not create or enlarge constitutional power" and could not justify action which was outside or beyond the constitutional powers of Congress. On the question of delegation of legislative authority, i.e., the adoption of codes by trades or industries and their promulgation by the president, Hughes called this a practice "unknown to our law . . . and utterly inconsistent with the constitutional prerogatives and duties of Congress."

On the issue of intrastate commerce, the chief justice found that the Schechter Corporation was not engaged to any meaningful extent in interstate commerce, and thus the "stream of commerce" doctrine did not apply. Therefore the poultry code had unconstitutionally attempted to impose federal regulation over intrastate commerce. Hughes also observed that, however laudable the motive, provisions of the code fixing hours and wages of employees of a business engaged in intrastate commerce were not a valid exercise of federal power. Conceding that some attempt to maintain wages in time of depression might be desirable, Hughes stated that "the recuperative efforts of the federal government must be made in a manner consistent with the authority granted by the Constitution."

On the basis of these conclusions, the Court found that the code provisions of the NIRA were unconstitutional, and the conviction of the Schechter Corporation was reversed. The effect of this unanimous decision was to invalidate the NIRA. (Gerald O. and L. G. Dykstra, *Selected Cases on Government and Business*, 1937; Alfred H. Kelly and Winfred A. Harbison, *The American Constitution,* 1970; *Supreme Court Reporter*, LV:837–854, 1935.)

JOSPEH M. ROWE, JR.

SCHNEIDERMAN, ROSE Rose Schneiderman was born in Russia in 1882 and immigrated to the United States in 1890. Her family settled in New York City, and she worked in the garment trades, quitting school at the age of thirteen. By 1900 she was an active trade unionist, and in 1905 she joined the Women's Trade Union League, an association which was a passion for the rest of her life. Schneiderman became an organizer for the WTUL in 1910 and then a national organizer for the International Ladies Garment Workers Union in 1915. She also became an active suffragette. During the 1920s, Schneiderman became president of the WTUL and at that time became a close associate of Eleanor Roosevelt.* Between 1933 and 1936, she was a member of the Labor Advisory Board* of the National Recovery Administration,* and in 1937 she became secretary of labor for New York. Schneiderman kept that position until 1943. She also continued as president of the WTUL until its dissolution in 1950. Rose Schneiderman died in 1972. (Susan Ware, *Beyond Suffrage: Women in the New Deal*, 1981.)

SECOND EXPORT-IMPORT BANK (See EXPORT-IMPORT BANK.)

"SECOND HUNDRED DAYS" The term "second hundred days" refers to the summer of 1935 when President Franklin D. Roosevelt* successfully directed Congress to pass a series of unprecedented relief, recovery, and reform measures. With Congress about to adjourn, the Supreme Court* handed down the *Schechter** decision on May 27, 1935, outlawing the National Industrial Recovery Act.* Angry about the destruction of the NRA* and committed to a new burst of legislation, the president kept Congress in session through the rest of the summer of 1935, during which time the National Resources Committee* and National

Youth Administration* were created by executive order and Congress passed the National Labor Relations Act,* Motor Carrier Act,* Social Security Act,* Banking Act of 1935,* Public Utility Holding Company Act,* Farm Mortgage Moratorium Act,* Wagner-Crosser Railroad Retirement Act,* Guffey-Snyder Bituminous Coal Stabilization Act,* and Wealth Tax Act.* The "second hundred days" proved to be a major portion of Roosevelt's "Second New Deal."* (William E. Leuchtenburg, *Franklin D. Roosevelt and the New Deal, 1932–1940*, 1963.)

"SECOND NEW DEAL" For two generations, historians have conveniently divided the first two administrations of Franklin D. Roosevelt* into the "First New Deal"* and "Second New Deal." They have confined the "First New Deal" to 1933 and 1934 when the president and Congress were focusing on relief and recovery measures, hoping to end the depression through coordinated national planning between business, labor, and government. The NRA,* AAA,* and TVA,* along with the CCC,* CWA,* and FERA,* were the legislative symbols of the "First New Deal," and people such as Hugh Johnson,* Lewis Douglas,* Rexford Tugwell,* and Raymond Moley* were its major advocates. The "Second New Deal" replaced the "First New Deal" after the end of the 73rd Congress. Serious political problems emerged as large corporations and big farmers took control of the NRA and AAA and began criticizing the Roosevelt administration. Business criticism of the New Deal,* the persistence of the depression, and the Supreme Court's* 1935 *Schechter** decision all forced policy changes on Roosevelt and led to the "Second New Deal."

In contrast to the "First New Deal," the "Second New Deal" abandoned the goal of national planning in favor of social reform, anti-trust policy, and Keynesian finance. Historians have debated the meaning of the policy change. Some have seen it as a move to the left because of such social legislation as the Social Security Act* and the National Labor Relations Act,* and the abandonment of budget balancing for Keynesian economics; but others have seen it as a conservative move, a defeat of national planning in favor of more traditional, Brandesian anti-trust policies embodied in such laws as the Public Utility Holding Company Act of 1935.* In the "Second New Deal," the influence of people like Raymond Moley and Hugh Johnson disappeared as their policies waned in power. The "Second New Deal" brought new people and new ideas to the forefront of American public policy. During the years of the 74th Congress in 1935 and 1936, the "Second New Deal" was dominated by neo-Brandesian lawyers like Felix Frankfurter,* Thomas Corcoran,* and Benjamin Cohen* who recommitted the federal government to faith in a competitive economy, supported by anti-trust policies, old-age pensions, and labor union rights. During the 75th Congress in 1937 and 1938, the "Second New Deal" maintained its commitment to anti-trust policies through such vehicles as the Temporary National Economic Committee* but also began to add the influence of such Keynesian economists as Marriner Eccles,* Lauchlin Currie,* and Alvin Hansen.* Although the move to deficit spending as conscious economic policy was hesitant during the late 1930s, it nevertheless distinguished the "Second New Deal" from the "First New Deal." (Arthur M. Schlesinger, Jr., *The Age of Roosevelt. Vol. III. The Politics of Upheaval, 1935–1936*, 1960.)

SECURITIES ACT OF 1933 The stock market crash of 1929 forced leading politicians to recognize the fact that private investors needed protection. Tremendous paper losses, as well as the collapse of large numbers of fraudulent investment companies, had brought the government into the investigation of dishonest securities representations, high pressure salesmanship, and the exaggeration of the returns an investor might expect. By 1932 President Herbert Hoover* had become convinced that corruption and greed on the securities exchanges had helped trigger the crash of the stock market, and he was convinced that public exposure of the fraud might stop similar speculation in the future. Senator Peter Norbeck* of North Dakota began the investigation in April 1932, and in November he hired Ferdinand Pecora,* a Theodore Roosevelt progressive and converted Democrat who had served for twelve years as assistant district attorney of New York, to direct the investigation. During 1932, 1933, and part of 1934, the "Pecora investigation" made headlines, exposing an enormous variety of securities fraud and corruption involving broker loans, holding companies, fictitious securities, margin buying, and gross misrepresentation. Out of his investigation came intense public demands for regulation of the securities markets.

On March 29, 1933, President Franklin D. Roosevelt* sent a message to Congress demanding full disclosure of all new securities issues and placing the burden of responsibility on securities sellers to properly inform the public. Raymond Moley,* a member of Roosevelt's "brain trust,"* asked Samuel Untermyer, a veteran of the Pujo hearings, to draft a securities bill, and President Roosevelt asked Huston Thompson, a former chairman of the Federal Trade Commission,* to do the same. Thompson's bill, which called for the Federal Trade Commission to review and disapprove the issuance of new securities, was introduced to the House of Representatives by Sam Rayburn,* the Texas Democrat. When severe Wall-Street opposition surfaced in response to the Thompson bill, Moley invited James M. Landis* and Benjamin Cohen* of the Harvard Law School to draft an alternative. The bill required full disclosure of all material and the right of the Federal Trade Commission to postpone the issuance of new securities if full disclosure had not been made. Thomas Corcoran helped lobby in Congress. Out of House and Senate negotiations, led by Congressman Sam Rayburn as well as Senators Joseph Robinson* of Arkansas and Duncan Fletcher* of Florida, came the Securities Act of 1933, which President Roosevelt signed on May 27, 1933.

The Securities Act of 1933, commonly known as the Fletcher-Rayburn Bill, required that companies issuing stock file the fullest possible information concerning new securities with the Federal Trade Commission. The sworn statement had to include all commissions or discounts to be paid, directly or indirectly, by the issuer to the underwriter, full description of all factors surrounding the physical issuance of the securities, the names of officers and directors of the issuing company, names of holders of 10 percent or more of prior securities issued by that company, and a detailed description of the business and financial conditions of the company, plus the salaries of its officers. The information was part of the public record, except that the FTC could keep material confidential which might affect the welfare of a company. After the sworn statement had been filed, twenty days had to elapse before the securities could be promoted and sold. Even with FTC approval, a company was not relieved of future liability. Evidence of untrue statements could be made the basis of criminal prosecution and civil suits by investors against the company. Similar restrictions were imposed on foreign securities, except that liability rested on the domestic agent of the issuer. Penalties for misstatement or misrepresentation included up to five years imprisonment, a fine of up to $5,000, or both. The only exceptions to these regulations were for federal, state, and municipal bonds; railroad securities; and the securities of religious, charitable, and educational groups.

The Securities Act of 1933 gave the Federal Trade Commission a number of new powers, including the power to summon witnesses, subpoena evidence, require production of any books, papers and necessary documents, obtain injunctions against a company for selling a particular security, and hold hearings to gather information. The FTC could issue stop orders to suspend the effectiveness of a registration statement if it did not comply with the law. Any sales of the security after the stop order were illegal. The Securities Act of 1933 was designed to prevent further exploitation of the public through sale of fraudulent or worthless securities. It placed before investors adequate information about new securities and protected honest securities dealers from guilt by association. For the first time, the federal government directly entered the securities markets in a regulatory capacity.

The business community severely criticized the bill, arguing that it effectively stopped the flotation of new securities by industry because of three aspects of the law: (1) the sweeping scope of civil and criminal liabilities and penalties that it contained, which included even accidental errors and omissions as grounds for action and which reached even to members of corporate boards of directors; (2) the time and expense required for corporations to assemble and make available the information required before an issue of securities could be approved; and (3) the ambiguous language of the act, which, for example, provided stiff penalties for the omission of "material facts," without defining what constituted a material fact. This third aspect of the law was typical of much New Deal* legislation, which took the detailed writing of laws from the hands of Congress and entrusted it to administrative bodies capable of issuing rules and regulations with the force of law. The Securities Act of 1933 was refined, in face of much criticism, with the Securities Exchange Act of 1934,* when the scope of liabilities and penalties was narrowed and administration of the law moved from the FTC to the new

Securities and Exchange Commission.* (Michael Parrish, *Securities Regulation and the New Deal*, 1970; Donald A. Ritchie, *James M. Landis. Dean of the Regulators*, 1980.)

GARY DEAN BEST

SECURITIES AND EXCHANGE COMMISSION Few institutions more fully exemplified the reform spirit of the New Deal* than the Securities and Exchange Commission, created by an act of Congress in 1934. For most of the 1930s and for several decades thereafter, the SEC's activities and the quality of its personnel set a standard of excellence for federal independent regulatory commissions. But despite its record of accomplishments, critics of the agency also suggested that the SEC displayed the inherent weaknesses of this method of business regulation which traced its roots back to the founding of the Interstate Commerce Commission* in 1887.

Franklin D. Roosevelt* and the New Dealers came to power in 1933, having pledged to reform the many abuses associated with the underwriting and the buying and selling of corporation securities. Among liberal politicians and academic experts, the stock market crash of 1929 was widely blamed for the contraction of credit, the collapse of commercial banks, and the economic depression that followed in its wake. The stock market debacle, in turn, was blamed upon the lavish extension of credit that supported unjustified speculation, the reckless behavior of investment bankers who marketed securities of dubious value, and the unethical manipulations of "insiders" on the stock exchanges who fleeced unwary investors through various tactics.

The New Deal's initial efforts to legislate against these abuses took the form of the Securities Act of 1933,* written largely by Professor Felix Frankfurter* of the Harvard Law School and several of his former students, especially James M. Landis* and Benjamin V. Cohen.* The Securities Act, which Congress passed during the hundred days,* vested power over the marketing of new corporate securities in the old Federal Trade Commission,* an independent regulatory commission created during the Wilson years. Under the 1933 law, corporations and banking syndicates were prohibited from selling securities in interstate commerce unless they had filed a detailed financial statement with the FTC, disclosing the company's assets and liabilities.

Designed basically to encourage what Roosevelt called "truth telling" in the marketing of securities, the law provided stiff criminal and civil penalties for corporate officers, accountants, and lawyers who intentionally withheld information or who filed false registration statements. Many Wall-Street bankers and attorneys denounced the statute as an unwarranted intrusion of governmental power into their private affairs and predicted a "drying up" of the nation's capital markets because of the complicated disclosure provisions. Supporters of the legislation, including some members of the investment banking fraternity, believed that the law would restore confidence in their industry and drive out of business their more disreputable, "fly-by-night" competitors.

Cohen, Landis, and another Frankfurter protégé, Thomas (Thomas the Cork) Corcoran,* provided the legislative impetus for the Securities Exchange Act, which Roosevelt sent to Congress a year later. As originally drafted by these New Dealers, the law would have given the FTC sweeping powers over the individual stock exchanges, completely prohibited the buying and selling of stocks by many exchange members for their own personal accounts, and given the commission the authority to regulate all margin transactions by means of which customers purchased stocks on credit. In this form, the proposal came under withering attack from the stock exchanges especially the floor traders who would have been put out of business and several important senators and congressmen who believed the measure to be too radical. In response to these protests, committees of the Congress modified the Cohen-Landis-Corcoran bill significantly before its final passage.

The most dramatic change vested administrative powers in a new, independent Securities and Exchange Commission, to be appointed by the president. The SEC was given jurisdiction over the 1933 Securities Act as well. Instead of prohibiting certain exchange activities by statute, the revisions gave the SEC broad discretion to adopt specific rules of trading on a case-by-case basis. At the insistence of Senator Carter Glass* of Virginia, the new agency lost all control over margin requirements. These important credit controls were given instead to the governors of the Federal Reserve System, who managed the nation's monetary policy.

The watering down of the administration's original stock exchange control bill was part of a larger compromise in 1934 through which Roosevelt hoped to revive a dormant investment market often paralyzed by the business community's fears that the new laws exposed them to intolerable civil liability. Through a series of legislative amendments and administrative rules, the disclosure and liability provisions of the 1933 law were modified. In addition, Roosevelt named as the first chairman of the SEC, Joseph P. Kennedy* of Boston, himself a legendary stock market speculator in the 1920s. As a sop to the more radical New Dealers, he also named Landis to the new agency.

The compromises of 1934 succeeded in reviving private capital investment. Despite the fears of Wall-Street conservatives, who had resisted any legislative reforms, the SEC under Kennedy cautiously implemented changes in trading rules and accounting practices. Self-regulation, relying upon the leaders of the exchanges and the accounting profession to generate reforms, became the SEC's dominant style of administration. On the other hand, despite the anxiety of liberals that Kennedy would be too tolerant of the industry, the SEC during his chairmanship did not hesitate to prosecute securities fraud; and it began a long, hard-hitting investigation into the conduct of bondholders' protective committees. Landis, who followed Kennedy as chairman in 1936–1937, carried forward this strategy of moderate reform.

The SEC experienced a renewed burst of regulatory zeal at the end of the 1930s under the leadership of William O. Douglas* and Jerome Frank,* two loyal New Dealers who displayed considerable skepticism about the progress of self-regulation. When the leaders of the New York Stock Exchange failed to promptly implement new trading rules or to revise by-laws to give greater voice in administration to public stock brokers, Douglas threatened to invoke the SEC's powers to impose these changes. That threat, plus a revolt of major brokerage houses against the exchange's old guard, produced internal reforms that placed the day-to-day management of the institution into the hands of younger professionals led by William McChesney Martin. The Douglas-Frank regime also brought a degree of order to the volatile over-the-counter markets by sponsoring the growth of a powerful, self-regulating trade association of brokers who specialized in this area.

In addition to enforcing the nation's basic securities laws, the commission was also given the stupendous task after 1935 of implementing the Public Utility Holding Company Act,* which compelled the reorganization of dubious corporate financial structures that had grown up in the industry during the 1920s. This task, involved the SEC in protracted litigation with the utility companies until after World War II and diverted the agency from its main task with respect to the stock exchanges and the securities industry.

By the end of the New Deal era, the SEC had developed a well-deserved reputation for administrative efficiency and absolute integrity, but it had not realized the dreams of many New Dealers, who hoped for a complete restructuring of the nation's securities industry. Devoted to the concept of self-regulation whenever possible, the SEC became, in the judgement of some critics, far too patient with the industry and with trade practices that continued to work against the interests of investors and the general public. On the other hand, given its limited administrative resources, it was not clear that the SEC could have accomplished more. (Michael Parrish, *Securities Regulation and the New Deal*, 1970.)

MICHAEL E. PARRISH

SECURITIES EXCHANGE ACT OF 1934 (See SECURITIES AND EXCHANGE COMMISSION.)

SENTINELS OF THE REPUBLIC Founded by Alexander Lincoln and headquartered in Boston, the Sentinels of the Republic was a bitterly anti-New Deal, anti-Semitic organization active in the mid-1930s. Financed by a number of important American families and corporations, but especially by the Du Ponts, the Sentinels of the Republic campaigned against Franklin D. Roosevelt* and called for destruction of the New Deal*—particularly such measures as the Social Security Act,* Public Utility Holding Company Act,* and Wealth Tax Act of 1935*—and demanded alteration of the general welfare clause of the Constitution. The Sentinels of the Republic was one facet of the American fascist movement which declined rapidly in the late 1930s. (Arthur M. Schlesinger, Jr., *The Age of Roosevelt. Vol. III. The Politics of Upheaval, 1935–1936*, 1960.)

SHAHN, BENJAMIN Benjamin Shahn was born September 12, 1898, in Kaunas, Lithuania, to Jewish parents who immigrated to Brooklyn in 1906. His father was a woodcarver and carpenter, and the family's Misnagdim Judaism put a high premium on craftsmanship, a value which the young Shahn shared and which propelled him into an artistic career. At the age of fifteen, Shahn apprenticed himself to a commercial lithographer, and he remained in the business for seventeen years, attending night art classes at New York University, the City College of New York, and the National Academy of Design. He travelled widely in Europe in 1925 and 1927 to 1929 and in 1930 had his first one-man show at the Downtown Gallery in New York. Shahn rejected the "passionless amorality" of modern art and preferred a style expressing his social liberalism. His series of paintings on Sacco and Vanzetti and Tom Mooney in 1931 and 1932 impressed Mexican muralist Diego Rivera, and Shahn went to work with him on the "Man at the Crossroads" fresco for the RCA Building at Rockefeller Center. Shahn's later work was influenced by his association with Rivera. During the late 1930s, Shahn painted for the Federal Art Project* of the Works Progress Administration,* and his most memorable work was the mural on immigration at the Jersey Homesteads, New Jersey, housing project. He also painted murals at the Bronx Central Avenue Post Office and the Social Security Building in Washington, D. C. His major themes involved poverty, immigration, and working-class problems. During World War II, Shahn designed posters for the Office of War Information, and in 1944 he worked for the Political Action Committee of the Congress of Industrial Organizations.* Benjamin Shahn died on March 14, 1969. (*New York Times*, March 15, 1969.)

SHARE-OUR-WEALTH (See LONG, HUEY P. or SMITH, GERALD L. K.)

SHELTERBELT PROJECT Dust storms had been common throughout the history of the Great Plains, but during the 1930s the drought, erosion, and storms were especially severe. Because of his longstanding interest in conservation and years of tree planting at Hyde Park, President Franklin D. Roosevelt* became interested in a small-scale "shelterbelt" program the Department of Agriculture had operated since 1913. Under the program, North Dakota farmers had planted tree belts around their exposed fields to control wind erosion. In July 1934 Roosevelt tried to get $15 million from existing drought relief funds to finance a large-scale "shelterbelt." Although he managed to get only $1 million, he had the Forest Service conduct a study of the potential program and at least start the "Great Plains Shelterbelt." The original plan called for a single belt of 3 billion trees in a 100-mile strip of land running from the Canadian border into central Texas. Within the strip, the Forest Service would plant tree belts one-mile long and eight rods wide at half-mile intervals. In 1935 the Forest Service planted 125 miles of shelterbelts, usually on AAA* land withdrawn from production. Paul Roberts was named director of the Shelterbelt Project. Despite opposition to the program from nurserymen and eastern foresters, the president authorized $1.9 million for the trees in 1936. In 1937 he made the Shelterbelt Project part of the Works Progress Administration.* Although the president never managed to get permanent funding, the planting went on. By the time of World War II, they had planted 217 million trees on 232,212 acres surrounding 30,000 farms. (Thomas R. Wessel, "Roosevelt and the Great Plains Shelterbelt," *Great Plains Journal*, VIII:57–73, [January 1969].)

SHIPSTEAD, HENRICK Henrick Shipstead was born in Burbank, Minnesota, on January 8, 1881; and after graduating from the state college at St. Cloud, he went on to Northwestern University and received a degree in dentistry in 1903. Shipstead practiced dentistry in Glenwood, Minnesota, between 1904 and 1920 and became active in local politics, serving as mayor of Glenwood (1911–1913) and a term in the state legislature (1917). He moved to Minneapolis in 1920, practiced dentistry there for two years, and joined the budding Farmer-Labor political movement, where his progressive views about government-business relations found a comfortable home. In 1922 Shipstead won a seat in the United States Senate on the Farmer-Labor party* ticket. He was re-elected in 1928 and 1934, and during the New Deal* generally allied himself with the coalition of progressive Republicans and liberal Democrats in the Senate. Shipstead endorsed Franklin D. Roosevelt's* re-election in 1936* but began to distance himself from the New Deal later in the 1930s, opposing increases in relief spending and the executive reorganization plan. With the Farmer-Labor coalition disintegrating in the late 1930s, Shipstead declared himself a Republican and won re-election in 1940.* He was an unsuccessful candidate for renomination in 1946, retired from public service, and died on June 26, 1960. (*New York Times*, June 27, 1960.)

SHOUSE, JOUETT Jouett Shouse, a leading anti-New Deal Democrat during the 1930s, was born in Woodford County, Kentucky, on December 10, 1879. He attended the University of Missouri and the University of Miami, studied for the law, and entered private business in Lexington, Kentucky, between 1898 and 1911. In 1911 Shouse moved to Kansas to begin a career as a commercial farmer and stock raiser, served a term in the Kansas state legislature (1913–1915), and in 1914 was elected as a Democrat to Congress. He left Congress in 1919 and became assistant secretary of the treasury until late in 1920 when he returned to private law practice in Washington, D. C. Between 1928 and 1932 Shouse served as chairman of the Democratic National Executive Committee. Shouse supported Franklin D. Roosevelt* in 1932, but early in 1933 grew frightened of the New Deal.* Although a Democrat, Shouse's politics were quite conservative, and his philosophical views rested with the propertied, Wall-Street legal fraternity, not with those of poor, working-class people. Dismayed about the large-scale spending and massive bureaucracy of the early New Deal, Shouse became a founder of the anti-Roosevelt American Liberty League*; he served as president of the league from its inception in 1934 to its dissolution in 1940. During those years Shouse remained a sharp critic of the New Deal, supported

Alf Landon* in 1936 and Wendell Willkie* in 1940, and served as a spokesman for conservative business interests. After the demise of the league, Shouse continued his law practice, and died in Washington, D.C., on June 2, 1968. (*New York Times*, June 3, 1968; George Wolfskill, *The Revolt of the Conservatives: A History of the American Liberty League, 1934–1940*, 1962.)

"SICK CHICKEN CASE" (See SCHECHTER POULTRY CORPORATION V. UNITED STATES.)

SILVER PURCHASE ACT OF 1934 Despite the general prosperity of the 1920s, western mining and farming interests had suffered economically. Agricultural and metals prices declined while production costs climbed. The economic squeeze on producers of cotton, wheat, and silver was especially difficult and became disastrous during the 1930s. Western senators began demanding federal assistance, arguing that expanding the stock of monetary silver would ease the gold shortage, expand the money supply, increase the price of silver, and, as so many westerners believed, increase farm purchasing power because commodity prices were so closely tied to silver. Issuing silver certificates in exchange for silver bullion would provide employment in the mining industry. These arguments by such "silver senators" as Burton K. Wheeler* of Montana, Key Pittman* of Nevada, William Borah* of Idaho, and William King* of Utah attracted strong support from other congressmen in the West, South, and Midwest. Their demands verged on the radical. After 1932 Senator Wheeler was calling for free coinage of silver at the ratio of sixteen to one with gold, a throwback to the Populist days. Congressman Martin Dies* of Texas wanted the export of agricultural surpluses in exchange for silver. Congressman William Fiesinger of Ohio demanded the purchase of 50 million ounces of silver each month until 1 billion ounces had been acquired.

President Franklin D. Roosevelt* rejected such extreme proposals, but he did accept two measures to appease the "silver senators" as well as to supplement the "gold-buying"* theory of recovery—that by expanding the money supply and manipulating its value the federal government might be able to stimulate purchasing power. First, Roosevelt approved Senator Elmer Thomas'* amendment to the Agricultural Adjustment Act of 1933* authorizing the Treasury Department to exchange silver certificates for silver bullion. Roosevelt then ordered the purchase of all newly-mined domestic silver, ratifying the Silver Agreement of 1933 signed at the London Economic Conference.* Second, the president signed the Silver Purchase Act of 1934 which declared that the proportion of silver to gold in the monetary system should be increased until the monetary stock was one-third that of gold or until the market price of silver reached $1.29 per ounce; that the Treasury Department issue silver certificates to equal the amount paid for the silver; that the president could nationalize silver stocks at a price not to exceed $.50 per ounce; and that all profits above original costs on the transfer of silver carry a 50 percent tax.

The silver speculation did little to aid agriculture; indeed, it was a boon to silver producers but not to consumers, since silver prices rose in the absence of legitimate demand. President Roosevelt had no real commitment to the program. He was generally skeptical of the merits of monetary tinkering but had to appease the silver bloc. The silver program had unfortunate international consequences, for nations with a silver monetary system saw their bullion flowing to the United States and creating monetary crises at home. By 1935 most of the silver senators agreed to stabilize silver prices and stop the speculation generated by the Silver Purchase Act of 1934. (John A. Brennan, *Silver and the First New Deal*, 1969.)

SILVER SHIRTS Led by William Dudley Pelley, the Silver Shirts was one of the more prominent fascist organizations of the 1930s. Pelley was born in Massachusetts in 1890. After years of working for various newspapers he claimed to have died and gone to heaven for "seven minutes" in 1928, where he was told about the imminent rise to power of Adolf Hitler. He launched the Silver Shirts in 1933 after Hitler's installation as chancellor in Germany. In his magazine *Liberation*, Pelley and his Silver Shirts campaigned against the "Dutch Jew Franklin Rosenfelt" and the "Communist New Deal." He wrote that the New Deal* "has been naught but the political penetration of a predominantly Christian country and Christian government, by predatory, megalo-maniacal Israelites and their agents." In 1934 Pelley tried to promote a Silver Shirt march on Washington, but he got into legal difficulties in North Carolina over securities fraud. Pelley and the Silver Shirts remained faithfully pro-Hitler and anti-New Deal throughout the 1930s, and in 1942 Pelley was convicted of sedition. He spent the next eight years in federal penitentiaries, during which time the Silver Shirts disappeared. William Pelley died on July 1, 1965. (George Wolfskill and John A. Hudson, *All but the People. Franklin D. Roosevelt and His Critics, 1933–1939*, 1969.)

SIMPSON, JOHN John Simpson, leader of the National Farmers' Union,* was born in Salem, Nebraska, on July 4, 1871. He graduated from the University of Kansas in 1896 and then taught in the public schools for four years. He also worked as an accountant for the state of Nebraska. Simpson entered the banking business in 1907 and gradually became involved in local farm politics because of his association with marketing cooperatives. Simpson was elected president of the Oklahoma Farmers' Union in 1917, and he remained in that position until his election as president of the National Farmers' Union in 1931. Enraged about the plight of farmers during the 1920s, Simpson became an advocate of federal legislation guaranteeing prices providing for at least the "cost of production" and a "fair profit." Simpson resented the American Farm Bureau Federation* because he felt it represented the interests of large commercial farmers and agribusinesses, while the National Farmers' Union advocated the interests of family farmers. During the early 1930s, he supported the Agricultural Adjustment Act of 1933* but criticized the fact that its greatest benefactors were large commercial farmers. He also advocated legislation to relieve farmers of pressing mortgage and credit problems. While sympathetic to the demands of radical farm organizations like the National Farmers Holiday Association,* Simpson nevertheless kept the National Farmers' Union from endorsing the movement. John Simpson died on March 15, 1934. (William P. Tucker, "Populism Up-To-Date: The Story of the Farmers' Union," *Agricultural History*, XXI:198–208, 1947.)

SINCLAIR, UPTON BEALL Upton Sinclair was born September 20, 1878, in Baltimore, Maryland. He graduated from the City College of New York in 1897, supporting himelf as a freelance writer. In the literature of social criticism, Upton Sinclair remains an important novelist and a prominent historical figure. During his lifetime of ninety years, he wrote 90 books of fiction and nonfiction, as well as plays and countless articles, the bulk of which represent his socialist ideals and his vigorous criticism of venality and tyranny in American big business and government. *The Jungle* (1906), his exposé of the meatpacking industry, directly influenced the passing of the Pure Food and Drug Act. Although critics have often deprecated the lack of complexity in Sinclair's plots and characterizations, his best novels are praised for their graphic depiction of social and political abuses widely celebrated in their day. Such novels are *King Coal* (1917), about Colorado coal mining conditions; *Oil* (1927), tracing the Teapot Dome scandals of the Harding Administration; and *Boston* (1928), a bitter indictment of the Sacco-Vanzetti trial. Other novels that show the range of his targets of reform include *Metropolis* (1908), about upper-class New York society; *The Profits of Religion* (1918); *The Brass Check* (1920), about American journalism; *Mammonart* (1925), class bias in the arts; *The Flivver King: A Story of Ford America* (1937); and *Little Steel* (1938), stories of plutocracy and the suppression of organized labor.

Sinclair's dedication to socialism was the prime mover, if not the theme, of almost all his writing, especially that of the first five decades of his career. Although never a systematic political theorist, he was dedicated to economic justice and was sensitive to class hegemony. His ideals were more often romantic or Utopian than Marxist, his indictments of capitalism accompanied by highly generalized visions. Class conflicts, he believed, could be diffused and transposed into cooperative communities; plutocratic tyranny could be converted into altruistic reform. In the final chapters of *The Jungle*, Sinclair's tone is typically one of redemption and exhortation, when his protagonist Jurgis Rudkis converts to the Socialist dream. Although the novel's excellence derives from its realistic portrayal of the victimization of workers, Sinclair clearly avoids a polemical, vindictive tone.

During the 1930s Sinclair's foray into electoral politics was dramatic. Finding his socialism compatible with the Democratic party* in California, especially during the depression, he ran for governor of the state in 1934 with the slogan "End Poverty in California" (EPIC). His platform urged production for use, not for profit; an end to state unemployment by means of state-owned industrial co-ops; and confiscatory taxation of the wealthy. His personal style and indefatigability won him so impressive a following that Republican Frank Merriam was forced to wage a vicious press campaign in order to defeat him.

In 1936 Sinclair's novel *Co-op* converted his ideas of state-owned industrial co-ops into the fictional colony San Sebastian. Since he had been founder, in 1906, of his own much-publicized colony Helicon Hall (which burned during its first year) and later had been a resident of other co-operatives (three years at Arden, Delaware), Sinclair's enthusiasm for non-profit and equitable labor had certain veracity. *Co-op* also showed, however, that bureauratic ineptness could impede government support of such colonies, thus revealing Sinclair's balanced view of early New Deal* programs that were sometimes as ineffectual as they were ambitious.

Sinclair's largest readership was no doubt won by the "Lanny Budd" novels he published between 1940 and 1953. Beginning with *World's End*, the eleven-volume series traces the history of the world from 1913 to 1949 through the simplistic device of a world-travelling Lanny, who is a weathervane and news headliner for all major world events. Critically unsuccessful, the novels interpreted history in too simple a dichotomy of progressive and repressive "forces," but they show that Sinclair's appetite for the world's drama had a healthy longevity, as did his belief in an evolving democratic socialism of the future.

Winner of the Pultizer Prize in 1943 for his anti-fascist novel *Dragon's Teeth*, Upton Sinclair has always been respected for his influence on mass culture, less so for his artistic merit or social-political thought. He is classed with Frank Norris, Jack London, and Theodore Dreiser as one of the fathers of American social criticism; and his work influenced, by their own testimony, such leaders and spokesmen as Robert McNamara, Allen Ginsberg, Daniel P. Moynihan, Walter Cronkite, and Norman Mailer. In the 1960s two important additions to his prodigious body of work were *My Lifetime in Letters* (1960) and *The Autobiography of Upton Sinclair* (1962). Upton Sinclair died in 1968. (William A. Bloodsworth, Jr., *Upton Sinclair,* 1977; Leon Harris, *Upton Sinclair, American Rebel*, 1975.)

BARBARA M. TYSON

SLATTERY, HARRY Harry Slattery was born in Greenville, South Carolina, on June 13, 1887. Slattery attended Mt. St. Mary's College in Maryland, as well as Georgetown University and George Washington University; and in 1909 he became secretary to Gifford Pinchot, head of the U. S. Forest Service. An avid progressive and conservationist, Slattery served as Pinchot's secretary until 1912, leaving federal government service with his chief after the Ballinger-Pinchot controversy. Slattery then became secretary to the National Conservation Association and remained there until 1917 when he became special assistant to Franklin K. Lane, secretary of the interior in the Wilson administration. In 1918 he switched over to the staff of William Wilson, secretary of labor. During the 1920s, Slattery practiced law in Washington, D. C., and worked as general counsel to the National Boulder Dam Association and the National Conservation Committee. In 1931 Slattery became the Washington representative to the New York Power Authority. Over the years he had earned a great reputation as an advocate for public power and progressive regulation of utilities. In March 1933 Secretary of the Interior Harold Ickes* named Slattery as his personal assistant, a position Slattery maintained until 1938 when he became under secretary of the interior. In 1939 President Franklin D. Roosevelt* named Slattery as the new administrator of the Rural Electrification Administration* to fill the vacancy created by the resignation of John Carmody.* Slattery was an aggressive leader of the REA, and between June 1939 and the end of 1941 he almost doubled its loans to more than $434 million. Slattery resigned from the REA in 1944 and died on September 1, 1949. (*New York Times*, September 2, 1949.)

SLOAN, ALFRED PRITCHARD, JR. Born on May 23, 1875, in New Haven, Connecticut, Alfred P. Sloan, Jr., was a prominent corporation executive and philanthropist who headed General Motors during the New Deal* era. Graduating from MIT in 1895 with a degree in electrical engineering, Sloan joined the Hyatt Roller Bearing Company and became president and general manager in 1898 when his father purchased the firm. In 1909 Hyatt Roller Bearing Company became a supplier to both General Motors and Ford. General Motors formed United Motors Corporation in 1916 as a holding company for the purchase of firms making auto parts, and Sloan sold Hyatt to them. He then became president of United Motors and vice-president and director of General Motors. During 1919 and 1920, Sloan completed three internal reports recommending major changes in transfer pricing, capital budgeting, and organizational structure. When Pierre du Pont became president of General Motors in 1920 he quickly implemented the recommendations. The reorganization created autonomous operating divisions, producing and selling different makes of cars in vertically integrated activities, with delegated authority to act, coordinated by central staff units. Corporate management was freed to turn its attention to major policy and planning. The General Motors approach, still largely in place, is the basic pattern for large industrial firms today. In 1923 Sloan became president and chief executive officer of General Motors.

During the Great Depression, Sloan turned his attention to philanthropy and emerged as a major spokesman for the business community, expressing concern about the growth of the federal government. At the same time, many New Dealers focused on Sloan as an example of the incredible wealth existing in an impoverished America. Secretary of Commerce Daniel Roper* had recruited Sloan to serve on the Business Advisory Council* in 1933; but Sloan was among the more conservative businessmen, and in 1934, upset about the drift of the New Deal, he resigned from the council, along with John J. Raskob* and Pierre du Pont, to help form the American Liberty League.* In 1937 Sloan became chairman of the General Motors board. He retired as chief executive officer in 1946 and finally retired from the board in 1956. During his tenure of office, General

Motors grew from 25,000 to over 600,000 employees, from under 3,000 to over 1,000,000 shareholders; from 205,000 ($270 million) to over 5 million ($14.6 billion) unit sales annually; and from $100 million to $6.9 billion in total capital. Alfred Sloan died on February 17, 1966. (Alfred D. Chandler, Jr., *Giant Enterprise: Ford, General Motors, and the American Automobile Industry*, 1964; Kim McQuaid, ''The Frustration of Corporate Revival during the Early New Deal,'' *Historian*, XLI:682–704, 1979.)

DUANE WINDSOR

SMALL BUSINESS CONFERENCE OF 1938 (See NATIONAL SMALL BUSINESS MEN'S ASSOCIATION.)

SMITH, ALFRED EMMANUEL Born on December 30, 1873, in New York City, Al Smith grew up in the social atmosphere of immigrant Irish-America—Roman Catholic, hardworking, and Democratic. He was a devout Catholic and attended parochial school, but his father died in 1886 and Smith had to go to work in a variety of laboring jobs. He also became involved in the religion of politics in New York City's Fourth Ward. Smith dutifully performed the errands of ward politicians as a young man, and in 1903 he won a seat in the state assembly. He proved to be an excellent politician, solicitous of constituent needs, loyal to party leadership, and adept at legislative maneuvering. In 1911 he was named majority leader of the assembly and then Speaker of the Assembly in 1912. After the Triangle Shirtwaist fire of 1911, Smith became a vocal advocate of strong social welfare responsibilities for the government, including labor standards laws, child labor restrictions, workmen's compensation, and regulation of business monopolies. His political stature grew, and he won the governorship of New York in 1918, lost in 1920, and then won again in 1922, 1924, and 1926. There he presided over a reorganization of New York state government, a conservation program, a comprehensive housing program, workmen's compensation improvements, public health, limits on child labor, and public works jobs development. In the process, Al Smith became a national political figure.

He was a prominent candidate for the Democratic presidential nomination in 1924, representing the urban, ''wet,'' northern wing of the Democratic party,* struggling against the ''dry,'' southern and Klan-supported candidacy of William G. McAdoo.* Both of them eventually lost out to the dark horse, compromise candidacy of John W. Davis.* By 1928, however, the urban wing had come to dominate the Democratic party, and Smith won the nomination. But his Roman Catholicism, opposition to Prohibition, and immigrant sympathies, and the prevailing ''Republican prosperity'' cost him the election, putting Herbert Hoover* in the White House. Smith went into private business after the election but gradually grew resentful of Franklin D. Roosevelt's* growing status as the new governor of New York. He doubted Roosevelt's political convictions and wanted the presidential nomination again in 1932. But Roosevelt won the nomination and the presidency, and Smith drifted into alienation. As a 1920s liberal, he had fought for civil liberties, individual rights, freedom from government interference in people's lives, and against bureaucracy and Prohibition. By the 1930s, jealous of Roosevelt and appalled at the New Deal* bureaucracy, Smith began calling for repudiation of the New Deal, joining the American Liberty League* and endorsing Alf Landon* in 1936 and Wendell Willkie* in 1940. Alfred E. Smith died on October 4, 1944. (Oscar Handlin, *Al Smith and His America*, 1958.)

SMITH, BLACKWELL Blackwell Smith was born in Albuquerque, New Mexico, on April 4, 1904. He graduated from Pomona College in California in 1925 and then took a law degree at Columbia in 1929. After practicing law for four years with a leading Wall-Street firm, Smith came to Washington, D. C., to take control of the Legal Division of the National Recovery Administration.* There Smith had the responsibility for drafting all of the NRA industrial codes, a thankless and difficult task which Donald Richberg* was grateful to let him have. Smith rose quickly through the NRA bureaucracy, serving successively, between 1933 and 1935, as assistant general counsel, associate counsel, acting general counsel, assistant administrator for policy, legal adviser to the National Industrial Recovery Board,* and general counsel. During the latter part of 1934, Smith met weekly with President Franklin D. Roosevelt* to review the code-writing progress and to select cases of code violation for administrative action. Smith left the National Recovery Administration after the *Schechter** decision in 1935 and returned to private law practice. He came back to the federal government in 1940 as legal counsel to the Industrial Materials Division of the National Defense Advisory Commission, assistant director of priorities for the Office of Production Management (1941), and director of the urgency rating division of the War Production Board (1942–1943). Smith travelled to New Zealand as head of the Lend Lease Mission later in 1943 and then returned to private affairs. (Peter H. Irons, *The New Deal Lawyers*, 1982; *Who's Who In America*, II:2941,1972.)

SMITH COMMITTEE (See NATIONAL LABOR RELATIONS BOARD.)

SMITH, ELLISON DURANT Born in Lynchburg, South Carolina, on August 1, 1864, Ellison Durant Smith was raised in his native state and graduated from Wofford College. Since he grew up during Reconstruction, he remained throughout his life a prominent advocate of southern causes, especially the welfare of cotton farmers. Early in his career, Smith was active as a cotton farmer and as a farm organizer and played a major role in establishing the Southern Cotton Association in 1905, an important trade group. In fact, his support of cotton interests was so intense that he acquired the nickname "Cotton Ed" Smith, a term which followed him throughout his political career. A loyal southern Democrat, Smith served as a member of the House of Representatives of South Carolina from 1896 to 1900, and in 1908 he won election to the United States Senate. His tenure there was one of the longest in American history, for he won re-election six times.

During the 1930s, Smith gained the reputation as one of Franklin D. Roosevelt's* most bitter Democratic critics. His senatorial career had been maintained by consistent appeals to racial prejudice, class consciousness, and sectional pride; and he lived in the past. Smith proved unable to adjust to the rapid changes in public policy characteristic of the New Deal.* Until 1935 he was an irritant to most New Dealers; as chairman of the Senate Agriculture Committee, he enjoyed a great deal of power, but his opposition was rather limited. After 1935 Smith openly broke with the New Deal, opposing the Public Utility Holding Company Act,* denouncing the attempted ''court-packing''* scheme, and viewing all minimum wage and pro-union laws as bald attempts to destroy southern industry.

In the election of 1938,* Roosevelt decided to make Smith a prime target of his ''purge'' of disloyal Democrats. In May 1938 the president permitted South Carolina's Democratic Governor Olin Johnston, to denounce Smith from the steps of the White House. In the election, Roosevelt openly campaigned against Smith, channeled federal patronage away from him, and endorsed Johnston. But although personally popular in South Carolina, Roosevelt could not transfer his popularity to Johnston. In what many interpreted as a political backlash, Smith won the primary with 55 percent of the vote and naturally went on to win the general election. Many people even believed that had Roosevelt not intervened, Smith might have lost the primary. ''Cotton Ed'' Smith went on to serve another term in the Senate and was re-elected again in 1944, but he died on November 17, 1944. (James T. Patterson, *Congressional Conservatism and the New Deal*, 1967.)

SMITH, GERALD LYMAN KENNETH Gerald L. K. Smith was born in Pardeeville, Wisconsin, on February 27, 1898, to a third-generation circuit-riding minister of the Church of the Disciples of Christ. He graduated from Valparaiso University in 1917 and studied briefly at Butler University in Indianapolis. While living in Indiana, Smith became active in the Ku Klux Klan, protesting the mass immigration from Europe. He moved to Shreveport, Louisiana, in 1928 and became minister at the Kings Highway Christian Church. Sympathetic with the living conditions of poor, working peoole, Smith soon began attacking the wealth, corruption, and exploitation he saw in corporate America. When his attacks expanded to the utility companies headed by some of the rich people in his own congregation, his job came into jeopardy. Still, he enjoyed enough political influence in northern Louisiana to convince Governor Huey P. Long* to stop local realtors from foreclosing on the homes of destitute people. When Huey P. Long was elected to the United States Senate in 1930, Smith became his full-time assistant. He wrote speeches for Long and became the national organizer for the network of ''Share-Our-Wealth'' clubs. The ''Share-Our-Wealth'' movement was a Populist crusade to redistribute income and to build public projects as a means of employing people unable to find jobs elsewhere.

When Huey P. Long was assassinated in September 1935, Smith assumed command of the ''Share-Our-Wealth'' movement, but he had no political base in Louisiana and was unable to keep control. He had no influence with the Long machine, and his political opponents in Louisiana had him arrested and deported from Louisiana. For several months he tried to maintain a high public profile by making speeches on behalf of the presidential candidacy of Governor Eugene Talmadge* of Georgia. Afraid of Smith eclipsing his own popularity, Talmadge soon insisted that he leave the state. He then went to Washington, D. C., and by assisting Dr. Francis E. Townsend* during congressional hearings, he found a new political vehicle. Townsend's crusade for old-age pensions was becoming increasingly popular, and Smith and Townsend soon joined forces, as Smith said, to rid the country of the ''communist dictatorship in Washington.'' Smith was a bitter opponent of Franklin D. Roosevelt,* calling him ''Franklin Delano Jewsvelt.'' By 1936 Smith had joined the coalition of Father Charles Coughlin's* National Union for Social Justice, Townsend's Old-Age Revolving Pensions, Ltd., and the Share-Our-Wealth remnants to form the Union party.*

Smith's position of prominence in the Union party was short-lived. His bitter anti-Catholicism, matched only by his hatred for Jews, disturbed Father Coughlin, even though Smith tried to soft-peddle it for a while. What proved more disturbing to Coughlin, Townsend, and Union party presidential candidate William Lemke* was Smith's proto-fascism. In the fall of 1936 Smith began calling for an army of healthy, pro-American young men to ''seize the government of the United States.'' His group, the Committee of One Million, accused the New Deal* of being a Communist conspiracy to destroy American capitalism. Afraid of Smith's fascism, Coughlin, Townsend, and Lemke expelled him from the Union party.

Smith continued to tour the country giving speeches, secured 1 million signatures against American entry into World War II, organized the America First Party, and in 1942 began publishing a pro-fascist newspaper, *The Cross and the Flag*. The America First Party ran him as its presidential candidate in 1944. To realize his dream of a ''white, Christian America,'' Smith organized the Christian Nationalist Crusade in 1947, calling for deportation of all Jewish Zionists, destruction of Jewish organizations, shipment of blacks back to Africa, and dissolution of the United Nations. On the basis of his continuous appeals for funds from followers, Smith had accumulated a fortune by 1960. He moved to Eureka Springs, Arkansas, in 1965 and erected a seven-story statue of Jesus Christ which, along with an anti-Semitic passion play on the nearby mountain, attracts thousands of tourists each year. Gerald L. K. Smith died in Glendale, California, on April 15, 1976. (David H. Bennett, *Demagogues in the Depression. American Radicals and the Union Party, 1932–1936*, 1969.)

SMITH, HAROLD DEWEY Harold D. Smith was born in Haven, Kansas, on June 6, 1898. He graduated from the University of Kansas with a degree in engineering in 1922 and took a master's degree in public administration at the University of Michigan in 1925. Smith worked on the staff of the League of

Kansas Municipalities between 1925 and 1928 and was director of the Michigan Municipal League between 1928 and 1937. Smith then joined the Michigan state government as director of the state budget between 1937 and 1939 and then became director of the federal Bureau of the Budget* in 1939. Smith stayed in that position until 1946. He died on January 23, 1947. (*Who Was Who In America,* II:495, 1950.)

SMITH, HILDA WORTHINGTON Hilda Worthington Smith was born in 1888 and graduated from Bryn Mawr in 1910. She received a master's degree from Bryn Mawr in 1911 and then completed more graduate work at Columbia University and the New York School of Social Work. Smith was an active suffragette and during the 1920s worked as an academic dean at Bryn Mawr and founder of the Bryn Mawr Summer School for Industrial Workers. Between 1933 and 1943, she worked as director of the Workers' Service Program of the Federal Emergency Relief Administration* and then the Works Progress Administration.* She was also in charge of the FERA and WPA summer camps for unemployed women. In 1943 Smith left the WPA and joined the Federal Public Housing Authority. She retired from the federal government in 1945. (Susan Ware, *Beyond Suffrage: Women in the New Deal*, 1981.)

SMITH, HOWARD WORTH Howard Worth Smith, one of the most bitter Democratic opponents of the New Deal* during the 1930s, was born in Broad Run, Virginia, on February 2, 1883. Smith attended Bethel Military Academy and graduated from there in 1901. He then went on to the University of Virginia Law School, taking his degree in 1903. He practiced law privately between 1904 and 1917, served as an assistant general counsel with the office of the Alien Property Custodian in 1917 and 1918, and served as commonwealth attorney of Alexandria, Virginia, between 1918 and 1922. Smith was a judge of the corporation court of Alexandria from 1922 to 1928 and judge of the sixteenth judicial circuit of Virginia between 1928 and 1930. In 1930 he was elected as a Democrat to the House of Representatives and became a member of the Rules Committee in 1933. In Virginia politics, Smith was part of the Glass-Byrd machine and viewed himself as a true Jeffersonian Democrat—a believer in states rights and social conservatism. Smith resented the New Deal's support of labor organization, deficit spending, black rights, and social welfare; and he opposed most major New Deal legislation. Although he was very frustrating to President Franklin D. Roosevelt,* Smith's congressional district was considered the most "safe" in the country, so there was little hope of unseating him. New Dealers tried to do so in the election of 1938,* but Smith was renominated and re-elected. He attacked the executive reorganization plan in 1939, bitterly denounced deficit spending, and along with Martin Dies* of Texas launched a hostile investigation of the National Labor Relations Board.* Smith eventually became one of the most powerful congressmen in American history, serving in the House of Representatives from 1931 to his defeat in the election primary of 1966. Smith then retired from public life, and he lived in Alexandria, Virginia, until his death on October 3, 1976. (*New York Times*, October 4, 1976; James T. Patterson, *Congressional Conservatism and the New Deal*, 1967.)

SNELL, BERTRAND HOLLIS Bertrand H. Snell, House Republican leader during the 1930s, was born on December 9, 1870, in Colton, New York. Snell graduated from Amherst College in 1894, and went to work as a bookkeeper and then manager of the Racquette River Paper Company in Potsdam, New York. Snell became president of the York State Oil Company and then expanded his business interests into banking and insurance. In 1914 he was elected as a Republican to Congress, and he served in the House of Representatives from 1915 to his retirement in 1939. A typical critic of the New Deal,* Snell resented the size of the federal bureaucracy, the budget deficits, the waste on relief programs, and what he considered Franklin D. Roosevelt's* desire for power, manifested in the "court-packing"* proposal and the executive reorganization plan. After his retirement, Snell stayed active in local New York politics until his death on February 2, 1958. (*New York Times*, February 3, 1958.)

SOCIAL DEMOCRATIC FEDERATION The Social Democratic Federation was founded in 1936 when several people dissatisfied with the leadership of Norman Thomas* left the Socialist party of America.* The two early leaders of the Social Democratic Federation were Jasper McLevy, mayor of Bridgeport, Connecticut, and Algernon Lee, president of the Rand School of Social Science. The Social Democratic Federation called on all liberals, radicals, and socialists to merge and form a third party, but they had no more success than several other left-wing movements in forming a new third party during the 1930s. The Social Democratic Federation gradually declined during the 1940s and in 1956 merged back into the Socialist party of America. (Frank A. Warren, *Alternative Vision: The Socialist Party in the 1930s*, 1974.)

SOCIALIST LABOR PARTY Founded in 1877 in Newark, New Jersey, the Socialist Labor party was the first nationally organized Marxist party in the United States. Between 1890 and 1914 the SLP was dominated by Daniel DeLeon, a doctrinaire ideologue whose law degree combined with Marxist theories to produce a rigid approach to American industrial problems. Because DeLeon insisted the Marxist revolution must come only from a worker-dominated party independent of all other groups, the SLP was never really to make significant gains in even the Socialist community. In 1932, with the economy in a state of collapse, the Socialist Labor party was convinced that revolution was imminent. Verne L. Reynolds carried the SLP presidential banner, with John W. Aiken as his running mate, but they received only 34,028 votes. The New Deal* then undermined even that pitiful following, for in 1936 the SLP candidates—John W. Aiken for president and Emil F. Teichert for vice-president—received only 12,790 votes. In 1940 Aiken did little better, winning only 14,883 votes. The

American people were simply not interested in the Socialist message. (Edward L. Schapsmeier and Frederick H. Schapsmeier, *Political Parties and Civic Action Groups*, 1981.)

SOCIALIST PARTY OF AMERICA Founded in 1901 in Indianapolis, Indiana, the Socialist party eventually became the most prominent advocate of Marxism in the United States. The major figure behind the fusion of the Social Democratic party and a group of the Socialist Labor party* opposing Daniel DeLeon was Eugene V. Debs, former head of the American Railway Union. Debs dominated the Socialist party until his death in 1926, when Norman Thomas* succeeded him as the leader of the party and perennial candidate for president. Thomas accepted the presidential nomination of the Socialist party in 1928, and he ran for president every four years as the nominee until 1952. In the campaign of 1928, Thomas called for nationalization of major American industries, government ownership of all electrical utilities, the encouragement of cooperatives, withdrawal of American troops from Latin America, cancellation of all World War I debts, diplomatic recognition of the Soviet Union, and support of the Kellogg-Briand anti-war treaties. He polled 267,835 votes in the election which put Republican Herbert Hoover* in the White House.

The collapse of the economy in 1929 and its continuing slide gave Norman Thomas and the Socialist party of America a new hope that the people of the United States would finally take their message seriously. Seeing the Great Depression as the inevitable, Marxist-predicted collapse of capitalism, they offered socialism as the panacea. In the election of 1932,* Thomas campaigned on a platform demanding federal relief and public works; minimum wage and maximum hours legislation for workers; protection of labor unions and the right to bargain collectively; complete systems of unemployment, medical, and old-age insurance; government refinancing of farm and home mortgages; repeal of the Eighteenth Amendment; American entry into the League of Nations and the World Court; and arms reduction. Although Thomas and his running mate James Maurer conducted a vigorous campaign, they were disappointed when they received only 881,951 votes, about 2 percent of the total. Still, they had made great progress since 1928 and expected the future to be just as promising.

Franklin D. Roosevelt* and the New Deal* destroyed their dreams. Morris Hillquit, long-time national secretary of the Socialist party, died in 1933, precipitating serious internal struggles in the organization. The party's decision to welcome Communists and other radical groups into membership only exacerbated the bickering. But far more important, the New Deal's Federal Emergency Relief Administration,* Civilian Conservation Corps,* Public Works Administration,* Works Progress Administration* Social Security Act,* Agricultural Adjustment Act,* National Industrial Recovery Act,* National Labor Relations Act,* Public Utility Holding Company Act,* and Wealth Tax Act* stole much of the Socialist thunder, reducing the party in 1936 to claiming that the Socialist party had been first to demand much of what the New Deal had produced and to call for more relief spending, a thirty-hour workweek, foreign policy isolationism, and a guaranteed cost of production for farmers. Norman Thomas again was the presidential candidate, with George A. Nelson as his running mate. Claiming that the New Deal was bringing the nation closer to war while trying to save capitalism, Thomas and Nelson hoped to improve their 1932 results. But they were bitterly disappointed when the public gave them only 187,720 votes. By that time the welfare state of the New Deal had effectively destroyed much of the support the Socialist party ever had in the United States. During the presidential campaign of 1940, Thomas ran for president again on much the same platform as in 1936. His intense isolationism by then too was becoming a handicap as the public grew more and more threatened by events in Europe and Asia. In an election which saw Franklin D. Roosevelt win an unprecedented third term, Norman Thomas received only 99,557 votes for president, by far the lowest total in the history of the Socialist party of America. Norman Thomas was never able to overcome socialism's own internal squabbles, public suspicion of radical solutions to economic and social problems, and the widespread acceptance of the New Deal reforms. (David A. Shannon, *The Socialist Party of America*, 1955; Frank A. Warren, *An Alternative Vision: The Socialist Party in the 1930s*, 1974.)

SOCIALIST WORKERS PARTY The Socialist Workers party was founded in Chicago in 1938 by James P. Cannon, a Marxist and Trotskyite. When Joseph Stalin expelled Leon Trotsky from the Soviet Union, the American Communist party* expelled its own Trotskyites. James Cannon then founded the Socialist Workers Party to promote Marxism as interpreted by Leon Trotsky. The party proved to be radical, militant, ideological, and totally ineffective in the United States; its membership never increased beyond several hundred people. Between 1948 and 1980, they ran a presidential ticket in the four-year elections but never polled more than around 40,000 votes. Their program for world revolution fell on deaf ears in the United States. (Constance Ashton Myers, *The Prophets Army: Trotskyites in America, 1928–1941*, 1976.)

SOCIAL SECURITY ACT OF 1935 On August 14, 1935, President Franklin D. Roosevelt* signed the Social Security Act into law. The act created a Social Security Board to provide for unemployment compensation, old-age insurance, assistance to the destitute blind, and assistance for homeless, crippled, dependent, and delinquent children. The act established a cooperative federal-state system of unemployment compensation, financed by a federal tax on employer payrolls equal to 1 percent in 1936, 2 percent in 1937, and 3 percent thereafter. The program was administered by each state, which received a credit up to 90 percent of the federal tax. A program for old-age and survivor's insurance was financed by equal taxes on employers and employees of 1 percent in 1937 and increasing to 3 percent by 1949. The old-age and survivor's insurance was exclusively a federal program. A national fund would accumulate until January 1, 1942, when pensions would begin being paid to eligible people sixty-five years of age and over. Benefits ranged from $10 to $85 a month, depending on how many years the employee contributed to the program. The Social Security Act also provided for federal grants to states to assist them in meeting the cost of state old-age pension systems as well as payments to the blind and eligible children.

The origins of the Social Security Act reach back to the early twentieth century. German and English models of health, old-age, and unemployment insurance had emerged in the late nineteenth century, but the American social insurance movement was not really launched until the early 1900s. The American Association for Labor Legislation, led by people like John R. Commons* and Isaac M. Rubinow,* began calling for unemployment and old-age insurance as a means of income maintenance in industrial economies. By the 1920s compulsory unemployment insurance had spread throughout Europe, and bills were introduced to many American state legislatures. Wisconsin enacted an unemployment compensation program in 1932 using an AALL model with employer funds providing the resources. To some social insurance advocates like Isaac M. Rubinow, the Wisconsin plan was inadequate because it rested on too narrow a financial base. They preferred instead a federal program financed by general revenues as the best way of maintaining purchasing power during periods of economic decline. The AFL* endorsed unemployment insurance in 1932. By 1935 Wisconsin was the only state to have compulsory unemployment insurance.

The first state old-age pension programs of the early twentieth century were diverse and sporadic and usually confined to police, firemen, and teachers. By the late 1920s municipal retirement plans were universal for firemen and police, and teacher pension systems were common. Several states had comprehensive retirement systems for all state employees by the late 1920s, and by 1930 there were more than 400 corporate pension systems in the United States. Abraham Epstein* had founded the American Association for Old-Age Security in 1929 to campaign for a comprehensive federal insurance program. Like Isaac M. Rubinow on unemployment insurance, Epstein wanted the program to be comprehensive, compulsory, and funded out of general revenues as a means of sustaining purchasing power and redistributing income. During the 1920s several congressmen, including William P. Connery, Jr.,* of Massachusetts and Senator Clarence Dill of Washington, submitted old-age insurance bills to Congress, but they could not prevail against the popular bias in favor of voluntarism.

The onset of the Great Depression all but destroyed faith in voluntarism and generated even more intense demands for unemployment and old-age insurances. In June 1934 President Roosevelt established the Committee on Economic Security,* headed by Secretary of Labor Frances Perkins,* to develop a social insurance program. They studied the issue and quickly came to agree on a national system of contributory old-age and survivor's insurance. The Townsend movement's growing popularity, represented by Congressman John McGroarty's bill providing for monthly pensions of $200, helped them decide on a comprehensive old-age security system. The unemployment insurance question was more difficult because the administration was divided. National planners like Henry A.

Wallace* and Rexford Tugwell* wanted a uniform, national system, while the president favored the Wisconsin plan for a federal-state system. The committee ultimately endorsed the latter. In January 1935 Senator Robert Wagner* of New York and Congressman David Lewis of Maryland introduced the measure to Congress.

The bill encountered intense opposition from a variety of sources. Business conservatives argued that it was un-American, a "cradle to the grave" welfare measure leading the country down the road to socialism. Some southerners did not like the fact that blacks would also be eligible to receive pensions. More liberal followers of Francis Townsend* and Huey Long* felt the bill was too stingy, that it did not offer enough to old people. Social insurance advocates like Isaac M. Rubinow and Abraham Epstein bitterly criticized the federal-state nature of the unemployment provisions and the contributory method of financing benefits. In their view, such provisions would prevent the Social Security Act from maintaining purchasing power or redistributing income. Indeed, they found the regressive tax on payrolls counter-productive. Still, the public sentiment for some type of unemployment and old-age insurance was overwhelming, and the bill passed the House in April and the Senate in June. After conference committee hearings, Congress approved the bill and the president signed it on August 14, 1935. In the summer of 1939, a series of amendments then created the modern social security program for unemployment compensation and old-age insurance. The date for starting monthly payments was advanced to January 1, 1940; supplementary benefits were provided for aged wives; average wages replaced total wages as the means for determining the size of benefits; increased payroll taxes were postponed until 1943; the maximum federal grant for each destitute blind person and each aged person not covered by social security was increased by $15 to $20 per month; and the federal share of state aid to dependent children went from 33 percent to 50 percent of the amount granted to each individual. (Roy Lubove, *The Struggle for Social Security 1900–1935*, 1968.)

SOIL CONSERVATION ACT OF 1935 The severe droughts which devastated the Great Plains in 1934 and 1935 and the subsequent flooding and soil erosion led to demands for a federal program to deal with the problem. There was a Soil Conservation Service, headed by Hugh Hammond Bennett,* which functioned in the Department of the Interior; and in 1935, with passage of the Soil Conservation Act on April 27, Congress put it on a permanent basis and transferred it to the Department of Agriculture. The law also authorized the establishment of soil conservation districts throughout the country. With CCC* and WPA* labor, the soil conservation districts began providing a variety of programs to farmers, including research on wind and water erosion; model projects; land-use planning for general areas as well as for farms and ranches; financial and technical advice to farmers; loans or gifts of seed, supplies, and conservation equipment; removal of steep slopes from cultivation; use of grasses and thick-growing crops; implementation of strip cropping, terracing, and crop rotation;

and widespread wind and water control projects. The Soil Conservation Service, under Hugh Bennett's dynamic leadership, was one of the New Deal's* most successful programs. In October 1938 Secretary of Agriculture Henry Wallace* added substantially to its responsibilities, including the program to develop submarginal land under the Bankhead-Jones Farm Tenancy Act of 1937;* flood control programs under the Flood Control Act of 1936;* development of small-scale farm and range water storage facilities under the Water Facilities Act of 1937; and the farm forestry work of the Farm Forestry Act of 1937. (Richard Lowitt, *The New Deal and the West*, 1984.)

SOIL CONSERVATION AND DOMESTIC ALLOTMENT ACT OF 1936 By the early 1930s, the ideas of Professors John Black* and Milburn Wilson,* who advocated raising farm prices through acreage and production reductions, were becoming increasingly popular among agricultural economists. With passage of the Agricultural Adjustment Act of 1933,* the "domestic allotment plan"* received congressional and bureaucratic life. But on January 6, 1936, in the *U. S. v. Butler** decision, the Supreme Court* invalidated the Agricultural Adjustment Act because of its federal controls on farm production and the processors' tax which financed the acreage reductions. Enraged about the latest Supreme Court assault on the New Deal,* the Roosevelt administration immediately responded with new legislation. Congress rushed the Soil Conservation and Domestic Allotment Act through committee to the floor of both houses, and President Franklin D. Roosevelt* signed the measure on February 29, 1936. Because of the quick passage of the new law, most farmers did not miss a check from the Department of Agriculture.

Although the Soil Conservation and Domestic Allotment Act was full of reassurances that it was not designed to discourage agricultural production, it was still a rather carelessly veiled attempt to keep acreage out of production. It also differed from the early Agricultural Adjustment Act in its provision that congressionally-appropriated funds, rather than a processing tax, would finance the "soil conservation." Two payments were provided to farmers. One was an allotment payment which could be made for not growing "soil-depleting" crops such as corn, cotton, tobacco, and wheat. Instead, farmers were to raise on AAA-idled acres a "soil-conserving" crop like grasses, clover, or hay. The second payment, known as an Agricultural Conservation Payment, was to provide farmers with money to purchase lime, potash, and phosphate fertilizers to restore fertility or money for terracing and anti-erosion measures. Farmers were invited to participate. Payments averaged about $10 an acre for taking land out of production, and soil-depleting crops were usually those found in surplus quantities. The law also provided $500 million to finance the "soil conservation."

The Soil Conservation and Domestic Allotment Act did not succeed in restricting production. Actual acreage planted increased, for many farmers simply took their poorest, marginal land out of production and increased yields on their better land. The combination of production increases in 1937 as well as the price collapse of 1938 led to new legislation, the Agricultural Adjustment Act of 1938.* (Dean Albertson, *Roosevelt's Farmer. Claude R. Wickard and the New Deal*, 1961.)

SOKOLOFF, NIKOLAI Born in Russia in 1886, Nikolai Sokoloff was a child prodigy, playing the violin in 1896 with the Kiev Municipal Orchestra under the musical direction of his father. He immigrated to the United States when he was twelve, and the next year he won a scholarship to study violin at the Yale University School of Music. After studying at Yale for three years, Sokoloff became a violinist for the Boston Symphony Orchestra. In 1920, already enjoying a national reputation, Sokoloff took the position of director of the Cleveland Orchestra, where he stayed for fifteen years until becoming director of the Federal Music Project* of the Works Progress Administration.* By that time, he was known not only as a gifted musician but as an advocate of music education in the public schools. Committed to technical artistry as well as mass appeal, Nikolai Sokoloff made the Federal Music Project the most artistically successful of the WPA professional programs. In the end, he probably became too concerned with technical artistry and performance. He tended to be disinterested in non-orchestral music and did not really spend enough time developing orchestral programs in areas where none had existed. In cities like New York where great orchestral talent existed, he expanded their programs and musical education associated with them. But he did not encourage music education as an amateur activity. As a result, the FMP was strong on orchestral performance but weak on community music development. It was not until 1939, when Sokoloff left the Federal Music Project and it was transferred to state control, that the project under the direction of Earl Vincent Moore began to emphasize community music education and amateur music development. Nikolai Sokoloff died in La Jolla, California, on September 24, 1965. (William F. McDonald, *Federal Relief Administration and the Arts*, 1969; *New York Times*, October 11, 1965.)

SOUTHERN TENANT FARMERS' UNION Rural poverty was catastrophic during the 1930s, and the Southern Tenant Farmers' Union began in the cotton fields of the Arkansas Delta where the misuse of the Agricultural Adjustment Act of 1933* was particularly widespread. Under the AAA,* cotton planters were paid 3 1/2¢ per pound of the average yield for every acre removed from production. In addition, the planter received 1¢ per pound as a parity* price. Half of this price was to be shared with his tenant. Thus the planter received 4¢ out of the 4 1/2¢ paid by the government. For example, on a farm producing 200 pounds of cotton per acre at 5¢ per pound, the owner and his sharecropper would each realize $5.00 an acre from the sale of the cotton. Under the AAA, the planter received $8.00 and the sharecropper received 50¢ for each acre taken out of production. From 1932 to 1934 one planter increased his gross income from $51,000 to $102,200. Unfortunately, many of the planters found ways to defraud the poor sharecropper and tenants of all payments, forcing them to live on what they could make from the cotton left in production. Compounding the problem was the fact that reduced cotton acreage also reduced the number of tenants required for production. Although difficult to document, it has been estimated that 20 percent of all sharecroppers and tenants were displaced as a result of the AAA program. There was little that the unorganized and often illiterate cropper could do to correct these injustices.

In the midst of suffering and displacement, two young men arose to speak for the tenants and croppers, Henry Clay East, a gasoline station owner in Tyronza, Arkansas, and Harry Leland Mitchell, owner of a dry cleaning establishment next door to East's station. In 1932 East and Mitchell organized a small Socialist group in Tyronza that evolved into the Southern Tenant Farmers' Union. The credit for the idea of creating the STFU goes, however, to Norman Thomas* who originally made the suggestion to East.

The STFU was formally organized on July 26, 1934, in Searcy, Arkansas. This small group held widely divergent opinions as to what form their union should take. Some wanted a brownshirted fascist military organization, while others wanted a planter-controlled company union. Mitchell and East eventually directed the STFU into focusing on the AAA. Blacks as well as whites were welcomed into the union, but at first they were segregated into individual locals organized along racial lines. Black leaders such as Edward Britt McKinney soon gained widespread respect among white members. This respect led to the joining of the two segregated locals in Marked Tree, Arkansas.

At first the union engaged in little more than letter-writing campaigns to government agencies and prominent individuals. It did, however, serve as a collection point for evidence and complaints against planters who abused the provisions of the AAA. The mere existence of such an organization soon brought a reaction by the planters. Union members were arrested on charges of anarchy, while nightriders riddled their homes with gunfire. Some members were murdered, while others simply disappeared.

The most successful accomplishment of the STFU occurred during the summer of 1935, when its members struck for higher wages for picking cotton. The strike, at the height of picking season, came as a complete surprise to the planters. The planters, unable or unwilling to delay the sale of their cotton, quickly settled with the STFU. Under the terms of the settlement, pickers wages were increased from 41¢ to 75¢ for each 100 pounds. The strike was settled, but the violence continued.

One incident more than any other brought the STFU's struggle to national prominence. When a group of planters spanked the bottom of Memphis socialite Willie Sue Blagdon for her participation in STFU affairs, southern newspapers were enraged. Beating a white woman was going too far. Ironically, it was this event and not the beating or killing of blacks which brought on a national outcry for action on the behalf of the tenants. President Franklin D. Roosevelt* announced that he was appointing a special commission on farm tenancy. An embarrassed AAA very quietly asked the FBI* to investigate the situation. The STFU suddenly became a celebrated cause.

The principal outgrowth of the investigations was an admission that something had to be done about the tenant problem. No one, however, could agree on a solution. Senator John Bankhead* and Representative J. Marvin Jones* introduced a bill that, had it been left in its original form, would have provided loans for homes and farm land. Although the bill had Roosevelt's support, Congress balked at the cost and trimmed the measure down to the point that it would have taken over 1,000 years to help purchase small farms for the approximately 3 million tenants and sharecroppers. The resulting Bankhead-Jones Farm Tenancy Act of 1937* did however lead to the creation of the Farm Security Administration.* This agency was to administer the Bankhead-Jones Act, but more interesting was its experimentation in the establishment of cooperative farms.

Just when the STFU looked as if it might become a power to be reckoned with, a number of events occurred which spelled its demise. The first disaster to befall the STFU was a membership split over which faction to support in the feud between the United Cannery, Agricultural, Packing, and Allied Workers of America (a part of the Congress of Industrial Organizations) and John L. Lewis* of the CIO.* The Communists within the STFU favored affiliation with UCAPWA, and the Socialists demanded affiliation directly with the CIO. This split was its undoing, and the outbreak of World War II was the final stroke. By 1943 the STFU was dead.

Historian and STFU expert, Donald H. Grubbs, placed this organization in the best historical perspective when he theorized that had something been done to give displaced tenants meaningful employment during the late 1930s, the anguish of Harlem and Watts in the decades to come might have been averted. (David E. Conrad, *The Forgotten Farmers: The Story of Sharecroppers in the New Deal*, 1965; Donald H. Grubbs, *Cry From the Cotton: The Southern Tenant Farmers' Union and the New Deal*, 1971.)

DAVID L. CHAPMAN

SPECIAL COMMITTEE ON FARM TENANCY In November 1936, because of continuing economic problems on the farm and the displacement of tenant farmers in the South as a result of AAA* acreage reductions, President Franklin D. Roosevelt* created the Special Committee on Farm Tenancy, under the chairmanship of Secretary of Agriculture Henry A. Wallace.* At the urging of Rexford Tugwell,* head of the Resettlement Administration,* Wallace toured the South and came back astounded at the extent of rural poverty in the United States. The special committee made its report to the president in February 1937, and Congress responded with the Bankhead-Jones Farm Tenancy Act of 1937* and creation of the Farm Security Administration.* (Samuel I. Rosenman, ed., *The Public Papers and Addresses of Franklin D. Roosevelt*, VI:81–85, 1941.)

SPRAGUE, OLIVER MITCHELL WENTWORTH O. M. W. Sprague was born in Somerville, Massachusetts, on April 22, 1873. He took all of his degrees at Harvard (A. B., 1894; A. M., 1895; Ph.D., 1897) and then joined the economics faculty there. Sprague became the Edmund Cogswell Converse Professor of Banking and Finance at Harvard in 1913 and held that position until 1941. Sprague had taught economics to Franklin D. Roosevelt* during the president's undergraduate days, and in June 1933 Secretary of the Treasury Henry Morgenthau, Jr.,* hired him as an adviser and executive assistant. Although Sprague was sympathetic to much of the New Deal* program, he seriously questioned the economic theories of George Warren* and therefore took exception to the gold-buying program* of the fall of 1933. Roosevelt lost patience with Sprague, concluded that he was a tool of large, eastern financial interests, and essentially forced his resignation. Sprague left the Treasury Department staff on November 22, 1933, and returned to the Harvard economics faculty. He retired from Harvard in 1941. Sprague was the author of several books, including *History of Crises Under the National Banking System* (1910), *Banking Reform in the United States* (1911), *Theory and History of Banking* (1929), and *Common Sense* (1934). Oliver Sprague died on May 24, 1953. (*New York Times*, May 25, 1953.)

STEAGALL, HENRY BASCOM Henry B. Steagall was born in Clopton, Alabama, on May 19, 1873. After taking a law degree at the University of Alabama in 1893, he practiced law in Ozark, Alabama. Imbued with Populist values, Steagall was a devoted Democrat and follower of William Jennings Bryan. In 1898 Governor Joseph Johnston appointed him county solicitor, and Steagall served one term in the Alabama legislature in 1906–1907 where he accumulated a record as a progressive. In 1914 Steagall was elected to the 64th Congress, and his seat was never seriously threatened from that time until his death twenty-eight years later.

Steagall was assigned to the House Committee on Banking and Currency, a natural forum for his concerns with bank regulation and the extension of rural credits and other assistance to his farmer constituents. He was an early proponent of federal deposit insurance, which several states tried unsuccessfully to implement during the 1920s. When the Democrats won control of Congress in 1930, Steagall became chairman of the committee and cooperated with Herbert Hoover's* administration to secure emergency legislation creating the Reconstruction Finance Corporation.* Finding that administration measures seemed too limited to secure economic recovery, he sponsored the Glass-Steagall Act of 1932, which broadened the acceptability of commercial paper for rediscount in the Federal Reserve System.

Steagall supported the presidential candidacy of Franklin D. Roosevelt* in 1932 and then established a personal rapport with the new president. Steagall helped rush through the Emergency Banking Act of 1933,* and after the crisis passed, sponsored the Glass-Steagall Banking Act* as a step toward reforming the banking system. In part, this reform was to be achieved through Steagall's long-advocated federal insurance of bank deposits: the bill provided for creation of the Federal Deposit Insurance Corporation.* Although the American Bankers'

Association opposed the measure, it proved effective in protecting depositors and creating confidence in the banking system.

Party loyalty led Steagall to support most administration measures, although sometimes reluctantly. Convinced that government aid for housing programs was socialistic and that such programs would benefit only urban communities, he did not vote Senator Robert Wagner's* housing bills out of committee in 1935 and 1936. However, in 1937 he responded to Roosevelt's urging and released the Wagner-Steagall Housing Act* for passage.

During his remaining years in Congress, Steagall devoted attention to agricultural matters, supporting the Bankhead-Jones Farm Tenancy Act of 1937,* maintaining close ties with the American Farm Bureau Federation,* and working to ensure that wartime economic controls did not have an adverse effect on prices for farm products. He died on November 22, 1943. (Jack Brien Key, "Henry B. Steagall: The Conservative as Reformer," *Alabama Review*, XVII:198–209, 1964.)

JANE A. ROSENBERG

STEINBECK, JOHN Born in 1902 in Salinas, California, John Steinbeck attended Stanford University off and on between 1920 and 1925. After a brief stint working and writing in New York, he returned to California and in 1929 published his first novel, *A Cup of Gold*, a romantic, quasi-historical melodrama about the Caribbean exploits of Sir Henry Morgan. In 1935 he achieved success with the publication of *Tortilla Flat*, a humorous novel about the paisanos of Monterey which satirizes middle-class values. His fiction then took a proletarian turn as he began to focus on the struggles between large farms and underpaid farm workers. Steinbeck had been introduced to one of the officials of the Communist-dominated Cannery and Agricultural Workers' Industrial Union by the well-known leader of the American muckraker movement, Lincoln Steffens. His interviews with this official and his contact with other farm-labor organizers in the Salinas area furnished material for *In Dubious Battle* (1936), considered by many the finest American strike novel. Although the work drew some criticism from doctrinaire radicals for its unflattering portrayal of Communist organizers who cynically exploit workers' miseries for their own political ends and from conservatives for its indictment of greedy growers resorting to vigilante violence to deny workers decent pay, it was more widely acclaimed by commentators from both the political left and right as even-handed.

In a more lyrical work—his short novel *Of Mice and Men* (1937)—Steinbeck depicts two itinerant California ranch workers, one of them retarded, whose impoverishment and hard work is made bearable through their modest dream of farming their own small plot of land. Just when the pair appear on the verge of realizing their dream, the moronic partner, in a state of befuddlement, strangles the flirtatious wife of a ranch boss's son, and his friend shoots him to forestall a lynching.

Shortly before *Of Mice and Men* was published, Steinbeck, intending to write a series of newspaper articles, had begun travelling up and down California's

Central Valley, visiting the squalid camps and shanty towns of migrant farm laborers. Mostly former inhabitants of southern Great Plains states who had lost their farms and businesses to drought and economic depression, these workers and their families were lured to California during the 1930s by promises of agricultural jobs. Unfortunately, they had arrived in such numbers that those who found jobs were lucky to receive subsistence wages. Dismayed by the workers' misery and disgusted by the growers exploitation of it, Steinbeck soon determined to treat the problem in a novel which would focus on the tribulations of a typical immigrant family and the social conditions which cause them. The result was *The Grapes of Wrath*, the publication of which in 1939 was a national cause célèbre. Praised by literary critics and liberals and condemned by such disparate factions as the California growers' associations and Oklahoma Chambers of Commerce (who believed that their state, the homeland of the central family of the novel, had been defamed), Steinbeck once again found himself the cynosure of a political storm.

By the summer of 1940 Steinbeck felt secure enough as a literary luminary to write a letter to President Franklin D. Roosevelt* requesting a personal meeting. He wanted to alert the president to the dangers of Nazi Bund activities in Latin America. They met briefly on June 26, 1940. After Pearl Harbor, Steinbeck worked in various government information and intelligence agencies, including the Writers' War Board, the Office of War Information, and the Office of Strategic Services. He aided the war effort by contributing two book-length works of propaganda: *Bombs Away: The Story of a Bomber Team* and *The Moon is Down*, both published in 1942.

From the end of the war until his death in December 1968, Steinbeck published stories, travelogues, film scripts, plays, and a number of novels—some of them best-sellers. But the consensus of critical opinion is that his postwar period was one of decline, his 1962 Nobel Prize notwithstanding. Steinbeck's career, in fact, closely paralleled the New Deal:* it began in the early 1930s, reached its zenith at the end of the decade, and began to decline during the war. Moreover, the best of Steinbeck's work—the social realism he wrote between 1936 and 1939—affirms the basic New Deal principles of equal justice and shares its commitment to humanitarian reform. (Jackson J. Benson, *The True Adventures of John Steinbeck, Writer,* 1984; Warren French, *John Steinbeck*, 1961; Thomas Kiernan, *The Intricate Music: A Biography of John Steinbeck*, 1979.)

DONALD V. COERS

STEPHENS, HAROLD MONTELLE Harold M. Stephens was born on March 6, 1886, in Crete, Nebraska. He attended the University of Utah between 1904 and 1906 but graduated from Cornell University in 1909. Stephens then attended the Harvard Law School and came to the attention of Felix Frankfurter.* He graduated from Harvard in 1913. Openly seeking a federal judicial appointment, Stephens practiced law in Salt Lake City and then Los Angeles between 1912 and 1933. At Frankfurter's suggestion, President Franklin D. Roosevelt* appointed Stephens assistant attorney general with control over the Anti-trust Division in 1933. Under his stewardship, the division did little, primarily because Stephens hated litigation and because the National Industrial Recovery Act of 1933* had virtually suspended the anti-trust laws and left the division without much power. Eventually, because he did not like litigation and because he worried about other government agencies pre-empting the Department of Justice in their own formation of administrative law, Stephens became a critic of the National Recovery Administration,* the Agricultural Adjustment Administration,* and the National Labor Relations Board.* His criticism was primarily internal, but because of his views, Roosevelt removed him in 1935 by appointing him associate justice of the U.S. Court of Appeals for the District of Columbia. Stephens remained there until 1948, when President * Harry S Truman appointed him chief justice of that court. Harold M. Stephens died on May 28, 1955. (Peter Irons, *The New Deal Lawyers*, 1982; *Who Was Who In America*, III:817, 1960.)

STERN, ROBERT Robert Stern was born in New York City in 1908. After graduating from Williams College in 1929, he took a law degree from Harvard in 1932. Stern began his career with the Petroleum Administrative Board* in 1933 where he worked on the ''hot oil'' cases. In 1934 he moved to the Justice Department and joined the staff of the Anti-trust Division. Stern's 1934 article ''That Commerce Which Concerns More States than One'' in the *Harvard Law Review* proved to be very influential and was widely circulated among government lawyers in the major New Deal* agencies. In the article, Stern argued that the courts would have to abandon their mechanical view of commerce as the simple movement of goods to a more fluid concept emphasizing the effect of local practices and institutions on a highly integrated national economy. Stern also worked closely with the staff of the solicitor general's office preparing briefs on commerce cases. Stern formally joined the solicitor general's staff in 1941 when Charles Fahy* received that appointment. Stern left government service in 1954 to join the Chicago law firm of Mayer, Brown, and Platt. (Peter H. Irons, *The New Deal Lawyers*, 1982; Katie Louchheim, ed., *The Making of the New Deal. The Insiders Speak*, 1983.)

STETTINIUS, EDWARD REILLY, JR. Edward R. Stettinius, Jr., was born on October 22, 1900, in Chicago. His father was Edward R. Stettinius, Sr., a business partner of J. P. Morgan. Edward R. Stettinius, Jr., attended the University of Virginia, but just prior to graduating in 1924 he took a position as a stock clerk with Hyatt Roller Bearings, a division of General Motors. He soon rose to the position of administrative assistant to General Motors President Alfred P. Sloan, Jr.* In May 1931 Stettinius became vice-president of General Motors. He was also an outspoken supporter of Franklin D. Roosevelt's* presidential campaign in 1932. After Hugh Johnson* became director of the National Recovery Administration,* Roosevelt asked Stettinius to serve as chief liaison between the NRA and American business. His major objective was to secure business support for the codes of the National Recovery Administration. Within a few months, Roosevelt named Stettinius to a position on the policy board of the National Recovery Administration. During the fall of 1934, Stettinius resigned from the policy board and took a post with the United States Steel Corporation as vice-president of its finance committee. President Roosevelt, convinced that Stettinius' presence in the New Deal* was critically important, prevailed on him in October 1934 to serve as a special adviser to the policy board. Stettinius accepted the advisory role and at the same time helped revive U. S. Steel's finances. Although the business response to the New Deal deteriorated over the years, Stettinius' loyalty was consistent. He brought to the New Deal a credibility among businessmen it could not have achieved in another way. His reputation for business acumen did not decline. At the end of 1937 the able industrialist was named as chairman of the U. S. Steel Corporation finance committee. Throughout 1938 he continued to increase the economic power of U. S. Steel and to advise the president on industrial policy.

Events in Europe, however, eventually brought Stettinius back into government service. In 1939 he took the post of chairman of the War Resources Board (1939–1940), directing the stockpiling of key materials. In 1940 President Roosevelt appointed him as a member of the National Defense Advisory Commission (1940–1941). The attack on Pearl Harbor in December 1941 thrust the United States into World War II, and Roosevelt consequently restructured the government to meet the challenge. In 1941 Stettinius was named director of priorities in the Office of Production Management and later in that same year he took over the administration of Lend-Lease. Stettinius fulfilled both assignments for President Roosevelt with much foresight and dedication. Stettinius then entered the State Department in 1943 and quickly reorganized its administration to make it more efficient. On December 1, 1944, he succeeded Cordell Hull* as secretary of state. During his tenure as secretary of state, Stettinius' major contribution was promoting the creation of the United Nations. He headed the United States delegation to the Dumbarton Oaks Conference (1944), accompanied the president to Yalta (1945), and signed the Act of Chapultepec (1945). Stettinius subsequently led the United States delegation to the San Francisco Conference (1945). He departed from the State Department in July 1945 and became the chairman of the United Nations Preparatory Commission. After 1946 Stettinius retired to private life and on October 31, 1949, he died of a coronary thrombosis in Greenwich, Connecticut. (William E. Leuchtenburg, *Franklin D. Roosevelt and the New Deal, 1932–1940*,1963; *New York Times*, November 1, 1949; Daniel Yergin, *The Shattered Peace*, 1979.)

JOHN S. LEIBY

STIMSON, HENRY LEWIS Born on September 21, 1867, in New York City, Henry L. Stimson was raised amidst material plenty. His grandfather, Henry C. Stimson, was a prominent Wall-Street financier, and his father, Lewis Stimson, a well-known surgeon. Henry L. Stimson attended private schools, including

Phillips Academy in Andover, Massachusetts, and then Yale University, where he graduated in 1888. He went on to the Harvard Law School, finally joining the law firm of Elihu Root in New York City in 1901. During the 1890s, Stimson became engaged in reform politics as a Republican, focusing most of his energies on reducing the power of the urban machines. Elihu Root had gone to Washington D. C., as secretary of war in 1899, so Stimson had friends in high places. His reputation as a progressive also served him well, and in 1906 President Theodore Roosevelt appointed him United States district attorney for the southern district of New York. He came to view a strong central government as the most effective tool in regulating the industrial establishment. In 1911 Stimson accepted President William Howard Taft's appointment as secretary of war. With the triumph of Woodrow Wilson and the Democrats in 1912, he returned to private law practice in New York.

During the 1920s, Stimson served as a foreign policy observer to the Philippines and Nicaragua, and in 1927 President Calvin Coolidge appointed him governor general of the Philippines. He served there until 1929 when newly elected President Herbert Hoover* named him secretary of state. When Japan invaded Manchuria in 1931, Stimson urged a policy of restraint as well as non-recognition of the puppet government there, an approach which became known as the Stimson Doctrine. During the years of the New Deal,* Stimson had a sympathetic attitude toward Franklin D. Roosevelt's* goals, publicly supporting him on the Reciprocal Trade Agreements Act* while privately criticizing the bureaucratic operations of the Securities Act of 1933* and the National Recovery Administration.* He opposed the Neutrality Acts of the 1930s and worried about the prevailing isolationist sentiments in the United States. To bolster his re-election bid in 1940, President Franklin D. Roosevelt named Stimson secretary of war, a post he held until 1945. Henry L. Stimson died on October 20, 1950 of heart failure. (Elting E. Morison, *Turmoil and Tradition. A Study of the Life and Times of Henry L. Stimson,* 1964.)

STONE, HARLAN FISKE Harlan Fiske Stone, the eleventh chief justice of the Supreme Court,* was born in Chesterfield, New Hampshire, on October 11, 1872. He graduated from Amherst College in 1894 and from the Columbia University Law School in 1898. Stone came from a Republican political tradition, but he developed a flexible pragmatism which later characterized his years on the Supreme Court. He opened a law practice in New York City and became a member of the Columbia law faculty in 1899. He was appointed dean of the law school in 1910 and served there until 1923. President Calvin Coolidge, amidst the wake of the Harding political scandals, appointed Stone as attorney general of the United States in 1924, and Stone quickly undertook a reform of the Federal Bureau of Investigation,* appointing J. Edgar Hoover as acting director to replace William J. Burns. Stone also helped reform the federal prison system and the Alien Property Custodian's office. In the process, he gained a national reputation as a loyal Republican with impeccable credentials for honesty and scholarship. President Coolidge named him to replace Justice Joseph McKenna on the Supreme Court in 1925.

Stone's judicial philosophy was well-developed by the mid-1920s. At Columbia University he had developed a reputation as a defender of civil liberties and as a believer in "sociological jurisprudence"—the conviction that the law must adjust to changing social and economic conditions. A Victorian liberal by instinct and sympathy, Stone resented the rigid, legal formalism of the conservative justices during the 1920s. He came to feel the Court was too zealous in protecting property rights from legislative encroachment of Congress and state legislatures. Indeed, Stone viewed the Constitution as a living document subject to changing interpretation. It was not a product of rigid judicial formulas. By the late 1920s and early 1930s Stone was clearly identified with Justices Oliver Wendell Holmes, Jr., and Louis Brandeis* as the "liberal minority" on the Supreme Court.

Although a close personal friend of President Herbert Hoover,* Stone grew impatient during the early years of the Great Depression with Republican conservatism. He hated laissez-faire economic principles in the face of massive social and economic dislocation, nor did he agree with the majority decisions of the Court invalidating many state taxation and regulatory statutes in the 1920s. In his view, state legislatures did not automatically violate Fifth Amendment property rights by passing progressive tax laws. During the years of the New Deal,* Stone generally sympathized with the governmental activism of the Roosevelt administration, even though he sometimes disliked specific measures, such as the currency tinkering of 1933. He also felt Franklin D. Roosevelt* was a terrible administrator. On the court, Stone regularly sided with Louis Brandeis and Benjamin Cardozo,* who had replaced Holmes in 1932, but they were usually a minority of three in the early New Deal. When the court assaulted the New Deal by invalidating the AAA* and NRA,* Stone was outraged at the presumptuousness of the conservative justices, for their willingness to prevent the federal government from dealing economically with the depression. During the "court-packing"* dispute of 1937, Stone took a curiously neutral role. Roosevelt eagerly used his written dissents to show how narrow-minded the Court had been in the early 1930s; and although Stone did not like the idea of expanding the Court, he welcomed the switch in loyalties of Chief Justice Charles Evans Hughes* and Justice Owen Roberts,* which frequently put Stone, Brandeis, and Cardozo in the majority in upholding New Deal legislation after 1937. President Roosevelt named Stone chief justice in 1941, and he served until his death on April 22, 1946. (Alpheus Thomas Mason, *Harlan Fiske Stone: Pillar of the Law*, 1956.)

SUBSISTENCE HOMESTEAD DIVISION By the early 1930s, because of cultural tension over the place of the city in American life, large numbers of people had joined the "back-to-the-land" movement, a naive dream about the possibility of creating homestead communities where the mystique of landed villages could survive. In the New Deal,* people like Franklin D. Roosevelt,*

Eleanor Roosevelt,* Henry Wallace,* and Rexford Tugwell* became enamored with the idea. In 1933 the president asked Senator John H. Bankhead* of Alabama to write a small section of the National Industrial Recovery Act* providing $25 million to relocate urban families on the farms. The proposal became part of Title II of the NIRA, under Secretary of the Interior Harold Ickes* and the Public Works Administration.* Ickes set up a Subsistence Homestead Division in the PWA and appointed M. L. Wilson* to head the agency. Wilson hoped to relocate 25,000 city families or farm families living on submarginal land. With limited funds, the Subsistence Homestead Division tried to start pilot projects across the country where the government would purchase land, machinery, houses, and livestock and then resell it to the homesteaders on thirty-year mortgages. In those pilot projects the government would also try to attract small handicraft industries to provide supplemental employment and income. The most well-known of the Subsistence Homestead Division's projects was at Arthurdale, West Viriginia, but by 1935 the agency had started fifty other projects and Harold Ickes had approved forty-five more on paper. By that time the Subsistence Homestead Division was absorbed into the new Resettlement Administration.* (Thomas H. Coode and Dennis E. Fabbri, "The New Deal's Arthurdale Project in West Virginia," *West Virginia History*, XXXVI:291–308, 1975.)

SULLIVAN, MARK Mark Sullivan was born September 10, 1874, in Avondale, Pennsylvania, and educated at Harvard, graduating from there with a bachelor's degree in 1900 and a law degree in 1903. He began his career in journalism while still in high school and while in law school continued to write for newspapers and magazines. After 1903 he wrote regularly for the *Ladies' Home Journal*, *McClure's*, and *Collier's*, finally becoming editor of the latter. Sullivan was one of the first of the "muckrake" journalists of the early twentieth century. Like many progressive journalists during World War I, he found much in Herbert Hoover's* activities to admire and joined the "Hoover-for-President" boom in 1920. Sullivan remained a close friend with Hoover throughout his life.

During the 1920s Sullivan became one of the first syndicated columnists, and during the New Deal* years he was ranked as one of the "big four," along with David Lawrence, Walter Lippmann,* and Frank Kent.* His close friendship with Hoover led him to oppose Franklin D. Roosevelt's* election in 1932,* but during Roosevelt's "honeymoon" after the inauguration Sullivan joined in the general support for New Deal policies. Nevertheless, Sullivan remained highly skeptical of Roosevelt's capacity for the office, and his contacts with New Dealers around the president convinced him that, whether Roosevelt was aware of it or not, many of them were intent on revolutionizing America. People like Henry A. Wallace,* Rexford Tugwell,* and Mordecai Ezekiel,* he thought, were "the most mild-mannered gentlemen in the world. But their state of mind is that of dictators. They have the theory that this must be a country with 'controlled' industry. . . . And how they lust to do the 'controlling.' "

Sullivan's legal training enabled him to perceive in the early New Deal legislative implications not readily apparent to other journalists, and he worried about the ''dictatorial'' potential of so much Roosevelt and his advisers were doing. But he did not openly oppose Roosevelt. Some of his readers, in fact, questioned whether he had not become a Roosevelt booster, but Sullivan was only giving the new president a chance to prove himself. ''It would be ungracious,'' he wrote, '' . . . to make it difficult for Roosevelt to carry out the measures which he honestly thinks will get the country out of the hole.'' By the fall of 1933, however, Sullivan had become convinced that the New Deal's emphasis on reform was retarding recovery from the depression. A talk with Roosevelt convinced him that the president's mind was dominated by a determination to push ahead with reform even if at the expense of recovery.

Because Sullivan's columns were so frequently critical of the early New Deal, it is difficult to fix the exact point at which he went from a ''constructive critic'' to an opponent of the New Deal. His column became more and more popular after 1933, and Sullivan remained a consistent opponent of New Deal domestic policies and feared that Roosevelt was bent on assuming dictatorial power. After 1937 many other journalists began echoing his concerns. Mark Sullivan died on August 13, 1952. (Mark Sullivan, *The Education of an American*, 1938.)

GARY DEAN BEST

SUMNERS, HATTON WILLIAM Hatton W. Sumners was born near Fayetteville, Tennessee, on May 30, 1875. He moved to Garland, Texas, in 1897, studied law privately, and was admitted to the bar in 1897. Sumners was elected prosecuting attorney of Dallas County in 1900 and served two terms, and in 1912 he won a seat in the House of Representatives. Sumners served in the House until 1947, becoming one of the most powerful figures in the Texas delegation. During the 1930s he was considered one of the more unreliable Democratic congressmen, at least in terms of his willingness to support New Deal* legislation. Sumners was a conservative Democrat uncomfortable with the growing power of labor unions and the federal government. After 1935 especially, he frequently balked at New Deal relief programs and deficit spending; and, as chairman of the House Judiciary Committee, his opposition to the court-packing* proposal was critical to its failure. Sumners also unsuccessfully opposed the executive reorganization plan in 1938 and 1939. He decided not to run for renomination in 1946 and retired from public life. Sumners died on April 19, 1962. (*New York Times*, April 20, 1962.)

SUPREME COURT During the 1930s, the Supreme Court occupied a conspicuously public role in American politics because of its philosophical differences with the New Deal.* When Franklin D. Roosevelt* took office in 1933, the Supreme Court was sharply divided into two camps. Justices Pierce Butler,* James McReynolds,* Willis Van Devanter,* and George Sutherland* were quite conservative, construing the powers of government very narrowly and limiting its capacity to deal with complex social and economic problems.

Justices Louis Brandeis,* Benjamin Cardozo,* and Harlan Stone* took a liberal position, interpreting the powers of government generously. Occupying a middle-ground, albeit a conservative one, were Chief Justice Charles Evans Hughes* and Justice Owen J. Roberts.* In 1934, for example, the Court upheld by a 5 to 4 vote the constitutionality of a Minnesota law giving courts the power to postpone mortgage foreclosures. Hughes and Roberts agreed with the liberal members that emergency conditions justified modest alterations in the contractual obligations. In 1935, however, the Court overturned, in *R. R. Retirement Board v. Alton R. R.*,* the federal law requiring carriers to establish a pension fund for employees. Justice Roberts joined the conservative bloc in denying that the law fell within the commerce clause. Hughes, Brandeis, Stone, and Cardozo dissented.

The Court's assault on the New Deal continued in May 1935 with the *Schechter v. U. S.** decision, a unanimous opinion setting aside the National Industrial Recovery Act of 1933.* The court argued that the law was an unconstitutional delegation of legislative power and a violation of national commerce authority. In a separate opinion, Justices Stone and Cardozo said it simply was poorly drafted and had been an unconstitutional delegation of Congress's power to the president. In January 1936 the cleavage in the Court came with the *United States v. Butler** decision invalidating the Agricultural Adjustment Act of 1933.* Justices Hughes, McReynolds, Van Devanter, Butler, Roberts, and Sutherland were the majority; and Cardozo, Brandeis, and Stone, the minority. Later in 1936 the same alignment declared the Guffey-Snyder Bituminous Coal Conservation Act* of 1935 unconstitutional. The court also set aside a New York minimum wage law for women in *Morehead v. Tipaldo** on the grounds that the law was an unconstitutional violation of an individual's right to "enter into contracts."

As far as President Roosevelt was concerned, the Court had put a straight jacket on the New Deal, using a narrow view of the Tenth Amendment to completely block the exercise of national power. He consistently agreed with the minority opinions of Brandeis, Cardozo, and Stone that the federal government must have the authority to deal with the Great Depression—that it must enjoy the "power to govern." Although conservatives hailed the Court's stand, Roosevelt in frustration decided on a major reform of the federal judiciary. His scheme to "pack" the Court by expanding its size and retiring elderly justices was the only way he felt confident of gaining the power he needed to deal with the economy. In a storm of protest throughout 1937, the "court-packing"* proposal was defeated, but Roosevelt won the war even while losing that battle. In the midst of the court fight, Chief Justice Charles Evans Hughes and Justice Owen J. Roberts shifted their allegiances, probably out of a fear that any more judicial intransigence might threaten the Court's existence. In *West Coast Hotel v. Parrish** (1937) the Court upheld a Washington minimum wage law by a 5 to 4 vote, with Hughes and Roberts joining Brandeis, Cardozo, and Stone in the majority. In April 1937 the same majority upheld the National Labor Relations Act of 1935* in *NLRB v. Jones & Laughlin Steel Corporation*,* using a broad interpretation of the interstate commerce clause. The Court also upheld the old-age pension and unemployment insurance provisions of the Social Security Act of 1935* in May 1937. In addition to the philosophical transformation, the Court also underwent major personnel changes in the late 1930s and early 1940s which made the New Deal triumphant. In June 1937 Justice Willis Van Devanter retired and Roosevelt replaced him with Senator Hugo Black* of Alabama. Black had been a strong supporter of the New Deal. In January 1938 Justice George Sutherland retired and Roosevelt replaced him with Stanley Reed,* former general counsel of the RFC* and solicitor general of the United States. Reed had defended major New Deal decisions before the Court during the mid-1930s. Liberal Justice Benjamin Cardozo died in July 1938, and Roosevelt replaced him with Felix Frankfurter* in January 1939. Frankfurter had long been a major figure behind the scenes in the New Deal, and his support of civil liberties and labor legislation was well known. Louis Brandeis resigned in February 1939, and the president replaced him with William O. Douglas,* then head of the Securities and Exchange Commission* and a former professor at the Yale Law School. Justice Pierce Butler died in November 1939, and Roosevelt appointed Frank Murphy,* attorney general and former governor of Michigan, in his stead. Murphy's credentials as a supporter of labor and civil liberties were impeccable. When Justice James McReynolds retired in January 1941, Roosevelt filled the vacancy with Senator James F. Byrnes* of South Carolina. Byrnes had been a long-time Roosevelt supporter in the Senate. Chief Justice Charles Evans Hughes resigned in June 1941, and the president named Harlan Fiske Stone as the new chief justice and filled the Court vacancy with Attorney General Robert Jackson,* an ardent New Dealer. Roosevelt's reform of the Supreme Court was complete. (Alpheus Thomas Mason, *The Supreme Court from Taft to Warren*, 1958; C. Herman Pritchett, *The Roosevelt Court. A Study in Judicial Politics and Values, 1937–1947*, 1948.)

SURVEY OF FEDERAL ARCHIVES Known as Federal Project No. 4 of the Works Progress Administration,* the Survey of Federal Archives existed from January 1936 through June 1937 as an independent program. The act creating the National Archives had required a description of federal records outside Washington, D. C., and in 1935 the National Archives requested a WPA grant to conduct the survey. President Franklin D. Roosevelt* approved the survey, and the WPA authorized the expenditure of $1,176,000. Philip M. Hamer, deputy examiner at the National Archives, headed the survey. The country was divided into thirty-four regions, each headed by a regional supervisor, usually selected from university faculties or the staffs of local historical societies. After June 1937 the Survey of Federal Archives continued under the auspices of the Historical Records Survey* and the National Archives. When the surveys were finally completed in 1942, 506 volumes of the inventory of federal archives had been published. (William F. McDonald, *Federal Relief Administration and the Arts*, 1969.)

SUTHERLAND, GEORGE George Sutherland was born on March 25, 1862, in Buckinghamshire, England. His parents, converts to the Mormon Church, immigrated to Utah in 1863; and Sutherland grew up in Springville. He left school at the age of twelve to support his family economically but in 1878 entered Brigham Young Academy in Provo, Utah. Sutherland spent three years there and then worked for one year on the Rio Grande Western Railroad. He entered the University of Michigan Law School in 1883, studied there for one year, and then returned to Provo to start his law practice. Sutherland moved to Salt Lake City in 1894; and when Utah achieved statehood in 1896, he won a seat in the state senate as a Republican. In 1900 Sutherland was elected to the House of Representatives of the United States, declined to run for a second term, and then was elected to the Senate in 1904. During his career in the senate, Sutherland built a mixed reputation, favoring such progressive measures as the Pure Food & Drug Act of 1906 and workmen's compensation while opposing the Federal Reserve Act, the Sixteenth Amendment, the Clayton Anti-trust Act, and the Federal Trade Commission Act. In 1916 he failed to gain renomination by the Utah Republican party* but stayed on and practiced law in Washington, D. C. He was a close friend and adviser to Senator Warren G. Harding of Ohio. In 1922, when Supreme Court* Justice John H. Clarke suddenly resigned, then President Harding appointed Sutherland to fill the vacancy.

Sutherland's political and judicial philosophy focused on the individual and personal freedom as the only political reality. In his mind, anything that enhanced personal liberty was good, and anything restricting it was bad. The key to guaranteeing personal freedom, he believed, was restricting government to an absolute minimum. He was proud of the Constitution because it so divided up power that it was impossible for the federal government to undermine personal liberties. During the 1930s, however, Sutherland saw that diffusion of power threatened by the New Deal,* particularly the growth of the executive branch and the expansion of congressional control over interstate commerce. Consequently, Sutherland aligned himself with the conservative majority before 1937, usually voting with Chief Justice Charles Evans Hughes* and Justices James McReynolds,* Pierce Butler,* Owen J. Roberts,* and Willis Van Devanter* in those decisions overturning major New Deal legislation. After the "revolution of 1937" involving the "court-packing"* scheme, Sutherland found himself in the minority. He retired from the Court on January 17, 1938, and died on July 18, 1942. (Joel Francis Paschal, *Mr. Justice Sutherland. A Man Against the State*, 1951.)

SWOPE, GERARD Gerard Swope, prominent businessman and an early architect of the idea of business and government cooperation, was born in St. Louis, Missouri, on December 1, 1872. In 1895 he graduated from the Massachusetts Institute of Technology with a degree in electrical engineering and went to work for Western Electric Company. Swope rose quickly through the company, becoming general sales manager of the New York office in 1908 and vice-president of the national office in 1913. Swope was elected president of General Electric in 1919 and chairman of the board in 1922. He kept that position until his retirement in 1939. During the 1920s and 1930s, Swope rose to a position of national prominence as a spokesman for the interests of the business community.

But Swope was hardly a symbol of laissez-faire conservatism. He had worked for years with Greenwich House in New York and was a friend of Jane Addams, and he had a sense of sympathy for the needs of poor workers and the unemployed. Swope was also a prominent figure in the trade association movement and believed in industrial self-regulation. As the first president of the National Electrical Manufacturers Association, Swope was a great believer in the capacity of industry to regulate itself. During the 1920s he became a close associate of Herbert Hoover,* who as secretary of commerce worked to encourage trade associations as a means of rationalizing the industrial economy, eliminating wasteful competition, and improving productivity. When the depression swept through the country, Swope believed its roots were embedded in the problem of overproduction. He began urging the federal government to adopt a plan of industrial self-regulation through trade associations, suspension of anti-trust laws, and national economic planning through the establishment of codes of "fair competition." Swope's ideas found fruition in the New Deal's* National Recovery Administration.*

During the early New Deal, Swope was one of the most influential businessmen, at least in terms of public policy, in the United States. He was first chairman of the Business Advisory Council* in the Department of Commerce in 1933, chairman of the Coal Arbitration Board* in 1933, a member of the first National Labor Board,* the Committee on Economic Security* in 1934, and the Advisory Council on Social Security in 1937 and 1938. Although Swope eventually came to believe the NRA machinery should be scrapped and turned over to an administrative council of the U. S. Chamber of Commerce,* he was a temperate, effective representative of the business community while an active participant in the New Deal. He was the author of three books—*Stabilization of Industry* (1931), *Futility of Conquest in Europe* (1943), and *Some Aspects of Corporate Management*. Gerard Swope died on November 20, 1957. (Kim McQuaid, *"The Frustration of Corporate Revival during the Early New Deal," Historian*, XLI:682–704, 1979; *New York Times*, November 21, 1957.)

T

TABER, JOHN John Taber, long-time congressman from New York, was born in Auburn, Cayuga County, New York, on May 5, 1880. He came from a small town background, graduated from Yale in 1902, and attended the New York Law School in 1903. Taber then began practicing law in Auburn, was supervisor of Cayuga County in 1905 and 1906, and special judge of the county court between 1910 and 1918. Taber cultivated his relations with businessmen in Auburn and developed a chamber of commerce mentality about politics. A faithful Republican, Taber chaired the Cayuga County Republican State Committee between 1920 and 1925 and was elected to Congress in 1922. He remained in Congress until 1962, when he decided not to stand for renomination. During the New Deal* years, Taber was a powerful opponent of Franklin D. Roosevelt.* With his pro-business, small-town background, he saw the New Deal as a dramatic change of course in American public policy, one which was taking the country down a one-way road to bureaucracy and centralization. Because of his rural, small-town constituency, he had absolutely no sympathy for the needs of organized labor and the urban poor. Taber consistently opposed increased relief expenditures, labor standards legislation, executive reorganization, and deficit spending. After his retirement from Congress, he practiced law in Auburn until his death on November 22, 1965. (*New York Times*, November 23, 1965.)

TAFT, ROBERT ALPHONSO Robert A. Taft, the senator from Ohio who was commonly called "Mr. Republican," was born on September 8, 1889, in Cincinnati, Ohio. He was the elder son of William Howard Taft, later president of the United States and chief justice of the Supreme Court.* The young Taft travelled widely with his parents on their diplomatic assignments, and he graduated from Yale in 1910. Three years later Taft graduated first in his class at the Harvard Law School. He practiced law for several years in Cincinnati and then worked under Herbert Hoover* in the Food Administration during World War I. Taft returned to his Ohio law practice in 1920 and served in the lower house of the state legislature between 1921 and 1930 and in the state senate between 1930 and 1936. He was the favorite son of the Ohio delegation at the

1936 Republican National Convention, and in 1938 he won a seat in the United States Senate. In the Senate, Taft quickly emerged as an implacable opponent of New Deal* programs and agencies and consistently voted to reduce their appropriations to insignificance. In foreign policy, Taft was regarded as an isolationist, voting against the selective service, lend-lease, the destroyer-for-bases deal, extension of the draft, and revision of neutrality legislation. As late as 1943, Taft continued to question the reasons for American involvement in the European war and seemed to favor a negotiated peace with Hitler, even if it meant German domination of the continent.

Re-elected in 1944, Senator Taft set a mixed course for the postwar world. He favored the United Nations but continued to oppose the continuation or expansion of most New Deal-type programs. Because of his urban constituency in Ohio, however, he took an active interest in social welfare legislation, favoring federal aid to education, federal housing and slum clearance programs, and some form of national health program. In the Republican-controlled 80th Congress, Taft established himself as a major power in the party. He was chosen to the powerful position of chairman of the Republican Steering Committee. In that Congress, his name was most prominently associated with the anti-labor Taft-Hartley Act of 1947. During the Korean War, Taft was an outspoken critic of Harry S Truman's* administration, accusing him of losing China, of being "soft" on communism, and of subverting the war process by firing General Douglas MacArthur. Many Republicans viewed Taft's denunciations as irresponsible. Although Taft had a keen eye set on the presidential election of 1952, he had made himself too controversial. He may have been "Mr. Republican," but eastern Republicans and pragmatists in the party regarded him as too burdened by his political past to be elected. Delegates at the Republican National Convention rejected Taft and turned instead to General Dwight D. Eisenhower, a national hero unembarrassed by any political history.

As Senate majority leader, Taft continued to play a major role in party affairs, but by April 1953 his health was failing. Exploratory surgery in July revealed that Taft was in an advanced stage of cancer. He died on July 31, 1953. (James T. Patterson, *Mr. Republican: A Biography of Robert A. Taft*, 1972.)

JOSEPH M. ROWE, JR.

TALLEY, LYNN PORTER Lynn P. Talley was born in Belton, Texas, on October 30, 1881. After graduating from high school in Temple, Texas, in 1898, Talley attended the Galveston Business College and then went to work as a stenographer for several railroads. Between 1903 and 1911 Talley worked for the City National Bank in Dallas as a teller, assistant cashier, and cashier, then he moved to Houston in 1911 and went to work for the Lumberman's National Bank. While in Houston Talley came to know Jesse H. Jones,* and their friendship became most important to him in later years. Talley returned to Dallas in 1915 as deputy governor of the Federal Reserve Bank of Dallas, became a vice-president of Southwest National Bank of Dallas in 1921, and returned to the

Federal Reserve Bank of Dallas in 1923 as director, chairman of the board, and governor. In 1931 and 1932 Talley moved out to San Francisco to become chairman of the board of the Bank of America during its financial crisis, and at Jesse H. Jones' suggestion, he came to Washington, D.C., in 1932 as a special assistant to the directors of the Reconstruction Finance Corporation.* When President Franklin D. Roosevelt* decided to establish the Commodity Credit Corporation* in 1933 to assist farmers in marketing and storing crop surpluses, he listened to Jesse H. Jones and named Talley president of the new agency. Talley stayed with the Commodity Credit Corporation until his health began to fail him in 1939. He submitted his resignation in 1939 and formally retired early in 1940. Talley died on October 8, 1942. (*New York Times*, October 9, 1942.)

TALMADGE, EUGENE Eugene Talmadge was born on September 23, 1884, in Forsyth, Georgia. His father, though active in politics, was a cotton farmer, but his son's interests were more academic. Talmadge attended the Hilliard Institute for Boys. He graduated from the University of Georgia and immediately went into public school teaching in 1904, working one year. He took a law degree at the university in 1907. Talmadge practiced law for some time, returned to work the family farm, and in 1918 became solicitor at the city court in McRae, Georgia. During the early 1920s, he tried to win elective office, but he was not successful until he began adopting a neo-Populist stance promoting the needs of poor cotton and corn farmers and condemning the state political machine. Talmadge won election as the state agricultural commissioner in 1926, and in 1933 he became governor of Georgia.

But as governor, Talmadge found himself increasingly alienated from the New Deal,* primarily because of its social activism and centralizing bureaucracy. He refused to institute any "little New Deal"* in Georgia and openly opposed union organization drives there. He also opposed the Bankhead Cotton Control Act of 1934* as "socialistic" and became personally critical of President Franklin D. Roosevelt.* Talmadge was too devoted to the idea of states' rights and viewed the New Deal as a frightening aberration from American political tradition. But his conservatism proved contrary to the wishes of the Georgia majority. In 1936 a coalition of New Deal Democrats under Eurith Rivers* took over Georgia politics, and Talmadge was ousted. He lost a race for the United Sttes Senate against Walter George* in 1938, won the governorship in 1940 after accommodating himself to the New Deal, and then lost again in 1942 to Ellis Arnall. Eugene Talmadge died on December 21, 1946. (William Anderson, *The Wild Man from Sugar Creek. The Political Career of Eugene Talmadge*, 1975.)

TAYLOR, EDWARD THOMAS Edward T. Taylor, longtime chairman of the House Appropriations Committee, was born on a farm near Metamora, Illinois, on June 19, 1858. He moved to Leadville, Colorado, in 1881, served as a principal of Leadville High School in 1881 and 1882, and then received a law degree from the University of Michigan in 1884. He began practicing law in

Leadville and served as superintendent of schools in 1884, and then he was elected deputy district attorney in 1885. Taylor moved to Glenwood Springs, Colorado, in 1887, became district attorney of the ninth judicial district between 1887 and 1889, and won a seat in the state legislature as a Democrat in 1896. He stayed in the state senate until 1908, simultaneously serving as city attorney between 1896 and 1900 and county attorney in 1901 and 1902. Taylor won a seat in the House of Representatives in 1908 and remained there until his death. During the New Deal,* Taylor was chairman of the powerful House Appropriations Committee and was generally a reliable supporter of Franklin D. Roosevelt.* In 1934, concerned about the interests of his farming and ranching constituents, Taylor made a major shift in policy and came around to the idea of government intervention into the agricultural crisis, writing the Taylor Grazing Act.* Taylor made a major shift in policy and came around to the idea of government intervention into the agricultural crisis, writing the Taylor Grazing Act.* Taylor died on September 3, 1941. (*New York Times*, September 4, 1941.)

TAYLOR GRAZING ACT OF 1934 The Taylor Grazing Act of 1934 virtually closed the era of homesteading and free use of the public domain and established a system of districts and permits for grazing on federal lands.

The general policy of the federal government since its inception had been to provide for an orderly passage of title to public lands from the government to individuals, meanwhile allowing grazing and other public use of lands still owned by the government. Long before the passage of the Taylor Grazing Act it was evident that uncontrolled grazing on the public lands had led to abuses—deterioration of the range because of overstocking and instability in the livestock industry because of intense competition for grass. Still, congressional coalitions representing local interests blocked reform with arguments of states' rights and individual opportunity.

A number of causes contributed to passage of the Taylor Act in 1934. One was a change in attitude by Congressman Edward T. Taylor* of Colorado, for whom the act was named. Long an advocate of local control, he finally concluded that federal regulation was necessary for conservation of the range. He introduced a bill to that effect in 1933 which failed to pass, but by 1934 he had powerful allies to secure its approval. President Franklin D. Roosevelt* supported the bill, as did Secretary of Interior Harold Ickes* and Secretary of Agriculture Henry A. Wallace,* thereby stilling earlier disputes as to whether control of grazing should be lodged in Interior or Agriculture Departments. Finally, drought in the West helped to impress upon Congress the urgency of action.

The act empowered the secretary of interior to create grazing districts, to issue permits to stockmen, and to collect fees for grazing. The total acreage of the grazing districts was limited to 80 million (increased by amendment in 1936 to 142 million), and the term of permits was to be no more than ten years. The bill created a grazing service within the Department of Interior to administer the grazing districts. The grazing service was to consult and cooperate with local stockmen's associations and to give preference in permits to nearby landholders with the capacity to carry stock during the season when they were not grazing on public lands.

The Taylor Grazing Act did not specifically close the public domain to homesteading, but it had that effect. Shortly after its passage President Roosevelt withdrew all remaining public lands in the West from entry so that they might be classified for proper use.

Under the original act and subsequent amendments, the grazing service had a degree of flexibility in the creation and management of districts. The service could dispose of small isolated tracts; exchange public lands for private lands; lease lands from private holders to round out a district; lease isolated lands not included within a grazing district to stockowners; and even reopen lands suitable for the raising of crops to homesteading. District, state, and national advisory boards of stockmen made policy recommendations to the service. Of grazing fees collected, shares were allocated to the state in which the district was located, were spent for range improvement in the district, and were remitted to the federal treasury.

Administrative reorganization in 1946 converted the grazing service into the Bureau of Land Mangement. (Wesley Calef, *Private Grazing and Public Lands: Studies of the Local Management of the Taylor Grazing Act,* 1960; Philip O. Foss, *Politics and Grass: The Administration of Grazing on the Public Domain*, 1960; Roy M. Robbins, *Our Landed Heritage: The Public Domain, 1776–1970*, 1976.)

THOMAS D. ISERN

TECHNOCRACY MOVEMENT From June 1932 through the first several months of 1933, the technocracy movement, advocating a government run by technical experts, held the attention of the American public. Howard Scott, the self-styled engineer who led the movement, maintained that capitalism was gasping for its last breath. He predicted total collapse of the "price system" within eighteen months because increasingly efficient production and decreasing manpower requirements had precipitated a crisis in the society. Scott was engaged in what he called "The Energy Survey of North America," a statistical study charting the effects of technological growth on employment in 3,000 major industries. The Architects Relief Committee had supplied thirty-six unemployed architects and draftsmen to complete the enormous undertaking while Columbia University offered Scott some financial assistance. Scott predicted a millenium of prosperity after the collapse of capitalism because the natural resources and technological capabilities of North America could be shared through a system of distribution based upon "energy certificates." The certificates, representing the yearly conversion of resources to energy, would be equally distributed among the population, improving the general standard of living.

Technocracy's critics called it socialism, fascism, or communism, and argued that it was based on several false premises. Mechanization was not advancing at the rate technocracy alleged; the proposal for a currency based on energy rather than gold was unworkable; and technocracy was hardly new, just a plagiarized distillation of the ideas of people like Thorstein Veblen, Frederick Soddy, and John Maynard Keynes.* Scott then sealed his own fate. On January 3, 1933, he alleged that Franklin D. Roosevelt* would use technocracy to justify a program of fascism. Nicholas Murray Butler, president of Columbia University, promptly disavowed any connection with Scott. In March 1933 a journalist published an exposé claiming Scott was a fraud, with no university degrees and a record of being fired as a foreman at a World War I munitions plant on suspicion of being a German spy. Though no longer a source of public interest, Scott went on to found Technocracy, Inc., which developed as a paramilitary organization throughout the 1930s and early 1940s, but the scandal surrounding his own career and the extent to which the New Deal* did employ technical expertise in government destroyed the movement. (William A. Akin, *Technocracy and the American Dream; The Technocrat Movement 1900–1941*, 1977.)

BERNARD K. DUFFY

TEMPORARY NATIONAL ECONOMIC COMMITTEE Concerned about the concentration of economic power and its effect on declining business competition, President Franklin D. Roosevelt* delivered a monopoly message to Congress on April 29, 1938, calling for an investigation of anti-trust enforcement. Congress formed the Temporary National Economic Committee, which sat between late 1938 and early 1941. Establishment of the TNEC reflected confusion within the administration over economic recovery, since the debate there raged between the traditions of anti-trust, industrial self-government, and federal compensatory spending. Roosevelt's message to Congress came after an intense lobbying effort on the part of anti-trusters Thomas Corcoran* and Benjamin Cohen,* whom Roosevelt trusted and admired. All this came at a time during the recession of 1937–1938* when Roosevelt was moving away from the budget balancing ideas of Henry Morgenthau, Jr.,* toward the compensatory spending ideas of Harry Hopkins* and Lauchlin Currie.*

Roosevelt had wanted a study of economic concentration conducted by the FTC,* SEC,* and Department of Justice, but Congress assumed its prerogatives. Senator Joseph O'Mahoney* of Wyoming led the fight for creation of the TNEC. Hostility over the "court-packing"* bill had already increased tensions between Congress and the president. Final composition of the TNEC reflected this tension with the addition of three senators and three congressmen as well as representatives of the SEC, FTC, and the Departments of Justice, Treasury, Commerce, and Labor. Committee members came primarily from the Middle West and the West. The majority of them held anti-trust sentiments. Politically, members ranged from independent Republicans to liberal New Deal* Democrats. All of them came from well-to-do, middle-class professional backgrounds: nine were lawyers, two were economists, one was an engineer and business manager, five had been university professors. Alternate members from the executive departments and members of the technical staff held diverse economic views ranging from anti-trust through industrial self-government to compensatory spending.

The TNEC held fifteen separate hearings between December 1, 1938, and March 11, 1941. Testimony of witnesses filled thirty-seven volumes and regarded such subjects as patents, life insurance, savings and investment, industrial insurance, war and prices, cartels, interstate trade barriers, and technology. Individual industries were examined including liquor, milk and poultry, construction, petroleum, iron and steel, and investment banking. Advocates of various economic policy alternatives held forth in the public hearings to mirror positions which had divided politicians and New Deal advisers since 1933. While billed as the most thorough investigation of economic practices in American history, the TNEC only managed to transfer the recovery debate from the internal advisory circles of the New Deal to the hearing rooms of the Congress. As a political move, creation of the TNEC took much of the heat off Roosevelt. As an economic investigation searching for a viable policy, the study resolved little. Policy advisers and scholars ever since have searched the testimony to find confirmation of their own preconceptions. Keynesian economists later claimed inaccurately that Harvard University economist Alvin Hansen* set forth the ideas of the new economics in justification of Roosevelt's resumption of federal spending in the spring of 1938. But other witnesses spoke of the need for stronger enforcement of anti-trust laws; legislative revision of tax, patent, and financial laws; and renewal of the experiment in industrial self-government.

The TNEC staff produced forty-three technical research monographs of interest to historians, but most of these were quickly buried in light of changing circumstances between 1938 and 1941. The committee's final report released in April 1941 proved unoriginal and lacking in inspiration. The Congress took up revision of patent laws recommended by the TNEC, but no other recommendations received legislative attention. Internally, the failure of the TNEC to generate policy recommendations stemmed from differences of opinion evident before the committee began its work.

The Roosevelt administration already had begun to rebuild links of cooperation with big business while the TNEC conducted its study. Assistant Attorney General Thurman Arnold,* appointed head of the Anti-trust Division in the Department of Justice in March 1938, met with Edward R. Stettinius, Jr.,* chairman of the board of the United States Steel Corporation, in the fall of 1938 to encourage that firm to lower prices without lowering wages in order to stimulate employment. Stettinius wrote in his private notes that Arnold was more concerned with proper anti-trust proceedings than "any damn fool monopoly investigation." But Arnold knew that the public would want a "show," so he obliged as the representative of the Department of Justice on the TNEC. If the most prominent advocate of anti-trust took this attitude toward the TNEC, then the study takes on diminished historical importance.

External changes between the spring of 1938 and completion of the TNEC's work in March 1941 also undermined the impact of the study. Roosevelt's own focus shifted away from domestic reform toward more active consideration of foreign policy events in Europe and the Far East. Recognizing that he would need big business support in the war mobilization effort, Roosevelt had begun steps to conciliate big businessmen through the Business Advisory Council* and the various war agencies established after the fall of France in June 1940. High unemployment, the major policy concern of the 1930s, became less important as the country moved toward full employment under the impetus of war-related production. While the federal government implicitly moved toward acceptance of compensatory spending policy, the older policy of anti-trust took a back seat. During World War II, economic concentration of power in the hands of big business continued under the stimulus of government contracts. By the spring of 1941, the TNEC was no longer news. As Ellis Hawley writes, creation of the TNEC "was not so much a victory for the anti-trusters as it was a way of avoiding the issue, a means of minimizing the policy conflict within the Administration and postponing any final decision." The final decision came by default with the war production effort which both instituted massive governmental compensatory spending and renewed cooperation between the federal government and big business. (Robert Collins, *The Business Response to Keynes, 1929–1964*, 1981; Ellis Hawley, *The New Deal and the Problem of Monopoly: A Study in Economic Ambivalence*, 1966; David Lynch, *The Concentration of Economic Power*, 1946; Dwight MacDonald, "The Monopoly Committee: A Study in Frustration," *The American Scholar*, VIII:295–308, 1939; Kim McQuaid, *Big Business and Presidential Power from FDR to Reagan*, 1982.)

PATRICK D. REAGAN

TENNESSEE VALLEY AUTHORITY In April 1933 President Franklin D. Roosevelt* asked Congress to create an agency to plan for the use, development, and conservation of the Tennessee River Valley. Congress responded the next month, and on May 18, 1933, the president signed legislation creating the Tennessee Valley Authority. The TVA was charged with improving navigability of the river, providing for flood control, planning reforestation and marginal lands programs, assisting industrial and agricultural development, and aiding the national defense by operating government nitrate and other properties at Muscle Shoals in northern Alabama. Establishment of the Tennessee Valley Authority was rooted in government ownership of Muscle Shoals, where the Tennessee River drops 140 feet in some thirty miles. Because of its hydroelectric potential, the government began constructing two dams and two nitrate plants there, but the war ended before the dams were completed and the plants operational. During the 1920s the issue of the disposal of the Muscle Shoals properties resulted in conflicts over proper use of the site and whether it should be publicly or privately controlled. Senator George W. Norris* of Nebraska led the fight for government retention of the properties, but his plans for the region were not endorsed by the White House until Franklin D. Roosevelt's election.

The controversy in the 1920s foreshadowed the TVA struggles of the 1930s. Although the TVA was run by a three-man board and was an independent, decentralized agency responsible directly to the president and to Congress, it was a government creation financed with federal funds. The strongest opposition came from power companies who resented the cheaper energy available through the authority. They charged that TVA was an unconstitutional extension of federal power, and they instituted a number of lawsuits against it. Although these were eventually resolved in the authority's favor, the fear that the authority as it existed would be declared unconstitutional led to amendment of the original act. The amendments, which emphasized navigation and flood control, brought the TVA activities in line with more traditional areas of federal development. Other conflicts arose over condemnation of property to create TVA reservoirs and lakes, competition with private fertilizer plans, the use of general tax revenues to benefit a specific geographical region, and whether TVA lured business from other areas to the valley with its cheap electrical power.

A major battle raged on the TVA board between 1933 and 1938 and reflected the shifting nature of New Deal* policy. The first chairman of the TVA board was Arthur Morgan,* former president of Antioch College and a utopian visionary whose multipurpose dream for TVA rested on his faith in cooperative planning between government and business. Arthur Morgan wanted to keep TVA power rates at levels consistent with those of private industry in order to prevent any sense of competition and its accompanying bitterness. Arthur Morgan also wanted to eliminate poverty in the valley. Morgan was joined on the board by Harcourt Morgan* and David Lilienthal,* both of whom came to disagree with his visions for the TVA. Harcourt Morgan was a longtime advocate of the needs of large, commercial farmers and strongly suspicious of centralized planning from the federal government, whether or not it involved the cooperation of business. David Lilienthal was a powerful advocate of public power and wanted the TVA to compete directly with the private power interests. On the TVA board, Harcourt Morgan and David Lilienthal formed a coalition against Arthur Morgan. Arthur Morgan hated their opposition to planning and what he considered overemphasis on public power, and between 1936 and 1938 he castigated them publicly. Roosevelt fired Arthur Morgan in 1938 because of his public charges of impropriety against Harcourt Morgan and David Lilienthal, but Arthur Morgan's decline was also a symbol of the end of the planning panacea in the New Deal and the transition toward anti-trust and government spending formulas.

Despite the opposition from private power companies, led by Wendell Willkie* and his Commonwealth and Southern Company, and the internal bickering on the TVA board, the Tennessee Valley Authority accomplished many of its objectives. A series of nine main river dams, augmented by dams along tributaries, converted the Tennessee River into a series of large lakes which provided a navigation channel 300 feet wide and capable of handling ships of nine feet draft from Knoxville, Tennessee, 640 miles north to the Ohio River at Paducah, Kentucky. Flood control was implemented along the Tennessee River and its tributaries in the lower Ohio and Mississippi River Valleys. Chemicals for fertilizer and defense were manufactured; reforestation and other erosion work began; recreational facilities were constructed; experimental farms were established to test crops, fertilizers, and agricultural methods; industrial development and education was encouraged; roads, bridges, and model cities were built; and, during the Great Depression, jobs were created in an area of 3 million people whose income was but 45 percent of the national average.

In 1938 Harcourt Morgan became the new head of the Tennessee Valley Authority, and in 1941 he was followed by David Lilienthal. By then the TVA was the largest producer of electrical power in the United States. TVA produced nitrates for munitions and power to manufacture aluminum during World War II, and after that its growth was exponential. By 1980 TVA power sales exceeded 120 billion kilowatt-hours, still the largest for any utility in the United States, and grossed over $3 billion. (Gordon R. Clapp, *The TVA: An Approach to the Development of a Region*, 1955; Wilmon H. Droze, *High Dams and Slack Waters: TVA Rebuilds a River*, 1965; Preston J. Hubbard, *Origins of the TVA: The Muscle Shoals Controversy, 1920–1932*, 1961; Marguerite Owen, *The Tennessee Valley Authority*, 1973.)

VIRGINIA F. HAUGHTON

TEXTILE LABOR RELATIONS BOARD Established on September 26, 1934, by President Franklin D. Roosevelt* to replace the Cotton Textile National Industrial Relations Board,* the Textile Labor Relations Board proved to be little more than a pro-mill government agency. The new board was established after the collapse of the United Textile Workers of America strike in the summer of 1934. President Roosevelt appointed Judge Walter P. Stacy, James Mullenbach, and Admiral Henry Wiley to the Textile Labor Relations Board, but during the nearly three years of its existence it actually slowed down the union movement. The board devoted most of its time to handling labor complaints about management dismissals of striking workers and usually found in favor of business, claiming they had no obligation to rehire strikers after an unsuccessful strike. In fact, the Textile Labor Relations Board had essentially become an ally of George A. Sloan and the Cotton-Textile Institute. The Textile Labor Relations Board was discontinued on July 1, 1937. (Bernard Bellush, *The Failure of the NRA*, 1975.)

THOMAS, ELMER Elmer Thomas was born in Greencastle, Indiana, on September 8, 1876. He graduated from Central Normal College in 1897 and from DePauw University in 1900. Thomas studied law privately and was admitted to the Indiana bar in 1897 and to the Oklahoma bar in 1900. He practiced at Lawton, Oklahoma, between 1901 and 1911 and served in the state senate between 1907 and 1920. Thomas won election as a Democrat to Congress in 1922 and in 1926 won a seat in the United States Senate. By 1933 Thomas had become a leading figure in the Senate inflationary bloc, a group of western farming and mining interests convinced that devaluing the dollar and eliminating the gold standard would trigger a price rise and an economic boom. In April 1933 President Franklin D. Roosevelt* called Thomas into the White House and, in order to temper western demands, asked him to draft a piece of legislation allowing the president to devalue the dollar, monetize silver, and print more money. Thomas agreed, and the measure was passed as an amendment to the Agricultural Adjustment Act of 1933.* Thomas generally became an administration Democrat loyal to most New Deal* issues, even though he had to adopt a conservative stance that was consistent with Oklahoma interests. Still, because Roosevelt had responded to Thomas' near fanatical commitment to monetary inflation in 1933 and 1934, he had a loyal follower. Roosevelt endorsed Thomas' renomination bid in 1938; and when the senator was re-elected, it was viewed as a victory for the New Deal. Thomas remained in the Senate until 1951. He died on September 19, 1965. (*New York Times*, September 20, 1965; James T. Patterson, *Congressional Conservatism and the New Deal*, 1967.)

THOMAS, NORMAN MATTOON Norman Mattoon Thomas was born on November 20, 1884, in Marion, Ohio, to a deeply religious Presbyterian family. He graduated as valedictorian from Princeton in 1905, travelled widely for several years, and entered Union Theological Seminary, then a center of the Social Gospel movement. While studying there, Thomas worked at Christ Church, which was located on the edge of Hell's Kitchen in New York City. He was ordained a minister in 1911 and went to work in East Harlem with poor immigrants. He held that position until World War I, when his outright opposition to the conflict forced him to resign. He became editor of *The World Tomorrow*, a left-wing magazine many Americans considered subversive. After the war, Thomas left behind his religious connections and devoted himself to the Socialist party.* He became co-director of the League for Industrial Democracy, the main promoter of the party, and in 1923 became editor of *The New Leader*. He ran on the Socialist ticket for governor of New York in 1924 and mayor of New York City in 1925. He also ran for president of the United States in the elections of 1928, 1932,* 1936,* 1940,* 1944, and 1948. During the 1930s, Thomas openly advocated public works, a shorter workweek, agricultural relief, unemployment insurance, elimination of child labor, old-age pensions, slum clearance, low-cost housing, nationalization of basic industries, and higher taxes on corporations and the wealthy. In 1938 he also organized the Keep America Out of War Congress. Thomas fully recognized the irony of the Socialist party's dismal showing in the national elections of the 1930s, arguing that President Franklin D. Roosevelt's* New Deal* was responsible for the party's decline in popularity. In 1928 Thomas had received only 267,835 votes, but that increased to 881,951 in 1932 because of the severity of the Great Depression. Socialists had great hope that Thomas would make major gains in the presidential elections of 1936, but he garnered only 187,720 votes. The New Deal had stolen much of the Socialist thunder. A compassionate, dedicated man, Norman Thomas was perhaps the nation's most consistent advocate of the welfare state, and over the years he saw most of his proposals implemented. He was just always ahead of his time. Thomas wrote several books, including *As I See It* (1932), *The Choice Before Us* (1934), *After the New Deal, What?* (1936), *Socialism on the Defensive* (1938), *Keep America Out of War* (1938), *Socialist's Faith* (1951), *The Test of Freedom* (1954), and *The Choices* (1968). Norman M. Thomas died on December 19, 1968. (James C. Duram, *Norman Thomas*, 1974.)

THORNHILL V. STATE OF ALABAMA Byron Thornhill was arrested on a charge of "loitering about the premises" of the Brown Wood Preserving Company during a labor strike. He was charged under an Alabama statute which prohibited loitering about or picketing a place of business. Trial before the Inferior Court of Tuscaloosa County resulted in conviction. Upon appeal, the case was heard in the state circuit court. Thornhill's defense was based on the complaint that the state law was unconstitutional in that it denied the defendant's freedom of speech, right of peaceful assemblage, and right to petition for redress of grievances. The circuit court denied motion for dismissal on the grounds of unconstitutionality, affirmed conviction, and even increased the sentence which had been imposed by the inferior court. The Alabama Supreme Court denied a petition for certiorari, but the Supreme Court* of the United States granted a writ of certiorari because of the importance of the issues involved in the case.

The case was argued before the Supreme Court on February 20, 1940, and judgment was handed down on April 22, 1940, with Mr. Justice Frank Murphy* writing for the majority. After discussing the particulars of the case and the historical background of freedom of speech and freedom of the press, Justice Murphy turned his attention to the Alabama law in question. He found the provision of the statute overly broad and its terminology vague and undefined. He ruled, therefore, that the statute did infringe upon basic freedoms guaranteed by the Constitution. "The freedom of speech and of the press guaranteed by the Constitution embraces at the least the liberty to discuss publicly and truthfully all matters of public concern without previous restraint or fear of subsequent punishment. . . . In the circumstances of our times the dissemination of information concerning the facts of a labor dispute must be regarded as within that area of free discussion that is guaranteed by the Constitution." The Alabama statute was declared unconstitutional, and the conviction of Thornhill was reversed. The Court thus restricted the power of the states to interfere with the right of labor to peaceful picketing. (Alfred H. Kelly and Winfred A. Harbison, *The American Constitution*, 1970; *Supreme Court Reporter*, LX:736–746, 1940.)

JOSEPH M. ROWE, JR.

TOLLEY, HOWARD ROSS Howard R. Tolley was born in Howard County, Indiana, on September 30, 1889. He graduated from Indiana University in 1910 and taught in the public schools until 1912. Between 1912 and 1915 he worked for the Department of the Interior on the coast and geodetic survey. He joined the Department of Agriculture in 1915, working in the Bureau of Agricultural

Economics. Tolley became assistant chief of the bureau in 1928 and served there until 1930 when he joined the staff of the University of California. In 1936, at the suggestion of Secretary of Agriculture Henry A. Wallace,* President Franklin D. Roosevelt* appointed Tolley to head the Agricultural Adjustment Administration,* replacing Chester Davis.* A superb economic planner, Tolley had contributed to every major New Deal* farm program, but he proved to be a poor administrator of the AAA, refusing to give any room to political considerations in formulating economic policy. Wallace replaced Tolley as head of the AAA in 1938, appointing Rudolph M. Evans* in his stead and naming Tolley chief of the Bureau of Agricultural Economics. Tolley remained with the Department of Agriculture until 1946, when he joined the United Nations as chief economist for the Food and Agriculture Organization. Tolley stayed with the UN until 1951 when he became a consultant for the Ford Foundation. He died on September 18, 1958. (Dean Albertson, *Roosevelt's Farmer. Claude R. Wickard in the New Deal*, 1961.)

TOWNSEND, FRANCIS EVERETT Francis E. Townsend was born near Fairbury, Illinois, in 1867 into a deeply religious, poor farm family. They moved to Nebraska, and eventually Townsend went on to southern California in search of productive land. He worked a number of jobs, finally settling in Omaha, Nebraska, attended the University of Nebraska Medical School, and graduated in 1903. He practiced medicine in Bear Lodge, South Dakota, for twenty years. After serving in the army during World War I, Townsend moved to Long Beach, California, in 1920. His medical practice proved so limited that he had to work part-time for a realtor, Robert Earl Clements. A former classmate helped Townsend secure a job in the Long Beach Health Office, but he was laid off a short time later. Townsend was nearly seventy years old and destitute, so he began calling for a plan where the government would give $200 per month to everyone over the age of sixty not enjoying that income. Although the money would come from a business tax, Townsend felt it would pump money into the economy, help end the depression, and create jobs for the young.

Townsend wrote a letter to the People's Forum column of a local newspaper late in 1933 and received a petition with more than 2,000 signatures in a few days. The realtor, Robert Earl Clements, joined forces with Townsend in setting up a headquarters on January 1, 1934. They founded the Old-Age Revolving Pensions, Ltd., to promote their scheme. Within two months they were sending out 1,500 pamphlets a week at 25¢ each. They started a newspaper, *The Townsend National Weekly*; hired an office staff of ninety-five people; and by September 1934 were receiving more than 1,000 letters a day. "Townsend Clubs" began to form; and by January 1935 there were more than 3,000 of them, with a membership of more than 500,000 people. The clubs were based on congressional districts and designed to serve as lobbying organizations for old-age pensions.

The Townsend plan appeared at a time when only twenty-eight states had any type of old-age pension, running from $7.28 per month in Montana to $30 per month in Maryland. In 1935 there were more than 7 1/2 million people in the United States over the age of sixty-five, and large numbers of them were in desperate financial condition. Most economists believed Townsend's plan was folly, but it struck a responsive chord among the American people. To the faithful, Townsend promised that old people "had more buying experience than those of younger years . . . they could become a research, educational, and corrective force in both a material and spiritual way." Club meetings were always patriotic and religious in tone.

While Townsend was campaigning on behalf of the elderly, Robert Clements was turning the movement into a promotional enterprise. He marketed Townsend buttons, badges, banners, license plates, tire covers, radiator emblems, pictures, pamphlets, and songs. The newspaper circulation reached 300,000 and was reaping a profit of $200,000 a year, mostly from ads for products to alleviate the discomforts of the elderly. The advertising companies gave Clements and Townsend a cut of the profits on merchandise sold.

With such a public profile, political action was inevitable. Townsend became somewhat of a threat to Franklin D. Roosevelt* by 1934 and 1935. John Steven McGroarty introduced the Townsend Plan into Congress in January 1935. Within three months more than 20 million signatures were collected in support of the bill, but Congress rejected the bill because of its impracticalities. Instead, they turned to the administration's Social Security Bill as a way of appealing to Townsend's supporters without enacting the Townsend Plan. Passage of the Social Security Act in 1935* took some of the wind from Townsend's sails. He threw his support to the Union party*—a coalition of his supporters and those of Father Charles Coughlin,* Gerald L. K. Smith,* and William Lemke*—in 1936 in a third-party effort to oust Franklin D. Roosevelt from the White House. One month before the election, Townsend switched allegiances and endorsed Alfred M. Landon* for president. Congress found Townsend guilty of contempt for refusing to testify before a committee investigating Old-Age Revolving Pensions, Ltd., but President Roosevelt commuted the sentence. For the remainder of his life, Townsend supported Republican candidates, but the passage of social security and the prosperity of the 1940s made his demands for old-age pensions seem anachronistic. He died in Los Angeles on September 1, 1960. (David H. Bennett, *Demagogues in the Depression. American Radicals and the Union Party, 1932–1936*, 1969.)

TRANSPORTATION ACT OF 1940 Although the Motor Carrier Act of 1935* had tried to set minimum rates for motor carriers and help railroads remain competitive in the freight industry, the railroads seemed doomed by the late 1930s, caught in an impossible squeeze between intense competition, depressed rates and economic activity, and huge fixed costs because of overwhelming debt burdens. After a March 1938 conference of ICC,* RFC,* treasury, commerce, and agriculture officials to examine the railroad crisis, President Franklin D. Roosevelt* appointed a Committee of Three, headed by ICC Chairman Joseph

Eastman* to summarize the conference. They recommended that in addition to RFC equipment and credit loans to troubled railroads, the ICC should be authorized to consolidate and unify American railroads, to do what the Emergency Railroad Transportation Act of 1933* had failed to do. Both labor and management resisted the proposal; labor because it would eliminate thousands of jobs and management because it would destroy several corporate entities. Congress rejected the measure. Later in the year, President Roosevelt appointed a committee of labor and railroad management to make an alternate proposal, but they jointly agreed to leave the problem out of the hands of the federal government. Not until 1940 did Congress pass the Transportation Act, but it did not really address the problem. Indeed, it relieved the ICC of its 1920 obligation to develop a consolidation plan. But the Transportation Act did give the ICC jurisdiction over coastwise, intercoastal, inland, and Great Lakes common and contract water-carriers in interstate and foreign commerce. Still, Congress exempted bulk shipments, which comprised most of inland waterway traffic. Finally, the act created a Transportation and Research Board to determine the place of rail, motor, and water carriers in the national transportation system. (Ari Hoogenboom and Olive Hoogenboom, *A History of the ICC. From Panacea to Palliative*, 1976.)

TRAYLOR, MELVIN ALVAH Melvin A. Traylor was one of the more prominent American businessmen in the early 1930s who were loyal Democrats. He was born in Breeding, Kentucky, on October 21, 1878, graduated from public high school in Adair County, Kentucky, and moved to Texas in 1898. Traylor taught school for a while, studied law privately, and was admitted to the Texas bar in 1901. He served as assistant attorney in Hill County, Texas, in 1904 and 1905 and rose to the presidency of the Citizens National Bank of Ballinger, Texas, between 1907 and 1910. Traylor succeeded in executive positions at several other banks, including the Stock Yards National Bank in East St. Louis and the Live Stock Exchange National Bank in Chicago, before joining the First National Bank of Chicago as vice-president in 1919. By 1925 Traylor was president of the bank. One year later he was elected president of the American Bankers' Association. Active in Democratic politics, Traylor remembered his own poverty-stricken roots in rural Kentucky, maintained a strong sympathy for dirt farmers, and ran as a "darkhorse," "favorite-son" candidate for the presidential nomination in 1932. When Franklin D. Roosevelt* won the nomination, Tralyor enthusiastically campaigned for him, just as he had done for William Jennings Bryan in 1896. During the banking crisis of 1933, he served as an informal adviser to New Deal* financial experts. Melvin Alvah Traylor died on February 14, 1934. (*New York Times*, February 15, 1934.)

TREASURY RELIEF ART PROJECT A contemporary of the Federal Art Project,* the Treasury Relief Art Project of 1935–1938 was a separate entity, funded by the WPA* and administered by Edward Bruce, the Treasury Department official who had presided over the Public Works of Art Project* between 1933 and 1934. The Treasury Relief Art Project produced murals and sculptures for federal buildings which had no funds for art projects. At its peak, the TRAP employed 356 artists who produced eighty-five murals, thirty-nine sculptures, and 10,215 easels. The Treasury Relief Art Project was transferred to the Federal Art Project in June 1938. (William F. McDonald, *Federal Relief Administration and the Arts*, 1969.)

TRUMAN, HARRY S Harry S Truman was born on May 8, 1884, in Lamar, Missouri. He attended public schools in Missouri, worked the family farm near Independence, and served in the American Expeditionary Force in France during World War I. After the war, Truman studied law at night school in Kansas City, became active in local Democratic politics, and gained the post of Jackson County judge in 1922 because of his support from ''Boss'' Tom Pendergast.* He was presiding judge of the Jackson County court between 1926 and 1934 and then secured the Democratic nomination for the U. S. Senate. In the Roosevelt landslide, Truman defeated Republican Roscoe C. Patterson. During his freshman term, Truman was an obscure but loyal New Deal* Democrat, representing an anti-trust progressivism combined with the mentality of the Missouri Democratic machine. He was re-elected in 1940 and then achieved prominence as chairman of the Senate Committee to Investigate the National Defense Program. President Franklin D. Roosevelt* turned to Truman as a compromise running mate in the election of 1944, and Truman became the 33rd president of the United States on April 12, 1945, after Roosevelt's sudden death. He brought the war to a successful conclusion and tried to promote his ''Fair Deal'' legislation involving civil rights, full employment, and stable prices. Truman surprised the nation in 1948 with the ''underdog'' victory over Governer Thomas E. Dewey, and that second term was consumed by foreign policy questions involving Korea, China, and the Soviet Union. Truman retired from political life in 1953 and returned to Missouri, where he died on December 26, 1972. (Alfred Steinberg, *The Man from Missouri. The Life and Times of Harry S. Truman*, 1962.)

TRUTH-IN-SECURITIES ACT (See SECURITIES ACT OF 1933.)

TUGWELL, REXFORD GUY Born on July 10, 1891, in Sinclairville, New York, Rexford Tugwell was recruited at the age of forty-two from Columbia University to help design and implement the New Deal.* He earned his B. S., A. M., and Ph.D. (1922) in economics from the Wharton School of Finance and Commerce at the University of Pennsylvania. From 1920 he taught economics at Columbia University, rising to the rank of full professor in 1931. He had a reputation for expertise in agricultural economics and his advocacy of national planning and government regulation of private enterprise. Before joining the Roosevelt administration, Tugwell had written the following books: *The Economic Basis for Public Interest* (1922), *The Trend of Economics* (1924),

American Economic Life (1925), *Industry's Coming of Age* (1927), *Soviet Russia in the Second Decade* (1928), and *The Industrial Discipline* (1933).

Tugwell received appointment as assistant secretary of agriculture under Secretary Henry A. Wallace,* but informally his major role was economic adviser to President Roosevelt. Tugwell was part of a growing school of economists who had long since abandoned the idea of laissez-faire and a market economy. Since the Industrial Revolution, economic organizations had become increasingly national and international in scope, operating from highly centralized corporate establishments. The Progressive movement had partially recognized that change by deciding in its anti-trust programs to regulate big business. But for Tugwell, the time had come to transcend progressivism by using the federal government not just as a bureaucratic regulator but as the only central institution in the society capable of establishing national economic goals, organizing national resources, and achieving those objectives. He saw those goals as full employment, price stability, and increasing incomes for the disadvantaged. Tugwell found himself considerably to the left of most New Deal economists, primarily because of his willingness, even enthusiasm, to use the federal government as the major vehicle for economic and social change.

Roosevelt appointed Tugwell under secretary of agriculture in 1934, and he served there until 1935. During the first "hundred days,"* Tugwell had played a major role in drafting the Agricultural Adjustment Act.* The basic goal of the AAA* was to restore farm prices to parity* with non-agricultural prices. By levying a tax on processors, the federal government would generate the revenue to subsidize farm income. The Agricultural Adjustment Administration would pay farmers to restrict production, a step which would curtail farm surpluses and shore up farm prices. Only then could farmer purchasing power be restored and a rash of farm mortgage foreclosures be prevented. The law, passed in May 1933, became the source of contemporary farm price support programs.

In 1935 President Roosevelt named Tugwell to head the newly-created Resettlement Administration.* Because of his views of economic planning and social change, Tugwell was a natural pick for the post. Between 1935 and 1937 the Resettlement Administration worked to assist poor farmers to resettle in other areas, provide government programs to prevent soil erosion and stream pollution, establish flood control and reforestation projects, grant loans to enable poor farmers to purchase better land and agricultural equipment, and establish subsistence homestead communities with low-income housing called "Greenbelt towns."* The Resettlement Administration proved quite controversial, especially among middle- and upper-class property interests who feared the loss of tenant and sharecropper labor and the undermining of rental rates from government housing. In 1937 the Resettlement Administration was absorbed by the Farm Security Administration,* and Tugwell resigned, accepting the position of chairman of the planning department with the New York City Planning Commission. He became chancellor of the University of Puerto Rico in 1941, and Roosevelt shortly thereafter named him governor of Puerto Rico. Tugwell stayed there throughout World War II, writing *The Stricken Land* in 1946. After leaving government service, Tugwell returned to academia as professor of political science (1946–1957) and director of the Institute of Planning (1946–1952) at the University of Chicago. Loyal to his faith in federal economic planning, he backed the Progressive party ticket of Henry Wallace in the election of 1948. During the 1950s and 1960s, Tugwell's writings continued to support national economic planning and included: *The Place of Planning in Society* (1954), *A Chronicle of Jeopardy* (1955), *The Democratic Roosevelt* (1957), *The Art of Politics* (1958), *The Brains Trust* (1968), and *Tugwell's Thoughts on Planning* (1975). Rexford G. Tugwell died on July 21, 1979. (Bernard Sternsher, *Rexford Tugwell and the New Deal*, 1964.)

DUANE WINDSOR

TULLEY, GRACE GEORGE Grace Tully was born on August 9, 1900, in Bayonne, New Jersey, to an Irish family steeped in the traditions of the Roman Catholic Church and the Democratic party.* Educated in a series of Catholic parochial schools, Tully went to work in 1918 for Bishop Patrick Hayes, auxiliary bishop and head of the church's Military Ordinate. She served as Hayes' secretary until 1928 when she went to work for the Democratic National Committee during Al Smith's* campaign for the presidency. The committee assigned her to work as secretary to Eleanor Roosevelt.* After Franklin D. Roosevelt* was inaugurated as governor of New York, she became his private secretary, a position she held until his death in 1945. After his death, Tully stayed active in Democratic politics, working as a member of the Roosevelt Campobello International Park Commission. (Grace Tully, *F. D. R. My Boss*, 1949.)

TWENTY-FIRST AMENDMENT The Democratic party* platform of 1932 had advocated the repeal of the Eighteenth Amendment. The plank called for immediate action by Congress to propose such an amendment to the states. After the Democratic victory, the lame-duck Congress submitted on February 20, 1933, the proposed amendment to the states.

Section 1. The eighteenth article of Amendment to the Constitution of the United States is hereby repealed.
Section 2. The transportation or importation into any state, territory, or possession of the United States for delivery or use therein of intoxicating liquors, in violation of the laws thereof, is hereby prohibited.
Section 3. This article shall be inoperative unless it shall have been ratified as an amendment to the Constitution by convention in the several states, as provided in the Constitution, within seven years from the date of the submission thereof to the states by Congress.

There was some controversy about procedures because this was the first amendment to be submitted by Congress for ratification by conventions in the states. The selection of delegates differed from state to state. In most cases, delegates were pledged simply for or against ratification. Thus, in the conventions there was little or no debate; delegates voted as they had pledged to vote. Approval was swift and the Twenty-first Amendment was proclaimed on December 5, 1933. (Alfred H. Kelly and Winfred A. Harbison, *The American Constitution*, 1970; *Proceedings of the Democratic National Convention of 1932*, p. 146.)

JOSEPH M. ROWE, JR.

"TWO-THIRDS RULE" Ever since 1836, when the Democratic party* first held a national convention, a two-thirds vote of all the delegates had been required to select a presidential candidate. At that time the party had been divided between the solid South and the northern machines of people like Martin Van Buren. Committed to its own institutions and suspicious of northern intentions, the southerners viewed the two-thirds rule as a protective veto over any unsuitable candidates. During the Civil War and postwar years, the two-thirds rule became sacrosanct to the South. They felt they needed that minority veto on the party ticket. On several occasions, the rule had become very controversial. In 1912 Senator Champ Clark of Missouri had held a majority of the delegates over eight ballots, but he could not get the two-thirds, and Woodrow Wilson eventually wrested the nomination from him. Twelve years later, the party went through the trauma of 102 ballots as Al Smith* and William Gibbs McAdoo* struggled for the nomination. In the end, John W. Davis* got the lead spot on the ticket. Franklin D. Roosevelt's* forces contemplated an attack on the two-thirds rule in the campaign of 1932. The growing strength of the Democratic party in the urban north gave them some leverage, but they abandoned the attempt once they felt confident of getting the nomination. Roosevelt was nominated on the fourth ballot. When the time came for the 1936 election,* however, Roosevelt's renomination was not even an issue, so he decided to eliminate the two-thirds rule. James Farley* engineered the move, and Senator Joel Bennett "Champ" Clark* of Missouri led the fight against the rule. Convinced that his father should have had the nomination back in 1912, Clark led the movement with a passion. In the end, it was no battle at all. President Roosevelt's power at the convention was overwhelming; the delegates eliminated the rule by voice vote, symbolizing the shift of the party from its historical southern to an urban northern base. (Arthur M. Schlesinger, Jr., *The Age of Roosevelt. Vol. III. The Politics of Upheaval, 1935–1936*, 1960.)

TYDINGS, MILLARD EVELYN Millard E. Tydings was born in Havre de Grace, Maryland, on April 6, 1890. He graduated from the Maryland Agricultural College in 1910 and then received a law degree from the University of Maryland in 1913. Tydings practiced law privately in Havre de Grace, served a term in the state legislature in 1916–1917, and then joined the army during World War I. He saw action with the American Expeditionary Force in France. Tydings returned from the war and regained his seat in the state legislature, serving as speaker between 1920 and 1922. He won election as a Democrat to Congress in 1922 and remained there until 1927, when he began his long career in the United States Senate.

Tydings had very cosmopolitan tastes, with interests in drama, painting, and music; and he did not carry the racial animosities of so many other southern Democrats of the era. He was also a strong anti-prohibitionist, believing firmly that the Eighteenth Amendment was a violation of individual rights. But Tydings also proved to be a very conservative Democrat and anti-New Dealer, a thorn in President Franklin D. Roosevelt's* side. In one of his first acts as a U. S. senator in the 1920s, he opposed all federal government development of Muscle Shoals* and during the "hundred days"* he fought the AAA,* NRA,* and TVA.* Later in the New Deal,* Tydings vocally opposed the "court-packing"* scheme and executive reorganization plans as a subterfuge for Roosevelt's dictatorial inclinations. He was so consistently an opponent of the New Deal that by 1938 even James Farley,* who opposed most of the president's "purge"* plans, agreed that Tydings should be targeted as a Democrat to have defeated in the senatorial primaries. His hatred of New Deal labor and housing policies, as well as his opposition to so much of the early New Deal, had left him with no support in the administration. The president openly supported Tydings' Democratic opponent, former coal miner and Congressman David J. Lewis. Although Tydings did not openly attack Roosevelt or the New Deal, he did criticize the president for interfering in local politics. In the end, Roosevelt's "purge" backfired, and Tydings handily defeated Lewis and later won re-election. Tydings then served in the Senate until 1951. He died on February 9, 1961. (James T. Patterson, *Congressional Conservatism and the New Deal*, 1967.)

U

UNEMPLOYED COUNCILS Late in the 1920s, energetic young Communist activists began seeking out the jobless throughout the country. With the onset of mass unemployment in 1930, such organizing activities became a top priority for Communists. In Chicago, for example, Communists participated in over 2,000 mass demonstrations between 1930 and 1935. The protests were used to build a core of local activists around whom the Unemployed Councils were organized. A Communist-led unemployed movement had emerged by February 1930 and burst dramatically on the public scene on March 6, 1930—International Unemployed Day, when the Unemployed Councils sponsored demonstrations across the country which led to the eventual arrest of more than 4,000 people in the ensuing five months. Unemployed workers in many cities began forming loosely-organized, neighborhood-oriented councils with a Communist-led Unemployed Councils of the USA directing them. Led by Herbert Benjamin, the Unemployed Councils of the USA sponsored "hunger marches" in 1931 and 1932 and petition drives for unemployment insurance. On the local level, the Unemployed Councils often forced concessions from relief authorities through demonstrations at relief offices, city halls, and state capitals. In Chicago, for example, the Unemployed Councils on several occasions blocked citywide relief cuts and, by handling complaints from thousands of people, helped establish important precedents on the adequacy and quality of relief. Unemployed councils also worked for the prevention of evictions. Members blocked the entrance of sheriffs or police, returned furniture, and packed courts to pressure judges in order to stop evictions. In Detroit especially, the Unemployed Councils were effective in stopping evictions.

The national organization of the Unemployed Councils strengthened and solidified in the years after 1933. Yet these same years saw the loss of some of the vitality and spontaneity of the unemployment movement, particularly on the local level. The local councils settled down as a more orderly movement that sought to represent the jobless in their dealings with relief authorities; they became in many areas the bargaining agent for both relief recipients and (starting in 1935) WPA* workers. Large demonstrations and eviction resistance flared up at times, but more often the unemployed organizations quietly carried out their trade union functions. These same years saw the disappearance of the Unemployed Councils as a distinct entity. In 1936 in the spirit of unity of the Popular Front era, the councils merged with the Socialist-led Workers' Alliance and the merged group took the name of the Socialist organization. Nevertheless, Communist leaders like Herbert Benjamin as well as the original councils in many areas remained a major force within the unified Workers' Alliance.

The Unemployed Councils along with other unemployed organizations of the depression era can be credited with several achievements. They resolved the immediate individual grievances of their members, won higher levels of relief and more equitable and less degrading relief practices, and mobilized pressure for the passage of unemployment insurance legislation. Perhaps even more important, the Unemployed Councils helped raise the political and social consciousness of the thousands of workers who passed through its ranks and learned the power of organization as a political economic weapon. Many of those who organized the CIO* came directly out of the Unemployed Councils. Although the councils never attracted more than a minority of the jobless, they constituted the most powerful movement of unemployed workers in American history and significantly advanced the cause of the forgotten man and woman of the 1930s. (Roy Rosenzweig, "Organizing the Unemployed: The Early Years of the Great Depression, 1929–1933," *Labor History*, X:37–60, 1976.)

ROY ROSENZWEIG

UNEMPLOYED LEAGUES In the summer of 1931 Carl Branin, a labor editor, joined with students and teachers at the Seattle Labor College to organize the Unemployed Citizens' League of Seattle. Through barter and the exchange of labor, UCL members obtained 120,000 pounds of fish, 10,000 cords of firewood, and eight carloads of potatoes, pears, and apples. By early 1932 over 6,000 families were organized into what one commentator called "The Republic of the Penniless." Soon the dream of a self-help cooperative faded, and the Seattle group turned to politics and direct action, using its political clout to take control of the city's relief apparatus and to successfully back candidates for mayor and county commissioner. At the same time, some segments of the UCL began to experiment with such insurgent tactics as physically resisting evictions and restoring cut-off electric and gas services.

The Conference on Progressive Labor Action closely followed the UCL. The CPLA, whose members were usually referred to as the "Musteites" after their leader A. J. Muste, aspired to develop an independent left-wing working-class movement and sensed the political potential of jobless organizations. Local Musteite organizers began to copy the Seattle model: organizing groups around self-help projects and then pushing them toward political militancy. Between 1932 and 1934 thousands of unemployed people from the industrial and mining towns of Ohio, the steel mills of Pittsburgh, the coal fields of eastern Pennsylvania and West Virginia, and the textile mills of North Carolina enlisted under their banners. By linking their unemployed leagues with such patriotic symbols as the Rattlesnake Flag and the slogan "Don't Tread on Me," they won strong local support in many communities.

The strength of these Musteite unemployed associations lay in local organization and local actions—sit-ins in relief offices, resistance to evictions, and petitions to local officials as well as self-help projects. But the groups did develop a formal national structure in July 1933 when 800 delegates from thirteen states convened in Columbus, Ohio, and created the National Unemployed League. Nevertheless, the Unemployed Leagues never expanded beyond the regional base and the approximately 150,000 members they had attracted by mid-1933. Indeed, the organization gradually declined over the next few years because of the emergence of New Deal* relief and reform programs, the problems of maintaining an organization of unemployed people who frequently moved looking for work, political attacks from the right, and shifting Musteite interests as they formed the American Workers party and then the Trotskyite Workers party. The Unemployed Leagues had a notable success in 1934. Members of the Lucas County, Ohio, Unemployed League defied an injunction against picketing at the Toledo Auto-Lite works, joined plant workers on the picket lines, and helped them win their strike.

Still, the Unemployed Leagues declined throughout the 1930s. The growing importance of New Deal relief programs meant that jobless workers employed on the WPA* and similar projects needed a national organization that could deal effectively with officials in Washington. An extreme internal factionalism sapped the energy of leading Musteite organizers. So in April 1936 the NUL merged with the Socialist-led Workers Alliance and the Communist-led Unemployed Councils* to form the Workers Alliance of America. The Workers Alliance of America continued to be an effective lobbying agency for the jobless through the rest of the 1930s, but this merger marked the disappearance of the Unemployed Leagues as a distinct social and political force. Nevertheless, its activities in the first half of the 1930s had not only improved the lot of the jobless but also demonstrated the effectiveness of a flexible, grass roots protest movement of the unemployed. (Roy Rosenzweig, "Radicals and the Jobless: The Musteites and the Unemployed Leagues," *Labor History*, XVI:52–77, 1975.)

ROY ROSENZWEIG

UNION PARTY By 1934, despite the abundance of relief and recovery legislation, the New Deal* was beginning to attract serious criticism from the right and the left. The left-wing critics were a curiously mixed lot, ranging from Huey Long* and his Share-Our-Wealth program to Norman Thomas* and the Socialist party,* and generally criticized Franklin D. Roosevelt* for not having done enough to ease the suffering caused by the depression. The greatest political threat, as far as Roosevelt was concerned, was posed by four groups in particular: Huey P. Long and the Share-Our-Wealth plan; Francis E. Townsend* and Old-Age Revolving Pensions, Ltd.; Father Charles Coughlin* and the National Union for

Social Justice; and William Lemke* and the Nonpartisan League.* After Huey P. Long's assassination in 1935, Gerald L. K. Smith* took over the Share-Our-Wealth movement. In the most general way, all four had, on the surface at least, a similar approach to the depression. Coughlin wanted to take monetary control out of the hands of private bankers and print large amounts of paper currency from a new central bank. Long and Smith wanted to confiscate large fortunes and redistribute the money to poor families. Townsend wanted to provide pensions to the elderly which they would have to spend, increasing circulation and stimulating recovery. Lemke wanted to print large volumes of paper currency and refinance farm and home mortgages. Above all else, they hated Roosevelt and the New Deal, and in 1936 they united to oppose his re-election, forming the Union party. They nominated William Lemke of North Dakota for president and Thomas C. O'Brien of Massachusetts as vice-president. The Union party platform was a composite of the four groups. In addition to promoting economic protectionism and foreign policy isolationism, they called for inflation of the currency, refinancing of all farm and home mortgages, old-age pensions, increased levels of work relief, high taxes on the rich, and anti-trust action against monopolies.

The Union party proved to be a fiasco, victimized by the competitive egos and political excesses of its leaders. Each man was reluctant to give much money to the party; they preferred to keep it in their own particular organizations. Without a political base in Louisiana, Smith found his hold on the Share-Our-Wealth movement slipping. His anti-Catholic, Ku Klux Klan background began to worry Charles Coughlin. In October, when Smith announced his intention of forming a paramilitary group to take over the United States government, the others expelled him from the Union party. In September the Vatican denounced the political activities of Coughlin; and Bishop Michael J. Gallagher, who brought back the message from Rome, even endorsed Roosevelt. Francis Townsend then all but destroyed the Union party in October by endorsing Republican Alf Landon* for president.

The election was anti-climactic. With little money and even less local organization, the party made a dismal showing. Lemke polled only 882,479 votes, to 16,674,665 for Landon and 27,752,869 for Roosevelt. The Union party was dead. Lemke tried to keep it alive, working to establish clubs in rural communities and city precincts, and holding the National Conference of the Union party on December 19, 1936, but he gathered little support. By 1938 the party was broke, and it officially dissolved in 1939. (David H. Bennett, *Demagogues in the Depression. American Radicals and the Union Party, 1932–1936*, 1969.)

UNITED STATES CHAMBER OF COMMERCE Formed in 1912 to promote business cooperation and economic growth in the United States, the U. S. Chamber of Commerce became one of the most powerful interest groups in the country. A response of the organizational demands of the Progressive era, the chamber evolved into the recognized voice of the general business community. During the New Deal,* although at first sympathetic to the National Recovery Administration* and the idea of a business commonwealth, the Chamber of Commerce soon became Franklin D. Roosevelt's* most bitter and consistent critic. Henry I. Harriman* had led the chamber during the first years of the New Deal and had tried to work closely with the administration, but in 1935 Harper Sibley became president and the chamber became openly anti-New Deal. Unlike the Business Advisory Council,* the U. S. Chamber of Commerce was a bastion of laissez-faire and openly opposed the National Labor Relations Act,* Social Security Act,* Walsh-Healey Act,* Robinson-Patman Act,* Guffey coal acts,* Banking Acts of 1933* and 1935,* anti-trust policy, and all forms of labor standards legislation. At their 1935 convention, the U. S. Chamber of Commerce formally censured Franklin D. Roosevelt and the New Deal and in 1936 launched a pamphlet campaign blaming him for the persistence of the depression. The president openly chastised them for their parochial, self-serving attitudes. Although a tenuous truce existed between them after 1936, the chamber still demanded "fiscal responsibility" and balanced budgets as the answer to the problem of unemployment. (Robert M. Collins, "Positive Business Response to the New Deal: The Roots of the Committee for Economic Development, 1933–1942," *Business History Review*, LII:369–391, 1978.)

UNITED STATES EMPLOYMENT SERVICE The United States Employment Service, the Department of Labor agency that manages the federal-state system of public employment offices, was permanently chartered by the Wagner-Peyser Act* of 1933. This legislation legally terminated a United States Employment Service dating from 1914, when Secretary of Labor William B. Wilson converted a bureau of information at Ellis Island into a "Bureau of Employment" that aspired to match workers and jobs. During World War I this bureau became the U. S. Employment Service and managed the selection and placement of workers in war industries. Rather than permanently charter the agency, Congress slashed its budget after the war; yet the agency continued as a budget line during the 1920s and primarily served the market for agricultural labor. Its appropriations ever sensitive to dramatic labor market change, the USES budget trebled by 1932—after Congress had sent to the White House Senator Robert Wagner's* legislation to abolish and reconstitute the agency.

Two months before President Franklin D. Roosevelt* signed the Wagner-Peyser Act, Secretary of Labor Frances Perkins* administratively disbanded Herbert Hoover's* USES. Her associate, Mary La Dame* (herself an expert on public employment offices) became the interim director of the reconstituted USES, and Frank Persons* (an industrial relations expert and officer in the New York Charity Organization Society) served as its permanent director during most of the New Deal.* They set for the agency a professional, reform-minded tone, emphasizing the necessity of merit selection for federal and state officials. They also moved quickly in 1933 on two fronts: first, to establish the role of the Labor

Department in emergency federal relief efforts; and second, to conclude agreements with each state establishing a permanent federal-state employment office network.

For three years, most USES activity revolved around the relief programs. The Special Board for Public Works agreed to vest the USES with all responsibility for recruiting labor for Public Works Administration* projects; the Department of Labor created the National Reemployment service under USES auspices to operate federally managed local labor exchanges for the PWA. By the fall of 1933, half the nation's counties had an NRS office; within a month after the creation of the Civil Works Administration* in November, the NRS expanded into most of the nation's counties. The NRS thereafter waxed and waned with the federal relief effort. It contracted in 1934 with the termination of the CWA, only to expand with creation of the Works Progress Administration* in 1935. In 1938 the NRS was liquidated, as most states had signed compacts joining the United States Employment Service.

The extension of the permanent state-federal system proceeded at a deliberate pace until the imminent start-up of the unemployment benefits under the Social Security Act* spurred state action. A number of states signed agreements with the USES in 1933 and 1934, but the growth of state-run offices was slow; barely 300 existed in December 1935. The Social Security Act in 1935 stipulated that unemployment compensation benefits would be paid through state employment offices or other approved agencies; at the federal level, the Social Security Board and USES agreed to channel benefits through the latter. By 1938 most states had come to terms with the USES and joined the system; while 348 state offices existed at the end of 1936, the states managed more than 1,000 (many former NRS offices) only a year later.

In 1939, under a federal reorganization, the USES was moved from the Labor Department to the new Federal Security Agency;* in December 1941, Roosevelt federalized the 1,500 state-run employment offices for the duration of the war. (Raymond C. Atkinson et al., *Public Employment Service in the United States*, 1938.)

DAVID BRIAN ROBERTSON

UNITED STATES FILM SERVICE The United States Film Service was established on August 13, 1938, at the request of President Franklin D. Roosevelt.* The president had been impressed with the work of Pare Lorentz,* whose two films, "The Plow That Broke the Plains" and "The River" had been sponsored by the Resettlement Administration* and the Farm Security Administration.* To give Lorentz more formal administrative support, Roosevelt created the United States Film Service and placed it under the umbrella of the National Emergency Council.* Pare Lorentz was named director of the service, with Arch Mercey as assistant director and Floyd Crosby as director of photography. The service was charged with making films to educate government employees and inform the public about current social and economic problems. Funding came from relief appropriations in the WPA,* PWA,* and Farm Security Administration.

The life of the U. S. Film Service was short-lived. Although Lorentz was able to produce "The Fight for Life" (1940) and "Power and the Land" (1940), the service encountered the opposition of the private film industry, which resented such federal intervention into their domain, and New Deal* opponents who viewed it as a vehicle for administration propaganda. In 1939 the House of Representatives failed to fund the U. S. Film Service, so the president once again took about $350,000 from other relief agencies to continue the work. He also placed the U. S. Film Service in the Office of Education, which was transferred to the new Federal Security Agency* in 1939. Congress then formally stripped it of all funds in 1940. (Robert L. Snyder, *Pare Lorentz and the Documentary Film*, 1968.)

UNITED STATES FOREST SERVICE During the New Deal,* two pieces of legislation affected the U. S. Forest Service. President Franklin D. Roosevelt's* lifelong interest in forest and wildlife conservation gave the Forest Service a real power base in the White House. Although the Forest Service spent a good deal of time fighting off Harold L. Ickes'* attempts to transfer it from the Department of Agriculture to the Department of the Interior and did not manage to substantially increase the size of the federal forest reserve, it did advertise the dual necessity of conservation and sustained yield. On August 29, 1935, Congress passed the Fulmer Act permitting the federal government to cooperate with the states in managing and developing state forests and in federal forest management. Federal funds were available for the expansion of state forest land, with proceeds from the land returning to the federal government until the amount equaled the cost of the land. States would then receive title. The Farm Forestry Act of May 18, 1937, authorized the government to develop a program of farm forestry and to continue tree planting on the Great Plains—what became known as the Shelterbelt Project.* Finally, the Forest Service tried to work closely with private timber operators during the 1930s in order not to compete with them and further depress lumber prices. The Forest Service restricted its cutting and then tried to sell timber only in non-competitive markets. By the late 1930s and early 1940s, with commercial demand up substantially, the competition of the past between the Forest Service and private timber producers had turned to cooperation. (Richard Lowitt, *The New Deal in the West*, 1984.)

UNITED STATES HOUSING AUTHORITY (See WAGNER-STEAGALL HOUSING ACT OF 1937.)

UNITED STATES V. BUTLER ET AL. Under sections 9 and 16 of the Agricultural Adjustment Act of 1933,* the federal government attempted to collect a claim from the receivers (William H. Butler et al.) of the bankrupt Hoosac Mills Corporation for processing and floor taxes on cotton. The receivers rejected the claim and the case went to the federal district court. That court found the government's claim valid and ordered the taxes paid. The decree was appealed to the 1st Circuit Court of Appeals, which reversed the order. The United States brought certiorari, and the Supreme Court* accepted the appeal.

The case was argued on December 9 and 10, 1935, and decided on January 6, 1936. By a decision of six to three, the AAA* was declared unconstitutional. Writing for the majority, Mr. Justice Owen J. Roberts* set forth a rather disjointed opinion. After a minute examination of the language and intent of the Agricultural Adjustment Act of 1933, Justice Roberts agreed with the circuit court that the processing tax was not a "tax" at all in the sense of the constitution but "a mere incident in the scheme of regulation." Although that did not in itself invalidate the act, Justice Roberts then proceeded to ask if such regulations could be justified under the general welfare clause of the Constitution. He defended Hamilton's broad construction, i.e., that the clause gave Congress a general grant of power to tax and appropriate funds for the general welfare. But Roberts then reached the startling conclusion that agricultural overproduction and the resultant collapse of the farm economy were local and not national problems. Therefore, the AAA violated the 10th Amendment to the Constitution.

Justice Roberts also protested that the system of voluntary crop reduction provided for in the AAA was not in fact voluntary, but coercive. "Congress has no power," he asserted, "to enforce its command on the farmer to the ends sought by the Agricultural Adjustment Act. It must follow that it may not indirectly accomplish those ends by taxing and spending to purchase compliance." Roberts warned that if such powers were affirmed, Congress could seize control over every aspect of American life. And to demonstrate his point, he adduced several examples of Congress run amuck. Thus, speaking for the majority, Justice Roberts affirmed the judgment of the circuit court striking down the AAA.

Writing for the minority (Harlan Stone,* Louis Brandeis,* Benjamin Cardozo*), Mr. Justice Stone sharply criticized the majority opinion of Justice Roberts. He demonstrated that Roberts' arguments not only lacked consistency and logic but that they misconstrued the language and intent of the AAA. Justice Stone accused the majority of invalidating the AAA not because Congress lacked constitutional power to enact it, but because the majority justices disapproved of the policies inherent in the AAA. In a parting shot, Justice Stone observed that "a tortured construction of the Constitution is not to be justified by recourse to extreme examples of reckless congressional spending." (Gerald O. Dykstra and L. G. Dykstra, *Selected Cases on Government and Business*, 1937; Alfred Kelly and Winfred Harbison, *The American Constitution*, 1970; *Supreme Court Reporter*, LVI:312–329, 1936.)

JOSEPH M. ROWE, JR.

UNITED STATES V. DARBY Fred W. Darby of Georgia was indicted for violation of the Fair Labor Standards Act* for failure to pay the minimum wage, for failure to abide by the maximum hours provision, and for failure to keep records showing the hours and wages of labor. The Federal District Court of the

Southern District of Georgia sustained a demurrer to the indictment and quashed the indictment on the grounds that the Fair Labor Standards Act was unconstitutional. The government appealed to the Supreme Court,* where the case was argued on December 19 and 20, 1940. Judgment was handed down on February 3, 1941 (amended February 17, 1941). Mr. Justice Harlan Stone* delivered the unanimous opinion of the Court.

Justice Stone addressed the two principal questions raised in the case. (1) Did Congress have the power to prohibit from interstate commerce lumber manufactured by Darby's employees who were paid less than the minimum wage; and (2) could Congress compel employers manufacturing goods for interstate commerce to keep records showing wages and hours of employees? In short, were such provisions of the Fair Labor Standards Act constitutional?

Justice Stone first determined that Darby's lumber business was manufacturing lumber for distribution in interstate commerce, although some lumber was confined to intrastate commerce. Did Congress have the constitutional power to prohibit shipment of such goods in interstate commerce? Citing the Marshall Court (*Gibbons v. Ogden*, 1824) Justice Stone affirmed that the power of Congress over interstate commerce "is complete in itself, may be executed to its utmost extent, and acknowledges no limitation, other than are prescribed by the constitution." Responding to the lower court's use of the Tenth Amendment, Justice Stone asserted that "the power [on Congress] can neither be enlarged nor diminished by the exercise or non-exercise of state power." The power of Congress included not only those measures which stimulate and protect commerce, but measures which might prohibit commerce as well. Justice Stone also observed that since the constitution placed no restrictions on congressional regulation of interstate commerce, the courts had no power to restrict congressional action. Thus, Congress had complete power to bar from interstate commerce goods produced in violation of congressional regulations. And to see that employers were complying with such regulations, Congress could require employers to keep accurate records showing that compliance.

In conclusion, the Court ruled that "the Act is sufficiently definite to meet constitutional demands. One who employs people without conforming to the prescribed wage and hour conditions, to work on goods which he ships or expects to ship across state lines, is warned that he may be subject to the criminal penalties of the Act." The decision of the district court was reversed; the constitutionality of the Fair Labor Standards Act was upheld. (Alfred H. Kelly and Winfred A. Harbison, *The American Constitution*, 1970; *Supreme Court Reporter*, Vol. LX1:451–463, 1941.)

JOSEPH M. ROWE, JR.

U.S. MARITIME COMMISSION Established by the Merchant Marine Act of 1936,* the U. S. Maritime Commission was a five-member, bi-partisan, quasi-judicial, independent regulatory agency charged with implementing that act. Each of the five members served staggered six-year terms. The commission enjoyed a great deal of independence and a complex array of duties, including research into current maritime operations, setting export rates, sponsoring a tramp fleet, cooperating with industry on engineering research, regulating merchant marine practices, and proposing additional legislation. President Franklin D. Roosevelt* nominated Joseph P. Kennedy* as chairman of the U. S. Maritime Commission, with H. A. Wiley, Rear Admiral Emory Land,* Thomas Woodward, and Edward Moran as members. Admiral Land succeeded Kennedy as chairman after the latter's appointment as ambassador to Great Britain in 1937.

The new commission enthusiastically tried to implement the Merchant Marine Act. The mail subsidies of the Merchant Marine Act of 1928 were terminated, and the commission initiated a number of investigations and surveys. They planned to build fifty new ships every year for ten years; but of the other functions detailed to the U. S. Maritime Commission, most had to wait until after World War II. The commission had barely got under way when the war transformed its peacetime role into a much more complicated, expensive operation. But during the 1930s the commission was instrumental in identifying several problems with the Merchant Marine Act of 1936. For example, the commission found that the difference between foreign flag shipping costs and U. S. flag shipping costs could not be consistently ascertained. Even if the data could be assembled, it would be immediately out of date due to rapidly changing conditions. The commission also observed that it was importent in the face of one of the root causes of the American merchant marine decline—higher costs and inefficiency. Since the operating cost differentials represented the parity payment, the government was subsidizing inefficiency as well as higher costs. The commission also found itself mired in labor-management relations and labor disputes which threatened to undermine effectiveness. Joseph P. Kennedy was convinced that industry survival was tied to stability in labor relations, and Congress created the Maritime Labor Board in 1938. The three-member board possessed only conciliation and fact-finding functions. Facing suspicion from maritime labor unions, the board expired in 1942. Finally, the U. S. Maritime Commission found itself at odds with several other federal agencies, such as the Department of Labor, which exercised similar authority. Still, the commission had some admirable accomplishments. Under Admiral Land, its wartime record of constructing over 5,000 ships was outstanding. Like the Merchant Marine Act of 1936, the U. S. Maritime Commission proved fundamental to all subsequent maritime policy. (Samuel A. Lawrence, *United States Merchant Shipping Policies and Politics,* 1966.)

DONALD H. DYAL

V

VANDENBERG, ARTHUR HENDRICK Arthur H. Vandenberg was born on March 22, 1884, in Grand Rapids, Michigan, to a once prominent but recently impoverished family. With powerful entrepreneurial instincts, Vandenberg rose from poverty to become a journalist, editor, and publisher of the Grand Rapids *Herald*. A conservative Republican, he wrote three books on Alexander Hamilton and was appointed to the United States Senate in 1928 to fill the seat vacated by the death of Democrat Woodbridge N. Ferris. Vandenberg remained in the Senate until his death on April 18, 1951. During the 1930s, although not a leader of the anti-New Deal opposition, Vandenberg opposed and voted against such measures as the TVA,* AAA,* National Labor Relations Act,* Fair Labor Standards Act,* Wealth Tax Act,* and the WPA* appropriations. In 1933, however, with Congressman Henry Steagall* of Alabama, Vandenberg sponsored the guaranteed bank deposit plan which became the Federal Deposit Insurance Corporation* in the Banking Act of 1933.*

Although his tenure in the Senate spanned the New Deal* era, Vandenberg's activities and reputation centered principally in the area of foreign affairs. A leading isolationist, Vandenberg, with Senator Gerald P. Nye* of North Dakota, led a major investigation into the munitions industry in 1934 and 1935. Vandenberg was also a prominent member of the Senate Foreign Relations Committee. After the attack on Pearl Harbor, however, he experienced a substantial change of sentiment and subsequently supported the war effort and the increased stature and role of the United States in world affairs. Indeed, Vandenberg was appointed by President Franklin D. Roosevelt* in 1945 as a delegate to the San Francisco meeting of the United Nations. Ironically, Vandenberg, the one time ardent isolationist, is given some credit for drafting Article 51 of the United Nations Charter supporting international peace and security through regional arrangements of collective defense. Arthur H. Vandenberg died on April 18, 1951. (C. David Tompkins, *Senator Arthur H. Vandenberg: The Evolution of a Modern Republican*, 1970.)

JAMES L. CARTER

VAN DEVANTER, WILLIS Willis Van Devanter was born in Marion, Indiana, on April 17, 1859. He attended the Indiana Asbury University (DePauw) between

1875 and 1878 and took a law degree at the University of Cincinnati Law School in 1881. Van Devanter practiced law privately in Marion, Indiana, and then in Cheyenne, Wyoming, between 1881 and 1886. He served as commissioner to revise Wyoming statutes in 1886 and then as city attorney of Cheyenne between 1887 and 1888. Van Devanter served one term in the territorial legislature in 1888 and then was appointed chief justice of the Supreme Court of Wyoming. A conservative, McKinley Republican, Van Devanter was chairman of the Republican State Committee between 1892 and 1894 and a member of the Republican National Committee between 1896 and 1900. President William McKinley appointed him assistant attorney general of the United States, with an assignment in the Department of the Interior. He stayed there until 1903 when President Theodore Roosevelt appointed him as a circuit judge in the 8th United States Judicial Circuit. In 1910 President William Howard Taft named Van Devanter an associate justice of the U. S. Supreme Court.*

During the years of the New Deal,* Van Devanter was one of the "nine old men" who proved most frustrating to President Franklin D. Roosevelt.* Although widely respected for the thoroughness of his opinions and their careful expression, Van Devanter had one of the most conservative judicial philosophies on the Court. Along with Justices Pierce Butler,* George Sutherland,* and James McReynolds,* Van Devanter had clearly aligned himself with those Americans who felt the New Deal was a dangerous, radical departure from traditional public policy. Interpreting the Tenth Amendment as backbone of states' rights and narrowly construing the commerce clause, Van Devanter had voted to overturn the Agricultural Adjustment Administration,* National Recovery Administration,* Guffey-Snyder Bituminous Coal Conservation Act, Tennessee Valley Authority,* Securities and Exchange Commission,* and the National Labor Relations Act.* For Van Devanter, there was really no such thing as "sociological jurisprudence" where the law was adjusted to economic and social circumstance. The law existed to protect property, contracts, and states' rights from arbitrary government action during times of social and economic emergency. The New Deal, with its amassing of federal power and bureaucracy, constituted one such emergency, and it was the obligation of the Supreme Court to protect traditional rights against legislative and executive intervention.

During Franklin D. Roosevelt's "court-packing"* scheme in 1937, Van Devanter agreed with Chief Justice Charles Evans Hughes* that the move was politically-designed and not because the court was overburdened. Afraid that the president might succeed with his plan and drastically alter the nature of the Supreme Court, Van Devanter agreed to go along with the suggestion of Chief Justice Hughes and Senator William Borah* of Idaho that he retire. Already seventy-eight years old, Van Devanter was ready for retirement, and felt the announcement of his resignation might stall the court-packing scheme by relieving the pressure: with a new appointment at his disposal, the president might be less inclined to push ahead with his proposal. On May 18, 1937, on the day the Senate Judiciary Committee was to vote on the proposal, Van Devanter announced his retirement, effective June 2. He then retired to his home in Washington, D. C., and died on February 8, 1941. (Alpheus Mason, *The Supreme Court from Taft to Warren*, 1958; *New York Times*, February 9, 1941.)

VANN, ROBERT LEE Robert Lee Vann was born on August 27, 1879, in Ahoskie, North Carolina. The son of ex-slaves, Vann graduated from high school in 1901, attended the Wayland Academy in Richmond, Virginia, between 1901 and 1903, and then entered the Western University of Pennsylvania in Pittsburgh. He edited the school newspaper, graduated in 1906, and then received a law degree in 1909. To supplement his income, he served as legal counsel to the new black newspaper, *The Pittsburgh Courier*, and in 1910 became editor, a position he held until his death in 1940. During the 1920s, the *Courier* became the most prominent black newspaper in the country; and Vann, the most prominent black journalist. A Republican, Vann supported Franklin D. Roosevelt* in 1932 after becoming disenchanted with Herbert Hoover's* ''feeble attempts'' to relieve the suffering. Roosevelt rewarded Vann with a position as special assistant to the United States attorney general and a spot on the unofficial ''black cabinet.''* In 1936 Vann urged black people throughout the country to switch their political allegiances—to ''turn Lincoln's picture to the wall. That debt has been paid in full.'' Eventually, Vann's position in the Justice Department proved to be more symbolic than real, and he came increasingly to feel that he was being used as a token instead of a real participant in the New Deal.* Vann also began feeling that the New Deal had not really done much for black people. Early in 1936 he resigned his Justice Department position and worked throughout the year to help elect Democratic candidates in Pennsylvania politics. In 1940, however, he broke with the New Deal and endorsed Wendell Willkie's* presidential candidacy. By then he felt that Roosevelt and the New Dealers were really only exploiting the black vote. Robert Vann died of cancer on October 24, 1940. (Andrew Buni, *Robert L. Vann of the Pittsburgh Courier: Politics and Black Journalism*, 1974.)

W

WADSWORTH, JAMES WOLCOTT, JR. James W. Wadsworth, Jr., was born in Geneseo, New York, on August 12, 1877. He graduated from Yale University in 1898, served in Battery A of the Pennsylvania Field Artillery during the Spanish-American War, and became a farmer and rancher in Geneseo after his return from the war in 1899. Wadsworth was elected to the state legislature in 1904 and served until 1910, when he moved to Texas to manage a large ranch. He stayed in Texas until 1915 and then returned to New York. Wadsworth had been elected to the United States Senate as a Republican from New York in 1914, and he served until 1927. He had not been re-elected in 1926. He resumed his agricultural pursuits until winning a seat in Congress in the election of 1932.* Wadsworth kept that congressional seat until 1951. During the 1930s he was a bitter opponent of the New Deal* and a founding member of the American Liberty League.* Wadsworth consistently criticized the New Deal as conservative, anti-business, and anti-American; and he hoped to build a coalition of anti-New Deal northern Republicans and southern Democrats. His visions were never realized. Wadsworth was not a candidate for renomination in 1950 and died on June 21, 1952. (*New York Times*, June 22, 1952.)

WAGNER-CONNERY ACT (See NATIONAL LABOR RELATIONS ACT OF 1935.)

WAGNER-COSTIGAN BILL (See FEDERAL ANTI-LYNCHING BILL.)

WAGNER-CROSSER ACT OF 1935 (See RAILROAD RETIREMENT ACT OF 1935.)

WAGNER-PEYSER ACT Signed by President Franklin D. Roosevelt* in June 1933, the Wagner-Peyser Act established the statutory authority of the U.S. Employment Service.* The bill, said Senator Robert Wagner* of New York, would provide "a really adequate free employment service nationwide in scope." The law authorized federal matching grants to the states for creating and managing such offices; it also placed the USES in the Department of Labor and charged it with providing technical information to the states, maintaining services for veterans and farmers, and developing a system for the interstate matching of workers and jobs. Wagner had a more ambitious vision for the offices, looking forward to a system of local labor market centers that would guide vocational training and industrial location. A number of the bill's proponents saw the measure as an essential prerequisite to a national system of unemployment compensation.

During the hundred days,* the measure seemed to require as little effort as it attracted notice. But no small effort brought the measure to the president's desk. As early as 1914, progressives in Congress introduced a vague measure proposing a full federalized network of labor exchanges. In the same year, the American Association for Labor Legislation made such a system a top priority in its influential ''Practical Program for the Prevention of Unemployment.'' In 1918 an advisory committee to the wartime U. S. Employment Service drafted legislation to charter a federal-state system of public labor exchanges for the postwar period. The basic outlines of the bill came from the experiences of public employment office managers and from the ideas of social welfare intellectuals like John R. Commons* and some of his students. Sponsored by Senator William Kenyon, Republican from Iowa, and Republican Representative John I. Nolan of California, the bill died in the rush to demobilize and privatize during 1919 and 1920. While Nolan and later his widow reintroduced the bill throughout the early and mid-1920s, it was denied even a committee hearing until the Great Depression.

Robert Wagner reopened congressional debate on permanent solutions to unemployment in 1928. He introduced three proposals to that end, including a version of the Kenyon-Nolan measure virtually identical to the original. In 1929 and 1930 the mounting toll of joblessness gave the proposals a new urgency. The Senate Commerce Committee reported the public employment office bill and the Senate approved it by a 34 to 27 vote in May 1930. Supported by liberal groups, such as the AALL and by the AFL,* and opposed by the National Association of Manufacturers,* the bill became a lightning rod for the conflict between Herbert Hoover's* administration and the growing, bi-partisan liberal coalition in Congress. Approved by the House Judiciary Committee, the legislation was bottled up in the Rules Committee until, pressured by the deteriorating economy, imminent adjournment, and intense lobbying by the AALL and others, the committee released Wagner's bill early in 1931. After defeating a last minute administration substitute (182–84), the House approved the bill by voice vote. President Herbert Hoover* then pocket vetoed the bill in March.

Hoover's veto did little more than render the bill a New Deal* measure. Wagner reintroduced it in 1932 and again in 1933, when freshman Representative Theodore Peyser, Democrat from New York, introduced it in the House. Both chambers approved the Wagner-Peyser Act on voice votes in June. On three occasions during the 1930s, Congress amended the legislation. An amendment in 1935 guaranteed small states a minimum federal appropriation, and another in 1938 eliminated a strict percentage of three-quarters of total appropriations earmarked for states. Other important changes occurred in the Social Security Act of 1935,* which singled out the public employment offices as distribution points for unemployment compensation, and Reorganization Plan No. 1 of 1939, which removed the USES from the Department of Labor and placed it in the Bureau of Employment Security of the Federal Security Agency.* Although amended on several occasions after the New Deal, the Wagner-Peyser Act remains the basic charter of the U. S. Employment Service. (Paul Douglas and Aaron Director, *The Problem of Unemployment*, 1931; *Employment Security Review*, June 1953.)

DAVID BRIAN ROBERTSON

WAGNER, ROBERT FERDINAND Born in Hesse-Nassau, Germany, on June 8, 1877, Robert Wagner and his family immigrated to New York City when he was eight. His political education, in the turn-of-the-century Tammany machine, helped forge an urban, progressive, pragmatic approach to domestic reform. Sent to the state legislature in 1904, he served as president pro tem of the state senate by 1911. With House Speaker Alfred E. Smith,* Wagner served on the New York Factory Investigating Commission and guided fifty-six industrial and labor reforms through the legislature by 1914. As a legislator, he emphasized the rights of organized labor and the need for government intervention for economic stability. A political realist, he preferred compromise to failure and, in Congress, focused his attention on a few proposals in each session.

After his election to the U. S. Senate in 1926, Wagner focused on the problem of unemployment, introducing three measures to establish federal responsibility for stabilizing labor markets. Herbert Hoover* signed one of the bills, to improve statistics gathering, in early 1930. The following year the president approved the establishment of a Federal Employment Stabilization Board, but this organization had little ultimate effect on American labor markets. The third measure reconstituted and extended the U. S. Employment Service;* although Hoover vetoed the bill in 1930, Franklin D. Roosevelt* signed it as the Wagner-Peyser Act* in June 1933.

As unemployment rose after 1929, Wagner concentrated on federal efforts to relieve immediate economic distress. In December 1931 he put forward a plan for a $2 billion emergency public works program; though cut to 1.5 billion dollars and limited to self-liquidating projects, the program became part of the Emergency Relief and Construction Act approved by Hoover in 1932. The following year provided much greater opportunity. As relief funds threatened to run out, Wagner sponsored the Federal Emergency Relief Act* of 1933, providing grants rather than loans to states for emergency relief. Public works remained his preferred response to distress; he succeeded in his very active efforts to include a $3.3 billion public works provision in the National Industrial Recovery Act.*

Roosevelt's administration also offered new opportunities for Wagner's ideas about national planning. In 1932 his staff had studied the effect of anti-trust on economic instability. In the first two months of the New Deal,* a group centered in Wagner's office developed a proposal to guarantee collective bargaining and to establish codes of industrial conduct meant to regularize wages, hours, production, and pricing on an industry by industry basis. Soon, adherents of this plan combined it with another developed in the Commerce Department. In May Roosevelt in turn demanded that the plan's proponents work out differences with yet another proposal developed by Hugh Johnson* and Donald Richberg.* Wagner's personal imprint on the National Recovery Administration* that emerged is clearest in his consistent advocacy of a strong collective bargaining guarantee in Section 7(a) of the NIRA.

His defense of labor rights made Wagner a natural choice to head the National Labor Board,* set up under the NRA in August 1933. Occupying a peculiar dual role of legislator and administrator, he worked energetically to create, through NLB decisions, a body of "common law" for labor disputes. Though the NLB handled nearly 2,000 cases within six months, NRA administrator Johnson preempted NLB authority in February 1934, creating a separate board for the crucial auto industry.

While Wagner's administrative role lapsed after early 1934, he redoubled his efforts to strengthen Section 7(a). Without administration support, he offered legislation in 1934 to create an independent NLB to mediate labor disputes and prevent unfair labor practices. The administration instead restructured the agency, renaming it the National Labor Relations Board* in mid-year. Wagner reintroduced his bill in 1935, dropping the mediation role and defining the NLRB role solely as the final enforcer of labor rights, arguing that such a body would "round out the program for a balanced economic system." Roosevelt's distance from the measure allowed a Senate vote, and the Senate approved; that action sparked outright administration support and success in the House. Roosevelt signed the bill most closely associated with Wagner's name, the National Labor Relations Act,* on July 5, 1935.

The senator was more a sponsor than an architect of social security laws. Consistent with his emphasis on labor markets, he introduced an exploratory unemployment compensation plan in 1932 and sponsored a measure for a railroad retirement system in that year. The latter became law in 1934 (but required new legislation in 1935 and 1937 in the face of court challenges). In the same year, Wagner and Representative David Lewis, Democrat from Maryland, introduced an unemployment compensation plan flexible enough to include systems that were being established in such states as Wisconsin and Ohio. The Committee on Economic Security* largely incorporated the Wagner-Lewis bill into its plan for a more comprehensive social insurance and relief system, and the senator introduced the Social Security Act* in 1935.

After 1935 he continued to press for an expanded welfare state, even as Congress grew less friendly to liberal proposals. He had included a plan for public housing in the NIRA and introduced a separate public housing bill in 1935. Revised in consultation with Democratic Congressman Henry Ellenbogen of Pennsylvania, he reintroduced the legislation in 1936 and 1937. With Roosevelt's late endorsement, the bill emerged only with difficulty and watered-down as the Wagner-Steagall Housing Act of 1937,* establishing a U. S. Housing Authority.* In the same year, he unsuccessfully advanced a federal anti-lynching law.* In 1938 and 1939 Wagner focused on health care, offering a proposal in 1939 to establish health care grants to the states. Effectively shelved by Roosevelt, the proposal informed the Wagner-Murray-Dingell bill of 1943, a most comprehensive plan to unify and nationalize such components of the New Deal as the U. S. Employment Service, unemployment compensation, and health insurance.

The ideas in Wagner's bills owed most to social welfare intellectuals in such organizations as the American Association for Labor Legislation, the Russell Sage Foundation, and the Brookings Institution. In his success at drawing together and advocating these ideas as contributions to a planned economy marked by a balance of labor and business power, Wagner should be considered a major architect of the American welfare state. Wagner remained in the Senate until 1949, and he died on May 4, 1953. (J. Joseph Huthmacher, *Senator Robert F. Wagner and the Rise of Urban Liberalism*, 1968.)

DAVID BRIAN ROBERTSON

WAGNER-STEAGALL HOUSING ACT OF 1937 When the Wagner-Steagall Housing Act became law in 1937, it marked the initial success for a long struggle to achieve government recognition of housing as a social need. Public housing existed for the first time in the United States during World War I, but those programs ended with the war. Urban housing reformers, labor leaders, and social workers revived the idea when the Great Depression allowed them to propose government housing as a means of reviving the construction industry. The major political impetus came from Senator Robert Wagner* of New York.

Despite the appeal of housing as a means of increasing employment, real estate and construction interests opposed it as government encroachment on private industry. Congressmen and senators from rural districts also opposed Wagner's proposals, believing that public housing would primarily benefit residents of large cities. Such opposition effectively prevented any large-scale public housing projects under the National Housing Act of 1934.* These protests, added to those of fiscal conservatives who feared the budgetary implications of costly housing programs, served to curtail financial obligations in the act.

Wagner introduced housing bills into three sessions of Congress. Each bill ran into opposition in the House, and the 1935 and 1936 measures never were reported out of the Banking and Currency Committee because chairman Henry Steagall* opposed public housing. By 1937 President Franklin D. Roosevelt* had been persuaded to lend support to the bill, and his help proved decisive in getting the measure to the floor. The Wagner-Steagall Housing Act became law on September 1, 1937.

The law created the United States Housing Authority,* a public corporation under the Department of the Interior, and provided $500 million in loans for low-cost housing. The U. S. Housing Authority was empowered to advance loans amounting to 90 percent of project costs. The president appointed Nathan Straus, an old friend and a Wagner protégé who had served on New York City's Public Housing Authority, to head the agency. Aware of the need to demonstrate that the authority would assist small as well as large communities, Straus saw to it that towns with populations of less than 25,000 received more than one-fourth of the project awards. By the end of 1940, 511 USHA projects were in progress or had been completed, but the agency could not hope to make significant progress toward ending urban blight. Available funding was not sufficient to alleviate urban problems; and banking, real estate, and construction interests continued to denounce the program. The total value of USHA loan contracts by the end of 1940 was $691 million, with 344 projects of 188,045 units completed and another 167 in planning stages. The U. S. Housing Authority extended low-interest sixty-year loans to local public agencies for the projects. During World War II, the USHA became active in planning, building, and maintaining defense housing projects. (J. Joseph Huthmacher, *Senator Robert F. Wagner and the Rise of Urban Liberalism*, 1968.)

JANE A. ROSENBERG

WALKER, FRANK COMERFORD Frank C. Walker was born in Plymouth, Pennsylvania, on May 30, 1886. He studied at Gonzaga University between 1903 and 1906 and then took a law degree at Notre Dame in 1909. After receiving his law degree, Walker moved west to Silver Bow County, Montana, where he began practicing law. He was assistant county attorney between 1909 and 1912 and won a seat as a state legislator in 1913 on the Democratic ticket. Walker joined the army during World War I and served with the American Expeditionary Force in Europe and then returned to Montana and his law practice. During the New Deal,* Walker served as executive secretary of the President's Executive Council in 1933 and then as executive director of the National Emergency Council* in 1935. In 1940, after James Farley* resigned in opposition to Franklin D. Roosevelt's* run for a third term, Walker replaced him as postmaster general. He kept that cabinet post until 1945 and served as chairman of the Democratic National Committee in 1943 and 1944. Frank C. Walker died September 13, 1959. (*New York Times*, September 14, 1959.)

WALLACE, HENRY AGARD Born near Orient in Adair County, Iowa, on October 7, 1888, Henry A. Wallace was the son of Henry Cantwell Wallace, a highly regarded agriculturalist of progressive Republican leanings who edited the family-run farm journal, *Wallace's Farmer*, and served as secretary of agriculture under Harding and Coolidge. As a boy, Henry A. Wallace took an interest in the scientific study of plants; and when he was sixteen, he conducted his first significant experiment with seed corn, embarking on a course of scientific inquiry that eventually earned him worldwide recognition as a plant geneticist. In 1910 Wallace graduated from Iowa State College (Ames). From 1910 to 1933 Wallace was an associate editor and (after 1924) senior editor of *Wallace's Farmer* and its successor, *Iowa Homestead and Wallace's Farmer*. In that capacity he became an authority on agriculture and was an influential advocate of agrarian interests. His genetic experiments with corn culminated in 1923 with the first successful hybrid seed corn for commercial use and led to the founding, in 1926, of the Hi-Bred Seed Company (later renamed the Pioneer Hi-Bred Seed Company) of which Wallace was president until 1933.

Wallace also had a profound interest in agricultural economics. Influenced by the ideas of Thorstein Veblen and self-taught in statistical techniques, Wallace probed the economics of farm production and falling farm income in the hard times of the 1920s, frequently making recommendations—for crop storage, collective action, planned production, and government assistance—which boldly challenged the laissez-faire thinking of the day. From 1924 to 1928 Wallace vigorously supported the McNary-Haugen Bill, a measure designed to boost farm prices by authorizing the government to buy up surpluses and sell them abroad. Though the McNary-Haugenites failed to achieve their purpose, Wallace emerged from the struggle as a seasoned veteran of farm politics and a respected farm leader of national importance.

Although a life-long Republican, Wallace endorsed Democrat Al Smith* instead of Herbert Hoover* in 1928. It was a decision prompted by Wallace's distrust of Hoover on farm matters and by his growing disillusionment with the Republican party.* During the next four years, Wallace was a trenchant critic of the Hoover administration. Needless to say, the rural poverty and suffering that followed in the wake of the Great Depression profoundly affected Wallace and moved him to speak out forcefully against an economic order that allowed hard working farmers to go broke in the midst of the plenty they had produced.

In 1932 Franklin D. Roosevelt,* seeking to initiate contacts with important farm leaders, arranged a meeting with Wallace and was impressed with his views on the need for basic social and economic reforms. Wallace, equally impressed with Roosevelt, enlisted in the New Deal* campaign, contributing ideas and advice on farm policy and providing vigorous editorial support that helped put conservative Iowa in the Democratic column.

After the election, Roosevelt asked Wallace to become secretary of agriculture. Wallace accepted and confronted at once the immense responsibility of implementing a program to relieve hardpressed American farmers. With Rexford Tugwell* as his assistant secretary, Wallace guided the preparation and passage of the Agricultural Adjustment Act of 1933.* The implementation of the Agricultural Adjustment Act was not without controversy. When the law was passed, 1933 crops were already in the field; and the country faced the impending disaster of another bumper harvest. Wallace quickly ordered the destruction of 10 million acres of growing cotton and the slaughter of 6 million baby pigs and 200,000 sows. These decisions created a storm of public protest and weighed heavily upon Wallace; but the alternative of even greater surpluses would have endangered both the New Deal farm program and economic recovery.

Further complaints resulted from the fact that millions of tenant farmers and sharecroppers were deprived of land and livelihood when southern landowners reduced cotton acreage in order to receive AAA* benefits. Critics like Norman Thomas* demanded radical measures to remedy the situation. In 1935 a number of liberal and radical lawyers, headed by Jerome Frank,* general counsel for the AAA, were "purged" from the Department of Agriculture by Wallace when their militant efforts to benefit dispossessed tenants antagonized powerful conservative politicians and threatened to undermine the New Deal coalition in the South. As chairman of the president's Special Committee on Farm Tenancy,* however, Wallace helped formulate proposals which became the basis for the Bankhead-Jones Farm Tenancy Act of 1937.*

Wallace also encountered difficulties with George Peek,* the first administrator of the AAA. Peek disputed Wallace's authority over him and openly disagreed with AAA policy he was supposed to execute. An economic nationalist and an unreconstructed McNary-Haugenite, Peek favored high tariffs, opposed crop reduction, and instead advocated all-out farm production and the dumping of surpluses abroad. At odds with the economic philosophy underlying the Wallace program, Peek was eased out of the AAA by Roosevelt in 1933 and given a new post; but he broke completely with the administration in 1935, thereafter bitterly attacking the New Deal and denouncing the AAA as "socialist farming." In spite of such problems, Wallace persevered; and by the mid-1930s the Agricultural Adjustment Act, with the aid of a severe drought, had brought about a rise in crop prices and a sharp reduction in rural debt.

Early in January of 1936, however, the Supreme Court's* *United States v. Butler et al.** decision invalidated the Agricultural Adjustment Act, declaring its processing tax and production control provisions unconstitutional. Wallace labored to piece together a stop-gap farm measure that would permit the government to maintain control over agricultural production and would satisfy at the same time the convoluted requirements of the conservative Court. Within two months Wallace won congressional approval for the Soil Conservation and Domestic Allotment Act,* which was signed into law by the president on February 29, 1936. This act, in which crop reduction was skillfully disguised as a conservation measure, authorized benefit payments to farmers who agreed to plant soil-conserving crops, like soybeans, and not to plant soil-depleting commercial crops, like corn, cotton, tobacco, and wheat.

During the recession of 1937–1938,* the Soil Conservation and Domestic Allotment Act, which depended upon the voluntary cooperation of farmers to limit production, failed to curb farm surpluses and halt the decline of prices. Wallace meanwhile, pushed for a new, more comprehensive farm program; and in February 1938 he secured his objective with the passage of the second Agricultural Adjustment Act.* This legislation revived elements of the AAA of 1933 (acreage restriction and the parity* payment principle), continued conservation payments, and provided for compulsory marketing quotas, federal crop loans, crop insurance (for wheat), and crop storage. At the heart of the new act was the principle of "the ever-normal granary,"* Wallace's idea of storing up surpluses in times of abundance in order to achieve stability in farm prices and to guarantee plentiful supplies of food in times of scarcity. Wallace did not solve the farm surplus problem with his new program—the coming of World War II did that. Nevertheless, the huge stocks of food stored as a consequence of the "ever-normal granary" legislation contributed significantly to the Allied cause during World War II. In the Agricultural Adjustment Act of 1938, Wallace believed he had successfully reconciled the interests of the American farmer with the welfare of the nation in general, and he considered enactment of that legislation his most important achievement as Roosevelt's secretary of agriculture.

By 1940 the New Deal had run its course, but Wallace's political career was not yet over. In that year, Roosevelt picked Wallace to be his vice-presidential running mate, largely to offset the Midwestern and rural appeal of the Willkie-McNary ticket. During his term as vice-president, Wallace played an important role in the making of foreign policy—he participated in decisions that culminated in the development of the atomic bomb, and he served as chairman of the Supply Priorities and Allocations Board and the Board of Economic Warfare. In 1944, however, due to pressure from southern conservatives and big-city political bosses, Wallace was dumped from the Democratic ticket in favor of Harry S Truman.* Roosevelt appointed Wallace secretary of commerce in 1945—an office he held until September 1946, when he was asked to resign because of his public criticism of Truman's "get tough" policy toward the Soviet Union. After a brief tenure as editor of the *New Republic* (1946–1947), Wallace entered the race for president in 1948 as the nominee of the newly formed Progressive party, which fell increasingly under the control and direction of Communists and fellow travellers. Although Wallace was well-intentioned in his desire to halt the cold war and secure world peace and was manifestly not a Communist, the red-tinged Progressive campaign damaged his public image and effectively put an end to his active involvement in politics. In his remaining years, Wallace devoted his energies chiefly to scientific work, conducting genetic experiments to develop improved strains of strawberries, corn, gladiolas, and chickens. He died on November 18, 1965, at the age of 77, a victim of amyotrophic lateral sclerosis. (Edward L. Schapsmeier and Frederick H. Schapsmeier, *Henry A. Wallace of Iowa: The Agrarian Years, 1910–1940*, 1968.)

ROBERT L. SHADLE

WALLGREN, MONRAD CHARLES Monrad Wallgren was born in Des Moines, Iowa, on April 17, 1891. His family moved to Galveston, Texas, in 1894 and then to Everett, Washington, in 1901, where he graduated from high school. Wallgren graduated from the Washington State School of Optometry at

Spokane in 1914, went into the retail optical and jewelry business, and served with the Coast Artillery Corps of the National Guard during World War I. After the war Wallgren resumed his business career; but the suffering of the unemployed during the Great Depression touched him deeply, and he began demanding federal relief programs. His pleas struck a responsive chord among the Unemployed Leagues* in Washington state, and in the election of 1932* he won a seat in the House of Representatives as a Democrat. Wallgren immediately allied himself with other House insurgents like Maury Maverick* and Thomas Amlie,* demanding more and more federal relief legislation for the poor, aged, and industrial workers. In 1940 Wallgren was elected to the United States Senate, where he served until 1945. He resigned that year to become governor of Washington. Wallgren was governor of Washington until 1949 and then accepted a position on the Federal Power Commission.* He resigned from the FPC in 1951 to pursue his citrus farming interests in California and his uranium claims in California and Nevada. Wallgren died in an automobile accident on September 18, 1961. (*New York Times*, September 19, 1961.)

WALSH-HEALEY PUBLIC CONTRACTS ACT OF 1936 When the Supreme Court* released the *Schechter** decision in May 1935 declaring the National Industrial Recovery Act* unconstitutional, it also invalidated the wages and hours provisions enforced by the National Recovery Administration.* The decision caught the administration by surprise, and their anger created a series of legislation to resurrect the NIRA with several "Little NRA"* laws. Secretary of Labor Frances Perkins* was particularly concerned about questions of labor standards and suggested that the least the administration could do was insist that minimum wages and maximum hours provisions be established in all federal contracts. Out of her concern came the Walsh-Healey Public Contracts Act of 1936. Sponsored by David I. Walsh of Massachusetts, chairman of the Senate Labor Committee, and Representative Arthur Healey of Massachusetts, the act was signed by President Franklin D. Roosevelt* on June 30, 1936. It required that all people employed by business contractors dealing with the federal government could not be paid less than the prevailing minimum wage established by the Department of Labor. All federal contractors for supplies and equipment exceeding $10,000 had to pay overtime for more than eight hours a day or forty hours a week. Both child labor and convict labor were prohibited in all federal contracts. The Walsh-Healey Act played an important role in maintaining labor standards between the *Schechter* decision in 1935 and passage of the Fair Labor Standards Act of 1938.* (Arthur M. Schlesinger, Jr., *The Age of Roosevelt. Vol. III: The Politics of Upheaval, 1935–1936*, 1960.)

WARBURG, JAMES PAUL Born on August 18, 1896, to a wealthy family in Hamburg, Germany, James P. Warburg graduated from Harvard University in 1917 and entered the New York financial community with the National Metropolitan Bank. He moved to the First National Bank of Boston and rose quickly through Wall-Street circles, becoming president of the International Manhattan Company in 1929. But in political terms, Warburg was considered a renegade, at least among his Wall-Street peers. A loyal Democrat, Warburg was not a laissez-faire ideologue but a brilliant, economically flexible pragmatist who saw in the federal government a means of stabilizing the economy. At first he was suspicious of Franklin D. Roosevelt's* monetary views, so he turned down an offer to become the under secretary of the treasury in the new administration. He became, however, a close economic adviser to Roosevelt during much of 1933, working carefully on the draft versions of the National Industrial Recovery Act* and serving as a delegate to the World Monetary Conference in London.

Warburg's break with the New Deal,* however, came with the gold-buying* scheme of late 1933. When Roosevelt became enamored with the "commodity dollar"* ideas of economist George Warren,* Warburg grew frightened and critical, afraid the proposal would destroy business confidence and prolong the depression. He pleaded with the president, but Roosevelt tired of the debate, deciding that Warburg was too tradition-bound and insensitive to the suffering of the poor. Warburg left the administration and publicly began attacking New Deal monetary policies. In 1935 and 1936 he wrote two pamphlets—*Hell Bent for Election* and *Still Hell Bent*—attacking the Roosevelt administration's economic policies and accusing the president of leading the country down the road to socialism and dictatorship. For a time in 1936 Warburg served as an economic adviser to Frank Knox, the old Bull Moose progressive seeking the 1936 Republican presidential nomination. When the Republicans nominated Alf Landon,* however, Warburg returned to the New Deal fold and endorsed Roosevelt's re-election bid.

Although he had lost the opportunity to be of much influence in the New Deal, Warburg continued his financial successes, serving as president of the Bydale Company and the longtime director of the Polaroid Corporation. During World War II, he served as a special assistant to the Coordinator of Information and as deputy director of the Overseas Branch of the Office of War Information. James P. Warburg died on June 3, 1969. (*New York Times*, June 4, 1969.)

WARREN, GEORGE FREDERICK George Frederick Warren, professor of farm management and monetary adviser to Franklin D. Roosevelt,* was born on February 16, 1874, at Harvard, Nebraska, the son of George Frederick and Julia Colista (Stanley) Warren. The father had moved to Nebraska as a homesteader after the Civil War. The son grew up on the family farm and worked his way through the University of Nebraska, graduating in 1897 with a degree in farm management. Warren received his M. S. A. (1904) and his Ph.D. (1905) from the New York State College of Agriculture at Cornell. For a year he was a horticulturist with the New Jersey Experiment Station, after which he went back to Cornell as assistant professor of agronomy. In 1920 Warren became professor of agricultural economics, a position he held until his death.

Franklin Roosevelt, before his inauguration as president, had been introduced to Warren and to Dr. Frank A. Pearson, Warren's Cornell colleague, by Henry Morgenthau, Jr.,* who had studied under Warren at Cornell. Warren and Pearson were co-authors of *Prices* (1933), a book in which they argued that the prices of wheat, cotton, and other commodities went up and down automatically with the price of gold in relation to paper currency. Therefore, the authors believed, if the government purchased gold in large amounts and raised the price gradually, this would lower the value of the dollar and raise the prices of commodities. President Roosevelt, fascinated by both Warren and the theory, brought him to Washington as a monetary adviser with an office in the Department of Commerce Building. In the end, the Warren plan failed, and in 1934 Warren returned to Cornell. He became ill in December 1937 and began making plans to retire as administrative head of his department and devote full time to teaching and research. He did not live to carry out his plans. On May 24, 1938, he died of multiple tumors of the liver. (*New York Times*, May 25, 1938; Arthur M. Schlesinger, Jr., *The Age of Roosevelt. Vol. II. The Coming of the New Deal, 1933–1934*, 1959.)

JOHN PAYNE

WARREN POTATO CONTROL ACT OF 1935 Like cotton and tobacco farmers participating in AAA* contracts, potato growers too were concerned about the planting of non-contract farmers. They feared their production would scuttle the AAA's crop reduction goals. The only answer seemed to be compulsory production quotas. The Bankhead Cotton Control Act* and Kerr-Smith Tobacco Control Act* had imposed compulsory quotas on cotton and tobacco, even though Secretary of Agriculture Henry Wallace* had opposed them. Potato farmers in Idaho, Maine, Virginia, and North Carolina were demanding compulsory quotas; and Senator William Borah* of Idaho was especially vocal. Congressman Lindsay Warren of North Carolina submitted a bill to Congress, and it passed as Title II of the Agricultural Adjustment Act Amendments on August 24, 1935. Although the act imposed a heavy tax on all non-contract potatoes, the Agricultural Adjustment Administration never really implemented the law. (Edwin G. Nourse, *Marketing Agreements Under the AAA*, 1935.)

WATSON, EDWIN MARTIN Edwin Martin Watson, army officer and secretary to President Franklin D. Roosevelt,* was born in Eufaula, Alabama, on December 10, 1883. Edwin grew up in Martinsville, Virginia, where his father was in the tobacco business and, for a time, used a picture of his son riding a pony to advertise a new brand of chewing tobacco. Watson entered West Point in 1902 but soon realized that his weakness in mathematics would have to be remedied by intensive outside study. After two resignations and two reappointments, he graduated in 1908. During his sporadic West Point career he became a star on the football team and acquired the enduring nickname "Pa," to distinguish him from another cadet named Watson, who was dubbed "Ma."

For seven years Watson's career was much like that of other regular army officers in peacetime. He served at many army posts in the United States and for three years was stationed in the Philippines. In 1915 President Woodrow Wilson made the popular officer his junior military aide; but when the country entered World War I, he granted Watson's request for active service. Watson commanded an artillery batallion attached to the second division and fought at Belleau Wood and St. Mihiel, rising to the rank of major. After the armistice, Watson became chief of the military section of President Wilson's personal staff at the peace conference and helped arrange the president's travels in France, England, and Belgium. Watson served from 1927 to 1931 as military attaché at the American embassy in Brussels.

In 1933, when Watson was a colonel serving in New York as an artillery instructor, Admiral Cary Grayson, who had been put in charge of Roosevelt's presidential inauguration, asked Watson to come down to Washington to help with the arrangements. Roosevelt liked the genial colonel and soon named him to the White House staff. In April 1939 he made Watson presidential secretary. In this position he skillfully protected the president from bothersome callers, supported him with his right arm in public, accompanied him on fishing trips, and entertained him with humorous stories. While his main job was to serve and protect the president, Watson, a keen judge of public opinion, occasionally influenced Roosevelt's political decisions. (In 1944 Watson and Steve Early* opposed the move to renominate Vice-President Henry Wallace*.)

During World War II, Watson, despite his poor health, accompanied the president on trips to the important conferences. He suffered one heart attack at the Teheran Conference in November 1943 and another one at the second Quebec Conference in September 1944. In early 1945 he insisted on going to the Yalta Conference. On the return trip he flew with the president to Egypt, where they boarded the cruiser *Quincy*. On February 20, two days out of Algiers, Watson died of congestive heart failure and a cerebral hemorrhage. (James MacGregor Burns, *Roosevelt: The Soldier of Freedom*, 1970; *New York Times*, February 28, 1945; *Who Was Who in America*, II:560.)

JOHN PAYNE

WEALTH TAX ACT OF 1935 On June 19, 1935, President Franklin D. Roosevelt* called for a major revision of the federal tax laws, saying that they were too complex and had operated "to the unfair advantage of the few" while not preventing an "unjust concentration of wealth and economic power." He sought a revenue measure which would redistribute wealth to alleviate the depression and provide funds to finance federal relief programs. Roosevelt's message was motivated by: recent Supreme Court* decisions which overturned key New Deal* measures; business and conservative opposition to New Deal programs; and pressure from radicals such as Huey Long,* Francis E. Townsend,* and Father Charles Coughlin.* It was also a response to such traditional advocates of social welfare legislation as Senators William E. Borah,* Robert M. La Follette, Jr.,* George W. Norris,* Gerald P. Nye,* and Hiram W. Johnson.*

The bill as proposed would curb the transmission of great wealth through inheritance and gift taxes, increase surtaxes on large personal incomes, and extend the principle of graduated taxation to corporations. Roosevelt also requested a constitutional amendment which would allow the federal government to tax interest income from future state and local security issues. The measure was enthusiastically received by the progressive insurgents and many other members of Congress, by radicals such as Long, Townsend, and Coughlin, and by the American Federation of Labor.* Conservatives were disturbed by the proposal, asserting that the measure was social not fiscal in nature, designed to confiscate wealth.

The Revenue Act of 1935, as passed, increased estate taxes and individual surtax rates (from a top of 59 percent to one of 75 percent on incomes over $50,000) and placed graduated net income taxes on corporations and a tax on incorporated dividends. Corporations could deduct gifts to charitable organizations up to 5 percent of their net income. Instead of the existing 13.75 percent tax on corporate income, the law imposed a 12.5 percent rate on small corporations and a 15 percent rate on corporations making more than $50,000 per year. An excess profits tax imposed a levy of 6 percent on corporate profits over 10 percent and 12 percent on profits over 15 percent. An amendment also allowed deductions prior to taxation for the amount of value lost by an estate within one year of death, the result of the rapid decline of fortunes in the 1929 stock market crash. Neither Roosevelt's proposed inheritance tax nor his constitutional amendment passed.

The act neither redistributed wealth nor raised significant additional revenues. It was not all the president asked for, though it was unpopular among those in high tax brackets. Liberals saw the measure as a landmark in the use of taxation for the decentralization of wealth, although the bill actually did little in this regard. Conservatives viewed it as unfair and unconstitutional. Both groups overreacted. While it pacified insurgents and radical reformers, the act did little to offset the effects of the Social Security Act* passed the same year. Lower income groups continued to pay a disproportionate share of the income tax. (Ronald A. Mulder, "The Progressive Insurgents in the United States Senate, 1935–1936: Was there a Second New Deal?," *Mid America* LVII:106–25, 1975; Randolph E. Paul, *Taxation in the United States*, 1954; Sidney Ratner, *American Taxation: Its History as a Social Force in Democracy*, 1942.)

VIRGINIA F. HAUGHTON

WEAVER, ROBERT CLIFTON Robert Clifton Weaver was born in Washington, D. C., on December 29, 1907. He attended local public schools in Washington, D. C., and then went on to receive a B. A. from Harvard University in 1929, an M. A. in 1931, and a Ph.D. in 1934. Between 1933 and 1937, Weaver served as an adviser on black affairs in the Department of the

Interior and was a member of Franklin D. Roosevelt's* "black cabinet."* Between 1937 and 1940 Weaver served as a special assistant for the U. S. Housing Authority.* His career in the field of public housing brought him appointments at Columbia Teachers' College in 1947, New York University later in 1947, and the J. H. Whitney Foundation in 1949. He served there until 1954 when he was appointed deputy commissioner of the New York State Division of Housing. Weaver was rent administrator for New York State between 1955 and 1959, when he joined the staff of the Ford Foundation. Weaver became administrator of the federal Housing and Home Finance Agency in 1961 and stayed there until 1966 when President Lyndon B. Johnson appointed him to the cabinet post of secretary of housing and urban development. Weaver remained there until 1969 when he became president of Bernard M. Baruch College. He is the author of a number of books, including *Negro Labor: A National Problem* (1946), *The Negro Ghetto* (1948), *The Urban Complex* (1964), and *Dilemma of Urban America* (1965). (John B. Kirby, *Black Americans in the Roosevelt Era: Liberalism and Race*, 1980.)

WEST COAST HOTEL V. PARRISH *West Coast Hotel v. Parrish*, decided on March 29, 1937, was the first major case of the Supreme Court* to reflect the shift of Chief Justice Charles Evans Hughes* and Justice Owen Roberts* away from the conservative majority which had dismantled the AAA* and NRA* in 1935 and 1936. The decision also came in the wake of President Franklin D. Roosevelt's* court-packing* reform proposal, when he unsuccessfully tried to retire justices and increase the size of the Court as a means of liberalizing its posture toward federal power. Although Chief Justice Hughes publicly condemned the proposal and Congress stopped it, the Court nevertheless made a major philosophical change in 1937, beginning with the *West Coast* case, when Hughes and Roberts joined Louis Brandeis,* Benjamin Cardozo,* and Harlan Fiske Stone* in upholding the Washington minimum wage law. Conservative Justices James McReynolds,* Willis Van Devanter,* Pierce Butler,* and George Sutherland* found themselves in the minority. Only a year before, in *Morehead v. Tipaldo*,* the Court had set aside a similar New York minimum wage law, arguing that private wage bargains were protected by the contract clause and therefore beyond even state legislative power. But Hughes reversed himself in the *West Coast* case, arguing that state legislation could protect "a class of workers who are in an unequal position with respect to bargaining power . . . and defenseless against the denial of a living wage . . . the community is not bound to provide what is in effect a subsidy for unconscionable employers." Historians have debated whether the switch of Hughes and Roberts was philosophically genuine or politically designed to save the Court from the president's assault, but Owen Roberts may have summed it up best when he offhandedly remarked, concerning the *West Coast* case, that a "switch in time saves nine." (Alpheus Thomas Stone, *Harlan Fiske Stone: Pillar of the Law*, 1956.)

WHEELER, BURTON KENDALL Born on February 27, 1882, in Hudson, Massachusetts, Burton K. Wheeler received a law degree from the University of Michigan in 1905 and was admitted to the Montana Bar. In 1910 Wheeler was elected to the Montana legislature and served there until 1913, when President Woodrow Wilson appointed him U. S. attorney for Montana. In 1918 Wheeler resigned to prepare a campaign for the governorship of Montana in 1920. He lost in the general election but was elected U. S. senator from Montana in 1922 and served continuously until 1947. He was defeated for renomination in the primary of 1946.

Wheeler was Robert M. La Follette's vice-presidential running mate for the presidency in 1924 on the Progressive party ticket. After the landslide victory of Calvin Coolidge over Robert La Follette and Democratic party* candidate John W. Davis,* Wheeler returned to the Democratic party. In the 1930s Wheeler was at first considered "a usually-reliable Roosevelt man." He vigorously championed early New Deal* legislation to control the banking system, establish the SEC,* and strengthen the Federal Reserve System. He termed the average banker "crooked" and advocated "treating them like we did Al Capone." After defeat of his free-coinage bill in 1933 and his 1-billion-ounce silver purchase bill in 1934, Wheeler seemed to undergo a radical political change. He opposed Franklin D. Roosevelt's* "court-packing"* bill but advocated an amendment to the Constitution permitting Congress to override judicial vetoes of its acts. Roosevelt had deliberately avoided constitutional amendment remedies as a recourse to his dilemma with the Supreme Court* because of the perceived difficulty in getting any amendment resolution passed by the Congress. Wheeler's advocacy of an amendment alienated many otherwise supporters of Roosevelt's plans and stopped any action by the Congress. It was Chief Justice Charles Hughes'* letter in reply to Wheeler's request for Court comment and suggestion, read openly in the Congress, that "put the death knell" to the Roosevelt court-packing bill. From 1938 on, Wheeler became an opponent-in-fact if not in voting of almost every piece of legislation introduced by the "Roosevelt faction" of the New Deal.

Wheeler apparently did not favor Roosevelt's non-candidacy for a third term in 1940. He became the Democratic party favorite son from Montana, and he quietly opened a presidential candidate office in Chicago and maintained it until Henry Wallace* was nominated as Roosevelt's running mate. He fought strenuously to include the 1940 party plank that pledged not to send "our boys" outside of the United States unless the country was attacked, even though he knew that Roosevelt had seriously opposed the plank.

Wheeler's ultimate break with Roosevelt and the mainstream of the New Deal came after his strenuous efforts to defeat the Selective Service Act of 1940; when it passed Wheeler seemed to undergo another internal political change. He made an impassioned plea against the act and said that "the draft will slit the throat of democracy." He also openly fought revision of the Neutrality Acts and opposed lend-lease legislation. He railed against sending United States naval vessels to escort supplies to Great Britain through German sub-infested waters. Wheeler's wife joined forces with retired General Robert Wood* of Sears, Roebuck and Company to incorporate the America First Committee, and she publicly welcomed Father Charles Coughlin* and his followers into membership.

After his defeat for the Senate in 1946, Wheeler operated a private law firm in Washington, D. C., with his son Robert. He died there on January 7, 1975. (*New York Times*, January 8, 1975; James T. Patterson, *Congressional Conservatism and the New Deal*, 1967.)

AUSTIN N. LEIBY

WHEELER-HOWARD ACT OF 1934 (See INDIAN REORGANIZATION ACT OF 1934.)

WHEELER-RAYBURN BILL (See PUBLIC UTILITY HOLDING COMPANY ACT OF 1935.)

WHITE HOUSE CONFERENCE ON THE EMERGENCY NEEDS OF WOMEN In November 1933 approximately 50,000 women in the United States were receiving work relief assistance from the Federal Emergency Relief Administration* and the Civil Works Administration,* but Harry Hopkins* estimated that another 300,000 to 400,000 needed assistance. At the urging of Eleanor Roosevelt* and under the planning of Ellen Woodward* and Mary Dewson,* the White House convened the conference on November 20, 1933. With Eleanor Roosevelt presiding, New Deal* administrators and women leaders addressed the need for more available jobs, the necessity of designing more acceptable work projects for women, and the need for more federal funds. Representatives from the National Consumers' League, League of Women Voters, American Red Cross, and the Women's Trade Union League also participated in the conference. (Susan Ware, *Beyond Suffrage: Women in the New Deal*, 1981.)

WHITE, SUE SHELTON Sue S. White was born in 1887 in Tennessee. A radical suffragette, she became secretary to Senator Kenneth McKellar in 1920 and received a law degree in 1923 after attending night school. Active in Democratic politics, White became assistant chairman of the Consumers' Advisory Board* of the National Recovery Administration* in 1933. Later White worked under Mary Rumsey* on the National Emergency Council* and then became special assistant to Jack Tate, general counsel of the Social Security Board. White died in 1943. (Susan Ware, *Beyond Suffrage: Women in the New Deal*, 1981.)

WHITE, WALTER FRANCIS Walter Francis White was born in Atlanta, Georgia, on July 1, 1893. After graduating from Atlanta University in 1916, White went to work for the Atlanta Life Insurance Company. Because of his success in establishing an Atlanta chapter of the National Association for the Advancement of Colored People,* White was brought to New York as the assistant secretary of the NAACP in 1918. In 1931 he became secretary of the NAACP, succeeding James Weldon Johnson, and directed the organization until his death in 1955.

Walter White was a black man with blue eyes, fair skin, and reddish hair. He could have easily ''passed'' for white but chose to identify himself with America's oppressed black minority. In 1934 White persuaded Senators Edward Costigan* of Colorado and Robert Wagner* of New York to sponsor a NAACP-drafted federal anti-lynching bill.* Walter White and the NAACP spent an enormous amount of time and energy lobbying for the passage of this important bill. The anti-lynching bill was never passed.

As the head of the NAACP, White campaigned for laws guaranteeing voting rights, banning poll taxes, ending discrimination in the armed forces, and integrating public schools. Eleanor Roosevelt* frequently kept White appraised of President Franklin D. Roosevelt's* views on civil rights. White was even granted a conference with the president, in which Roosevelt expressed his reasons for not forcefully supporting civil rights legislation. White's greatest obstacle was not the president but the Great Depression, which had hurt black people more than any other group. His ability to help black people through the NAACP was made more difficult by a greatly depleted treasury. The NAACP itself had become a casualty of the depression.

White's achievements in civil rights were numerous, but his greatest achievement was giving civil rights a national focus. As a national spokesman for black people, White not only appealed to America's conscience, but he also appealed to the political interests of America's public officials. White sought to convince the Democratic party,* especially in two-party states, that the black vote could help them win elections. Although the Democratic party under Roosevelt did not live up to the expectations of black people, it was the only party that even symbolically supported the civil rights movement in the 1930s. Without the leadership of Walter White much of the NAACP's later successes would not have been possible. White died in 1955. (W. Augustus Low and Virgil A. Clift, eds., *Encyclopedia of Black America,* 1981.)

MICHAEL G. DENNIS

WHITE, WILLIAM ALLEN William Allen White, the noted journalist, was born in Emporia, Kansas, on February 10, 1868, and kept Emporia his home during his illustrious career. He attended the University of Kansas to study journalism and in 1895 became the owner and editor of the *Emporia Daily and Weekly Gazette*. A gifted writer and syndicated columnist, White wrote a number of books, including *Stratagems and Spoils* (1901), *The Old Order Changeth* (1910), *The Life of Woodrow Wilson* (1924), *The Life of Calvin Coolidge* (1925), and *Masks in a Pageant* (1928). Politics was his specialty, and he wrote with a passion. A loyal and progressive Republican during the 1930s, White found himself in a difficult political position. He found Franklin D. Roosevelt* a dynamic and charming public figure, and he believed that the New Deal* legislation for work relief, unemployment and old-age insurance, collective bargaining, and progressive taxation was long overdue. Indeed, he wrote, they were an "attempt to bring the American people up to the modern standards of English-speaking countries." White was also convinced that the Republican "old-guard," including ex-President Herbert Hoover,* would have to give way to new leadership if the party was to survive. As far as White was concerned, such laws as the Social Security Act,* National Labor Relations Act,* Securities Exchange Act,* and the Banking Act of 1935* were here to stay—modern political adjustments to a highly centralized industrial economy.

His personal relationship with Roosevelt was a cordial one, with the president accusing him of being a good friend for "three-and-a-half years out of every four." In 1936 White endorsed the election of Alf Landon* and tried an independent run at the Kansas governorship himself. Both were unsuccessful. During the late 1930s, White became increasingly insecure about Roosevelt's ambitions and was dismayed with the "court-packing"* proposal and the administrative reorganization program. But at the same time, he was becoming increasingly concerned about events in Europe and Asia and resentful of the isolationist wing of his party. White wrote *A Puritan in Babylon* in 1938 and in 1940 chaired the Committee to Defend America by Aiding the Allies. William Allen White died on January 29, 1944. (David Hinshaw, *A Man from Kansas. The Story of William Allen White*, 1945; *New York Times*, January 30, 1944.)

WHITNEY, RICHARD Richard Whitney was born in Beverly, Massachusetts, on August 1, 1888. He attended Groton and then graduated from Harvard in 1911. After leaving Harvard, Whitney worked for the J. P. Morgan & Company and then entered the family securities business, eventually becoming president of Richard Whitney & Company, a major Wall-Street investment firm. Shortly after the "Great Crash of 1929," Whitney became head of the New York Stock Exchange and presided over it during the sensational Pecora investigations of the early 1930s. Despite all the revelations of stock fraud and manipulation of the public, Whitney remained a staunch defender of the securities industry in the United States and just as staunchly opposed government regulation, including the Securities Act of 1933* and the Securities Exchange Act of 1934.* Whitney resigned as president of the New York Stock Exchange in 1935 and returned to private business. In 1938 his opposition to government regulation became more understandable after the SEC forced disclosure of his corporate condition, exposing embezzlement of funds from the New York Stock Exchange and the New York Yacht Club and forcing him into bankruptcy. Whitney spent more than three years in prison after conviction for fraud. He died on December 5, 1974. (*New York Times*, December 6, 1974; Michael Parrish, *Securities Regulation and the New Deal*, 1970.)

WICKARD, CLAUDE RAYMOND Claude Raymond Wickard was born on February 28, 1893, on a farm in Carroll County, Indiana. He came from a long line of Democratic farmers who worshipped Andrew Jackson and William Jennings Bryan. Against his father's wishes, Wickard left the family farm after high school and entered Purdue University in 1910. He graduated in 1915 with a degree in agriculture and then returned home to farm. In 1919 Wickard was elected vice-president of the Carroll County Farm Bureau. He suffered economically during the agricultural depression of the 1920s, became president of the county farm bureau in 1926, and vociferously supported the McNary-Haugen plan for exporting farm surpluses. The frustration of producing more and more on his own farm and receiving less and less income led Wickard into politics, and in 1932 he won a seat in the Indiana state senate. He did not stay there long. Early in 1933 Dr. A. G. Black,* chief of the Corn Hog Section of the Agricultural Adjustment Administration,* named Wickard as his assistant.

The AAA was soon caught up in a variety of ideological struggles, especially between the commercial farm interests of people like Chester Davis* and the urban liberalism of Alger Hiss* and Jerome Frank,* and between the domestic allotment views of Secretary of Agriculture Henry A. Wallace* and AAA administrator George Peek's* faith in marketing strategies. Wickard sided with commercial farming and domestic allotment, endeared himself to Davis and Wallace, and secured his own position in the Department of Agriculture. He became head of the AAA Corn Hog Section in 1935, and in 1937 Wallace named him head of the North Central Division of the Department of Agriculture. Wickard had extraordinary respect and devotion for Henry Wallace and his views on parity,* the "ever-normal granary,"* and acreage reduction. In 1940 Wallace selected Wickard as his under secretary of agriculture, and when Wallace became Roosevelt's vice-president after the inauguration in 1941, Wickard became the new secretary of agriculture. He served in the cabinet until just after Franklin D. Roosevelt's* death in 1945, when President Harry S Truman* appointed him to head the Rural Electrification Administration.* Wickard worked diligently as REA administrator until the Republican victory in 1952. In March 1953 Ezra Taft Benson, the new secretary of agriculture under Dwight D. Eisenhower, asked for Wickard's resignation. Wickard then returned to Indiana and unsuccessfully ran for the United States Senate in 1956; he could not overcome the Republican landslide that year. Claude R. Wickard died on April 19, 1967. (Dean Albertson, *Roosevelt's Farmer. Claude R. Wickard in the New Deal*, 1961.)

WILKINS, ROY Roy Wilkins, one of the leading civil rights advocates in American history, was born in St. Louis, Missouri, in 1903. After graduating from the University of Minnesota, Wilkins went to work for the black newspaper, the *Kansas City Call*. In 1931 he joined the staff of the National Association for the Advancement of Colored People* in New York City as an assistant secretary. When W. E. B. Du Bois resigned in 1934 as editor of *The Crisis*, official organ of the NAACP, Wilkins filled the position. His editorials were frequently critical of Franklin D. Roosevelt* and the New Deal.* He claimed that checks from the AAA* wound up in the hands of white landholders who withheld them from black tenant farmers and sharecroppers. He also protested the differential wage scales of the National Recovery Administration.* Wilkins also insisted that President Roosevelt "threw Negroes to the wolves" when he exempted them from the labor standards provisions of the Cotton Textile Code of the NRA. When farmers, domestics, and casual laborers were excluded from the benefits of the Social Security Act,* Wilkins declared the decision discriminated against millions of blacks. Throughout the 1930s Wilkins and the NAACP worked for a federal anti-lynching bill.* Roosevelt feared if he openly advocated an anti-lynching bill, the South would punish him in Congress by striking down his New Deal legislation. Wilkins was not sympathetic to the president's political problems. In 1940 and 1941, when the country began to mobilize for war, Wilkins excoriated the War Department for its segregated policies and pleaded with Roosevelt to end segregation in the military by executive order. Roy Wilkins became executive director of the NAACP in 1955 and worked to develop a powerful coalition that fought successfully for civil rights in the 1950s and 1960s. Roy Wilkins died on September 8, 1981. (Roy Wilkins with Tom Mathews, *Standing Fast*, 1982.)

ANITA PILLING

WILLIAMS, AUBREY WILLIS Born in Springville, Alabama in 1890, Aubrey Willis Williams was compelled by his father's meager earnings to work to supplement the family income and was unable to acquire a single year of formal education before his twenty-first birthday. Among the boy's earliest memories was the discriminatory treatment reserved for the town's black residents. Very early, he reached the conclusion that the effort devoted to "keeping the black man in his place" was both an outrage and an unbelievable endeavor, given the region's number one problem: poverty. Largely through the influence of his deeply religious mother and two Birmingham ministers, Williams absorbed a strong dose of the social gospel, especially its message of christian responsibility for the physical as well as the spiritual needs of the afflicted.

Williams applied these teachings in Europe during World War I. There he assisted with the work of the Red Cross and, viewing the war as a struggle between the forces of light and darkness, fought with the French Foreign Legion. In 1922 he accepted the position of executive secretary of the Wisconsin Conference of Social Work, an organization dedicated to preventing delinquency, poverty, crime, and child neglect. Williams' contribution to the conference included the principle that social workers must publicize need and must draft model legislation before petitioning for legal reform. He also threw his influence behind the philosophy that work relief was the only respectable form of public assistance.

Williams' efforts in 1932 and 1933 to centralize relief in Texas and Mississippi for the Reconstruction Finance Corporation* brought him to the attention of

Harry L. Hopkins,* who appointed him his deputy. The two shared parallel views on relief matters and forged a smooth working relationship throughout the New Deal.* Neither Hopkins nor Franklin D. Roosevelt,* however, was as committed as Williams to equal treatment for blacks, and neither seemed as optimistic as the southerner that the New Deal could bring far-reaching reforms to America. As Hopkins' deputy within the Federal Emergency Relief Administration* and Civil Works Administration,* Williams played a role second only to his chief in drafting legislation designed to put to work the able-bodied unemployed on relief under a federally controlled agency.

In 1935 Williams became both deputy director of the Works Progress Administration* and executive director of the National Youth Administration,* holding the latter post until shortly before the NYA ceased operation in 1943. While CCC officials found it expedient to establish segregated camps in both the North and the South, Williams insisted that blacks be given their fair share of NYA jobs and be included without discrimination in all the agency's social functions. Senators resented his advice to reliefers to ''vote to keep our friends in power'' and his role in helping draft the 1941 executive order creating the Fair Employment Practices Committee.* Unlike Hopkins or the president, Williams seldom placed politics ahead of principle. As a result, he was occasionally a liability to Roosevelt.

Yet, the mutual respect shared by the president and the NYA director disclosed much about the character of the New Deal. Roosevelt never rebuked Williams for his indiscreet comments, though they cost the Alabaman an appointment he coveted: successor to Hopkins as WPA director. In 1945, in the face of warnings that Williams could not be confirmed by the Senate as REA head and although there were other positions the southerner could have filled (not requiring senatorial confirmation), Roosevelt pressed forward with his appointment. Although defeated in his nomination, Williams never lost faith that the New Deal would make America over in the vision of a more just, equalitarian nation. He signed his letters to the president, ''Devotedly yours,'' and wrote: ''I'm without doubt prejudiced, but I think under your leadership rests the sole remaining hope for the continuation of freedom in our time.'' The longevity of Williams' New Deal career signalled that the New Deal created more than a ''broker-state.'' It serves notice that, for a brief time in American history, the New Deal forged an accommodation between the political center and an indigenously American, left-liberal idealism.

Williams spent his last twenty years publicizing racial discrimination in the South and speaking out against McCarthyism, activities which in 1954 brought on a politically-motivated investigation by the House Committee on Un-American Activities. Williams died in 1965. (Richard A. Reiman, ''Apprenticeship in Democracy: The Evolution of New Deal Youth Policies Through the Federal Emergency Relief Administration and National Youth Administration, 1933–1943,'' Ph.D. dissertation, University of Cincinnati, 1984.; John A. Salmond, ''Aubrey Williams: Atypical New Dealer?,'' in John Braeman, Robert H. Bremner, and David Brody, *The New Deal: The National Level*, 1975; John A. Salmond, *A Southern Rebel: The Life and Times of Aubrey Willis Williams, 1890–1965*, 1983; and Morton Sosna, *In Search of the Silent South*, 1977.)

RICHARD A. REIMAN

WILLIAMS, SAMUEL CLAY S. Clay Williams was born in Mooresville, North Carolina, on September 24, 1884. He graduated from Davidson College in 1905 and then received a law degree from the University of Virginia in 1908. Between 1908 and 1917, Williams practiced law privately in Greensboro and Winston-Salem, North Carolina, and in 1917 he became assistant general counsel for the R. J. Reynolds Tobacco Company. Williams became general counsel in 1921, vice-president in 1925, and president of R. J. Reynolds in 1931. At the beginning of the New Deal,* Williams was optimistic about the prospects for government-business cooperation, and he was appointed to Secretary of Commerce Daniel Roper's* Business Advisory Council.* He remained with the group throughout the 1930s. In 1933 Williams took a leave of absence from the R. J. Reynolds Tobacco Company to assume a position on the National Labor Board,* and from September 1934 to March 1935, he also served as head of the National Industrial Recovery Board, the agency which had replaced Hugh Johnson* as director of the National Recovery Administration.* In 1934 Williams also served as chairman of the Business Advisory Council. Williams then returned to R. J. Reynolds Tobacco Company as chairman of the board in 1935. He died on February 25, 1949. (*Who Was Who In America*, II:581, 1950.)

WILLKIE, WENDELL LEWIS Wendell Willkie, Republican presidential candidate in 1940, was born in Elwood, Indiana, on February 18, 1892. He graduated from Indiana University in 1913, taught school briefly, and then completed his law degree at Indiana in 1916. Willkie moved to Akron, Ohio, to work in the legal department of Firestone Tire and Rubber Company after graduation. From very early in his career, Willkie was an independent Democrat with conservative views on social and economic policy and internationalist views on foreign policy. He was very much in favor of United States entry into the League of Nations, denounced the Ku Klux Klan in the mid-1920s, and supported the presidential candidacies of Al Smith.* In 1929 Willkie moved to New York to join the law firm of Weadock and Willkie to handle the account of the new billion dollar utility empire of Commonwealth and Southern Corporation. By 1933 Willkie had become president of the company.

As a representative of the utility interests, Willkie became a leader in the unsuccessful struggle of the business community to oppose the Tennessee Valley Authority* and the Public Utility Holding Company Act of 1935.* Willkie did not question the right of government to regulate a public utility monopoly; he simply could not understand the desire of the New Deal* to compete directly with private enterprise and break up large, efficient business units. By the mid-1930s, Willkie was gaining a national reputation as an intelligent critic of the

New Deal. He spoke widely against deficit spending, confiscatory taxes, and bureaucratic waste, as well as against the philosophical implications of big government. He voted for Alf Landon* in 1936, and by the late 1930s a number of Republicans began looking his way as a possible GOP presidential candidate in 1940. The New Deal had simply gone beyond Willkie's essentially Wilsonian view of progress and reform. His presidential aspirations, seemingly unlikely because he had never held public office and had been a lifelong Democrat, were nevertheless boosted by a coalition of Wall-Street investors, anti-New Deal journalists, and anti-Roosevelt Democrats. Not until 1939 had Willkie even changed his party membership to the Republicans. But at the national convention, with the war in Europe becoming more and more ominous, Willkie's support grew in direct proportion to the decline of Governor Thomas Dewey's of New York. He won the nomination on the sixth ballot and then selected Senator Charles McNary* of Oregon as his running mate. During the campaign, Willkie skillfully attacked the New Deal for accumulating a massive bureaucracy without ever really solving the depression and for letting the state of national defenses deteriorate badly. Although his criticisms were to the point, international events were undermining his appeal. Increased war-goods spending by the federal government was creating tens of thousands of new jobs; and the public, afraid of the possibility of American entry into the war, became increasingly reluctant to change leaders. In the end, Willkie could never really find a campaign issue. Franklin D. Roosevelt* defeated him handily: 27,307,819 to 22,321,018 popular votes and 449 to eighty-two in the Electoral College. Four years later, on October 8, 1944, Wendell Willkie died of heart failure. (Mary Earhart Dillon, *Wendell Willkie, 1892–1944*, 1952.)

WILSON, MILBURN LINCOLN M. L. Wilson was born on October 23, 1885, in Atlantic, Iowa, and was educated at Iowa State College (B. S. A., 1907) and the University of Wisconsin (M. S., 1920), where he majored in agriculture. After working for a few years as a farmer, he joined the staff of Montana State College as an agronomist in 1910. Between 1910 and 1924, Wilson rose through the ranks of the county extension agent network, finally becoming the extension agricultural economist in 1922. In 1924 he spent two years as a consultant with the U. S. Department of Agriculture, specializing in large-scale wheat farming, and in 1926 he returned to Montana State as chairman of the department of agricultural economics. In 1932 Wilson read Professor John D. Black's* book *Agricultural Reform in the United States* and translated the ideas for controlled production into his own "domestic allotment plan."* At the 1932 meetings of farm economists in Chicago, Wilson promoted the idea; and it gained a wide following. Rexford Tugwell* picked up on the concept of acreage reductions to control overproduction and invited Wilson to come back to Albany and present the plan to Governor Franklin D. Roosevelt,* the Democratic nominee for president. Wilson met with the governor and told him of his plans to have farmers sign "production control contracts," reduce their production, and receive payments from processing taxes. Wilson published those ideas in *Farm Relief and the Domestic Allotment Plan* in 1933. They became the genesis of the Agricultural Adjustment Act of 1933.*

When the New Dealers came to Washington, D. C., in 1933, Milburn Wilson was among them. Secretary of Agriculture Henry A. Wallace* named him chief of the Wheat Production Section of the AAA,* and in September he became head of the Division of Subsistence Homesteads, a forerunner of the Resettlement Administration.* Between July 1934 and February 1940, Wilson served first as assistant secretary of agriculture and then as under secretary of agriculture. When Henry Wallace left the Department of Agriculture to serve as President Roosevelt's running mate in 1940, Wilson stepped down as the under secretary and became head of the department's extension work. Wilson stayed there until his retirement in 1953. He died on November 22, 1969. (Dean Albertson, *Roosevelt's Farmer. Claude R. Wickard in the New Deal*, 1961; Milburn L. Wilson, *Farm Relief and the Domestic Allotment Plan*, 1933.)

WINANT, JOHN GILBERT John Gilbert Winant was born on February 23, 1889, in New York City. He attended St. Paul's School in Concord, New Hampshire, and then Princeton and Dartmouth. Winant joined the U. S. Army during World War I and served with the American Expeditionary Force in France. A progressive Republican, Winant served terms in the New Hampshire House of Representatives in 1917 and 1923, as well as a term in the state senate in 1921. He also served as governor of New Hampshire from 1925 to 1927 and 1931 to 1934. After leaving the state house in 1934, President Franklin D. Roosevelt* appointed Winant to become the first chairman of the Social Security Board. When Alf Landon* criticized social security in the election of 1936,* Winant endorsed Roosevelt's re-election. In 1937 Winant was appointed assistant director of the International Labor Office in Geneva, and he was promoted to director in 1939. In 1941, on the eve of American entry into World War II, President Roosevelt named Winant ambassador to Great Britain. John Gilbert Winant died on November 3, 1947. (Bernard Bellush, *He Walked Alone: A Biography of John Gilbert Winant*, 1968.)

WISCONSIN PROGRESSIVE PARTY The Wisconsin Progressive party was founded in 1934 by Senator Robert M. La Follette, Jr.,* and his brother, Philip La Follete.* As progressive Republicans seeing their state move inexorably into the Democratic camp during the 1930s, they wanted to establish a political vehicle which would re-elect Robert to the Senate and give Philip a chance to win the governorship. Supported by such groups as the National Farmers' Holiday Association* and the Farmer-Labor Political Federation, the Wisconsin Progressive party denied any connection with either the Democratic* or Republican parties* and called for humane regulation of capitalism, refinancing of farm and home mortgages, veteran's bonuses, increased taxation of the rich, unemployment and old-age insurance, nationalization of monopolies, a minimum wage, soil conservation, and a congressional amendment requiring a public referendum for any declaration of war. In the election of 1934,* the Wisconsin Progressive party succeeded in re-electing Robert M. La Follette, Jr., to the Senate, elected Philip La Follette as governor of Wisconsin, placed seven people in Congress, and took control of the lower house of the state legislature. President Franklin D. Roosevelt* accepted their domination of Wisconsin politics and channeled federal patronage through Robert M. La Follette. The Wisconsin Progressive party came to an end in 1938 when Governor Philip La Follette absorbed it into the National Progressives of America.* (Roger T. Johnson, *Robert M. La Follette, Jr. and the Decline of the Progressive Party in Wisconsin*, 1964.)

WITT, NATHAN Nathan Witt, a 1932 graduate of the Harvard Law School, had been born to an immigrant family living on the Lower East Side of Manhattan. An admirer of Felix Frankfurter* because of the Harvard professor's work on behalf of Sacco and Vanzetti during the 1920s, Witt worked as a cab driver to pay his Harvard tuition. He attracted Frankfurter's attention in a third-year administrative law seminar, and Frankfurter urged him to go into Wall-Street legal work for a time, even though Witt's interests were in labor law and civil liberties. Witt went to work for the prestigious law firm headed by William Donovan and came to love the craft of legal drafting. Frankfurter then introduced him to Jerome Frank,* and Witt went to work for a year on the legal staff of the Agricultural Adjustment Administration.* In 1934, recruited by his friend Charles Wyzanski,* Witt joined the staff of the first National Labor Relations Board.* Zealously pro-labor, Witt consistently advocated enforcement of labor law and NLRB decisions and gained a reputation as a union advocate. Eventually, he became secretary to the second National Labor Relations Board before returning to private law practice with the firm Liebman, Leider, and Witt in 1939. (Peter H. Irons, *The New Deal Lawyers*, 1982).

WOLMAN, LEO Leo Wolman was born in Baltimore, Maryland, on February 24, 1890. After focusing his attention on economics, he graduated from Johns Hopkins University in 1911 and then completed a Ph.D. there in 1914. Wolman taught on the faculties of Hobart College, Johns Hopkins, and the University of Michigan before joining the faculty of the School for Social Research in 1919. During those early academic years he earned a scholarly reputation as an expert on labor relations with the publication of such works as *The Boycott in American Trade Unions* (1916). While teaching at the School for Social Research, Wolman also served as director of research for the Amalgamated Clothing Workers of America and became close to Sidney Hillman.* With leaves of absence over the years, Wolman had also served as chairman of the Interstate Commission on Unemployment Insurance (1914), a member of the U. S. Commission on Industrial Relations (1914), a member of the Council on National Defense (1917), chief of the section on production statistics for the War Industries Board (1918), a member of the American Peace Mission in Paris (1919), and a member of the U. S. Unemployment Conference (1921).

In 1933 Wolman became chairman of the Labor Advisory Board* of the National Recovery Administration* and in 1934 a member of the first National Labor Board.* Despite his background, Wolman's basic philosophical instincts tended toward the conservative, and he grew somewhat disturbed with the size of the New Deal* bureaucracy and the growth of the deficits. In 1934 Wolman chaired the Automobile Labor Board,* which for all intents and purposes suppressed the National Labor Board and found in favor of the automobile companies. Wolman had become a professor of economics at Columbia University in 1931, and he stayed there until 1958. Leo Wolman died on October 2, 1961. (*Who Was Who In America*, IV:1029, 1968.)

WOMEN'S REBELLION Women's Rebellion was a small, anti-New Deal group of the 1930s representing the interests of the upper class in the United States. Led by Sarah Oliver Hulswit, the Women's Rebellion warned of socialism and communism and called for the disfranchisement of all relief and welfare recipients and all WPA* employees. They accused Franklin D. Roosevelt* of being a "traitor to his class." (George Wolfskill and John A. Hudson, *All but the People. Franklin D. Roosevelt and His Critics, 1933–1939,* 1969.)

WOOD, ROBERT ELKINGTON Robert E. Wood was born in Kansas City, Missouri, on June 13, 1879. He graduated from the United States Military Academy in 1900 and immediately went into service in the Philippine Insurrection between 1900 and 1902. Wood then spent the next few years in domestic service before becoming assistant chief quartermaster, chief quartermaster, and director of the Panama Railroad Company on construction of the Panama Canal. He lived in the Canal Zone between 1905 and 1915. Wood entered private business in 1915 as assistant to the president of the General Asphalt Company. When World War I broke out, Wood returned to active service as acting quartermaster general for the United States Army. He left that post in 1919 to become vice-president of Montgomery Ward & Company. In 1924 Wood accepted the vice-presidency of Sears, Roebuck and Company, and became president of the company in 1928. He served as president of Sears until 1939, when he became chairman of the board, a post he filled until 1954.

During the early 1930s, Wood was an active follower of American politics and a participant in the New Deal.* Although his professional interests were definitely pro-business, Wood realized that the modern, industrial economy was an intricate, complex machine which needed government attention, if not regulation. He became an early proponent of the trade association movement and the idea of industrial self-government and consequently supported the National Industrial Recovery Act of 1933.* In June 1933 Wood was appointed by Secretary of Commerce Daniel Roper* to the New Deal's Business Advisory Council,* a group of prominent businessmen prepared to advise the administration on economic and business matters. Wood was enthusiastic about the National Recovery Administration,* even though he grew frustrated with its bureaucratic infighting. Before the *Schechter** decision in 1935, Wood actively promoted extension of the NRA. Wood was also a member of the Committee for the Nation to Rebuild Prices and Purchasing Power,* a group supporting the "commodity dollar"* theories of Irving Fischer* and George Warren.* Wood was therefore quite pleased when, late in 1933, President Franklin D. Roosevelt* began manipulating the value of the dollar by purchasing gold on world markets.

Wood's sympathies with the New Deal, however, changed dramatically after 1935. The demise of the NRA and the idea of national planning, the rise of Brandesian anti-trust activity in the New Deal, the tight regulation of the securities markets and holding companies, and the increased taxes on the wealthy dismayed Wood, as did continuing budget deficits and "wasteful relief spending." Later in the 1930s, he also became disturbed with the drift in American foreign policy. A committed isolationist, Wood became a founding member of the America First Committee in July 1940. By that time he had become completely alienated from Franklin D. Roosevelt and the New Deal. Wood retired from Sears in 1954 and died on November 6, 1969. (*New York Times*, November 7, 1969.)

WOODIN, WILLIAM HARTMAN Born on May 27, 1868, in Berwick, Pennsylvania, William Hartman Woodin studied at the Columbia University School of Mines until 1890 when he went to work at his father's business—the American Car and Foundry Company. He rose through various positions of responsibility, finally becoming president in 1916. He became chairman of the board in 1922 as well as president of the American Locomotive Company. Woodin's only public position before the New Deal* was a term as state fuel director of New York, an appointment he accepted in 1922 from Governor Nathan L. Miller. Woodin was a lifelong Republican, but during the 1920s he had become a close friend of Franklin D. Roosevelt* when they worked together for the Warm Springs Foundation. He had also supported Alfred E. Smith's* candidacy for presidency in 1928 and Roosevelt's in 1932. In February 1933 Roosevelt named Woodin as secretary of the treasury. Although there was some public criticism of the appointment because of Woodin's ties to the J. P. Morgan & Company, Woodin served well in 1933, presiding over the reconstruction of the banking system and consistently playing the role of fiscal conservative, urging restraint in New Deal spending policies. Because of ill health, Woodin took a leave of absence in October 1933, but on January 1, 1934, he had to resign. He died on May 3, 1934. (*New York Times*, May 4, 1934.)

WOODRUM, CLIFTON ALEXANDER Clifton A. Woodrum was born in Roanoke, Virginia, on April 27, 1887. He attended the University College of Medicine in Roanoke and graduated with a degree in pharmacy, but he then studied law at Washington and Lee University and was admitted to the bar in 1908. After practicing law privately for nine years, he was elected commonwealth attorney for Roanoke in 1917, judge of the Hustings Court of Roanoke in 1919, and to the House of Representatives in 1922. Woodrum served as a Democratic congressman until his resignation on December 31, 1945. A conservative Democrat who believed in economy in government, Woodrum frequently used his position on the House Appropriations Committee to cut relief spending. In 1939 his subcommittee on the appropriations committee launched an investigation of the Works Progress Administration,* particularly the programs of Federal One.* Woodrum accused the administration of using the WPA for political purposes and accused the WPA of being subject to left-wing influence. His subcommittee investigation led to a number of changes in WPA financing, including the requirement that 25 percent of project funds be generated locally, that all WPA expenditures be allocated on a monthly basis, and that the Federal Theatre Project* be eliminated in 1939. In 1945 Woodrum resigned his congressional seat to become president of the American Plant Food Council. He died on October 6, 1950. (Barbara Blumberg, *The New Deal and the Unemployed: The View from New York City*, 1979; *New York Times*, October 7, 1950.)

WOODWARD, ELLEN SULLIVAN As an assistant administrator of the FERA,* CWA,* and WPA,* Ellen S. Woodward was reputed to be the second most important woman in the New Deal* after Frances Perkins.* Born in Oxford, Mississippi, Ellen Sullivan grew up in Washington, D. C., and in Oxford in the shadow of her prominent father, William Van Amberg Sullivan, a Mississippi congressman (1897–1898) and United States senator (1898–1901). Through him she developed an early interest in public affairs which expanded following her marriage in 1906 to Albert Young Woodward, an attorney. After his sudden death in 1925, she succeeded him in the 1926 Mississippi legislature, becoming the second woman to serve in the lower house of that body. Subsequent employment as the director of civic development for the newly created Mississippi State Board of Development (1926–1929) and then as the board's executive director (1929–1933) provided Woodward with opportunities to administer programs to advance the industrial, agricultural and educational affairs of the state. Her associations with national economic consultants who came to Mississippi brought her competence, efficiency, and personal charm to the attention of public welfare associate Harry L. Hopkins.* In August 1933 she was appointed by him to direct the newly created Women's Division of the Federal Emergency Relief Administration. She remained the director of women's relief work activities under the Civil Works Administration and the Works Progress Administration.

Assisted first by Chloe Owings and later by Agnes Cronin, Woodward created a jobs program for women in every state and the District of Columbia, each directed by a woman. She was adamant that the state directors be given autonomy over their programs and that adequate funds be allocated to the women's projects. She insisted, too, that men and women in relief work should be given equal pay for equal work. Woodward was supported in her views by Hopkins and by Eleanor Roosevelt,* who became her strongest ally.

The Women's Division was successful in devising work for both skilled and unskilled women. In July 1935, when the WPA was created, Woodward's office became the Division of Women's and Professional Projects. Nearly 500,000 women were employed in work relief activities that included household training, sewing, school lunch preparation, gardening and canning, rural library development, and public health extension. In 1936 Woodward's duties expanded when she was named director of the WPA white-collar professional projects for writers, musicians, actors, and artists that employed an additional 250,000 persons. When congressional critics investigated the WPA arts programs, Woodward tenaciously defended them. When congressional cuts forced a retrenchment in WPA employment after 1937, she concentrated upon the retention of institutional service projects through which women on relief provided assistance in local social services such as school lunchrooms, county hospitals, libraries, and nursery schools.

In December 1938, at the same time that Hopkins left the WPA, Woodward was appointed to the three-member Social Security Board upon the resignation of Mary W. Dewson.* Reappointed by President Franklin D. Roosevelt* in 1943, she remained on the board until 1946. As a member of the board, Woodward continued to publicize the economic needs of women in her efforts to expand social security for working women, widows, and dependent children as well as the extension of unemployment insurance for women. Much of her work with the board lay in the area of international social welfare; from 1943 to 1946 she was a member of the United States delegation to the United Nations Relief and Rehabilitation Administration. In 1946 she became the director of the office of Inter-Agency and International Relations of the Federal Security Agency.* Woodward retired from government service at the end of 1953. She continued to live in Washington, D. C., and died at her apartment on September 23, 1971. (Martha H. Swain, " 'The Forgotten Woman': Ellen S. Woodward and Women's Relief in the New Deal," *Prologue*, XV:201–214, 1983.)

MARTHA H. SWAIN

WORKS PROGRESS ADMINISTRATION The Works Progress Administration was created by Executive Order No. 7034 on May 6, 1935, following the passage on April 8 of the Emergency Relief Appropriation Act.* The nearly $5 billion authorized by the act was the greatest single appropriation in United States history to that time, although only about $1.4 billion of the initial funding for relief employment was allocated to the WPA. The remainder went to employment functions in other New Deal* programs and executive department agencies. Both the WPA and the new social security system were intended to replace the emergency programs of the Federal Emergency Relief Administration* with a "permanent program" aimed at distinguishing unemployment relief from other types of assistance, i.e., for the aged, handicapped, and other unemployables. Care for the latter was to be returned to the states and locales. In short, the continuation of the dole and related poor relief was not to be a function of the Works Progress Administration. That policy was in compliance with a decision made by President Franklin D. Roosevelt* in January 1935 that the federal government "must and shall quit this business of relief."

The WPA inherited much of its national and state administration from the FERA, which officially ended on December 31, 1935. Harry L. Hopkins* became the head of the WPA; Aubrey Williams* remained his chief administrative assistant; and Ellen S. Woodward* continued as the director of the Women's and Professional Projects. State WPA directors were given strong direction from the national office through five regional offices, headed by field representatives and a staff of regional engineers and examiners; and they were expected to adhere closely to standardized procedures and issuances. Between 1935 and 1943 the WPA spent $11.4 billion and employed about 3.3 million people at its peak. During its existence project operation resulted in the creation or improvement of a wide variety of public facilities including more than 2,500 hospitals, 5,900 school buildings, 1,000 airports or landings, hundreds of thousands of miles of rural roads and urban streets and sidewalks, and thousands of public parks and utility plants. In the non-construction field WPA workers assisted communities in expanding educational, library, health, and related community services. Under the aegis of "federal one,"* professionals were employed in the Federal Writers',* Theatre,* Art,* and Music Projects* which together provided relief work for about 40,000 persons, the largest number being employed on the Federal Music Project. WPA writers produced state and regional guides, folklore and ethnic studies, and oral histories. Musicians gave concerts, composed pieces indigenous to American regions, and provided instruction to all levels of countless citizens. Artists indexed American designs, painted murals for public buildings, and operated community art centers. Federal Theatre troupes produced drama and musicals in forty states, reaching large numbers of people who had never seen a stage performance.

Despite the enormous productivity of the WPA and its success in providing some level of income for about one-third of the unemployed at an average monthly income of $50, it had its detractors. Welfare officials were disturbed that state and local governments could not adequately assist the large number of needy who were ineligible for WPA work. Although Hopkins did not create a political machine, the attempt of some governors, congressmen, and local officials to do so led to the Hatch Act* of 1939. Certification of the unemployed for relief and their subsequent discharge depended upon annual congressional appropriations which fluctuated (they were cut in 1937 and increased in 1938). Because the WPA relied upon social work staffs of state and local agencies to certify applicants for project assignments, local prejudices led to discrimination against women and minorities. Hence there was always dissatisfaction among a large number of workers who were either discharged or feared a discharge. Some dissidents formed the Workers' Alliance whose protests further alienated congressional critics and a segment of the public. Moreover, the make-work nature of some WPA projects led punsters to rename the agency the "We Piddle Around" and to ridicule expenditures as "boondoggling."* There is no doubt that many workers were inefficient. Conservatives in and out of Congress disliked the attention given by the Writers', Art, and Theatre Projects to themes of social protest and the economic dilemmas of the dispossessed. Many businessmen charged that the WPA competed unfairly with private industry, and organized labor complained that it undercut prevailing wages.

Congressional opponents of the WPA* succeeded in killing the Federal Theatre and reducing the WPA under the terms of the Emergency Relief Appropriation Act of 1939.* The Reorganization Act of 1939* renamed the Works Projects Administration* and placed it in the new Federal Works Agency.* After the resignation of Hopkins in late 1938, Col. Francis C. Harrington,* formerly the head of the WPA Engineering Division, became the administrator. With his appointment the emphasis of the WPA shifted even more to large-scale construction. Although the Women's and Professional Projects Division now under Florence Kerr* remained, its programs diminished. With the onset of preparation for war in 1941 the entire WPA shifted in focus as national defense became the chief administration goal. As employment opportunities increased within the private sector, WPA projects withered and the remaining programs were liquidated in July 1943.

The legacy of the WPA is tremendous. Many impressive public buildings, parks, and edifices remain although many have been destroyed or replaced by more modern structures. Only in recent years have the merits of the historical research of the professional projects been truly recognized. The national endowment for the arts and humanities, begun in the 1960s, is considered a legacy of the WPA cultural projects. The initials "WPA" are among the best remembered symbols of the 1930s. They are still visible in thousands of American communities as a reminder of the most ambitious undertaking of the federal government to provide employment for the jobless in time of economic stress. (Grace Adams, *Workers on Relief*, 1939; Federal Works Agency, *Final Report on the WPA Program, 1935–1943*, 1946; William F. McDonald, *Federal Relief Administration and the Arts*, 1969; Edward Ainsworth Williams, *Federal Aid for Relief*, 1939.)

MARTHA H. SWAIN

WORKS PROJECTS ADMINISTRATION Established in 1935 under authority of the Emergency Relief Appropriations Act,* the Works Progress Administration* functioned as an independent agency operating a wide variety of work relief programs. As part of the Reorganization Act of 1939,* the WPA was renamed the Works Projects Administration and transferred, along with several other work relief agencies, to the newly-created Federal Works Agency.* The new WPA began its work on July 1, 1939, with Colonel Francis Harrington* continuing as its commissioner, now under the direction of John M. Carmody,* head of the Federal Works Agency. Harrington designated all administrative personnel to continue in office, and all existing rules and regulations remained in force.

With the Reorganization Act of 1939, federal work relief no longer enjoyed extraordinary status, instead becoming part of regular government operations. (William F. McDonald, *Federal Relief Administration and the Arts*, 1969.)

WYZANSKI, CHARLES EDWARD, JR. Charles E. Wyzanski, Jr., was born in Boston on May 27, 1906. He graduated from Harvard in 1927 and from the Harvard Law School in 1930. After clerking for a year with U. S. Circuit Judge Learned Hand in 1932, Wyzanski became solicitor in the Department of Labor between 1933 and 1935. Wyzanski helped draft the National Industrial Relations Act in 1933,* but he came away with serious misgivings about the measure. A protégé of Felix Frankfurter,* Wyzanski was at once a social liberal and a constitutional conservative who had even voted for Herbert Hoover* in 1932. His Brandesian views of the economy left him extremely uncomfortable with the NIRA's suspension of anti-trust laws and the attempt to include small as well as large businesses seemed guaranteed to violate the line separating interstate from intrastate commerce. Wyzanski also believed the code-making authority of the law gave too much discretionary, legislative power to the president, and he felt the bill would not survive careful judicial scrutiny. Wyzanski also opposed Robert Wagner's* unsuccessful Labor Disputes Act of 1934 and worked to make the National Labor Relations Act* guarantee that unions as well as businesses not intimidate employees. Wyzanski's approach to the bill reflected the position of his boss, Secretary of Labor Frances Perkins,* who felt the National Labor Relations Act deemphasized mediation in favor of an adversary coalition between government and labor against the business community. In 1935 Wyzanski joined Stanley Reed's* legal staff in the solicitor general's office, where he prepared briefs on labor relations questions, helped prepare the Social Security Act of 1935,* and argued the social security case before the Supreme Court.* A brilliant attorney, Wyzanski was enraged at Roosevelt's "court-packing"* scheme in 1937, almost resigned immediately upon hearing of it, and then left the federal government at the end of the year to return to private law practice. Wyzanski returned to the federal government in 1941 as a member of the National Defense Mediation Board, but he resigned that position later in the year to accept appointment as a United States district judge for Massachusetts. In 1966 Wyzanski became chief judge of the U. S. District Court for Massachusetts. (Peter H. Irons, *The New Deal Lawyers*, 1982; Katie Louchheim, ed., *The Making of the New Deal. The Insiders Speak*, 1983; *Who's Who In America,* II:3651, 1982.)

Appendix A

A NEW DEAL CHRONOLOGY, 1933-1941

The following dates indicate the time when laws went into effect, agencies were established, court decisions were rendered, or executive decisions were implemented.

1933

March

5 Proclamation No. 2038 convened Congress in emergency session.
6 Proclamation No. 2039 declared the bank holiday.
9 Emergency Banking Act.
20 Economy Act.
22 Beer Tax Act.
27 Executive Order No. 6084 created the Farm Credit Administration.
31 Civilian Conservation Corps Reforestation Act.
Emergency Conservation Work Act.

April

5 Executive Order No. 6101 created the Civilian Conservation Corps.

May

12 Agricultural Adjustment Act.
Emergency Farm Mortgage Act.
Federal Emergency Relief Act.
London Economic Conference convened.
17 Tennessee Valley Authority created.
27 Securities Act (Fletcher-Rayburn Bill).

June

6 Wagner-Peyser Bill (National Employment Act).
13 Home Owners' Refinancing Act.
16 Banking Act (Glass-Steagall Bill).
Emergency Railroad Transportation Act.

Farm Credit Act.

National Industrial Recovery Act.

Executive Order No. 6174 established the Public Works Administration.

26 Consumers' Advisory Board appointed.

July

8 Executive Order No. 6198 named Harold L. Ickes Federal Emergency Administrator of Public Works.

9 Cotton Textile National Industrial Relations Board created.

11 Executive Order No. 6202A established the Emergency Council, later the National Emergency Council.

Executive Order No. 6199 prohibited the shipment of "hot oil."

27 Executive Order No. 6225 created the Central Statistical Board.

30 National Planning Board established.

August

4 Coal Arbitration Board established.

5 National Labor Board established.

10 Executive Order No. 6246 required all government purchases to be made from suppliers cooperating with NRA codes.

19 Executive Order No. 6252 defined the function and powers of the Public Works Administration.

28 Petroleum Administrative Board established.

October

16 Executive Order No. 6340 established the Commodity Credit Corporation.

November

9 Executive Order No. 6420B established the Civil Works Administration.

17 Executive Order No. 6433A established the National Emergency Council.

December

5 Executive Order No. 6474 established the Federal Alcohol Control Administration.

Twenty-First Amendment to the Constitution ratified.

Proclamation No. 2065 officially repealed the Eighteenth Amendment to the Constitution.

10 Public Works of Art Project established.

16 Executive Order No. 6511 authorized the National Labor Board to investigate and deal with the labor-management disputes.

19 Executive Order No. 6514 established the Electric Home and Farm Authority.

Petroleum Labor Policy Board established.

21 Proclamation No. 2067 ratified the London Agreement on Silver of 1933.

30 Proclamation No. 2070 restored to the jurisdiction of state banking authorities all state-chartered banks not members of the Federal Reserve System.

1934

January

30 Gold Reserve Act.

31 Farm Mortgage Refinancing Act.

Proclamation No. 2072 concluded the "gold-buying" program and set the price of gold at $35 per ounce.

February

2 Executive Order No. 6581 established the Export-Import Bank.

9 Executive Order No. 6591 authorized the army to begin carrying air mail.

23 Crop Loan Act.

March

7 Executive Order No. 6632 established the National Recovery Review Board.

10 Conservation of Fish Act.

12 Second Export-Import Bank established.

28 Independent Offices Appropriations Act.

April

7 Jones-Connally Farm Relief Act.

16 Johnson-O'Malley Act.

21 Bankhead Cotton Control Act.

27 Home Owners' Loan Act.

May

2 Proclamation No. 2082 extended Title I of the Emergency Railroad Act for one year.

9 Jones-Costigan Sugar Act.

18 Crime Control Laws.

Emergency Cattle Purchase Program.

24 Municipal Bankruptcy Act.

June

6 Securities Exchange Act.

7 Corporate Bankruptcy Act.

12 Reciprocal Trade Agreements Act.

18 Indian Reorganization Act.

19 National Labor Relations Board (the first board) established.

Silver Purchase Act.

20 Communications Act.

21 Railway Labor Act (Crosser-Dill Act).

26 Executive Order No. 6748 established the National Longshoremen's Board.

27 Railroad Retirement Act.

28 Federal Farm Bankruptcy Act (Frazier-Lemke Bill).
Executive Order No. 6751 established the National Steel Labor Relations Board.
Executive Order No. 6757 established the Committee on Economic Security
Kerr-Smith Tobacco Control Act.
National Housing Act.
Taylor Grazing Act.

30 Executive Order No. 6770 established the Industrial Emergency Committee.
Executive Order No. 6777 established the National Resources Board.
Federal Prison Industries, Inc. established.

July

5 National Power Policy Committee established.

August

9 Executive Order No. 6814 "nationalized" silver.

September

11 Proclamation No. 2098 extended provisions of the Agricultural Adjustment Act.

26 Textile Labor Relations Board established.

October

16 Federal Tender Board established.

December

11 Executive Order No. 6917 established the Federal Prison Industries, Inc.

1935

January

7 *Panama Refining Company v. Ryan* (293 U.S. 388).
Amazon Petroleum Corporation et al. v. Ryan (293 U.S. 388).

February

18 "Gold Cases": *Norman v. Baltimore & Ohio Railroad Company* (294 U.S. 240); *United States et al. v. Bankers' Trust Company* (294 U.S. 240); *Nortz v. United States* (294 U.S. 317); *Perry v. United States* (294 U.S. 330).

22 Connally Act.

April

8 Emergency Relief Appropriation Act.

27 Soil Conservation Act.

30 Executive Order No. 7027 established the Resettlement Administration.

May

6 Executive Order No. 7034 established the Works Progress Administration.

Railroad Retirement Board et al. v. Alton Railroad Company et al. (295 U.S. 330).

11 Executive Order No. 7037 established the Rural Electrification Administration.

27 *Louisville Joint Stock Land Bank v. Radford* (295 U.S. 555).

"Black Monday": *Schechter Poultry Corporation v. United States* (295 U.S. 495).

June

7 Executive Order No. 7065 established the National Resources Committee.

15 Executive Order No. 7074 re-established the National Labor Relations Board.

26 Executive Order No. 7086 established the National Youth Administration.

July

5 National Labor Relations Act (Wagner-Connery Bill).

31 Executive Order No. 7121 extended the power of the National Labor Relations Board.

August

2 Federal Art Project established.

Federal Music Project established.

Federal Theatre Project established.

Federal Writers' Project established.

9 Motor Carrier Act.

12 Executive Order No. 7139 created a new Electric Home and Farm Authority to replace the old EHFA.

14 Social Security Act.

23 Banking Act.

24 Warren Potato Control Act.

27 Indian Arts and Crafts Board established.

28 Farm Mortgage Moratorium Act.

Public Utility Holding Company Act (Wheeler-Rayburn Bill).

29 Federal Alcohol Administration Act.

Railroad Retirement Act (Wagner-Crosser Act).

Fulmer Act.

30 Guffey-Snyder Bituminous Coal Stabilization Act.

Wealth Tax Act (Revenue Act of 1935).

September

21 Executive Order No. 7186 increased the spending limit of the Emergency Relief Appropriation Act of 1935.

November

16 Historical Records Survey.

Federal Surplus Relief Corporation established.

December

21 Executive Order No. 7252 terminated the National Recovery Administration.

1936

January

6 *United States v. Butler et al.* (297 U.S. 1).

10 Proclamation No. 2153 extended the Gold Reserve Act of 1934 by one year.

27 Adjusted Compensation Act.

February

17 *Ashwander et al. v. Tennessee Valley Authority* (297 U.S. 288).

29 Neutrality Act.

Soil Conservation and Domestic Allotment Act.

March

8 Federal Dance Project.

April

3 Executive Order No. 7334 increased the spending limits of the Emergency Relief Appropriation Act of 1935.

6 *Jones v. S.E.C.* (298 U.S. 1).

20 Rural Electrification Act.

May

1 Alaska Reorganization Act. (PL 538-74th Congress).

18 *Carter v. Carter Coal Company* (198 U.S. 238).

June

1 *Morehead v. Tipaldo* (298 U.S. 587).

15 Flood Control Act.

20 Federal Anti-Price Discrimination Act (Robinson-Patman Act).

22 Flood Control Act.

Revenue Act (Undistributed profits).

26 Oklahoma Indian Welfare Act.

29 Merchant Marine Act.

30 Walsh-Healey Public Contracts Act.

November

17 Special Committee on Farm Tenancy established.

1937

February

7 "Court-packing" bill sent to Congress.

March

29 *West Coast Hotel v. Parrish* (300 U.S. 379).

April

12 *National Labor Relations Board v. Jones & Laughlin Steel Corporation* (301 U.S. 1).

26 Guffey-Vinson Bituminous Coal Act.

May

18 Farm Forestry Act.

27 Columbia River Basin Anti-Speculation Act.

June

29 Emergency Relief Appropriation Act.
Railroad Retirement Act.

July

22 Bankhead-Jones Farm Tenancy Act.

August

5 National Cancer Institute Act.

17 Miller-Tydings Act.

20 Bonneville Power Administration Act.

26 Revenue Act.
Judicial Procedures Reform Act.

28 Water Facilities Act.

September

1 Farm Security Administration established.
Wagner-Steagall Housing Act.

2 Pittman-Robertson Act.

16 Executive Order No. 7709A abolished the National Emergency Council.

October

12 Proclamation No. 2256 convened a special session of Congress.

27 Executive Order No. 7732 transferred all federal housing projects to the United States Housing Authority.

December

27 Executive Order No. 7776 extended the authority of the National Emergency Council to June 30, 1938.

1938

February

3 Housing Act.

10 Federal National Mortgage Association established.

11 Small Business Conference convenes.

16 Agricultural Adjustment Act.
Federal Crop Insurance Act.

May

27 Revenue Act.

June

16 Temporary National Economic Committee convenes.

21 National Gas Act.

22 Chandler Act.

23 Civil Aeronautics Act.

25 Fair Labor Standards Act.
Food, Drug, and Cosmetic Act.

August

13 United States Film Service established.

1939

January

14 Federal Real Estate Board established.

April

3 Reorganization Act.

May

16 Food Stamp Plan implemented.

June

5 *Hague, Mayor, et al. v. Committee for Industrial Organization* (307 U.S. 496).

30 Emergency Relief Appropriation Act.

July

1 Reorganization of the executive branch of the federal government is implemented.
Federal Loan Agency established.
Federal Security Agency established.
Federal Works Agency established.
National Resources Planning Board established.

6 Monetary Act.

August

2 Hatch Act.

4 Reclamation Project Act.

September

8 Executive Order 8248 broadly defined duties of Bureau of the Budget.

11 Proclamation No. 2361 suspended Title II of the Sugar Act of 1937.

November

4 Neutrality Act.

1940

April

22 *Thornhill v. State of Alabama* (310 U.S. 88).

June

24 Emergency Relief Appropriation Act.

July

19 Hatch Act (second act).

August

22 Investment Advisers Act.
Investment Company Act.

September

18 Transportation Act.

1941

February

3 *United States v. Darby* (312 U.S. 567).

17 *United States v. Darby* (amended).

June

25 Executive Order No. 8802 established the Fair Employment Practices Committee.

July

1 Emergency Relief Appropriation Act.

November

24 *Edwards v. People of the State of California* (314 U.S. 160).

ANN H. HOLDER

Appendix ***B***

A SELECTED BIBLIOGRAPHY OF NEW DEAL PROGRAMS

GENERAL STUDIES

Alsop, Joseph. *FDR: A Centenary Remembrance*. 1982.

Blum, John Morton. " 'That Kind of Liberal': Franklin D. Roosevelt after Twenty-Five Years." *Yale Review*, LX (Spring, 1982).

Brinkley, Alan. "The New Deal Prelude." *Wilson Quarterly*, VI (Spring, 1982).

Braeman, John, Robert H. Bremner, and David Brody. *The New Deal. The National Level*. 1975.

Burns, James MacGregor. *Roosevelt: The Lion and the Fox*. 1956.

———. *Roosevelt. The Soldier of Freedom*. 1970.

Conkin, Paul. *The New Deal*. 1967.

Flynn, John T. *The Roosevelt Myth*. 1948.

Freidel, Frank. *Franklin D. Roosevelt: Launching the New Deal*. 1973.

Frisch, Morton J. *Franklin D. Roosevelt: The Contribution of the New Deal to American Political Thought and Practice*. 1975.

Fusfeld, Daniel R. *The Economic Thought of Franklin D. Roosevelt and the Origin of the New Deal*. 1956.

Garraty, John A. "The New Deal, National Socialism, and the Great Depression." *American Historical Review*, LXXVIII (October, 1973).

Greer, Thomas H. *What Roosevelt Thought. The Social and Political Ideas of Franklin D. Roosevelt*. 1958.

Hearns, Charles R. *The American Dream and the Great Depression*. 1977.

Horowitz, Irving Louis. "From the New Deal to the New Federalism: Presidential Ideology in the U.S. from 1932 to 1982." *American Journal of Economics and Sociology*, XLII (April, 1983).

Humphrey, Hubert H. *The Political Philosophy of the New Deal*. 1970.

Irons, Peter H. *The New Deal Lawyers*. 1982.

Lee, Bradford A. "The New Deal Reconsidered." *Wilson Quarterly*, VI (Spring, 1982).

Leuchtenburg, William E. *Franklin D. Roosevelt and the New Deal, 1932-1940*. 1963.

———. "The Legacy of F.D.R." *Wilson Quarterly*, VI (Spring, 1982).

Lowitt, Richard. *The New Deal and the West*. 1984.

Louchheim, Katie, ed. *The Making of the New Deal. The Insiders Speak*. 1983.

Manchester, William. *The Glory and the Dream. A Narrative History of America, 1932-1972*. 1973.

May, Dean, *From New Deal to New Economics*, 1982.

McElvaine, Robert S. *The Great Depression. America, 1929-1941*. 1984.

Mitchell, Broadus. *Depression Decade, From New Era Through New Deal, 1929-1941*, 1947.

Moley, Raymond and Elliott A. Rosen. *The First New Deal*, 1966.

Patterson, James T. *Congressional Conservatism and the New Deal*. 1967.

Perkins, Dexter. *The New Age of Franklin D. Roosevelt, 1932-1945*. 1957.

Rauch, Basil. *The History of the New Deal*. 1944.

Romasco, Albert U. *The Politics of Recovery: Roosevelt's New Deal*. 1983.

Rosen, Elliott A. *Hoover, Roosevelt, and the Brains Trust: From Depression to New Deal*. 1977.

Rosenman, Samuel I., ed. *The Public Papers and Addresses of Franklin D. Roosevelt*. Vols. 1-9. 1937-1946.

Sargent, James E. *Roosevelt and the Hundred Days: Struggle for the Early New Deal*. 1981.

Schlesinger, Arthur M., Jr. *The Age of Roosevelt. Vol. I. The Crisis of the Old Order, 1919-1933*. 1957.

———. *The Age of Roosevelt. Vol. II. The Coming of the New Deal*. 1959.

———. *The Age of Roosevelt. Vol. III. The Politics of Upheaval, 1935-1936*. 1960.

Tugwell, Rexford G. *The Democratic Roosevelt*. 1957.

———. *FDR: Architect of an Era*. 1967.

———. *Roosevelt's Revolution. The First Year. A Personal Perspective*. 1977.

Wann, A. J. *The President as Chief Administrator: A Study of Franklin D. Roosevelt*. 1968.

Wolfskill, George and John R. Hudson. *All but the People: Franklin D. Roosevelt and His Critics, 1933-1939* 1969.

AGRICULTURE

Abrahams, Paul. "Agricultural Adjustment During the New Deal Period. The New York Milk Industry: A Case Study." *Agricultural History*, XXXIX (April, 1965).

Badger, Anthony J. *Prosperity Road: The New Deal, Tobacco, and North Carolina*. 1980.

Baldwin, Sidney. *Poverty and Politics: The Rise and Decline of the Farm Security Administration*. 1968.

Brown, D. Clayton. *Electricity for Rural America: The Fight for the REA*. 1980.

Bulkley, Peter B. "Agrarian Crisis in Western New York: New Deal Reinforcement of the Farm Depression." *New York History*, LIX (October, 1978).

Campbell, Christiana McFadyen. *The Farm Bureau and the New Deal: A Study of the Making of National Farm Policy, 1933-1940*. 1962.

Case, H. C. M. "Farm Debt Adjustment during the Early 1930s." *Agricultural History*, XXXIV (October, 1960).

Clawson, Marion. "Conserving the Soil." *Proceedings of the Academy of Political Science*, XXXIV (1982).

———. "Resettlement Experience on Nine Selected Resettlement Projects." *Agricultural History*, LII (January, 1978).

Dethloff, Henry C. "Missouri Farmers and the New Deal: A Case Study of Farm Policy Formulation on the Local Level." *Agricultural History*, XXXIX (July, 1965).

Ellis, Clyde T. *A Giant Step*. 1966.

Feder, Ernest. "Farm Debt Adjustment during the Depression—The Other Side of the Coin." *Agricultural History*, XXXV (April, 1961).

Fite, Gilbert C. "Farmer Opinion and the Agricultural Adjustment Act, 1933." *Mississippi Valley Historical Review*, XLVIII (March, 1962).

Guth, James L. "The National Cooperative Council and Farm Relief, 1929-1942." *Agricultural History*, LI (April, 1977).

Hoag, W. Gifford. *The Farm Credit System: A History of Financial Self-Help*. 1976.

Hunter, Robert F. "The AAA between Neighbors: Virginia, North Carolina, and the New Deal Farm Program." *Journal of Southern History*, XLIV (November, 1978).

Kirkendall, Richard S. *Social Scientists and Farm Politics in the Age of Roosevelt*. 1966.

Koppes, Clayton, R. "Public Water, Private Land: Origins of the Acreage Limitation Controversy, 1933-1953." *Pacific Historical Review*, XLVII (November, 1978).

Kramer, Randall A. "Federal Crop Insurance, 1938-1982." *Agricultural History*, LVII (April, 1983).

Lambert, C. Roger. "The Drought Cattle Purchase, 1934-1935." *Agricultural History*, XLIV (October, 1970).

———. "The Illusion of Participating Democracy: The AAA Organizes the Corn-Hog Producers." *Annals of Iowa*, XLII (Fall, 1974).

———. "Texas Cattleman and the AAA, 1933–1935." *Arizona and the West*, XIV (Spring, 1972).

———. "Want and Plenty: The Federal Surplus Relief Corporation and the AAA." *Agricultural History*, XLVI (July, 1972).

May, Irvin R., Jr. "The FSRC and Emergency Work Relief." *Agricultural History*, XLVI (July, 1972).

McDean, Harry C. "Federal Farm Policy and the Dust Bowl: The Half-Right Solution." *North Dakota History*, XLVII (Summer, 1980).

———. "Social Scientists and Farm Poverty on the North American Plains, 1933-1940." *Great Plains Quarterly*, 3 (Winter, 1983).

Morgan, Robert J. *Governing Soil Conservation: Thirty Years of the New Decentralization*. 1966.

Nelson, Lawrence J. "New Deal and Free Market: The Memphis Meeting of the Southern Commissioners of Agriculture, 1937." *Tennessee Historical Quarterly*, XL (Fall, 1981).

———. "Oscar Johnson, the New Deal, and Cotton Subsidy Payments Controversy, 1936-1937." *Journal of Southern History*, XL (August, 1974).

Nourse, Edwin G. *Marketing Agreements Under the AAA*. 1935.

Perkins, Van L. *Crisis in Agriculture. The Agricultural Adjustment Administration and the New Deal, 1933*. 1969.

Saloutos, Theodore. *The American Farmer and the New Deal*. 1983.

———. "New Deal Agriculture Policy: An Evaluation." *Journal of American History*, LXI (September, 1974).

———. "The New Deal and Farm Policy in the Great Plains." *Agricultural History*, XLIII (July, 1969).

Schapsmeier, Edward L. and Frederick H. Schapsmeier. "Farm Policy from FDR to

Eisenhower: Southern Democrats and the Politics of Agriculture.'' *Agricultural History*, LIII (January, 1979).
———. *Henry A. Wallace of Iowa: The Agrarian Years, 1910-1940*. 1968.
Shover, John L. ''Populism in the Nineteen-Thirties: The Battle for the AAA.'' *Agricultural History*, XXXVIII (October, 1964).
Stokes, W. N., Jr. *Credit to Farmers. The Story of the Federal Intermediate Credit Banks and Production Credit Associations*. 1973.
Stout, Joe A., Jr. ''Cattlemen, Conservationists, and the Taylor Grazing Act.'' *New Mexico Historical Review*, XLV (October, 1970).
Tugwell, Rexford G. ''Some Aspects of New Deal Farm Policy: The Resettlement Idea.'' *Agricultural History*, XXXIII (October, 1959).

ARTS

Clark, B. '' 'To Preserve Local History': The WPA Historical Records Survey in Oklahoma, 1936-1942.'' *Chronicles of Oklahoma*, LXI (Summer, 1983).
Dieterich, Herbert R. ''The New Deal Cultural Projects in Wyoming: A Survey and Appraisal.'' *Annals of Wyoming*, LII (Fall, 1980).
Hendrickson, Gordon O. ''The WPA Writers' Project in Wyoming: History and Collections.'' *Annals of Wyoming*, XIL (Fall, 1977).
Jones, Alfred H. *Roosevelt's Image Brokers: Poets, Playwrights, and the Use of the Lincoln Symbol*. 1974.
Lally, Kathleen. ''History of the Federal Dance Project.'' Ph.D. Thesis, Texas Women's University, 1978.
Mangione, Jerre. *The Dream and the Deal: The Federal Writers' Project, 1935-1943*. 1972.
Marling, Karal Ann. *Wall-to-Wall America: A Cultural History of Post Office Murals in the Great Depression*. 1982.
Mathews, Jane De Hart. ''Arts and the People: The New Deal Quest for a Cultural Democracy.'' *Journal of American History*, LXII (September, 1975).
———. *The Federal Theatre, 1935-1938: Plays, Relief, and Politics*. 1967.
McDonald, William F. *Federal Relief Administration and the Arts*. 1969.
McKinzie, Richard D. *The New Deal for Artists*. 1973.
Noggle, Burl. *Working With History: The Historical Records Survey in Louisiana and the Nation, 1936–1942*. 1981.
O'Connor, Francis V. *The New Deal Arts Projects: An Anthology of Memoirs*. 1972.
Penkower, Monty Noam. *The Federal Writers' Project: A Study in Government Patronage of the Arts*. 1977.
Randle, Mallory B. ''Texas Muralists of the PWAP.'' *Southwestern Art*, I (Spring, 1966).
Rhoads, William B. ''The Artistic Patronage of Franklin D. Roosevelt: Art as Historical Record.'' *Prologue*, XV (Spring, 1983).
Rollins, Peter C. ''Ideology and Film Rhetoric: Three Documentaries of the New Deal Era.'' *Journal of Popular Film*, V (No. 2, 1976).
Ruby, Christine Nelson. ''Art for the Millions: Government Art during the Depression.'' *Michigan History*, LXVI (January/February, 1982).
Smiley, David L. ''A Slice of Life in Depression America: The Records of the Historical Records Survey.'' *Prologue*, III (Winter, 1971).
Snyder, Robert L. *Pare Lorentz and the Documentary Film*. 1968.

Taber, Ronald W. "Vardis Fisher and the 'Idaho Guide': Preserving Culture for the New Deal." *Pacific Northwest Quarterly*, LIX (April, 1968).

———. "Writers on Relief: The Making of the Washington Guide, 1935-1941." *Pacific Northwest Quarterly*, LXI (October, 1970).

Warren-Findley, Jannelle. "Musicians and Mountaineers: The Resettlement Administration's Music Program in Appalachia, 1935-1937." *Appalachian Journal*, VII (Autumn/Winter, 1979-1980).

York, Hildreth. "The New Deal Art Projects in New Jersey." *New Jersey History*, XCVIII (Fall–Winter, 1980).

COMMUNITIES

Arnold, Joseph L. *The New Deal in the Suburbs: A History of the Greenbelt Town Program, 1935-1954*. 1971.

Conkin, Paul K. *Tomorrow a New World: The New Deal Community Program*. 1959.

Collins, Robert M. "Positive Business Responses to the New Deal: The Roots of the Committee for Economic Development, 1933-1942," *Business History Review*, LII:369-391, 1978.

Coode, Thomas H. and Dennis E. Fabbri. "The New Deal's Arthurdale Project in West Virginia." *West Virginia History*, XXXVI (July, 1975).

Fairbanks, Robert B. "Cincinnati and Greenhills: The Response to a Federal Community, 1935-1939." *Cincinnati Historical Society Bulletin*, XXXVI (Winter, 1978).

Holley, Donald. *Uncle Sam's Farmers: The New Deal Communities in the Lower Mississippi Valley*. 1975.

ECONOMIC POLICY

Anti-Trust and Regulation

Barnouw, Erik. *The Golden Web: A History of Broadcasting in the United States, 1933 to 1953*. 1968.

Benston, George J. "Required Disclosure and the Stock Market: An Evaluation of the Securities Exchange Act of 1934." *American Economic Review*, LXIII (March, 1973).

Burns, Helen M. *The American Banking Community and New Deal Banking Reforms: 1933-1935*. 1974.

de Bedts, Ralph F. *The New Deal's SEC: The Formative Years*. 1964.

Eaton, Michael M. "The Robinson-Patman Act: Reconciling the Meeting Competition Defense with the Sherman Act." *Antitrust Bulletin*, XVIII (Fall, 1973).

Funigiello, Philip J. *Toward a National Power Policy: The New Deal and the Electric Utility Industry, 1933-1941*. 1973.

Jackson, Charles O. *Food and Drug Legislation in the New Deal*. 1970.

———. "Muckraking and Consumer Protection: The Case of the 1938 Food, Drug, and Cosmetic Act." *Pharmacy in History*, XIII (1971).

Kennedy, Susan Estabrook. *The Banking Crisis of 1933*. 1973.

Komons, Nick A. *Bonfires to Beacons: Federal Civil Aviation Policy Under the Air Commerce Act, 1926–1938*. 1978.

Miscamble, Wilson D. "Thurman Arnold Goes to Washington: A Look at Antitrust Policy in the Later New Deal." *Business History Review*, LVI (Spring, 1982).

Parrish, Michael. *Securities Regulation and the New Deal*. 1970.

Wagner, Susan. *The Federal Trade Commission*. 1971.

Whitnah, Donald R., *Safer Skyways: Federal Control of Aviation 1926-1966*. 1966.

Economic Recovery

Bellush, Bernard. *The Failure of the NRA*. 1975.

Brand, Donald R. "Corporatism, the NRA, and the Oil Industry." *Political Science Quarterly*, XCVII (Spring, 1983).

Fine, Sidney. *The Automobile Under the Blue Eagle: Labor, Management, and the Automobile Manufacturing Code*. 1963.

Fricke, Ernest B. "The New Deal and the Modernization of Small Business: The McGeary Tire & Rubber Company, 1930-1940." *Business History Review*, LVI (Winter, 1982).

Galambos, Louis. *Competition & Cooperation: The Emergence of a National Trade Association*. 1966.

Hawley, Ellis W. *The New Deal and the Problem of Monopoly: A Study in Economic Ambivalence*. 1966.

Himmelberg, Robert F. *The Origins of the National Recovery Administration: Business, Government, and the Trade Association Issue, 1921-1933*. 1976.

Holmes, Michael S. "The Blue Eagle as 'Jim Crow Bird': The NRA and Georgia's Black Workers," *Journal of Negro History*, LVII (July, 1972).

Johnson, James P. *The Politics of Soft Coal: The Bituminous Industry from World War I through the New Deal*. 1979.

Koeniger, A. Cash. "Carter Glass and the National Recovery Administration." *South Atlantic Quarterly*, LXXIV (Summer, 1975).

Lear, Linda J. "Harold L. Ickes and the Oil Crisis of the First Hundred Days." *Mid-America*, LXIII (January, 1981).

Longin, Thomas C. "Coal, Congress, and the Courts: The Bituminous Coal Industry and the New Deal." *West Virginia History*, XXXV (January, 1974).

Nash, Gerald D. "Experiments in Industrial Mobilization: WIB and NRA." *Mid-America*, XLV (July, 1963).

Olson, James S., *Herbert Hoover and the Reconstruction Finance Corporation, 1931-1933*. 1977.

Robbins, William G. "The Great Experiment in Industrial Self-Government: The Lumber Industry and the National Recovery Administration." *Journal of Forest History*, XXV (July, 1981).

Rosenof, Theodore. *Dogma, Depression, and the New Deal: The Debate of Political Leaders over Economic Recovery*. 1975.

Skocpol, Theda and Kenneth Finegold. "State Capacity and Economic Intervention in the Early New Deal." *Political Science Quarterly*, XCVII (Summer, 1982).

Ware, James. "The Sooner NRA: New Deal Recovery in Oklahoma." *Chronicles of Oklahoma*, LIV (Fall, 1976).

Foreign Trade

Adams, Frederick C. *Economic Diplomacy: The Export-Import Bank and American Foreign Diplomacy, 1934–1939*. 1976.

McHale, James M. "National Planning and Reciprocal Trade: The New Deal Origins of Government Guarantees for Exporters." *Prologue*, VI (Fall, 1974).

Schatz, Arthur W. "The Reciprocal Trade Agreements Program and the 'Farm Vote', 1934-1940." *Agricultural History*, XLVI (October, 1972).

Government Spending

Collins, Robert M. *The Business Response to Keynes, 1929–1964*. 1981.

Critchlow, Donald T. "The Political Control of the Economy: Deficit Spending as a Political Belief, 1932–1952." *Public Historian*, III (Spring, 1981).

Lekachman, Robert. *The Age of Keynes*. 1966.

Sargent, James E. "FDR and Lewis Douglas: Budget Balancing and the Early New Deal." *Prologue*, VI (Spring, 1974).

———. "Roosevelt's Economy Act: Fiscal Conservatism and the Early New Deal." *Congressional Studies*, VII (Winter, 1980).

Stein, Herbert. *The Fiscal Revolution in America*. 1969.

Monetary Policy

Brennan, John A. *Silver and the First New Deal*. 1969.

Chandler, Lester V. *American Monetary Policy, 1928–1941*. 1971.

Howson, Susan. "The Management of Sterling." *Journal of Economic History*, XL (March, 1980).

Moore, James R. "Sources of New Deal Economic Policy: The International Dimension." *Journal of American History*, LXI (December, 1974).

Wicker, Elmus R. "Roosevelt's 1933 Monetary Experiment." *Journal of American History*, LVII (March, 1971).

EXECUTIVE REORGANIZATION

Fish, Peter Graham. "Crises, Politics, and Federal Judicial Reform: The Administrative Office Act of 1939." *Journal of Politics*, XXXII (August, 1970).

Karl, Barry Dean. *Executive Reorganization and Reform in the New Deal: The Genesis of Adminstrative Mangement, 1900-1939*. 1963.

Polenberg, Richard. *Reorganizing Roosevelt's Government: The Controversy Over Executive Reorganization, 1936–1939*. 1966.

LABOR

Auerbach, Jerold S. *Labor and Liberty: The La Follette Committee and the New Deal*. 1966.

Bernstein, Irving. *Turbulent Years: A History of the American Worker, 1933-1941*. 1970.

Conrad, David Eugene. *The Forgotten Farmers: The Story of Sharecroppers in the New Deal*. 1965.

Cortner, Richard C. *The Wagner Act Cases*. 1964.

Daniel, Cletus E. *The ACLU and the Wagner Act: An Inquiry into the Depression-Era Crisis of American Liberalism*. 1980.

———. "Agricultural Unionism and the Early New Deal: The California Experience." *Southern California Quarterly*, LIX (Summer, 1977).

Derber, Milton and Edwin Young, eds. *Labor and the New Deal*. 1957.

Gross, James A. *The Making of the NLRB: A Study in Economics, Politics and the Law*. 1974.

Grubbs, Donald H. *Cry from the Cotton: The Southern Tenant Farmers' Union and the New Deal*. 1971.

Lorwin, Lewis L. and Arthur Wubnig. *Labor Relations Boards*. 1935.

McFarland, C. K. *Roosevelt, Lewis, and the New Deal*, 1933-1940. 1970.

Schwartz, Bonnie Fox. "New Deal Work Relief and Organized Labor: The CWA and the AFL Building Trades." *Labor History*, XVII (Winter, 1976).

Vittoz, Stanley. "The Economic Foundations of Industrial Politics in the United States and the Emerging Structural Theory of the State in a Capitalist Society: The Cases of New Deal Labor Society." *Amerikastudien*, XXVII (No. 4, 1982).

LOCAL LEVEL

Arrington, Leonard. "The New Deal in the West: A Preliminary Statistical Inquiry." *Pacific Historical Review*, XXVIII (August, 1969).

———. "The Sagebrush Resurrection: New Deal Expenditures in the Western States, 1933-1939." *Pacific Historical Review*, LII (February, 1983).

Bitton, Davis. "The New Deal in Pocatello." *Idaho Yesterdays*, XXIII (Summer, 1979).

Braeman, John, Robert H. Bremner, and David Brody, eds. *The New Deal. Vol. II. The State and Local Level*. 1975.

Burke, Robert E. *Olson's New Deal for California*. 1953.

Heinemann, Ronald L. *Depression and New Deal in Virginia: The Enduring Dominion*. 1983.

Ingalls, Robert P. *Herbert H. Lehman and New York's Little New Deal*. 1975.

Judd, Richard M. *The New Deal in Vermont: Its Impact and Aftermath*. 1979.

Keller, Richard C. "Pennsylvania's Little New Deal." *Pennsylvania History*, XXIX (October, 1962).

Koeniger, A. Cash. "The New Deal and the States: Roosevelt versus the Byrd Organization in Virginia." *Journal of American History*, LXIII (March, 1982).

Larsen, T. A. "The New Deal in Wyoming." *Pacific Historical Review*, XXXVIII (August, 1969).

Long, Durward. "Key West and the New Deal, 1934-1936." *Florida Historical Quarterly*, XLVI (January, 1968).

Lowitt, Richard. "George W. Norris and the New Deal in Nebraska, 1933-1936." *Agricultural History*, LI (April, 1977).

Lowry, Charles B. "The PWA in Tampa: A Case Study." *Florida Historical Quarterly*, LII (April, 1974).

Malone, Michael P. *C. Ben Ross and the New Deal in Idaho*. 1970.

Minton, John Dean. *The New Deal in Tennessee, 1932-1938*. 1979.

Patenaude, Lionel V. *Texans, Politics, and the New Deal*. 1982.

Patterson, James T. *The New Deal in the States: Federalism in Transition*. 1969.

———. "The New Deal in the West." *Pacific Historical Review*, XXXVIII (August, 1969).

Reading, Don C. "New Deal Activities and the States, 1933-1939." *Journal of Economic History*, XXXIII (December, 1973).

Trout, Charles H. *Boston, the Great Depression, and the New Deal*. 1977.

Wickens, James F. *Colorado in the Great Depression*. 1979.

MINORITIES

Blacks

Bauman, John F. "Black Slums/Black Projects: The New Deal and Negro Housing in Philadelphia." *Pennsylvania History*, XLI (July, 1974).

Bunche, Ralph J. *The Political Status of the Negro in the Age of FDR*. 1973.

Clayton, Ronnie W. "The Federal Writers' Project for Blacks in Louisiana." *Louisiana History*, XIX (Summer, 1978).

Craig, E. Quita. *Black Drama of the Federal Theatre Era: Beyond the Formal Horizons*. 1980.

Holley, Donald. "The Negro in the New Deal Resettlement Program." *Agricultural History*, XLV (July, 1971).

Holmes, Michael S. "The New Deal and Georgia's Black Youth." *Journal of Southern History*, XXXVIII (August, 1972).

Kalmar, Karen L. "Southern Black Elites and the New Deal: A Case Study of Savannah, Georgia." *Georgia Historical Quarterly*, LXV (Winter, 1981).

Kirby, John B. *Black Americans in the Roosevelt Era: Liberalism and Race*. 1980.

Mertz, Paul E. *New Deal Policy and Southern Rural Poverty*. 1978.

Reed, Merl E. "The FEPC, the Black Worker, and the Southern Shipyards." *South Atlantic Quarterly*, LXXIV (Autumn, 1975).

Ross, B. Joyce. "Mary McLeod Bethune and the National Youth Administration: A Case Study of Power Relationships in the Black Cabinet of Franklin D. Roosevelt." *Journal of Negro History*, LX (January, 1975).

Ross, Ronald. "The Role of Blacks in the Federal Theatre, 1935-1939." *Journal of Negro History*, LIX (January, 1974).

Sitkoff, Harvard. *A New Deal for Blacks: The Emergence of Civil Rights as a National Issue. Vol. I. The Depression Decade*. 1978.

Weiss, Richard. "Ethnicity and Reform: Minorities and the Ambience of the Depression Years." *Journal of American History*, LXVI (December, 1979).

Wolters, Raymond. *Negroes and the Great Depression: The Problem of Economic Recovery*. 1970.

Wye, Christopher G. "The New Deal and the Negro Community: Toward a Broader Conceptualization." *Journal of American History*, LIX (December, 1972).

Indians

Gower, Calvin W. "The CCC Indian Division: Aid for Depressed Americans, 1933-1942." *Minnesota History*, XLIII (Spring, 1972).

Hauptman, Laurence M. *The Iroquois and the New Deal*. 1981.

Kelly, Lawrence C. *The Assault on Assimilation: John Collier and the Origins of Indian Policy Reform*. 1983.

———. "The Indian Reorganization Act: The Dream and the Reality." *Pacific Historical Review*, LXIV (May, 1975).

———. *The Navajo Indians and Federal Indian Policy, 1900-1935*. 1968.

Koppes, Clayton R. "From New Deal to Termination: Liberalism and Indian Policy, 1933-1953." *Pacific Historical Review*, XLVI (November, 1977).

Parman, Donald L. "The Indian and the Civilian Conservation Corps." *Pacific Historical Review*, XL (February, 1971).

———. *The Navajos and the New Deal*. 1976.

Philp, Kenneth R. *John Collier's Crusade for Indian Reform, 1920-1954*. 1977.

Schrader, Robert Fay. *The Indian Arts and Crafts Board: An Aspect of New Deal Indian Policy*. 1983.

Stefon, Frederick J. "The Indians' Zarathustra: An Investigation into the Philosophical Roots of John Collier's Indian New Deal Educational and Administrative Programs (Part I)." *Journal of Ethnic Studies*, XI (Fall, 1983).

Taylor, Graham D. *The New Deal and American Indian Tribalism: The Administration of the Indian Reorganization Act, 1934-1945*. 1980.

Weeks, Charles J. "The Eastern Cherokee and the New Deal." *North Carolina Historical Review*, LIII (July, 1976).

Wright, Peter M. "John Collier and the Oklahoma Indian Welfare Act of 1936." *Chronicles of Oklahoma*, L (Autumn, 1972).

Jews

Dinnerstein, Leonard. "Jews and the New Deal." *American Jewish History*, LXXII (June, 1983).

Mexicans

Hoffman, Abraham. *Unwanted Mexican Americans in the Great Depression: Repatriation Pressures, 1929–1939*. 1974.

Women

Scharf, Lois. *To Work and to Wed: Female Employment, Feminism, and the Great Depression*. 1980.

Swain, Martha H. " 'The Forgotten Woman': Ellen J. Woodward and Women's Relief in the New Deal," *Prologue*, XV (December, 1983).

Ware, Susan. *Beyond Suffrage: Women in the New Deal*. 1981.

———. *Holding Their Own: American Women in the 1930s*. 1982.

PLANNING AND CONSERVATION

Conservation

Barrett, Glen. "Reclamation's New Deal for Heavy Construction: M-K in the Great Depression." *Idaho Yesterdays*, XXII (Fall, 1978).

Calef, Wesley. *Private Grazing and Public Lands: Studies of the Local Management of the Taylor Grazing Act*. 1960.

Cart, Theodore W. " ' New Deal' For Wildlife: A Perspective on Federal Conservation Policy, 1933-1940." *Pacific Northwest Quarterly*, LXIII (July, 1972).

Droze, Wilmon H. "The New Deal's Shelterbelt Project, 1934-1942." In Harold M. Hollingsworth and William Holmes, eds. *Essays on the New Deal*. 1969.

Saindon, Bob and Bunky Sullivan. "Taming the Missouri and Treating the Depression: Fort Peck Dam." *Montana. The Magazine of History*, XXVII (Summer, 1977).

Swain, Donald C. "The Bureau of Reclamation and the New Deal, 1933-1940." *Pacific Northwest Quarterly*, LXI (July, 1970).

———. "The National Park Service and the New Deal, 1933-1940." *Pacific Historical Review*, XLI (May, 1972).

Wessel, Thomas R. "Roosevelt and the Great Plains Shelterbelt." *Great Plains Journal*, VIII (January, 1969).

Planning

Christie, Jean. "The Mississippi Valley Committee: Conservation and Planning in the Early New Deal." *Historian*, XXXII (May, 1970).

———. "New Deal Resources Planning: The Proposals of Morris L. Cooke." *Agricultural History*, LIII (July, 1979).

Clawson, Marion. *New Deal Planning: The National Resources Planning Board*. 1981.

Graham, Otis L., Jr. "The Planning Ideal and American Reality: The 1930s." In Stanley Elkins and Eric McKitrick, eds. *The Hofstadter Aegis*. 1974.

Tennessee Valley Authority

Clapp, Gordon. *The TVA: An Approach to the Development of a Region*. 1955.

Droze, Wilmon Henry. *High Dams and Slack Water: TVA Rebuilds a River*. 1965.

———. "TVA and the Ordinary Farmer." *Agricultural History*, LIII (January, 1979).

Hubbard, Preston. *Origins of the TVA: The Muscle Shoals Controversy, 1920-1932*. 1961.

McDonald, Michael J. and John Muldowny. *TVA and the Dispossessed: The Resettlement of Population in the Norris Dam Area*. 1982.

McGraw, Thomas K. *Morgan versus Lilienthal: A Feud within the TVA*. 1970.

———. *TVA and the Power Fight, 1933-1939*. 1971.

Morgan, Arthur E. *The Making of the TVA*. 1974.

Owen, Marguerite. *The Tennessee Valley Authority*. 1973.

RELIEF

Argersinger, Jo Ann E. "Assisting the 'Loafers': Transient Relief in Baltimore, 1933-1937." *Labor History*, XXIII (Winter, 1982).

Baldridge, Kenneth W. "Reclamation Work of the Civilian Conservation Corps, 1933-1942." *Utah Historical Quarterly*, XXXIX (Summer, 1971).

Blumberg, Barbara. *The New Deal and the Unemployed: The View from New York City*. 1979.

Bremer, William W. "Along the 'American Way': The New Deal's Work Relief Program for the Unemployed." *Journal of American History*, LXII (December, 1975).

Burran, James. "The WPA in Nashville, 1935-1943." *Tennessee Historical Quarterly*, XXXIV (Fall, 1975).

Church, Verne V. "CCCs and Fire Fighting." *Forest History*, XIV (January, 1971).

Dubay, Robert W. "The Civilian Conservation Corps: A Study of Opposition, 1933-1935." *Southern Quarterly*, VI (April, 1968).

Erickson, Herman. "WPA: Strike and Trials of 1939." *Minnesota History*, XLII (Summer, 1971).

Hendrickson, Kenneth E., Jr. "The Civilian Conservation Corps in Pennsylvania: A Case

Study of a New Deal Relief Agency in Operation.'' *Pennsylvania Magazine of History and Biography*, C (January, 1976).

———. ''The Civilian Conservation Corps in South Dakota.'' *South Dakota History*, XI (Winter, 1980).

———. ''The National Youth Administration in South Dakota: Youth and the New Deal, 1935-1943.'' *South Dakota History*, IX (Spring, 1979).

———. ''Relief for Youth: The Civilian Conservation Corps and the National Youth Administration in North Dakota.'' *North Dakota History*, XLVIII (Fall, 1981).

Holland, Reid. ''The Civilian Conservation Corps in the City: Tulsa and Oklahoma City in the 1930s.'' *Chronicles of Oklahoma*, LIII (Fall, 1975).

Johnson, Frederick K. ''The Civilian Conservation Corps: A New Deal for Youth.'' *Minnesota History*, XLVIII (Fall, 1983).

Ober, Michael J. ''The CCC Experience in Glacier National Park.'' *Montana. The Magazine of History*, XXVI (July, 1976).

Richardson, Elmo R. ''Was There Politics in the Civilian Conservation Corps?'' *Forest History*, XVI (July, 1972).

Salmond, John A. *The Civilian Conservation Corps. 1933–1942: A New Deal Case Study*. 1967.

Schuyler, Michael W. ''Federal Drought Relief Activities in Kansas, 1934.'' *Kansas Historical Quarterly*, XLII (Winter, 1976).

Stetson, Frederick W. ''The Civilian Conservation Corps in Vermont.'' *Vermont History*, XLVI (Winter, 1978).

Walker, Forrest A. *The Civil Works Administration: An Experiment in Federal Work Relief*. 1979.

Wallis, John Joseph and Daniel K. Benjamin. ''Public Relief and Private Employment in the Great Depression.'' *Journal of Economic History*, XLI (March, 1981).

Williams, Edward A. *Federal Aid for Relief*. 1939.

SOCIAL SECURITY

Altmeyer, Arthur J. *The Formative Years of Social Security*. 1966.

Brown, J. Douglas. *An American Philosophy of Social Security: Evolution and Issues*. 1972.

Fisher, Jacob. *The Response of Social Work to the Depression*. 1980.

Leff, Mark H. ''Taxing the 'Forgotten Man': The Politics of Social Security Finance in the New Deal.'' *Journal of American History*, LXX (September, 1980).

Lubove, Roy. *The Struggle for Social Security, 1900–1935*. 1968.

McKinley, Charles and Robert W. Frase. *Launching Social Security*. 1970.

Nelson, Daniel. *Unemployment Insurance: The American Experience, 1915-1935*. 1969.

Sanders, Daniel S. *The Impact of Reform Movements on Social Policy Change: The Case of Social Insurance*. 1973.

SUPREME COURT

Baker, Leonard. *Back to Back: The Duel Between FDR and the Supreme Court*. 1967.

Cortner, Richard C. *The Jones & Laughlin Case*. 1970.

Dawson, Nelson Lloyd. *Louis D. Brandeis, Felix Frankfurter, and the New Deal*. 1980.

Dunne, Gerald T. *Hugo Black and the Judicial Revolution*. 1977.

Leonard, Charles A. *A Search for a Judicial Philosophy: Mr. Justice Roberts and the Constitutional Revolution of 1937*. 1971.

Leuchtenburg, William E. "Roosevelt's Supreme Court Packing Plan." In Harold M. Hollingsworth and William Holmes, eds. *Essays on the New Deal*. 1969.

Lowitt, Richard. "Only God Can Change the Supreme Court." *Capitol Studies*, V (Spring, 1977).

Mason, Alpheus Thomas. *The Supreme Court from Taft to Warren*. 1958.

Morrison, Rodney J. "Franklin D. Roosevelt and the Supreme Court: An Example of the Use of Probability Theory in Political History." *History and Theory*, XVI (No. 2, 1977).

Patenaude, Lionel V. "Garner, Sumners, and Connally: The Defeat of the Roosevelt Court Bill in 1937." *Southwestern Historical Quarterly*, LXXIV (July, 1970).

Pritchett, Herman. *The Roosevelt Court. A Study in Judicial Politics and Values, 1937-1947*. 1948.

Appendix C

NEW DEAL PERSONNEL, 1933-1941

The list of New Deal officers and agency personnel is inclusive for 1933 through 1941. Some of the individuals listed may have continued to serve after 1941, but these tables do not indicate that service. Also, the major sources for the names are *The United States Official Register* (1933 and 1934) and *The United States Government Organization Manual* (1935-1941). The years of service for each individual listed were drawn from those sources, so in many cases the individual may have served somewhat earlier or later but not appeared in the particular manual at the time.

Agricultural Adjustment Administration

George N. Peek, Administrator (1933)
Chester C. Davis, Administrator (1934-1935)
Howard R. Tolley, Administrator (1936-1938)
Rudolph M. Evans, Administrator (1938-1941)

Attorney General of the United States

Homer S. Cummings (1933-1938)
Frank Murphy (1939)
Robert H. Jackson (1940)
Francis Biddle (1941)

Automobile Labor Board (three members)

Richard Byrd (1934)
Nicholas Kelley (1934)
Leo Wolman (1934)

Bureau of Indian Affairs

John Collier, Commissioner (1933-1941)

Bureau of the Budget

Daniel W. Bell, Acting Director (1933-1938)
Harold D. Smith, Director (1938-1941)

Civil Aeronautics Authority

Edward J. Noble, Chairman (1938)
Robert H. Hinckley, Chairman (1939)
Donald H. Connolly, Administrator of Civil Aeronautics, (1940-1941)
Harllee Branch, Chairman, Civil Aeronautics Board (On June 30, 1940, the Civil Aeronautics Authority was transferred to the Department of Commerce and its functions split between the Administrator of Civil Aeronautics and the Chairman of the Civil Aeronautics Board.)

Civil Works Administration

Harry L. Hopkins, Administrator (1933-1934)

Civilian Conservation Corps

Robert Fechner, Director (1933-1939)
J. J. McEntee, Director (1940-1941)

Commodity Credit Corporation

Lynn P. Talley, President (1933-1938)
Carl B. Robbins, President (1939-1940)
J. B. Hutson, President (1941)

Comptroller of the Currency

J. F. T. O'Connor (1933-1937)
Preston Delano (1938-1941)

Cotton Textile Board (three members)

John G. Winant, Chairman (1934)
Marion Smith (1934)
Raymond V. Ingersoll (1934)

Cotton Textile National Industrial Relations Board

Robert W. Bruere, Chairman (1933-1934)
George L. Berry (1933-1934)
B. E. Green (1933-1934)
C. M. Fox (1934)
Arthur Dixon (1934)

Electric Home and Farm Authority

Emil Schram, President (1936-1940)
A. T. Hobson, President (1941)

Export-Import Bank of Washington

George N. Peek, President (1935)
Warren Lee Pierson, President (1936-1941)

Farm Credit Administration

Henry Morgenthau, Jr., Governor (1933)
William I. Myers, Governor (1934-1937)

F. F. Hill, Governor (1938-1939)
Albert G. Black, Governor (1940-1941)

Farm Security Administration

Will W. Alexander, Administrator (1937-1939)
C. B. Baldwin, Administrator (1940-1941)

Federal Alcohol Administration

Franklin Chase Hoyt, Administrator (1935)
Wilford S. Alexander, Administrator (1936-1940)

Federal Art Project

Holger Cahill, Director (1935-1941)

Federal Bureau of Investigation

J. Edgar Hoover, Director (1933-1941)

Federal Communications Commission

Eugene O. Sykes, (1935-1938), Chairman (1934)
Anning S. Prall, Chairman (1935-1936)
Frank R. McNinck, Chairman (1937-1938)
James Lawrence Fly, Chairman (1939-1941)
Thad H. Brown (1934-1939)
Norman S. Case (1934-1941)
Hampson Gary (1934)
George Henry Payne (1934-1941)
Irvin Stewart (1934-1936)
Paul A. Walker (1934-1941)
T. A. M. Craven (1936-1941)
Frederick I. Thompson (1939-1940)
R. C. Wakefield (1941)

Federal Crop Insurance Corporation

Leroy K. Smith, Manager (1938-1941)

Federal Dance Project

Don Becque, Supervisor (1935-1936)
Lincoln Kirstein, Supervisor (1937, resigned after one day)
Stephen Karnot, Administrative Assistant (1937-1938)
Evelyn David, Co-ordinator of Dance Activities (1938-1939)

Federal Deposit Insurance Corporation

Walter J. Cummings, Chairman (1933)
Leo T. Crowley, Chairman (1934-1941)

Federal Emergency Relief Administration

Harry L. Hopkins, Administrator (1933-1938)

Federal Farm Mortgage Corporation

William I. Myers, President (1934-1937)
F. F. Hill, President (1938)
A. T. Esgate, Executive Vice-President (1939)
J. H. Guill, Vice-President (1940-1941)

Federal Housing Administration

James Moffett, Administrator (1934)
Stewart McDonald, Administrator (1935-1940)
Abner H. Ferguson, Administrator (1941)

Federal Loan Agency

Jesse H. Jones (1939-1941)

Federal Music Project

Nikolai Sokoloff, Director (1935-1939)

Federal National Mortgage Association

Sam H. Husbands, President (1938-1941)

Federal Power Commission

Frank R. McNinch, Chairman (1933-1936)
Herbert H. Drane (1933-1936)
Claude L. Draper (1933-1941)
Basil Manly (1933-1941)
George O. Smith (1933)
Clyde L. Seavey (1934-1939), Chairman (1937-1939)
John W. Scott (1937-1941)
Leland Olds (1939-1941), Chairman (1940-1941)
Leon M. Fuquay (1939-1941)

Federal Prison Industries, Inc.

Sanford Bates, President (1935-1941)

Federal Real Estate Board

D. H. Swayer, Chairman (1939-1941)

Federal Reserve Board

Eugene R. Black, Governor (1933)
Charles S. Hamlin (1933-1935)
George R. James (1933-1935)
Adolph Miller (1933-1934)
M. S. Szymczak (1933-1941)
J. J. Thomas (1933-1935)
Marriner S. Eccles, Chairman (1934-1941)
Joseph A. Broderick (1936)
Chester C. Davis (1936-1940)

John K. McKee (1936-1941)
Ronald Ransom (1936-1941)
Ernest G. Draper (1938-1941)

Federal Savings and Loan Insurance Corporation

Nugent Fallon, General Manager (1934-1940)
Oscar R. Kreutz, General Manager (1941)

Federal Security Agency

Paul V. McNutt, Administrator (1939-1941)

Federal Surplus Commodities Corporation

Chester C. Davis, President (1935)
Francis R. Wilcox, President (1936)
Jesse W. Tapp, President (1937-1938)
Milo Perkins, President (1939), Administrator (1940-1941)

Federal Surplus Relief Corporation

Harry L. Hopkins (1934)

Federal Theatre Project

Hallie V. Flanagan, Director (1935-1939)

Federal Trade Commission

Charles H. March, (1934-1940), Chairman (1933, 1936, 1941)
Garland S. Ferguson, (1933-1941), Chairman (1934, 1938)
Ewin L. Davis, (1933-1941), Chairman (1935, 1940)
William A. Ayres, (1934-1941), Chairman (1937)
Robert E. Freer, (1935-1941), Chairman (1939)
William E. Humphrey (1933)
Otis Johnson (1933-1940)
Raymond Stevens (1933)

Federal Works Agency

John M. Carmody, Chairman (1939-1941)

Federal Writers' Project

Henry G. Alsberg, Director (1935-1939)

First Export-Import Bank

George N. Peek, President (1934-1935)

First National Labor Relations Board

Lloyd Garrison, Chairman (1934)
Francis Biddle, Chairman (1935)
Harry A. Mills (1934)
Edwin S. Smith (1934)

Historical Records Survey

Luther H. Evans, National Director (1935-1939)
Sargent P. Childs, National Director (1940-1941)

Home Owners' Loan Corporation

William F. Stevenson, Chairman (1933)
John H. Fahey, Chairman (1934-1938)
Charles A. Jones, General Manager (1939-1941)

Indian Arts and Crafts Board

Louis C. West, General Manager (1936-1937)
Rene d'Harnoncourt, General Manager (1937-1941)

Interstate Commerce Commission

Patrick J. Farrell, (1933-1934), Chairman (1933)
William E. Lee, (1933-1941), Chairman (1934)
Hugh M. Tate, (1933-1936), Chairman (1935)
Charles D. Mahaffie, (1933-1941), Chairman (1936)
Carroll Miller, (1933-1941), Chairman (1937)
Walter M. Splawn, (1934-1941), Chairman (1938)
Joseph B. Eastman (1933-1941), Chairman (1939-1941)
Ezra Brainerd, Jr. (1933)
Balthassal Meyer (1933-1938)
Clyde B. Atchison (1933-1941)
Frank McManamy (1933-1938)
Claude Porter (1933-1941)
Marion Caskie (1935-1938)
John Rogers (1937-1941)
J. Haden Alldridge (1939-1941)
William J. Patterson (1939-1941)
J. Monroe Johnson (1940-1941)

Maritime Labor Board

Robert W. Bruere, Chairman (1938-1941)
Louis Block (1938-1941)
Claude E. Seehorn (1938-1941)

National Bituminous Coal Commission

C. F. Hosford, Jr., Chairman (1935-1936)

National Bituminous Coal Labor Board

Judge J. D. Acuff (1933-1935)
John M. Carmody (1933-1935)
T. S. Hogan (1933-1935)
M. S. Johnson (1933-1935)
John A. Lapp (1933-1935)

National Emergency Council

Donald Richberg, Executive Director (1934)
Frank C. Walker, Executive Director (1935)
Eugene S. Leggett, Acting Executive Director (1936–1937)
Lowell Mellett, Executive Director (1938-1939)

National Institute of Health

George W. McCoy (1933-1937)
Lewis R. Thompson (1938-1941)

National Labor Board

Senator Robert Wagner, Chairman (1933-1934)
Henry S. Dennison (1933-1934)
Ernst Draper (1933-1934)
Pierre S. du Pont (1933-1934)
William Green (1933-1934)
Dr. Francis J. Hass (1933-1934)
Louis E. Kirstein (1933-1934)
John L. Lewis (1933-1934)
Leon C. Marshall (1933-1934)
Walter C. Teagle (1933-1934)
S. Clay Williams (1933-1934)
Leo Wolman (1933-1934)

National Longshoremen's Labor Board

Archbishop Edward J. Hanna (1934-1935)
Edward F. McGrady (1934-1935)
D. K. Cushing (1934-1935)

National Planning Board

Frederic A. Delano, Chairman (1933-1934)

National Recovery Administration

Hugh S. Johnson, Administrator (1933)
Clay Williams, Administrator (1934)
Laurence J. Martin, Acting Administrator (1935)

National Resources Board

Harold L. Ickes, Chairman (1934)
Frederic A. Delano, Chairman (1935-1938)

National Resources Planning Board

Frederic A. Delano, Chairman (1939-1941)

National Steel Labor Relations Board

Judge Walter Stacy, Chairman (1934-1935)
Dr. James Mullenback (1934-1935)
Rear Admiral Henry Wiley (1934-1935)

National Youth Administration

Aubrey Williams, Executive Director (1935-1941)

Petroleum Labor Policy Board

Nathan R. Margold, Chairman (1933-1934)
Seth W. Candee (1933-1934)
H. C. Fleming (1933-1934)
Charles C. Jones (1933-1934)
R. H. Ivory (1933-1934)
Dr. George W. Stocking (1933-1934)
R. R. Zimmerman (1933-1934)
Dr. John A. Lapp (1935-1936)

Postmaster General of the United States

James A. Farley (1933-1939)
Frank C. Walker (1940-1941)

Public Works Administration

Harold L. Ickes, Administrator (1933-1938)
Col. E. W. Clark, Commissioner of Public Works (1939–1940)
Maurice Gilmore, Commissioner of Public Works (1941)

Reconstruction Finance Corporation

Jesse H. Jones, Chairman (1933-1938)
Emil Schram, Chairman (1939-1940)
Charles B. Henderson, Chairman (1941)

Resettlement Administration

Rexford G. Tugwell, Administrator (1935-1936)

Rural Electrification Administration

Morris L. Cooke, Administrator (1935-1936)
John M. Carmody, Administrator (1937-1938)
Harry Slattery, Administrator (1939-1941)

Second Export-Import Bank

George N. Peek, President (1934-1935)

Second National Bituminous Coal Commission

C. F. Hosgood, Chairman (1937)
Percy Tetlow, Chairman (1938)
Howard A. Gray, Director (1939-1941)

Second National Labor Relations Board

Joseph Warren Madden, Chairman (1935-1939)
Harry A. Mills, Chairman (1941)

John M. Carmody (1935)
Edwin S. Smith (1935-1941)
Donald W. Smith (1936-1938)
William Leiserson (1939–1941)

Secretary of Agriculture

Henry A. Wallace (1933-1939)
Claude R. Wickard (1940-1941)

Secretary of Commerce

Daniel C. Roper (1933-1938)
Harry L. Hopkins (1938-1940)
Jesse H. Jones (1941)

Secretary of Labor

Frances Perkins (1933-1941)

Secretary of State

Cordell Hull (1933-1941)

Secretary of the Interior

Harold L. Ickes (1933-1941)

Secretary of the Navy

Claude Swanson (1933-1938)
Charles Edison (1939-1940)
Frank Knox (1940-1941)

Secretary of the Treasury

William A. Woodin (1933)
Henry Morgenthau, Jr. (1934-1941)

Secretary of War

George H. Dun (1933-1936)
Harry Woodring (1936-1940)
Henry L. Stimson (1940-1941)

Securities and Exchange Commission

Joseph P. Kennedy, Chairman (1934)
James M. Landis, Chairman (1935-1936)
William O. Douglas, Chairman (1937-1938)
Jerome N. Frank, Chairman (1939-1940)
Edward C. Eicher, Chairman (1941)

Social Security Board

John G. Winant, Chairman (1935-1936)
Arthur J. Altmeyer (1935-1941), Chairman (1937-1941)

Vincent M. Miles (1935-1936)
George E. Bigge (1937-1941)
Mary Dewson (1937-1938)
Ellen S. Woodward (1939-1941)

Tennessee Valley Authority

Arthur E. Morgan, Chairman (1934-1937)
Harcourt A. Morgan (1934-1941), Chairman (1938-1941).
David Lilienthal (1934-1941)
James P. Pope (1939-1941)

Textile Labor Relations Board

Judge Walker P. Stacy, Chairman (1934-1935)
James Mullenback (1934)
Admiral Henry Wiley (1934-1935)
Frank P. Douglass (1935)

United States Employment Service

W. Frank Persons, Director (1933-1939)

United States Film Service

Pare Lorentz (1938-1940)

United States Housing Authority

Nathan Straus, Administrator (1937-1941)

United States Maritime Commission

Rear Admiral Henry A. Wiley, Chairman (1936)
Joseph P. Kennedy, Chairman (1937)
Rear Admiral Emory S. Land, Chairman (1938-1941)

Works Progress Administration

Harry L. Hopkins, Administrator (1935-1938)
Col. F. C. Harrington, Commissioner of Work Projects (1939)
Howard Hunter, Commissioner of Work Projects (1940–1941)

ANN H. HOLDER

Appendix ***D***

NEW DEAL ACRONYMS

AAA: Agricultural Adjustment Administration.
AALL: American Association for Labor Legislation.
AAPA: Association Against the Prohibition Amendment.
AFBF: American Farm Bureau Federation.
AFL: American Federation of Labor.
ALB: Automobile Labor Board.
ALL: American Liberty League.
BAC: Business Advisory Council.
BB: Bureau of the Budget.
BIA: Bureau of Indian Affairs.
BPA: Bonneville Power Administration.
CAA: Civil Aeronautics Authority.
CCC: Civilian Conservation Corps.
CIO: Committee for Industrial Organization. Congress of Industrial Organizations (after 1938).
CPLA: Conference on Progressive Labor Action.
CWA: Civil Works Administration.
EHFA: Electric Home and Farm Authority.
EIB: Export-Import Bank.
FAP: Federal Art Project.
FBI: Federal Bureau of Investigation.
FCA: Farm Credit Administration.
FCC: Federal Communications Commission.
FCIC: Federal Crop Insurance Corporation.
FDIC: Federal Deposit Insurance Corporation.
FDP: Federal Dance Project.
FEPC: Fair Employment Practices Committee.
FERA: Federal Emergency Relief Administration.
FFMC: Federal Farm Mortgage Corporation.
FHA: Federal Housing Administration.
FLA: Federal Loan Agency.
FNMA: Federal National Mortgage Association.
FPC: Federal Power Commission.
FRB: Federal Reserve Board.

FSA: Farm Security Administration.
FSCC: Federal Surplus Commodities Corporation.
FSLIC: Federal Savings and Loan Insurance Corporation.
FSRC: Federal Surplus Relief Corporation.
FTC: Federal Trade Commission.
FTP: Federal Theatre Project.
FWA: Federal Works Agency.
FWP: Federal Writers' Project.
HOLC: Home Owners' Loan Corporation.
HRS: Historical Records Survey.
ICC: Interstate Commerce Commission.
IEC: Industrial Energy Commission.
NAM: National Association of Manufacturers.
NBBC: National Bituminous Coal Commission.
NEC: National Emergency Council.
NFU: National Farmers' Union.
NIRA: National Industrial Recovery Administration.
NLB: National Labor Board.
NLRB: National Labor Relations Board.
NPA: National Progressives of America.
NPB: National Planning Board.
NRA: National Recovery Administration.
NRB: National Resources Board.
NRPB: National Resources Planning Board.
NRS: National Reemployment Service.
NSLRB: National Steel Labor Relations Board.
NYA: National Youth Administration.
PAB: Petroleum Administrative Board.
PCA: Production Credit Association.
PLPB: Petroleum Labor Policy Board.
PWA: Public Works Administration.
PWAP: Public Works of Art Project.
RA: Resettlement Administration.
REA: Rural Electrification Administration.
RFC: Reconstruction Finance Corporation.
SEC: Securities and Exchange Commission.
STFU: Southern Tenant Farmers' Union.
TNEC: Temporary National Economic Committee.
TRAP: Treasury Relief Art Project.
TVA: Tennessee Valley Authority.
UCL: Unemployed Citizens' League.
UMW: United Mine Workers.
USDA: United States Department of Agriculture.
USES: United States Employment Service.
USFS: United States Film Service.
USHA: United States Housing Authority.
WPA: Works Projects Administration.

INDEX

CONTRIBUTORS

LENA ALLRED received her undergraduate degree from Brigham Young University and possesses master's degrees from the University of Houston and Sam Houston State University. She is currently working toward the Ph.D. in history at the University of Texas.

LORRAINE A. BROWN received her Ph.D. from the University of Maryland in 1968. She is the author with John O'Connor of *Free, Adult, Uncensored: The Living History of the Federal Theatre Project* (1978). Professor Brown is the Administrator of the Institute on the Federal Theatre and New Deal Culture and teaches in the English Department at George Mason University in Fairfax, Virginia.

GARY DEAN BEST received the Ph.D. in history from the University of Hawaii at Manoa in 1973. He is the author of *The Politics of American Individualism* (1975), *To Free A People* (1982), and *Herbert Hoover: The Post-Presidential Years* (2 volumes) (1983), and numerous scholarly articles. Professor Best is chairman of the history department in the University of Hawaii at Hilo.

ROBERT S. BROWNING III received the Ph.D. from the University of Wisconsin in 1981. Currently a lecturer in history at Sam Houston State University in Huntsville, Texas, Browning is the author of *Two If By Sea* (1983), a study of American coastal defense policy.

DAVID BURNER earned his A.B. at Hamilton College and his Ph.D. at Columbia University. He has published several books, most recently *The Torch Is Passed: The Kennedy Brothers and American Liberalism* (1984) with Thomas R. West. Professor Burner teaches at the State University of New York at Stony Brook.

JAMES L. CARTER received the Ph.D. from Texas Tech University and teaches political science at Sam Houston State University in Huntsville, Texas.

ART CASCIATO is a Ph.D. candidate in English at the University of Virginia. His dissertation-in-progress is a history of the League of American Writers. Casciato is also the co-editor of *Critical Essays on William Styron* (1982) and author of articles in *American Literature, Mississippi Quarterly*, and *Agenda*. He teaches in the English department of Northeastern University in Boston, Massachusetts.

DAVID CHAPMAN received the Ph.D. in American History from Texas A & M University. He is currently employed as an Assistant Professor in the Texas A & M University Archives.

DONALD V. COERS received the Ph.D. in English from Texas A & M University in 1974. He teaches English at Sam Houston State University in Huntsville, Texas, and is currently Associate Editor of *The Texas Review*.

CHARLES E. DARBY, JR. received his B.A. and M.A. from Sam Houston State University in Huntsville, Texas. He is currently teaching in the Conroe Independent School District in Conroe, Texas.

EDWIN S. DAVIS received the Ph.D. from Texas Tech University. He is currently associate professor of political science at Sam Houston State University in Huntsville, Texas. Davis is also editor of the *Texas Journal of Political Studies*.

MICHAEL G. DENNIS received the M.A. in history from Sam Houston State University. He is team leader in the history department at Cypress-Fairbanks I.S.D. in Houston, Texas.

E. LARRY DICKENS is professor of political science at Sam Houston State University in Huntsville, Texas. He received the Ph.D. from Texas Tech University and is co-author of *Fundamentals of Texas Government* and *Introduction to American and Texas Government*.

BERNARD K. DUFFY received his Ph.D. from the University of Pittsburgh. He has published a number of articles regarding public address, rhetorical theory, and cultural history. Professor Duffy teaches in the English department of Clemson University, Clemson, South Carolina.

DONALD H. DYAL is an associate professor and head of Rare Books and Special Collections at Texas A & M University Library. He has studied at the University of Washington, Brigham Young University, and Texas A & M University, where he received the Ph.D. in American History in 1980.

CATHERINE P. EGGERS received her M.A. in history from Sam Houston State University. Ms. Eggers is currently teaching history at Booker T. Washington Junior High School in Conroe, Texas.

PATRICIA L. HASELBARTH received her master's degree from Sam Houston State University in 1983. She is a founding member of PoDan Sam, a professional company combining poetry and dance, and holds certification in Labanotation. Ms. Haselbarth teaches in the dance department of Sam Houston State University.

VIRGINIA F. HAUGHTON received the Ph.D. in history from the University of Kentucky in 1973. She is the author of several articles, including "John Worth Kern and Labor Legislation" (*Mid-America*, 1975). Dr. Haughton has recently joined the history department of Memphis State University, following several years with the history department of the University of Texas at Arlington.

ELLIS W. HAWLEY received the Ph.D. from the University of Wisconsin (Madison). He is the author of *The New Deal and the Problem of Monopoly* (1966), *The Great War and the Search for a Modern Order* (1979), and a number of essays, articles, and contributions to multi-author works. Professor Hawley teaches in the history department of the University of Iowa in Iowa City, Iowa.

ANN H. HOLDER holds master's degrees from George Peabody College for Teachers and Sam Houston State University. She currently is Reference Librarian and Social Science Bibliographer, Newton Gresham Library, Sam Houston State University, Huntsville, Texas.

THOMAS D. ISERN is associate professor of history at Emporia State University, Emporia, Kansas. He received the Ph.D. in history from Oklahoma State University. His publications include *Custom Combining on the Great Plains: A History* (1981).

WILLIAM LASSER received his Ph.D. in political science at Harvard University. He is currently teaching in the political science department at Clemson University and writing a book on the Supreme Court in periods of crisis.

AUSTIN N. LEIBY completed his Ph.D. in history and political science at Northern Arizona University. He is the author of several articles on the people and cultures of the Southwest, including "The Mormon Battalion and the Apache Campaign of 1885," Rio Grande Westerners Brand Book (Santa Fe Chapter), 1973. He is currently associated with the Migrant Child Tutor Program of the Phoenix Union High School District in Arizona.

JOHN S. LEIBY earned the Ph.D. at Northern Arizona University and is the author of *Report to the King: Colonel Juan Camargo y Caballero's Historical Account of New Spain* (1984).

H. CARLETON MARLOW received his Ph.D. in history from the University of Oklahoma. He is the author of the *American Search for Woman* (1976), *The*

Bibliography of American Women (1978), and *Americans and the Women's Rights Movement* (1981). Professor Marlow teaches in the history department at Brigham Young University.

IRVIN M. MAY, JR. holds a Ph.D. from the University of Oklahoma. In addition to many articles, he is the author of *Marvin Jones: The Public Life of an Agrarian Advocate* (1980). Formerly a professor of history at Texas A & M University, May is now legal historian for the law firm of Vinson & Elkins in Houston, Texas.

JAMES S. OLSON received the Ph.D. from the State University of New York, Stony Brook. He has taught at Sam Houston State University in Huntsville, Texas, since 1972. Olson's publications include *Herbert Hoover and the Reconstruction Finance Corporation, 1931–1933* (1977) and *The Ethnic Dimension in American History* (1979).

MICHAEL E. PARRISH received his Ph.D. in history from Yale University. He is the author of *Securities Regulation and the New Deal* (1972) and *Felix Frankfurter and His Times* (1982). He teaches in the department of history at the University of California, San Diego.

JOHN PAYNE received the Ph.D. from the University of Texas and is currently a professor of history at Sam Houston State University.

F. ROSS PETERSON obtained his Ph.D. in American Studies from Washington State University. He has written several books and articles, including *Prophet Without Honor: Glen H. Taylor and the Fight for American Liberalism* (1974) and *Idaho: A Bicentennial History* (1976). Professor Peterson teaches history at Utah State University in Logan, Utah.

ANITA PILLING has an undergraduate degree from Brigham Young University and master's degrees from Brigham Young University and Sam Houston State University. She currently teaches at Willis High School in Willis, Texas.

PATRICK D. REAGAN received his Ph.D. in history from Ohio State University. He is the author of articles in *Ohio History* and *Business History Review*. Currently he is working on a history of national planning in the United States from 1900 to 1945. Professor Reagan teaches in the history department of Tennessee Technological University in Cookeville, Tennessee.

RICHARD A. REIMAN received his Ph.D. in history from the University of Cincinatti. His dissertation was an analysis of the National Youth Administration. Professor Reiman teaches in the history department of the University of Alabama.

RANDY ROBERTS received the Ph.D. from Louisiana State University. He is the author of *Manassa Mauler: The Life of Jack Dempsey* (1979) and *Papa Jack: Jack Johnson and the Era of White Hopes* (1983). Professor Roberts is an assistant professor of history at Sam Houston State University in Huntsville, Texas.

DAVID BRIAN ROBERTSON is assistant professor of political science at the University of Missouri-St. Louis. Since receiving his Ph.D. from Indiana University, he has published articles on policy design and labor market policy in such journals as *Policy Studies Review*. He is currently working on a manuscript tracing the evolution of federal labor market programs in the development of the welfare state.

JOSEPH M. ROWE, JR. studied at Kent State University and the University of Michigan, and received his Ph.D. from Texas A & M University. He now teaches history at Sam Houston State University, Huntsville, Texas.

JANE A. ROSENBERG has master's degrees from Indiana University and Kent State University. She is currently working for The Council on Library Resources in Washington, D.C. and completing a Ph.D. in history at the University of Michigan. Ms. Rosenberg has written articles for *Choice*, the *OAH Newsletter*, and the *History Teacher*.

ROY ROSENZWEIG received his Ph.D. from Harvard University. He is the author of *Eight Hours for What We Will: Workers and Leisure in an Industrial City, 1870–1920* (1983). Professor Rosenzweig teaches in the history and American studies departments at George Mason University in Fairfax, Virginia.

LOIS SCHARF received the Ph.D. from Case Western Reserve University. She is the author of *To Work and to Wed: Female Employment, Feminism, and the Great Depression* (1980) and co-editor of *Decades of Discontent: The Women's Movement, 1920–1940* (1983). Ms. Scharf is the executive director of National History Day and teaches American history at Case Western Reserve University.

JAMES C. SCHNEIDER received the Ph.D. at the University of Wisconsin-Madison. He specializes in modern United States history and currently teaches at the University of Texas-San Antonio.

J. CHRISTOPHER SCHNELL received his Ph.D. in history from Kansas State University. He is the author of many articles, including the prize-winning "Missouri Progressives and the Nomination of F.D.R.," *Missouri Historical Review* (April, 1974). Professor Schnell teaches in the history department of Southeast Missouri State University in Cape Girardeau, Missouri.

JORDAN A. SCHWARZ earned the Ph.D. in history from Columbia University. He is the author of *The Speculator: Bernard M. Baruch in Washington, 1917–1965* (1981) and *The Interregnum of Despair: Hoover, Congress and the Depression* (1970). He is completing a book about Adolf A. Berle and is professor of history at Northern Illinois University.

ROBERT L. SHADLE, a Woodrow Wilson Fellow in 1960, did his graduate work in history at the University of Iowa and teaches in the history department of Sam Houston State University, Huntsville, Texas.

MARTHA H. SWAIN received her Ph.D. in history from Vanderbilt University. She is the author of *Pat Harrison: The New Deal Years* (1978) and a number of articles on southern women in politics and New Deal relief programs for women. Professor Swain teaches in the department of history and government at Texas Women's University, Denton, Texas.

BARBARA M. TYSON took her Ph.D. at the University of Texas and is currently an associate professor of English at Sam Houston State University, Huntsville, Texas.

DAN K. UTLEY holds a master's degree in history from Sam Houston State University. Since 1982, he has served as the Director of Research for the Texas Historical Commission.

ROBERT A. WALLER received his Ph.D. in history from the University of Illinois-Urbana. He is the author of *Rainey of Illinois* (1977) and numerous articles. Currently he is dean of the college of liberal arts at Clemson University, Clemson, South Carolina.

RAYMOND WILSON received his Ph.D. in history from the University of New Mexico. His books include *Ohiyesa: Charles Eastman, Santee Sioux* (1983) and *Native Americans in the Twentieth Century* (1984). Professor Wilson is a member of the history department at Fort Hays State University in Hays, Kansas.

DUANE WINDSOR received his Ph.D. in political economy from Harvard University. He is author or co-author of a number of books, including *Housing Development and Municipal Costs* (1973), *Fiscal Zoning in Suburban Communities* (1979), *The Changing Boardroom* (1982), and *The Foreign Corrupt Practices Act: Anatomy of a Statute* (1982). Professor Windsor teaches in the Jesse H. Jones Graduate School of Business Administration at Rice University, Houston, Texas.

GEORGE WOLFSKILL received the Ph.D. in history from the University of Texas-Austin. He is the author of several books, including *The Revolt of the Conservatives* (1962), *All But the People* (1969), and *Happy Days Are Here Again!* (1974). Dr. Wolfskill is professor emeritus at the University of Texas-Arlington.